The Impact of the National Curriculum on the Teaching of Five-Year-Olds

Theo Cox and Susan Sanders

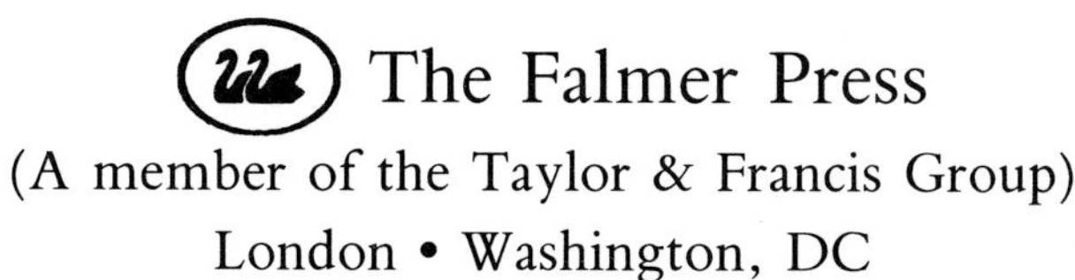

The Falmer Press
(A member of the Taylor & Francis Group)
London • Washington, DC

UK The Falmer Press, 4 John Street, London WC1N 2ET
USA The Falmer Press, Taylor & Francis Inc., 1900 Frost Road, Suite 101, Bristol, PA 19007

First published in 1994

A catalogue record for this book is available from the British Library

Library of Congress Cataloging-in-Publication Data are available on request

ISBN 0 7507 0250 8 cased
ISBN 0 7507 0251 6 paper

Jacket design by Caroline Archer

Typeset in 12/14pt Bembo
Graphicraft Typesetters Ltd., Hong Kong

Printed in Great Britain by Burgess Science Press, Basingstoke on paper which has a specified pH value on final paper manufacture of not less than 7.5 and is therefore 'acid free'.

The Impact of the National Curriculum on the Teaching of Five-Year-Olds

Contents

List of Tables and Figures

Acknowledgments

The research study upon which this book is based was funded by the University of Wales Faculty of Eduction. The authors would like to thank the Director of Education of the LEA in which the study was carried out for his permission to carry out the study, and the county council officers who provided background information on the participating schools and on the county INSET programme concerning the National Curriculum. Our special thanks are due to the headteachers and Year 1 class teachers of the participating schools for their cooperation with the research project at a time when they were fully occupied in meeting the new demands of the National Curriculum and other changes stemming from the 1988 Education Reform Act.

In addition we wish to thank Richard Daugherty, former Chairman of the Curriculum Council for Wales, for his helpful advice concerning policy developments within the council, and for making available various Council publications. We also wish to thank Miss Frances Wood, Librarian of the University College of Swansea Department of Education Library, and her staff, for their helpfulness in locating and obtaining various publications. Our thanks are also due to members of staff in the Education Department of University College Swansea, namely: Alan Dobbins (Senior Lecturer), for his help in the data analysis; Alice Laing (Departmental Research Fellow) and Gill Harper Jones (Lecturer), for reading and commenting on Chapters 10 and 11 respectively; and Jackie Curry and Sian Davies for their secretarial assistance.

Finally, but by no means least, we record our thanks to Jane Evans, our Project Research Officer, for carrying out all of the teacher interviews.

Theo Cox
Susan Sanders
October 1993

Chapter 1

Introduction: The National Curriculum and the 1988 Education Reform Act

Since the 1944 Education Act, until the introduction of the National Curriculum primary teachers have enjoyed considerable freedom of educational thought and practice, and, in contrast to their secondary school colleagues, their work has not been constrained by the requirements of a national system of formal examinations. (The eleven-plus selection procedures did constrain the upper primary curriculum of some schools, it is true, but these procedures were largely abandoned in the 1960s.) Despite this enviable degree of autonomy, however, primary schools have been subject to a greater or lesser degree of control of their curriculum planning, teaching and classroom organization by the policies of their respective LEAs. At its best the influence of such policies has been of great benefit to primary schools in providing sound guidance and support, while respecting teachers' professional independence. However, such influence has been damaging in those cases where the strong advocacy of a particular LEA philosophy or approach to primary teaching has foisted upon teachers practices which they have neither understood fully nor accepted into their own thinking (see Alexander, 1992, for example).

The passing of the Education Reform Act (ERA) in 1988 marked a strikingly new phase in education characterized by central government control of the content of the curriculum across the 5 to 16 year age range. This was coupled with a deliberate weakening of the powers of local government in educational matters through the enforced delegation of their responsibilities for management and budgeting to the schools themselves. Chitty (1992) provides a lucid analysis of the political background to the introduction of this Act. His view of the Act is summed up in the following statement:

> It increased the powers of the Education Secretary to a quite alarming degree, and restored to central government a control over the school curriculum which had been surrendered in the inter-war period. While gathering more power to the centre, it simultaneously introduced important limitations on the functions of LEAs, who were forced to give greater autonomy to schools, heads and governing bodies. Above all, it effectively ended that ill defined partnership between central government, local government and individual schools which had been such a prominent feature of the educational scene since the settlement of 1944. (Chitty, 1992: 37)

However Chitty argues that the origin of the National Curriculum lay partly in Prime Minister James Callaghan's celebrated speech in October 1976 at Ruskin College, Oxford, which launched the 'great debate' in education. Amongst other things Callaghan advocated the need for a core curriculum of basic knowledge, greater teacher accountability, and the direct subordination of the secondary curriculum to the needs of the economy (for a collection of papers written to celebrate the tenth anniversary of that speech see Williams *et al.*, 1992).

As Chitty states, the major provisions of the 1988 Education Reform Act are:

1 the introduction of a National Curriculum for all state schools alongside a national system of assessment for pupils from 5 to 16 years. The Act defines mathematics, English and science as 'core subjects' (plus Welsh in Welsh medium schools in Wales), with a second group of 'foundation' subjects, namely: a modern foreign language (for secondary pupils only); Welsh as a second language for schools in Wales; technology; history; geography; art; music; and physical education.[1] Religious education was added later as a 'basic subject'.

For most subjects the Act stated that there would be attainment targets for children aged 7, 11, 14 and 16, which would provide standards against which pupils' progress and performance could be assessed by the individual teacher and also, through a national system of tests (Standard Assessment Tasks or SATs). The detailed content of the National Curriculum, including the attainment targets, was laid down in subject orders (often referred to as 'National Curriculum folders' by teachers), supplemented by non-statutory programmes of study for each subject;

2 the introduction of a system of local management of schools (LMS) under which school budgets for staffing, premises and services were delegated from the LEA to individual schools;

3 the creation of a new tier of schooling comprising City Technology Colleges (CTCs) and grant maintained schools. The latter would choose to opt out of LEA control and receive direct funding from central government. The Act allowed the governors of all secondary schools and primary schools with over 300 registered pupils to apply to the Secretary of State for grant maintained status.

As enshrined in the ERA the content of the National Curriculum, although not its principle, has been the subject of considerable criticism (see, for example, Chitty, 1992; Lawton, 1988). Certainly, at the primary level, its strong subject orientation seems incompatible with the view of the curriculum expressed in the Plowden Report (Central Advisory Council for Education, England, 1967). This argues that the extent to which subject matter ought to be classified, and the headings under which such classifications are made will vary very much with the age of the children, with the demands made by the structure of the subject matter to be studied, and with the circumstances of the school. Pointedly the report states that 'Any practice which predetermines the pattern and imposes it upon all is to be condemmed' (para. 538). The report goes on to suggest that for young children the broadest division of the curriculum is suitable, e.g.

language, science, mathematics, environmental studies and the expressive arts. For older children (9 to 12) more subject divisions can be expected, although 'experience in secondary schools has shown that teaching of rigidly defined subjects, often by subject specialists, is far from suitable for the oldest children who will be in middle schools' (para. 538).

As recently as 1985 HMI proposed a curriculum model for children aged 5 to 16 which was based upon areas of learning and experience rather than traditional subjects, as follows:

> aesthetic and creative;
> human and social;
> linguistic and literary;
> mathematical;
> moral;
> physical;
> scientific;
> spiritual;
> technological. (DES, 1985, para. 33)

These areas were not suggested as discrete elements to be taught separately and in isolation from one another and were not equated with particular subjects, although it was acknowledged that some subjects would contribute more to some areas than others.

The National Curriculum guidance document entitled *A Framework for the Whole Curriculum 5–16 in Wales* (CCW, 1989) puts forward a list of eight 'elements of learning' which correspond closely to the areas of learning just listed. It is advocated that the discrete subjects of the National Curriculum should be subsumed within these elements which should facilitate planning on a cross-subject basis and 'help to break down a still prevalent tendency to develop the teaching of individual subjects in isolation from others' (CCW, 1989: 5). However, the fact remains that this document, together with an equivalent document published by the National Curriculum Council (1990) is for guidance only while the full legislative weight of the ERA is channelled through separate subject orders.

Despite the fact that it seems somewhat at odds with earlier, alternative curriculum models, the National Curriculum could still be said to represent a careful analysis of the knowledge, skills and understanding which children need to learn, albeit within a narrow subject framework. It does not prescribe *how* this content should be taught so that, at the primary level, for example, it should be possible to teach it through a thematic, topic approach to some extent. Indeed the guidance document produced by the Curriculum Council for Wales (CCW, 1989) states that the primary curriculum will be designed in an integrated manner and often implemented through topic or thematic work (but see Chapter 9 of this book on this question).

Further, it was not intended that the National Curriculum should constitute the whole of the primary or secondary school curriculum. Indeed the National Curriculum Council (NCC) argued that the National Curriculum alone could not provide the broad and balanced curriculum to which all pupils were entitled; it identified five broad themes which underpinned the curriculum, particularly at the secondary school level. These were: economic and industrial understanding, careers education and guidance, health education, education for citizenship, and environmental education (NCC, 1990). In addition, this NCC document stressed the importance of the dimensions of equal opportunities for all pupils and their preparation for life in a multicultural community as underpinning all teaching in schools.

In his recent interim report on the revision of the National Curriculum Sir Ron Dearing (NCC, 1993b)[2] proposes to increase the amount of teaching time available for discretionary use by the teacher. Such a move would clearly allow schools more scope to teach beyond the confines of the National Curriculum.

A central element of the National Curriculum was an elaborate system for the assessment of children's performance and progress. This was designed to provide both formative information, which would enable teachers to match the learning tasks more closely to individual's level of knowledge, skill and understanding, and summative information, which would provide a summary of a child's level of achievement in a given area of skill or knowledge. Formative assessment was to be carried out by the teacher using a self-designed or school-designed system, while summative assessment was to be carried out by means of nationally prescribed Standard Assessment Tasks (SATs). These were designed to reflect normal teaching practice as far as possible, and were to be given by the class teacher, but they were standardized in their method of administration and scoring and would yield results that were comparable from school to school. As such they could be used to provide overall pupil performance data for the national 'league tables' of school performance which were introduced by the 1988 Act.

This assessment system was based on the work of a Task Group on Assessment and Testing set up by the government under the leadership of Professor Paul Black. Their recommendations were contained in a main report (DES/Welsh Office, 1988a) and three supplementary reports (DES/Welsh Office, 1988b). The overseeing and subsequent development of the National Curriculum assessment system was entrusted to the School Examinations and Assessment Council (SEAC) set up by the government at the same time as the National Curriculum Council (NCC) in England and the Curriculum Council for Wales (CCW). (NCC and SEAC were merged into a new body called the School Curriculum and Assessment Authority on October 1st 1993, while the CCW is being replaced by a new Assessment and Curriculum Authority for Wales from April 1994.)

It could be argued that the time scale for the phased introduction of the National Curriculum and its associated apparatus for assessment was very tight in terms of allowing teachers sufficient time to adapt to each element as it came on stream. At Key Stage 1, for example, the full National Curriculum, comprising nine subjects, plus Welsh for schools in Wales, and religious education, was introduced during the period 1989 to 1993. However the demands placed upon the teachers at this key stage were significantly increased by a succession of changes to existing subject orders and assessment arrangements which took place during this period. One example is that the mathematics subject order was revised in 1991.

While these additional changes were likely to be very frustrating to hard pressed teachers trying to get to grips with the essentials of the National Curriculum it has to be said that, in some measure, these changes were made by the present government in response to concerted action by the teachers themselves. This was especially so in the case of the national assessment arrangements which are currently being streamlined.

The recent *post hoc* changes to the National Curriculum have now culminated in a full scale review of the whole system which has been entrusted by the Education Secretary to Sir Ron Dearing, currently Chairman of the SEAC, and also to the Chairman of the Curriculum Council for Wales. The overall aim of the review is to achieve a slimming down of the National Curriculum and its assessment procedures but, in the course of conducting it, Dearing is raising a number of key issues upon which he is inviting the views of teachers in a commendably frank and consultative fashion (see his series of five articles in the *Times Educational Supplement* commencing 17 September 1993 (Dearing 1993 a, b, c, d, e)). He has already produced an interim report (NCC, 1993b) and is to make his final recommendations in December 1993. In one of these articles he states his view that teachers wished 'to take time to get things right and, meanwhile, put a brake on the rate of change' (Dearing, 1993a: 21). Accordingly he has recommended that no further curricular changes should be made before September 1995. He has made it clear that he is seeking to lighten and rationalize the present over-cluttered structure of the National Curriculum without going back to the drawing board. He is keen not to jettison those elements which teachers have worked so hard to implement to date.

Studying the Impact of the National Curriculum at Key Stage One

The aim of our research study, which was funded by the University of Wales, was to study the impact of the National Curriculum upon the teaching of 5-year-old children, i.e. those in Year 1 of this curriculum, as judged by the teachers themselves. We decided to focus upon this age group in particular since they were the very first to experience the National Curriculum. The study was conducted in a representative sample of the primary and infant schools of a South Wales LEA from 1989 to 1990, with a short follow-up study in 1991. The focus of the study was upon the National Curriculum as such but, inevitably, the responses of the teachers at interview were partly coloured by their perceptions of the effects of other innovations introduced by the ERA, including LMS.

It is important to bear in mind that the study was carried out in Wales, which has its own independent body, the Curriculum Council for Wales (CCW). There are certain differences between the National Curriculum in Wales from that in England which, taken together, constitute a distinctive 'Welsh dimension'. The most important of these is the fact that, in Wales, the Welsh language is an additional core or non-core subject, depending on whether the school teaches through the medium of Welsh or English. The consequence of this, of course, is that the weight of the National Curriculum is greater in Wales than in England and the lack of fluency in Welsh of many primary school teachers in Wales poses some difficulty. In addition, four non-core subjects, namely history, geography, art and music, have been given separate orders, the result of which pupils in schools in Wales will follow somewhat different programmes of study from their peers in England.

The LEA within which the study was carried out had its own distinctive policies for primary education which were transmitted through its team of primary advisors and advisory teachers, and also through a series of policy documents published from 1987 onwards. The latter state the basic principles of that policy and their detailed application in the various areas of the primary curriculum. In addition the schools received all of the statutory and non-statutory National Curriculum guidance documents produced by the CCW.

Structure of the Book

Part I of this book starts with the essential background information on the schools, teachers and children in the study sample and details of the research questionnaires. This is followed by a detailed presentation of the study findings in Chapters 3 to 7. Chapter 8 provides a summary of the main findings, a discussion of them in the light of other National Curriculum studies and reports, and our conclusions.

In Part II we discuss in greater depth selected major issues arising from the study in the light of the wider literature. These are pedagogical and curricular issues (Chapter 9), the education of slower learning and socially disadvantaged pupils (Chapter 10) and the education of under-5s (Chapter 11).

Notes

1 Strictly speaking these subjects are described in the Act as 'non-core' subjects, since all of the subjects, including the 'core subjects', are foundation subjects. Throughout this book we have used the term non-core subjects, in line with correct usage. However, where teachers have used the term 'foundation subjects' (meaning non-core subjects) we have retained their wording.

2 Sir Ron Dearing's final report advising changes to the National Curriculum, School Curriculum and Assessment Authority, 1994 was published too late to be incorporated in detail in our book. However his recommendations regarding Key Stages 1 and 2 appear to be broadly in line with those in his interim report which are referred to in the following chapters. The only exception to this is the fact that the final report recommends that, at Key Stages 1–3, the National Curriculum should be slimmed down to free some 20 per cent of teaching time for use at the discretion of the school, whereas the interim report suggested a lower percentage of discretionary time at Key Stage 1 (10–15 per cent). (See Chapter 8, page 129).

Part I

The Study

Chapter 2

Aims and Conduct of the Research Study and Background Information on the Schools

Selection of Sample Schools

The study was carried out in a South Wales LEA which was predominantly urban in character but included some rural areas containing village communities. Our aim was to draw up a representative sample of the LEA's 142 primary and infant schools. This would be small enough to enable the team's research officer to carry out structured interviews with the headteachers and Year 1 class teachers. The first step was to obtain background information from the LEA on its primary and infant schools in terms of their roll size, type (infant or primary), catchment area, status (maintained or voluntary) and their linguistic medium of teaching (Welsh or English). Then, using a method of random selection, we drew a sample of twenty-eight schools, approximately one in five, which reflected the range of variation of the LEA's schools in terms of the features just described. Each of these schools was approached and if a headteacher felt unable to take part in the project, as a number of them did, owing to great pressure of work, an alternative, equivalent school was approached. Just before the commencement of the study, two schools from the group of twenty-eight withdrew, reducing the final sample to twenty-six schools (between one in five and one in six of the total number of schools). Background information on these schools now follows.

School size

Table 1 shows the distribution of school size in terms of number of pupils on roll. The cut-off points between the divisions of size

Table 1 Roll size of sample schools

No. of pupils on roll	No. of schools
Small : 161 or fewer	9
Medium: 162–250	9
Large : 251–400	8
Total	26

Table 2 School type

Type	No. of schools
LEA Infant	4 (20)
LEA Primary	19 (102)
LEA Welsh-medium (Primary)	1 (10)
Voluntary Aided	2 (10)

Note: The numbers in brackets refer to the LEA's primary/infant schools as a whole.

were obtained by ordering the sizes of all 142 of the LEA's schools and then marking off equal thirds.

Type of School

Table 2 shows the distribution of schools in terms of their type, with the numbers of equivalent schools throughout the LEA in brackets for comparison.

It will be seen from Table 2 that the LEA Welsh-medium primary schools were slightly underrepresented in our sample. Otherwise the distribution of schools seems satisfactory.

Catchment Area

With the aim of obtaining a representative spread of sample schools in terms of their type of catchment area, the LEA was asked to indicate, for each of its schools, whether it served a mainly middle-class, a skilled working-class or lower working-class area. On the basis of this information the sample of twenty-eight schools (subsequently twenty-six) was drawn up so as to reflect the distribution of types of catchment found in the LEA

Table 3 Catchment areas of sample schools

Type of area	*No. of schools*
Mixed middle-class/skilled working-class	17 (113)
Skilled working-class/lower working-class (i.e. semi or unskilled or unemployed)	9 (29)
Total	26 (142)

Note: The figures in brackets refer to the LEA's primary/infant schools as a whole.

schools overall. It should be stressed that the LEA information was based upon the professional knowledge of a senior officer who knew the schools well.

Once the final sample of schools had been selected the headteachers were asked to indicate the nature of their school catchment areas in the same terms as those described above. In the event some of them found difficulty making an objective judgment of the social composition of their areas and it was therefore decided to use a cruder classification as shown in Table 3.

Table 3 shows that the distribution of sample schools in terms of their catchment areas was reasonably representative of that in the LEA as a whole but perhaps with a slight overweighting of schools serving 'lower working-class' catchments. However, given the subjective nature of this information the figures in the table should be regarded with caution. Of the nine schools serving predominantly lower working-class areas five had been designated by the LEA as 'social priority area' schools before that practice was discontinued.

Research Procedure: Aim and Method

The primary aim of the study was to obtain the views of a representative sample of primary headteachers and Year 1 class teachers in the chosen LEA on the impact of the National Curriculum upon the education of 5-year-old children. To achieve this aim we judged that the use of structured interviews, based upon questionnaires, would be the most appropriate research technique. The use of a postal questionnaire would have allowed us access to a much bigger sample but this would have limited the scope of the types of question that we could ask and, more importantly, would have precluded the possibility of probing and elaborating the teachers' initial responses to questions (Oppenheim, 1992). Limited project resources precluded the use of direct observation of teachers and children working in their classrooms, desirable as that would have been as a complementary technique to that of interviewing the teachers. The research team comprised the two co-authors and a part-time research officer who was an experienced primary teacher.

The First Round of Interviews

Separate questionnaires were drawn up for the headteachers and Year 1 class teachers respectively. Year 1 teachers were defined as teachers of all infant classes containing children eligible for Year 1 of the National Curriculum, i.e. between 5 and 6 years of age.

The headteachers' questionnaire (1989) covered the following topics:

- the school and its background;
- organization and staffing;
- home–school links;
- children with special needs/learning difficulties (identification and provision);
- curriculum planning prior to the National Curriculum (including assessment and record keeping;
- preparing for the National Curriculum (curriculum development and INSET);
- anticipated problems in delivering the National Curriculum and its anticipated effects on the teaching of the core subjects and on the teaching of children with special needs;
- support and resources needed.

The class teacher's questionnaire (1989) covered the following topics:

- class composition, classroom organization and staffing;
- curriculum and teaching methods (including assessment and record keeping and the use of free play);

curriculum development and INSET (preparation for teaching the National Curriculum);
anticipated effects of the National Curriculum on the teaching of core subjects and on teaching children with special needs;
anticipated problems in teaching the National Curriculum;
support and resources needed.

In addition to the above questions the questionnaires included a short fourteen-item scale designed to measure teachers' attitudes to the National Curriculum to be completed in writing by the teachers themselves (see Appendix 1). This yielded an overall attitude score but the teachers' responses to each item could also be analysed separately (see Chapter 7 for further details).

Prior to their use in the study both questionnaires were piloted on a small sample of headteachers and class teachers from another LEA. As a result of this exercise some of the original questions were eliminated or rephrased to make them clearer. In addition it was suggested by the pilot sample teachers themselves that, in order to cut down on valuable interview time, the more factual questions could be completed by the teachers before the interview. In accordance with this suggestion the questionnaires were circulated to the sample teachers about two weeks in advance of their interviews with a request for them to complete specified questions in writing beforehand.

The first round of interviewing took place during the summer term of 1989, i.e. the term immediately preceding the introduction of the National Curriculum at Key Stage 1 in September 1989. (A few interviews had to be postponed until the following term.) On average each interview lasted about an hour for headteachers and three-quarters of an hour for class teachers.

The Second Round of Interviews

The second round of interviews took place approximately one year after the first round, during the summer term of 1990, i.e. toward the end of the first year of the implementation of the National Curriculum. The interview questionnaires were closely related to those used in the first round, suitably adapted to take account of the fact that the National Curriculum had been in operation for nearly one year.

The headings of the headteachers' questionnaire were as follows:

general information (updating that obtained in 1989);
children with special needs/learning difficulties (identification and provision);
curriculum planning and INSET under the National Curriculum (including assessment and record keeping);
effects of the National Curriculum on:
curriculum, organization and teaching of the four core subjects,
thematic, cross-curricular work,
teaching children with special needs and under-5s;
views on the impact of the National Curriculum:
preparedness for teaching the National Curriculum,
problems and difficulties experienced,
benefits and disadvantages of the National Curriculum,
further support and resources needed.

The headings for the class teachers' questionnaire were as follows:

class composition, classroom organization and staffing;
curriculum and teaching methods (including assessment and record keeping and the use of free play);
curriculum development and INSET under the National Curriculum;
effects of the National Curriculum on:
curriculum, organization and teaching of the core subjects,
teaching children with special needs and the under-5s;
views on the impact of the National Curriculum:
preparedness for teaching the National Curriculum,
problems and difficulties experienced,
benefits and disadvantages of the National Curriculum,
further support and resources needed.

Table 4 The sample of teachers

	Headteachers	Class teachers	Total
1989 (lst interviews)	26	31	57
1990 (2nd interviews)	24	34	58
1991 (follow-up)	21	31	52

The two sets of questionnaires covering the first year of implementation of the National Curriculum comprised the main body of data for the study. However, during the following year (1990–91) it was decided to ask the participating schools if they would be willing to complete short written follow-up questionnaires concerning the impact of the National Curriculum and their views on it. Nearly all of the schools agreed to do so and the follow-up questionnaires were therefore sent to the participating schools for completion by the headteachers and Year 1 class teachers respectively in the summer term 1991. Each questionnaire (headteachers' and class teachers') contained selected questions from the questionnaires used for the second round of interviews in 1990 plus the short attitude scale. In this way the scope of the study was extended by a further year.

The Sample of Teachers

Table 4 shows the size of the teacher sample for the first and second round of interviews and also for the administration of the written follow-up questionnaire. The questionnaires were completed by the headteachers in the sample schools and the teachers of all infant classes which contained some Year 1 children.

As might be expected there was some turnover in the composition of the class teacher sample over the three occasions on which data were gathered, due to staffing changes within the schools. In contrast the composition of the headteachers sample remained virtually unchanged over the period, apart from five withdrawals from the study owing to pressure of work or retirement. Table 5 shows the extent to which the same teachers were involved in two or more years of the study. These teachers can be thought of as comprising a 'core sample' although they are

Table 5 The 'core sample' of teachers

	Headteachers	*Class teachers*	*Total*
Present in 1989/1990	24	26	50
Present in 1989/1990/1991	21	14	35

only separated out in the analyses of the attitude scale data (see Chapter 7).

A comparison of Tables 4 and 5 shows that the majority of headteachers and class teachers who took part in the first round of interviews in 1989 were also present for the second round of interviews in 1990 but, by 1991, just under half of the original sample of class teachers were still present in the study.

Background Information on the Sample Schools

Background information on the sample schools was provided by the headteachers in the first interview questionnaire completed at the outset of the study. This was updated, where appropriate, in the second interview questionnaire completed in 1990. In addition some information about home–school links was provided by the class teachers in their questionnaires.

General information

Of the twenty-six schools four operated on the 'open plan' system with free access between open teaching areas. Twenty-one schools had nursery classes attached to them which were mostly attended by 3 to 4-year-old children on a half-time basis. In the smallest schools four of the headteachers had full teaching responsibility for a class although they received some teaching support to enable them to carry out their headship duties. Of the remaining twenty-two headteachers twelve stated that they regularly engaged in some form of teaching (ten in 1990).

The status of Welsh in the schools

In twenty-two of the twenty-six schools Welsh was a non-core subject in the National Curriculum. In the remaining four schools it was a core subject which meant that the children attending these schools would be tested in Welsh rather than English at the end of Key Stage 1. Of the latter schools one was a designated Welsh-medium school while the remainder used a combination of English and Welsh for teaching purposes.

Classroom Organization and Staffing

Regarding the location of the Year 1 children, in seventeen classes they were taught in single age group 'I1' classes for 5 to 6-year-olds. In the remaining thirteen classes they were taught in combination with one or more other age groups. (Information was missing for one class teacher.)

In 1989 only eight of the headteachers reported that their infant teachers engaged in any form of team teaching and nine in 1990. This mainly appeared to take the form of combining classes for certain practical activities such as music and drama, but also Welsh, in order to capitalize upon the expertise of particular members of staff.

Of the twenty-two primary schools, eleven had a teacher with designated responsibility for the infants department but the remainder did not and this situation did not change in 1990. Four of the headteachers stated that the curriculum for infant children was planned separately from that for juniors but, by 1990, this number had dropped to two.

On the question of pattern of infant classroom organization the majority of headteachers stated either that they recommended a pattern to the class teacher, e.g. an 'integrated day', but left the final choice to her or him, or they expected the infant teacher to decide on their own preferred pattern.

In 1989 nearly half of the primary head teachers (ten) claimed that the pattern of infant classroom organization was different from that in the junior department, referring to such features as their greater informality and their more practical, play based approach. Other differences mentioned were the use of the integrated day pattern of organization in infant classes and the fact that in some cases they contained mixed age groups. However, by 1990 the number of schools where the pattern of classroom organization was described as different had dropped to five. This could possibly be a reflection of academic and other pressures exerted upon the schools' infant departments but this is speculative.

Children with Special Needs and Learning Difficulties

In 1989 nine headteachers reported having one or more children in their infant departments with statements of special need, with most of the classes involved having only one such pupil. One headteacher commented that the policy of the LEA seemed to be not to issue formal statements in respect of children under 7.[1] In 1990 there were six statemented children at the infant stage but eleven headteachers stated that they were planning to refer particular children with a view to their being statemented. Again it is possible that this reflected a change in the educational climate in some schools following the introduction of the National Curriculum and other changes stemming from the ERA.

Regarding school procedures for the early detection of children's learning difficulties seventeen headteachers reported that these were based upon teacher observation and discussion with other staff, including the headteacher, and eleven headteachers mentioned discussion with or referral to the district educational psychologist. Only six headteachers mentioned specifically that any cases of learning difficulty would be discussed with the parents, although this does not necessarily mean that the other headteachers would not have done so.

By the the following year (1990) the detection procedures appeared to have changed very little but one headteacher reported the appointment of a member of staff as a coordinator for special needs who would prepare a written policy document on the school's provision for special needs. (Hitherto very few primary schools within this LEA appeared to have made such appointments but this situation was beginning to change with the appointment of a new county adviser for special needs.) In 1989 only two headteachers reported that their schools had produced written guidelines on their policies concerning children's special needs and in 1990 this number had increased by one with another two headteachers stating their intention of producing them.

The children in the sample schools with statements of

special educational need would, of course have received special provision and support as of right. On the question of support for non-statemented children with learning difficulties, twenty-one headteachers reported that some form of support teaching was available in addition to any extra help that the class teacher managed to offer. The support teachers typically worked with small groups of children with learning difficulties, either within the children's classrooms or by withdrawing them or by a combination of these arrangements.

Parental Involvement

The headteachers were asked whether parents were encouraged by the school to help in the education of their children and, if so, in what ways. As might be expected all of them stated that they encouraged parental involvement, particularly in the area of children's reading and language skills. In addition some schools set the children homework (but not necessarily for infant pupils) and encouraged the parents to support their children in doing this. Many of the schools were operating within a LEA organized scheme aimed at directly involving parents in the development of their children's reading skills. Under this scheme, known as 'Children and Parents Enjoy Reading' (CAPER), the LEA provided the participating schools with attractive reading books for the children to take home to read with their parents on a regular basis. In addition it provided advisory support for schools taking part in the scheme. (See also Chapter 11.)

The headteachers were also asked if parents assisted directly in the work of the school. Well over half of them (fifteen) reported that they did so and another three headteachers planned for their parents to do so. Parental contributions included assistance in the school library, accompanying children on school trips and assistance in practical curricular activities such as cooking, art and craft. Only five headteachers mentioned any parental involvement in the teaching of the core subjects, such as listening to children reading or assisting in science work.

The class teachers were also asked whether the parents were involved in the teaching of the core subjects either at home or at school. The majority of teachers reported that the parents listened to their children reading at home, although with varying frequency. A few teachers mentioned some problems in this respect such as the non-return of school reading books loaned by the school to the parents, or lack of parental interest in such involvement despite the school's encouragement.

In reply to a question concerning the parents' direct involvement in the teaching of core subjects at school twenty teachers indicated that parents were not involved, although some parents assisted in non-core classroom activities such as art or cookery. Only six teachers stated that parents were involved directly in children's core curricular activities. Their involvement ranged from listening to children reading; assisting the teacher in maths or reading; helping in the teaching of Welsh (Welsh speaking parents); and supporting a specific core subject activity if requested by the teacher.

In summary all of the schools claimed to have a policy of encouraging parents to be actively involved in the development of their children's reading skills at home but parental assistance within the school, when it occurred, appeared to be confined to non-core curricular activities in all but a few schools.

The Sample Teachers and Their Classes

The following information on the Year 1 infant classes was provided by the teachers through the questionnaires which they completed in 1989 and 1990.

Class size and age range

In 1989 the majority of the teachers (twenty-one) reported class sizes of between twenty and thirty pupils, with seven having smaller classes and three having larger classes. The distribution was similar in 1990. Regarding age range, over half of the teachers (seventeen) had classes containing only Year 1 children, i.e. 5 to 6-year-olds; seven had classes of 4 to 6-year-olds (i.e. Reception and Year 1 children); three had classes of 5 to 7-year-olds, and three had classes of 4 to 7-year-olds. (Information was missing for one teacher in the sample.) The distribution was similar in 1990.

The majority of classes (twenty-six in both 1989 and 1990) consisted solely of children whose first language was English and only five classes (six in 1990) contained some children with a different mother tongue. (Half of the latter children were Welsh-speaking and the remainder spoke one of a range of languages from Europe, the Middle East or the Indian subcontinent.)

Range of children's abilities

The teachers were asked to indicate the range of abilities shown by their children in respect of mathematics and language. In both subjects the range was very wide. For example, in English, children's levels of reading ranged from the recognition of just a few words to reading fluently with good comprehension. In mathematics (number) the range covered little or no recognition of written number to competence in addition and subtraction to 20, or even 100. The skill range would no doubt be wider in those classes with a wider age range.

Children with special needs

In 1989 five teachers reported having a child in their class with a statement of special need but there appeared to be only one such case in 1990. However a much larger number of teachers in both years claimed to have children in their classes with suspected special educational needs (nineteen teachers in 1989 and twenty-two teachers in 1990). The main problems associated with such needs were speech and language or reading difficulties, generally slow progress, difficulties in vision or hearing, or behaviour difficulties, sometimes linked with social immaturity.

Method of classroom organization

The teachers were asked to indicate which of the three following patterns of organizing classroom activities they used:

Pattern 1: Whole class engaged in the same curriculum activity (maths, language, etc.) at the same time, whether working in groups or individually, and switched to another common activity at the teacher's direction;

Pattern 2: Class divided into fixed groups and each group worked on a different curriculum activity from other

Table 6 Regular support for the class teacher

Type of support	1989 (N=31)	1990 (N=34)
None	5	10
Qualified helper (e.g. nursery nurse)	9	10
Unqualified helper (e.g. parent)	7	6
Other teacher (e.g. support teacher)	10	12
Student teacher	1	2
Secondary school pupil	10	7

groups (e.g. one group worked on maths, another on writing, etc.);

Pattern 3: Individual decisions were made on each activity time, either by the child or the teacher as to which particular activity the child will engage in.

In 1989 four teachers used Pattern 1, seven used Pattern 2 and the remaining teachers used a combination of the above patterns. One teacher, for example, stated that the whole class might be engaged in the same curriculum activity which might then be followed by 'integrated groups'. A similar distribution emerged in 1990 except that only one teacher claimed to be using Pattern 1 and one teacher used Pattern 3.

Teacher support

The teachers were asked what regular forms of classroom support they received. Their responses are summarized in Table 6.

The total numbers in Table 6 exceed the total number of teachers since each teacher might record more than one form of support. It will be noted that the number of teachers apparently without a regular form of classroom support was five in 1989 and ten in 1990.

Team teaching

The teachers were asked if they engaged in any form of team teaching or shared teaching. In 1989 ten teachers reported that they did and this number rose to sixteen in 1990. The forms of collaboration ranged from the complete sharing of combined classes by two or more teachers, to lesson sharing with other teachers for the more specialized subjects such as music or physical education. In addition, some teachers referred to their collaboration with other teachers in curriculum planning and organization, including the planning of cross-curricular topics.

Note

1 This may have been due to pressures of work on the LEA's team of educational psychologists. The LEA carried out an annual screening survey of the basic attainments of all 7-year-old children in order to identify those with possible special needs/learning difficulties.

Summary

The Schools

On the basis of the objective data provided in this chapter we consider that our sample of schools was representative of the infant and primary schools within this particular LEA with regard to their size (number of pupils on roll), type (infant or primary, voluntary or state maintained), and type of social catchment area. The schools ranged in size from small village schools, where Year 1 pupils were taught in classes containing two or even three age groups, to large urban schools with single age group classes. Amongst the smaller schools were some where the headteacher had teaching responsibility for a class. Nearly all of the schools in the sample had a nursery class or classes attached to them.

The Classes

Most of the classes taught by the Year 1 teachers in the sample contained between twenty and thirty children. Their age ranged from four to seven years but over half of the classes contained only Year 1 children (five to six-year-olds). The range of the children's attainments in the basic skills was wide: at one extreme there were children with virtually no formal attainments in reading writing or number, and at the other, there were children whose attainments were well above average for their age. Although only a handful of children had formal statements of special educational need well over half of the teachers in the sample judged that their classes contained children with some form of special need with regard to their academic progress, general development or behaviour.

The majority of teachers appeared to use some form of 'integrated day' pattern of classroom organization, i.e., where groups of children work concurrently on different curricular activities, as well as other patterns of organization at certain times. Most teachers received some form of classroom assistance but less than one-third received help from a qualified worker. Between one-half and one-third of teachers engaged in some form of team teaching.

The Research Enquiry

The research procedure was based upon structured personal interviews carried out with the headteachers and Year 1 class teachers during the summer term immediately preceding the introduction of the National Curriculum at Key Stage 1 in September 1989. The teachers were reinterviewed approximately one year later, in the summer of 1990. In addition a short follow-up enquiry was carried out in the summer of 1991 by means of a written questionnaire. On the basis of these interviews the teachers' predictions of the impact of the National Curriculum on a variety of aspects of the schools' curricula, methods of classroom organization, teaching and assessment could be compared with their subsequent judgments of its actual impact. Also the nature and content of the INSET received by the teachers, or considered to be needed by them, could be compared before and after the introduction of the National Curriculum, as well as their needs for staffing and resourcing. Finally, changes in the teachers' general attitudes to the National Curriculum, and their views towards particular aspects of it could be compared over the period of the study. The results from all of these comparisons are presented in the next five chapters.

Chapter 3

Preparing for the National Curriculum

Introduction

In the past new curriculum initiatives have, in the main, come through the development of materials for classroom use, e.g. the development of software for mathematics by the SMILE project[1] or the coming together of enthusiastic teachers to disseminate 'good practice', e.g. the area groups run under the auspices of the Nuffield Mathematics Trust. In the secondary schools changes have also been driven by new examination syllabuses, of which the General Certificate of Secondary Education (GCSE) is a recent example. With the introduction of the National Curriculum, perhaps for the first time, changes were now to be driven by legislation. What should or could be provided to ensure that the legislation would be translated into classroom practice?

The rhetoric prior to the introduction of the National Curriculum emphasized the autonomy of the teacher to decide *how* to teach the content that would be laid down by it. It would have been incongruous for materials to have been developed centrally since the politics of privatization and insistence on market driven competition prevalent in government at that time would not had sat comfortably with the provision of official classroom materials. (Work on assessment was put out to tender, which might have been an option for curriculum materials too.) Publishers were extremely quick to produce textbooks and materials supposedly in line with National Curriculum directives, although on closer scrutiny, the early revisions appeared to have been in the main new covers and new publicity.

What fitted with the notion of the autonomous teacher was the notion of 'empowering' INSET in which the teachers' professional knowledge was valued, developed and shared with others. The 'cascade' model that had been tried and found varying success with the Technical and Vocational Education Initiative (TVEI) and with GCSE was used again in many local education authorities (LEAs). Curriculum 'specialists' attended INSET of varying lengths and returned to school to lead the implementation of the National Curriculum. HMI (DES, 1991: 10) appraising this INSET subsequently reported that 'Too little attention was given to training key people to be trainers of others.' The time scale of the production, the various subject documents and the costs of such INSET were obviously strong factors in the LEA's prioritization. Some subjects were familiar in the curriculum and also within typical LEA advisory support structures. Mathematics for example had received substantial funding in the post-Cockcroft days of the mid-1980s; others traditionally received less support, such as Welsh in non-traditionally Welsh-speaking areas or little support in the primary phase, such as Technology. Existing support structures and lead time in setting up new structures and new costs would be factors in the prioritization of LEA INSET programmes.

However the National Curriculum was not just about content. The second main prong, and to some extent the fundamental new element that was pedagogically difficult for teachers of younger pupils, was the notion of formalized and reported assessment procedures. Not only would the pupils be judged, but the politicians spoke of weeding out weak teachers and of parental choice as a result of league tables, leading to the running down of 'below standard' schools.

Satisfied that they were not going to be told *how* to teach and that the *what* would not necessarily be vastly different from current work, teachers' anxieties clustered around the assessment procedures (details of our findings appear in the next chapter). The preparation of teachers would need to allay these fears if only to contain the ground swell of resistance to the formal testing of 7-year-olds that followed the announcements.

The LEA Programme

Despite the fact that the next few years were to see the erosion of the powers of LEAs by the government, the onus of the preparation for the National Curriculum fell on them. Some provision was made centrally, for example, by those commissioned to produce assessment materials but with the purpose that 'trained' LEA representatives would do the subsequent work within the locality. Provision was split between assessment and individual subjects. Table 7 gives a brief description of the INSET programme devised by the LEA from which our research sample of schools was drawn.

Individual school programmes
In addition to the LEA-run INSET and the subsequent cascade, many schools used non-contact time to work on the implementation of the National Curriculum. Often these sessions were run totally in-house but from time to time there would be input from an outside agency such as the local university or higher education institution.

Written guidance
In addition to the INSET programme indicated above, schools also had access to a wide range of written materials. These varied from those produced centrally in England (DES) and those produced in Wales (CCW, Welsh Office) to those produced by the LEA and in some instances, those produced in-house by the school or cluster of schools.

An LEA Rationale

One of the LEA primary advisors, with particular responsibility for early years' education, was interviewed in a mostly non-structured way to unpick the LEA thinking behind the programme of INSET that was provided between 1988 and 1992. She was interviewed in 1989, 1990 and 1991. Documentation was also collected from the LEA.

The LEA had produced a series of policy statements that covered both the teaching of individual subjects and the ideology of primary school teaching in the eighteen months prior to 1989. With the arrival of the National Curriculum the LEA view was that 'the National Curriculum should fit in with the LEA policy

Table 7 LEA INSET programme 1988–1992

1988–1989

* Seminars for headteachers. 35 headteachers per day.

* Spring Term: Core subjects 2 representatives per school. Curriculum specialist and one other. 1 had to be an infant teacher. 2 days per subject.

* Headteachers' conference focussing on Thematic approaches.

1989–1990

* Programme informed by information gathered by visits by advisory team to every school in the LEA. Focus on assessment. 20 Headteachers are seconded part time in Autumn Term to develop INSET for Spring Term.

* Spring Term: Teaching of core subjects to rising 5-year olds. 2 by 1 workshops for 75 teachers (total 150).

1990–1991

* National Curriculum Assessment for all primary school teachers. 3 by 1 days during Autumn and Spring Terms. Topics: Teacher Assessment, Record Keeping, Standard Assessment Tasks.

* Design and Technology. 2 teachers from each school. 3 by 1 days.

* History and geography. 2 teachers from each school. 2 by 1 days.

* Welsh

* Headteachers' meetings. Schools grouped by LEA into clusters. Meetings led by a primary advisor.

1991–1992

* Sessions for music, art and PE. 2 teachers from each school.

* Number of staff development days increased from 3 to 6 because of need for training in use of SATs and teacher assessment.

and not the other way round!' The cascade model was to be used. There was a commitment to continuity and progression with staff development days on the LEA documents being run jointly for primary and secondary schools. The message from the LEA to the schools, was 'It is not going to be right at the start — it will be a question of trial and error and we will all learn and benefit from hindsight and experience.'

The Effectiveness of the Support

The purpose of the INSET programmes was to prepare the teachers and the schools for the smoothest implementation of the National Curriculum possible. In order to consider how successful this programme was, headteachers and class teachers in our research sample were asked questions about the preparation they received and how prepared they felt as a result.

The success of the programmes is evaluated in terms of how the teachers felt rather than how they performed. Neither is it evaluated in terms of the teachers' comments about individual courses or tutors. The outcomes of the INSET concern us here.

The Headteachers' Views

In 1989 the headteachers were asked how well prepared they thought they and their staff were for the introduction of the National Curriculum for 5-year-olds in the next September. Under one-third felt well prepared. The large majority, nearly three-quarters, felt fairly well prepared and only one respondent felt poorly prepared. Whether this was due to good INSET provision or blissful ignorance remained to be seen.

> There is much enthusiasm on the part of staff which is tinged with apprehension!

Reasons for feeling well prepared included a notion of 'it's only what we are doing anyway'.

School is already running along the lines required by the National Curriculum.

Our last seven years have been good preparation!

Our existing methodology and approach is comparable to that which will be required.

We have tried to prepare ourselves over the past two years with the information available to us.

In the main it's an extension of the practice which should be going on.

There were also strong indications of being overwhelmed with material from all sources. The LEA produced materials, while considered to be of good quality, added to this feeling.

The cascade of material from DES, LEA and other advisory/statutory bodies is overwhelming.

Not enough time has been given to absorb, assimilate and evaluate.

What is due to come in may make all [our] planning out of date. [It's been] too much too quickly.

There was also a feeling that the issues concerning infant education had not really been tackled. This was not an uncommon feeling amongst teachers of younger pupils. They often reported that their area was overlooked.

Not enough time has been given to developing the infant element in the curriculum.

There has been little opportunity for infant teachers to get together to discuss problems.

The special problems of a small school were also highlighted.

[All] the work has to be spread between three people and this puts extra pressure on them.

By 1990 the headteachers were reporting a shift in confidence. Whereas three-quarters had felt only fairly well prepared now nearly one-half said they were well prepared, with the rest feeling fairly well prepared.

One headteacher reported that

> The staff are moving slowly along the path. Change cannot be enforced — it has to happen gently. [It is a] gradual process to build up to the National Curriculum.

Another headteacher reported that the staff now had a greater awareness and familiarity with the documents and was therefore able to put them into perspective a little, and that this had helped with future planning

In 1991 confidence dropped with only one-third of headteachers reporting that they were well prepared for the next year. Two-thirds reported feeling fairly well prepared commenting in particular on the proposed further changes to the mathematics and science orders.

Headteachers were also asked what additional INSET they felt was necessary both for themselves and for the class teachers. This gives us an indication of their notions of readiness. There was a wide range of needs suggested with many headteachers citing unique needs. However nearly half the headteachers mentioned training in assessment and record keeping for both themselves and their teachers.

How true a picture did the headteachers have of their schools' readiness and needs? We next looked at how the class teachers felt about their own preparation.

The Teachers' Views

The class teachers questioned in 1989 had similar feelings to the headteachers. Under one-third felt well prepared; around three-quarters felt fairly well prepared and only one felt poorly prepared. This was not in the same school as the headteacher who felt poorly prepared.

By 1990 half of classteachers were feeling well prepared with the rest fairly well prepared. Nearly one-third were feeling much better prepared than the year before and two-thirds felt better prepared. Reasons given for this were predictably to do with familiarity and having had personal experience or having learnt from the personal experience of a colleague. There had also been a building up of resources and opportunities within courses and school based activities for planning.

By 1991, as with the headteachers, there was an apparent drop in confidence. Now just over one-third rather than one-half of class teachers reported feeling well prepared. Why should this have been? Between 1989 and 1990 the subjects that had been introduced were mathematics, science and English. Between 1990 and 1991 technology and Welsh were introduced. It may have been that these subjects were 'newer' in many respects than the earlier ones and this had led to the drop in confidence. The original orders in mathematics, science and English were already under review. Teachers may have felt that their efforts towards competency in those subjects were wasted. It may have been that teachers could see that soon more subjects (history and geography) would be added and that they would need to tackle an ever-broadening curriculum. It could have been that the adverse comments of politicians and the media left teachers feeling inadequately prepared for their teaching role in general. Whatever the cause, the drop in the level of confidence about preparation for teaching the National Curriculum was worrying.

Perceived Additional Needs

Headteachers and class teachers were also asked what support and resources they needed to implement the orders.

1989: Headteachers

In 1989 headteachers saw human resources as being most important. Equipment was the next priority with emphasis given to science equipment. Although calculators and computers were specifically mentioned in the mathematics orders only two headteachers mentioned them specifically. While this is not too surprising given the prominence given to computers within the LEA, there had been no marked adoption of calculators. The LEA had not been part of the Primary Initiatives in Mathematics Project (PRIME)[2] and there appeared to be marginal use of calculators in many schools. While six schools had computers available in every classroom and eight schools reported that they were in regular use, only two schools were using calculators regularly in mathematics lessons.

Support from LEA advisory staff was also seen as desirable by eight headteachers. Rather surprisingly in retrospect, the need for more time to carry out the tasks required by the National Curriculum was only mentioned by two headteachers.

1989: Class teachers

The class teachers placed strong emphasis on both human resources and equipment. In particular the extra human resources were seen in terms of supporting the assessment process.

> Can teachers teach and assess simultaneously?

> . . . teaching support especially for assessment with split age classes.

In fact assessment and record keeping featured strongly.

> More time for assessment and record keeping.

> More support and training for assessment and record keeping in all areas.

> Tape recorders for taping children for assessment.

Technology, science and Welsh received specific mention alongside support for the teaching of the core subjects in terms of INSET, advisory teacher support and specialized equipment.

1990: Headteachers

In 1990 the emphasis had shifted away from human resources towards equipment. Once again science equipment was in most demand with technology now overtaking mathematics as the second need. INSET in Welsh, technology and assessment were mentioned as was continued support from the LEA advisory staff in terms of school based and centrally based INSET. There was still little interest in extra calculators or computers. However eleven schools reported change in their use of calculators compared with five reporting a change in their use of computers.

1990: Class teachers

In 1990 sixteen teachers specifically mentioned the need for 'an extra pair of hands' in the classroom. This was not specifically for the assessment procedures. Several teachers mentioned working with small groups. It appears that differentiation was now taking place and that teachers felt that children needed more individual teaching in order to 'achieve the ATs' (attainment targets).

Equipment for technology and computers received specific mention but once again it was the need for equipment for science (in particular expendable resources) that predominated.

Advisory support was seen as desirable but in terms of advice and discussion rather than criticism or written documentation.

Once again the need for specific support with the teaching of Welsh received mention.

1991: Headteachers

By 1991 the human resource emphasis had returned. The need was seen in terms of the classroom (pupil/teacher ratio, adult help, non-contact time) and in support from the LEA.

> [We need] more help from the advisers; [they are] rarely seen in schools today.

> This school seriously needs additional support at infant level in basic subjects.

> [We need] advisory school based support for foundation [non-core] studies.

> Support [is] needed from advisors [and] advisory teachers to come to school to give encouragement to staff and help when needed.

Now that the assessments were being carried out a need was seen for extra staffing and time to allow for this.

> Teacher support for Y2 teacher [is needed] so that they can conduct the teacher assessment more fairly on a one to one basis and when involved in small group tasks.

> [An] additional teacher [is] required during SATs.

> Non-contact time to teach and assess individuals and small groups of children.

However there was still a need for other resources. What was noticeable was a new emphasis on money.

> A strong injection of cash would be appreciated!

> More money! We cannot buy new materials to implement all the new work developing from the National Curriculum.

> This year we have had to provide money from school funds to get books from the prescribed booklist for reading.

There were also pleas for time.

> [We need] time to consider where we are, what needs to be done and where we are going. After school is not the answer.

> [I need time] to digest all the new documents to enable me [headteacher] to support staff.

1991: Classteachers

Once again there was a strong need for human support within the classroom. Sometimes this was of the 'extra pair of hands' variety, sometimes it was in terms of smaller classes. This need was both to help with the teaching as well as to allow the assessment procedures to be undertaken. Welsh once again received specific mention for advisory teacher support and courses. The teachers too mentioned money in a way that they had not done before. Science equipment was again mentioned. Teachers also saw a need for books for teachers as well as pupils, particularly for non-core subjects.

One class teacher said that there was never enough money for the resources that were required in every subject. Another said that her school was well equipped both in human and material resources. It is not clear whether this was a difference in expectations or that the schools were in fact differently resourced.

Conclusions

The report by HMI (England) on in-service training for the introduction of the National Curriculum 1988–90 comments

> By the end of the report period the majority of teachers were better informed and more confident about implementing the core subjects of the National Curriculum. However, anxieties about assessment, recording and reporting were largely undiminished. The teachers' training needs changed once they had started to implement the National Curriculum by becoming more specifically related to the difficulties they were encountering. (DES, 1991: 9)

Barber and Graham (1993) attribute the substantial degree of success with which the National Curriculum has been implemented in part to LEAs.

> One [reason] is that LEAs, on the whole, have provided effective assistance, support and training to schools, yet their continued existence remains doubtful. All the evaluations of National Curriculum implementation are strongly positive about the role of the LEAs, and particularly their advisory or curriculum support teachers, have played. (Barber and Graham, 1993: 14)

This reflects the overall findings of the research project.

The initial feelings that teachers had of being overwhelmed with information were somewhat alleviated as it became apparent that the subject orders were not going to arrive simultaneously. We believe that it was the subsequent revision of the core subjects of mathematics and science that led to a drop in confidence.

Initially the requests for more resources were often tied in with concerns over the management of the assessment procedures. As these became more familiar the required resources were to do with aspects of the curriculum such as calculators for mathematics. Class teachers still looked for extra pairs of hands to help with wider aspects of teaching than formal assessment procedures. As might have been expected the particular subjects highlighted by teachers changed as new subject orders came on line. Emphasis on money increased as schools became more familiar with the implications of local financial management.

Teachers articulated concerns about assessment and record keeping in our research. This was also reported by Bennett *et al.* (1992) and Broadfoot *et al.* (1991a). These findings raise a number of questions regarding assessment including the following:

- Were their concerns partly fuelled by the emphasis that the LEA placed on assessment by focusing on INSET for this or was the LEA responding to the teachers' needs?
- What role did the emphasis in the media and by the politicians of the need for accountability and the role of the National Curriculum in raising standards play?
- How new was the notion of a formal assessment procedure to primary school teachers and, in particular, teachers of the rising 5-year-olds?

- Where did the emphasis lie between teacher assessment and the more formal SATs?

The fact that the LEA did focus much of the early INSET on the assessment side of the National Curriculum may in part account for the fact that the teachers reported feeling to some extent prepared in that area.

The next chapter which examines the teaching of the core subjects reports a strong feeling that it was in assessment and record keeping that most change took place.

Notes

1 SMILE was a mathematics curriculum development project set up in 1972 by the Inner London Education Authority.

2 The Primary Initiatives in Mathematics Education was a Schools Curriculum Development Committee (during the course of the project the work of this committee was taken over by the National Curriculum Council) funded project that ran from 1985 to 1989 and was based at Homerton College, Cambridge. It was directed by the late Hilary Shuard.

Chapter 4

Teaching The National Curriculum

Introduction

This chapter reports some effects of the structure and content of the National Curriculum on the teaching at Key Stage 1. Although traditionally there has been some discrete subject teaching in the primary school even at Key Stage 1 (mathematics, music and PE for example) there has been a strong emphasis on the teaching of themes and topics without subject boundaries. Within the LEA in which we did our research the advisory service held a strong commitment to such an approach. Although not all teachers embraced the approach with equal enthusiasm, often because the message was picked up as the dogmatic interpretation that everything should be taught through the thematic approach, there was an overall sympathy with cross-curricular teaching. A concern voiced early on in the life of the National Curriculum was the effect that single-subject orders might have on such approaches. It was obvious to us that this should be a focus of our research.

The choice of science as a core subject alongside English (or Welsh) and mathematics, while not particularly controversial, was a change in emphasis. This then led us to another important area for research.

Class Teachers and the Core Subjects[1]

This section considers the class teachers' views first because they were actively involved with the day to day teaching. Headteachers' views are considered later as their responses may be seen to be also concerned with policy and informed by a variety of elements as well as personal experience. There are also more comments from class teachers than headteachers. This reflects the results of the interviews.

In 1989 the teachers were asked questions about the planning, organization, assessment and record keeping of various subjects. They were then asked to predict the effects of the National Curriculum in mathematics, English, Welsh and science. We were interested in particular in how they thought their day to day class-based work would be affected. We asked them specific questions about thematic and cross-curricular work. In 1990 the class teachers were in general asked the same questions again but this time they were asked to reflect on the effects that the National Curriculum had had on their work. A comparison of their projections and reflections follows.

In 1989 class teachers felt that the greatest impact of the National Curriculum would come in the areas of record keeping and assessment. This was fairly consistent across the subjects with mathematics and science being seen as likely to be marginally more affected than English and Welsh. In science and Welsh the message was that teachers were expecting major change. However in English and mathematics there was little difference between the numbers of teachers expecting minor change and those expecting a more substantial change. If we think about the traditional role of English and mathematics in our English-medium primary schools this is understandable. The time and energy put into record keeping focused on the 'Basics', the three Rs, in other words English and mathematics. The approach to science and Welsh was less formal, less firmly structured and hence there was less emphasis on assessment and record keeping.

> Assessment and record keeping of science has been very informal and sketchy in the past.
>
> We have no real science assessment at the present.
>
> Records [in science] will need to be more detailed and individual.
>
> Very little [science] is recorded at present.

> The main change will be in assessment and record keeping since it is so difficult to assess science with infants — so much depends on the teacher's knowledge of individual children — I fear that these professional skills may be lost if everything has to be formally recorded.

With Welsh the trend seemed to be very informal with four teachers stating that no written records were kept at present. Five teachers reported that there was no Welsh for infants at all.

> Time allocation to Welsh is very haphazard at present.

> There will be lots of change overall since the approach has always been rather vague.

Reflecting in 1990 the teachers felt that the impact had been less than they had envisaged in all subjects but particularly so in science and Welsh. Eighteen teachers reported that record keeping and assessment in Welsh still needed to be developed as no formal records were kept. This obviously had not been prioritized as a task and therefore the teachers had not noticed a change. It appears that the main energies were put into the development of science teaching with seventeen teachers reporting more (time being spent on?) science teaching than before and hence there was less impact on the other subjects than teachers had envisaged.

However in mathematics nine teachers reported that assessment and record keeping had changed and was now more detailed. One teacher speculated

> I wonder what more this detail really tells you about a child's progress?

Two teachers reported that they had always kept detailed records of mathematics and these had been easy to adapt for the National Curriculum.

In English the emphasis appeared to be on an increase in record keeping.

The changes in record keeping varied from subject to

subject. In English and mathematics where records may have been kept in the past they were now more detailed and directly related to the National Curriculum attainment targets. In science and Welsh, where it was much less likely that records had been kept, formal detailed records were developed.

Assessment became more formalized and detailed with teachers anticipating the style of the standardized assessment tasks that would be introduced in 1989/90. Teachers were quite used to assessing pupils' performance in some areas of English and mathematics. The same was not true for science or second language Welsh. The teachers would have to transfer skills developed in assessing reading, arithmetic etc., to the assessment of communication, using and applying mathematics, etc. as well as to science and Welsh.

In 1989 teachers had envisaged that their classroom organization and teaching methods would only change in a minor way or not at all and this was what they felt had happened when asked to reflect in 1990. When reporting what type of changes had taken place, teachers tended to comment on the allocation of time to different subjects and to some slight adjustment of methods to include more practical work.

> I am now doing more practical work in science hence there has been some change in organization, time spent and teaching methods.
>
> In order to fit in the science some of the maths [*sic*] time has been reduced.
>
> . . . more time spent on practical activities [in mathematics] hence a change in teaching methods and organization — it takes more time to organize and carry out.
>
> To be meaningful science needs to be done in small groups; this takes more time.
>
> Plenty of practical work has always been school policy.
>
> There's been no real change in time or methods.

When it came to considering the curriculum in terms of content and time allocation the teachers had envisaged minor or no changes in English and mathematics with more change in science and major changes in Welsh.

> We will need more time for core subjects to cover the work.

> We will need more time for observing throughout the year.

> I'm recording everything at present due to the fact that I'm unsure what is expected. Eventually I will know what to record/what not to record.

In 1990 more teachers felt there had been changes in English and mathematics and even more in science. In Welsh fewer had perceived a change than had been expecting it. Once again this suggests to us that the energies had focused on science.

In 1989 there was a tendency for teachers to think that they would not have to change their teaching methods — although they were split equally between no change and some change in the teaching of English. A third were expecting change in mathematics.

> More investigative work will have to take place than at present — this is bound to affect the teaching of mathematics.

> More practical work, more problem solving [AT1 and 8].

A third were expecting major changes in the teaching of science and Welsh. Up to then Welsh appears to have been taught informally or by visiting teachers.

In 1990 very few teachers reported major changes in their teaching methods. This contrasts with the findings of the Primary Assessment Curriculum and Experience (PACE) team. In 1990 45 per cent of their teachers perceived some loss of autonomy over teaching methods. However nearly half felt no change in their freedom to select teaching methods. (Osborn *et al.* 1993)

In Welsh nearly two-thirds reported no change at all. The changes that were reported were in the area of planning.

> The only changes will be to include all attainment targets when planning — a great deal of Welsh is done cross-curricularly already.

In science over a third of the teachers reported some change but over another third reported no change. The reported changes were an increase in practical work and more detailed planning.

> Every child does practical work for every experiment. Previously the class teacher may have demonstrated and the children observed.

> The class teacher needs to be more aware and plan in more detail.

In mathematics nearly one-half felt that they had made no changes at all with an identical number reporting some change. Those changes too mentioned practical work.

> . . . more practical work now — everything else has just been altered slightly to meet the National Curriculum requirements.

> I now do more games, discussions and investigational work.

> There's more discussion before and after the activity now.

In English nearly one-half reported some change with just over one-third reporting no change. The changes in English teaching were more varied than those reported above. The comments reported below give a flavour of that variety.

Nothing drastic!

. . . more time on drama and listening skills.

. . . not as structured as it was.

With a split class [mixed age] I feel I'm pushing them further to meet the attainment targets.

The school has decided to drop the reading scheme so all the work is now centred on the topic.

. . . much more language work based on picture books.

The class teachers were contacted again in 1991. They were asked to comment on any problems or difficulties they had experienced in the implementation of the National Curriculum in the same four subjects. Four out of five teachers reported no difficulties or problems in implementing English. A very large majority also reported no problems or difficulties with the implementation of the mathematics National Curriculum but two teachers mentioned that they felt that there was too much to cover in-depth in the time available. However over one-third reported some problems or difficulties with the implementation of the science curriculum.

Two teachers felt that some attainment targets, e.g. AT 10 Level 3 (*sic*) were not easily achievable.

Some of the attainment targets were difficult for children to understand.

Four teachers reported a lack of equipment and five teachers felt there were too many attainment targets.

There are too many attainment targets to cover them in any depth.

There are too many attainment targets to ensure depth as well as breadth.

Some non-Welsh speaking class teachers (six) made comments about their own deficiencies such as:

> I'm not very good but I'm learning.
>
> As a non-Welsh speaker it is difficult to extend the children's vocabulary or their fluency or sentence construction.
>
> I'm relying on the peripatetic teacher too much.
>
> I'm English born and bred!

Despite this very nearly all teachers reported no problems or difficulties with implementing the Welsh curriculum.

It appears that three years into the National Curriculum teachers had found the implementation of English, mathematics and science less problematic than they had envisaged at first. This perhaps supports the NCC's 'teething problems' theory (NCC, 1993a: 7). Non-Welsh speakers felt that they were struggling somewhat with the Welsh but this is understandable given their lack of knowledge and skill.

The Headteachers' Views

The headteachers were asked in 1989 to predict the effects of the National Curriculum in each of the four core subjects. As with the class teachers the headteachers were expecting the biggest change to be in connection with Welsh but when they reflected in 1990 it was in science that they had perceived the greatest change. Overall it was with record keeping and assessment that they were consistently expecting the most changes and in 1990 it was with record keeping and assessment of science and Welsh that the headteachers felt there had been the greatest changes. There were also changes in record keeping in English and mathematics but there was more of a balance/spread as to the extent of the change. There was much less change reported in the curriculum, class organization and teaching methods in Welsh and

English. The responses in mathematics were more or less balanced between no change and some change. In science the emphasis was towards some change with much change in the curriculum being more commonly reported. Other than in science, headteachers observed less change in the curriculum than they had expected in 1989.

With English nearly two-thirds of the headteachers were expecting no change in classroom organization with all of them expecting change in assessment methods and record keeping. Nearly one-third were expecting no change in teaching methods and three-quarters expecting change in the curriculum. In 1990 half reported no change in curriculum, class organization or teaching methods and all of them reported change in assessment and record keeping.

In mathematics one-third were expecting no change in the curriculum, one-half no change in teaching methods, with all expecting change in assessment and all but one change in record keeping. In 1990 more reported no change in teaching methods; the other reports were more or less consistent with the predictions.

In science the greatest change between 1989 and 1990 was in classroom organization with two-thirds of headteachers predicting some change in 1989; whereas in 1990 one quarter actually reported that much change had taken place.

In Welsh there was much less change reported in curriculum, classroom organization and teaching methods than had been predicted. Nearly all headteachers reported change in record keeping and assessment although the emphasis shifted slightly from much change to some change.

The details of the changes the headteachers reported in all of the above were similar to those reported by the class teachers: more formalized or new assessment methods; more detail in the record keeping; and organizational changes driven by the need to find time for new subjects or new elements of existing subjects.

> There is now more variety and practical work; teaching methods have had to change to accommodate this.
>
> Assessment in English has to take account of all the attainment targets.

> Science is now an integral part of infant work whereas previously it was much more incidental.
>
> In the past science was much less structured.
>
> There was no real assessment or record keeping in science before the National Curriculum.
>
> Record keeping is now much more detailed [in mathematics].
>
> There is more emphasis on problem solving and games [in mathematics] than before.
>
> Welsh will be brought into as many aspects of cross-curricular work as possible.
>
> Teaching methods [in Welsh] will remain mainly oral with some written work.

Thematic Work

As well as following reactions to the individual subjects teachers and headteachers were asked about cross-curricular/thematic/topic work. One aspect of topic work for consideration is what curriculum subjects are touched by the topic work. This is subtly different from 'teaching' a curriculum subject through a topic, thematic or cross-curricular approach. For example many topics include the use of mathematical skills such as the drawing of graphs. Sometimes a new type of graph, pie charts for example, will be introduced using data gathered from the topic. On other occasions the children will have learnt how to draw pie charts by using their published mathematics scheme with some data provided by the authors and later they will use that skill to display data collected as part of a topic. In its 1992 review of primary education CCW (1992c) reported that, in general, skill getting was achieved with discrete teaching and skill usage was practised in topic work (p. 17).

Class Teachers' Views

Teachers were asked how often certain subjects were included in the planning of topic work. We did not ask them to distinguish between use or consolidation of skills and concepts and the introduction of new skills or concepts.

In 1989 thirty teachers responded. Twenty-nine always included English and mathematics, twenty-eight science, twenty-seven expressive arts, twenty environmental studies, nineteen religious education and nine (including two in Welsh-medium schools) Welsh in their topic planning. Five never included Welsh and one teaching in a Welsh-medium school never included English in their planning. The English-medium schools included Welsh to varying degrees: seven always, five frequently, six sometimes, five rarely and five never.

In 1990 thirty-three class teachers responded. There was little change in the inclusion of English, mathematics and science. However now twenty-two teachers were always including Welsh in their topic planning. One was including it frequently, six sometimes, five rarely and five never. Expressive arts had dropped to nineteen always including it, four frequently, two sometimes and one rarely. Environmental studies was included to more or less the same extent as in 1989. Religious education had changed slightly with twenty-two including it always, four frequently and seven sometimes.

In 1989 three-quarters of the teachers were expecting that the National Curriculum would affect their cross-curricular approach. However the majority of those were only expecting that there would be minor changes. Two-fifths of the schools stressed that they were already using a thematic approach. One-fifth were adamant that the National Curriculum would not affect that thematic approach.

> This school already runs a thematic approach to teaching and this will not change.

There, however, were feelings that the thematic work would have to become more focused.

It should not affect it but teachers will have to be careful to relate what is being done to what is required by the National Curriculum.

There will have to be more precise planning.

We will need to think in subject areas in order to achieve targets; that is work out a flow chart around a theme but split it into subjects to ensure that all attainment targets are covered.

It is going to be easier to link maths [*sic*] and language into a science topic linked to the National Curriculum therefore there might be less choice [of subjects] than before.

Themes which cover attainment targets in core subjects will obviously be chosen in preference to others.

In the past we have always been able to choose freely, now we will be selecting with attainment targets in mind.

In 1990 teachers' reflections were similar to their 1989 predictions. Well over three-quarters reported some effect on their cross-curricular approach with well over one-half of those teachers reporting little change. Under one-fifth reported no change at all. Practically half of the teachers commented on the need to relate this work to attainment targets. There was support for the view that work *had* to be cross-curricular in order to cover the National Curriculum.

I am more aware of the need for a cross-curricular approach. How else would teachers fit everything in?

However one teacher reported:

It is difficult to cover the whole range of activities within the thematic approach — some have to be taught separately.

There was also a feeling that the choice of topic or theme *was* now constrained.

> Themes are laid down now whereas prior to the National Curriculum the class teacher could chose her [*sic*] own theme — now if she wants to change them she has to consult the other infant staff.

> Now I chose a theme on science and fit the other curriculum areas to it. I felt free before. Now I'm constrained in my choice.

The Headteachers' Views

There was only marginal change in headteachers' views about a thematic approach between 1989 and 1990 with the vast majority predicting and then recording little or some change, with a small number recording no change or substantial change.

In 1990 headteachers were also asked if they expected a shift in the balance between cross-curricular and subject specialist work. Over one-half replied no and over one-third replied yes.

In 1992 CCW (1992c) reported:

> While many schools approached the issue [planning] thematically, some because it was the method currently favoured by HMI Inspectorate [*sic*] and the advisory service, others explained that a broad theme moving towards a more subject specific delivery was being used more frequently . . . in many cases schools were committed to the ideology of working thematically. (p. 16)

In 1993 OFSTED (1993a) went further: 'The vast majority of primary schools remain firmly committed to grouping different subjects together to be taught as topics' (para. 7).

Back in 1990 the headteachers reported:

> Staff feel the pull towards subject based teaching.

> Where NC requirements don't fit in naturally with themes these must be covered separately.

It is not possible to teach via a subject approach. Teachers would be swamped and not able to keep track of what children were getting out of it. With a thematic approach teachers will know what's been touched upon.

Most work will be covered within topics but there may be occasions when subjects will have to be taught as one-offs.

It's difficult to answer until we know what history and geography require.

When headteachers were questioned in 1991 about the shift from cross-curricular work 50 per cent were now reporting a shift.

Attainment targets not covered in the theme are taught separately. The introduction of the National Curriculum subjects makes the integration of these into one theme extremely difficult if not impossible. We are concerned that the view that subject basics cannot be tackled in a thematic approach is spreading. We are trying for a balance between what is integrated and what must be done separately.

The NC itself being subject orientated has not helped — we continue a thematic approach but with core subject areas being dealt with in a more subject orientated fashion.

The balance has been to science over the last three years. This might well change to history and geography this coming year.

In 1992 CCW (1992c) reported that the most common approaches to planning were:

- subject specific topics developed within themes, e.g. history in particular, also geography;

- subject specific topics used to fill in gaps, to reinforce, used as mini topics;
- discrete subject planning as more subjects come on-stream, e.g. maths, science and some English;
- linking the broad theme to individual schemes of work (the topic web!). (para. 7)

Conclusions

The introduction of the National Curriculum appears to have affected the teaching of core subjects mainly in the areas of assessment and record keeping. Some teachers also reported changes in their methods of teaching and classroom organization to accommodate the subject order requirements, for example, more practical work in mathematics and science. Despite past rhetoric of CCW and advisers, headteachers were noticing a shift away from cross-curricular work as did OFSTED (1993a: 6):

> Over the year however there was a noticeable shift towards designing topics that were more focused on a single subject such as history or science; fewer schools than previously used broad topics to teach all or most of the subjects.

Classteachers were reporting (as did CCW in 1992c: 17) much more structuring of topic work to take in as much National Curriculum work as possible.

There was also evidence of a trend towards science led topics although CCW reports (1992c: 16) (after the introduction of the history and geography orders) that the trend is towards topics led by those subjects. CCW (1992c) reported that

> In more than a few primary schools there were differences in the approaches used at infant and junior level. Subject specific tasks were used less frequently in infant schools who were more likely to plan over the whole of KS1.

It is possible that our primary school headteachers were reporting more generally about the 4–11 phase than specifically about Key Stage 1.

There is a consensus then between our research, CCW's consultation findings and those reported by OFSTED. There is already a move away from thematic/cross-curricular work towards discrete subject teaching, topics are no longer broad multi-subject studies but tend to focus on science or history or geography.

The key questions arising from our research and reports both formal and informal are

1 Are there similar trends in the impact on the teaching of core subjects and the thematic approach in Key Stage 1 and Key Stage 2?
2 Are these trends continuing, becoming more pronounced or returning to the pre-National Curriculum status quo?
3 How are single subject/specialist teaching and cross-curricular work viewed now?

We address these questions in Chapter 9.

Note

1 We have included Welsh alongside English, mathematics and science because of its dual role as both a core and non-core subject. When comments refer to Welsh-medium schools this will be made explicit.

Chapter 5

Differentiating the National Curriculum

In this chapter we examine ways in which teachers in the sample sought to differentiate their teaching so as to meet the perceived needs of their individual pupils with regard to their differing age, maturity or ability levels. Further we look at the impact of the National Curriculum on this process of differentiation as judged by the teachers. The findings are presented under the following headings:

- Differentiation in free play activities;
- Teaching under-5s;
- Differentiation according to ability:
  - The class teachers' views on the teaching of more able learners and slower learners;
  - The headteachers' views on the teaching of more able learners and slower learners.

Differentiation in Free Play Activities

During their interviews prior to the introduction of the National Curriculum the Year 1 class teachers were asked the following questions concerning free play in their classrooms:

1 On average during each day how much time does each child spend in free play activities?
2 Does this vary according to the age or ability of each child?
3 Does this amount change over the course of each year?
4 What role do you take in these free play activities?

5 Are these activities linked to the more formal work in the various curriculum areas?

These questions were repeated approximately one year later during the first year of the implementation of the new curriculum.

In the following presentation of findings it should be remembered that, while the majority of the teachers were responsible for either a single age class (5 to 6-year-olds) or a twin age group (4 to 6-year-olds), a minority of teachers taught classes with a wider age range, from 4 to 7-year-olds.

On average, in both years, the children spent between one half hour to one hour daily in free play activities, although some teachers were unable to quantify the amount which fluctuated for various reasons. In both years most of the teachers stated that the amount of time spent in free play varied according to the age and ability of each child. Where there was a mixed age range in the class the younger children, particularly the under-5s, would spend more time in free play and several teachers reported that, as children developed during the year and were increasingly able to tackle more structured work they spent less time in free play. As one teacher put it:

> The older they get the less they play and the more formal their work becomes their need for play is less.

However there seemed to be some divergence of practice regarding the amount of free play time accorded to the slower developing, 'less able' children. In those classrooms where the opportunities for free play were conditional upon the children completing teacher directed tasks beforehand, the slower children were reported as spending less time in free play than their age peers. In contrast some other teachers made a point of giving these children *additional* free play since their ability to carry out more formal work was limited. In the words of one of these teachers:

> The poorer ability children play more, the brighter pupils move towards work which demands more of them.

Despite this concern to meet the perceived developmental needs of the slower learning children the introduction of the National Curriculum appeared to reduce the teacher's scope to allow them more free play time, at least in some classrooms. The following comments express some teachers' concern at this trend:

> Children now have a lot less free play than before the National Curriculum as the result of the teacher cramming in work.
>
> Play time has decreased due to National Curriculum demands and this can be detrimental to some pupils who need to play to learn social skills and to develop language.
>
> Slow pupils [now] work most of the time in order to meet attainment targets. Before the National Curriculum they played much more in order to develop language and oral skills.
>
> Less able children spend more time on work but really they are the ones who need more play.

In some other classrooms though, despite the need to work towards the National Curriculum attainment targets, the teachers were able to continue to arrange for slower learning children to have more opportunities for free play than their peers. One teacher, for example, said that she required them to complete fewer teacher directed tasks than the more able children before being allowed to engage in free play. This was done in order to motivate them to complete the more structured tasks.

In both years nearly all of the teachers reported that their children's free play activities were linked to the more formal curriculum at least sometimes. This linking took various forms and ranged across the whole curriculum. For example, children might act out a scene from a novel they had been studying in their English curriculum. Similarly their sand and water play and their constructional play with Unifix, Multilink or Lego bricks was thought to help them in developing important mathematical concepts.

One-third of the teachers mentioned that the children's free play sometimes reflected a topic being dealt with in their more formal work, as when setting up a classroom shop following a visit to a supermarket. However there was some disagreement among the teachers regarding the principle of deliberately linking free play with the more formal curriculum. Those rejecting the principle made comments such as:

> Free play is linked to topic work occasionally but in the main free play is exactly that.
>
> Play is not part of the forward planning of the class teacher.

The teachers appeared to vary widely in the extent to which they became directly involved in their children's free play activities. A number of them used free play times as an opportunity to listen to children reading or for teaching groups of children. A few expressed the view that free play should be kept as free as possible from 'adult interference', other than to sort out disputes or to encourage children to engage in some form of free play activity if they were not doing so. Other teachers seemed to be more actively involved in the free play activities insofar as their time allowed this. Such involvement ranged from directly observing the children's free play to advising and helping them in their play and initiating such activities where necessary. When observed, good social behaviour would be praised and encouraged. Teachers might engage in discussions with children in the free play context in order to develop their language.

Clearly those teachers fortunate enough to have the regular help of a nursery assistant or other qualified aide were in a much better position to support their children's free play activities if their wished to do so, although this point did not actually arise in our interviews with them.

There was relatively little explicit reference by the teachers to the impact of the National Curriculum on the nature of their professional involvement in their children's free play. One commented that she now sometimes deliberately structured a free play activity so as to work toward a particular attainment target and two other teachers reported that they now had much less time to sit with children as they played, due to the demands of the National Curriculum upon them.

In summary, during the year following the introduction of the National Curriculum, there did not appear to be a major shift in the amount of time devoted to free play, the extent to which it was linked to more formal teaching, or in the nature of the teacher's involvement in it. Nevertheless the class teachers reported a decrease in the amount of time available for free play and some of them were particularly concerned about the adverse consequences of this for the development of slower learning children.

Teaching Under-5s

The Views of the Class Teachers

Approximately one year after the introduction of the National Curriculum the class teachers were asked at interview what effect they felt the National Curriculum had had on the teaching of children under age 5. Such children would have been in separate reception classes for 4 to 5-year-olds in the medium sized or large infant schools/departments, but in the smaller schools, they would be taught alongside 5-year-olds (Year 1) and sometimes older children (see Chapter 2). Of the thirty-four teachers involved at this time, twenty-seven did not have any under-fives in their classes and therefore did not respond to the question.

The comments of the seven remaining teachers referred to both positive and negative effects of the National Curriculum upon the teaching of these children, although a few teachers stated that there had been no noticeable effect since the children worked at their own level. Regarding benefits, one teacher felt that starting the National Curriculum at a younger age would benefit the child in the long run. Another teacher said that, while she felt that she expected too much of this group because they were in a class with older pupils, it could be an advantage for them since they were developing alongside the Year 1 pupils and they progressed toward the attainment targets despite their age. The latter teacher clearly felt that the younger children could be subjected to some pressure towards the achievement of attainment targets as did a number of other teachers.

Further feedback from class teachers on the question of the effect of the National Curriculum upon under-5s came from a seminar held by the authors in the summer of 1993. The twenty-four infant teachers who attended came from several LEAs within the region and one or two of them came from schools that had participated in the study. The teachers were put into small groups to discuss several questions, including the effect of the National Curriculum upon under-5s. In contrast to the somewhat mixed responses to this question from the teachers in our study reported above, the teachers in the seminar groups reported predominantly adverse consequences for under-5s. These included the premature formalization of the curriculum for these children and increased pressure upon them to work towards the achievement of National Curriculum attainment targets. Such pressure had led to a reduction in their opportunities for free play and less time for their teachers to talk with them and thereby help to enrich their language.

Particularly worrying was the increased emphasis reported by these teachers upon the production of written work by the children. As one group commented

> The National Curriculum has influenced our perception of what is respectable, bona fide work.

Another group described the 'worksheet syndrome' which was now squeezing out forms of learning, including the more practical, which the teachers regarded as being of higher quality. Such formalization of their learning could cause children to come to dislike school, it was thought.

Finally there was some reference to the negative effects on this age group of the heavy preoccupation of some infant teachers with the administration of SATs during the summer term. According to one group this created tensions within the (mixed age) classroom and a possibly adverse environment for the younger children. Whereas the summer term was traditionally a period of rapid development for infants, including under-5s, it was now largely occupied with SATs in mixed age classes.

The Views of the Headteachers

In their interviews the headteachers were not asked any questions directly about children's free play activities but, in the second interview, and in the written follow-up questionnaire they completed one year later, they were asked about the effect of the National Curriculum upon the teaching of the under-5-year-olds in their schools, whether in Year 1 or in nursery or reception classes. In 1990 approximately one-third of them felt that little or no change had occurred in such teaching following the introduction of the National Curriculum. By 1991, this proportion had risen to over half of the group. Comments from this group were along the following lines:

> Individual children are given work to do regardless of age. The National Curriculum has not changed this;
>
> With mixed age classes the children have always followed the same curriculum as older children but at their own level and this has not changed with the introduction of the National Curriculum;
>
> The quality remains intact and is being developed. The classroom atmosphere remains warm and friendly with all committed to the various tasks.

Some of these headteachers spoke of the pre-5 curriculum (including nursery education) as preparing children for Key Stage 1. One headteacher went further than this by announcing that the school would be making a start with the Key Stage 1 curriculum for the under-5s in the reception class later that year. Another commented as follows concerning this age group:

> They have started work on the National Curriculum and a far more structured approach has resulted.

The responses of the remaining headteachers to this question mentioned both the benefits and the possible dangers to the under-5s of the introduction of the National Curriculum. The benefits noted included a broader curriculum, with more science than previously and more confident teaching associated with this. The dangers concerned the premature introduction of very young children to more formal, National Curriculum-led teaching. One headteacher, for example, expressed the fear of starting the National Curriculum too early.

> The aims and needs of the individual child in early childhood education should be protected. They should be allowed to progress at their own rate of development.

Another felt that care should be taked not to 'turn off' 4-year-olds by an over-emphasis upon written work. The teaching headteacher of a class of 3 to 7-year-olds, worried by the problem of catering for the under-5-year-olds in such a situation had decided to split the class in the afternoons, with the latter forming a separate teaching group. Such views regarding the need to preserve the distinctive, 'child centred' character of the teaching of pre-5 children appear to contrast with the view of other headteachers, illustrated earlier, that a firmer structuring of the curriculum, following the introduction of the National Curriculum, was to be welcomed for these children.

One or two headteachers expressed concern about the effects of formalizing the curriculum for pre-5 children from disadvantaged home backgrounds. The following comment echoes the worry of some class teachers, reported earlier, that the introduction of the National Curriculum had resulted in less free play for these children:

> Too much is demanded of our young pupils who do not receive a lot of parental support. A lot of time was spent previously on social skills, constructive play and developing relationships. However, as a result of the National Curriculum there is insufficient time for this nowadays and pupils have to develop these skills and attitudes at the same time as they are being pressured to progress through levels of attainment.

In summary, while only one-third to one-half of the headteachers reported any impact of the National Curriculum upon the teaching of children under 5, opinion was sharply divided amongst them as to whether this was positive or negative. Those stressing its benefits described the firmer structuring of the curriculum that had resulted, while others viewed the National Curriculum as a threat to the distinctive, child centred nature of the early years' curriculum. The latter view was reinforced by the conclusions of a group of infant teachers attending an INSET seminar after the completion of the study. These teachers reported that their under-5 pupils were being subjected to more formal work in preparation for the National Curriculum, with a consequent reduction in their opportunities for free play, talk, and various practical activities.

Differentiation According to Ability

As reported in Chapter 2 the majority of Year 1 classes represented in the study sample contained either 5 to 6-year-old children only or the latter group plus 'reception infants' aged 4 to 5-years old. Despite this concentration in age the range of children's academic attainment appeared to be wide.

During their interviews prior to and following the introduction of the National Curriculum the Year 1 class teachers were asked about the extent to which they individualized the curriculum and their teaching methods to meet the individual learning needs of their children. Many teachers claimed to be doing this 'always' or 'as much as possible', whether in the context of whole class or group teaching. Such individualization of work was clearly essential for those teachers in small schools whose infant classes catered for a very wide age range. It took the form of either allowing children to work at their own pace and level on tasks set for the whole class or of the setting of different tasks by the teacher according to the children's abilities or attainments. The latter was achieved partly through the use of published schemes for the core subjects and also, for some teachers, by the preparation of work cards or work sheets specially designed for individual children or groups.

In their interviews before the introduction of the National Curriculum both the Year 1 class teachers and the headteachers were asked what effect the National Curriculum might have on the more able children and the slower learning children in their classes, including those with special educational needs respectively. At interview in the following year they were asked to judge the effect of the introduction of the National Curriculum upon these groups of children in the light of their experience of teaching it for a year. In addition the headteachers, but not the class teachers, were asked to report the effects of teaching the National Curriculum on these children after a further year, in a written follow-up questionnaire. The views of the class teachers and of the headteachers will be reported separately and then compared.

The Class Teachers' Views

More able learners

Half of the class teachers expected the introduction of the National Curriculum to have little or no effect upon their teaching of the more able children, claiming that all infants work at their own individual rates and that the more able children were already fully extended. The other half anticipated that there would be some effect or made no prediction, perhaps reserving their judgment. Some of the latter teachers thought that the National Curriculum attainment targets would provide examples of how to stretch the more able children, making it easier to plan for their needs. Their comments included the following:

> They will succeed by following a curriculum which will stretch and enrich them.

> They will be pushed further because the National Curriculum will give the teacher direction.

Another prediction was that the wider content and variety of work in the new curriculum would create interest amongst these children.

One year later approximately half of the teachers judged that the introduction of the National Curriculum had had little or no effect upon the more able children in their classes; a similar proportion to those predicting such an outcome, as reported above. Again, there were comments from some teachers to the effect that these children would always cope whatever was presented to them. Those reporting observable effects mainly mentioned positive benefits, in particular the richer variety of subject matter to which the children were exposed, including more science and the greater opportunity for pupils to carry out investigations themselves. Teacher benefits included the tighter curriculum planning which gave them more direction in extending the more able children and the improved quality of teacher teamwork and staff collaborative planning.

There were relatively few negative effects noted and these centred on the pressure placed on the children and their teachers to cover the new extended curriculum and the possible danger that the more able pupils might suffer a loss of teacher attention as teachers spent more time with slower learning pupils in order to help them achieve their attainment targets. On the whole, therefore, the teachers' original predictions of either no significant impact, or mainly beneficial effects of the introduction of the National Curriculum on the teaching of more able pupils appeared to be borne out, at least in their own judgment.

Slower learners

It was pointed out in Chapter 2 that over half of the class teachers in the study judged that they had some children in their classes whom they suspected of having special educational needs, although very few children had been formally statemented.

With regard to slower learning children, including those with recognized special educational needs, approximately half of the teachers did not expect that the introduction of the National Curriculum would significantly affect them since they were judged to be fully catered for within the existing curriculum.

The consequences predicted by some of the remaining teachers were almost entirely negative, reflecting their concern about these children's capacities to cope with the increased demands of the new curriculum, as illustrated in the following comments:

> I wonder if they will get lost in the work load. How do you get children who cannot read and write to do the work required?

> When Welsh becomes compulsory [in Wales] it could cause problems. They find it difficult enough to cope with number and English.

Other concerns focused upon the possibly damaging effects on these children's self-esteem of being labelled as failures at an early age with regard to the meeting of attainment targets, and upon the increased demands likely to be made on the teacher in helping the slower learners to achieve them.

One year later only three teachers reported that the introduction of the National Curriculum had had little effect upon the slower learning children, in contrast to the larger number (approximately half) of teachers who had predicted this, as reported above. For the remaining majority of teachers the observed impact of the National Curriculum was broadly in line with the earlier predictions of mainly negative consequences. There were frequent references to the greater curriculum pressure on these children to achieve the National Curriculum attainment targets with the result that the teachers were having to push them harder than before at the expense of the quality of the children's conceptual grasp and the degree of their skill mastery. The following comments illustrate these negative effects:

> I worry about pushing the slow learners too hard without going through the stages of learning a concept just to meet the attainment target.

> They receive a wider range of subject matter but may be put under more pressure than they should be to meet the attainment targets and are possibly not given enough time to absorb ideas fully before moving on to the next stage.

A small number of teachers reported that some of their slower learning children could not always comply with the demands of the new curriculum and were struggling to meet the new pressures upon them, for example, by not finishing set tasks and consequently having less time for free play. One teacher found herself unable to spend as much time with these children as before and worried a great deal about this. As in the interviews held one year previously some teachers expressed concern about the damaging effect on a child of a formal signalling of the failure to reach a particular attainment target.

> There is no safety net built in. The slower child will be labelled earlier on.

Despite the predominantly negative nature of the perceived consequences for slower learners of the introduction of the National Curriculum, there were some observations of benefits. One teacher commented that they were stretched more than before and experienced a richer curriculum at their level which included science and technology. Another felt that the National Curriculum made it easier for the teacher to see the next logical step in the teaching sequence, while the explicit sequence of attainment targets and their levels was seen as a benefit by the teacher who made the following remark:

> The National Curriculum makes the class teacher more aware of what slower learning children cannot do when it is all set out in front of you.

The importance of parental support for children's learning was expressed in the following comment by one of the teachers:

> It depends very much on the home background and parental support. The National Curriculum has had no real effect on their performance or the work presented to them. Children who receive support at home tend to make more progress than those who don't.

Finally one teacher appeared to adopt a somewhat philosophical attitude to the pressure to get these children to reach the relevant attainment targets.

> It may be better to spend more time discussing and talking with these children and training them to concentrate rather than worrying about covering attainment targets.

The Headteachers' Views

More able learners

When asked to predict the impact of the National Curriculum upon the more able children in the interview; prior to its introduction; well under half of the headteachers (nine) expected it to have little or no effect, citing similar reasons to those given by the class teachers to the same question reported earlier; for example, that the school was already catering fully for children's individual needs or that more able children will cope with anything whatever method or curriculum is employed. A similar number of headteachers expected the National Curriculum to bring some benefits to these children for a variety of reasons. These included: the possibility of accelerating the pace of their learning through the National Curriculum, perhaps with the help of secondary school teachers; a sharper focus upon individual capability than before which would enable children to reach their full potential and attain higher levels of attainment; and the motivational benefits of carrying out more investigative, problem solving work. Benefits to the class teachers were expected to come from the curriculum planning guidance provided by the National Curriculum, particularly with regard to planning for progression.

Only four headteachers thought there might be possible adverse effects. These included the danger that the more able children would not be so fully extended as before since the teacher might now pitch her or his teaching more at the average ability level of the class, threatening the concept of mixed ability teaching. Other comments referred to the prescriptive nature of the new curriculum which might reduce the opportunities for more able children to follow their own interests.

After one year of implementing the National Curriculum approximately half of the headteachers (fourteen) judged that it had made little or no impact upon the learning of the more able pupils. Their comments echoed those reported above in support of this predicted outcome, stressing the adaptability of these children in their learning. A few headteachers wished to reserve judgment after only one year and the number reporting positive outcomes was lower than expected on the basis of the earlier predictions. One of the latter headteachers commented that all children had benefited through working at their own levels in each curriculum area, while others mentioned the curricular planning benefits predicted earlier. As one headteacher put it,

> By the teacher examining each [curriculum] area in turn the children are receiving confident teaching and a broader curriculum.

In their responses to a written follow-up questionnaire presented after two years of implementing the National Curriculum, the proportion of headteachers reporting little or no impact on the learning of more able children remained unchanged compared with that after one year. The following comments indicated these headteachers' apparent satisfaction with this outcome:

> These pupils have adapted to the demands of the National Curriculum and have coped well with the programmes of study. They are capable of independent learning and progress at their own pace.

> Our work has not significantly altered and such children are still encouraged and stretched.

One headteacher went so far as to claim that these children coped easily with the demands of the National Curriculum.

As during the previous year only four headteachers referred to positive gains from the introduction of the National Curriculum for these children. Their comments were predominantly concerned with the curriculum planning benefits for the teacher which enabled them to plan more effectively in order to extend the learning of the more able children. No adverse effects were reported.

To sum up, as in the case of the class teachers, the headteachers' original predictions of mainly beneficial effects of the introduction of the National Curriculum appeared to have been borne out up to two years afterwards, at least in terms of their own perceptions, although fewer headteachers reported benefits compared with the number predicting them. The class teachers and headteachers reported similar kinds of benefits and very few teachers (and only one headteacher) reported any negative effects upon the more able learners.

Slower learners

The pattern of headteacher predictions about the likely impact of the National Curriculum upon the teaching of slower learning children, including those with special educational needs, was appreciably different from that reported above with regard to more able learners since a higher proportion predicted possible adverse consequences for these children. Approximately one-third of them expected the National Curriculum to have little or no impact, five predicted possible benefits and just over one-third predicted a negative impact due to the greater pressure to achieve which the National Curriculum was expected to exert upon slower learning children, coupled with reduced class teacher time to devote to supporting them. One headteacher felt that the practice of mixed ability teaching was now under threat.

The actual impact of the National Curriculum, as judged by the headteachers after one year, accorded with their predictions with regard to the different outcomes. Those teachers reporting little or no impact claimed that their slower learning pupils were continuing to work at their own pace and level and that the work was sufficiently differentiated to meet their learning needs. The few references to positive benefits stressed the breadth of the new curriculum, one teacher commenting that the National Curriculum would ensure that this group would have access to the whole curriculum. The reported negative effects, like the predictions, stressed the new pressures now placed on slower learning pupils, either directly or indirectly as a result of pressures upon their teachers. The following comments reflect the obvious concern of these particular headteachers about the dangers for these children:

> There is more pressure on teachers to get this group up to standard [for example, level 1] at least for the sake of the parents who will become more familiar with the levels.

> The National Curriculum has had a dramatic effect on them. The school can no longer give them the attention that they need. They are culturally deprived and just need the 'real basics'. Teachers are now under pressure to analyse what children are learning and when they review it and the children are not making great progress it is demoralizing for the whole staff. (Headteacher of a Social Priority Area school)

> These children don't have enough time to get through the tasks. Pressure of time creates disadvantages for slower learners.

> Failure could be reinforced earlier if the ethos of the school is wrong.

> They find it difficult to cope with the work and assimilate it in so many subjects.

One year later the pattern of the headteachers' responses to the same question in the written follow-up questionnaire was broadly similar to that reported after one year. Six headteachers judged that the National Curriculum had made little impact upon the slower learners. Two of the few headteachers reporting benefits referred to the greater effort and determination of their teachers to work harder with their slower learning pupils to enable them to reach the attainment targets, and one claimed that a far more structured approach to the teaching of these children had now been adopted. The description of negative outcomes once again referred to the pressure now being placed on these pupils to progress towards the attainment targets but, on this occasion, some headteachers expressed the view that insufficient time was now being spent upon the 'basic skills' of reading and number to meet these children's needs.

> These pupils are badly served by the demands of the National Curriculum as the time spent on the basic subjects has been reduced to fulfil the demands of a much more rigid curriculum.

One headteacher reported his staff's concern that children with difficulties in reading and number were being left behind, while another reported that the difference between the more able and the slower learning children was becoming more marked.

In summary it is clear that, for both class teachers and headteachers the number of reported adverse effects of the National Curriculum upon the teaching of the slower learning children exceeded that of reported benefits. The quality of these children's grasp of basic skills and concepts was seen to be threatened by the weight of the wider curriculum demands and the drive to work towards average levels of performance in the various attainment targets was putting undue pressure upon these children. Also the consequences of their failure to reach the expected target levels were likely to damage their self-esteem.

Chapter 6

The Teachers' Views on the Impact of the National Curriculum

In this chapter we look at the views of the teachers on various aspects of the National Curriculum in the light of their experience of implementing it over two years. The reponses of the Year 1 class teachers will be followed by those of the headteachers.

The Year 1 Class Teachers' Views

Problems in Delivering the National Curriculum

The Year 1 class teachers were asked whether they had experienced any particular problems or difficulties in implementing the National Curriculum during the first year (1989–90). All but seven teachers (twenty-six out of thirty-three) stated that they had done so. The most frequently mentioned problem was finding the time to meet the demands of the new curriculum in terms of its coverage (range of attainment targets) and the required assessment and record keeping, while at the same time keeping abreast of the statutory and non-statutory curriculum documents as they appeared. One teacher commented that much more time was needed for planning as there was so much to cover and, since she was not familiar with the documents she continually had to refer to them, which took up valuable teaching time. Several teachers referred to the problem of striking the right balance between teaching, assessment and recording. A different problem mentioned by a teacher in a school serving a disadvantaged area was that of getting poorly motivated learners to complete the prescribed work.

Several teachers expressed concern at the sheer scope of the new curriculum and felt that this increased coverage was being achieved by 'skimming the surface' at the expense of teaching in reasonable depth, or, in one teacher's words, the problem of 'fitting it all in knowing that justice is being done in each area'. Making an objective judgment of the breadth versus depth issue was difficult to do when one was engaged in ongoing teaching of the new curriculum according to another teacher.

The above problems were some of those actually experienced by the teachers during the first year of the implementation of the National Curriculum but, prior to this year (i.e. during the summer term 1989), the same teachers had been asked what problems they anticipated when implementing the National Curriculum in the coming school year. The anticipated and actual problems can therefore be compared. There is of course a danger in asking about anticipated problems, namely that the person asked will be predisposed to perceive subsequent problems in a self-justifying pattern. To counter the effects of such a possible bias it would be necessary to have, for comparison, a group of teachers who were not asked what, if any, problems they anticipated, but merely what, if any, problems they had actually experienced. However the inclusion of such a comparison group of teachers was not feasible in this study. In the event there were some differences in the nature of the problems reported and those anticipated which suggests that if there was a 'self-justifying' effect it did not operate strongly.

The number of teachers who anticipated some problems (twenty-seven out of thirty-three) was almost identical with the number subsequently reporting such problems. Amongst the anticipated problems, that of finding time to meet all of the demands of the National Curriculum was again prominent but, at this stage, the teachers saw these as focusing upon the difficulty of finding time to cope with the demands of assessment and record keeping, particularly in classes with a wide age or ability spread, including classes containing nursery-aged children. This particular concern was understandable given the relative lack of official information about the nature of the required assessments at that time. One teacher felt that she would need to be far more aware of the individual child in order to be able to assess and record his or her development and progress.

The fact that there were fewer specific references to actual, as opposed to anticipated, problems associated with assessment and record keeping might be taken to suggest that, on the whole, the Year 1 teachers coped better with these demands than they had anticipated, although it should be pointed out that, at this stage, the shools were not involved in the administration of the SATs. However an indication that such problems were still of concern to some of the teachers came from their responses to a question in the questionnaire completed by the teachers toward the end of the first year of implementation of the National Curriculum (that is, in 1990).

In this questionnaire the teachers were asked what problems they anticipated during the following year. While only eleven out of the thirty-three teachers responding expected any problems, most of those mentioned were again concerned with the management of time with particular regard to meeting assessment and record keeping requirements. One teacher put it as the problem of 'managing the time to do all that the government requires and to *teach* the children'. Concern was also expressed by a few teachers about achieving full curriculum coverage, particularly in the light of the introduction of some of the National Curriculum non-core subjects during the following year. The timing of the latter was commented on by some teachers, for example,

> It would have been nice to have had a year to reinforce the core subjects *before* the introduction of the foundation subjects.

The fact that only one-third of the teachers anticipated any problems during the second year of the National Curriculum might be taken as an indication that they were feeling more confident in their ability to meet its demands. (It also lends support to the view expressed earlier that the teachers' reported problems were not simply a reflection of the problems they anticipated.) Evidence for such a gain in the teachers' confidence also came in their responses to a question in the follow-up questionnaire which asked them to compare their current feelings about the National Curriculum with those approximately one year earlier.

The majority of the teachers (twenty out of thirty-three) felt 'more happy' regarding the National Curriculum, with only eight teachers feeling unchanged in their views and two teachers feeling less happy than before. Their spontaneous comments on this question suggest the reasons for their generally more positive feelings. The fact that the teachers had by now had a year's experience of delivering the National Curriculum and were more familiar with the documents was clearly a major confidence building factor. There was a feeling amongst some teachers that their earlier fears had been unfounded, two of them commenting that it is the unknown which causes anxiety, and another stating that thinking about it is worse than doing it.

The experience of teaching the new curriculum had obviously helped them to come to terms with the practical demands of planning and timing. As one teacher put it,

> It's all more familiar after working with the documents for a year and knowing areas of weakness and the timing of the work. Even with the [forthcoming] introduction of the foundation subjects there is much less anxiety than this time last year.

Effect of the National Curriculum on the Teacher's Role, Methods of Teaching and Classroom Organization

Toward the end of the first year of the introduction of the National Curriculum the Year 1 teachers were asked at interview about its effects upon their role as class teachers and upon their methods of teaching and classroom organization. The same question was completed in the written follow-up questionnaire repeated approximately one year later. On both occasions the majority of teachers indicated that there had been significant changes in these respects but a minority (thirteen teachers each time) felt that their work had not changed in any significant way. On each occasion there was a mixture of positive and negative responses, with the latter being more numerous than the former.

On the positive side a few teachers commented that their planning was far more meticulous than previously because of the

National Curriculum. One said that she was experimenting with various teaching methods to accommodate the amount of work the National Curriculum requires and to execute it successfully to the benefit of all children. For another the National Curriculum had made her more aware of her role as class teacher in ensuring that the core subjects were not taught as separate subjects but were interrelated so that breadth, depth and relevance were demonstrated. The greater breadth of the new curriculum was reflected in the response of the teacher who said,

> It made me realize that I hadn't provided certain subjects in the past to the required depth and I have made a determined effort to include the subjects into my everyday teaching and to give children more opportunities for their own discoveries.

Another teacher commented that the National Curriculum had made her more aware of the importance of providing a structured, balanced form of learning with progression and continuity as a major factor.

Associated with this more detailed and careful planning was a greater degree of collaboration between teachers within a school, mentioned by some. These comments related more to curriculum planning than methods of teaching as such, about which there were relatively few statements, apart from a few references to the increased amount of group work amongst pupils taking place since the introduction of the National Curriculum.

On the negative side there were frequent references on both occasions to the increased pressure on class teachers resulting from the introduction of the National Curriculum and its associated assessment and record keeping requirements. In particular this pressure was perceived as stemming from the requirement that teachers should help all pupils to meet the full range of attainment targets at the appropriate levels. One teacher referred to the 'pressure to meet deadlines and to keep pushing the children forward even if they are not ready'. Another redefined her role as 'someone who has to teach the National Curriculum and balance time as best as possible to cover as many attainment targets as possible'. In contrast the teacher who stated that she found it 'a little difficult' to cover the attainment targets due to having a mixed class sounded only a mildly critical note.

The pressure brought on by the new demands for assessment and record keeping were reflected in comments such as the following:

> The role is far more demanding in the amount of record keeping which places increasing demands on the teacher's already overburdened workload. As a class teacher I am more restricted in my planning for the year with the National Curriculum and more time is spent recording assessments of children as 'proof' for any HMIs.

This pressure was felt by a number of teachers to extend into their domestic lives as indicated by comments such as

> There is more pressure outside of the classroom and in family life because of the time teachers need for all the paper work. The National Curriculum seems to be continually on one's mind. I never switch off from school.

For some teachers at least the increased pressures had detracted from their former enjoyment of their work, leading to responses such as

> The enjoyment of child based teaching has gone. We haven't time to spend on the things the children bring in. I feel bogged down with form filling and writing files and records. This gives less time for real teaching for which I was trained.

Another teacher commented that the pastoral role of the infant teacher had changed because there was now little time to listen to children's problems. A teacher who had been involved in the administration of SATs to Year 2 children saw herself as 'more of an assessor and examiner, a deliverer of the National Curriculum now, as opposed to a reactor to the needs and interests of children'.

Several teachers clearly regretted the constraints which the

National Curriculum had placed upon their former flexibility in curriculum planning in reponse to children's spontaneous interests. As one put it

> The aims of the teacher to act as a catalyst and to encourage and show children how to learn and ask questions are restricted now because of the attainment targets I have to teach. Interesting opportunities are sometimes lost and not pursued because of the time element in which to achieve my attainment targets.

One teacher even felt that she was no longer in (curricular) control as the National Curriculum had taken control of her.

Even some of the teachers who felt that the introduction of the National Curriculum had not significantly affected their teaching role or methods acknowledged the restrictions now placed upon their planning freedom, for example:

> My methods haven't changed in respect of treating children according to their own individual needs but my scope has been restricted because of the statements of attainment I have to teach to now.

Not all of these teachers shared this feeling of restriction however, as exemplified in the response

> I have always taught cross-curricular, therefore the National Curriculum hasn't affected me greatly, only to increase record keeping. Even though the National Curriculum is subject based, with careful planning, the subjects can be brought together into cross-curricular work quite effectively.

Benefits and Disadvantages of the National Curriculum

In addition to the above questions asked at the 1989 and 1990 interviews the teachers were asked to state the benefits and disadvantages of the newly introduced curriculum. This question was repeated in the written follow-up questionnaire completed in 1991. Some of the response themes already noted appear again in the class teachers' responses to this question. On both occasions the majority of teachers listed both benefits and disadvantages, with only a handful noting either one or the other or neither. It is encouraging that around half of the teachers proposed curricular benefits of some kind. Some of these were associated with the wider curriculum content of the National Curriculum, particularly with regard to science and technology, and the wider range of activities engaged in by the children, including more practical work and more collaborative group work.

A number of teachers clearly felt that the National Curriculum provided a valuable planning framework which enabled them to see continuity and progression in each curriculum area and to plan in a more structured way than before. Typical comments in this respect were:

> Progression is more evident to the teacher when planning work and this can only be of benefit to the children. We know where to go from stage to stage.

Also the planning framework provided by the statements of attainment and programmes of study was seen by some as an important guide in assessing children's progress, as reflected in the following comments:

> There are far stricter guidelines to follow. It is easier to plan work and see where the children are. The assessments make you think about what you have done and where you are going.

The new National Curriculum assessments were seen by some teachers as providing a more precise measure of children's levels of attainment in the core subjects than hitherto, as exemplified in the comment, 'I am able to see exactly which stage each child is at in each curriculum area.' Some teachers felt that the planning and assessment framework provided by the National Curriculum enabled them to plan work more effectively to meet pupils' individual curricular needs. The benefits of the National Curriculum were felt by a number of teachers to apply particularly to more able children, for whom it was seen as offering considerable scope, for example by giving them a wider range of experiences and greater independence.

The disadvantages of the National Curriculum were perceived especially with regard to the pressures it put upon both teachers and children. Some teachers clearly felt themselves to be under strong pressure to maximize their children's progress towards the many attainment targets in the core subjects. This, in turn, raised anxieties in some teachers about the depth and quality of their teaching and also about the effects of the pressures they were putting on their pupils.

> As there are so many attainment targets to cover within the year I am finding myself having to skim the surface of some attainment targets rather than spending more time teaching them so that the children will achieve a better understanding. Young children are expected to reach a certain level of achievement at a certain date in the year and this shows little consideration of the fact that early development is along different paths and at different times, depending on the child's readiness in the different skills.

Slower pupils were felt by some teachers to be particularly vulnerable to the pressures exerted by the National Curriculum.

> Slower children may be pushed towards levels of attainment when they are not ready and I worry that if they fail to meet them this will be seen as a reflection of bad teaching.

In a similar vein another teacher, in a school serving a socially disadvantaged area, commented on 'the immense pressure to get poorly motivated children to a reasonable standard' and felt worried that the poor standard of their work might be interpreted as due to poor teaching on her part. Another, working in a similar school, commented on the difficulty of setting her children more science and practical tasks when they were unable to read.

Regarding children's failure to reach particular attainment targets, two teachers raised the question of whether the work should be repeated until the children did understand it. Their concern appeared to be that slower children would suffer if the teacher forged ahead regardless of how quickly they grasped concepts.

Several teachers responded that the increased breadth of the curriculum would lead to insufficient time being spent on the 'basic skills' of reading, writing and number. A teacher working in a disadvantaged area school commented that her children needed constant practice on 'the basics' since many had no books or pencils at home, but the National Curriculum made no allowance for this. At least one teacher found that she could not hear children read on a daily basis, as before, but now only once a week.

Summary of the Class Teachers' Views

Most of the Year 1 class teachers in the study had experienced some problems in implementing the National Curriculum during the first year. The greatest concern was expressed about the sheer range of the attainment targets in the core subjects (those in the non-core subjects being still to come) and the fear that this increased curriculum coverage could only be achieved at the expense of the depth and quality of teaching and of increased pressure on the children, particularly the slower ones, to reach the desired attainment targets. Additionally some teachers regretted the perceived loss of flexibility in the infant curriculum which had hitherto allowed them to exploit children's spontaneous interests as they arose. The demands on the teacher's time and class management skills made by the new assessment and record keeping requirements were another focal point of concern, with some teachers feeling that such demands interfered with the 'real job' of teaching, making the teacher's role more stressful and less enjoyable than before.

Despite these strongly expressed concerns it was encouraging that many teachers appeared to have gained in confidence in their ability to implement the National Curriculum as a result of their first year's experience of teaching it and well over half of them felt 'somewhat happier' about the National Curriculum at the end of the second year of its implementation than during the first year. The greater breadth of the new curriculum and the fact that it provided a clear curriculum planning framework with built-in continuity and progression were perceived as positive gains by a number of teachers. Some teachers also reported that the introduction of the National Curriculum had led to a greater degree of collaboration and teamwork between teachers within their schools.

The Headteachers' Views

Problems in Delivering the Curriculum

The majority of headteachers (twenty out of twenty-six) had anticipated that their schools would experience some difficulties in implementing the National Curriculum during its first year. Nineteen out of twenty-four subsequently reported having experienced some problems when interviewed toward the end of that year. These problems were focused on the demands of assessment and record keeping, on the pressure on their staffs and upon the difficulties in obtaining adequate resources to support the new curriculum. Regarding assessment and record keeping, the relative lack of official guidance on what to assess and record and the time such processes would take, especially since teachers had no free periods, were particular worries. One headteacher wondered whether the class teacher had the necessary expertise to carry out the finely graded type of teacher assessment that he anticipated. The comment by another headteacher that assessment and record keeping were administrative rather than teaching functions echoed the views of some class teachers, presented earlier, who contrasted such functions with 'real teaching.'

In both years some headteachers clearly felt that their schools had been under considerable pressure to keep abreast of the National Curriculum documents as they appeared and to formulate their schools' curricular policies in the light of these, although such pressures may have eased somewhat after the first year. In contrast, a few headteachers felt that as a result of prior discussion and planning their schools had been well prepared to accommodate the new curricular demands. The increased workload of the class teacher was noted by some headteachers, one of whom commented upon the many hours of extra work involved and the consequent increase in teacher stress.

Regarding other problems, shortages of material resources, especially for the practical activities required by the new curriculum, worried some headteachers, as did the lack of books (especially for the non-core subjects), of library space and also space for storing materials. In at least one school, which served a disadvantaged area, these problems were compounded by that of vandalism. Some headteachers commented upon their teacher's relative lack of confidence to teach certain subjects such as science, technology and Welsh for which the need for further training was recognized. At least one headteacher saw it as part of her role to build the confidence of her staff to meet the new curricular demands.

The problems facing small rural schools were highlighted by a number of headteachers, due to the wide age and ability ranges that typified classes to be found there and the inevitable limitations within small staffs in the teacher expertise needed to cover all aspects of the curriculum. At least one headteacher working in such a school felt a sense of isolation in knowing what was going on in other schools and worried whether his school was working along the right lines in its attempts to implement the National Curriculum.

Effects of the National Curriculum on the Headteacher's Role

As with the class teachers, the headteachers were asked about the effects of the National Curriculum upon their professional role towards the end of each of the first two years of its implementation. The majority of headteachers felt that there had been some changes in their role, some of which were clearly regretted. Increased pressure in some form was noted by several headteachers although some of them commented that this was partly due to other coincidental developments, particularly the introduction of local management of schools (LMS). In the words of one headteacher,

> Pressures have increased considerably because of constant changes and demands in all directions. The introduction of the National Curriculum is only a small part of this.

The statutory responsibility which headteachers had acquired for the effective implementation of the new curriculum appeared to be a particular source of challenge and, in some cases, stress to them as the following quotation indicates:

> I feel more accountable for every aspect of my work, especially for the effective delivery of the curriculum. The constraints which can impede any progress in my work cause grave concern, especially if out of my control.

The need for headteachers and class teachers to share the responsibility for implementing the new curriculum was stressed by one headteacher as follows:

> They [headteachers] become leaders of teams and teachers need a different attitude to the headteacher as the National Curriculum is nationally prescribed and they cannot blame the headteacher for schemes of work. It has to work for the school and the staff have to pull together to make it work.

Associated with this increased sense of accountability was the perception by some headteachers of an increased demand upon them to support and sustain the confidence and ability of their staffs to meet the demands of the National Curriculum. As one headteacher put it

> The headteacher must give confidence to staff and boost their morale that they are on the right track and find relevant help for areas of weakness. This puts pressure on the headteacher who must know the National Curriculum in detail to reassure staff and keep up to date with changes in it.

Another headteacher felt that, although his views about education had not changed, his role had as a result of the National Curriculum and of LMS which had caused him worry and pressure to make his role effective. He now saw himself as a 'facilitator and motivator' to his staff in respect of the implementation of the National Curriculum.

Increased administrative duties concerned some of the headteachers as illustrated in the following examples:

> My role as headteacher has changed significantly over the last few years. I have less time to attend to curriculum matters because of administrative work and a great deal of curricular responsibility has been delegated.

> . . . a feeling that greater emphasis on administration such as form filling, record keeping and achieving goals is necessary rather than the previous philosophical approach where values held seem different from those current.

> My office has changed. We are no longer teachers but financiers, accountants and diplomats.

Associated with this increase in administration was a sense of regret, expressed by some headteachers about the reduced teaching contact that they now had with children. However, although many headteachers reported increased burdens and stress in their post-National Curriculum roles, not all of their comments were negative in tone. As mentioned earlier, six headteachers felt that there had been little or no change in their role. Another felt that although the National Curriculum appeared 'threatening and overwhelming', confidence to cope with it should grow in time.

Changes in Methods of Infant Class Teaching and Classroom Organization

At the end of the first and second years following the introduction of the National Curriculum about half of the headteachers felt that it had resulted in little change in the methods of teaching or classroom organization in their infant schools or departments. Of the changes reported by the remaining headteachers, the tighter structuring of classroom activities in order to work toward specific attainment targets received frequent mention. Like their class teacher colleagues, whose views were presented earlier, some headteachers regretted the relative loss of spontaneity of infant education. The loss of 'fun time' in the primary curriculum was regretted by another.

Associated with these changes was the reduced opportunity for play in Year 1 and Year 2 classes, which the headteacher of one of the schools serving a disadvantaged area saw as particularly regressive since 'many of our pupils do not know how to play usefully'. As regards teaching method the only change noted was the increased use of group work in the classroom, a trend also reported by the class teachers.

The headteachers were also asked to note whether the introduction of the National Curriculum had affected their schools in any other respect. The increased pressure on staff arising from a greater work load and increased responsibility were mentioned by several headteachers, one of whom commented graphically as follows:

> The National Curriculum has put tremendous demands on an already hard-working and conscientious staff. There never seem to be enough hours in the day and 'Adds hours' at the end of the day deliver the final killing blow.[1]

Another headteacher noted more discernible mood swings in her staff due to this pressure, adding that 'the children are often the saving grace'.

On the positive side, the increased need for coordinated planning prompted by the introduction of the National Curriculum led the staff to collaborate more closely than before according to several headteachers. One stated that it had helped staff to become more of a team, supporting and sharing with each other, thus creating continuity of planning. This planning framework had increased the sense of professionalism and confidence in some of the schools, as reflected in the following comments:

> The National Curriculum has standardized what is being taught in schools and this gives teachers reassurance that they have been working in the right way.

> The curriculum is far more organized. There is more whole school planning to accommodate sequential subjects like history and geography.

Benefits and Disadvantages of the National Curriculum

Like the Year 1 class teachers, the headteachers were asked to state what they perceived to be the benefits and disadvantages of the introduction of the National Curriculum toward the end of each of the first two years. As regards benefits only a handful of headteachers on each occasion appeared unable or unwilling to suggest any, although this did not necessarily reflect a negative view of the National Curriculum since, as mentioned earlier, some headteachers felt that the introduction of the National Curriculum had made relatively little difference to the curriculum they had already been offering. As one of these headteachers put it,

> There is little benefit as such since the children are receiving much the same now as previously — perhaps science and experiments have increased and are more varied.

The benefits suggested by the majority related to curriculum planning, curriculum breadth and variety and to assessment and evaluation. Concerning the former, the National Curriculum had led to more thorough and coherent planning, with more continuity than before, according to a number of headteachers, as indicated in the following comments:

> The National Curriculum helps teachers in their planning by giving targets to work towards.

> What has to be done is stated clearly for staff to follow. Things which teachers have always done are now in black

> and white and in order. This is bound to be easier, particularly for the young inexperienced teachers.

> Children follow a well defined programme of study in all curriculum areas. It has probably given a greater balance to the curriculum as staff plan to incorporate all strands of the National Curriculum in their lessons.

The broader curriculum and greater variety of curriculum activities such as practical work in mathematics, science and technology, were welcomed by several headteachers, as they had been by some of the class teachers. One headteacher commented that a wider range of subjects and approaches to learning were now available to children, who were more stimulated as a result.

Perceived positive aspects of the newly introduced methods of assessment and record keeping were identified by some headteachers as the following comments show:

> Teachers can see how well they are doing. For the first time staff can actually state levels of attainment which they could not do before.

> The National Curriculum gives a yardstick by which slower children can be measured to see how far behind they are.

> Teachers can measure progress against specific objectives and statements with common criteria for all pupils.

The stated disadvantages of the National Curriculum fell mainly under the headings of increased pressure on teachers and children and reduced flexibility in curriculum planning. As with the benefits, a handful of headteachers on both occasions failed to state any disadvantages. The increased pressure upon school staffs was described in comments such as the following:

> There is constant pressure to complete programmes of work across a wide range of subjects. Children are too

> young to be subjected to this pressure and meeting so many new subjects in a short space of time.

Such pressure was felt by some headteachers to be falling particularly on slower pupils, as illustrated in the following comment:

> There is no real disadvantage for bright pupils but I feel anxious for slower pupils and under-achievers. I feel there *may* be too much pressure too early on. Young children need time to play, socialize and mix and these aspects of the infant curriculum may suffer as a result of the National Curriculum, thus disadvantaging the children.

The increased pressure upon teachers already discussed was thought likely by some headteachers to have negative effects upon the children in time, for example,

> Teachers are over-worked and over-stressed and their low morale cannot be of help to the children. The intense pressure must be relaxed so that the true benefits of an exciting new curriculum can be realized.

Part of the pressure on teachers was judged by some headteachers to have resulted from too many curriculum changes at one time, threatening teachers' confidence and expertise.

The constraining effect of the National Curriculum on the primary teachers' traditional freedom and flexibility of curriculum planning was particularly mentioned by some headteachers in their responses to the follow-up questionnaire completed after the second year of implementation of the National Curriculum. This might reflect the cumulative impact of the introduction of the non-core subjects on top of the core subjects already in place. The sense of an overcrowded curriculum was conveyed in such comments as:

> There isn't enough time in the day to do everything required plus following a thematic approach. Teachers find themselves pulled in all directions, particularly with the humanities. A free interest based approach is impossible when targets have to be reached.

> The curriculum has been narrowed and there is a lack of spontaneity created by over-planning. It should be remembered that these children are only five!

Other disadvantages mentioned related to the reduction of teaching resulting from the demands of record keeping and assessment and the dilution of the curriculum at the expense of its greater breadth, a theme that emerged strongly in the class teachers' responses. The following list of disadvantages of the National Curriculum provided by one headteacher usefully summarizes the comments of many headteacher colleagues in the research sample:

- subjects overloaded with statements of attainment;
- too many attainment targets;
- little time for reflection and evaluation;
- record keeping is time consuming;
- the National Curriculum is subject based.

Toward the end of the first National Curriculum year the headteachers were asked to compare their feelings towards the National Curriculum with those expressed a year previously. Half of them (twelve) felt happier about its introduction than before, ten responded that their feelings were unchanged and two felt less happy. The stated reasons for feeling happier about the National Curriculum included the headteachers' perception of an increase in their class teachers' confidence in their approach to it and the realization that the new curriculum did not differ drastically from that which had operated prior to its introduction. The following comments illustrate these positive feelings:

> It is continuing good practice and making everyone better at planning the activities provided for the children.

> The staff realize that it's work they have been doing before in any case. The more familiar they become with the National Curriculum levels the easier it will be.

Such references to curriculum continuity need to be juxtaposed with both class teachers' and headteachers' comments reported earlier about the greater breadth and scope of the National Curriculum in relation to the schools' existing curricula, particularly with regard to science and technology.

The increased confidence amongst some school staffs appeared to stem partly from their perception of curriculum continuity just noted and also from their realization, based upon a year's experience, that they could meet the challenges posed. The following comments echo the views of some class teachers reported earlier:

> We are coming to terms with it. It's not as frightening as first appeared.

> We've met the challenges — the staff are much happier because of the self support system within the school.

Some of the headteachers whose feelings remained unchanged stressed the preparation that their schools had made for the introduction of the National Curriculum, as illustrated in comments such as,

> The school was quite well prepared last year and the National Curriculum has not made any dramatic difference to our way of working. The National Curriculum has been absorbed.

Several headteachers wanted to reserve judgment about the impact of the National Curriculum, given the relatively early stage of its implementation and their awareness that more work needed to be done on it by them.

The following two comments expressed the difficulty felt by some headteachers in making objective judgments about the quality of their school's implementation of the National Curriculum:

> It is hard to judge the school's delivery of the National Curriculum until it is reviewed by an outside body.

> It is difficult to be objective about your own school.

Headteachers' Overall Views about the National Curriculum

In addition to stating the benefits and disadvantages of the National Curriculum, the headteachers (but not the class teachers) were asked for their overall comments on the effects of its introduction toward the end of the first and second years respectively. On both occasions, but particularly the later one, the negative comments tended to outweigh the more positive ones although this should not be interpreted as indicating a predominantly negative view towards the National Curriculum on the part of the headteachers (see Chapter 7). Predictably there was some overlap between their responses to the two different questions. Positive comments, such as the following, corresponded with some of the stated benefits of the National Curriculum in stressing the improved team work and collective planning by school staffs:

> A greater sharing is taking place of ideas, resources and talents.

> It has made teachers work as a team. Teachers are looking closely at what is being done in the classroom and their own method. It has helped the teachers to look more closely at individual children and to develop ways of observing children at work.

> Teachers are rising to the challenge. They *have* to work as a team and not as individuals as before.

Other positive comments made by the headteachers referred to the dedication of their staffs and to their own efforts to maintain their teachers' morale and positive attitudes in the face of the challenges they were facing:

> Infant staff have worked extremely hard to ensure the success of the introduction.

> We have tried to be positive — always looking on the bright side — morale must be kept high.

> Initially it affected the morale of teachers. Pressure of work and time left teachers thoroughly exhausted. I have committed staff who have always worked above and beyond what was expected of them.

Some of the negative comments centred upon the increased work load and pressure on teachers, particularly with regard to assessment and record keeping and echoed those reported earlier. One such reponse highlighted the particular pressure placed upon staff in small rural schools:

> Because it is a small school there is too great a pressure and expectation on teaching staff in delivering the National Curriculum. They have to take on too many responsibilities which in a larger school would be spread around.

Other negative comments expressed strong disapproval of the rate of change imposed on schools by the introduction of the National Curriculum, particularly in conjunction with other changes stemming from the Education Reform Act. Amongst such changes the daunting effect that the sheer volume of documentation can have on teachers was clearly reflected in the following comment:

> The rapid and ever increasing amounts of materials bombarding schools is leading teachers to become dispirited and tending not to read the plethora of written recommendations and instructions. Clearer guidelines, of which there appears to be a better appreciation at the Welsh Office, need to be issued to replace the piles of documents already issued so that they can be dumped.

In their responses to the follow-up questionnaire completed toward the end of the second National Curriculum year, a few headteachers expressed particular frustration at the further changes that had been made to attainment targets in the core subjects of maths, English and science and resented the lack of oppportunity for consolidation and long term planning that resulted from them:

> The fact that the maths and science attainment targets are being reorganized confirms my view that the National Curriculum is being introduced in haste. More time in planning and introducing would provide a more solid foundation on which schools and teachers could build with confidence. A great deal of work in planning a suitable recording system in this school has been wasted effort in view of these changes.

> I think that everything has been rushed and we have been overwhelmed with new ideas too quickly. We have spent a lot of time working out our policies only to find that they are out of date as something else has taken their place. Changes are being made in maths, English and science again. This is very frustrating — things are far too unsettled.

Finally a number of critical comments referred to the rigidifying effect of the National Curriculum on curriculum planning stated earlier by some headteachers as a disadvantage of the National Curriculum. In particular its subject orientation was attacked, as in the following comments:

> A considerable amount of time, effort, sweat and tears has been put in to make the implementation of the National Curriculum work only to find that its subject based approach does not weld with the thematic approach. The subjects are overloaded and there is no perception of how the whole curriculum will fit together.

> I believe the National Curriculum has distinct benefits. Now it must be made to work. Every subject is overloaded. We must try to ensure that each subject does not become a separate entity.

Summary of the Headteachers' Views

The majority of headteachers reported that their schools had experienced some problems in implementing the National

Curriculum during the first two years, including increased pressure on class teachers to achieve the relevant attainment targets and to meet the demands of assessment and record keeping, and a shortage of the material resources needed. Like their class teacher colleagues most of them felt that their professional role had changed to some degree as a result of the introduction of the National Curriculum, coupled with other changes stemming from the ERA. Apart from a greater administrative workload the main changes were a sharper sense of professional accountability arising from the new legal responsibility for delivering the new curriculum, and a heightened awareness of their role in leading and supporting their staff and maintaining their confidence during a time of stress and challenge. Opinions were evenly divided about the impact of the National Curriculum on methods of teaching and organization in infant classrooms but those who felt there had been some change reported a tighter degree of structuring of classroom activities and reduced flexibility in curriculum planning resulting from the drive to meet the various attainment targets across the curriculum. The reduced opportunity for free play, particularly for disadvantaged children, was a strong concern of some headteachers.

The perceived benefits of the National Curriculum included better curriculum planning with greater continuity and progression than before and a broader, more varied curriculum and range of learning experiences. Disadvantages were felt to arise mainly from the increased pressure to achieve the relevant attainment targets which affected both teachers and children, particularly the slower learners who needed time to consolidate their learning. Nevertheless, as with the class teachers, half of the headteachers reported feeling happier about the National Curriculum one year after its introduction.

The headteachers' overall comments on the National Curriculum ranged from very positive to strongly negative. The favourable comments stressed the greater collaboration now taking place amongst teachers within their schools and the dedication and hard work of those teachers in trying to implement the National Curriculum effectively. On the negative side strong disapproval was expressed about the greatly increased workload and pressure on class teachers arising from the demands of the

National Curriculum, and also about the rapid pace at which it had been introduced at Key Stage 1. Particular frustration was expressed at the sheer weight of documentation and the fact that changes were already being made to some of the core subject attainment targets so soon after their introduction. A further criticism of some headteachers concerned the over-loaded nature of the new curriculum, both within and across subjects.

Overall the views of the headteachers and Year 1 class teachers regarding the positive and negative features of the National Curriculum broadly corresponded, with differences in emphasis which appeared to reflect the differences in their respective roles. Both groups felt that it provided a helpful planning framework, with clear aims and objectives, but strongly regretted the pressure which it engendered toward meeting the wide range of attainment targets and the consequent loss of flexibility and spontaneity in curriculum planning.

In this chapter the spontaneous views of the headteachers and class teachers towards the National Curriculum, based upon two years' experience of implementing it, have been presented. In the following chapter the overall attitudes of the teachers towards the National Curriculum are examined, using a specially devised attitude measurement scale. While the content of that scale was somewhat different from that of the questions asked in the teacher interviews, some comparisons between the results of the two forms of enquiry will be made.

Note

1 The term 'Adds hours' is a local one referring to the statutory non-teaching contact time which all teachers are now required to spend as part of their contracts.

Chapter 7

Teachers' Attitudes to the National Curriculum

In this chapter we explore the attitudes and views of the teachers towards the National Curriculum using a specially designed attitude scale. This enabled us to compare the attitudes of the headteachers and Year 1 class teachers on three occasions, to see if they showed any significant changes over the three years of the study. The three occasions were approximately one year before the introduction of the National Curriculum (1989) and towards the end of the first and second years following its introduction (1990 and 1991).

An attitude can be defined as the organization of a person's psychological processes with respect to some aspect of the world which she or he distinguished from other aspects. These processes include thoughts and beliefs (cognitive processes), feelings (affective processes) and dispositions to behave in certain ways toward the object of the attitude (conative processes). Attitudes are learned and modified as the result of experience, often incidentally rather than systematically, and some are significantly related to an individual's personality, particularly her or his fundamental values and motives. Although an attitude will predispose us to behave in a certain way towards its object, our behaviour in a specific, real life situation will be subject to other important influences. This means that we cannot predict precisely how a given individual will behave in a particular context simply from a knowledge of her or his attitudes. In the case of teachers, therefore, even if we can accurately measure their attitudes to the National Curriculum we cannot assume that they will directly act out their beliefs toward it in the classroom since their behaviour will also be subject to other powerful influences, including the expectations of others. Even so it is important to try to measure teachers' attitudes to a reform as fundamental as the National Curriculum since they have a statutory commitment to its successful implementation and that is likely to be helped by positive attitudes and hindered by negative ones.

The written attitude scale devised for this study comprised fourteen statements about the National Curriculum, seven positive and seven negative, which the teachers were asked to respond to using a five-point scale ranging from 'strongly agree', through 'uncertain', to 'strongly disagree' (see Appendix 1). (Technical details about the scale can be found in Cox *et al.*, 1991). The selection of statements for the scale was made from a reading of the current educational press and from discussions with teachers at INSET and other meetings. The scale was piloted in two primary schools not included in the study sample. For the purpose of calculating a total attitude scale score, only ten of the fourteen items were used since, for the remaining four items it was found that the teachers' scores on those items showed little relationship to their total scores derived from all items in the scale. (The four items omitted from the total attitude scale score were items numbered 1, 2, 11 and 12 respectively.) However these four items were retained for the item by item analysis of results presented later in this chapter. Since the scores for each of the items ranged from 1 to 5 (i.e. from 'strongly disagree' to 'strongly agree' in the case of positively worded items and the reverse for negatively worded items) the minimum and maximum scale total scores were 10 and 50 respectively, with an arithmetical mid-point or 30.

The attitude scale was completed in writing by the teachers immediately prior to their interviews in 1989 and 1990 and as part of the written follow-up study carried out in 1991. Thus we obtained a measure of their attitudes to the National Curriculum approximately one year before its introduction and toward the end of the first and second years following that. We can therefore compare the results for each year to see if there are any significant changes over the study period. Before doing that, however, we will present the results for each year separately.

Year By Year Results

The distribution of the teachers' total attitude scale scores for each of the three years are shown in Figures 1 to 3 in which we have combined the scores of the headteachers and class teachers since they were found not to differ significantly (see Appendix 2, Table A.1 for the mean scale scores for headteachers and class teachers on each occasion). It is clear that in each year there is a wide spread of attitude scores ranging from strongly negative to strongly positive but on each occasion the scores tend to cluster around the arithmetical scale mean of 30.

While it is tempting to regard the middle of the score range on this scale as reflecting a neutral or moderate overall attitude toward the National Curriculum, one must be cautious in making such an interpretation because of the nature of the type of attitude scale used. Thus, in some cases, the total scores in the middle range may have resulted from a combination of both positive and negative scores on the various scale items, but in other cases the same total scores could have resulted from a high proportion of 'neutral' responses, that is, scoring 3 in the response scale. Thus the same middle range scores could reflect a consistently moderate or neutral attitude toward the National Curriculum, or, in contrast, an inconsistent attitude in which positive and negative views cancel each other out. However the more extreme total attitude scale scores are easier to interpret since they are likely to reflect the respondents' stronger, more consistent views. While it is encouraging to infer from Figures 1 to 3 that some of the sample teachers had strongly positive overall attitudes to the National Curriculum, it is somewhat alarming that there are other teachers whose overall attitudes appear to be strongly negative, even though, as we pointed out earlier in this chapter, we must not assume a direct link between a teacher's attitude and his or her classroom behaviour.

Trends in the Teachers' Attitudes over Time

It can be seen from Figures 1 to 3 that, while the attitude score distributions for each of the three years show a wide spread around the scale mean, those for 1990 and 1991 show a bias toward the

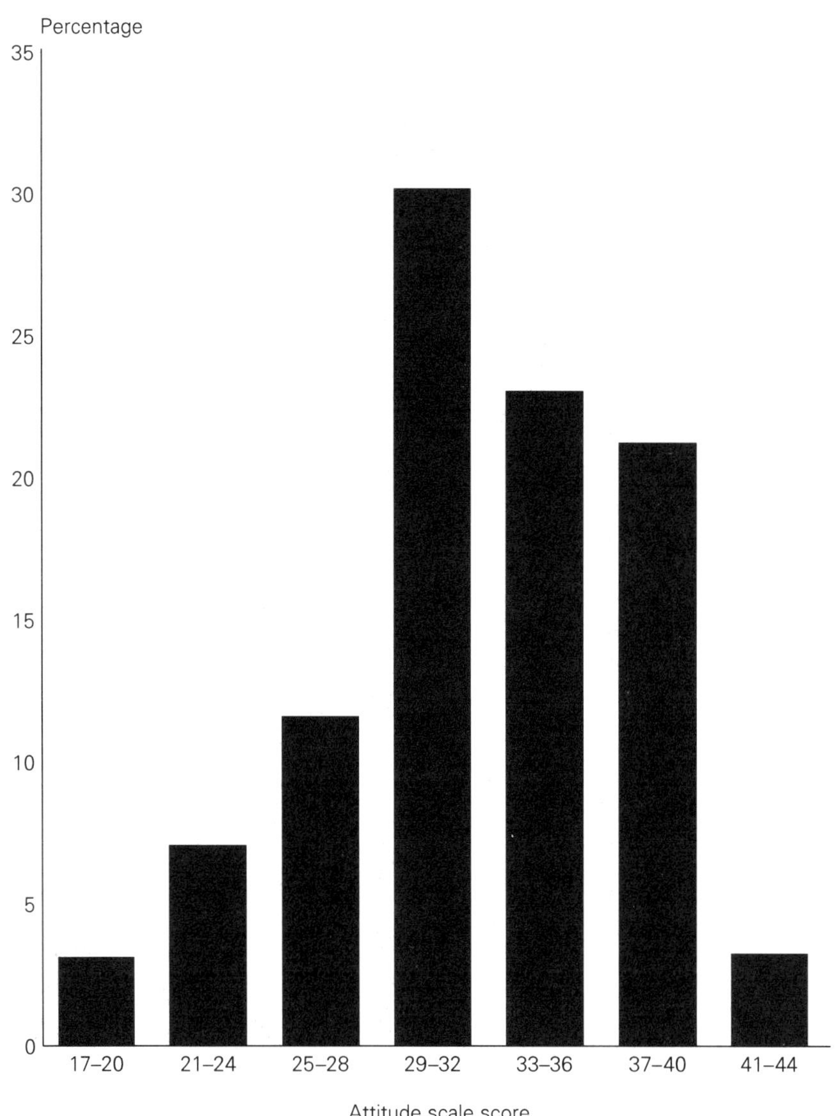

Figure 1 Teachers' attitude scale scores in 1989
Note: N = 57; Mean = 32.00

negative end of the score range. Statistical testing confirmed that the teachers' mean scores for each of those years were significantly lower than that for 1989, although there was no significant difference between the means for 1990 and 1991 (see Appendix 2, Table A.2.) Since the composition of the sample of Year 1 class teachers had changed somewhat during the three years

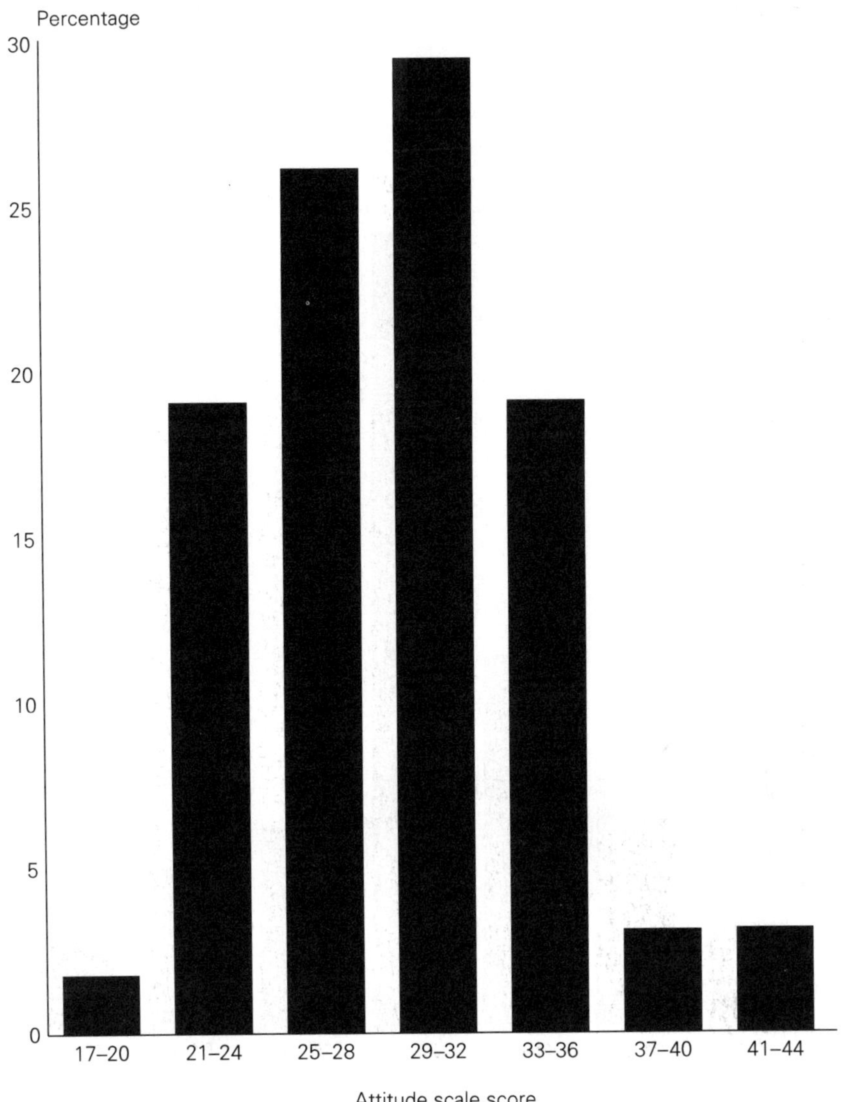

Figure 2 Teachers' attitude scale scores in 1990
Note: N = 58; Mean = 29.33

of the study, we must be cautious about attributing this downward trend in the mean scores to a 'hardening' of teachers' attitudes to the National Curriculum. (The composition of the headteachers' sample remained stable over the three years, apart from minor changes.) In order to made a strictly fair comparison between the teachers' year to year scores it is necessary to identify those teachers

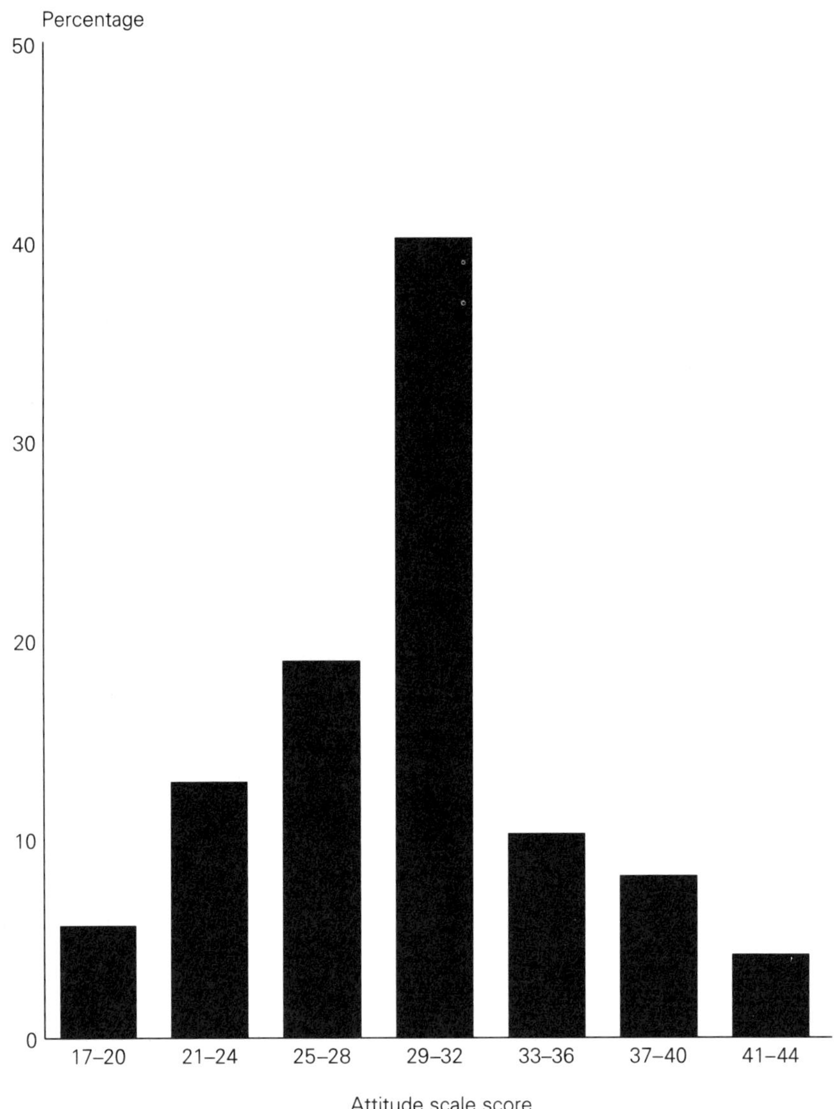

Figure 3 Teachers' attitude scale scores in 1991
Note: N = 52; Mean = 29.58

who responded to all three attitude questionnaires. This 'core sample' comprised thirty-five teachers, made up of twenty-one headteachers and fourteen Year 1 class teachers. The total attitude scale score distributions for this sample were plotted and were found to be very similar to those of the full sample and also to show the same negative trend over the three occasions (see

Appendix 2, Figures A.1 to A.3). Moreover the same pattern of between group differences emerged from the statistical testing as for the total sample. We can state with confidence then that, as a group, the teachers in this study appeared to become more negative in their overall attitudes toward the National Curriculum during the first two years of its implementation. We must emphasize though that this shift is a limited one for the teachers' attitude scores remained widely distributed about the mean on each occasion and at no time became predominantly negative.

One might expect this apparently negative shift in the teachers' attitudes to the National Curriculum to be reflected in their spontaneously expressed views reported in the previous chapter. In fact there is conflicting support for, on the one hand, at least half of the class teachers and headteachers judged that they felt happier about the National Curriculum one year after its implementation, but, on the other hand, negative views about the National Curriculum expressed by the headteachers in each of the first two years after its introduction tended to outweigh the more positive views, as did those of the class teachers regarding the impact of the National Curriculum upon their professional role. Since the attitude scale was made up of fourteen separate items it is worth examining the teachers' responses to each of these on each occasion to see if they can tell us something about the nature of the negative shift in the teachers' overall attitudes. For this analysis all fourteen of the attitude scale items will be used, not only the ten items used to compute the total attitude scale scores.

The full sample teachers' responses to each of the fourteen items of the attitude scale are shown in Table 8, from which we can identify those items where there appears to be a trend in the teachers' response patterns over the three occasions, either in the positive or the negative direction. Amongst the ten items which were used to compute the total attitude scale score there appears to be a negative shift in the response pattern over time for seven items (numbers 3, 5, 6, 7, 8, 9, and 10), with a similar shift for two of the four items not contributing to the total attitude scale score (numbers 2 and 12). In view of the changes in the composition of the teachers' sample over the study period mentioned earlier the responses of the 'core sample' of thirty-five teachers were also examined and these showed a similar negative shift on the same items as in the full sample.[1] Since the 'core sample' provides a more reliable guide to trends in the teachers' responses over time the following results are drawn from that sample only.

Of the items in which a statistically significant negative shift occurred two were concerned with National Curriculum assessment and reporting. In 1991, compared with 1989, more teachers endorsed the view that the formal assessment of attainment targets at age seven is too early and educationally unsound (item 10) and fewer endorsed the view that the SATs of the National Curriculum are essential to back up the teachers' own assessments (item 12). On the other items concerned with this topic the negative trends fell short of statistical significance. Two other scale items showed a statistically significant negative trend. First more teachers in 1991 agreed with the view that the National Curriculum posed a serious threat to cross-curricular (project) work because of its subject emphasis (item 2). Second fewer teachers in 1991 than in 1989 endorsed the view that the National Curriculum is broad, balanced and relevant to children's needs (item 9). There were no significant changes in the positive direction although there was a slight trend for more teachers in 1991 than in 1989 to disagree with the view that the introduction of the National Curriculum would lead to a concentration on 'the basics' (item 11).

A direct comparison between the teachers' views on the specific items of the attitude scale and their views expressed at interview is not possible since the questions guiding the latter were more concerned with the impact of the introduction of the National Curriculum, including its formal assessments, upon the teachers' professional role and methods rather than with its educational merits *per se*, although the latter sometimes received mention in the teachers' responses to the more open-ended questions. However the increased concern about the possible threat posed by the National Curriculum to cross-curricular work shown by the teachers in their responses to item 2 of the attitude scale was certainly reflected in the spontaneous comments of some of the teachers at interview.

On balance the evidence reported above indicates that, as a

group, the teachers in the sample became somewhat more negative in their attitudes to the National Curriculum, particularly with regard to the educational consequences of formal assessment. However this should not be taken to imply that their attitudes to the new curriculum were wholly negative for this was certainly not the case. Reference back to Table 8 shows that on some of the attitude scale items not concerned with formal assessment the majority (over 50 per cent) of teachers showed a positive view on each occasion. Thus, in each year, around 80 per cent of teachers welcomed the fact that the National Curriculum allowed them to decide how to achieve its aims (item 4), over 70 per cent disagreed with the view that the National Curriculum would mean a concentration on the 'basics' (item 11), and nearly 60 per cent disagreed with the view that the National Curriculum would seriously deprive the class teacher of professional freedom and scope for initiative (item 6). Finally, in both 1989 and 1990, over half of the teachers rejected the view that the National Curriculum was a backward educational move (item 13).

One might expect that as teachers gained experience in implementing the new curriculum they would become more definite in their views about it and that this would be reflected in fewer of them using the 'uncertain' response when completing the attitude scale subsequent to its first administration. From Table 8 it can be seen that there is indeed a trend for the percentage of respondents using this category to diminish between 1989 and 1991, although not between 1989 and 1990. This trend proved to be statistically significant for the full sample, but not for the 'core sample' although the latter teachers showed a similar downward trend in their use of this category. Two of the scale items showing a marked reduction in the proportion of uncertain responses were concerned with the formal assessment of children's attainments (items 10 and 12), which is consistent with the trend already reported for the teachers to become more negative in their views on this topic. On these particular questions the teachers' views certainly appeared to be crystallizing.

There were, however, three scale items where the proportion of teachers expressing uncertainty remained relatively high, i.e., over 25 per cent on all three occasions. These were item 9,

Table 8 Teachers' views on the National Curriculum over three years

Attitude Scale Item	Date	strongly agree	agree	uncertain	disagree	strongly disagree
		Percentage Responding				
1 We will find the NC helpful because it tells us what to teach and when.	1989	3	39	26	23	9
	1990	0	41	26	31	2
	1991	4	40	17	36	2
2 The NC poses a serious threat to cross-curricular (project) work because of its subject emphasis.	1989	5	16	17	44	17
	1990	5	29	17	45	3
	1991	15	33	15	36	0
3 The NC will force teachers to concentrate on teaching those skills/attitudes that are most easily measured at the expense of those that are less easy to assess.	1989	2	26	23	39	10
	1990	3	48	29	17	2
	1991	6	52	21	21	0
4 I welcome the fact that the NC still allows us to decide *how* to achieve its aims.	1989	28	51	12	7	2
	1990	29	50	15	5	0
	1991	17	67	6	8	2
5 The reporting of pupils' performance will mean that teachers will not be able to get away with poor teaching.	1989	5	35	21	32	7
	1990	0	15	36	34	14
	1991	4	13	23	48	11
6 The NC will seriously deprive the class teacher of professional freedom and scope for initiative.	1989	3	16	17	53	10
	1990	3	22	15	52	7
	1991	4	25	13	52	6
7 The formal assessment of children at age 7 will have a narrowing effect on the primary (infant) curriculum.	1989	16	26	25	32	2
	1990	15	50	21	10	3
	1991	11	48	21	17	2

8	The NC assessments will be helpful in backing up our judgments when discussing pupils with parents.	1989	7	72	10	10	0
		1990	2	52	24	22	0
		1991	6	52	17	25	0
9	The NC is broad, balanced and relevant to children's needs.	1989	5	49	39	7	0
		1990	2	34	41	22	0
		1991	0	38	40	19	2
10	The formal assessment of attainment targets at age 7 is too early and educationally unsound.	1989	32	23	30	16	0
		1990	36	38	15	7	3
		1991	35	38	17	8	2
11	The introduction of the NC means that we can concentrate on the basics and forget about the airy fairy subjects that have crept into primary education.	1989	2	2	23	39	35
		1990	0	5	5	62	28
		1991	2	2	10	56	31
12	The standard assessment tasks (SATs) of the NC are essential to back up the teachers' own assessments.	1989	0	51	39	7	3
		1990	0	15	38	34	12
		1991	0	6	15	58	21
13	The introduction of the NC is a backward move educationally.	1989	3	7	39	51	0
		1990	5	14	43	36	2
		1991	2	15	27	52	4
14	The introduction of the NC means that all pupils will get the same breadth and depth of curriculum regardless of which school they attend.	1989	2	40	26	30	2
		1990	2	28	26	29	15
		1991	2	27	29	35	8

Note: N = 57 (1989), 58 (1990) and 52 (1991)

stating that the National Curriculum was broad, balanced and relevant to children's needs, item 13, stating that the National Curriculum was a backward move educationally and item 14, stating that under the National Curriculum all pupils would get the same breadth and depth of the curriculum regardless of which schools they attended.

One can understand that some teachers might consider that two years is not long enough to decide whether the introduction of the National Curriculum really is a backward educational move. This relatively short time scale may also explain why a substantial proportion of them were still undecided about whether the new curriculum was broad, balanced and relevant to children's educational needs, or whether pupils were likely to gain its full curricular benefits regardless of which schools they attended. During the period of the study, the non-core subjects of, history, geography, music, technology, physical education and (in Wales) Welsh were successively introduced and the teachers were still in the very early stages of incorporating the new programmes of study into their curricula and teaching methods. Some teachers' spontaneous comments reported in the previous chapter indicated that they appreciated the scope and breadth of the full new curriculum but felt strong anxieties about the consequent danger of superficiality in the teaching of it.

Summary

In each of the three years when their attitudes were measured the teachers (headteachers and class teachers combined) showed a wide range of attitudes to the National Curriculum, ranging from the strongly positive to the strongly negative, with the majority of teachers lying between those extremes. There was a strong tendency for the teachers' attitudes to become less positive during the three years of the study, particularly with regard to the formal assessment of children's attainments. In addition the proportion of teachers regarding the National Curriculum as a serious threat to cross-curricular teaching significantly increased during this period. Associated with this pattern was a clear trend towards greater certainty amongst the teachers in their responses to the scale items, with the exception of three items. This apparently negative shift in attitudes towards the National Curriculum appeared to conflict with the finding reported in the previous chapter that at least half of the teachers reported feeling happier about the introduction of the National Curriculum in the second year of the enquiry but this could be due to the fact that the attitude scale addressed some educational issues not covered in the teachers' questionnaires. Despite this negative trend in overall attitudes the majority of teachers continued to express positive views regarding some aspects of the National Curriculum, agreeing that it provided a useful planning framework which still allowed them scope for professional initiative and they strongly rejected the view that the introduction of the National Curriculum would lead to an over-concentration on 'the basics'.

Note

1 In the full teachers' sample only items 2, 5, 8, and 12 showed a statistically significant negative shift when tested by the Chi-squared technique (1989 vs 1991). In the core sample only items 2, 5, 9, 10 and 12 showed a significant difference.

Chapter 8

Summary, Discussion and Conclusions

The following is a summary of the main findings of the study. These will then be discussed in relation to the findings of other relevant National Curriculum studies and reports from HMI and government agencies, with the exception of the findings concerning the education of under-5-year-old children, and the education of slower learning and socially disadvantaged children which will be discussed in Chapters 10 and 11 respectively.

1 In each of the three years of the study the headteachers and class teachers combined showed a wide range of measured attitudes towards the National Curriculum ranging from strongly positive to strongly negative but with the majority lying within these extremes. There was a strong tendency for the teachers' overall attitudes to become somewhat less positive during the first two years of the implementation of the National Curriculum than in the year prior to its introduction. This trend stemmed mainly from those items in the attitude scale which were concerned with the formal assessment of children's attainments. On the remaining items of the scale the majority of teachers responded positively on each of the three occasions when they completed the scale.

2 While there was recognition of the breadth and variety of the National Curriculum many teachers expressed concern about the sheer number of attainment targets and statements of attainment to be covered in the core subjects and felt that this wider curriculum coverage could only be achieved at the expense of the depth and quality of children's learning in these subjects.

3 Many class teachers, supported by their headteachers,

expressed serious concern about the heavy demands upon their time and class management skills made by the new assessment and record keeping requirements which were felt by some teachers to reduce the time available actually to teach their pupils the new curriculum.

4 Many headteachers expressed strong disapproval about the greatly increased workload and pressures upon their class teachers arising from the demands of the National Curriculum and the rapid pace of its introduction at Key Stage 1. Particular frustration was expressed at the fact that changes had already been made to some core subject attainment targets and programmes of study soon after their introduction.

5 Despite the pressures exerted on them by the demands of the National Curriculum many teachers appeared to gain in confidence in their ability to meet these demands during the first year of its implementation. This was coupled with the recognition, by both class teachers and headteachers, of the fact that the National Curriculum provided a clear curriculum planning framework with built-in continuity and progression.

6 Headteachers reported feeling a sharper sense of professional accountability arising from their schools' responsibility to implement the new curriculum and a heightened awareness of their role in leading and supporting their staff in this process and in maintaining their morale during a period of stress and change.

7 There was a fairly even split amongst the headteachers in their responses to the question of whether the introduction of the National Curriculum had made an impact upon the methods of classroom organization and teaching at the infant stage. The view that the impact had been slight contrasted with reports of a tighter structuring of classroom activities, reduced flexibility in curriculum planning and a greater degree of collective staff planning and collaboration than previously.

8 In some classrooms the introduction of the National Curriculum appeared to reduce the scope for Year 1 teachers to engage in their children's free play activities,

although this trend was not strong when the amounts of free play time were compared in 1989 and 1990 in the teachers' sample as a whole. This was a source of concern to those teachers reporting such a reduction, especially with regard to slower learning children and those from socially disadvantaged backgrounds since free play activities were seen as providing the vital foundation for the development of these children's language, cognitive and social development.

9 Headteachers were divided in their views about the consequences of the introduction of the National Curriculum for the teaching of under-5-year-old children (including those in Year 1 classes). Some appeared to view the 'pre-5' curriculum in terms of preparing children for Key Stage 1 work and welcomed the opportunity to impose a firmer structure upon it than before. Others, however, expressed concern at what they saw to be the premature introduction of very young children to more formal National Curriculum-led teaching and stressed the importance of preserving the distinctive child centred character of early years education. The views of the latter were strongly supported by those of a group of infant teachers, drawn from several LEAs in the region who were invited to state their views on this question at an INSET seminar held after the completion of the study.

10 The majority of head and class teachers judged that the National Curriculum had made no major impact upon the teaching of more able pupils, claiming that these children continued to work at their own individual rates and levels and that they had been fully extended in their learning prior to the introduction of the National Curriculum. Where teachers did report some impact of the new curriculum upon these children's quality of learning only benefits were mentioned.

11 A substantial proportion of teachers reported that the introduction of the National Curriculum had put greater pressure upon slower learning children in order to reach the appropriate attainment targets. There was concern that the quality and depth of such children's learning

might suffer as the result of this pressure. Some teachers also voiced the concern that an early and public failure of certain children to reach the attainment targets would have a damaging effect upon their motivation and self-esteem. A further worry was expressed that teachers would be unable to spend sufficient time in teaching these children the basic skills because of the wider curricular demands of the National Curriculum. Some class teachers themselves felt under pressure in their efforts to help slower learning children to reach the prescribed attainment levels.

12 Teachers' perceived needs for INSET and their confidence in being able to deliver the National Curriculum varied during the study. Initially their concerns focused on assessment and record keeping but, after relevant INSET, they felt better prepared in this regard. As new subject orders became available teachers looked for appropriate INSET focusing on the teaching of non-core subjects.

13 Over the study period both headteachers and class teachers perceived a change in the status and nature of the topic or cross-curricular approach to teaching. Topics became more focused, with a trend towards science, and the choice of topics appeared to be constrained by the emphasis upon whole school planning. Class teachers expressed diverse views about the suitability of a cross-curricular approach to the teaching of the National Curriculum, some considering that it was the only way to cover its breadth, while others thought that it would be impossible to cover the whole of the National Curriculum in this way. However, amongst the headteachers there was an increasing acknowledgment that discrete subject teaching would have a place in the teaching of the National Curriculum.

14 Anxieties about assessment and record keeping were expressed throughout the period of the study. After relevant INSET, however, teachers felt better prepared to undertake these activities; they then began to see the need for added resources, time and classroom help in order to

be able to carry out the procedures. Teachers also reported that it was in the area of assessment and record keeping that most change had taken place.

Discussion

Up to this point we have simply presented the findings of our study largely without comment and have tried faithfully to reflect the views of the teachers in our sample, based upon their experience of implementing the National Curriculum over two years. It is now necessary to examine these findings from the wider perspective of the outcome of other contemporaneous research studies and the literature on educational theory and practice.

The Research Background

We must first of all stress that our sample of teachers and primary schools was drawn from just one LEA in South Wales and involved only Year 1 class teachers and headteachers. While we are confident that the sample of schools was representative of primary schools in this particular LEA we cannot claim that it was equally representative of primary schools across England and Wales nationally. Moreover the study focused upon the implementation of the National Curriculum at Key Stage 1 only and in particular in Year 1. We must therefore relate our findings to those emerging from other studies which were somewhat wider in their scope and were based upon samples which may be more representative nationally.

For this purpose our main data sources were two ongoing large scale research studies of the impact of the National Curriculum on primary schools and teachers and also reports issued by various government-funded agencies such as Her Majesty's Inspectorate (HMI), now the Office for Standards in Education (OFSTED), the National Curriculum Council (NCC), and the Curriculum Council for Wales (CCW). The latter reports provide empirical data concerning the implementation of the National Curriculum at Key Stages 1 and 2 based upon HMI and

OFSTED surveys and school inspections, as well as the results from specially convened teachers' conferences and from other consultation exercises directed at schools and LEAs.

The first large scale research project is entitled 'Primary Assessment Curriculum and Experience' (PACE) and is centred at the Universities of Bristol and of the West of England. It was based upon a sample of forty-eight primary and infant schools drawn from eight LEAs in England and Wales. Its overall aim was to evaluate the impact of the National Curriculum upon infant children and their teachers. Data were gathered from two rounds of structured interviews with 150 headteachers and infant teachers, the first of which was carried out in 1990, shortly after the introduction of the National Curriculum at Key Stage 1. The second round of interviews was carried out in 1992. In addition the research team made direct classroom observations of teachers and pupils working in a sub-sample of project schools.

The second major study was carried out at the University of Exeter under the title of the Leverhulme Primary Project (LPP). As part of this wide ranging study a written questionnaire survey of the views of 901 teachers from 152 primary schools in England and Wales was carried out in 1989. This sample was judged to be a nationally representative one since it closely matched the distribution of primary schools in England and Wales according to size and region. (see Wragg *et al.*, 1989). This study was followed by a more recent survey of teachers from a representative sample of 131 primary schools, some of which had participated in the original survey, using a modified version of the original postal questionnaire which included a section addressed specifically to teachers of Key Stage 1 children.

Teachers' Overall Response to the National Curriculum

One of the main findings of our study was that, in terms of their measured attitudes, the headteachers and Year 1 class teachers in the sample appeared to be predominantly positive toward the National Curriculum in principle, although they were seriously concerned about aspects of the formal assessment of young children's attainments. This finding is very strongly supported by those from the PACE and Leverhulme studies respectively (Osborn and Pollard, 1991; Bennett *et al.*, 1992). It was also strongly backed up by the reported observations of HMI and other government appointed agencies in the report by the Office for Standards in Education (OFSTED) published in 1993a. Indeed we have not encountered any publication which claims that primary teachers are opposed to the National Curriculum *in principle.*

Similarly our finding that the teachers welcomed the planning framework offered by the National Curriculum, with its built in progression is supported by the results of other studies. The PACE project reported that most of the teachers in the study welcomed at least some aspects of the National Curriculum, particularly the curriculum clarification and focus it provided (Osborn and Broadfoot, 1991; Osborn *et al.*, 1993), and the Leverhulme Project found that the primary teachers were using the National Curriculum widely as a planning framework, through its statements of attainment and programmes of study (Bennett *et al.*, 1992). This is perhaps the most encouraging finding from the various studies which suggests that, despite being imposed upon teachers and schools by government decree, the National Curriculum has met a long standing need for detailed curriculum guidance.

The Manageability of the National Curriculum

Despite their positive acceptance of the National Curriculum in principle, the teachers in our study expressed two very serious concerns about its implementation in practice. The first of these was about the sheer scale of curricular prescription in terms of the number of attainment targets and statements of attainment which they saw as a threat to the quality of the children's learning. This concern was echoed by HMI in their published response to the 'three wise men' consultative document sent to all primary schools and LEAs in England (Alexander *et al.*, 1992). In their report (OFSTED, 1993a) HMI state that, while expressing strong support for the National Curriculum in principle and acknowledging the better balance and greater breadth which it had brought to children's educational experience, teachers in England showed strong concern over its manageability with regard to capacity of primary schools to teach all subjects in the necessary depth. Manageability was seen as a particular problem at Key Stage 1 where the fundamental and time-consuming introduction of young children to the learning of literacy and numeracy had to be undertaken together with the work on the full range of the National Curriculum core and non-core subjects. The report explicitly warned that if schools were overstretched to provide the National Curriculum then the depth of children's learning was likely to be sacrificed in pursuit of breadth, thus supporting the views of many teachers in our own study.

Objective evidence for the increased workloads of infant teachers during the year following the introduction of the National Curriculum was also provided in a study of teacher time and curriculum manageability at Key Stage 1 carried out by Campbell and Neill (1992) for the Assistant Masters and Mistresses Association (now the Association of Teachers and Lecturers). This was based on written evidence from over 100 infant teachers from sixty-one LEAs in England and Wales, although the authors did not claim that this constituted a nationally representative sample. The sample was heavily biased towards 'Year 2' infant teachers (that is, of 6 to 7-year-old children) since they comprised nearly two-thirds of it.

The teachers kept a detailed record of their time spent on work for a period of seven consecutive days in 1992. The study found that, on average, the teachers worked a fifty-two hour week in 1992 (ten hours per day). This was a slight increase upon the average times recorded in previous phases of the study carried out in 1990 and 1991, and a major increase upon the average figure of forty-four hours recorded in a separate study carried out in 1971. The authors attributed the infant teachers' heavy workload partly to the demands of the National Curriculum but also to their 'personal sense of conscientiousness'.

Despite this degree of teacher commitment, Campbell and Neill concluded that as it stood, the Key Stage 1 curriculum (core and non-core) was unmanageable in terms of the times officially allocated for teaching the various subjects. This, they claimed, created an impossible dilemma for conscientious teachers and was a cause of stress and a reduced sense of achievement amongst them, although no supporting evidence for the latter assertion was provided. With further educational reforms still on-stream the authors saw no reason to predict any significant reduction in the teachers' workloads. Their report also provided evidence that the workload of Year 2 teachers was significantly heavier than that of other infant teachers, probably because of the extra demands placed on them by the administration of SATs at the end of this Key Stage.

No doubt as a direct consequence of such widespread concern amongst teachers and researchers about the manageability of the National Curriculum the National Curriculum Council (NCC), in its advice to the Secretary of State for Education, recommended that each subject order should be reduced to an 'essential core' of knowledge, skills and understanding appropriate to each Key Stage (NCC, 1993a). By contrast the Chairman of the Curriculum Council for Wales (CCW) argued against making such major changes at this relatively early stage in the implementation of the National Curriculum on the grounds of the costs, uncertainty and disruption that this would cause (Daugherty, 1992).

Assessment and Record Keeping

The second major concern of our teachers was over the heavy demands upon their time and their class management skills made by the new assessment and record keeping requirements of the National Curriculum, which were seen by some teachers as reducing the time available for actually teaching the National Curriculum. Coupled with this was the view of a majority of the teachers that the formal assessment of children's knowledge and understanding at age 7 was inappropriate. This concern was also highlighted in the other research studies of the impact of the National Curriculum and in other reports. The Leverhulme Project for example reported that concerns about national assessment were dominant amongst the sample of teachers (Bennett *et al.*, 1992), and the PACE project reported the frustration and anger expressed by many teachers over the amount of time now demanded by record keeping and assessment and their fears that these activities were beginning to take over from 'real teaching' (Osborn and Pollard, 1991).

The Leverhulme Project included a sample of teachers of 5 to 7-year-old children in order to study their views on and experiences of National Curriculum assessment and testing. A large proportion of these particular teachers felt that their time for 'normal classwork' was substantially reduced by the new assessment requirements and most teachers felt themselves to be under additional stress as a consequence. Well over half of these teachers reported having to make changes in their methods of classroom organization in order to manage these new requirements. In similar vein, the NCC advice document reported widespread concern amongst teachers that arrangements for assessment and record keeping were having an unhelpful impact on curricular decisions and were cutting disproportionately into teaching time (NCC, 1993a). Also HMI (England), in a review of the implementation of the National Curriculum in its second year (1990–91), reported that the time taken up by assessment and record keeping remained a concern for many teachers and had not so far led to a general increase in the standards of teaching and learning (DFE, 1992). The specially commissioned study of infant teachers' workloads by Campbell and Neill (1992) also highlighted the disproportionate amount of time taken up by National Curriculum testing and recording.

The Pace of Change

In our own study strong concern was expressed by the headteachers about the greatly increased work load and pressure upon their class teachers following the introduction of the National Curriculum. Some headteachers also voiced their resentment at the rapid pace at which the curriculum orders had been introduced at Key Stage 1 and, in particular at the fact that significant changes had been made in some subject orders soon after their introduction. Similarly critical views were expressed by teachers in other studies and reports. The Leverhulme Project and PACE studies reported that the teachers in their samples had reacted negatively to the compressed time scale for the introduction of the National Curriculum and the stress and higher teacher work loads resulting from it (Osborn *et al.*, 1993; Bennett *et al.*, 1992). Similarly Vulliamy and Webb (1993) reported that the primary teachers in their sample of teachers attending a global education INSET project, while generally accepting the principles and content of the National Curriculum, made explicit criticisms about the speed of its implementation and the increased volume of paper work resulting from its introduction.

Learning to Cope with the National Curriculum

The positive finding of our own study that, despite the demands and pressures exerted by the National Curriculum, many of the teachers appeared to gain in confidence in their ability to meet its requirements during the first year of its implementation finds support in the HMI review of the implementation of the National Curriculum during 1990–91 (DFE, 1992). This concluded that many primary teachers were becoming more confident about the assessment of pupils' work within the National Curriculum and that curriculum planning in Key Stages 1 and 2 continued to improve as teachers began to collaborate more and as clearer and more effective subject teaching guidelines were written. In their discussion of the survey findings from the Leverhulme Primary Project Bennett *et al.* (1992) stated that, following the implementation of the National Curriculum on a highly compressed time scale, with the accompanying stress for teachers, more certainty had appeared in the system as implementation proceeded and the process of accommodation to its requirements continued to take place. This process was reflected in the changing nature of the teachers' concerns as monitored in the study.

In the light of such findings it might be suggested that as teachers' confidence in their ability to manage the requirements of the National Curriculum grows, through improved curriculum planning and classroom organization and teaching methods, the disruptive and demoralizing effects of the over-rapid introduction of the National Curriculum will prove to have been only transitory. While in our own study the headteachers were fairly evenly split in their views concerning the impact of the National Curriculum on their schools' methods of teaching and classroom organization at the infant stage it might be predicted that, as the full range of non-core subject orders comes on-stream, with the accompanying assessment, record keeping and reporting requirements, then all schools will have to make major adaptations to their existing methods. Support for this view comes from a more recent finding of the PACE Project that the proportion of class teachers who felt that they had less freedom in their choice of teaching methods than previously increased between 1990 and 1992 (Osborn *et al.*, 1993).

The Future of Cross-curricular Teaching

The trends picked out in our research study concerning the effects of the National Curriculum upon teachers' use of the topic approach were also reported by the Curriculum Council for Wales (1992c) and by Webb (1993). The PACE project also found that teachers' ability to respond to topics introduced by children and to create teaching activities around them was being eroded (Osborn *et al.*, 1993). There is no doubt that the National Curriculum is constricting the choice of topic in thematic work but there is also evidence that much more careful thought is now being given to planning the structure and progression of this work than hitherto. The 'three wise men report' (Alexander *et al.*, 1992) contained a sharp critique of the quality of much of the cross-curricular, thematic work being carried out in primary schools and one might speculate whether this would have been the case if their report had been written a year or so later. We think not; neither do we believe that the improvement in the structure and planning of this work, which we and others have reported, are wholly due either to the report or to attacks upon 'woolly progressive education'. On the contrary we believe that it is a positive outcome of the introduction of the National Curriculum and the INSET which has been provided in its support.

There is evidence from some of the studies described earlier, including our own, that teachers are now talking of the need for discrete subject teaching to complement thematic work when it is not possible to cover all of the National Curriculum content through such an approach. This could be because they now see themelves as accountable in terms of the National Curriculum orders, whereas, in the past, they might have seen themselves as accountable to the thematic approach traditionally endorsed by many LEA primary advisory services (see Alexander, 1992). Also, as part of the improved curriculum planning, groups of teachers are meeting and working collaboratively. This has improved progression and led to a consideration of the curriculum over a Key Stage as a whole. There is a sharing of specialisms and skills that benefits both teachers and pupils. We see this as another positive outcome of the National Curriculum.

In our opinion the recent questioning of the capacity of the thematic, cross-curricular approach to teaching to carry the full burden of the National Curriculum work means a re-evaluation of the notion of 'good primary practice'. For some any decline in the amount and status of thematic work would be a negative outcome of the National Curriculum. Nevertheless, while we would deplore the loss of this approach completely we see advantages in the exploration of other ways of curriculum planning. This debate about cross-curricular vs discrete subject teaching is discussed in more detail in Chapter 9.

The Role of the Headteacher

Our findings that the headteachers reported a sharper sense of their own professional accountability arising from their schools' legal responsibility for delivering the new curriculum, coupled with a heightened awareness of their role in leading and supporting their staffs, finds endorsement in two reports produced as part of the National Curriculum consultation exercises mounted in England and Wales. In the first of these, OFSTED reported that educational leadership was considered to be central to the headteacher's role and that the demands of LMS and administration were subordinate to this task. Considerable professional overload was reported by headteachers as they managed the demands from LEAs, governors, teachers and parents (OFSTED,

1993a). In a document of advice and guidance produced for primary schools in Wales, the Curriculum Council for Wales (CCW, 1992a) also draws attention to the constraints upon headteachers as they strive to discharge their role as the leading professional in the school. The document recommends that high priority should be given to providing management training for headteachers in relation to their leadership roles in the management of schools, of classroom practice and of curriculum development.

The PACE Project reported that the great majority of headteachers in the study had experienced a reduction in autonomy and felt themselves subject to more constraints and controls. This sense of loss of autonomy grew between 1990 and 1992 (Croll *et al.*, 1993). The study also found that, during this period, a minority of headteachers had moved toward a rather more directed, managerial strategy for accomplishing change, although other headteachers achieved a more collaborative, 'collegial' style.

Conclusions

Our main conclusions drawn from our own study, but supported by the literature we have reviewed in this chapter are as follows:

1 While there was a general welcome by teachers for the clear planning framework provided by the National Curriculum this was offset by their widespread concern at the over-loaded curriculum, with the sheer number of attainment targets threatening the depth and quality of the children's learning.
2 Teachers of Key Stage 1 of the National Curriculum have reported a significant increase in their workloads following the introduction of the new curriculum and a strong feeling of being under pressure to reach the many attainment targets relevant to their pupils. This pressure may be adversely affecting the teaching of slower learners and children under 5 because of a reduction in their opportunities for play based, experiential learning.
3 The assessment and record keeping requirements of the National Curriculum were a major focus of the concerns

of class teachers and headteachers alike because of the demands they made upon the time and managerial skills of class teachers at the expense of their teaching time. This deep concern was coupled with the view of the majority of teachers that the formal assessment of children's educational attainments at age 7 was educationally unsound.

4 Teachers' use of thematic/topic work changed over the period of the research. Topic work became more structured in order to take in as much National Curriculum work as possible. Topics also became more focused with a trend towards science-led topics. There was also something of a move away from cross-curricular work towards discrete subject teaching, even at Key Stage 1.

Future Developments

It is vitally important to continue the process of monitoring the impact of the National Curriculum in the years to come, in order that we may be able to assess its longer term effects. This process will be complicated by the fact that further major changes to it are already in the pipeline. Such monitoring will need to be carried out at all levels from the individual school upwards. At the national level the new agencies soon to be set up by the present government, the Schools Curriculum and Assessment Authority in England, and the Curriculum and Assessment Authority in Wales, together with OFSTED, will clearly have a major role to play in this process. At the same time there will be a continuing need for independent research studies of the kind reviewed in this chapter, at least some of which should include an element of classroom based observation, preferably involving teachers themselves as researchers.

At the time of writing, the Dearing Report (NCC, 1993b) has been published as an interim response to the Secretary of State for Education's commission to look into the scope for slimming down the National Curriculum and its associated assessment and record keeping. Amongst this report's recommendations which bear upon Key Stage 1 are the following:

1. Each National Curriculum subject order should be revised to distinguish between a statutory core which must be taught, and optional studies to be carried out at the discretion of the individual teacher;
2. As a result of this restructuring teachers should be allowed a specified margin of teaching time after the requirements of the National Curriculum and Religious Education have been met. The smallest margin (10 to 15 per cent) should be specified for Key Stage 1 because of the high priority accorded to the learning of the basic skills within the core subjects.
3. Standard national assessment should be retained but with a reduction in the time it requires and equal status should be given to teacher assessment in reporting to parents and others.

It is clear that, as a result of the accumulated evidence about the unmanageability of the National Curriculum in its present form and the recommendations of the Dearing Report (although interim at this stage), the next few years will see a significant easing of the demands placed upon Key Stage 1 teachers both in teaching and assessment under the National Curriculum. However many of the major educational issues raised by our study and by other studies reviewed in this chapter will remain and will need to be resolved, especially at the school level. What is now needed is a rational debate, informed by the theoretical and research literature on the one hand and by a critical self-analysis by teachers of their professional philosophies, beliefs and classroom practices on the other (see Alexander, 1992, for a useful model designed to guide the conceptual analysis of what constitutes 'good primary practice'). These issues include the relationship and balance between the teaching of the so-called basic skills and the rest of the curriculum at Key Stage 1; the relationship between the curriculum for under-5s and the National Curriculum; the identification of and provision for slower learners under the National Curriculum; and the future of cross-curricular, thematic teaching and of discrete subject teaching at the primary school stage. These issues are explored further in Part II of this book.

Part II

Selected Issues Arising from the Study

Chapter 9

Pedagogical and Curricular Issues

Introduction

Since the introduction of the National Curriculum the debate in education has expanded to include attacks on 'primary practice' and the initial training of teachers. As the formal assessment procedures spread into the secondary sector they met strong opposition culminating in the teaching unions refusing to administer the tests and the Headteachers' Association refusing to report results. As an attempt to defuse the situation a review of the National Curriculum was announced. This review was to be led by Sir Ron Dearing and was to have a short time scale. In May 1993 Sir Ron invited those interested in education to respond to four questions. (In Wales a fifth question on the order for Welsh was included.) The questions addressed the two main criticisms of the National Curriculum: the detail within the subject areas and the complexity of the assessment procedures. There was some debate, particularly in Wales, following the lead of the Chair of CCW Richard Daugherty that a period of 'no change' during which evidence was collected for a wide ranging review was a preferable path.

> In conclusion, I would therefore ask those who, for various reasons, find current Orders unsatisfactory to have patience while, with goodwill and the professional insights gained from experience, we work towards a more satisfactory framework — a second generation of curriculum Orders . . . Are you, and more to the point, are primary teachers ready to contemplate another upheaval in the framework? The ultimate test for me is would pupils be best served by a further period, lasting several years, of fundamental change? Should we not, while that debate is

> in progress, concentrate all our energies on making as much of a success as we can of the current framework? (Daugherty 1992: 15)

This caution in the face of the possibly destabilizing effects of further change was reiterated by some of the associations and organizations approached specifically for a response, for example the Mathematical Association.

Duncan Graham, who had served as Chair of the NCC from 1988 to 1991, comments on the fact that the NCC was not

> permitted to undertake the broad, disinterested research which I had envisaged when appointed. Changing and updating of the curriculum needs to be on the best available evidence, commissioned from reputable bodies. (Graham, 1993: 9)

In a research project instigated by the Association of Teachers and Lecturers, Rosemary Webb (1993) found that a large majority of headteachers, class teachers and advisers were convinced that what was needed now was a period of consolidation without further changes. However this was not to be.

Pedagogical Issues

Although our research focused on Key Stage 1 it is difficult to discuss this stage in isolation. In many areas Key Stage 1 and Key Stage 2 pupils attend the same schools. In some schools they may be in the same class. The headteachers who interpret the policies are often responsible for pupils in both stages and may not distinguish between them as clearly as early years experts might. Not all headteachers will have had extensive experience of teaching at Key Stage 1. For these reasons we widen the discussion in this chapter to include the whole of the primary phase.

What to Teach or How to Teach?

Despite the rhetoric that the National Curriculum was about what to teach rather than how to teach (as illustrated in the following quotation) there were pedagogical issues that arose from it.

> The National Curriculum is not a straitjacket. It provides for greater clarity and precision about *what* should be taught while enabling schools to retain flexibility about *how* they organise their teaching. (NCC, 1989a: 1; our emphasis)

The presentation of the curriculum as discrete subject packages appeared to conflict with the thematic and cross-curricular approaches beloved of the primary practitioner and advanced by such initiatives as the Technical and Vocational Education Initiative (TVEI). Despite the fact that early supporting material such as *Policy into Practice* (DES, 1989b) and *A Framework for the Whole Curriculum in Wales* (CCW, 1989) emphasized such approaches and cross-curricular themes, dimensions and competences (skills in England) were a much heralded element of the National Curriculum, they were never really treated as seriously as the individual subjects in many quarters. For example when the Council for the Accreditation of Teacher Education (CATE) queried the suitability of undergraduate degrees of students on an initial teacher training (ITT) course they indicated that relevance to the primary school curriculum did not necessarily include subjects such as economics despite the inclusion of economic awareness as a cross-curriculum theme (personal communication from CATE to Susan Sanders, 1991)

Several initiatives were run to develop materials for the teaching of such themes and dimensions but by 1993 they received only four pages of mention in CCW (1993) compared with twenty-three pages on individual subjects and appear under the heading 'other opportunities'. However Rosemary Webb reports that

> Most of the LEAs regarded the cross-curricular themes (economic and industrial understanding, careers education and guidance, health education, education for citizenship and environmental education) as important. (Webb, 1993: 75)

Teaching Methods

Robin Alexander's report on the Primary Needs Initiative in Leeds (Alexander, 1991) followed by the government-commissioned report by Alexander, Rose and Woodhead (1992) were instrumental in raising the debate about the efficacy of 'good primary practice'. Good primary practice is something that is rarely defined but has a meaning for practitioners.[1]

It is perhaps because of this lack of explicit definition that it has proved easy to attack it and to undermine teachers' confidence in it. This debate about primary practice, tied with the notion that the National Curriculum and its associated formal assessment procedure would raise standards within schools, led to re-examination of the way that younger school pupils are taught. Out of this came calls for 'subject specialist' teaching and this was backed up by the new proposals for the initial training of teachers (DFE, 1993). As these proposals also included provision for non-graduate teachers of nursery and Key Stage 1 pupils it could have been possible for the curriculum implications to have been lost.[2]

A simple way to change practice within the primary school is to prepare teachers to teach only in a certain way. The pedagogy of institutions had been under concerted attack with limited success. By legislating for a narrower curriculum and more time spent on the basic elements of the core subjects the government might expect to end up with a teaching force with a totally different notion of 'good primary practice'.

In this chapter we suggest ways that the manner in which the National Curriculum is taught is being influenced and manipulated. We highlight implications of both a curricular and pedagogical nature for educationalists and teachers of Key Stage 1 pupils in particular.

Single Subjects or Whole Curriculum?

In 1989 the Early Years Curriculum Group wrote

> The documents published by the National Curriculum Council are very encouraging in the way in which they

> explicitly endorse good primary practice. A number of ideas which permeate these documents assert and affirm the very principles on which the early years curriculum is founded. (Early Years Curriculum Group, 1989: 21)

The group's writing indicates a wholesale commitment to a cross-curricular approach.

However we have argued in Chapter 4 that this belief may be at best dated and at worst naive. The interest in Robin Alexander's work in particular, from the report into primary education in Leeds in 1991 which led to the report on curriculum organization and classroom practice in primary schools by Alexander, Rose and Woodhead (the 'three wise men'), focused media attention on the obvious shortcomings of some thematic, topic and cross-curricular approaches. Unfortunately the media attention was not balanced and in many instances the positive findings were ignored.

The report described topic work as 'very undemanding' with negligible opportunities for progression. The quality of planning was questioned. Monitoring and assessment of topic work were described as weak.

As an alternative way of meeting such criticisms we were offered the notion of subject specialist teaching in the primary school: 'Subject teaching has an essential place in modern primary education' (Alexander *et al.*, 1992: 35, para. 123). However the paragraph goes on to say

> When topic work focuses on a clearly defined and limited number of attainment targets it, too, can make an important contribution to the development of pupil learning.

Our research indicates that this is the new style of topic work, highly focused and carefully planned with attainment targets in mind.

Duncan Graham (1993) is more sceptical in his evaluation of the three wise men's suggestions for subject specialism.

> How much of the talk of specialism was politically inspired and was it educationally sound? The arguments must

> be as strong for extending primary methods upwards into secondary schools — as so many successful middle-schools do — as for the introduction of earlier specialisation. (Graham 1993: 123)

Whether politically inspired or not there is certainly evidence that groups have begun to explore other ways of 'delivering the curriculum'.

Webb (1993: 69) reports

> In one authority the message on the courses over the past year, which was initially disseminated at a headteachers' conference, has been that 'the global topic planned through flow diagrams is outdated and doesn't take account of the structure of the National Curriculum'.

As primary teachers struggle to cover the breadth of the National Curriculum they try various strategies.

Tyler (1992) discusses what he sees as the 'bipolar construct "cross-curricular" versus "single subject" '. He reports two views coming across from primary teachers. On the one hand there is a group of teachers who feel that the only way to manage the 334 statements of attainment so far detailed is by a cross-curricular approach. On the other hand there is another group of teachers who argue for a 'more discrete approach to the primary curriculum'. It is because of the complex nature of the documents that they see the task of meshing them together as too great. They take the fact that the documents are single subject in nature that the curriculum should be taught in the same way. We too heard these two views expressed by teachers (see Chapter 4).

For Tyler (1993) the two views come from different teachers, but how many teachers struggle to reconcile what they perceive to be pedagogically sound but unmanageable as against a style with which they have little faith pedagogically but makes the everyday running of their teaching so much easier to manage? The conflicting messages over time from the NCC, the CCW, etc. only serve to confuse.

Tyler (1993: 4) identifies three main curricular styles in current use.

> These three styles can be characterised by the differing degrees of integration and differentiation in the curriculum; they are approaches which emphasise (i) individual subjects, (ii) subject specific topics or (iii) thematic planning.

Graham (1993: 119) does not see the pressures to change teaching methods as coming from the nature of the National Curriculum but from

> a tide of romantic traditionalism, a gut response to ministers' own school-days, and an over reaction to anecdotal evidence of the perceived dangers of extreme teaching methods.

Whatever the government's reasons for pushing for change in teaching methods (and we do not necessarily disagree with Graham's interpretation) they have cleverly chosen not to legislate the methods of teaching but to subtly influence them.

Changing Pedagogy

The Collins English Dictionary defines pedagogy as 'the principles, practice or profession of teaching'. All of these have been subject to pressure to change since the introduction of the National Curriculum. In the next part of this chapter we focus on several ways in which this pressure has been exerted.

The Role of Curriculum Guidance (NCC, CCW and the LEAs) as Change Agent

Tyler (1992) reports that some of the guidelines suggest the use of curriculum specialists. He comments as we do in Chapter 4 that initially and now superficially the non-statutory guidelines support a cross-curricular approach. This support can be seen as strong and directive initially but now superficial and soft. Topic work had a similar fate (see Chapter 4).

We argued in Chapter 4 that this support changes over time so that by the time of writing (summer 1993) the support is minimal from both NCC and CCW. In fact we interpret this as these bodies 'selling out' the primary practitioners who followed their earlier directives, for the sake of the rhetoric of the New Right. Rosemary Webb (1993) highlights one LEA's strong anti-thematic approach for Key Stage 2 (see above).

To what extent can teachers at Key Stage 1 hold on to the thematic approach? The formal testing procedures crumbled not because of the sensible and measured reactions of the Key Stage 1 teachers who had tried them out but because of the strongly unionized Key Stage 3 teachers' response *before* they had tried them out. How empowered do Key Stage 1 teachers feel to withstand the explicit and implicit pressures to move away from thematic, cross-curricular approaches and towards single subject teaching?

As the support for thematic, topic and cross-curricular approaches from the likes of NCC, CCW and LEAs diminishes how can the demoralization of teachers be stemmed? So far the arguments for the maintenance of such approaches have been based on dogma: for instance the romantic image of young children and teachers tripping through the wet grass was used by Gammage during a lecture defending 'good primary practice' at University College, Swansea in 1992. (Gammage, 1992) What is needed is extensive and rigorous research into the benefits of such approaches. The evidence has to be of a quality to dispel the hysteria of the New Right. Teacher organizations and individual teachers can support and participate in such research.

The Role of Assessment as Change Agent

The government knew that it is often the assessment procedures that drive the teaching approach. Despite the rhetoric of the guidelines and the 'hands off' approach of the orders in terms of teaching styles influence is exerted through the formalized assessment procedures. Kelly (1990) in his discussion of the assessment and testing programme within the National Curriculum refers to the 'backlash effects' that testing has on the curriculum.

Caroline Gipps, writing in 1988, had no doubts that 'on the

basis of what we know already about the effects of testing' that regular and significant testing would affect several elements of primary school practice. These included

— a variety of teaching and learning approaches,
— the integration of some subjects into topic work,
— [few] lessons in formal subjects, other than maths [*sic*]. (Gipps, 1988: 71)

The change in the approach to teaching of mathematics (away from the purely didactic; including investigative and problem-solving approaches) is attributed by many not to the Cockcroft Report or to the work of the advisory teachers but to the inclusion of a coursework element in GCSE.[3]

The impact of testing on teaching was recognized in 1988 by the National Society for the Study of Education in the USA.

> In recent years, it seems that the aims of education, the business of our schools, and the goals of educational reform are addressed not so much in terms of curriculum — the courses of study that are followed — as they are in terms of standardized tests. It is testing, not the 'official' stated curriculum, that is increasingly determining what is taught, how it is taught, what is learned, and how it is learned. (Madeus, 1988: 83)

The testing procedures for Key Stage 1 (and for Key Stagc 2) are *not* cross-curricular in nature. Individual subjects are tested separately. What message does this send to teachers?

Nigel Proctor warned in 1990 that the focus on subject testing suggested to him that cross-curricular issues could face extinction. To what extent will his prediction prove correct? Will Key Stage 1 become a conservation area for such issues until former primary practice grows strong and flourishes in captivity, able to defend itself against the criticisms of Alexander *et al.* (1992) and others and thence to re-populate Key Stage 2 and beyond? Or will Key Stage 1 become the Galápagos or Madame Tussauds' of the thematic approach, visited with nostalgia by past practitioners and young teachers but, like steam railways, an enjoyable pastime with little relevance in the real world of the big school? The choice is ours, not just that of the teachers of Key Stage 1 pupils.

Topic work can certainly be like Alexander *et al.*'s (1992) worst scenario. However they were criticizing the current implementation of the approach, not the approach itself. Unfortunately much of the defence was erroneously centred on the sentiment 'Oh no it isn't like that', which was not strictly true, rather than a focus on putting it right. Defendants appeared to be defending the indefensible — poor classroom practice. They did the approach no service.

The National Curriculum has allowed the professionals to do what Alexander *et al.* suggested it could, namely improve the delivery without rejecting the approach. NCC and CCW should recognize this fact and make explicit their support for the approach when it is used well. This would increase Key Stage 1 teachers' confidence in their use of this approach and would legitimize it.

Teachers need to be confident in their commitment to thematic, topic and cross-curricular approaches. Tyler (1992: 8) concludes that

> Despite the current modifications to the assessment programme at Key Stages 1 and 2, the main emphasis in testing will continue to be on individual subjects within the curriculum. The danger is that the current cross-curricular and thematic approaches which are used so effectively in many schools will be replaced by a highly differentiated, and possibly fragmented, curriculum.

In August 1993 Sir Ron Dearing published the results of his review of the National Curriculum. At Key Stage 1 only English and mathematics are to be assessed by external tests. Science is to be tested only by statutory teacher assessment. The elements of English and mathematics to be tested are much reduced (NCC, 1993b). The possible impact of this on the curriculum is discussed in the second part of this chapter.

Initial Teacher Training as an Agent of Change

Another way in which the government has sought to influence the teaching of the curriculum has been through the regulations governing the training of teachers. If teachers are trained to teach a certain content in a certain way, then they may well hold on to that, whatever the accepted craft knowledge in the schools in which they teach. By regulating the training that teachers receive, a government may well expect eventually to change the practice within schools.

From 1989 onwards the CATE regulations stipulated the number of hours that students should study and be taught English (and Welsh in Welsh-medium schools), mathematics and science — the core subjects of the National Curriculum. This limited the number of hours available for the rest of the primary school curriculum and led to debates, particularly within the PGCE programme, as to the feasibility of training students to teach all the subjects within the time span of the existing training programme. This coupled with the attack on the philosophy and experience of teacher trainers leading to calls for more school based work (and the resulting depletion in available hours in college) is reflected in the new proposals (Welsh Office, 1993; DFE, 1993).

There is an emphasis in the HMI report (OFSTED, 1993b: 2) on the time problem within ITT courses.

> Poor quality provision often resulted from inadequate time allocation rather than poor preparation or delivery. The content of a few courses did not fully cover the National Curriculum content required in primary schools.

The new proposals for the training of primary school teachers (DFE, 1993) introduce the notion of subject specialist teachers and teachers not being trained to teach all the subjects in the curriculum. However with the latter there are conflicting messages, particularly as the proposals refer on occasions to the National Curriculum (for example DFE, 1993: 7, para. 11) and on other occasions to the primary curriculum (for example DFE, 1993: 7, para. 12). Indeed in paragraph 21 both are used without any definition or distinction being made.

> . . . wishes to encourage the use of specialist teaching in primary schools, particularly at Key Stage 2[4] (Welsh Office, 1993: para. 13)

> Newly qualified teachers should be able to demonstrate relevant knowledge and understanding of the National Curriculum, including testing and assessment arrangements, in the core subjects and those other foundation subjects *covered by their course.* (Welsh Office, 1993: Annex A, para. 2.3) (our italics)

> The new criteria do not therefore require all courses to cover all subjects of the primary curriculum . . . (Welsh Office, 1993: para.15)

However some clarification is offered:

> It is expected that, for the time being, most courses will continue to prepare students to teach the full primary curriculum. (Welsh Office, 1993: para. 14)

The statements of competences included in the 1993 proposals for initial teacher training require the new teachers to demonstrate relevant knowledge and understanding of the National Curriculum. As the National Union of Teachers (1993) response to those proposals pointed out there was no reference to the need for new teachers to demonstrate knowledge of the *whole* curriculum. Alexander *et al.* (1992: 35, para. 121) commented

> The subject knowledge required by the National Curriculum makes it unlikely that the generalist primary teacher will be able to teach all subjects in the depth required. This is particularly the case in Key Stage 2, but is true also in Key Stage 1.

The new proposals emphasize the fragmented curriculum rather than the curriculum as an entity. Will this lead to a generation of teachers who see the curriculum not as a coherent whole but as made up of discrete packets of subjects that do not support, overlap or interact with each other? Is there an over-emphasis on subject as curriculum orders? Course evaluations from last year's primary phase PGCE students at the authors' institution included requests for more emphasis on the National Curriculum document in mathematics. One author's efforts to teach the students about mathematics as a *context* for the orders had not worked. They saw mathematics as the orders.

Students quite rightly perceive practising teachers as experts in the delivery of the National Curriculum. Teachers working with students can help. They can 'hold the dream' of good primary practice, and help students to work in a variety of ways by interpreting the National Curriculum Orders while maintaining their integrity. We should not forget the rhetoric from NCC quoted on page 134 that the National Curriculum is about what to teach rather than how to teach it.

The initial teacher training (primary) proposals also allow for the development of new courses; 'However, more courses may be developed to cover parts of the primary curriculum in greater depth' (Department for Education, 1993: para. 14). Such courses will have to be developed by higher education institutions in partnership with schools. If neither are willing is the government prepared to instruct or influence with funding? We note a lack of success with such tactics in recent months. Secondary schools were instructed to carry out Key Stage 3 testing; most did not. Opting out was accompanied by financial benefits; to date many schools have rejected opting out of LEA control.

Curricular Issues

The Effect on the Curriculum

To some extent it is inappropriate to separate pedagogical and curriculum issues and in the preceding part of this chapter we have dealt with some curriculum aspects. However there is a fundamental issue which we have left to deal with separately and this is the way in which aspects of the National Curriculum change our overall view of what the curriculum, the primary school curriculum and the early years curriculum, might be.

Let us imagine for the moment a national curriculum which accounts for 100 per cent of the content. The subjects of this national curriculum are art, drama, music and dance for the first three years, then the humanities are included and finally when pupils reach the age of 11 mathematics, science and language and literature are taught as well. What does this tell us about the society? Which subjects does that society perceive as the most important? Which subjects would parents ask about on open evenings? What skills are employers looking for?

Now let us imagine that the government of that country wants, for whatever reason, to embrace a broader curriculum but not to lose sight of the traditional values of the society. Why not insist that all the subjects are taught from the beginning of formal education but only test art, drama, music and dance at the end of the first three years and so on? Would that not serve your purpose? If a subject is tested it must be important!

Now to return to our own National Curriculum. Never mind the rhetoric; what will the effect of the new testing procedures be on the early years' curriculum? What distortions will appear? Will teachers continue to struggle with technology or Welsh if the pupils are not to be formally tested in those subjects (see Chapter 11)?

Our teachers told us in 1993 that subjects that have to be formally tested have a heightened focus and that 'teaching to the tests' is already happening. The curriculum is already changing under the pressure of the formal assessment procedures. How will history view the outcomes of revisions driven by the teachers' concerns?

If the amount of time that has to be spent on the orders is cut down, as Dearing (NCC, 1993b) proposes, will teachers use the saved time for thematic work, for example, or will they fill all the available time with the National Curriculum? What are the tensions between Key Stage 1 and Key Stage 2? Do they still have distinctive elements? Should the approach to teaching be different in each Key Stage? Should there be a different, more limited curriculum for Key Stage 1 with greater emphasis upon learning the basic skills (see Chapters 10 and 11, and Dearing, 1993)?

Do teachers have a view of assessment as distinct from

teaching? Do they need to remind themselves that assessment is part of teaching? Certainly some of the teachers in our study seemed to have (see Chapters 3 and 4) but they may have been referring to the summative kinds of assessment rather than the formative when they made statements contrasting testing with teaching. Would this remove some of their concerns? Teachers found the management of the earlier pedagogically sound assessment procedures difficult. They may have found themselves accepting tests that were easier to manage but pedagogically unsound. Dearing helps as he raises the status of teacher assessment and acknowledges some of the failings of standardized assessment tasks.

Conclusions

During the course of our study there was a change from the almost automatic acceptance by teachers of the thematic approach as *the* approach during the primary years. Different approaches such as focused topic work, discrete subject teaching and teaching by subject specialists are being explored. The wider debate about the breadth of curriculum available at Key Stage 1 may just be beginning. An explicit debate is to be welcomed; manipulation of the curriculum by other means is not.

Notes

1 For an extensive discussion readers could refer to Chapter 11 in Alexander, 1992.
2 This is particularly possible as much of the discontent at the proposals focused on this element with the teacher unions also questioning the partnership proposals between schools and higher education institutions.
3 We have heard this sentiment attributed to Professor Hugh Burkhardt several times but have never seen it written. Broadfoot *et al.* (1991b: 153) quote 'What you test is what you get' and attribute it to Burkhardt (1989). However no publication details are provided in the references and this particular reference could not be traced despite personal correspondence with the authors.
4 This encouragement is not exclusively at Key Stage 2, however!

Chapter 10

Slower Learners and Socially Disadvantaged Children

In our study well over half of the class teachers, both in 1989 and 1990, judged that they had some pupils in their classes with special educational needs, even though only a handful of Key Stage 1 children in the sample schools had been formally statemented (see Chapter 2). The reported learning difficulties of these children were particularly related to speech, language and reading and some children were described as showing behaviour difficulties which affected their concentration and sometimes caused disruption in class. In terms of the Warnock Report (DES, 1978) and the 1981 Education Act, the majority of these 'slower learners' would probably be described as having mild or moderate learning difficulties, with a smaller number perhaps showing specific learning difficulties in language, reading or number. Some of them would, in addition, show emotional or behavioural difficulties. In some cases these children's learning problems may have been caused, at least in part, by factors such as specific learning difficulties, physical or sensory difficulties or limited general ability (DES, 1978).

However, given that one-third of the sample schools served predominantly working-class or lower working-class areas (including five schools formerly designated as social priority area (SPA) schools), it is also very likely that many of the children would have come from socially disadvantaged home backgrounds. Such homes, for reasons of poverty, family disruption or lack of parental awareness, do not provide the parental and family support for their learning which is such a crucial component in children's early education, with the result that these children enter school with a low level of pre-literacy and other skills and knowledge upon which infant school teachers can build. Starting from a lower educational base than children from more favoured backgrounds, these children are more likely to make comparatively slower progress in learning the basic skills, and the 'achievement gap' between them and the former may widen progressively during their primary and secondary school years (Cox, 1982). While it is very important not to equate working-class membership with social disadvantage, the majority of disadvantaged children tend to come from families characterized by lower occupational status or long term unemployment (Davie *et al.*, 1972; Wedge and Essen, 1982).

Effects of the National Curriculum on Slower Learners

Access to the National Curriculum

Both the class teachers and the headteachers were asked how they thought the introduction of the National Curriculum was affecting the slower learning children. Their responses were summarized in Chapter 5. While a proportion of the teachers claimed that these children were largely unaffected by the introduction of the National Curriculum and continued to work at their own pace and level as before, many more expressed serious concern about its impact upon their learning. In particular they were worried that pressure was being placed upon them to achieve the relevant attainment targets at the same time as their classmates and that this pressure undermined the quality of their learning with respect to understanding and level of skill mastery. Further, the requirement that these children should be taught the full range of National Curriculum subjects, including Welsh as a second language since the schools were located in Wales, meant that there was insufficient time to teach them the basic skills of reading, writing, spelling and number to an adequate level of mastery. As reported in Chapter 6, both of these concerns were expressed by some teachers with regard to Year 1 children in general but, presumably, the level of concern was greater with regard to slower learning children.

At least some of the teachers voicing such concerns were

anxious that their slower learning pupils should not be disadvantaged in relation to their classroom peers when it came to formal assessment (through SATs) of their attainments at age 7. They felt that if these children performed relatively poorly in the tests, their 'failure' would be public and consequently more damaging to their self-esteem. These teachers appeared to be caught in the dilemma that pushing the slower learners too hard would impair the quality of their learning, particularly of the basic skills, but not pushing them hard enough would lead to their subsequent low achievement in formal assessment and damaged self-esteem.

Such concerns regarding the prospects for the slower learning children find support in a document produced by the NCC (1993c) on the topic of special needs and the National Curriculum which was based on the views of teachers in special schools, special units in ordinary schools and in special support services. The document distinguishes between 'exceptionally severe' (profound and multiple) learning difficulties and 'other' learning difficulties of the kind described earlier in this chapter. While strongly endorsing the principle of the entitlement of all pupils to a broad, balanced and relevant curriculum, including the National Curriculum, the teachers identified several issues of concern regarding the teaching of slower learning children, including the following:

1 The links between the Key Stages and chronological ages are reported to be unrealistic for this group of pupils. Many need to work at National Curriculum levels below those designated for the Key Stage, whilst still having access to age-appropriate programmes of study;
2 Although these pupils may progress more slowly than their peers, they could still gain full access to the National Curriculum programmes of study at a later date;
3 Other priorities, such as speech therapy, extra time on reading and mathematics and life skills, mean that the time available for National Curriculum subjects is reduced;
4 Teachers suggest that there should be non-mandatory Standard Assessment Tasks for this group of pupils and much greater emphasis on teacher assessment. (NCC, 1993c: 5)

Clearly, like some of the teachers in our study, these teachers appear to be seeking official acknowledgment of the slower pace of learning of pupils with a variety of learning difficulties that are not accompanied by a formal statement of special educational need under the 1981 Education Act, and more flexibility in the framework of the National Curriculum to accommodate their needs. Under present regulations the processes available to schools for adapting the requirements of the National Curriculum to meet individual learning needs involve making formal statements of special educational needs or formal exemptions (disapplications) or modifications to it. All of these are somewhat bureaucratic processes and, as Lewis (1991) points out, the heavy statutory emphasis upon these procedures sits uneasily with the rhetoric of the National Curriculum which stresses its suitability for all children. Lewis argues that if the National Curriculum is really attuned to individual learning needs then there should be no need for formal disapplications or modifications. It should be stressed, however, that in an earlier publication focusing upon children with special educational needs, the National Curriculum Council envisaged that only a few pupils should require exceptional arrangements for modifications or exemptions and only when the NC requirements prove impossible to achieve or are inappropriate to the pupil's very specialized needs (NCC, 1989b). In its later (1993c) publication it reports teachers' rejection of the 'negative concept of disapplication' and their request for a more positive approach to access to the National Curriculum for pupils with special educational needs.

Pending some rewriting of the National Curriculum orders and regulations to provide the necessary flexibility in responding to the wide variety of children's individual learning needs, teachers will have to continue to work under the present legislative framework but they will need advice and support in resolving the dilemma outlined above. Perhaps their concerns about the public 'failure' of slower learning children to achieve the same attainment target levels as their classmates at the end of Key Stage 1 would be eased by their own acceptance of the fact that the range of variation in children's learning needs and capabilities will be reflected in different levels of attainment when these are formally assessed. This acknowledgment would by no means justify teachers holding low expectations of their slower learning pupils' potential levels of attainment but it would perhaps help them to avoid over-pressurizing these children.

Learning Basic Skills

It is a fundamental aim of primary (infant) education to secure in all children the foundations of the skills of language, literacy and numeracy, upon which so much of the learning in other curriculum areas is built. To achieve this aim, infant teachers need to allocate sufficient time in the curriculum to provide the necessary learning experiences, both informally at the level of pre-literacy and pre-numeracy skills and awareness, and in a more direct and structured fashion in the later stages. Our study findings have raised the question of whether the wider subject requirements of the National Curriculum have unduly constrained the time available for the teaching of the basic skills, particularly for slower learning children.

On this question reports from government-appointed agencies seem somewhat conflicting. In its recent advice to the Secretary of State for Education the NCC (1993a, para. 2.3) expressed the particular concern of teachers that the breadth of the National Curriculum meant that 'there is now insufficient time to teach the basics of reading, writing, spelling and arithmetic which are essential to all future learning'. Such concern was probably one of the factors which led this body to recommend that the various subject orders of the National Curriculum should be slimmed down to an 'essential core' of knowledge, understanding and skills appropriate to each Key Stage. Similar concern was voiced by infant teachers throughout Wales as reported in a document produced by the CCW compiled in the process of carrying out consultations with schools, teachers and LEAs concerning the National Curriculum (CCW, 1992c). In contrast OFSTED, in its report in 1993, based upon HMI school inspections and consultations with teachers and schools, made the following observation: 'Although there was some concern that as a result of introducing the National Curriculum, the time for teaching the basic skills of literacy, and to a lesser extent numeracy, was being "squeezed", most teachers in Key Stages 1 and 2 *devoted at least sufficient time to these aspects of the work.*' (OFSTED, 1993: 7. Our italics). However this report also commented that intakes of pupils varied markedly in respect of readiness for school work, making it necessary for some schools, mainly those serving disadvantaged areas, to give more attention and time to teaching reading than elsewhere.

In a specially commisioned study Campbell and Neill (1992) analysed the working week of a sample of infant teachers. They found that, far from there being a shortage of time for English and mathematics, the large amount of teaching time devoted to the core subjects, and to English in particular, did not leave enough time for teaching the non-core subjects and religious education. In one of their analyses 56 per cent of the teacher's week, on average, was spent on core subjects, 30 per cent on non-core subjects and 12 per cent on teacher assessment and SAT administration. In their view the teachers' emphasis on core subject teaching was squeezing out reasonable time for other subjects and thus making it impossible to deliver a balanced and broadly based curriculum as required by the 1988 Education Reform Act.

At the time of writing, the Secretary of State for Education has announced plans for a slimming down both of the subject orders and of the associated testing procedures. This should certainly help teachers in their task of balancing the need to spend sufficient time in teaching the basic skills to slower learning and other pupils with that of simultaneously covering the whole curriculum. Even so schools serving socially disadvantaged areas will still need to devote relatively more time to teaching reading and other basic skills than other schools, as the OFSTED (1993a) report made clear. However, as perhaps was hinted in that report, there is a danger that teachers can spend *too much* time on teaching the basic skills to slower learning and socially disadvantaged children, with the result that these children may not experience the full range of the wider curriculum which is their entitlement. In our own study, although few teachers reported benefits from the National Curriculum for slower learning children, some of those who did so mentioned that these children were experiencing a richer curriculum than before, which now included science and technology.

As Lewis (1991) points out, curricula for children with learning difficulties in both mainstream and special schools have in the past been criticized as being too restricted and concentrated on the narrow teaching of the basic skills. In his analytical study of the work of the schools participating in the Leeds Primary Needs Project, many of which served socially disadvantaged areas, Alexander (1992) concluded that too much time was allocated to language and maths, given that the children were observed to be spending less of their time working and more time being distracted in these subjects than in others. This may have been partly due to the formal nature of the basic skills work being required of them which emphasized reading and writing at the expense of listening and speaking. Despite the the greater allocation of time and resources to the teaching of the basic skills in these project schools there was no evidence of a subsequent rise in the children's measured reading standards.

Another negative consequence of an over-concentration of curriculum time on the teaching of basic skills is that valuable opportunities for the children's developing writing and reading skills to be reinforced in the context of other curriculum learning, such as in science or history, are reduced.

The planned reduction of the National Curriculum load should benefit all children, but particularly slower learners for whom the pressures to progress on all fronts, described by our teachers, should be eased. However the reduction of curriculum overload and the allocation of sufficient, but not too much time to the teaching of the basic skills will not in themselves be enough to ensure the successful learning and progress of these children.

Assessment and Recording

What is also needed is a skilful and sensitive exploration of each child's learning difficulties and strengths in a given curriculum area and a careful matching of the learning tasks chosen to each child's profile of skills and understanding at any given stage. In addition the teacher must also select teaching methods that are appropriate both to the task and to the child's learning needs. All this represents a challenge to the class teacher's professional skills and curricular knowledge. In its report on the implementation of the National Curriculum during its second year, for example, HMI found that the principal difficulty facing teachers at all Key Stages and in all subjects was the matching of learning tasks to the abilities of individual pupils (DFE, 1992), although they comment that teachers were becoming more aware than before of the precise level of pupils' achievements and needs through improved curriculum planning and assessment. In the NCC document on special needs and the National Curriculum referred to earlier (NCC, 1993c), the teachers consulted identified a need for guidance on differentiating teaching across all ability ranges but particularly for pupils with special educational needs and the exceptionally able.

As Alexander (1992) points out, a satisfactory matching of curriculum task to individual learning needs requires, amongst other things, that the teacher has an adequate depth of curriculum knowledge in the given subject to be able to diagnose each child's learning needs. While this requirement applies equally strongly to both core and non-core subjects it seems to be in the latter that primary teachers feel most insecure in this respect (Bennett *et al.*, 1992). Nevertheless, for all subjects, including those concerned with the teaching of the basic skills, an adequate level of INSET provision and back-up classroom advisory support for the teacher is essential if the challenge of meeting children's individual learning needs within the framework of the National Curriculum is to be met. In this connection it is disturbing to note HMI's comment that the reduction in the number of advisory teachers and the need for the latter to concentrate on other issues, in consequence of other changes stemming from the ERA, has deprived schools of valuable support (DFE, 1992).

While it cannot make up for a shortfall in good INSET provision and back-up advisory support, the class teacher can find some helpful guidance in publications dealing with the teaching of children with special needs within the framework of the National Curriculum, such as the NCC's (1989b) document entitled *A Curriculum for All*. This states that, in the process of giving pupils with special educational needs the opportunity to demonstrate their performance levels on the statements of attainment, teachers will often find it necessary to structure their schemes of work in such a way as to provide a series of intermediate goals. They will also need to adapt their record systems to reflect these small steps towards the statements of attainment. This approach of breaking down teaching sequences into smaller than usual steps to meet the needs of slower learning children is generally known as curriculum based teaching, or sometimes objectives based teaching, and it has many advocates (for example Solity and Bull, 1987). However, as the NCC's (1989b) document points out, some attainment targets are more difficult to break down into smaller steps than others. Moreover, Lewis (1991) argues that in planning teaching activities designed to help children with learning difficulties to reach particular statements of attainment, it is more profitable to focus on the relevant programmes of study, rather than simply to break down the former.

The book by Lewis is a valuable source of practical guidance to the teacher on teaching children with special needs. Another useful source is the book by Chazan *et al.* (1991) on helping 5 to 8-year-olds with special educational needs. This includes a good discussion of the construction of individual learning programmes for children and is illustrated with case studies.

In addition to the diagnostic assessment of children's strengths and weaknesses in a particular aspect of learning which was discussed earlier, teachers will need to carry out regular assessment and recording of their children's progress towards the various core curriculum statements of attainment. Given that the three levels of performance reflected by these statements at Key Stage 1 are relatively crude, it is important for the teacher to devise a finer graded system for recording the progress of slower learning pupils. Otherwise there is a real danger that the more subtle, but nevertheless real progress made by such children towards a particular statement of attainment will go unrecorded, which could be demotivating for the teacher as well as the pupil. Checklists can be useful in this respect but some of these have been criticized as superficial by HMI (DES, 1990a). The curriculum or objectives based methods of teaching referred to earlier have their own built-in assessment and recording systems which can be readily adapted to the National Curriculum. Also Lewis (1991) provides helpful suggestions concerning the use of classroom observation by the teacher in identifying children's individual learning needs, and the use of individual records as a means of recording the progress of slower learning pupils towards particular learning objectives within the National Curriculum.

The Role of the Teacher

The problems discussed so far in this chapter have largely focused on the effects of the National Curriculum upon slower learning children. Equally important is the impact of the National Curriculum upon the teachers since their morale, attitudes and professional skills are the crucial determinant of the children's academic progress. There was evidence from our own study of a concern by teachers in schools serving predominantly socially disadvantaged areas that their professional skills were being called into question in the light of the new climate of the schools' public accountability for their pupils' academic achievement and progress. As one teacher put it,

> Teachers are under pressure to analyse what children are learning and when they review it and the children do not make progress it is demoralizing for the staff.

Another teacher referred to the 'immense pressure on the class teacher to get poorly motivated children to a reasonable standard' and expressed the concern that poor work by the children would be interpreted as poor teaching. The headteacher of a socially disadvantaged area school expressed his concern that in view of the low level of attainment by most pupils in the school and the lack of parental support, the publication of formal test results (SATs) would in no way reflect the hard work and dedication of the staff. Taking this point further, another headteacher working in a similar school pointed out that in order to interpret the Key Stage 1 test results fairly it is necessary to know the children's starting levels on school entry so that the children's progress can be evaluated. Ironically, given the current strong backlash amongst both teachers and parents against all formal

National Curriculum testing, this would argue for the creation of some form of testing of school entry skills at age 5.

The relatively low academic attainments of socially disadvantaged children have been well documented in Britain (Davie *et al.*, 1972; Cox and Jones, 1983) and one cannot deny that schools serving predominantly disadvantaged areas face a formidable challenge to their professional skills in ensuring that their pupils reach acceptable levels of academic achievement across the full range of the National Curriculum subjects. A particular burden falls upon infant teachers in such schools since they are teaching children whose entry skills in many cases are relatively low and their task is to lay the foundations of oracy, literacy and numeracy upon which the children's future school progress depends. However it is vital that, in trying to meet this challenge, teachers should maintain positive attitudes and expectations towards their socially disadvantaged pupils and not prejudge their capabilities. Indeed the so called 'three wise men' report (Alexander *et al.*, 1992) stresses the importance of all schools having the highest expectations of their pupils and claims that standards in primary schools will not rise until teachers expect more of their pupils, in particular the more able and the disadvantaged children.

There is a good deal of evidence that many teachers underestimate the capabilities of their socially disadvantaged pupils, for example from the study of the progress of children attending infant schools in the inner London area (Tizard *et al.*, 1988) and in the study of Leeds primary schools by Alexander (1992) already referred to. Alexander concluded that the way in which the Leeds Primary Needs Project was being implemented encouraged a deficit view of disadvantaged children which concentrated on what they could not do rather than on what they were capable of. In their joint discussion paper Alexander *et al.* (1992) claim that in some schools there has been a tendency to stereotype children and assume that social disadvantage inevitably leads to educational failure. It may be that some of the teachers in our own study were falling into this trap. Further evidence came in OFSTED's (1993a) report on curriculum organization and practice in primary schools. This states that amongst the issues raised in the follow-up conferences,

> there was surprisingly little sense of the urgency to need to know in some detail the existing standards of pupils' performance in literacy and numeracy and the direction in which standards were moving. Nor was there sufficient appreciation of how assessment information could be used to plan programmes of work for individuals, groups or classes. (OFSTED 1993: para. 28)

If one accepts such evidence for the widespread under-expectation by many teachers of the capabilities of their socially disadvantaged and slower learning pupils, the urgent question arises as to what can be done to eradicate it. Part of the solution, as has already been discussed, lies in enhancing teachers' diagnostic skills and curricular knowledge so that they match learning tasks more closely to individual children's needs without pre-judging their future capabilities. For Alexander (1992) this is the key requirement in the raising of teachers' expectations. Other pointers come from the study carried out by Mortimore *et al.* (1988) into the differential effectiveness of a sample of inner London primary/junior schools in raising their pupils' educational attainments. This study found that, while the social class grouping of the parents was the most powerful determinant of the children's initial attainments at age 7, their subsequent progress up to age 11 was more closely related to the quality of the education they received in their primary/junior schools. Despite the fact that they served similar catchment areas, some schools were more effective than others in boosting the educational performance of their socially disadvantaged pupils as well as that of children from more advantaged home backgrounds. The authors stress that while the more successful schools were characterized by their smaller size, good physical environment, stability of teaching staff and covered the full primary age range, as well as having voluntary status, these were not the crucial factors accounting for their better overall performance. The most important factors accounting for the academic success of these schools included intellectually challenging and clearly focused teaching, good record keeping, parental involvement and the creation of a postive school ethos.

Parental Involvement

The inclusion of parental involvement in Mortimore *et al.*'s (1988) list of key factors underpinning successful primary school teaching comes as no surprise given all the evidence we have for the importance of parents in fostering their children's early development and education. In the next chapter we discuss the value of pre-school and early school intervention projects designed to sharpen the awareness of (lower) working-class parents that they have much to contribute to their children's education and to develop their skills in doing so. The success of such projects can be measured in terms of the level of educational skills which children have acquired by the time of their entry into Key Stage 1 of the National Curriculum, including their attitudes and motivation towards school learning. In addition to such projects, however, there is much that primary schools can do to encourage and develop active partnerships with the parents, including those from socially disadvantaged backgrounds (Wolfendale, 1987).

By far the main thrust of schemes to encourage the active involvement of parents in their children's education has been in the area of reading and language, following the pioneering Haringey Reading Project which was centred on a number of infant schools serving lower working-class areas (Hewison and Tizard, 1984). In the LEA in which our own study took place some of the primary schools had been participating in a county-wide programme designed to enhance the role of parents in helping to develop their children's reading and language skills. This scheme, entitled Children and Parents Enjoy Reading (CAPER) has achieved considerable success in the judgment of its authors (Branston and Provis, 1986) and has its counterpart in other schemes operating throughout England and Wales.

In Chapter 2 we described the findings of our enquiry into the partnership links between our sample schools and their parents. Not surprisingly, all schools claimed that they encouraged their parents to help in the education of their children at home but our data do not allow us to judge the strength or quality of the schools' parental links, although there is likely to be some variation in these respects between the schools. A few class teachers from disadvantaged area schools referred to the problems they encountered in trying to encourage parental involvement in reading, such as the non-return of books loaned by the school to the parents, and some teachers described the level of parental response to their efforts as poor.

No one can deny that the challenges facing schools serving predominantly socially disadvantaged areas in their efforts to engage the active support of their parents are considerably greater than in schools serving more favoured areas. Acknowledging this it is vital that the staffs in such schools should be united in their efforts through the development of whole school policies, and should try to maintain a steady expectation of a positive outcome despite setbacks and discouragement. At the same time they will need adequate levels of staffing and resources to meet the challenges they face, a fact that was recognized in the now defunct practice by LEAs of designating selected schools as social priority area schools and funding them more generously. Also it must be recognized that the role of the school in combating the multiple problems of deprivation which characterize such areas is necessarily limited. Their main task is to try to ensure the optimum development, academically and socially, of their pupils, within the framework of the National Curriculum. More than that should not be expected.

In our enquiry we also asked the schools whether, in addition to encouraging parents to be actively involved in their children's education at home, they involved them directly in the work of the school, within the classroom or elsewhere. As reported in Chapter 2, while over half of the headteachers reported that they did encourage parents to assist directly in the work of the school, the roles that they were asked to play were largely ancillary in nature and provided support of one kind or another for the school's curricular activities, such as helping in the school library or accompanying children on school trips. Only a handful of schools actually encouraged parents to assist directly in teaching activities such as hearing children read or talking to them in the context of other activities.

Given that socially disadvantaged children typically do not experience adequate levels of purposeful talk with adults in learning contexts, the need to maximize their opportunities to engage in such talk in their classrooms is all the greater. While the use of parents to help in instructional contexts can arouse anxieties in teachers about their loss of control of the teaching process, properly managed, parental support in classroom teaching activities can be of real benefit both to pupils and their teachers, for whom parents represent a valuable resource (Tizard *et al.*, 1981; Wolfendale, 1988). Indeed, in the context of adult–child dialogue, the observational studies of Tizard and Hughes (1984) and Wells (1985) show that the educational quality of the conversations between working-class mothers and their young children in domestic contexts can sometimes be higher than that between teachers and their pupils, where the teacher's attention has to be spread over a large group. Similarly the carefully managed use of older pupils, or more capable age mates in the 'peer tutoring' of slower learners in key areas such as reading represents another potential valuable resource for the hard pressed teachers (Topping, 1987).

The Need for a Whole School Policy

If effective parental involvement and other necessary features of good educational provision for slower learning children are to be secured it is essential that they should be built into an agreed whole school policy for teaching pupils with special needs. Indeed it is part of their statutory duties for governing bodies of all maintained schools to draw up and report on the school's policy on special educational needs (DFE/Welsh Office, 1993). This should be designed to inform, guide and coordinate the work of teachers and other staff, parents and governors in their efforts to meet these children's learning and developmental needs. Useful suggestions for the content of such a policy are contained in a publication by the CCW (1992b) which identifies some of the principles and practical considerations which schools should take into account when reviewing their provision for children with special needs. These are presented under the headings of 'Classroom Management' and 'School Management and Organization' respectively. Classroom management covers matters of curriculum planning to meet individual pupil's learning needs, assessment, and the organization of the classroom and its resources to provide full access for these children to the learning tasks of the National Curriculum.

School management and organization deals first with school policy and planning, which includes a policy statement on the way the school caters for children with special needs, and also a statement on how the educational requirements of these children are incorporated into the school's overall development plan. This section of the statement also needs to make clear how priorities are to be decided regarding allocation of the school's resources. Second, the policy should establish clear channels of communication relating to children with special needs, both within the school and between the school, parents, governors and outside agencies. The role of a designated staff coordinator for special needs is clearly very important in this respect.

The remaining subsections of the CCW whole school policy document (1992b) concern staff development, including INSET relating to educational provision for special needs; the involvement of external support services, including special needs support teachers and LEA advisors; community links; and assessment and evaluation at the school level. Surprisingly, educational psychologists are not specifically mentioned in connection with support services although they have a vital role to play at all stages of the processes of identifying, assessing, and providing for children's special educational needs (Wolfendale, 1987). They are also well qualified to assist schools in the development of overall policies for meeting children's special needs and in the evaluation of the effectiveness of those policies in action.

Following the passing of the 1993 Education Act the Department for Education and Science and the Welsh Office have published a draft code of practice on the identification and assessment of special educational needs and draft regulations on assessments and statements (DFE/Welsh Office, 1993). The regulations prescribe the issues to be addressed in a school's special educational needs policy which include:

> Basic information about the school's educational provision, including the name of the school's special educational needs coordinator;

Information about the school's policies for identification, assessment and provision for all pupils with special educational needs, including policy on access to the National Curriculum;

Information about the school's staffing policies, special educational needs in-service training policy, and partnership with outside bodies such as external support agencies, special schools and voluntary organizations.

The draft code also states that the annual report for each school shall include a report containing such information as may be prescribed about the implementation of the governing body's policy for pupils with special educational needs. The importance of the fullest possible liaison between schools and parents is strongly emphasized, together with the need for schools to recognize the unique contribution which parents can make to the assessment and educational provision for their children with special educational needs.

Summary and Conclusions

The teachers in our study expressed serious worries concerning the impact of the National Curriculum upon their slower learning pupils, particularly those from socially disadvantaged home backgrounds. While accepting these children's entitlement to the breadth and balance of the National Curriculum they showed genuine concern that the progress and well being of these pupils, particularly in the basic skills, were being threatened by the pressures engendered by curriculum overload and having to push the children towards specified levels of attainment. The recently announced plan to review the scope and content of the whole curriculum and its associated testing requirements will undoubtedly help to relieve these pressures to the benefit of pupils and teachers alike. However such a development, welcome though it is, will not alone ensure the optimal educational progress of slower learning children. Drawing upon analytical studies of the work of urban primary schools serving disadvantaged catchment areas and also reports from various government-appointed agencies, we have highlighted what we judge to be the crucial features of a high quality educational programme for these children. These are as follows:

- the maintenance of high expectations by teachers of their children's capabilities;
- the provision of focused teaching that is matched to children's curricular needs, as revealed by careful diagnostic assessment;
- the selection of appropriate teaching methods and resources;
- the regular assessment and recording of progress towards particular learning objectives;
- the maximum involvement of parents in the teaching process both at home and in the school;
- the provision of high quality INSET focusing on the differentiation of teaching to meet individual learning needs;
- the provision of adequate levels of staffing and resources.

These features are unlikely to be present in a school's educational provision for its slower learning pupils unless they form part of an agreed whole school policy for pupils with special needs which will inform and guide the work of its staff. This policy should, in turn, be integrated within the wider educational policy of the school if the provision for children's special needs is to have the status and priority that it deserves.

Subject to these considerations, the introduction of the National Curriculum should prove to be positively beneficial in raising the educational attainment of slower learning pupils within the framework of a broad, balanced and relevant curriculum. Some potentially beneficial features of the National Curriculum in this regard have been described by Lewis (1991). These are:

1 a shared curriculum framework which means that, potentially, such children are more likely to be working within mainstream classes alongside peers;
2 a shared curricular language;
3 the National Curriculum should lead to such children

receiving a broad curriculum which incorporates non-core as well as core subjects;

4 the acknowledged importance of assessing children's learning at regular intervals, seeing this as being an integral part of teaching rather than providing merely an 'add-on' measure of the end products of learning.

Finally, it should be acknowledged that the National Curriculum and the Education Reform Act which gave rise to it pose some potential threats to the quality of provision for special educational needs as well as potential benefits. The teachers in our study pinpointed some of these, including undue pressures upon pupils to achieve National Curriculum attainment targets and the likely demoralizing effects on the children and teachers alike if they fail to do so and thereby depress the school's published SAT record. In a recent overview of provision for meeting special needs in the ordinary schools, Hegarty (1993) is critical of the limited attention paid to special educational provision in the ERA and also of the piecemeal way in which the various reforms have been introduced, with further significant changes still to come. Together with the threat to such provision which he regards as inherent in the new climate of open competion between schools, such factors make for uncertainty in the education sector and undermine the ability of schools to plan their provision for children's special needs in the medium and longer term.

In the light of these potential threats it will be essential to continue to monitor the impact of the National Curriculum and other changes stemming from the ERA into the forseeable future. Evidence of any damaging effects upon the education of children with special needs could well be instrumental in persuading the government of the day to take the necessary action to counter these effects and to ensure that these children receive the quality of education that they deserve.

On a more hopeful note there is much that could be done during the early years of children's development, particularly during the pre-school years, to reduce the chances that children from socially disadvantaged backgrounds will enter the stage of statutory schooling destined to be slower learners. Such measures are discussed in the next chapter.

Chapter 11

Educating Children Under Five

Introduction

The term 'early years', in the educational context, refers at its broadest to the age range 0 to 7 or even 8 years (e.g. Early Years Curriculum Group, 1989), with the terms 'pre-school', and 'under-5' being used for children in the 0 to 5 age range. In the context of teacher training the phrase usually refers to the 3 to 7 or 8 age range (DES, 1990b). The fact that, in Britain at least, children enter into the period of statutory schooling at age 5 provides a legal distinction between between the age ranges of 0 to 5 and 5 to 7 or 8 respectively. This distinction, which of course is not necessarily significant in psychological or educational terms, has now been reinforced by the National Curriculum. This starts officially at age 5 (Year 1), although, in practice, 4-year-olds within an infant class composed predominantly of 5-year-olds or even older children are likely to be working closely within its framework.

Many official reports and other publications on education in the early years, such as the HMI report entitled *The Education of Children Under Five* (DES, 1989a), and more recently, the Rumbold Report, *Starting with Quality* (DES, 1990b), concentrate specifically upon this more restricted age range. Certainly the principles underlying early years' education discussed later in this chapter seem to be based upon our knowledge of children's patterns of learning and development during these particular years. Nevertheless, if healthy continuity between the education of children under *and* over 5 is to be achieved, it makes good sense to consider the educational needs of young children across the wider age range. In this chapter however, the discussion will focus upon the education of children under 5, in particular 4 to

5-year-olds in infant classes, since this relates to the context of our study.

Basic Principles of Early Childhood Education

There seems to be widespread agreement as to what the basic principles of early childhood education are. In its document entitled *Under-Fives in School* the Curriculum Council for Wales (CCW, 1991) expounds the following principles for the education of children aged from 3 to 5:

1. The curriculum will contribute to the all-round growth and development of every child.
2. Learning through structured and spontaneous play is the springboard into the curriculum.
3. There will be plenty of active involvement and relevant first-hand experiences in an environment rich with possibilities.
4. Adults concerned with the under-5s have a particular responsibility for their care and safety.
5. The contribution which parents have made and continue to make to their child's education is valued.
6. Equal opportunities are offered to girls and boys, to children with special learning needs and to those from different cultures.

The above principles show appreciable overlap with the following principles put forward by the Early Years Curriculum Group (1989: 3), although the omission of any reference to play is somewhat surprising:

1. Early childhood is valid in itself, and is a part of life, not simply a preparation for work, or for the next stage of education.
2. The whole child is considered to be important — social, emotional, physical, intellectual and moral development are interrelated.
3. Learning is holistic and for the very young child is not compartmentalized under subject headings.

4 Intrinsic motivation is valuable because it results in child-initiated learning.
5 In the early years children learn best through first-hand experience.
6 What children can do, not what they cannot do, is the starting point in children's education.
7 There is potential in all children which emerges powerfully under favourable conditions.
8 The adults and children to whom the child relates are of central importance.
9 The child's education is seen as interaction between the child and the environment, which includes people as well as materials and knowledge.

Some of the above principles could be said to apply to all stages of learning but the reference to child-initiated learning, its holistic nature and the importance of concrete experience apply particularly to this stage. Although not putting it forward as a principle, the Early Years Curriculum Group's document emphasizes the central role of the teacher in ensuring opportunities for supporting and extending children's learning, particularly through their direct interaction with the children.

Such principles as those listed above need to be supported by appropriate theory and research and conceptual analysis if they are not to remain at the level of mere ideology. Whitehead (1993) argues that the imposition of the National Curriculum has provided a great opportunity to debate the nature of the early years' curriculum and advocates what she calls a 'developmental curriculum' which is responsive to ways in which children learn and develop during this phase. Such a curriculum draws widely on research in child development in order to pick out key features of children's early learning. Drawing on the child development literature, the psychologist David Elkind has described three major principles which he claims should underlie the education of 4-year-old children (Elkind, 1989). One of these is that such teaching should be interactive and that, in any instructional context, the teacher should serve as 'matchmaker' between the child and the materials. An effective match depends on the teacher's knowledge of the cognitive demands of the materials and the child's cognitive strengths and weaknesses. Similar ideas have been put forward by Bruner (1966).

Educational Provision for Under-5s

The 1972 White Paper entitled *A Framework for Expansion* (Secretary of State for Education and Science, 1972) recommended that, within the following ten years, nursery education should be provided in Britain for 50 per cent of 3-year-olds and 90 per cent of 4-year-olds. These bold proposals seemed to provide the long awaited recognition by our society, through its government, of the vital importance of early years' education. However, successive governments have failed dramatically to achieve these ambitious targets. Instead of a major expansion in nursery education we have seen the growth of pre-school playgroups and an increase in the number of 4-year-olds being admitted early into infant school reception or other classes. With falling rolls most LEAs now admit children before statutory school age.

Study of the Rumbold Report on the education of 3 and 4-year-old children (DES, 1990) and the HMI report on under-5s (DES, 1989a), reveals that approximately 45 per cent of under-5s in England attended some form of maintained school provision in 1989. Of these approximately 24 per cent of 3 to 4-year-olds attended nursery schools or classes and around 20 per cent of children in this age group (62 per cent of 4-year-olds) attended infant reception classes. Of the remaining population of under-5s it was estimated that between 40 and 60 per cent attended private pre-school playgroups. In Wales there has been a strong tradition of children starting school before 5 and it is estimated that, during 1989–90, 70 per cent of all 3 and 4-year-olds in Wales were attending school either on a full or part time basis. Of the total number, just over 66 per cent of pupils under 5 were full time in primary schools (CCW, 1991).

The above statistics indicate that the majority of our 4-year-olds are not receiving the nursery education recommended in the 1972 White Paper but are being educated in pre-school playgroups or infant classes. In the context of the maintained sector, this raises the question of whether the quality of education provided in infant (reception) classes is comparable in quality to that received by children attending nursery schools or classes. The view of HMI, at least in 1989, was that it was not, as the following quotation indicates:

> The quality of education for children under five is greatly influenced by the type of provision within which it takes place. Taking all factors into account children under five in nursery schools and classes generally receive a broader, better balanced education than those in primary classes. The work is well planned with a suitable emphasis on purposeful play and exploratory activity. Other conditions associated with the more frequent occurrence of better quality education in nursery schools and classes include: a narrower age band of children; better adult/child ratios; accommodation which in the main is purpose built or well adapted to the age group; better material resources; and more teachers experienced in teaching three and four year old children. (DES, 1989a: para. 6)

The report went on to describe the quality of education provided in infant classes for under-5-year-olds as lacking in breadth and balance so that the curriculum was not well matched to the children's educational needs, for example, providing insufficient exploratory or practical work to support the children's developing ideas of language before they start on the more formal work appropriate to later stages of learning. However there were some notable exceptions where the teaching was characterized by well planned activities and the excellent interaction between adults and children was enhanced by effective parental cooperation. Moreover some recent signs of improvement in the quality of education provided for these young children were noted, which were associated with the provision of good curricular guidelines, backed up by good in-service training and good staffing and resources. The report refers to the government's LEA Training Grant Scheme which would help in the provision of suitable training in the teaching of this age group but, regrettably, this has now been discontinued.

The Teaching of 4-Year-Olds in Infant Classes

Classroom based research studies of the education of 4-year-olds in infant classes have, in general , supported the judgments of HMI in their 1989 report regarding its quality (DES, 1989a). Bennett and Kell (1989), for example, found that both the amount and the level of play observed in their sample of classrooms was very limited. Teachers appeared to have low expectations concerning children's play and often used it as a time filler. The play activities provided lacked clear purpose and challenge and the teachers made very little attempt to monitor them or to interact with the children during them. On the basis of her observations of infant classrooms Anning (1991) described the teachers' approach to their children's topic work, creative and play activities, as '*laissez-faire*'. Their non-interventionist stance to these activities contrasted sharply with their direct, heavy involvement in the teaching of the basic skills of reading, writing and number. However their tight control of these particular activities was at odds with their expressed beliefs in progressive, child centred education, which emphasized the importance of children's first-hand practical and play experiences. The role played by the Year 1 teachers in our own study in their children's free play varied along the interventionist to non-interventionist continuum, as described in Chapter 5.

In these and other classroom based studies it has also been found that the children spend up to two-thirds of their time in basic skills activities, which leaves relatively little time for the creative, play based activities which are central to the ideology of early childhood education. Our own study showed that, before the advent of the National Curriculum, it was common for the balance between play based and teacher directed and structured activities in classes for 5-year-olds to shift in the direction of the latter as the school year progressed. This seems to be a perfectly justifiable shift in emphasis provided that the children continue to have opportunities for free play activities that are appropriate to their stage of development. The other studies reported above indicate that the balance between the two types of activity is often very uneven. Indeed, in one observational study of classrooms for 6 to 7-year-olds it was difficult for the observers to record any recognizable play activities at all, for these accounted for only 1 per cent of the school day (Tizard *et al.*, 1988).

In Anning's (1991) view the teachers whose work she observed were experiencing an obvious dilemma in trying to reconcile their direct instructional role in the basic skills with their professed role as indirect nurturers of the spontaneous learning of their young pupils. She argued that in concentrating their work in the area of the basic skills they appeared to be, at least in part, responding to pressures from outside school, including parental pressure. Indeed, well before the introduction of the National Curriculum the need to raise national standards of reading, writing and number has been a long-running theme in the media and in the pronouncements of successive governments. The setting up of the now defunct Assessment of Performance Unit some years ago (1975) was a good illustration of this governmental concern.

Given that the infant school curriculum, even for 4-year-olds, showed a strong academic bias well before the onset of the National Curriculum we need to know whether, as might be predicted, this bias has been exacerbated since. At a broader level we also need to ask how the curriculum for children under 5 should relate to the National Curriculum.

The Impact of the National Curriculum on Under-5s in Infant Classes

The evidence to date concerning the impact of the National Curriculum upon the education of children under 5 in infant classes is extremely sparse and urgently needs strengthening. In our own study (see Chapter 5) up to half of the headteachers felt that the National Curriculum had made little or no impact, at least by 1991, while the remaining headteachers were sharply divided in their evaluation of its impact. It will be recalled that some of our headteachers appeared to welcome the 'firmer structuring' of the curriculum for these children that had resulted, while others were clearly concerned by the increasing formalization of the under-5 curriculum which they felt threatened the fundamental principles of early years' education. The latter, negative view of the impact of the National Curriculum was strongly reinforced by the judgments of a group of infant school teachers attending a research seminar held in conjunction with our research project. Collectively these teachers reported that the National Curriculum was leading to the increasing formalization of the curriculum for this age group, with a greater emphasis now being placed upon children's written work and an increase in the amount of teacher directed work at the expense of the children's opportunities for free play and practically based learning. Also, in mixed-age classes the under-5-year-old children were suffering from the preoccupation of the class teacher with formal National Curriculum assessment, particularly during the summer term. Especially worrying was the comment of one discussion group that the National Curriculum had altered their perception of what constituted 'bona fide work' for these children, that is, activities that they thought were validated by the National Curriculum.

The results from our study suggest that the over-concentration upon the teaching of the basic skills, already prevalent in infant classes containing 4-year-old children, may well have become more pronounced since the introduction of the National Curriculum. This would mean that infant teachers may be exerting even tighter control over these children's classroom activities, despite their avowed belief in the principles of child centred education. This view is supported by the findings of Bennett (1992) which described the work of a small authorities project which had been set up to examine the provision for 4-year-olds in infant schools in the north of England.

The study produced evidence that the teachers' classroom organization and control of their pupils' learning activities had become less flexible than before, with more limited time being allocated for children's self-chosen activities and stronger control over the composition of children's groups in accordance with their age and ability. In ten of the seventeen classes observed the children stayed in teacher-directed groups throughout the day, the time to be spent on various activities was carefully controlled and the children remained in the same groups throughout the day. Despite these trends the teachers in the project rated the development of children's personal qualities such as self-confidence, independence and a sense of achievement and enjoyment from learning as being more important than their language, social and physical development, which in turn was rated as more important than their learning of the basic skills.

Like Anning (1991), Bennett is sensitive to the pressures upon infant school teachers which result in a conflict between their stated policies and their practice.

> As learning objectives become clearly defined and attached to particular activities so the notion of choice and self-directed learning becomes harder to achieve. (Bennett, 1992: 42)

Indeed she goes on to suggest that it may now be asking infant teachers too much to offer a wholly appropriate curriculum for 4-year-olds with all of its demands. These demands now include: establishing a firm parent–school partnership; ensuring continuity between earlier learning experience and that provided from age 5; assessment and record keeping; and working with other professionals, especially within the context of the National Curriculum and the expectations of teacher colleagues and parents.

The Impact of the National Curriculum in Nursery Schools, Classes and Centres

In the context of the present discussion it is important to distinguish, within the maintained sector, between the educational provision for 4-year-old children in infant classes and that in separate nursery schools and classes. As discussed earlier there is evidence that the quality of provision and the levels of staffing, training and resourcing are generally better in nursery schools and classes than in infant classes. Separate nursery schools enjoy complete independence from primary schools and even nursery schools within the latter may be considered to have a distinctive ethos which is further removed from the requirements of the National Curriculum than that which characterizes many infant classes.

The evidence to date concerning the impact of the National Curriculum upon nursery education is just as sparse as that described above for infant classes. The most important study we have been able to find was a survey carried out by Sylva *et al.* (1992) in a sample of local authorities chosen to represent different geographical areas. The pre-school centres within these authorities were chosen to represent the most common forms of state provision for this age group, namely, half day nurseries in the education sector and full day nurseries in the social services sector. The survey, based upon written questionnaires completed by the nursery staff, found that most of the nursery workers believed that many of the attainment targets specified in the National Curriculum could be reached by some pre-school children. They also claimed to be regularly using classroom materials which were relevant to those attainment targets. Sylva *et al.* analysed the National Curriculum core subject attainment targets in terms of their compatibility with play-based nursery education and judged that many of them were compatible with the practice of nursery education, for example, listening attentively and responding to stories and poems (attainment target E1, level 1 (b)). However they were concerned to find that even those targets which they judged to be incompatible because they required formal teaching were regarded by at least one or more of the survey respondents as compatible with their practice.

Within the education sector nurseries the main changes reported were in assessment and record keeping which were more curriculum focused, in line with the headings and structures of the National Curriculum attainment targets, and increased continuity between the nursery (age 3 to 5) and infant (age 5 to 7) phases of children's education. This continuity was being achieved through increased liaison between nursery and infant school staffs and also through joint participation in in-service training courses. Both of these changes were regarded positively by the nursery staff in the survey. However, like their infant class teacher counterparts, they were aware of the potential threat to the traditional, play-based curriculum posed by the introduction of the National Curriculum, coupled with increased parental pressure for 'school-like achievements'. In the spontaneous comments made by the nursery staff during the survey the most cited drawbacks of the National Curriculum were the pressure to achieve placed upon the children, as well as the teachers, and the reduced emphasis upon learning through free play. Despite these fears most of the staff questioned felt that they had taken from the National Curriculum what was compatible with their customary practice and avoided aspects which they thought inappropriate for very young children.

It may be that parental pressure for children to achieve academically is increasing, even within the nursery sector, following the introduction of the National Curriculum. In a pilot project which compared views on educational provision for pre-school children in Belgium and the UK David (1992) reported that, compared with their Belgian counterparts, British parents were moving further from the concept of child development as a natural process and were increasingly seeking to shape their lives, for example, by attaching great importance to the acquisition of reading and writing skills at an early age. David interprets this as a challenge to nursery educators to demonstrate to parents that the informal learning experiences that characterize early childhood education yield real and observable benefits for the children, even though they precede the more formal achievements.

Achieving High Quality Education for the Under 5s

Perhaps the major challenge facing teachers and other adults involved in the education of children under 5 today is to achieve curricular continuity between this phase and Key Stage 1 of the National Curriculum in ways which do not violate the principles of early childhood education stated at the beginning of this chapter. In discussing this and other challenges facing early childhood education Drummond (1989) refers to 'an intellectual hole at the centre of the early years universe', namely the current inability of early years' educators to justify and explain their professional practices with convincing rigour. She argues that there is a need to develop a professional language which will enable early years' teachers to link theory with practice and research findings with their own classroom observations. In a similar vein Anning (1991) argues that early years' teachers have misunderstood and misapplied research findings on child development and learning because they have not critically analysed them from a professional, educational viewpoint. She considers that the teachers' own 'common-sense theories', developed through a critical reflection of what they already know, should provide them with the insights needed for them to address psychological and other theories in a more confident and receptive way. Anning provides a useful account of some of the relevant psychological and other research which bears upon the role of the early years' teacher.

Ways Forward

If early years' teachers, and particularly infant class teachers, are to meet the challenge of achieving high quality education for the under 5s which also links into the National Curriculum at Key Stage 1, they will need considerably more support at both the national and local level than they currently receive. Nationally the fundamental importance of early years' education should be given official recognition through the expansion of integrated education and services for children under 5 and their families (Pugh, 1990, 1992). This expansion should be supported by programmes of in-service training for all those working with this age group. The Rumbold Report (DES, 1990) recommends that, in order to provide properly for under-5s, reception classes should enjoy a more generous staff ratio with staff having received early years' training.

Regarding the curriculum for under-5s it is vital that this should remain distinct from, although clearly related to, the National Curriculum. The National Curriculum Council in its publication entitled *A Framework for the Primary Curriculum* (NCC, 1989a) comments on the inappropriateness of young children under 5 being taught separate subjects but also stresses that their teachers must be aware of what strands of learning underlie the collaborative, manipulative and imaginary play activities in which these children engage. In this way, they argue, the teacher can use the spontaneity and enthusiasm of young children to provide the starting points for further work while at the same time establishing a sense of continuity and progression with the National Curriculum framework. The Rumbold Report similarly warns against the direct downward extension of the National Curriculum into the curriculum for under-5s and urges educators in this sector to guard against pressures to engage in formal teaching directed towards a specific set of attainment targets.

The curriculum document produced by the Early Years Curriculum Group (1989) referred to earlier provides useful practical guidance for teachers in their task of forging links between early years' teaching and the National Curriculum. They emphasize the fundamental need for the teacher to interact with the young child in the context of the child's play activities. This requires that the teacher not only realizes the importance of such interaction in developing the child's understanding and competence, but is aware of the best strategies to use in the given situation. The Rumbold Report lists the following conditions which are necessary if children's play is to be educationally fruitful:

- sensitive, knowledgeable and informed adult involvement and intervention;
- careful planning and organization of play settings in order to provide for extended learning;
- enough time for children to develop their play;
- careful observation of children's activities to facilitate assessment and planning for progression and continuity. (DES, 1990: para. 90)

A number of classroom based research studies have examined the quality of teacher–pupil dialogue in various contexts and in the light of these have made suggestions regarding the most productive conversational strategies for the teacher (Wood, 1980; Wells, 1985). It is also necessary for the teacher to have sufficient resources and classroom management skills to create the necessary time to engage in such interaction at an individual level. In this connection Bennett and Kell (1989) recommend that teachers should make much greater use of small group teaching for instructional purposes since it is impossible to provide fully individualized teaching for each child.

As we have already stated, the teachers of infant classes containing 4-year-old children probably face the greatest challenge in achieving high quality education for the under-5s because of their closer exposure to the demands of the National Curriculum and strong pressures to concentrate their efforts upon teaching the basic skills. The recently announced proposals for a significant slimming down in the content of the National Curriculum, including Key Stage 1 and its associated assessment procedures should help the beleaguered infant teacher considerably, as would the provision of protected non-contact time. However the pressure on them to prepare the ground for their 4-year-old pupils to learn the basic skills of reading, writing and number is unlikely to diminish because of their central place in national priorities. Indeed the interim report by Sir Ron Dearing (NCC, 1993b: sect. 3.20) uncompromisingly states that 'The principal task of the teacher at Key Stage 1 is to ensure that pupils master the basic skills of reading, writing and number'. The same section also indicates that the content of these skills will need to be firmly prescribed. While accepting the great importance of these skills, infant class teachers should resist any pressure from colleagues or parents to teach their 4-year-old pupils these skills directly and formally.

The developments just described will significantly help teachers to raise the standard of educational provision for the under-5s but it will also be necessary for them to tap the considerable potential contribution that parents can make towards the education of their young children. Our own study revealed that, although the schools readily endorsed the policy of encouraging parents to actively help at home in the development of their children's reading and language skills, the direct use of parental assistance within the school was largely confined to assistance in non-core curricular activities. Nursery and infant schools are ideally placed to develop and implement programmes designed to achieve a high level of parental involvement in the development of pre-literacy and other cognitive and linguistic skills in the under-5s within both the home and school settings. Whether such parental involvement can truthfully be called a partnership has been questioned by Pugh (1990). Nevertheless, in the new climate of unprecedented accountability, nursery and primary schools need to face the challenge of engaging in a genuine dialogue with their parents regarding the education of their pupils to the highest level of quality.

There is a strong emphasis in the Rumbold Report on the importance of educators of under-5s working to establish a partnership with parents in the interests of their children, as the following quotation shows:

> What is needed is for educators to be able and willing to explain to parents how the experiences offered to children contribute to their learning, and to describe how their children are progressing. They need to be able to share responsibility with parents. This places considerable demands upon the educators: they need to be ready to spend time on it, and to exercise sensitivity; they also need to have enough confidence to invite parents to share in their children's education. They must ensure that they have the necessary skills to work effectively with parents. (DES, 1990: para. 100)

Early Education for Socially Disadvantaged Children

The need for socially disadvantaged children to receive a high quality early childhood education prior to their entry into the first stage of the National Curriculum is even greater than it is for children from more favoured backgrounds. This is because their educational and play experiences within the home setting will tend to be more limited than those of their more fortunate peers. Not only may they lack early exposure to a range of stimulating play materials, books and toys but, more crucially, they may have insufficient experience of cognitively stimulating interaction with a parent within the context of meaningful joint activities such as story telling. As a result they may fail to develop the basic educational concepts, skills and attitudes towards learning upon which the infant teacher hopes to build (see Cox, 1993, for a fuller discussion of educational disadvantage and educational provision needed to combat it). It was for this reason that the Plowden Report argued that attendance at a nursery school is desirable for most children but especially so for children from deprived backgrounds on account of their need for

> the verbal stimulus, the opportunities for constructive play, a more richly differentiated environment and access to good medical care that good nursery schools can provide. (Central Advisory Council for Education (England), 1967: para. 165).

The Committee recommended that their proposed increase in nursery school provision should begin within the

> educational priority areas and spread outward, with a minimum goal of part-time attendance for all 4 to 5-year-olds living in such areas, with perhaps 50 per cent of these children having full-time places.

As we have seen this recommendation, along with that for an expansion of nursery education generally, has not so far been implemented, although it is fair to point out that most, if not all, local authorities operate a policy of priority admission to their nursery schools and centres for the most socially disadvantaged children.

In Chapter 5 we reported the concern of some of our sample Year 1 class teachers that the pressure exerted by the National Curriculum towards more formal attainments was resulting in reduced opportunities for children's free play. This restriction was proving particularly damaging for the slower learning pupils who needed to play much more than other children in order to develop language and other skills. Such concern was shared by at least one headteacher whose school served a disadvantaged area. He deplored the fact that there was now insufficient time for the school to spend on the children's social skills, constructive play and attitudes to learning. However, as we have already argued, the mere provision of free play time in the nursery or infant class will not in itself meet such children's educational needs. The play opportunities need to be accompanied, wherever appropriate, by stimulating interaction with a teacher of other adult.

An important but so far unresolved issue concerning the early education of socially disadvantaged children is whether the traditional play-based nursery curriculum which characterizes most nursery schools and centres is capable of meeting all of these children's special educational needs. Proponents of the more sharply focused and teacher directed educational programmes that have been specially designed to develop children's cognitive and language skills in particular argue that these should complement the traditional nursery approaches or even replace them for a period. The federally funded pre-school intervention programmes in the USA which started in the early 1960s were aimed particularly at poor lower working-class black children and their families. These came to be known as 'Headstart' programmes and many of them continue to this day with state or federal funding. At first there was much disappointment with the finding that the short term cognitive and other gains recorded by the children taking part in these programmes 'washed out' after a time. However later rigorous analyses of the long term effects of a number of these programmes, selected for the quality of their planning and evaluation yielded much more encouraging results (see Woodhead, 1989, for a summary of these).

On the question of the design of these successful early intervention programmes Woodhead (1989) points out that they varied considerably in the curriculum models followed, and in their instructional or learning methods, ranging from a more traditional play-based nursery programme to more specialized programmes such as the 'High Scope Cognitively Oriented Curriculum' (Hohmann *et al.*, 1979) and the highly teacher-controlled 'Direct Instruction' programme of Bereiter and Engelman (1966). Despite this variation, all of the selected programmes shared certain features which Woodhead argues may have accounted for their success. All were carefully planned and implemented, were designed with the age group in mind and had clear aims. In addition they had low adult–child ratios and engaged the parents actively in their children's learning (see also Cox, 1993).

In Britain a number of studies have demonstrated short or medium term educational gains for children receiving specially designed early intervention programmes targeted on very young socially disadvantaged children (see for example Kellaghan, 1977). Some of these were specially designed to develop particular language and cognitive skills in disadvantaged children on the premise that the traditional nursery school curriculum was too diffuse to meet these children's special educational needs. However it has been found that the benefits associated with such programmes do not necessarily outstrip those which can be achieved through good quality traditional nursery education (Woodhead, 1976; Clark, 1988). Moreover a large scale study of the longer term benefits of pre-school education by Osborn and Milbank (1987) found that *all* forms of such provision were beneficial although the highest cognitive and other gains were recorded by children attending nursery schools or play groups. The lowest gains were found amongst the children attending nursery classes attached to primary schools. It was also found that pre-school education boosted the educational achievement of socially disadvantaged children at least as much as that of children from more favoured backgrounds.

The finding of relatively disappointing gains shown by children attending nursery classes attached to primary schools in Osborn and Milbank's study has attracted attention and discussion (see for example Woodhead, 1989). The authors speculate that this outcome may have been because the staffing levels and the curriculum in such classes were more akin to those in infant classes than to those in the nursery schools and play groups. Woodhead (1989) urges caution against taking this finding at its face value because of the complex nature of the methods of statistical analysis used in the study. He also refers to an observational study by Jowett and Sylva (1986) which found that children who attended a nursery class attached to an infant school showed a higher quality of play and learning behaviour in their infant classes than children who had previously attended a playgroup.

A possible advantage of a specially devised structured intervention programme for disadvantaged children is that it provides a clear curriculum framework and objectives to guide the teacher in her or his interaction with the children receiving it. Another possible benefit is that it ensures that teacher—pupil interaction time is built into the programme and not left to chance. As Woodhead (1976) puts it, traditional informal methods of nursery/

infant teaching require a very high degree of organizational skill on the part of the teacher if they are to meet the varying needs of individual children within the class. Their success depends on

> the ability of the teacher to maintain implicitly in the quality of her [*sic*] organisation of activities and interaction with children the structure, sequence and control which is maintained explicitly in a formal programme (Woodhead, 1976: 74)

The main disadvantage of such programmes lies in their separation from the normal curriculum and this may be one of the reasons why in general British nursery and infant teachers do not take kindly to them (see, for example, Quigley, 1971). Another possible reason for this resistance is the rather prescriptive nature of some programmes, although this can be exaggerated. With such considerations in mind the developers of some intervention programmes for disadvantaged children have tried to develop programmes which can more readily be incorporated into the traditional pattern of classroom organization and curriculum of the nursery or infant class. A good example of such a programme is that devised by Curtis and Blatchford (1981) for disadvantaged children which is based upon the broad curriculum theme of 'My World'. At the end of the day the choice as to whether to use a special programme for disadvantaged, or indeed any, young children must be left to the teacher in the light of her or his knowledge of the children's needs and capabilities as well as her or his own professional style and inclinations.

As we have stressed earlier in this chapter, a high quality early years' education needs the active support and involvement of parents, all the more so in the case of socially disadvantaged children. Nursery schools and units provide an ideal base for the encouragement and guidance of such involvement and the literature contains helpful accounts of successful intervention projects designed to achieve this (for example, Donachy, 1979; Hirst and Hannon, 1990). In the LEA from which our study schools were drawn a school based programme aimed at achieving the active participation of parents in the development of their children's reading and language skills was well established in many primary schools and this was extended to some nursery schools or classes (Branston and Provis, 1986). A useful source book for nursery and infant teachers wishing to involve parents more actively in their young children's education has been provided by Tizard *et al.* (1981).

Prominent writers on the needs of children under 5 such as Gillian Pugh (1990) often emphasize the need for an integrated service for children and their families which combines educational, social, health and other forms of provision. One way of achieving integrated service provision is through combined centres, which were advocated in the Plowden Report. A number of these have been developed in recent years (for an assessment by HMI of combined provision for under-5s see DES, 1989b). An interesting feature of one such centre in Scotland, described by Watt (1988), is that it was set up as part of a wider project in which a comprehensive school, designated as a community school, sought to develop its role in an area of multiple deprivation.

In her evaluation report on the work of this Scottish combined centre, Watt discusses the possibility that the way in which pre-school education helps children and adults to cope with stress and to enhance their motivation and self-concepts might turn out to be one of the most fundamental contributions it can make in support of disadvantaged children and their families. This contribution, she suggests, even more than the development of children's language and cognitive skills, may be the main reason for the long term beneficial effects of the early intervention projects described earlier in this chapter. The aim of developing in children what Bronfenbrenner (1979) calls the capacity to be 'self-directing' — to take one's own decisions and live one's own life — is certainly in tune with the expressed aims of early years' educators. It is also a worthy aim for all those who work with the parents of socially disadvantaged children since their self-concepts and capacity for self-directed action may also need development. As Watt (1988: 98) puts it:

> pre-school education even of the traditional 'best' kind can only be effective if it takes account of: opportunities for 'self-direction' in both children and mothers; links with

> other pre-school and community agencies; the total context in which young families lead their lives; the next educational stage to which children with their parents will progress.

In this quotation Watt encapsulates the essential features of the high quality early years' education which we have discussed in this chapter.

Appendix 1

The Teachers' Attitude Scale

VIEWS OF THE NATIONAL CURRICULUM

Please tick appropriate column

	Statement	Strongly agree	Agree	Uncertain	Disagree	Strongly disagree	
1	We will find the NC helpful because it tells us what to teach and when.						1
2	The NC poses a serious threat to cross-curricular (project) work because of its subject emphasis.						2
3	The NC will force teachers to concentrate on teaching those skills/attitudes that are most easily measured at the expense of those that are less easy to assess.						3
4	I welcome the fact that the NC still allows us to decide *how* to achieve its aims.						4
5	The reporting of pupils' performance will mean that teachers will not be able to get away with poor teaching.						5
6	The NC will seriously deprive the class teacher of professional freedom and scope for initiative.						6
7	The formal assessment of children at age 7 will have a narrowing effect on the primary (infant) curriculum.						7
8	The NC assessments will be helpful in backing up our judgments when discussing pupils with parents.						8
9	The NC is broad, balanced and relevant to children's needs.						9
10	The formal assessment of attainment targets at age 7 is too early and educationally unsound.						10
11	The introduction of the NC means that we can concentrate on the basics and forget about the airy fairy subjects that have crept into primary education.						11
12	The standard assessment tasks (SATs) of the NC are essential to back up the teachers' own assessments.						12
13	The introduction of the NC is a backward move educationally.						13
14	The introduction of the NC means that all pupils will get the same breadth and depth of curriculum regardless of which school they attend.						14

Appendix 2

Additional Tables and Figures

Table A.1 Headteachers' and class teachers' mean attitude scale scores

Year	HT/CT	N	Mean	SD	T Value	P
1989	HT	26	33.04	4.61	1.33	NS
	CT	31	31.13	6.00		
1990	HT	24	30.62	5.24	1.62	NS
	CT	34	28.41	5.06		
1991	HT	21	29.95	6.23	0.40	NS
	CT	31	29.32	5.10		

Key
HT: headteachers
CT: class teachers
NS: not significant
N: number
SD: standard deviation
P: probability

Table A.2 Teachers' mean attitude scale scores over three years: Headteachers and class teachers combined

1989 (N=57)		1990 (N=58)		1991 (N=52)	
Mean	SD	Mean	SD	Mean	SD
32.00	5.45	29.33	5.20	29.58	5.53

T values:
1989 vs 1990 T = 2.69, $p<.01$
1989 vs 1991 T = 2.30, $p<.05$
1990 vs 1991 T = 0.24, not significant

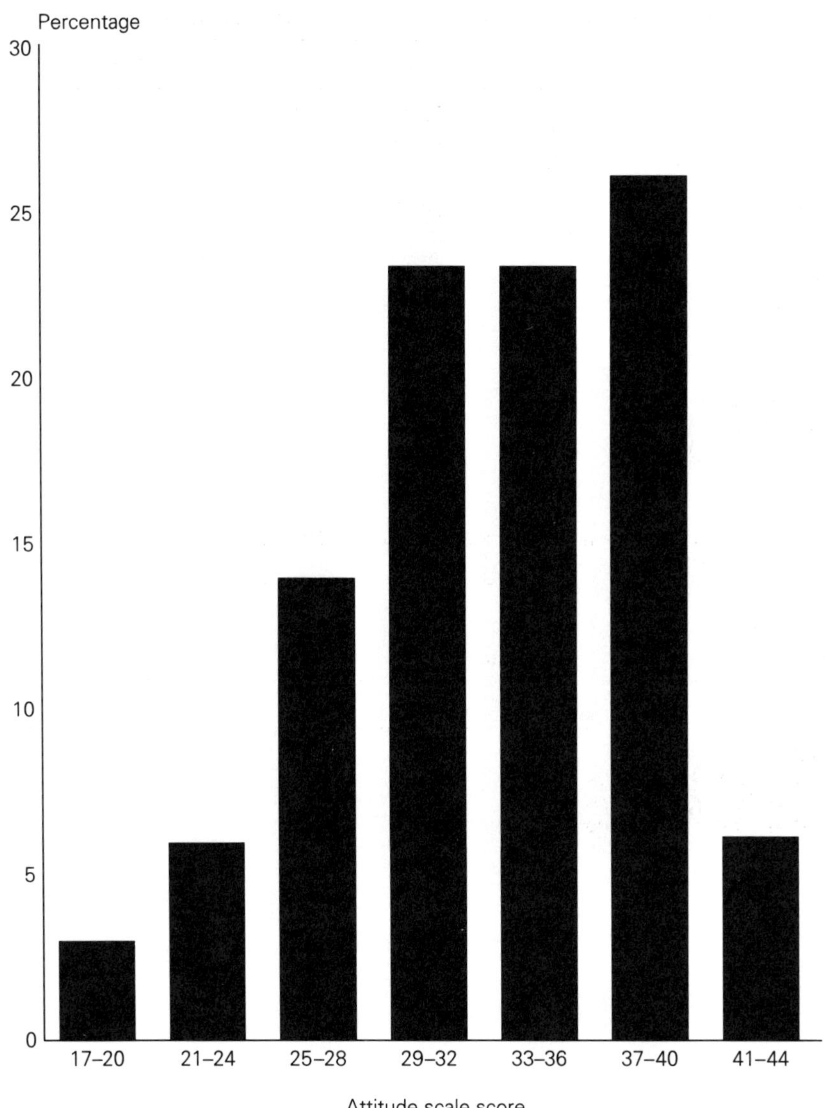

Figure A.1 'Core sample' teachers' attitude scale scores in 1989
Note: N = 35; Mean = 32.77

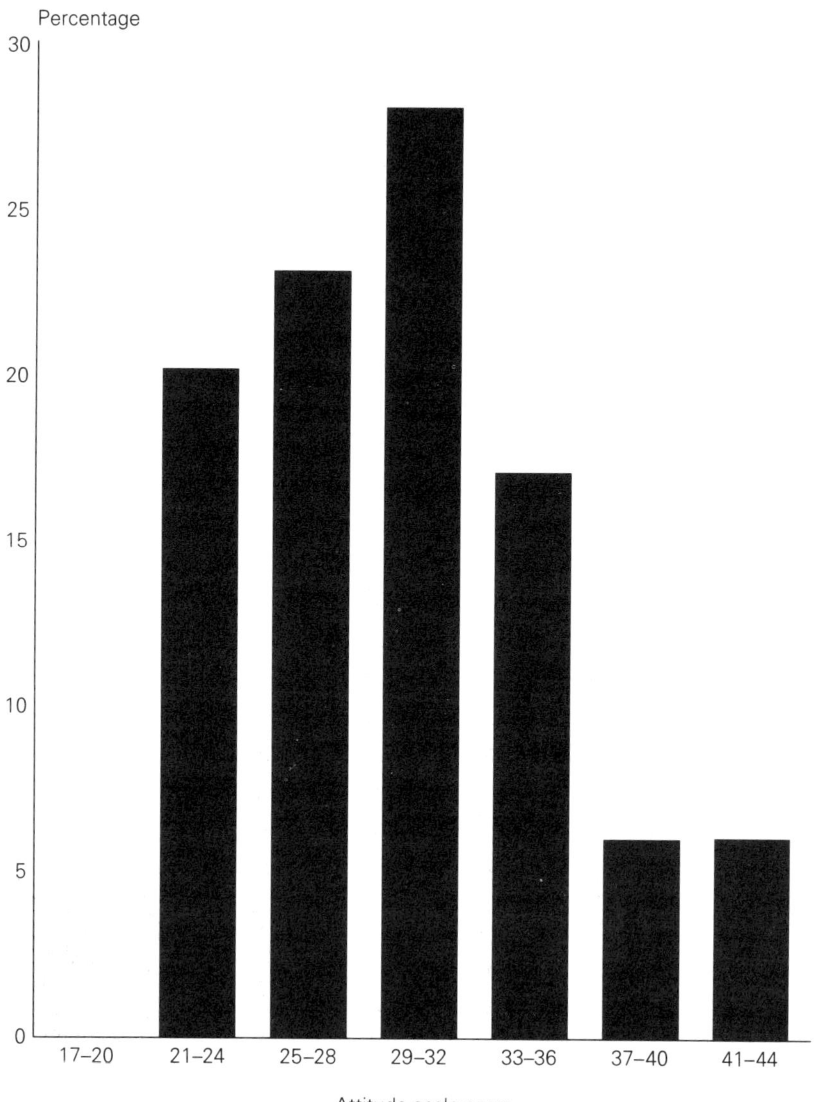

Figure A.2 'Core sample' teachers' attitude scale scores in 1990
Note: N = 35; Mean = 29.80

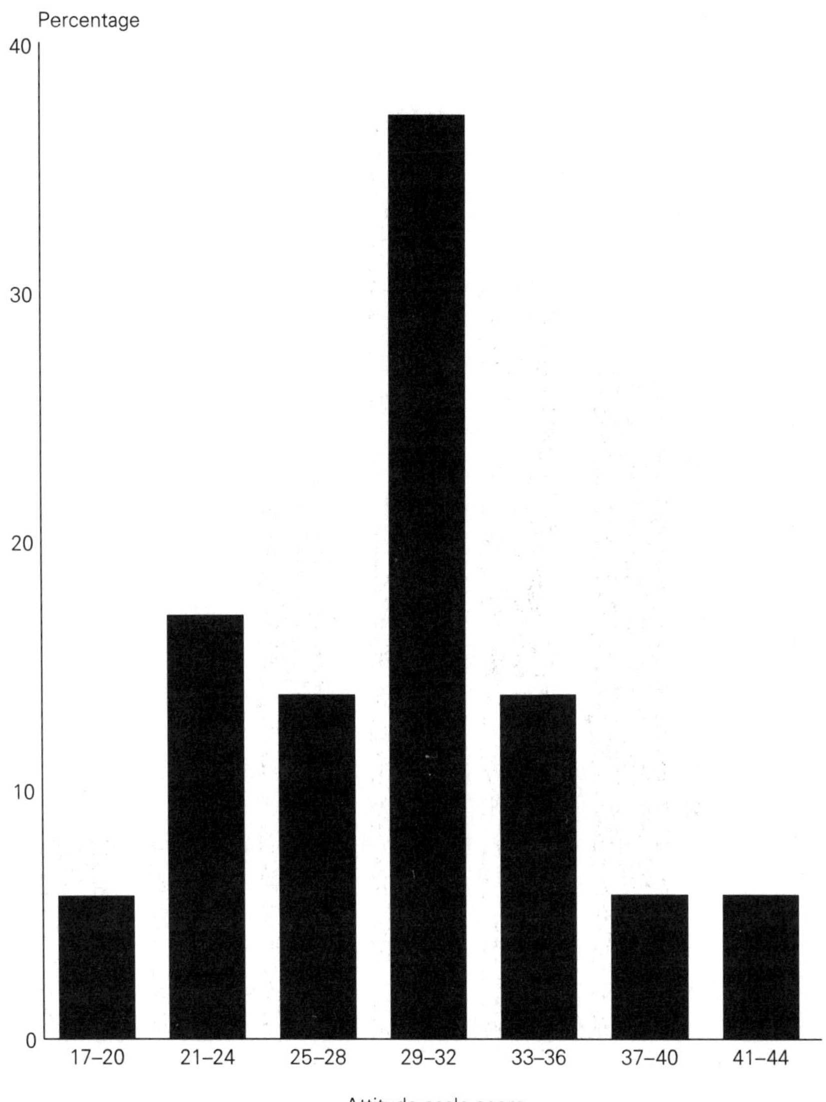

Figure A.3 'Core sample' teachers' attitude scale scores in 1991
Note: N = 35; Mean = 29.68

References

ALEXANDER, R. (1991) *Primary Education in Leeds*, Leeds: University of Leeds.

ALEXANDER, R. (1992) *Policy and Practice in Primary Education*, London: Routledge.

ALEXANDER, R., ROSE, J. and WOODHEAD, C. (1992) *Curriculum Organisation and Practice in Primary Schools: A Discussion Paper*, London: HMSO.

ANNING, A. (1991) *The First Years at School: Education 4 to 8*, Milton Keynes: Open University Press.

BARBER, M. and GRAHAM, D. (Eds) (1993) *Sense and Nonsense and the National Curriculum*, London: Falmer Press.

BENNETT, D. (1992) 'Policy and practice in the teaching of four-year-olds', *Early Years*, 13, pp. 40–44.

BENNETT, S.N. and KELL, J. (1989) *A Good Start?: Four-Year-Olds in Infant Schools*, Oxford: Basil Blackwell.

BENNETT, S.N., WRAGG, E.C., CARRÉ, C.G. and CARTER, D.G. (1992) 'A longitudinal study of primary teachers' perceived competence in, and concerns about, National Curriculum implementation', *Research Papers in Education*, 7, pp. 53–78.

BEREITER, C. and ENGELMAN, S. (1966) *Teaching Disadvantaged Children in the Pre-School*, Englewood Cliffs, NJ: Prentice Hall.

BRANSTON, P. and PROVIS, M. (1986) *Children and Parents Enjoy Reading: A Handbook for Teachers*, London: Hodder and Stoughton.

BROADFOOT, P. with ABBOTT, D., CROLL, P., OSBORN, M. and POLLARD, A. (1990) 'Reading the tea leaves: Teachers' reactions to changes in assessment under the National Curriculum', *Working Paper No. 3*, Bristol: PACE.

BROADFOOT, P. and POLLARD, A. with ABBOTT, D., CROLL, P. and

OSBORN, M. (1991a) 'The conduct and effectiveness of primary school assessment', *Working Paper No. 6*, Bristol: PACE.

BROADFOOT, P., ABBOTT, A., CROLL, P., OSBORN, M., POLLARD, A. and TOWLER, L. (1991b) 'Implementing national assessment: Issues for primary teachers', *Cambridge Journal of Education*, 21, pp. 153–68.

BRONFENBRENNER, U. (1979) *The Ecology of Human Development*, Cambridge, MA: Harvard University Press.

BRUNER, J. (1966) *Towards a Theory of Instruction*, Cambridge, MA: Harvard University Press.

CAMPBELL, R.J. and NEILL, S.R.St.J. (1992) *Teacher Time and Curriculum Manageability at Key Stage 1: Third Report of Research into the Use of Teacher Time*, Warwick: University of Warwick.

CENTRAL ADVISORY COUNCIL FOR EDUCATION (ENGLAND) (1967) *Children and their Primary Schools: Vol.1: Report*, (The Plowden Report) London: HMSO.

CHAZAN, M., LAING, F. and DAVIES, D. (1991) *Helping Five to Eight-Year-Olds with Special Educational Needs*, Oxford: Basil Blackwell.

CHITTY, C. (1992) *The Education System Transformed: A Guide to the School Reforms*, Manchester: Baseline Books.

CLARK, M.M. (1988) *Children Under Five*, London: Gordon and Breach.

COCKROFT, W.H. (Chair) (1982) *Mathematics Counts. Report of the Committee of Inquiry into the Teaching of Mathematics in Schools*, London: HMSO.

COX, T. (1982) 'Disadvantaged fifteen-year-olds: Initial findings from a longitudinal study', *Educational Studies*, 8, pp. 1–13.

COX, T. (1993) 'Coping with unhappy children who have educational disadvantages', in VARMA, V. (Ed.) *Coping With Unhappy Children*, London: Cassell.

COX, T. and JONES, G. (1983) *Disadvantaged 11-Year-Olds*, Oxford: Pergamon Press.

COX, T., EVANS, J. and SANDERS, S. (1991) 'How primary school teachers view the National Curriculum in one LEA', *Educational Review*, 43, pp. 273–81.

CROLL, P. and ABBOTT, D. with BROADFOOT, P., OSBORN, M. and

Pollard, A. (1993) 'Whole school change and the National Curriculum: Headteacher perspectives', paper presented to the British Educational Research Association Conference, Liverpool.

Curriculum Council for Wales (CCW) (1989) *A Framework for the Whole Curriculum 5–16 in Wales*, Cardiff: CCW.

Curriculum Council for Wales (CCW) (1991) *Under-Fives in School*, Cardiff: CCW.

Curriculum Council for Wales (CCW) (1992a) *Aspects of Primary Education in Wales*, Cardiff: CCW.

Curriculum Council for Wales (CCW) (1992b) *Developing Whole School Policies for Pupils with Special Educational Needs: Curriculum Bulletin No. 6*, Cardiff: CCW.

Curriculum Council for Wales (CCW) (1992c) *A Report on the Primary Education Review in Wales 1992*, unpublished but copies available from Cardiff: CCW.

Curriculum Council for Wales (CCW) (1993) *Developing a Curriculum Cymreig*, Cardiff: CCW.

Curtis, A. and Blatchford, P. (1981) *Meeting the Needs of Socially Handicapped Children*, Windsor: NFER Nelson.

Daugherty, R. (1992) 'The future development of the primary curriculum in Wales', speech given at Llandrindod Wells, Cardiff: CCW.

David, T. (1992) 'What do parents in Belgium and Britain want their children to learn in the early years?', paper read to the XX Congress of the World Organization for Early Childhood Education (OMEP) at Northern Arizona University, Flagstaff, AZ.

Davie, R., Butler, N.R. and Goldstein, H. (1972) *From Birth to Seven*, London: Longman.

Dearing, R. (1993a) 'Have your say', *Times Educational Supplement*, September 17, p. 21.

Dearing, R. (1993b) 'Well, what do you think?', *Times Educational Supplement*, September 24, p. 14.

Dearing, R. (1993c) 'Join the law and order debate', *Times Educational Supplement*, October 1, p. 10.

Dearing, R. (1993d) 'Time to search for a Key to Stage 4', *Times Educational Supplement*, October 8, p. 12.

Dearing, R. (1993e) 'And now the trickiest problem', *Times Educational Supplement*, October 15, p. 12.

Department for Education (DFE) (1992) *The Implementation of the Curriculum Requirements of the ERA: An Overview by HMI of the Second Year, 1990–91*, London: HMSO.

Department for Education (DFE) (1993) *Draft Circular for the Initial Training of Primary School Teachers: New Criteria for Course Approval*, London: HMSO.

Department for Education (DFE)/Welsh Office (1993) *Draft Code of Practice on the Identification and Assessment of Special Educational Needs. Draft Regulations on Assessments and Statements*, Cardiff: Welsh Office.

Department of Education and Science (DES) (1978) *Special Educational Needs: Report of the Committee of Enquiry into the Education of Handicapped Children and Young People*, (The Warnock Report) London: HMSO.

Department of Education and Science (DES) (1985) *The Curriculum from 5 to 16*, London: HMSO.

Department of Education and Science (DES) (1989a) *Aspects of Primary Education: The Education of Children Under Five: Report by HMI*, London: HMSO.

Department of Education and Science (DES) (1989b) *From Policy to Practice*, London: DES.

Department of Education and Science (DES) (1989c) *Combined Provision for the Under Fives: The Contribution of Education: Report by HMI*, London: HMSO.

Department of Education and Science (DES/HMI) (1990a) *The Implementation of the National Curriculum in Primary Schools. A Survey of 100 Schools*. London: DES.

Department of Education and Science (DES) (1990b) *Starting with Quality: The Report of the Committee into the Quality of the Educational Experience Offered to 3 and 4-Year-Olds: Chaired by Mrs Angela Rumbold, CBE MP*, (The Rumbold Report) London: HMSO.

Department of Education and Science (DES) (1991) *In-service Training for the Introduction of the National Curriculum: A Report by HMI*, London: HMSO.

Department of Education and Science (DES/Welsh Office)

(1988a) *National Curriculum Task Group on Assessment and Testing (TGAT). A Report*, London: DES.

Department of Education and Science (DES/Welsh Office) (1988b) *National Curriculum Task Group on Assessment and Testing (TGAT): Three Supplementary Reports*, London: DES.

Donachy, W. (1979) 'Parental participation in pre-school education', in Clark, M.M. and Pheyne, W.M. (Eds) *Studies in Pre-School Education*, London: Hodder and Stoughton.

Drummond, M.J. (1989) 'Early years education: Contemporary Challenges', in Desforges, C.W. (Ed.) *Early Childhood Education: British Journal of Educational Psychology Monograph Series No. 4*, Edinburgh: Scottish Academic Press.

Early Years Curriculum Group (1989) *The early years and the National Curriculum*, Stoke-on-Trent: Trentham Books Ltd.

Elkind, D. (1989) 'Developmentally appropriate education for 4-year-olds', *Theory into Practice*, 28, pp. 47–52.

Gammage, P. (1992) *The Tension Between Content and Process*, Lecture given at University College Swansea, Department of Education. 19th May 1992, in the series 'Primary Education-Planning for the Future', unpublished.

Gipps, C. (1988) 'What examinations would mean for primary education', in Lawton, D. and Chitty, C. (Eds) *The National Curriculum: Bedford Way Paper No. 33*, London: University of London Institute of Education.

Graham, D. (1993) *A Lesson for Us All: The Making of the National Curriculum*, London: Routledge.

Hegarty, S. (1993) *Meeting Special Needs in Ordinary Schools: An Overview*, London: Cassell.

Hewison, J. and Tizard, B. (1984) 'Parental involvement and reading attainment', *British Journal of Educational Psychology*, 50, pp. 209–15.

Hirst, K. and Hannon, P. (1990) 'An evaluation of a pre-school home teaching project', *Educational Research*, 32, pp. 33–39.

Hohmann, M., Banet, B. and Weikart, D.P. (1979) *Young Children in Action*, Ypsilanti, MI: High Scope Press.

Jowett, S. and Sylva, K. (1986) 'Does kind of pre-school matter?' *Educational Research*, 28, pp. 21–31.

Kellaghan, T. (1977) *The Evaluation of an Intervention Programme for Disadvantaged Children*, Windsor: NFER.

KELLY, A.V. (1990) *The National Curriculum: A Critical Review*, London: Paul Chapman.

LAWTON, D. (Ed.) (1988) *The Education Reform Act: Choice and Control*, London: Hodder and Stoughton.

LEWIS, A. (1991) *Primary Special Needs and the National Curriculum*, London: Routledge.

MADEUS, G.S. (1988) 'The Influence of testing on the curriculum', in TANNER, L. *Critical Issues in the Curriculum*, Chicago: University of Chicago Press.

MORTIMORE, P., SAMMONS, P., STOLL, L., LEWIS, D. and ECOB, R. (1988) *School Matters*, London: Open Books.

NATIONAL CURRICULUM COUNCIL (NCC) (1989a) *Curriculum Guidance 1: A Framework for the Primary Curriculum*, York: NCC.

NATIONAL CURRICULUM COUNCIL (NCC) (1989b) *Curriculum Guidance 2: A Curriculum for All: Special Educational Needs and the National Curriculum*, York: NCC.

NATIONAL CURRICULUM COUNCIL (NCC) (1990) *Curriculum Guidance 3: The Whole Curriculum*, York: NCC.

NATIONAL CURRICULUM COUNCIL (NCC) (1993a) *The National Curriculum at Key Stages 1 and 2: Advice to the Secretary of State for Education*, York: NCC.

NATIONAL CURRICULUM COUNCIL (NCC) (1993b) *The National Curriculum and its Assessment: An Interim Report*, York: NCC.

NATIONAL CURRICULUM COUNCIL (NCC) (1993c) *Special Needs and the National Curriculum: Opportunities and Challenge*, York: NCC.

NATIONAL UNION OF TEACHERS (1993) *Response of the National Union of Teachers to the Proposals of the Secretary of State for the Initial Training of Primary School Teachers*, London, NUT.

OFFICE FOR STANDARDS IN EDUCATION (OFSTED) (1993a) *Curriculum Organisation and Classroom Practice in Primary Schools: A Follow-up Report*, London: DFE Publications Centre.

OFFICE FOR STANDARDS IN EDUCATION (OFSTED) (1993b) *The Training of Primary School Teachers*, London: HMSO.

OPPENHEIM, A.N. (1992) *Questionnaire Design and Attitude Measurement*, 2nd Rev. Edn, London: Pinter Publications.

OSBORN, A.F. and MILBANK, J.E. (1987) *The Effects of Early Education*, Oxford: Clarendon Press.

OSBORN, M. with ABBOTT, D., BROADFOOT, P., POLLARD, A. and CROLL, P. (1993) 'Changes in teachers' professional perspectives', paper presented at the British Educational Research Association Conference, Liverpool.

OSBORN, M. and BROADFOOT, P. (1991) 'The impact of current changes in primary schools on teacher professionalism', paper presented to the American Educational Research Association Conference, Chicago.

OSBORN, M. and POLLARD, A. with ABBOTT, D., BROADFOOT, P. and CROLL, P. (1991) 'Anxiety and paradox: Teachers' initial responses to change under the National Curriculum', *Working Paper No. 3*, Bristol: PACE.

PROCTOR, N. (Ed.) (1990) *The Aims of Primary Education and the National Curriculum*, London: Falmer Press.

PUGH, G. (1990) 'Developing a policy for early childhood education: Challenges and constraints', *Early Child Development and Care*, 58, pp. 3–13.

PUGH, G. (1992) 'An equal start for all our children?' *The Second Times Educational Supplement Greenwich Lecture, 1992*, London: National Children's Bureau, Early Childhood Unit.

QUIGLEY, H. (1971) 'Nursery teachers' reactions to the Peabody Language Development Kit', *British Journal of Educational Psychology*, 41, pp. 155–162.

SCHOOL CURRICULUM AND ASSESSMENT AUTHORITY (1994) *The National Curriculum and Its Assessment: Final Report*, London: School Curriculum and Assessment Authority.

SECRETARY OF STATE FOR EDUCATION AND SCIENCE (1972) *Education: a Framework for Expansion; presented to Parliament by the Secretary of State for Education and Science*, London: HMSO (Cmnd. 5174), December.

SOLITY, J.E. and BULL, S.J. (1987) *Special Needs: Bridging the Curriculum Gap*, Milton Keynes: Open University Press.

SYLVA, K., SIRAJ-BLATCHFORD, I. and JOHNSON, S. (1992) 'The impact of the UK National Curriculum on pre-school practice, Some "top-down" processes at work', *International Journal of Early Childhood*, 24, pp. 41–51.

TIZARD, B. and HUGHES, M. (1984) *Young Children Learning: Talking and Thinking at Home and at School*, London: Fontana.

TIZARD, B., MORTIMORE, J. and BURCHELL, B. (1981) *Involving Parents in Nursery and Infant Schools*, London: Grant McIntyre.

TIZARD, B., BLATCHFORD, P., BURKE J., FARQUAHAR, C. and PLEWIS, I. (1988) *Young Children at School in the Inner City*, London: Lawrence Erlbaum.

TOPPING, K.J. (1987) *The Peer Tutoring Handbook: Promoting Cooperative Learning*, London: Croom Helm.

TYLER, K. (1993) *Curriculum Styles in the Primary School*, Loughborough: Loughborough University Department of Education.

VULLIAMY, G. and WEBB, R. (1993) 'Progressive education and the National Curriculum: Findings from a global education research project', *Educational Review*, 45, pp. 21–41.

WATT, J. (1988) *Evaluation in Action: A Case Study of an Underfives Centre in Scotland: Occasional Paper No. 3*, The Hague: Bernard Van Leer Foundation.

WEBB, R. (1993) *Eating the Elephant Bit by Bit*, London: ATL Publications.

WEDGE, P. and ESSEN, J. (1982) *Children in Adversity*, London: Pan Books.

WELLS, G. (1985) *Language Learning and Education*, Windsor: NFER Nelson.

WELSH OFFICE (1993) *Draft Circular: The Initial Training of Primary School Teachers: New Criteria for Course Approval*, Cardiff: Welsh Office.

WHITEHEAD, M. (1993) 'National Curriculum: Understanding the background', *Nursery World*, 93, pp. 10–11.

WILLIAMS, M., DAUGHERTY, R.A.D. and BANKS, F. (Eds) (1992) *Continuing the Education Debate*, London: Cassell.

WOLFENDALE, S. (1987) *Primary Schools and Special Needs: Policy, Planning and Provision*, London: Cassell.

WOLFENDALE, S. (1988) 'Parents in the classroom', in THOMAS, G. and FEILER, A. *Planning for Special Needs: A Whole School Approach*, Oxford: Basil Blackwell.

WOOD, D. (1980) *Working with Under Fives*, London: Grant McIntyre.

WOODHEAD, M. (1976) *Intervening in Disadvantage: A Challenge for Nursery Education*, Windsor: NFER.

WOODHEAD, M. (1989) 'Is early education effective?' in DESFORGES,

C.W. (Ed.) *Early Childhood Education: British Journal of Educational Psychology Monograph Series No. 4*, Edinburgh: Scottish Academic Press.

WRAGG, E.C., BENNETT, S.N. and CARRÉ, C.G. (1989) 'Primary Teachers and the National Curriculum', *Research Papers in Education*, 4, pp. 17–37.

Name Index

Subject Index

Tactical Management

Cookie
Cookies
Cookie

■ GLOBAL MANAGER SERIES ■

Tactical Management

A Management Model for Challenging Times

A comprehensive guide to support you in the achievement and maintenance of health for your organization

William Rice-Johnston

INTERNATIONAL THOMSON BUSINESS PRESS
I(T)P® An International Thomson Publishing Company

London • Bonn • Johannesburg • Madrid • Melbourne • Mexico City • New York • Paris
Singapore • Tokyo • Toronto • Albany, NY • Belmont, CA • Cincinnati, OH • Detroit, MI

Tactical Management

First published by International Thomson Business Press

A division of International Thomson Publishing Inc.
The ITP logo is a trademark under licence

British Library Cataloguing-in-Publication Data
A catalogue record for this book is available from the British Library

---

First edition 1999

Typeset by LaserScript Limited, Mitcham, Surrey
Printed in the UK by TJ International, Padstow, Cornwall

ISBN 1–86152–376–9

International Thomson Business Press
Berkshire House
168–173 High Holborn
London WC1V 7AA
UK

http://www.itbp.com

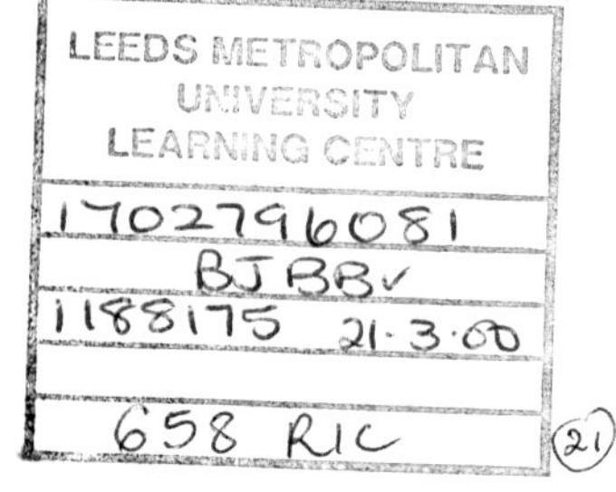

Dedication

To May
and
The Goobie Gang:
Alex, Adam, Louise, Kathryn, Faye, Matthew, Lewis, James

None but yourself, who are your greatest foe.

Henry Wadsworth Longfellow
Michael Angelo

We has met the enemy, and it is us.

Walt Kelly
Pogo

Contents

Acknowledgements

Books like this one nearly always include a section in which the author thanks a large number of people who supported him or her during its writing and publication, or who have otherwise contributed to its success. These acknowledgements typically also include the comment that it has not been possible to mention everybody individually.

I am not going to do that. Some of you are credited with your specific contributions in the text, the rest of you know who you are and have already been thanked by me personally. I would be ungracious, however, if I failed to extend my thanks to Mandy Little, my agent and Julian Thomas, my publisher. Two of you also deserve special thanks for having supported and guided this project from the beginning: Daphne Oxland and Simon Harbridge, thank you.

William Rice-Johnston
June, 1998

Preface

It '. . . was like giving someone a haircut.
It was a . . . lot harder than it looked'.

Stephen King
The Tommyknockers

Why this book?

'Gadzooks,' the reader thought, 'not *another* book by some ivory towered academician on how my life as a manager can become blissful, carefree and infinitely productive by applying some exciting new technique involving yet another use of the word "management"'.

Not likely. However:

1 Are you *totally* satisfied with present levels of customer service throughout your organization? Are all your *customers* totally satisfied with present levels of customer service? (Whether your customer is halfway around the world or in the next department the principle is the same.)
2 Are you *totally* satisfied with present levels of quality throughout your organization? Are all your *customers* totally satisfied with present levels of quality? (Whether you deliver a product or a service the principle is the same.)
3 Are you *totally* satisfied with present levels of profits for your entire organization? Are your board and shareholders, or others to whom you are responsible for your budget, totally satisfied with present levels of profits? (If you operate within a non-profit environment the principle is the same; you are still responsible for the effective and efficient management of all the resources under your control.)

If the answer to all these questions is yes, then your organization might be described as healthy. The health of your organization is the necessary first step on the road to the attainment of long-range organization objectives. You might then add, however:

- I seem to have to work awfully hard to achieve these results; or
- our markets are diminishing and changes will have to be made to maintain profit levels; or
- our competition is growing fiercer and fiercer and I don't know how much longer we can hold our own; or
- our equipment is old and worn out and operating costs are rising rapidly; or
- one of the clear ramifications of the move to a global economy is the need for a drastic upgrading of our quality standards; or
- any one of a dozen other reasons why you must examine every available source of information and inspiration to support you during your never-ending quest to maintain the health of your organization.

We live in challenging times. Only the well-managed business organization will remain healthy, and that health is crucial to survival. You must manage your organization successfully for the short-term within a framework that supports the consistent achievement of long-range organization objectives. You must develop a model that enables you to manage your organization effectively within a climate of rapidly accelerating change. The ability to deal effectively with this change is essential and you must equip yourself with processes and practices that enable you to do this. The rapidly accelerating pace of change in our lives is nowhere more apparent than in the business community. Writers far more eloquent than I have expressed this. Markets will continue to become more differentiated, customers will continue to become more demanding, the workforce will continue to become more vocal regarding its place in the organization, delivery times will continue to shorten, order quantities will continue to diminish *ad infinitum*.

In 1997 a total of 12,610 companies were liquidated, either on a compulsory or voluntary basis, within England and Wales. For 1996 the figure was 13,461: for 1995 14,536: for 1994 16,728 and for 1993 it was 20,708.[1] My thesis is that if each manager were successfully doing the job for which they are being paid and to which they have committed by acceptance of the position, these figures would be much lower.

Tactical Management is a management model: it will yield positive results for you when you apply the principles and practices systematically. It is applicable to any business; whether providing a product or service, profit or non-profit making, public or private, autonomous or part of a larger institution; to the management of a secretariat consisting of three people and the management of an engineering facility of 5000. It is applicable to the operation of a foundry and the claims department in an insurance company.

Utilizing present resources you can deliver more product or service, improve quality, reduce delivery times, improve staff morale, communications and workplace safety, and, finally, improve the profitability of your organization. Utilizing present resources you can improve the ability of your organization to achieve long-range objectives.

Tactical Management is all about *doing*. It is operations based, it is action oriented, it is confrontational, it is about dealing with change, it is about taking risks, it is even about an occasional failure – one of those risks. It is, finally, about improving the health of your organization.

Tactical Management is about looking systematically at parts of your organization, identifying something that could be done differently to improve that operation, laying out a process to address the change, then going out and *doing* it.

A productivity improvement goal of 100 to 200 per cent in the next two to four years is not only attainable but essential to the health of your organization.[2] This book is all about your professional objective for that improvement.

If you are a manufacturing organization you are spending 20 per cent or more of your sales revenues doing things wrong and doing them again; if you deliver a service you are spending 35 per cent or more of your total operating costs doing things wrong and doing them again.[3] You must reduce operating costs by these factors if your business is to remain healthy. This book is about this professional objective: to stop things from going wrong in the organization for which you are responsible.

The central thesis of *Tactical Management* is that if you can stop things from going wrong each day you can achieve short-range objectives, and if you can achieve short-range objectives consistently you can ensure the attainment of long-range organization objectives.

This is a book to be *used*

Think about this:

> You and one of the members of your management team are walking down the hall toward your office. You have just left a meeting chaired by this person. You, in your role of boss and coach, are discussing the results of the meeting.
>
> 'Hilary (or Hillary),' you say, 'you didn't control that meeting very well. You never really set out the objective clearly, nor did you ask for the commitment'.
>
> Hillary (or Hilary) replies, 'No, Boss, you're right. I let them talk all around the issue, but we never really identified the specific cause of the problem'.
>
> By this time you have arrived at your office and you both enter. You walk to the bookcase and take down your copy of *Tactical Management*: 'Here. Read the chapter on setting and achieving objectives. It will take you less than a half-hour and I think it will help you understand why we didn't accomplish anything today'.

This is a book to be *used. Tactical Management* is a work to be kept in a prominent spot on your desk or bookshelf and used, regularly and frequently, in your daily work. It is not intended to gather dust and never be opened again after the first reading. Nor should it be used to settle abstruse academic arguments raised in the bar or boardroom about the precise definition for an obscure term of management theory. This is a book to be read routinely in your efforts to address the problems you have to deal with and the specific actions you must take every day to keep the business running. This is not a book about strategic planning, finance or marketing, although we shall refer to those matters from time to time. This is a book about all the things you must do after the strategic, financial and marketing matters have been considered. It is based on an amalgamation of classical, traditional and current management thinking, blended with the author's twenty-six years of experience as a consultant practicing manager.

There is a great deal of literature available today on the subject of management. Most of it is good, some of it is excellent. Much of it, however, while relevant is not easily accessible to the practising manager; it is either too general or too arcane for the specific problems you encounter daily in the workplace. Furthermore, if you are the manager of a small or medium size enterprise, particularly if that enterprise is part of a larger entity, you usually have neither the time, the resources nor the discretion to experiment with textbook proposals.

As a busy manager, what you need is a book that will help you as you go about the business of managing your operation. It should:

- Provide you with easily accessible references to useful management principles and practices based on sound and lucid management theory, and offer you guidance on how those principles and practices can be tailored to the specific needs of your organization.
- Direct you to other sources, both secondary and primary, for those topics you wish to investigate in more detail.
- Suggest to you how the specific concepts and subjects that make up *Tactical Management* fit into a general framework of management theory and practice as presented by other authorities.
- Provide you with guidelines on possible limitations of the principles and practices under discussion.
- Offer you information on the general direction of current management thinking, and how that relates to your specific needs.
- Provide you with some glimpses of the future: on the direction in which the author and other contemporary writers on management think we are moving.
- Offer you a little comfort when you are about to face the consultant (or perhaps even worse: the seller of consultancy services), the bearer of the latest chalice for the eternal salvation of management, or a visit

from the currently most visible (and probably youngest) Head Office staff department high-flier.

- Provide you with a suitable framework into which you can fit all those little bits of information you regularly pick up on management subjects in your reading and during discussion with colleagues.
- Give you a basis for evaluating the usefulness and applicability of information gained from seminars and training sessions attended by you and other members of the management team and, finally;
- Communicate to you – with total integrity and some degree of humour and empathy, it is hoped – that the problems you face daily in the workplace, whether that workplace is the factory floor, the office, the council admin centre, the paediatric ward or the salesperson's route, are not unique to either you or your organization: that we are all in this together.

This book will do that for you. This is a book to be *used*.

Notes

1 *Financial Statistics*, No. 431, March 1998, Insolvencies in England and Wales, Table 6.1A. (London: The Stationery Office, Office for National Statistics, Natu Patel, Ed.) These figures are for liquidations. Other statistics describe business failures. I have elected not to use them because they are subject to many different interpretations.

2 Tom Peters, *Thriving on Chaos*. (New York: Harper & Row 1988.) One of Peters' theses is that improvements of this magnitude are possible. I agree with him.

3 Philip B. Crosby, *Quality Without Tears*. (New York: 1985.) I agree with Crosby that improvements of this scale are possible. You can easily document the potential within your own organization.

Introduction

> For management has to *manage*, and managing is not just passive, adaptive behaviour; it means taking action to make the desired results come to pass.
>
> Peter Drucker
> *The Practice of Management*

> The ingenuities of 'tactics' . . . are requisites to the accomplishment of the coordination of activities at proper places and times.
>
> Chester I. Barnard
> *The Functions of the Executive*

Tactical Management

Tactical Management is a set of practices a manager uses to achieve results: a body of activities that begin after a plan is formulated and end when the aim of the planning process is accomplished. Tactical Management converts a plan into a series of actions that result in completion of the objective defined by the plan.

The management cycle

'Management cycle' describes the total activity of managers. Specific elements in the cycle and terminology differ, depending on the model[1] you are using. A typical model begins with a plan, includes decision-making to identify actions to be taken, implementation of actions, measurement of progress toward the objective and a control process. Nearly all models are characterized as linear: the first element is the plan and subsequent elements are placed to the right, connected by arrows to represent the flow of information and sequence of activities.

The Tactical Management model is different from others. Within this model the cycle is characterized by a closed loop. Measurement of progress is followed by evaluation of that progress, then actions are identified to adjust the plan if any problems are interfering with your ability to meet the objective. The loop is closed when the plan has been adjusted and the cycle begins again. Moving toward an objective is always a continual process of closing one loop in the management cycle within another, larger loop, each more ambitious in scope, until the final objective is accomplished.[2] Consider a typical management cycle:

> A five-year strategic plan is developed for the organization, and this is used to generate a series of one-year business plans for operating units. Yearly budgets created at department level are monitored monthly. Work is planned monthly, and those plans are followed by production or service schedules and may be weekly or daily according to needs. Results are measured, reported and evaluated in reverse order. Actual production or service volumes are recorded daily or weekly and summarized monthly; revenues and costs are recorded monthly and summarized quarterly or yearly. At each step, planning at the next level is adjusted to reflect any negative variance between the plan and actual results that would interfere with achievement of the long-range or strategic objective.

The Tactical Management model is a useful description for the way managers really work. Management activity is never a linear process with a defined end; it is a cyclical process that does not end as long as the organization exists.[3]

This model also emphasizes the principle of control that is central to any body of management theory. While loops are being closed effectively and the organization is moving closer and closer to objectives, processes are in control; otherwise they are out of control. Tactical Management seeks to keep processes in control.

The Tactical Management model

Tactical Management includes all elements in the management cycle following from the original plan:

1. identifying resources needed to achieve the objective;
2. committing and assigning resources to the separate tasks that constitute total activity;
3. monitoring progress as tasks are completed;
4. reporting formally on progress;
5. evaluating progress with regard to schedule attainment;
6. quantifying variances to the schedule;
7. identifying specific causes of variances;
8. developing processes of corrective action to address the causes of variances;
9. taking corrective action to eliminate causes; and
10. adjusting the plan as necessary to keep the process moving toward the objective.[4]

It should be apparent after thoughtful examination of these elements that they include the bulk of the work of most managers most of the time. Even those managers whose primary responsibility is strategic planning, finance, sales, marketing, human resource management, training, public relations or information technology spend most of their time making decisions and taking actions to make things happen. It is thus appropriate to treat Tactical Management as a comprehensive body of management activity: we are justified in describing Tactical Management as a management model relevant to the work of all managers.

Tactical Management

Tactical Management is such an important part of the management cycle that it cannot be separated from other management activity. There is a discipline we describe as Tactical Management. There is, however, no set of practices that sets an individual apart as a Tactical Manager, distinct from other managers. Every effective manager must necessarily always be a tactical manager.

Tactical Management treats a collection of activities that are often examined in isolation as a unified discipline. It places equal consideration on interactions between elements in the cycle and on the dynamics of the individual elements themselves. It is customary, for example, to delegate the responsibility for making things happen, what we refer to as operations, to supervisors, their immediate superiors and the next level of management, collectively described as first line or front line managers. Planning processes, particularly for the medium term, are the responsibilities of another group described as middle managers. These are typically treated as two distinct disciplines with very little structured emphasis on how they interact. A further example concerns work assignments. Supervisors and first-line managers are trained in the importance of good work assignment practice as a specific issue within the greater context of general communications. The argument is that making effective assignments to staff will increase the likelihood that work will be completed on schedule and according to specification. Little formal consideration is given within the context of work assignment practice to the importance of how more (or less) effective planning will affect the assignment of work, and how more (or less) effective work assignments will affect later medium term or long-range planning.

It is easy to confirm that a manager is managing effectively: he or she consistently achieves results that support long-range objectives for the organization.[5] It is more difficult to understand what must be done when a manager is not managing effectively. This requires:

- recognizing that performance is below target: objectives are not being achieved;

- quantifying the problem: measuring how big the variance is – the gap between where we are and where we want to be;
- committing to actions to reduce the variance by eliminating the cause;
- adjusting the original plan as necessary to close the loop and begin a new management cycle; and
- confirming that actions taken and revisions to the plan are consistent with the original, long-range objective.

These are precisely the elements that are not examined in detail in most models as elements in a comprehensive system. Significant attention is paid to strategic skills appropriate to managing at long-range and medium-range levels. The rest of the cycle, including managing at the operational level and control at the shortest interval – usually referred to as scheduling, is treated as something managers, particularly middle and senior managers, absorb through osmosis: there is no need to address these elements in detail because the necessary skills will be accumulated over time and through practice.[6] Except for a cursory mention, most models ignore about three quarters of the management cycle. Few writers or practitioners examine in any detail the premise that the most carefully devised strategic plan will not accomplish objectives without all the decisions, actions and problem solving that must follow every day, in the workplace, at the tactical level.[7]

Tactical Management places primary emphasis on that part of the management cycle that keeps processes in control. Processes are kept in control when – and only when – every member of the management team accepts responsibility for identifying variances, then taking action to eliminate causes of problems. When processes are kept in control, the fundamental objectives of the organization are achieved. Monitoring daily work assignments and setting short-term objectives may not be as glamorous as strategic planning or strategic management, but consistently achieving long-range objectives for the organization is glamorous indeed.

Concerning the style of this book

In those situations where the manager responsible for providing a service must use an approach distinctly different from one providing a product, I make that clear. Otherwise the term 'product' rather than 'product or service' will be used simply because it contains fewer syllables. 'Costs' will be used generically to refer to either costs or expenses; at the tactical level it makes no difference. When I refer to profits I mean revenues minus costs. If you are responsible for the management of a non-profit operation, in most cases all the practices apply if you set a target of either zero profits or compliance with a budget forecast. As you become acquainted with the Tactical Management model you will find only a few situations where these distinctions are necessary.[8]

The text often refers to functions within the management structure at different levels: section leaders, supervisors and first-line managers through to middle and senior managers to executives – generically all referred to as management. We are interested in principles of management in the most general sense. One of my goals is to convince you that the similarities between the problems managers face at different levels in the organization are more important than the differences. Another consideration is that in the healthy company this distinction between management levels becomes blurred beyond usefulness, and in the truly excellent company it becomes almost meaningless.[9]

I often use the word process to refer to entities we have traditionally called programmes. This is deliberate. Programmes has evolved in our language to characterize activities that are detailed, specific and closed-ended. Processes seems to me to communicate more positively activities that are general, universal and open-ended. Processes will be more responsive to the needs of the organization of the future than will programmes.[10]

Another of my goals is to make you comfortable with the practice of developing your own management model and understanding that this is a crucial element in your professional growth. Therefore I promise not to define management within this book. That is one of your assignments.

All stories, cases and examples presented here are true (except for a few I have clearly noted as having been invented). Throughout I shall try to present them not only as accurately as I can recall, but also within the original context and with minimum hyperbole. The only editing has been that necessary to preserve anonymity for the actors. This is either to ensure privacy, prevent embarrassment or maintain a modicum of good taste according to circumstances. In particular, all quotations presented as having been heard by me are verbatim. It has not been necessary to embellish them to make my point. If you listen carefully during your workday you will hear them too. When you have finished this book I hope you will be more aware of these gems that reveal so much about how speakers perceive the organization and their places in it.

Most of the issues we examine in this book are very subjective. They relate either to the way people act in the workplace, how they communicate with each other or how they respond to unexpected, often rapid changes in the environment. One of my premises is that people do not operate their lives on facts but on their perceptions of facts. This distinction is important. If we all made decisions and took actions based on facts it would be easy to predict how other people were going to react in a particular situation. We might ask ourselves how *we* would react, then generalize this to somebody else under the assumption that we were all working with the same facts. People respond to their perceptions of the world around them. They do this within a framework of the total environment within which they are operating – there and then.[11] The result is that prediction is more difficult. We have to try to understand how the person with whom we are trying to communicate perceives the world. I think it is helpful when this occurs to step back and ask ourselves to define the issue at its most basic level. I shall do that occasionally in this book, sometimes leading you through the sequence of thoughts I am using to try to understand the fundamental problem. I shall also sometimes juxtapose apparently incongruous entities. I may, for example, talk about the manufacture of Swiss watches and the preparation of journal vouchers in the same paragraph, or the supervision of a foundry shakeout operation and a paediatric ward in the same context. These processes may seem pedantic and condescending but that is not my intention. It is my aim to address systematically a difficult, subjective matter; or one that is highly emotional and has been trivialised in the popular press or that could mean dramatically different things to different people.[12]

Finally, *Tactical Management* is presented in what I hope you perceive as a confrontational style. My good friend and associate, Steve Schroeder, says that: 'It must stand up to the "*Why?*" questions'. I intend to upset you occasionally; to cause you to sit bolt upright in your chair, fold your arms and ask whether this model it truly relevant to your organization and your particular operation. If you think a statement that I have made does not apply to you, I expect you to challenge it. I expect you to walk out there to where the work is actually done and convince yourself that it is as good as it is going to get – that it cannot be improved.[13] If reading this book motivates you to make just one trip out to the floor and ask just one '*Why?*' question, then I have succeeded.

Concerning theories and models

Throughout this book we will refer to the works of many other authors on management practice, behaviour, motivation, organization, leadership and related topics. Within that body of literature you will regularly encounter information that appears to be inconsistent with other things you have read, including parts of *Tactical Management*. This is because you are involved simultaneously with several models and with the attempts of different authors to create a model or theory that has utility for a specific situation.

Scientists like to work with things they call theories. To us a theory may sound like unintelligible professional jargon. To the scientist, however, in addition to sounding like unintelligible professional jargon a theory is a formal, unambiguous description of the way something works. This formal statement is to facilitate the process of observation and measurement; to test its validity. The value of any theory lies in its utilization as a tool to plan or predict the future. This is its only use, it has no other.[14] If you, for example, want to design and build a bridge, you will use theories from various disciplines such as the mechanics of structures and the strengths of materials. One of your objectives is probably to predict with some degree of confidence that your bridge will not fall down.[15]

A less intimidating word than theory is model. One good, everyday example of a model is a map. You use it to predict the future: to plan how you are going to get from Point A to Point B. From the perspective of understanding theories and models, your prediction about your move from Point A to Point B is no different from your prediction about how well the bridge will endure: both are your plans for the way you want something to happen based on an appropriate model.

Your choice of map depends on your means of transportation. You may use a road map, an Ordnance Survey map, an air chart or a sea chart. There is no single ideal or perfect map. You could certainly make your way from London to Glasgow by car using Ordnance Survey maps but the process would be cumbersome. The back seat of your car would be full of maps, the scale is wrong and there is far more detail than you need. Tourists in London occasionally come to grief by locating some point of interest then trying to walk there by scaling the familiar Pocket Tube Map. When you are trying to get from Kensington High Street to Tower Bridge by tube the tube map is a good model; when you are trying to walk from Covent Garden to Piccadilly Circus it is not, the *London A to Z* is a much better choice. In the matter of scale the two maps are inconsistent: the tube map is not to scale whilst the *A to Z* is. The tube map is a useful model so long as it is used with objective of finding your way by tube from one station to another. There is a problem if you attempt to use it to judge the walking distance between those two stations.

The singular test for a management model is whether it works for you. If, for example, a particular statement of leadership theory makes sense for you when developing your subordinates, it is a good model. If a theory articulated by another author appears to make your effort more effective, that is a better model. If you appear to be most effective by using one theory in one set of circumstances and another theory at another time, this is the best possible use of models. There is absolutely no ambiguity in this practice.

We describe Tactical Management as a management model. The purpose of this model is to assist you in your ability to plan, to predict the future for the operation of your business – and to enhance your effort to make certain things happen the way you want them to happen, when you want them to happen. When Tactical Management does this for you it is a useful model.

Isaac Newton did not discover some sort of fundamental truth about the universe; he offered us an explanation for the way something works. He created a model to explain the way certain physical things behave.

Albert Einstein did not discover a better or more fundamental truth about the universe; he offered us another explanation for the way something works. He created a different model to explain the way some of those same physical things behave. You use Newton's model every time you hit a golf ball or put a cue to a snooker ball. Einstein's model will work in those circumstances, but it is more complicated than necessary. Using Einstein's model for this application is analogous to trying to find your way from London to Glasgow using Ordnance Survey maps. On the other hand, if you want to predict the behaviour of light as it passes near a star, you should use Einstein's model. Newton's model will work after a fashion, but its limitations will introduce anomalies. This is analogous to using the tube map to plan a walk from one tube station to another.[16]

A thorough understanding of this issue is important in the development of your own management model. Development of your model began the day you decided to become a manager. It is evolving continually and that process will not stop until the day you cease to be a manager. Your model is unlike all others. You have assembled it from elements from a number of sources. These include your formal education, your hobbies and avocations, every bit of work experience, all your reading, your attendance at seminars, all your thinking and talking about your work and all the experiences you have accumulated throughout your life. By the time you have completed your reading of this book, *Tactical Management* will also be part of it. You accept parts of that experience and reject others. You will continue that process: now accepting concepts you earlier rejected, later rejecting concepts you earlier accepted, chopping and changing as you go, finally creating concepts original to you through the same thought processes. The sole criterion must be how well your model supports your efforts to manage the organization. If it is sometimes advantageous to use two concepts which in other contexts contradict each other, that will not diminish the usefulness of either concept or your model in general.[17]

We will variously use the words theory, hypothesis, thesis, premise, principle, occasionally postulate and sometimes even law in this work to provide a bit of interest. In each case, however, we are referring to a model.[18]

Do this: do this tomorrow

Tactical Management is about a set of actions – actions you and other managers on your team should be taking. If this effort is to be successful, it is important to understand why those particular actions will be effective and why they have not already been taken. It is appropriate to begin this process by asking you to examine your operation in a particular way.[19]

Devote the entire day, without interruption, to a comprehensive look at your organization. When I say 'the entire day', I mean *the entire day*, from very early in the morning to late at night. I do not mean the one hour between your weekly staff meeting and the daily damage limitation meeting with Sales and Quality. When I say 'without interruption', I mean *without interruption*; take no calls, no messages from your secretary or visits from head office staff.

Spend the time walking through the facility from one end to the other.[20] Stop from time to time, stand still and from that spot observe critically what is going on around you. It is important you do not look for causes, excuses, reasons or individuals to blame for what you see. That will interfere with the observation process. Evaluation will come later.

Talk to everybody: operators, junior clerks, engineers, section leaders, supervisors, secretaries, messengers and managers. Ask each what they like about the job and what they dislike. Find out what systems people really think about operations people and vice versa. Talk to union representatives. Ask what each would change if given the chance. You will discover that once the usual fulmination about more money is finished, the typical union representative will tell you what he or she thinks is really important, most of which relates to better communications, safety and improved methods.

Look at the flow of work, safety and housekeeping, scrap and rework. You will find scrap and rework in every area including Admin; often the cost is higher in Admin than in Operations. Examine the way people communicate. Sit in on a customer service meeting and a quality meeting. Visit the training centre and attend any session then in progress.

Spend one hour, no less, with whoever in your organization deals directly on the telephone with customers concerning problems, complaints, incomplete and incorrect orders, quality problems and late deliveries. Do not spend the time in the unit manager's office discussing football results, sit down beside the clerk who actually speaks with these customers. Listen as that clerk tries very hard to make excuses sound like plausible reasons why something did not happen the way it should have. Ask yourself if *you* would be satisfied with these excuses if you were on the other end of that telephone line. Talk to marketing and sales people; discover what they must do to keep customers happy. Visit the unit that deals with written customer enquiries and spend one half hour reading through a basket full of them. Ask yourself if you could afford to continue to do business with a company that provided this level of service.

Make some calculations: what percentage of total revenues for the past twelve months reflect something other than a complete, on-time, perfect delivery? What percentage of your total labour budget for that same period was paid to deal with customer complaints and enquiries? Ask Marketing for a realistic estimate of revenues lost to the business when customers went elsewhere in the past year. Ask Sales to tell you what part of their budget is allocated to trying to win those customers back. Calculate the cost of penalties for late or incomplete deliveries. Calculate the premiums you have paid for additional freight to expedite late shipments for the past year.

Count the number of people involved in institutionalised rework: people who routinely, day after day, are required to do things that have already been done once. Be objective about it. Include total costs: additional handling and set-ups – nearly always treated as indirect labour or overhead – a convenient means of distorting the true costs, premiums paid for extra material deliveries, overtime, delay time accrued to other units or lines and the extra floor space needed to quarantine material. Ask yourself how anybody can be expected to take pride in fixing something that should never have been broken.

Finally, identify an area somewhere in your factory or office where you can observe about fifteen people or more at a time. Select a time about mid-morning or mid-afternoon and spend exactly half an hour there. Find a spot where you can stand or sit unobtrusively and do the following:

Action

At five minute intervals throughout the half-hour count the total number of staff or operators you can see and record that number. Then count again, but this time record the number of people you *honestly* feel are working. For this study ignore the nature of the work you see; the one requirement is that a person is performing some kind of work. At the end of the thirty minute period calculate the total number of people working and a grand total of all occurrences observed. Now divide the number working by the total observed. If you are lucky, extremely lucky, performance will range between 60 and 65 per cent. If you are unlucky the number will be lower – it can be *much* lower. Now compare this performance with *that reported under your current work measurement system.* Look at the variance. Ask yourself why. Ask your supervisors and managers why.[21]

Throughout the half-hour period count the number of times every person you can see moves from the place of work, either bench or desk, and returns. Under typical circumstances you will record between 100 and 120 individual movements. If you really want to ruin your day try this in your word processing unit or secretariat. Ask yourself if labour hours are being utilized most productively when these people are required to move around that much. Ask yourself if they would not be quite so tired at the end of the shift if they did not have to jump up and down so many times each hour. Why do they seem to be doing so many things in batches of one? Ask your supervisors and managers why.[22]

Return to your office and close the door. Review your notes. Ask yourself if you saw any opportunities for improvement in customer service and quality. Did you see any opportunities for improvement in productivity – doing things right, or methods – doing the right things? Did you see any opportunities for improvement in profits? Did you see anybody doing the right things at the wrong time? Did you see anybody doing nothing all?[23]

Is this the best your organization has to offer your customers, staff, board, shareholders and other stakeholders. Is this the best *you* have to offer?

Why things go wrong (or don't go right)

Periodically you and the board sit down to develop a strategic plan for your organization. You might do this every five years and update it yearly, or you might develop a new five year plan every year. From this you create a series of business plans; probably every year. These are translated into budgets for each of your operating units, profit or cost centres.

If the assumption is made that each of these elements in the plan is reasonable and attainable, that should be the end of the process. Why would it be otherwise? All that should remain is for you, the rest of the management team and staff to go out and do it. But it seldom works out that way, does it? Things often go wrong somewhere between the agreement to a plan and the recording of actual results. This is true whether you are looking at a five year strategic plan, a monthly budget or a daily production schedule.

Do clerical staff *want* to make errors when preparing journal vouchers? Do you really believe that operators come to work prepared to do a bad job and make poor quality products? Do engineers schedule equipment breakdowns at inconvenient times? Do procurement people deliberately not order material or order incorrectly? Do your managers contrive not to provide you with the routine operating information they know you need regularly? Do systems people program the computer to crash? Do salespeople come to work and declare: 'I think I'll try *not* to sell anything today?'

Probably not.

If the clerk in accounts is trained for the job and neither plans nor wants to make errors on journal vouchers, and neither does the supervisor, why do errors occur? If the operator knows when the machine is producing bad parts, and so does the superintendent, why are bad parts produced? If the manager knows your report is due, and knows that you know, why is it not delivered on time?

Look at the notes you made during and after your one-day tour of the facility. Highlight some particularly odious examples of things going wrong, then sit down and prepare a detailed list of reasons why you think things go wrong. Itemize as objectively as possible the things you feel are interfering with the ability of the staff, managers and yourself to do the job you are being paid to do. Do not offer up platitudes such as poor communications, low morale, lack of training, tough competition, deregulation or bad tooling. Do not generalize. Make specific comments relevant to your operation.[24]

Now try to match the reasons you have just listed to the specific things you saw going wrong on your tour. When you reflect on it you realize that things do not usually go wrong for the reasons you think they do.

The clerk does not make errors because he or she is poorly trained or poorly motivated. Errors are made because that clerk's perception of the requirements of the job is that it is okay to make *some* errors, *sometimes*: 'Hurry up with that. We're not making Swiss watches, you know!' The operator does not let the machine make bad parts because he or she isn't paying attention or doesn't care. Bad parts are made because the operator's understanding of the requirements of the job is that making *some* bad parts, *sometimes*, is okay: 'Let that job run, we must ship today. I'll get somebody to sort them'. Your report is not received on time because your real message is that it is not really that important. Your supplier ships you inferior material because you accept inferior material. Your staff are not fully trained to do the job because you made the decision not to train them: not making a decision is a decision.

Please note my choice of words; it is not casual. Nobody orders the clerk to make errors or the operator to make bad parts. That, however, is the message sent by management. The people who work for you will usually try very hard to live up to your expectations of them.

Most things go wrong because people receive conflicting messages. When conflicting messages are sent the communication effort is a failure. The result is always poor decisions and ineffective actions – or no decisions or actions at all. Most things go wrong because priorities get garbled.

And what to do about it

You can do something about it if you understand how people react when they receive conflicting messages: why priorities get garbled.

Some of it happens because you and all the other people in the organization throughout every day are very, very busy trying to get the product out or deliver the service; you simply do not take the time to ensure that communications are received accurately. Sometimes you make assumptions that messages are understood, again because you are in a hurry. Occasionally you recognize that a problem exists but rather than deal with some unpleasantness, you ignore it and hope it will go away. Sometimes you know you do not have the resources to complete the work on schedule but you make the commitment anyhow – or coerce one of your subordinates into making the impossible commitment.

Most of the problem, however, has to do with the signals you broadcast. You talk convincingly about quality, for example, but soon after you bend the specification to ship an order on time. You talk assertively about managing costs and later blithely compensate for inadequate planning with overtime. This creates discrepancies between what you say and what you do.[25] If a conflict is perceived between what you are saying and what you are doing, the response from the person with whom you are trying to communicate will be to react to your action rather than to your verbal communication. In a typical face-to-face encounter in the workplace 83 per cent of the information transmitted is through non-verbal channels.[26]

Conflicting messages are received because conflicting messages are sent. If you want to stop things from going wrong the first thing you must do is to stop sending conflicting messages.

When a person receives conflicting messages he or she seeks to make sense out of the situation: within that person's mind the conflict *must* be resolved. All the messages you send are organized according to how important each is perceived to be *for that person*. They are prioritized in a way that makes that person comfortable at that time, within that environment. Actions are taken based on those messages that are placed at the top of the list. The messages that conflict are placed lower on the list and do not result in any action. In these circumstances the person may appear to take actions that make no sense to you, or more likely, appear deliberately contrary to the intention of your communication. To that person, however, the actions are justified.[27]

If you want to stop things going wrong and stop a person doing the wrong things, you must place doing the right things at the top of his or her priority list. This requires two distinct processes. A great deal of *Tactical Management* is concerned with these:

1 You must ensure the message received from you is unambiguous – clear and free from conflict. You must make the clerk understand fully what you want done: what the right thing is. Do you want vouchers produced with some errors or do you want error-free vouchers? In fact, producing error-free vouchers costs you less money, and it has nothing to do with Swiss watches.
2 You must ensure that your objective is as high on the priority list of the receiver as it is on yours. Is it more important, to you, to keep a machine running and produce bad parts or to make good parts? If making good parts is really more important to you, you must convince the operators that it should be important to them too. It usually turns out that this is usually not as difficult as it sounds. The operator, in fact, wants to make good parts. Much of your job is merely to remove any obstacles.

It follows that a great deal of what every manager must do is to communicate accurately to people in the workplace what is expected to happen. If communications are improved and conflicting messages are eliminated, the chances of things going wrong are reduced significantly.

You may argue that there are many other reasons why things go wrong: a plan you developed was not successful because it was based on incomplete information and vague or ambiguous assumptions. Inadequate training can be a factor for the lack of both technical and management skills. Machines do break down and tooling does fail from time to time. Suppliers can suddenly raise prices, fail to deliver or go out of business. Markets can decline rapidly, much quicker than you can respond effectively. The release of a competitor's new product can have a severe impact on sales. The government can impose costly revisions to safety regulations with little notice.

Review the notes from your tour again and you will realize that very little of what you saw out there was a result of any problem caused by situations similar to those described in the paragraph above. Nearly every one of the problems you observed was the result of people taking ineffective or incorrect actions based on inaccurate or conflicting information. This example is instructive:

> One of my recent projects was a detailed analysis of a large food processing operation. The analysis was to identify opportunities for implementing management team building, total quality systems, and in-process quality systems based on statistical process control (SPC). Many products manufactured at this facility had a very short shelf life and often the pressure on operations to ship daily was intense. During interviews with senior quality managers we were told that operations sometimes deliberately used ingredients that were out of date to complete an order, then informed quality after products had been shipped. A few weeks later production for one entire day, representing about 50 per cent of the factory's total capacity, was rejected and returned by a major customer (approximately 60 per cent of total facility revenues). The reason given was that out-of-date material had been identified in the product.
>
> Managers commented: 'You can't hire dependable people these days. Nobody cares about doing a good job anymore. Why wasn't anybody paying attention to dates on that material?'

My response is that people were doing precisely what they thought was expected of them. They had seen managers in the past make decisions to use out-of-date material. Why should it be any different this time? The difference this time, of course, was that the customer discovered it. The problem was not caused by operators who didn't care about doing a good job, but by managers sending conflicting signals. The operators resolved the conflict by acting the way they had seen managers act in the past.

The first, big, important step for you and the rest of the management team on the road to health for your organization is to be doing the right things consistently and to be *seen to be doing the right things*. This will be crucial in your effort to eliminate the communication of conflicting signals.

Notes

1 Model in this context is a synonym for theory. A theory is, fundamentally, an explanation for the way something works. See Page 6.
2 The idea of a closed-loop management cycle will be considered in detail in Chapter 7. The principle is central to the Tactical Management model. This cursory presentation is adequate for the present discussion.
3 There are organizations that cease to exist by design. We describe them as projects or task forces. Even here, however, there are hierarchies of management cycles: series of loops-within-loops closed by management actions that ultimately accomplish final project objectives.
4 Individual elements in the management cycle have not been rigorously defined. No problem should result for the reader if commonly accepted definitions are applied. These elements will be examined in detail in a number of places within this book.
5 This is not necessarily the best, or even a good, definition for manager or management. It is, however, the easiest and most objective technique for measuring how well a manager is managing.
6 This is not to ignore the vast literature and practice for such matters as communications, meeting management, supervisory development, production scheduling and time management. My argument is that literature and practice seldom attempt to place those disciplines within the greater context of a closed-loop management cycle.
7 If you doubt the accuracy of this statement review the syllabus for any MBA programme. Compare the number of courses addressing strategic planning, finance and marketing with the number of courses devoted to scheduling and assigning work and the appropriate actions to be taken by managers *at the tactical level* to deal with variances to the strategic plan.
8 The purist will say I should be using the phrase return on investment: that the word profits is being used naïvely. My objective is to examine how to make things happen at the tactical level. We are not concerned about how your accountant depreciates a piece of equipment or writes off damaged finished goods. Nor are we concerned about the most fundamental statement of organization objectives. You are being asked to manage your operation so that in the long-term, after you have paid all the bills, you have the most money left over and that you consistently achieve long-range strategic objectives. Profits is a word that will do the job.
9 The significance of this paragraph should become clear to you as we proceed.
10 Philip B. Crosby: 'Eating a sandwich is a programme, raising a child is a process'.
11 The difference between facts and perceptions will be considered in detail in Chapter 11.
12 One simple example of this is the discussion of profits versus return on investment which appears in Note 8 above.
13 If I really believed this were the case I would not have written this book.
14 There appears to be a general propensity among human beings to want to

understand how things work, but explaining the past is clearly of limited use to the practising manager.

15 If you think this statement is trivial, consider the Tacoma Narrows Bridge. Then the third longest suspension bridge in the world, it fell down, spectacularly, in the western United States in 1940.

16 You may have to think about this paragraph before you agree with it. You may choose not to agree with it at all. You may even choose to reject it with vigour. If that is the case my point has clearly been made.

17 How often do you say: 'The sun rises in the East?'

18 In formal scientific enquiry it is convenient to use these terms differently, but that is of no concern in this context.

19 If you do this properly it will not be easy. Carry your folio and be prepared to make plenty of notes.

20 This walk-through will be useful only if you allocate the entire day to a single facility. If you are responsible for several facilities this exercise will require one full day for each.

21 What you have just done is something called a ratio/delay study. It is completely unscientific and statistically unsound, but the resulting performance will be nearly identical to pure work performance calculated using traditional work measurement techniques.

22 What you have done now is known as a mobility study. Here there is no question of validity: what you see is what you get. A mobility study will not work well with an individual such as a messenger, set-up person or paediatric nurse, but you should have the idea by now.

23 I routinely make the assertion that if you were to give me a one hour tour of any part of your operation I could easily draft thirty '*Why?*' questions. You could answer ten without difficulty. Ten you could not answer, but the supervisor or area manager could. For the remaining ten the only answer would be: 'I don't know; that's the way we've always done it'.

24 An important premise of *Tactical Management* is the profound difference between a statement such as: 'One of my big problems is lack of staff training,' and 'I need X hours to train Y people in Z disciplines.' You can take no effective management action against the former, but you can with the latter. Developing processes for qualifying and quantifying training needs will be examined in Chapter 21.

25 Tony J. Watson, *In Search of Management: Culture, Chaos & Control in Managerial Work*. (London: International Thomson Business Press, 1996.) Watson characterizes these differences between what you say and what you do as a gap between the official and unofficial organization cultures.

26 Michael Argyle, *Bodily Communication* 2nd Edn. (London: Methuen, 1988.) Results of an admittedly limited amount of research in this area suggest a wide range of values for this ratio depending on the particular study examined. The 83 per cent ratio will.

27 Leon Festinger, *A Theory of Cognitive Dissonance*. (Stanford, California: Stanford University Press, 1957.) A working knowledge of this theory is not necessary for effective management. It is fun, however, to throw such references into your conversation at garden parties, etc.

■ PART ONE ■

The principles

> We don't need a systems analyst. The system here is perfect.
>
> Bill Vietor
> *USA TODAY* (1984)

Every author of a book such as this *must* offer you lists of various things you are expected to remember and quote at your next staff meeting or communications session. It is part of the genre. Here are the eight axioms of *Tactical Management*:

Within the scope of operational objectives – at the tactical level:

1 Managers and executives often do not do the things they should do, they do things they should not do, incorrectly or at the wrong time. The penalties for the organization are always poor customer service, poor product or service quality, or higher than necessary operating costs – usually all three.
2 It is within the responsibility, authority, skill, experience and expertise of those managers and executives to make appropriate changes in practices, processes and procedures necessary to resolve those problems effectively. Indeed, these are the obligations of their offices.
3 These changes can nearly always be made at zero cost[1] or very low cost, and they *always* result in significant net savings to the organization.
4 They can nearly always be made at very low risk to the staff and managers involved.
5 They can nearly always be implemented quickly and easily, evaluated promptly and adjusted readily if needed.
6 They *always* have an immediate positive impact on customer service, quality and cost management, and therefore on the health of the organization.

7 They therefore *always* enhance the achievement of long-range organization objectives.
8 They can always be managed through a process of simple, straightforward and relatively small actions taken in sequence. Even those actions that may be described as major can and must be broken down into a series of little steps or phases.[2]

I am not going to devote the first eight chapters of this book to a detailed examination of these eight axioms nor do I expect you to memorize them. You will be asked, however, to keep them in mind. Everything we are going to discuss as part of *Tactical Management* will in some way relate to at least one of them, and usually more than one.

The first six chapters consist of a review and discussion of what I believe to be fundamental principles of management at the tactical level. These are: change, customer service, quality, cost management, management theory and organization theory. You may be surprised by some of my choices. Customer service and quality, for example, are not usually considered principles. But think about it. If customer service and quality were deemed principles as essential to effective management as traditional sorts such as motivation and communications, perhaps our organizations would be healthier. Count the total number of hours people in your organization have spent in the past year on courses for customer service or quality then compare this to total hours spent attending seminars for communications or motivation.

I have chosen to begin this journey with a chapter about the management of change. Almost every action you take in your role as manager relates somehow to bringing about change in the organization. These include changing the way something is done, the way people function in the workplace, or the way you communicate or revise a plan to reflect changes in the environment. The management of change is an important part of the practice of management, and indeed everything else we do, and I feel it should be treated as a principle of management.

With these preliminaries out of the way, you can get on with making some positive things happen in your organization.

Notes

1 Throughout the book I will provide many cases of changes made at zero cost to the organization that resulted in immediate in-pocket savings.
2 We have given this process a name: short segment task control. See Chapter 8.

Managing Change: Dealing with menacing carnivores

There are going to be times when we can't wait for somebody. Now, you're either on the bus or off the bus. If you're on the bus, and you get left behind, then you'll find it again. If you're off the bus in the first place –

Ken Kesey
Quoted by Tom Wolfe in *The Electric Kool-Aid Acid Test*

Go, go, go said the bird: humankind
Cannot bear very much reality.

T. S. Eliot
Four Quartets

Introduction

Change is popular now. If you pick up a syllabus for any recent management development programme you are certain to see several courses that feature the word change prominently: *Managing Change in the Workplace, Living With Change, The Changing Marketplace, The Changing Workforce, Changing Information Needs*. Not to be outdone, this book begins with a discussion of change.

As a manager you are required to manage change routinely in a number of different situations:

- Any well-developed planning process, from a five-year strategic plan to a daily production schedule, necessarily includes provisions for adjustment or revision to address variances that inevitably occur. For the strategic plan it could be to respond to a volatile market or fluctuating interest rate. For the daily production schedule it could be to deal with raw material that is sometimes not delivered on time. In either case it is rare for any plan to be carried through to completion with no adjustment. This sort of adjustment represents change that must be managed if objectives are to be achieved.

- A decision is made to make a major change in the way something is done: to automate a manual operation, develop a production line for a new product, bring in work that was formerly done by outside resources, contract out work that was formerly done in-house or restructure the management team.
- Changes to the operation can be mandated by the environment: The government may legislate new product or workplace safety standards or pollution controls. The public may demand that you assume a new level of responsibility for the reliability of products or services. Negotiations with members of the workforce can require substantial changes in work rules.
- People in the organization are not doing something they should be doing; they are either not carrying out assigned duties, are not doing work to specification or are not completing other tasks correctly. One of your responsibilities as a manager is to change what people are doing to increase the likelihood that work will be completed as planned.[1]
- You have made decisions concerning how the overall climate in the organization should alter to increase the likelihood that long-range objectives will be achieved in a changing environment. These changes are usually described as relating to the culture of the organization. Implementing widespread change of this nature is often described as managing cultural change or changing the culture of the organization.[2]

When you think about these examples you realize that each requires asking somebody, including perhaps yourself, to change the way something is done. You must give directions such as: 'Change what you are doing because the plan has changed. If the objective is to be achieved you have to do something different', 'We have made the decision to do something different and that will require a change in what you do', or 'Change what you are doing because what you are doing is not what you should be doing'.

Resistance to change

If an important part of your total management effort is either to change what somebody is doing or the way they do it, then it is crucial to understand how people deal with change. You are familiar with the cliché: 'People have a natural resistance to change'. This sounds clever, but unless it can be applied in the workplace it means very little – people do, in fact, have a natural resistance to change.

Fight or flight

Think back to a time long ago. Imagine you are an early human being, a cave person, returning from the water hole to your rock shelter. As you step around the end of the big clump of trees next to the trail, suddenly you come face-to-face with a large, menacing carnivore. Instinctively you want to react in one of two obvious ways: you want to either attack or run away, negotiation does not appear to be a viable option. This is what we refer to as the 'fight or flight' response.[3] Even though many of us no longer live in rock shelters[4] and most of the larger menacing carnivores are gone, we still have an instinctive response to similar situations.

Imagine you are walking through the office, returning from the photocopying machine to your desk. As you step around the end of the big block of filing cabinets next to the aisle, you come face-to-face with a large, menacing boss. Instinctively you want to react in one of two ways: to either attack or run away – negotiation does not appear to be a viable option. In most situations you can do neither, which triggers dramatic reactions in your body. If this kind of situation occurs regularly it results in stress.

Orientation response

Although this is a simplified picture, the analogy is reasonably accurate. If you are driving down the street and you narrowly avoid a serious accident, your sympathetic nervous system reacts in a predictable way. Your heart goes thumpty-thumpty-thump, your stomach feels funny, your palms become sweaty and your muscles tense. You can feel all these symptoms, but it is important to understand that some other things that you cannot feel also happen. Your hearing becomes more acute, you lean in the direction of the danger – all your senses are directed toward the incident, the pattern of your brainwaves alters, your pupils dilate, blood flow to the brain increases, and adrenaline and noradrenaline are discharged into your bloodstream to prepare for the release of additional energy your body needs to cope with this situation. This reaction is called an orientation response or OR and it has implications for an understanding of our ability to deal with change.[5]

The orientation response is hypothesized as the preparation of the mind and body to deal with a novel situation: something new in our life. When we did live in rock shelters it was crucial to our survival that we handle things like the meeting with the large menacing carnivore successfully.

Adaptive reaction

While the OR is the mechanism that enables us to cope with one-off situations like encounters with menacing carnivores, the adaptive reaction syndrome enables us to deal with repetitive situations like menacing bosses. Adaptive reaction, like OR, manifests itself in dramatic changes in the brain and body. The conditions have enough similarities that OR can be seen as the first stages of the adaptive reaction.

The brain and body need a certain amount of time to recover from engagements with both menacing carnivores and menacing bosses. You recall that after your near road accident you needed a few minutes before your heartbeat returned to normal. If the incident had been scary enough you might even have pulled to the side of the road and stopped. The adaptive reaction is what we commonly call stress. Problems occur, both with OR and adaptive reaction but particularly with adaptive reaction, when there is not enough time between successive events for the body to recover. When this happens over time, physiological damage can result: too much stress can, indeed, damage your health.

The symptoms of both OR and adaptive reaction are present for every novel situation, not just spectacular and unpleasant ones like the near collision. Suppose, for example, you require one of your subordinates to work over the weekend to deliver a report that you need for an important meeting Monday morning. If you receive a telephone call late Sunday evening to inform you the report will not be ready as promised, you will react with symptoms identical to those resulting from the near collision. The difference is that they are less intense. You will not feel the changes, but they can be measured with sensitive instruments.[6] Adaptive reaction is present if a production line keeps going down and you have to defer other duties repetitively to deal with it, or the same irate customer keeps demanding to speak with you concerning the same troublesome order. These reactions have also been shown to be present for pleasant experiences, such as your move to a bigger and more prestigious office or the delivery of a new car.

It can be demonstrated that for every individual there is a range of the right amount of change or novelty. For reasons we do not understand fully, each individual has a different level at which there will be no unfavourable response. While we do not know why the level is different for different people, we can make some guesses when a person is presented with more change or novelty than he or she can handle.

Stability zones

Each person creates refuges from novelty or change, places we call stability zones.[7] Whether stability zones are created consciously or not is of no concern here but their existence is important, and the fact that a person reacts in a certain way to too high levels of change or novelty is crucial to our understanding of it. If the novelty a person is faced with is a change you have proposed for the workplace you must manage it successfully if you are to meet objectives.

People react to too little novelty in predictable ways: they become bored, and if there is too little change they eventually become apathetic, angry or even totally alienated. Of far more concern to us, however, is the reaction to high levels of novelty or change. When levels are high a person can actually be seen to retreat into one of those stability zones. It could be something fairly obvious such as a hobby, sport or the garden, or it could be far more subtle. Less obvious sorts of stability zones include the little habits and rituals we all engage in. If you look carefully you can see this process in action. And if you look carefully you can see also that the size of the zone varies from one individual to another, and for the same individual at different times. For reasons not understood some people need bigger stability zones than others. Think back to the time when the typing pool became the word processing unit. You recall that the conversion from typewriters to word processors created, apparently,[8] little turmoil for some operators but significant discomfort for others.

As a management consultant I have spent considerable time over the years on the road living in hotels and eating in restaurants. During most of that time my office has been a room somewhere within my client's premises; occasionally a very elegant conference room, more likely an unused records closet. When a project is kicked off on a Monday, part of the routine for the project team always is to go into the city centre for lunch and a look around. As team members stroll down the street looking for a restaurant a predictable reaction occurs. It will be impossible for them to walk past either a leather goods shop or an office stationer. They are all *compelled* to enter any shops they pass. Each consultant is mystically drawn to two categories of items; luggage and briefcases. They are part of each consultant's stability zone. The hotel room, the restaurant and the office can change, sometimes from week to week, sometimes even daily, but these two items do not.

Try this little experiment: if you think about one of the regularly scheduled meetings you chair that is attended by the same people every time, you realize that each person sits in nearly the same location at every meeting even when the venue is different. For the next meeting, arrange it so it is impossible for individuals to sit where they usually do. Observe the reactions. Some will be extremely uncomfortable, some less so, but at least one person and probably more than one will comment on the arrangement. What has happened is that you have tampered with stability zones. The premise is that by always choosing the same seat a person has removed a bit of novelty: this is part of the workday and workplace that does not change and the need to make a decision has been eliminated.[9]

Managing change in the workplace

The meaning for you as a manager should now be clear. It is a necessary part of your role that you manage change in the workplace proactively. Since change has both psychological and physiological implications for each person, including you, this must be addressed as part of every management action. The dilemma you face is that on one hand you must ask everybody in the organization, including yourself, to accept more and more change in the workplace as the norm, and to accept that the pace of change will continue to accelerate. On the other hand you must contend with the reality that everybody, again including you, can only be expected to respond positively to so much change. The central issue is when it becomes difficult for you to reconcile the two: when the needs of the workplace require more change from each individual than he or she can reasonably handle, or, alternatively, when stability zones have been too far reduced.

Several things can be done. The first must simply be to recognize that for all the reasons we have discussed you can expect a natural resistance to change and this resistance has absolutely nothing to do with age, intelligence, IT awareness, education, pig-headedness or place in the organization chart.[10]

Expect people to offer any number of arguments why the proposed change is not a very good idea. Some try to ignore the matter completely, and others try to delay implementation as long as possible. A few are obstinate and you occasionally encounter the individual who becomes blatantly belligerent or attempts to sabotage the effort. Possibly the most difficult of all, however, are those who present you with innumerable, elegant, flawlessly logical arguments why your proposal will not work.[11] Even those who appear to freely accept the change can initially display reservations or objections later during implementation.

Next remember that even positive changes result in some discomfort. Handle every matter involving change with sensitivity. Include as many people affected by the change as possible in planning processes. Explain the issues. Talk about it. Ask for the commitment. Allow enough time for them to become accustomed to the new – hammering in the change without any empathy for those concerned will not help.[12]

Acknowledge, for example, that although the new computerized record keeping system is far more effective and efficient, it provides better customer service and reduces operating costs, you still sometimes prefer to hold a bit of paper in your hand. You cannot make notes on the margin of a PC, stuff it in your pocket or carry it into a meeting. The usual argument is that 'My people can access the paper record quicker', but you know now it is more complicated than that.

Realize you are always face to face with whole people; as much as we wish it were so, they do not leave parts of themselves at home when they come to work. As well as all the things occurring on the job, everything going on in each person's personal life is at least as important, perhaps more so depending on circumstances. You routinely take this into account when you are aware that somebody is involved in some kind of personal problem, some crisis. Keep two things in mind, however: first, perhaps you do not know a situation exists; you are the boss, remember, and they do not tell you everything. Second, remember that positive changes also contribute to OR and adaptive reaction. They could be keeping up with the mortgage payments, but if their son is getting married next month and their daughter is going off to university the month after that, that could be all the change they are willing to accept at this point in their lives. If you happen to meet an unexpectedly high level of resistance from somebody for whom it seems out of character you must look a little deeper.

Recognize stability zones for what they are: places of refuge in a capricious universe. A few years ago somebody designed the perfect office – the office of the future. This humourless individual declared there was no place in the office for flowers, trinkets, photographs of loved ones or scenic calendars; these sorts of things detract from the business environment and interfere with efficient operations. Nonsense. These things represent unchange in a changing world. The office of the future should be full of them. That 'artwork' in the machine shop represents something more than voyeurism. Take a walk through any contemporary open plan office and look at the number of ingenious ways individuals have created stability zones. This can pose a particular problem for you if you are responsible for the management of a facility where either safety, hygiene or good work practices exclude the display of personal items. In a food processing area, operating theatre, integrated circuit clean room or space satellite assembly bay, people are usually prohibited from taking scenic calendars, ceramic cats or furry stuffed bunnies into the workplace. The design, maintenance and housekeeping in canteens, restrooms and lavatories probably become important in these situations. This is not an argument in favour of better housekeeping, but if there are few or no opportunities for an individual to create personal stability zones in the workplace, the canteen and restroom become more important in this respect.

Accept that continual change must become a way of life if your organization is to remain healthy: it cannot be avoided. It asks a great deal, perhaps too much, that you, the rest of the management team and all staff come to welcome massive doses of change: to thrive on chaos.[13] But it is essential to understand that for the business of the future, change must necessarily be part of everything that happens within the organization.

Risk

Several specific points concerning the management of change in the workplace call for a more detailed examination. The first of these is risk. Each time you change something you move from the known to the unknown. You exchange something that works, perhaps imperfectly, for something that does or does not work better; or does not work at all (remember the Tacoma Narrows Bridge).

Consider a methods change. The present method, in spite of its problems, provides you with a certain degree of predictability. When the revised procedure is introduced you cannot confirm beforehand that it will be an improvement over the old. You expect it will, of course; that is your plan. Depending on the scale of the revision you could waste a certain amount of time and money, and customer service could suffer for the short term. Regardless of the magnitude of the change, however, perhaps the greatest risk you run is the potential supercilious 'I told you so!' from the old hand on the line who argued against it from the beginning. This usually hurts appreciably more than any wasted resources.

Think about how *you* feel when going after a totally new market, purchasing a new mainframe, installing a completely redesigned production line or making a major revision to a process. The commitment of time, money and energy is much greater but the same concern for predictability occurs, and you still face the same risk from that old hand on the line. This one can have the added dimension, of course, that your job is on the line.

Delegation of authority automatically involves risk. As organizations of the future become broader and flatter, as the number of levels of management decrease and the span of control increases, and communications channels are simplified,[14] it is imperative that authority for completion of many tasks is delegated and assigned as a matter of routine farther and farther downward within the organization. Each time you delegate a duty you had yourself previously performed, you run the genuine risk that it will not be completed as well as you would have done it. When you remember that you are still responsible for successful completion of the task your concern for this type of change should be clear.

Ownership

A second specific change issue concerns loss of ownership. Another manifestation of the broader and flatter organization will be that more people from more disciplines will be involved in process development and implementation. A series of jobs that have previously been done by individuals sequentially will now be completed collectively by those individuals working as a team. Operations people as users will become more directly involved in computer program design, maintenance engineers will become more actively involved in new equipment specification and procurement and production people will interface more closely with both marketing and product development staff.

These kinds of changes inevitably result in some loss of ownership. If you had in the past been solely responsible for a particular activity, and in the future that activity is to be handled by you and others working as a team then you no longer wholly own it: you must share it with the others on the team. Is it not reasonable to predict resistance to a change that might result in having to share recognition for a success or a job well done?

Learning curve

Most changes, particularly those concerning methods or equipment, involve learning something new. Recall your first trip out after dark in your new car. Inserting the ignition key was an effort, the wipers moved each time you attempted to dip the headlights and adjusting the radio was an onerous chore. Nothing happened smoothly or automatically; you had to think about each of those actions.

Change always involves breaking old habits and learning new ones. This demands time and that time must necessarily be on the job. Initially tasks will not be completed as quickly or as well as they had under the old system. Think back to the example of the conversion from typewriters to word processors. If delivery schedules are tight it is not unreasonable to anticipate the argument that now is not the time to bring in a new procedure or new piece of equipment.

Cultural change

When we attempt to create a model for changing the culture of an organization we are moving into extremely subjective and difficult territory. While we can quote the Bible and Plato for references to organization development (OD), as a science OD is new. Because the science is new and the topic is complex, much of the writing is arcane, research results are often scarce and inconclusive, and models are convoluted.[15] To develop a theoretical understanding of cultural change it is necessary to describe the present culture, and to do this we must first explain what we mean by the organization and the culture of the organization. I have no intention of doing that here. What I shall do, however, is ask you to think informally about two examples of change in an organization that go well beyond straightforward alterations to methods, procedures or practices.[16] During your career it is likely you have experienced both these events, either as a participant or vicariously through one of your close professional colleagues.

First, consider the acquisition of a family-owned and family-managed business by a large conglomerate. When you think back to that experience the most graphic memories are not of the new organization chart, letterhead, logo or new members of the management team. Your most vivid memories are of the difficulties people in the acquired organization had adapting to the new regime imposed by the acquiring organization. No matter how carefully and thoughtfully the move was managed, even if facilitated by a team thoughtfully drawn from both organizations, the process was traumatic for nearly everybody. It was so traumatic for some that they chose to leave rather than adapt. The transition to the new corporate culture probably took significantly longer that planned. Those managers from the old culture that succeeded in adapting were still uneasy long after you would have expected them to be comfortable with the new order.[17]

Second, consider a business that has grown from a small to medium or medium to large size in a relatively short time, say over three, four or five years. You would expect everything about this sequence to be positive; after all, this is what business is supposed to be about. Growth means increased sales, increased sales mean increased revenues, economies of scale resulting from bigger orders reduce unit costs and this contributes to improved profits. But the business probably did not grow that smoothly. Mysterious sorts of gremlins crept into production processes as volumes increased. Supervisors who had been very good at managing manual lines were not as effective with automated processes even after extensive training on the new equipment. Messages that in the past had always been transmitted consistently began to get lost somewhere in the system. Quality for key customers deteriorated. Previously dependable delivery schedules slipped. Managers who used to be seen regularly on the floor disappeared into their offices, never to return. The door that was always open closed. What the organization was experiencing was a changing environment that demanded changes in organization culture. Problems resulted because managers did not recognize this and failed to manager the change proactively. The only difference between this situation and the acquisition in the previous paragraph is that here the transition took place much more slowly. The need to manage the change, however, was as important in both cases.

Factors important when managing cultural change in an organization are these:

1 Time is needed. Full assimilation of major cultural change by all participants requires time on the order of years, not weeks or even months.
2 Changing the formal organization is objective; changing the informal organization is subjective. When we talk about cultural change we are asking people not only to change the way they do something but to understand why they must change what they are doing.
3 If the change is going to be universal everybody affected must be involved and must commit to the change. When we talk about changing the culture we are necessarily talking about *everybody* in the organization. You cannot implement cultural change in one department.
4 Change must be led and must be seen to be being led by everybody on the management team, but especially by senior managers and executives.

Unless senior managers and executives demonstrate a total commitment to the change it will not succeed. Other organization processes such as delegation, time management or cascade communications can be developed through a pilot project in a selected area or department, but not this one. It can never be driven, it must always be led.

5 The entire management team must operate consistently within the new culture even when it seems awkward or artificial. Even tiny accidental lapses toward old practices must be addressed immediately.
6 The entire change effort must be made as visible as possible. Posters, slogans, newsletters and coffee mugs are not trivial frills, they are essential ingredients – they become temporary stability zones for the new culture.

Finally, recognize that the management of major cultural change demands a major effort. It will not succeed without major inputs of energy and commitment. Think about our two examples. You can easily remember at least one take over that was a complete disaster because responsible managers underestimated the scale of the task. You can easily recall at least one business with a promising future that failed because it grew too fast – that failed because responsible managers did not manage the growth.

Your personal menacing carnivore

Just when you thought it was safe to take a walk in the forest you are now confronted by your very own personal menacing carnivore. *Tactical Management* is all about changes you must make in the things you do in the course of managing your organization. It should by now be clear that you are going to be asked to do a number of things differently from the way you did them in the past. You have already been asked to spend an entire day looking at your operation in a way that no doubt is much different from any view you have taken until now. In every chapter in Part II I will counsel you to 'think about this, look at this, try this, do this'. I fully anticipate that each of these will represent a change for you.

After this discussion is it not reasonable that you, also, will be resistant to change? You, too, are more comfortable with things the way they are. Think about how *you* feel when you are asked to make a change: the committee meeting for which you prepared an elaborate presentation has been rescheduled from next week to this week – or even more devastatingly you have been asked to reduce your forty-five minute bells and whistles epic to a ten minute synopsis, your carefully prepared business plan for this year has been totally abrogated by a massive rise in raw material costs, or the board have decided the comprehensive management reorganization planned for next year should be completed within the next quarter. Why should you be expected to be better prepared, either psychologically or physiologically, to handle these changes than any other members of the management team or staff?

The succinct answer is that you are not. You are as susceptible to OR and adaptive reaction as anybody else; sometimes more so because of your position and the demands placed on you by the business. My final suggestion is to think about how *you* react to change and keep that in mind as you manage change throughout the organization.

Notes

1 Please note that I have not complicated this discussion by suggesting your job is to change somebody's behaviour.
2 Changing the entire culture of an organization is beyond the scope of this chapter, indeed, beyond the scope of this book. Chapter 27 is about a one-year project to *begin* the process in your organization.
3 There are many references to the fight or flight response. For a detailed discussion see, for example, Nicky Hayes, *Foundations of Psychology: An Introductory Text*. (London: Routledge, 1994.).
4 At the risk of appearing unromantic, we never, in fact, lived in caves.
5 Alvin Toffler, *Future Shock*. (London: Pan Books Ltd., 1971.) Toffler is a secondary reference for this subject. His discussion is particularly cogent.
6 This is the principle upon which a polygraph works.
7 Toffler, *Future Shock*; op. cit.
8 I say apparently because not all stability zones are obvious.
9 Toffler, *Future Shock*; op. cit. There is an argument that seat location is based on territorial behaviour. This could be true, but I believe only for the original choice.
10 There are numerous studies that purport to correlate resistance to change with such factors as age, intelligence or education. My experience has not convinced me the correlations are good enough to use as a basis for management decisions or actions.
11 The logic could, indeed, be flawless. See Pages 25–6, Risk.
12 Much of *Tactical Management* addresses team building, task teams and improved communications directly and indirectly. All these practices are structured specifically to support an organization where each individual has a better opportunity to work within a dramatically and constantly changing work environment.
13 Peters, *Thriving on Chaos*; op. cit. I disagree with Peters that we must *welcome* massive doses of change. His point must be taken, however, that we must learn to live with it.
14 The changing organization and simplified communications channels will be examined at several points in this book.
15 For an accessible introduction to the subject you might start with: D. S. Pugh, editor, *Organisation Theory: Selected Readings* 3rd Edn (London: Penguin 1990.)
16 Much of *Tactical Management* is about processes for managing cultural change in the organization, although I will place very little emphasis on definitions for either organization or organization culture.
17 This is clearly an oversimplification of a complex issue but I think it is adequate for this discussion.

■ CHAPTER 2 ■

Customer Service: The customer *is* always right (by definition)

Whilst I realize you have other customers, *I* am your most important customer.

The senior mechanical engineer of a steel processing company in a letter to a supplier

You don't *ever* want to agree a specification with the customer. That means you have to make it that way every time!

A marketing account manager of a food processing company during a discussion about the meaning of customer service

Introduction

Think for a moment about those phenomena that inevitably bring a lump to the throat, a tear to the eye and a good feeling deep down inside. They include: Queen and Country, cricket, the union flag, motherhood and . . . customer service. These stir powerful emotions within all of us and make us glad to be alive. We believe unerringly in these things, and woe to anyone who dares scorn our unquestioning devotion. We all agree customer service is important. Most of us preach it day in and day out throughout the organization. Like quality it somehow equates with goodness. Believing in it is good, and one would rather risk being seen eating red jam at breakfast than be heard to denigrate customer service.

Customer service is as difficult a concept to appreciate as quality. The problem is that unless you can define it and develop a process to measure it you have no means of knowing whether your customer service is working – well or at all. When something goes wrong, in the absence of a process you are left with nothing more than *post hoc* explanations: statements of what you think might have happened. If you define an unhappy or dissatisfied customer as one who has left and taken business to a competitor, that definition provides no tactical information and you have no useful knowledge to prevent a recurrence. If your sole measure of customer service is the direct cost of customer returns, you are only accounting for a small percentage of the total cost to your organization.[1]

However, if you can define customer service you can write a specification for it. If you can write a specification you can measure compliance and determine whether you have satisfied the customer: you can measure the results. You can develop a process, implement practices based on a plan and evaluate performance, then take effective management action whenever performance is below what was planned.

Customer service is such an important element in your management model that we want to treat is as a principle of management. Customer service has to do with the delivery of the products or services you are responsible for delivering.

Customer service and quality

In Chapter 3 we will investigate quality as a principle of management and how it applies to your organization. Effective use of the Tactical Management model requires a clear understanding of the difference between what I mean by quality and what I mean by customer service. Quality is defined as conformance to specification for whatever product or service your organization delivers. Quality processes encompass all activities, procedures and practices developed to ensure conformance to the specification. Quality is concerned with the product or service itself, but not with delivery times or delivery quantities.

Customer service is defined as the creation of the specification and agreement to it. Customer service processes include all activities, procedures and practices developed to ensure that creation and agreement effort is successful. Customer service is also concerned with issues such as delivery times and quantities and whether they conform to the customer's orders.[2]

The distinction is important: quality has to do with determining whether what we delivered is what the customer ordered. Customer service has to do with a complete, unambiguous understanding of what it is the customer ordered. Unless this division is drawn carefully, what usually happens in the real world is these two separate issues become mixed. The result is a confusion in the workplace with which you are familiar. There is one specification for a Swiss watch and there is another for a journal voucher. Whether responsible staff and managers are meeting the specification is a question of quality. Whether the customer ordered one or the other has absolutely nothing to do with quality, it has to do with customer service.

There is a further, tricky issue to address. Assume we have agreed the specification with the customer, manufactured the product strictly to specification, and delivered it according to the order quantity and delivery date. We have met our commitment to the customer fully with respect to both customer service and quality. The remaining question has to do with whether the customer can really use the product as it has been specified. Suppose the customer ordered a Swiss watch and we know what is really needed is a journal voucher. Not only is a Swiss watch not necessary, but based on our knowledge of the customer's needs it will not work for the planned application. Have we failed our customer in the matter of customer service or quality? My brief answer is that we have failed: our relationships with *all* our customers should be open and honest to the extent that we can refuse to produce and deliver something that will not work even when it is demanded. Further, committing to the production and delivery of a product or service that will not work for the customer contributes nothing to the long-term objectives of our organization.[3,4]

The definition for customer service

The *Tactical Management* definition for customer service is that you deliver goods or services to your customers according to these mutually agreed conditions:

1. Delivery schedules

You comply fully with delivery schedules; deliveries will be neither later nor earlier than specified. The problem of late deliveries needs no explanation. Early deliveries are as unacceptable as late ones, or they will be in the near future if they are not already in your particular business. Your customer wants deliveries at the specified time. In the automotive industry this window has been reduced to two hours for key items, in some retail operations the target is one hour. This requirement is equally important if you deliver a service. What is your reaction if a contract engineer or technician scheduled to perform work on a critical piece of equipment arrives either one day later or one day earlier than scheduled?

2. Delivery quantities

You comply with order quantities; shipments will be neither over nor short of the order quantity. All remarks concerning delivery schedules apply to delivery quantities. Both delivery schedules and quantities are becoming increasingly important in manufacturing operations as more organizations move to a JIT (Just In Time) culture. Under JIT processes the delivery of parts, sub-assemblies or components to a production line becomes critical. This is because your customers are refining production scheduling processes to reduce in-process inventories, improve process control and improve their own delivery schedules in the same way you are. This can be a problem for you too if you are responsible for the delivery of a service. Think about how you feel when you are standing in a long queue at the bank, building society, Post Office or supermarket asking yourself why there do not seem to be enough tills open.

3. Quality

You meet product specifications fully; compliance will be complete – with no deviations. Quality management principles are the subject of Chapter 3. This effort demands total compliance with the product specification. Otherwise, you have shipped the product in error: the customer has received something that was not ordered. Your processes should be capable of meeting the specification or you should not have committed to the order.[5] It is either to specification or it is not. If it is not, do not ship it. In Chapter 3 we will also address the issue of formal specifications for the quality of services. Yes, they can be implemented; and yes, if you deliver a service you will be expected to provide them as part of a comprehensive customer service process.

Some businesses have recurring problems because assumptions are made by customers in the absence of formally agreed specifications. Familiar examples include many retail products, toys and services such as health care and public transportation. How often have you known a child to be disappointed when a new toy either was not nearly as big as the picture on the box suggested, did not include any of the accessories shown or did not go half as fast as the advertisement implied? How often have you remarked that a product does not look anything like the description on the container? What happens in these situations is that the customer expects the product to conform to a clearly defined specification: a perception created by the supplier through advertising. The problem is that there has, in fact, been no agreement to a specification although in the mind of the customer there has.[6] This is not a discussion about advertising ethics. My thesis is that ambiguous, unclear or deliberately misleading specifications achieve nothing for your organization for the long term except to ensure a never-ending sequence of costly problems.

4. Quality and process documentation

You conform to all requirements for documentation of quality specifications and process history. In addition to meeting the quality specification itself there is a need to meet all conditions for quality and process documentation. Your customer is continually refining operational planning and scheduling processes in the same way you are. The customer wants to be confident that material leaving the receiving dock for the factory floor can be put on the line immediately. Part of the process to achieve this is to require that your process and outgoing inspection documentation are identical to the customer's incoming documentation.[7] In the future this will become increasingly important for all businesses, perhaps it already is in yours.

In industries such as drugs and pharmaceuticals, food processing and aerospace there is a need for product and ingredient traceability in the interest of either safety or hygiene. This requirement is contingent on accurate and complete process documentation. As the public demand that manufacturers assume more responsibility for product reliability this will become more important in other industries.

5. Packaging and handling requirements

You comply with all requirements for packaging and handling. Specifications for the packaging and handling of products you deliver can be as important as the product itself. In retail foods or cosmetics, for example, the presentation can be crucial to the sale, often more important than the product itself. Automated process control systems and inventory management systems increasingly include the use of OCRs (optical character readers) or bar-code readers[8] in many industries. Many customers now require suppliers to comply with strict specifications for printing on packaging materials.[9]

6. Order entry systems

You meet all requirements for the order entry system. Your order entry systems should be consistent with your all your customers' order-placing needs. At the most basic, you should design manual systems that are fully compatible with customers' manual systems. The opposite end of this spectrum is a totally compatible computer system that enables customers to operate an on-line, fully automated order entry system. Ideally your customers should be able to bring up computer screens in their order departments and type in information that generates production orders in your offices. When you can do this for a customer you have considerably reduced the likelihood that business will be taken to a competitor.

7. Information requirements

You conform to all information requirements. Your customer may want to format shipping documents and receiving papers, for example, in a special way to expedite information flow or ensure accurate inventory control and material handling. You make it convenient when you design statements and invoices to conform to the customer's practices and procedures. Actions such as these support increased effectiveness and efficiency and contribute to lower costs for your customers.

8. Warranties and service agreements

You provide comprehensive guarantees and warranty agreements. You should offer the most comprehensive warranties, guarantees and service agreements in your industry. This is true whether you deliver a product or service. You should strive to make this one of your organization's hallmarks throughout the business world. If your quality processes are effective, your costs for these services will be very low. You are thus in a position to market a very visible and attractive service at an extremely low cost.

9. Pricing and terms

You meet pricing and invoicing terms and you achieve full agreement on price. Confirm that your customers are happy with the price and terms, that they are not merely accepting them, grudgingly, because they feel they have no choice. If they are not happy, they will go somewhere else at the first convenient opportunity.

10. After-sales service

You provide suitable after-sales services and you meet your customers' requirements for service agreements. You should offer a range of service contracts that support your customers' processes. You should make available qualified service personnel for both on-site and telephone assistance. Again, if your total quality management processes are effective this will cost you very little.

11. Product utility

You provide products or services that fully meet your customers' needs. Both you and your customers must be satisfied the products you provide meet needs better than any other. You must be confident that your customers have not been coerced into accepting these products because they are the only ones available. Convince your customers it is the best you, or anybody else has to offer. Further, convince yourself products will work precisely the way customers expect them to work. There must be no surprises in this respect.

12. Technical and marketing support

You provide related support services such as technical assistance for the marketing of your customers' products or services. Give your customers assistance with marketing and sales effort, provide information and literature they can offer and arrange tours of your facilities for their customers. Make product managers and technicians available to visit their customers and help them to write product and service specifications. Make yourself available to your customers for those situations where there is a need to make a special effort to establish a level of comfort with a particular customer. This is important if your customers are retailers or if their customers are retailers. Your sales to them are limited by their abilities to sell on, no matter how successful your efforts. If you want to increase your sales you must help them increase their sales.

13. Options to existing products and product lines

You assist with the process of exploring other products, product lines or variations to present products. Work with your customers in a continuing process to investigate and develop opportunities to expand present product lines, create options to existing products and experiment with entirely new products and lines. They must be convinced that all possible options are being considered.

14. Flexible response to changing needs

You respond quickly to every customer's changing requirements. Make your customers confident that your organization offers the maximum flexibility and rapid response to every changing need. These include changes to the product itself, information and documentation requirements, delivery schedules, quality specifications, packaging needs, and technical and marketing support services. This range of services has been discussed above. The emphasis here is not on the services themselves, rather on the speed and flexibility of your responses to the customer's changing needs. This can provide an occasion for you to differentiate your product in a highly competitive industry or one where there are few opportunities to distinguish your products from those of your competitors.

15. Number and frequency of deliveries

You work continually to adjust the number and frequency of deliveries according to needs. Your customers are continually seeking ways to improve material handling efficiencies, reduce inventory carrying costs and improve production planning. You can support those efforts by reducing delivery quantities and increasing the frequencies of deliveries according to customers' requirements.

16. Refinements to product specifications

You work continually to refine product specifications. You must be engaged in a joint, formal, intensive, ceaseless project with every customer to refine and tighten product specifications.[10] This will reduce their operating costs and improve operating efficiencies. The result will be improved competitiveness for customers that will ultimately benefit you in increased orders.[11]

Measuring customer service

When you examine these sixteen requirements critically you discover the first eight can be measured easily: you have either delivered the correct quantities on time or you have not. When you think about the remaining eight, however, you realize they are more subjective. Happiness is involved. Perhaps the customer is happy with the price; perhaps not. Maybe it is simply that there seem to be no reasonable options. You need a definition for happiness that will submit to measurement. There is happiness if:

- The customer says, 'I am happy with your service.' The test is simple: ask.[12]
- The customer keeps doing business with you. Either little or no business is done with your competitors or the volume done with you keeps increasing.
- The customer keeps asking you to do more and more.

Now you have a definition for customer service. You have criteria that enable you to specify clearly, objectively and in writing what each customer wants – what the requirements are. You can evaluate. You can measure. Either you have met the specification, in which case attainment is 100 per cent; or you have failed, in which case attainment is zero. The target is full customer service: total compliance with the specification. Anything less is unsatisfactory and must be corrected immediately.

Some difficult questions answered

Is there such a thing as an awkward or difficult customer? No. If you are working within a mutually agreed specification for customer service, if you have agreed to deliver something, the customer is not being awkward when there is a demand that you deliver it. Review the specification.

Is it possible the customer can be unreasonable: that there is a demand to provide something you cannot possibly deliver? No. You are either able to deliver it or you are not. Review the specification.

Does the customer always know what is really needed? Not necessarily. You may be in a better position than the customer, either because of experience or technical expertise, to make a judgement that what is being requested is not the best for the planned application. Do not sell your customer something you know will not work; recommend options. Otherwise, do not make the commitment. Both you and the customer must agree all sixteen criteria for the specification.

Is the customer always right? Yes, so long as they require no more than that you operate to a mutually agreed specification.

Customer service and the profit equation

The profit equation must begin with the generation of revenues, and this occurs when a satisfied customer pays for the product or service that has been delivered. This statement is equally applicable to every non-profit operation where a product or service is exchanged for revenue: the more product you deliver and the better you serve your customers, the more revenue you generate.[13] Lest you think this statement is so obvious as to be condescending, think about this:

Example

Our analysis work in a large admin centre included the review of an operating department that was totally driven by customer telephone calls. All orders for one of the retail services delivered by this organization were placed through telephone calls to this department. Each day promptly at noon everybody walked out of the area to go to lunch. The phones rang and rang and rang until about 1.00 pm when staff returned. The department manager, recognized in this organization as a high flyer, was asked how this contributed to good customer service. He replied, defensively, 'My people are on flexi-time. I can't do anything about it if they all want to go to lunch at the same time.'

Did this manager have even the most basic understanding of the relationship of customer service to profitability? What was this organization losing in sales, and therefore profits, by ignoring potential customers during probably the most productive hour of the day? How would any one of your department or middle managers react to this situation?

A properly conceived, fully developed and carefully implemented customer service process is the first, crucial step in your quest for health for your organization. Two things must happen:

1 It is essential that reporting systems, data bases, process control mechanisms and operating procedures provide full and accurate information on the capabilities of processes and total costs. You cannot sit down with a customer and mutually agree a price that will be profitable if you do not know total costs or whether you can deliver the product according to the specification. Beyond that you cannot

consider the feasibility of new products or new product lines, variations to present products or tighter specifications. Much of Tactical Management is about developing systems and procedures to enable you to specify capabilities and identify total costs.

2 You must create a culture throughout the organization where every individual commits not only to the mechanics of an improved customer service process but also to the principles behind it. In addition to keeping customers happy it improves the management of costs.[14] Another prominent Tactical Management theme is that doing things right the first time is the most cost effective way to operate. It saves you money if you do it right the first time. Constantly strive for zero defects – no deviation from the specification. It saves you even more money when you do it *all* right the first time.

A commitment to customer service

Implementation of this total commitment to the customer demands that you lead your organization through cultural change: a new way of doing business based on a formal, measurable process and a discipline of full compliance with the specification:

- Consider the positive implications of having a measurable standard, a target, where none existed before. Relate this to the health of the organization. Understand the important contribution this will make to your ability to make decisions and take actions to manage operations effectively. Use this as a basis for selling this change to everybody in the organization.
- Create and publish a customer service charter in which the sixteen elements feature prominently. Revise my basic statements to reflect the special needs of your particular operation. Develop procedures to apply these elements to the needs of every customer. Develop the controls and practices needed to manage the processes.
- Make your customers full, active partners in this process. Make them comfortable with your new way of doing business. Explain in depth, through formal presentations, what you are doing. They will be extremely happy to work with you. For you these changes represent something new and exciting; for the customer they represent something fervently desired for a long, long time. Develop processes to facilitate both the creation of specifications and revisions to them. Implement procedures that enable you to confirm quickly and easily that both of you agree the specification. This entire effort demands that you work very closely with your customers – something you should be doing routinely anyhow.
- Communicate positively to every single individual in the organization that this is very important; that it must be at the top of everybody's

priority list. No deviation from the specification is acceptable: if even one of the sixteen criteria has not been fulfilled that particular customer service effort is unacceptable. The problem must be addressed immediately and effectively so it never occurs again.

The importance of this should not be difficult to communicate to those people who actually handle the product, deliver the service or come face-to-face with the customer. The commitment to the new customer service culture must, however, be given by *everybody* in the organization. This includes clerks in microfilm, mailroom staff and people who work in the canteen: everybody. This commitment will not be given unless you *ask* for it. That, too, is an essential element of the process.

- It is crucial that you are consistent and that you are seen to be consistent in all this: that your actions correlate perfectly with your words.[15] You can never deviate. You can destroy all your work in an instant. You have to do nothing more complicated than direct that, just this one time, the specification can be ignored: just this one time we can bend the specification and ship something the customer did not order. At that moment credibility for this entire new effort will have been reduced to zero: 'It's business as usual. Nothing has changed. Management, once again, are saying one thing and doing something else'.

Use these eight axioms as a starting point:

1 The only acceptable level of customer service is full compliance with the specification.
2 This is the most tactically effective way to increase revenues.
3 Full compliance will minimize long-term costs and therefore contribute to increased profits.
4 There is no such thing as an awkward, unreasonable or difficult customer.
5 The customer *is* always right.
6 Every action that every individual takes in the course of organization work should be evaluated according to its contribution to customer service.
7 Every order is your most important order.
8 Every customer is your most important customer.

Finally, this chapter is not about the dynamics of effective marketing, the development or management of a sales team or the principles behind those efforts. Those are not tactical issues. My purpose has been to discuss elements that contribute directly, tactically to the health of your organization – the creation of an objective customer service process. You should consider, however, how our thinking here can be integrated into your efforts to create and maintain effective marketing and sales teams.

The internal customer

Your organization has two sorts of customers, external and internal. External customers are the obvious ones we nearly always refer to when we discuss customer service. They are users or consumers of products or services delivered by your organization as its mechanism for achieving long-term objectives. Discussions and examples in this chapter have concentrated on the external customer and the model has been developed around the needs of external customers.

The needs of the internal customer in the context of customer service are less obvious. Organizations are not monolithic, they consist of large numbers of units or sub-organizations, each of which is an organization itself.[16] The most conspicuous example is probably an operating department, a less apparent example is a smaller unit such as a section or a workteam. Each of these units is, however, a customer of every other unit in the organization that is responsible for providing products or services to it. The assembly department is a customer of every unit responsible for providing it with raw materials, components or sub-assemblies. A workteam is a customer of all workteams that deliver work to it. Everybody who submits an engineering request form is a customer of the maintenance department, and anybody who eats in the canteen is a canteen customer.

Internal customers are customers in every sense of the word. Organization health demands that every internal customer must be treated with the same respect, concern and attention that you have in the past reserved for the one described as your most important customer. This is a fundamental element of a properly managed Total Quality Management (TQM) process. Indeed, most practitioners identify the concept of fully meeting the needs of the internal customer as part of the definition of TQM. All sixteen criteria apply to every area or department within the organization to whom you deliver a product or service. Everything we have said also relates directly to internal customers.[17]

A test of your commitment to customer service

Walk over to admin and identify the newest trainee clerk. Ask: 'Who is our most important customer?' If the answer is anything other than a sparkling clear: 'Every single one of them', then *you* have failed this test.

Notes

1 Review the notes from your one-day tour of the facility.

2 These introductory definitions are admittedly brief and incomplete. The complete definition for customer service is the entire content of this chapter and the complete definition for quality the entire content of Chapter 3.

3 It will probably be useful to review these last two paragraphs again after you have read this chapter and Chapter 3.
4 Establishing open and honest relationships with your customers is an important element of every effective customer service process. It will be examined in more detail later in this chapter.
5 It may be helpful to reread the second quotation at the beginning of this chapter.
6 In the public sector, various Customer Charters popular now are attempts to address this problem.
7 This has been standard in the US automotive industry since the early 1980s. At the time of writing it is assuming more prominence in the UK in both the automotive and aerospace industries.
8 Referred to as wedge readers in the US.
9 Several supermarket chains in the US now expect bar-codes on products to be read successfully with a single pass over the reader at the till. If the code is not read, the cashier is instructed to give the product to the customer free of charge. Costs are passed on to the supplier as a deduction from the invoice.
10 You should already be doing this independently of any other customer service effort. If you have not been doing so, begin immediately – today.
11 In Chapter 3 we will examine the principle that 'right the first time' as an element of total quality management processes saves you money: that a culture of zero defects is the lowest cost way to manufacture a product. When you and customers jointly tighten specifications, increased reliability for the products you supply enhances your customers' in-process quality efforts.
12 Thomas J. Peters and Robert H. Waterman, Jr., *In Search of Excellence*. (New York: Harper & Row, 1982.) One of the principles of the *Excellence* philosophy is that if you really want to find out what your customer is thinking, you ask.
13 There are at least two obvious exceptions where there is no revenue generated: the delivery of products or services that are (1) part of a government, military, municipal administration, school, charity or similar operation when there is no exchange of revenue, and (2) to an internal customer: to another department within the same organization. See Page 42, The Internal Customer.
14 This is the subject of Chapter 4.
15 In the Introduction we described this as not sending conflicting signals.
16 Chester I. Barnard, *The Functions of the Executive* 30th Anniversary Edn. (Cambridge: Harvard University Press, 1968.)
17 The implications of treating every unit in the organization as a valued customer will be discussed again in Chapter 27.

■ CHAPTER 3 ■

Quality: Painting white roses red

'Would you tell me, please, why you are painting those roses?'
'Why, the fact is, you see, Miss, this here ought to have been a *red* rose-tree, and we put a white one in by mistake;'

Lewis Carroll
Alice In Wonderland

Well, certainly we can credit your account tomorrow. But we're very busy, so if we do it tomorrow, it will be wrong. If you want us to be absolutely certain it is correct, you will have to wait until next week sometime . . . maybe.

Your bank manager[1]
discussing a credit to your account

Introduction

How many errors do you accept on your bank statement? That is a patently silly question; you expect it to be perfect. You want it free from error – you expect zero defects. If a mistake has been made, you expect people at your bank to take whatever actions are necessary at whatever cost to them to correct it. Further, if the error has cost you through, for example, a service charge or loss of interest you expect to be reimbursed. Why is it then that you expect your customers to:

- accept products or services that contain errors, are things that were not ordered, are not to the specification that was agreed;
- not be unhappy, or dissatisfied, about delay or inconvenience; and
- not ask for a reimbursement for costs incurred as a result?

Your bank manager's quotation seems absurd, but is it? Is this any different from your informing customers you can deliver the product nearly on time – only a little bit late – if they will agree to a deviation: if they will agree to accept material that was not ordered. The alternative is that you might be able to get it right if they accept a much longer, usually unspecified delay.

Quality means nothing more and nothing less than you make the product according to the specification you agreed with the customer.[2]

Quality as a principle of management

Quality must be perceived as a central principle of management. You must make quality management an integral part of every decision you make and every action you take to maintain the health of your organization. It must become as important in this respect as traditional fundamentals of management practice such as strategic planning, communications, motivation and organization development. Quality management is not an ancillary or support function, it is one of the core disciplines essential to effective management of every business organization.[3] Quality is directly related to the achievement of long-range organization objectives; it is a control mechanism. In the Introduction we said that processes are in control when they are moving the organization closer and closer to objectives. Properly managed quality processes support control for the organization.

The subject is often obfuscated by the silliness that has prevailed through the years: 'Hurry up with that; it's good enough. We'll ship it the way it is'. This statement is usually made to a relatively new machine operator or junior clerk who is trying very hard to get it right. The result is to communicate that making errors is not only acceptable but a necessary and routine part of the job. It also communicates that if you want to get to be the boss, the person who gives orders, you must really get tough: you must stop being soft on customers.

A proper understanding of quality is also usually hindered by the nearly universal feeling that words such as good quality, top quality or high quality somehow relate to perfection, fitness of purpose, niceness or goodness. A brief examination of the concept of zero defects should be helpful in this respect.[4]

Zero defects

Zero defects is a concept that is crucial to any consistent, totally effective quality management effort. Zero defects has nothing to do with fitness of purpose, niceness or goodness. Those are not issues of quality they are issues of customer service. Zero defects has to do with how close your operation is to meeting a specification fully. When you are delivering the product or service to all your customers fully according to the sixteen criteria in Chapter 2, you are operating a zero defect customer service process. When you are making a product with no rejections or rework anywhere along the line, you are operating a zero defect manufacturing process. When you never have to reject or return a raw material or sub-assembly to a supplier, you and they are jointly operating zero defect processes. Zero defects is not about perfection, it is about conforming to a specification.

Quality management

Quality management is the total effort by which you ensure the product you deliver to the customer is the product that was ordered. It is the complete process by which you:

Obtain the specification

Obtain a totally unambiguous, complete description for the product or service you are expected to deliver. The nature of this transaction will depend entirely on the needs of your particular business or industry. You must develop procedures to facilitate both the creation of specifications and revisions to them as needed. This approach is relevant whether you provide a product or service. If you provide a service, creating a specification may be more difficult than for a product. Your process must be capable of description, however. What is it you put on your sales brochure and tell people over the telephone that you do?[5]

This matter is so clearly the beginning of all quality management effort that little elaboration is needed. Many of the steps we examined in Chapter 2 as elements of customer service relate either directly or indirectly to obtaining information about specifications.

Confirm capability

Confirm that equipment and processes are capable of making the product to specification; confirm that practices and procedures are capable of delivering the service to specification. This is a technical matter that is specific to the product or service. Capability is confirmed through a series of steps that may begin in the design department or the research laboratory. Further work includes pilot runs or production trials. Throughout these steps careful measurements and analyses of results are used to establish how well the product will perform against the specification. The analysis is usually supported by statistically based sampling and evaluations of trial results.[6] This effort may include evaluation of the capabilities of suppliers to meet specifications for raw materials, packaging or sub-assemblies. Capability studies also provide information for product costing, estimates of resources needed for operator training and data on machine or line capacities. These can be translated into potential pricing and delivery schedules.

You must not agree to deliver something you are incapable of making. This should be obvious; it is not. Businesses often promise things they cannot deliver. When this happens it ensures employment for huge armies of inspectors. Their job is to sort through bins of finished product to separate it into three categories: good, extremely bad, and bad, but customers will accept these when they are really desperate. When you can fully define capability you are in a good position to start to attack that 20 per cent or more of your sales revenues or 35 per cent or more of your total operating costs discussed in the Preface.[7]

If you provide a service, defining capability can sometimes be labyrinthine. If you offer a service such as specialized equipment repair, that should be amenable to a clear statement of expected results. If you offer a service such as software development or programming, however, it may be more difficult to forecast capability or performance results accurately. In these circumstances you must be scrupulous in your statement of what you can deliver and be totally honest with your customers when capability cannot be clearly defined.

Agree the specification

Agree the specification with the customer. You cannot do this before you know your capability. In Chapter 2 we talked about making your customers full, active partners in this process. We said you must get close to them and they will be delighted to work with you in this way. Unless you are really close to customers, unless you convince them you completely understand their needs, it will never be possible for you to be assured fully that what you are delivering is what was ordered. Under those circumstances you always risk some returns and some unhappiness. The goal of your customer service process is zero returns and zero unhappiness.

There are some transactions for which the specification, or at least part of it, is not in writing or formally agreed. We discussed some examples in Chapter 2. There is, however, always an implied agreement. If you are responsible for an operation such as that you must confirm that sales presentations, advertisements, brochures and other promotion efforts accurately reflect the specification. Remove all ambiguities and misrepresentations from your presentations. Take whatever actions are necessary: formal or informal, written or oral, including the simple expedient of asking, to be certain the specification is agreed.

A full understanding of a specification supports the effective management of costs, although this is usually not obvious. On your tour you observed at least one process that was out of control. In an attempt to meet delivery schedules or keep a line running, operators, supervisors and first-line managers were performing some operations to tighter limits than necessary to compensate for a specification that was not clear. They were reaming a hole that could have been drilled, depositing extra cream because of unspecified sponge weights, checking paper advices against the input screen – twice, overfilling bottles or hand-finishing items after machining because the surface spec was vague. These extra steps always increase costs and do nothing to support improved customer service. On the contrary, they produce variances in the finished product that typically cause the customer to inspect more closely. This results in not only higher process costs but higher levels of returns.

Three crucial steps

Further elaboration for these first three steps is necessary. It is essential that quality management processes begin with these three steps taken in sequence. Unless every quality process begins this way it will almost certainly fail. You cannot deliver the product unless you know what you are expected to deliver, and you cannot do this unless you agree the specification with the customer. You cannot commit to the specification until you have confirmed you are capable of making the product and you cannot do this without an appropriate analysis of capability. And you cannot analyse capability until you have achieved a full understanding of what the customer requires. Unless you have taken these three steps you cannot know your total costs and without that information you cannot price the product profitably. It does not always occur this way, in some businesses it seldom occurs this way and in other businesses it never occurs this way. How often has this happened to you?

Example

The *New and Improved* had been in production now for a few months. The customer was relatively happy with it. You were experiencing some problems with deliveries because of in-process quality problems but by working weekends and producing on nights you were generally able to meet delivery schedules.

Head office were not pleased about current levels of labour and material variances throughout the plant. At the next board meeting they wanted to see your action plan to reduce these variances substantially over the next quarter. Your investigation revealed the *New and Improved* was responsible for a large percentage of the variances. Current actual direct costs were far higher than forecast, actual yields were well below estimates and rework costs for both materials and labour were rocketing. Overtime allocations for this product were obscene. You sensed vaguely that something was wrong prior to your investigation but you had no idea it was so serious until you put some numbers to it.

After this revelation, your next action was to call a meeting with sales, product development, production, quality, engineering and purchasing to apportion blame. During that meeting the salesperson responsible for the order related the following:

> 'At a regular monthly meeting with the customer we were told they were ready to purchase the *New and Improved* in high volume; could we make it? The salesperson was pleased to reply in the affirmative because we had been after this one for a long time. The customer asked whether we had made it before and was told we had not, but that was not a problem. We quoted a price of £1.29 each. We were told they could be purchased from our competitor for £1.27; so we said we could supply them for £1.26 each. Without communicating with anybody from product development, production, quality, engineering, purchasing or anybody else, the salesperson returned with a huge order for a product we had never produced at a price that was determined solely by what a competitor was quoting (well, after all, it did look a little bit like one we had made in the past)'.
>
> The rest, as they say, is history.

All quality management effort must begin with these three steps taken formally and in sequence. Details of the individual steps and specific actions will vary according to your particular business and the product, but you and your team must not ignore any part of this process. Pressures of time, competition or the desire to fill the order book must not become excuses for shortcutting either the statement of the specification, confirmation of capability or formal agreement to the specification. Each time you attempt to curtail the process, something like the above is certain to occur. The result is that in an attempt to meet delivery schedules and reduce costs you ship product that is not to specification. What you achieve are unhappy customers and increased costs.

Control the process

Implement all procedures and practices necessary to confirm that during manufacture or service implementation the product is in compliance with the specification. Process control, if it is to be effective, must occur during the process and not after it is complete. The difference is important. If you inspect finished product and evaluate it purely on the basis of compliance with no consideration of causes, your process is totally reactive – it is after the fact. You can accomplish nothing more than separating product into two categories: good and bad. You never obtain any knowledge of what to change to prevent bad product in the future.

If, however, you inspect not only the product but also the process you can make the procedure proactive; you can obtain knowledge about causes. You can obtain information to modify processes to eliminate sub-standard product entirely. This is the reason we talk about quality and quality management but not about quality control. In the past quality control programmes have often emphasized reactive product inspection rather than proactive process control.[8]

Process control includes two elements, one technical and the other organizational. The technical element is the set of practices and procedures to manage the process. The organizational element is at least as important although often ignored. Organizational practices must be established to enable those people responsible for process control to control processes. Operators, supervisors and first line managers must be empowered to confirm either that processes are in control or alternatively to take all actions necessary to bring them back under control quickly and effectively. It must be clear throughout the organization these individuals have authority to make operating decisions *then and there* to keep processes under control. There must be a total commitment from the entire management team to support them in this effort.

Identify variances

Implement procedures to identify when the specification is not being met. This is truly effective only when you have developed a system that tells you compliance is still good but action must be taken immediately if it is to remain so. Identification of variances is the technical component of ensuring compliance with the specification. This is a series of inspection techniques and action procedures developed to support the process.[9] They include steps to:

(a) Keep the process in specification throughout the entire production cycle. A properly structured SPC mechanism will identify problems with the process *before* it goes out of specification. This is the most cost effective option because no bad product has been made and it is fundamental to the zero defects principle.
(b) Bring it back into specification when it deviates. This is second best but sometimes necessary in the real world.
(c) Stop the operation *immediately* and not restart it until the cause of the variance is identified and corrected.[10] This is the point when most quality control programmes fall apart. The operator recognizes that bad product is being made and stops the machine, then Somebody From The Office runs out to the floor and gives instructions to keep it running.
(d) Remove from the system any products that are not to specification. If the first two procedures have been effective this requires minimum resources.

Developing and implementing in-process procedures for the identification of variances for a service organization or an admin operation can be particularly challenging. It is possible, however. Designing office towers, rebuilding rolling mills or inputting credit advices to an information system can be managed as effectively and profitably as the manufacture of widgets. Work from the basics. When you have been able to write a specification and determine capability you can establish in-process control.

Take corrective action

Implement formal procedures to take appropriate action to eliminate problems causing variances to processes. If you have procedures in place to identify the problem but no processes for taking action you are faced with the same cumbersome, costly triage discussed above. Your team will spend time sorting through bins of bad product, you will still have to deal with unhappy customers and your operating costs will continue to increase.

Included under this heading are organizational procedures to ensure that decision-making authority is vested in those people who are best able to take effective corrective action.[11] We describe taking effective corrective action as management action. Management action is a structured process to make certain that root causes are identified and solutions are enacted so that the problem does not recur. Without effective management action no problem is ever really solved. This is especially true for quality issues.[12]

Control material movement

Implement procedures to ensure that any component that is not to specification is removed from the process. Do not perform the next operation on any item that is out of specification. Be certain any product that is not to specification does not leave the facility. Do not ship anything the customer did not order. This element needs little discussion. It should be the lowest cost step in the process. If you are doing everything else correctly few resources will be necessary.

Document the production process

Implement procedures to ensure documentation of the entire process. This will support for both you and the customer full compliance with the specification. As we discussed in Chapter 2, this is an important element of every well-developed customer service process. It is helpful if this information is formatted so it is convenient for your customers to interpret.

Proper documentation is also a requirement for monitoring capability. Further, it supports another customer service goal: that of generating knowledge in order to identify opportunities to increase the flexibility of processes, to tighten product specifications and examine potential variations to present products and possibilities for new products.

At some point in this discussion you are going to ask me a question that usually goes something like: 'What about those situations where customers routinely accept a product that is not to spec? Why should we continually struggle to meet a ± 0.01 mm tolerance when customers will accept ± 0.02 mm every time they are desperate for a delivery?'

Read Chapter 2 again. You and the customer must mutually agree the specification. If the customer accepts, even once, items produced to the ± 0.02 mm tolerance the sales team must identify either that:

1 ± 0.02 mm is wholly acceptable. In this case you should be close enough to the customer to ask for a change to the specification. Customers ask for a tighter tolerance than they need because they lack faith in your operation. They ask for ± 0.01 mm because they know you will deliver ± 0.02 mm. They reason that if they ask you for the ± 0.02 mm they really need, you will ship them product to a tolerance of ± 0.04 mm.

2 ± 0.02 mm is not acceptable. This means customers are spending money to rework the item every time you ship to that tolerance. You have two choices:
   (i) make the product to the ± 0.01 mm tolerance, or
   (ii) watch customers take their business to your competitor at their first convenient opportunity.

Quality management and the profit equation

The profit equation begins with customer service and the generation of revenues, and quality is the bridge from there to the management of costs:

- *Quality management is an integral part of the customer service process.* It contributes immediately and directly to happy customers and thus to the generation of revenues.
- *Quality management is a powerful contributor to the management of costs.* A properly managed quality process is the crucial first step in the series of actions taken to ensure that products are manufactured and services are delivered at the lowest possible long-term cost.[13]

  A properly conceived, fully developed and carefully implemented quality management process is the second crucial step in your quest for organization health.[14]

A commitment to quality

Developing and implementing a comprehensive, effective quality management philosophy demands the same scale of effort we talked about in Chapter 2 in connection with customer service. It should be clear that the two are intimately related. You must recognize this represents a significant change in culture not only for the rest of the organization but also for you. You must create a vision and lead the team through the realization of that vision[15] to a process that achieves consistent, long-term results.

Everything I said in Chapter 2 about the introduction of a new way of operating the business is applicable here. You should be aware, however, of one important difference. Customer service is an almost totally external, outward-looking process. Emphasis is on the relationship between the customer and the organization. Customer service is about something as intangible and subjective as happiness. Quality management, on the other hand, is an almost totally internal, inward-looking process. Emphasis is entirely on the mechanics of getting it right. Quality management is very tangible and completely objective. Because of this distinction, quality management is generally easier to implement and manage. It is not difficult to specify the criteria to be evaluated and measure the results. A new culture of intensive quality management is typically not, however, easier to develop and promote. If you have allowed managers to operate in an environment where *almost* meeting the specification is good enough, significant effort will be necessary to change that. If you have let members of the management team convince themselves there somehow exists a law of diminishing returns with respect to taking that last step to get it right – that it would cost too much to meet the specification fully, you have some work to do. If you have made them comfortable making decisions to ship product that is not what the customer ordered – does not meet the specification, they are going to be uncomfortable with this new way of managing the business.

Please note my choice of words. I have referred to managers when perhaps you expected me to say staff and managers or the entire team. This is deliberate. When you begin to promote this process most of the resistance will come from managers: you will discover stronger support amongst staff. They have never been too keen on *almost* getting it right, probably because they are always the ones blamed when it goes wrong: 'You can't find dependable people anymore; nobody cares about doing a good job'.

Successful, totally effective quality management begins with you. It includes a number of elements:

- You must develop then actively and visibly promote a philosophy, a vision of quality. It must become a way of life in every part of the organization. Everybody must be totally committed, every person in the organization has a contribution to make, each person's every action must relate to quality. The importance of this should not be too difficult to communicate to those people who handle the product or deliver the service. This commitment, however, must be given by *everybody* in the organization; that includes word processor operators, messengers, accounting clerks and maintenance engineers: everybody. That commitment will *not* be given unless *you* ask for it.

- Consider that every area and department has products and customers: therefore every department has a requirement for quality management. Why should the maintenance department not actively create a comprehensive quality process for the services it provides? The print shop delivers a product. Why should it not have a complete quality system? Develop and implement formal quality management processes for these units.
- Think about a pilot scheme if the idea of immediate implementation of a total process across the entire organization appears overwhelming. Look inward to where customers are within the facility. Develop a quality management process for the canteen or bought ledger operation. This will be easy to control, easy to evaluate and the risk is low.
- The definition of quality must be the basis for this philosophy. Quality means compliance with the specification, nothing less. Everything you do will submit to description, measurement and specification, and therefore everything you do is amenable to this process.
- The target, the objective, the goal for every quality management effort is zero defects; nothing less is acceptable. There is no such thing as a law of diminishing returns where quality is concerned; getting it right the first time saves you money.
- Prevention rather than correction is the only meaningful way to manage quality. This must become a way of life in your organization. You cannot inspect quality into the product and hoards of inspectors at the end of a production line accomplish nothing. A customer service representative whose primary job is to try to placate unhappy customers should not exist.
- Prevention depends on early identification of potential problems and effective action to address the situation *before* bad product is made. A vigorous and effective management action philosophy is a crucial component of quality management.

Stop painting the roses red, or trying to convince customers that white roses are what they really want. Replace the white rose tree with a red rose tree. It will make customers happy and it will save you money.

Notes

1 This quotation is made up: I do not know your bank manager. Nor should anyone in the banking community take umbrage, this is nothing more than a convenient parody.

2 Philip B. Crosby, *Quality Is Free*. (New York: New American Library, 1980.) Crosby has removed much of the difficulty over quality issues with this definition.
3 The technical elements of effective quality management effort will be examined in detail in Chapter 24.
4 A thorough examination of the concept of zero defects would require an entire book. The process to implement a comprehensive zero defect culture in your organization might take two years. Part Three is about the first year of this process.
5 This chapter is not about writing specifications. Part Two will provide a great deal of information on structuring practices and activities so that objective measurement is possible. Particular emphasis will be given to services and subjective activities that do not easily lend themselves to objective description and measurement.
6 This is an element of the discipline known as SPC (Statistical Process Control) which will be examined in detail in Chapter 24.
7 Capability will be examined in detail in Chapter 24.
8 This principle is also fundamental to SPC.
9 This principle is also fundamental to SPC. See Chapter 24 for a discussion of inspection practices, their limitations and their contributions to quality management.
10 If you are still uncomfortable with this read Chapter 2 again.
11 Chapter 10 addresses some of the complications involved with effective decision-making under dynamic operating conditions.
12 Chapter 7 addresses management action in detail.
13 It is not difficult to demonstrate that 'right the first time' produces the product at the lowest total cost. Review the notes from your tour with particular emphasis on the *total* cost of not getting it right the first time.
14 In Chapter 24 we will examine the specific application of these principles to your operation.
15 Here I do not think vision and lead are too strong or hyperbolical. Indeed, Part Three of *Tactical Management* is all about vision and leadership of a very high order.

■ CHAPTER 4 ■

Cost Management: Show me your cost sheet

That's interesting, but show me your cost sheet.

Andrew Carnegie, quoted by Charles M. Schwab
What A Young Man Must Do To Succeed In Business

The shop managers don't have time to be concerned about costs; they're too busy taking care of customers.

The senior manager for training in a retail company (services)

We always deliver the aeroplane on time, regardless of the cost.

A senior operations manager in a UK aerospace company

Introduction

Cost management is a set of practices, processes and positive actions taken to manage organization resources. This chapter is about cost management: about the tactical utilization of resources.[1] This chapter is *not* about cost control, cost containment or cost reduction. Cost control, as the term is generally used today, is a negative series of actions taken to interfere with staff as they strive to provide good customer service and manage quality. The difference is important: the goal of the organization is not to save money, it is to meet long-term objectives. Tactically, the objective for cost management processes is not to spend less, but to ensure the organization is left with more at the end of the day.[2] This statement is applicable *in toto* whether you are responsible for a profit or non-profit operation and whether your customers are external or internal. It is true whether your spend derives from sales revenues or from a budget allocation. Good use of all resources supports the achievement of long-range organization objectives. You are in control of operations when you are meeting objectives; that is our definition of control. Effective control of operations requires competent management of all resources employed to meet those objectives.

Cost management as a principle of management

The management of costs must be seen as a fundamental principle of management. Consider a profit-making organization. If objectives are to be achieved revenues must be generated and costs managed so total costs are less than total revenues. When this is done according to forecast, what is left over is profit and this is what you planned.[3] When you look at a non-profit making organization there is the same need to deliver the product or service at the lowest possible total cost, usually against a budget forecast or target. If you make some relatively minor adjustments to cost/benefit or value chain analyses these principles apply fully for those situations where no revenues are exchanged. Effective use of this set of practices is crucial to organization health and ultimately the achievement of primary organization objectives. These practices are essential to organization objectives regardless of the nature of the organization and its primary objectives; they must be perceived as important enough that they are elevated to the status of a fundamental principle. Cost management as a principle is not about accounting practices, it is about an organization culture. It is about a culture that seeks to maximize the utilization of all resources available for the pursuit of objectives. Cost management practices achieve this through accurate information about costs, an understanding of how that information should be used and effective management action based on that information.

Cost control

The boundary between cost management and cost control can be indistinct. If a decision to select the lowest priced available raw material is based on a thorough analysis of production needs and the material meets specifications, that decision reflects good, proactive cost management practice. If, at the other extreme, a decision is based solely on price, the material does not meet specifications and you cannot make parts to standard, that decision reflects poor, reactive cost control practice. In the real world of the workplace many of your decisions probably fall somewhere in between.[4] It may therefore be useful to consider what cost management is not.

When the management of costs is seen simplistically as cost control, the immediate reaction to a drop in revenues or an increase in operating costs is to initiate a cost cutting programme. There is a feeling that the problem can be solved if the right kind of memos are written. People are instructed to stop using the telephone. This really means they must stop talking to customers. Training for staff and supervisors is cancelled. This is probably exactly the opposite of what should be done. People are directed to eliminate preventive maintenance for key equipment and cut the spares budget, eliminate scheduled enhancements to computer systems and despatch important correspondence to customers by second class post. Teambuilding sessions are cancelled. What is achieved is an increase in operating costs, which interferes with customer service and quality and usually exacerbates the specific problem the action was supposed to resolve.

These actions are not effective for the long term because:

- There is no plan or structure to the effort. This occurs, if understandably, because there is a panic and urgent orders, perhaps from the board or head office, to do something quickly. Sometimes an ultimatum is delivered: 'Reduce costs by the end of the fiscal year or seek employment elsewhere'.[5] Without a structured process it is impossible to plan actions well. In Chapter 7 we will examine formal processes for management action described as the tactical closed-loop management cycle. My premise is that if management action is to result in consistent results that support organization objectives it must be based on formal, structured practices. Think back over the past year for some examples from your own experience of panic orders from the board or head office that resulted in mass confusion and no substantive reduction in *total* operating costs.
- Symptoms of problems rather than root causes are addressed, or something that has no relevance at all is attacked. This, also, is a result of an unplanned, unstructured approach. Assaulting symptoms rather than root causes accomplishes nothing because the problem will recur. Assume, for example, that induction costs are over budget because staff turnover is higher than forecast. High induction costs are a symptom, high turnover is the problem.[6] Attempting to cut costs by reducing induction training from two days to one will not accomplish anything except to increase problems on the floor for supervisors and experienced operators. They are the people who have to complete the training you eliminated from the classroom. If you want to bring induction costs down to within target, you must reduce turnover to forecast levels or below.
- Total costs are not known; decisions are based on incomplete information. Under many accounting systems in a manufacturing operation, for example, direct labour costs may only represent half of the total, sometimes less. Without knowing total costs it is impossible, *ever*, to relate actions taken fully to profits generated as a result of those actions. I am familiar with business organizations where temporary and casual labour are paid out of personnel department budgets and at least one where payments are from the personnel petty cash account. Accounting for these costs is at best monthly as one gross total. There is no feedback to operating departments. How can you accurately determine the cost of a product under these circumstances? How can you price that product profitably?

Cost management

Effective cost management demands a formal discipline. You must have processes to furnish you with cost/benefit or value-chain analyses for all resources and activities and that information must be used as part of a systematic effort. Otherwise much of your decision-making and actions will be ineffective. You will always be reacting to situations, working after the fact, spending time trying to excuse why something happened rather than planning how to prevent it from happening in the future.

Effective cost management demands that you have formal processes in place to:

- develop and maintain a master schedule,
- identify total operating costs for individual operations and activities,
- prepare a budget: forecast specific costs for every operation and activity,
- evaluate current operating practices,
- investigate options to current practices and
- implement and evaluate selected options to operating practices when you recognize improvements can be made with respect to the management of costs.

Your present management effort already includes efforts within these six areas. I doubt, however, that you approach them in the way I recommend with respect to comprehensive management of costs. Much can be achieved when these six are amalgamated into a formal, fully integrated process.[7]

Developing and maintaining a master schedule[8]

You must have processes to enable you and your team to match the costs of resources with the revenues generated by those resources. This begins with a master schedule. You do this routinely for material costs. You attempt to calculate, sometimes to the fraction of a penny, the contribution of an individual lot of raw material to finished goods. Accuracy can vary dramatically depending, typically, on whether your yield percentage calculation is based on empirical studies or wishful thinking. You also try to do this with labour, but usually with far less accuracy because ordinarily you only have immediate access to direct costs. Truly effective cost management effort must enable you to relate all resource costs to revenues with the same accuracy you now seek to achieve for materials.

Develop a formal master schedule: a set of procedures to identify the contribution of every individual product or service to total forecast revenues. The initial yearly forecast is in revenue value, the master schedule is by product volume or service delivery. The precise point at which this conversion is made is determined by the needs of the operation. If your forecast consists of nothing more than one number, one revenue total for the entire year, it is useless. It will be impossible to use it to manage resources. Unless the forecast is converted into a detailed master schedule it will contribute nothing to effective tactical cost management effort.

The master schedule is developed around monthly forecast volumes for specific products or services. There is another need: it must be possible to convert forecast monthly volumes easily into monthly, then weekly production plans, and these must be according to an interval of control appropriate for your industry. The interval of control must be determined to be effective for your operation. In the past for many manufacturing operations, production plans were based on a monthly interval. Many manufacturing operations now operate with weekly plans; those serving the automotive industry or fresh food processors frequently work to a daily production plan. For most retail operations the interval is one day. For banks, building societies, supermarkets, fast food operations and others providing similar retail services to the public, the interval for scheduling cash tills must be one hour.

The other requirement for the master schedule is that you must be able to compare planned to actual values by individual product and by controlling interval. You must be able to do this quickly: within one interval, whether that interval is weekly, daily or hourly. You must be able to do it easily: the information must be accurate and the collection process must not be onerous. Only then can the master schedule support improved control for operations.

Identifying total operating costs for individual operations and activities

If cost management is to be effective you must have the ability to account for total costs. If you do not, something like this is certain to occur:

A parable

This is a true story. Some embarrassing details such as the name of the company have been omitted.

> Once upon a time there was a foundry. The founders were awarded a big government contract for a Thing, because their price was lower than all others. There was great joy as they went about supplying the government with hundreds of thousands of identical Things; But at the end of the year the chief accountant said: 'Verily, the numbers do not make sense. We have sold a great many Things, but still we seem to be losing money.' And it came to pass, it was discovered that the cost to make each individual Thing was nearly £1 more than the selling price.

> Sadly, *this* foundry is no more. And He said unto them, 'Blessed are they who know their true costs, for their enterprise shall remain profitable and their organization healthy'.[9]

You must have accurate base data. Accounting and reporting systems must provide complete and timely information for the total operation:

- Work standards, operating practices, methods and procedures must be current and accurate. They also must cover all activities – not just the principle ones or those that demand significant amounts of staff hours or key equipment time. Standards are sometimes established using a Pareto analysis: the 20 per cent of unit activities accounting for 80 per cent of total hours are studied. You cannot expect to identify total costs for any operation accurately if you have only considered 80 per cent of total activity content.
- Information has to take into account all unusual or off-standard situations such as the cost of computer system slowdown. It is usually possible to account for time when production lines or computer systems are down, but if labour costs increase and machine utilization decreases because certain activities require more time to complete, those costs must be included. Many mainframe systems slow down dramatically during mid-morning and mid-afternoon peak use times. Review the notes from your tour to identify what screen entries that should be completed in one minute are really costing your organization during those times.
- Accounting systems must not permit the burial of costs such as material handling or rework as indirect or overhead. Indirect costs and overheads can be a significant percentage of total operating costs and must not be omitted from calculations. For some accounting systems, casual and temporary labour are treated as part of overheads. I am familiar with a retail operation where indirect costs are reported quarterly, not by individual shop but by region. Clever shop managers reduce permanent staff hours to below target, on which they are paid a performance bonus, then operate with a large number of temporary staff whose costs are allocated to indirects. Head office accountants meanwhile sign bonus cheques early in the morning then spend the rest of the day trying to figure out why costs are up and profits are down.
- The reporting system must account for time when people are off the clock. When the line goes down and operators are assigned to housekeeping chores, for example, consider how this is recorded. If time off the clock is also treated as an indirect this can distort the calculations, especially in an operation with significant downtime or set-up time. Review the notes from your tour.
- Review the system for accounting for both materials and time related to rework and processing scrap. If staff have had to do something twice

to get it right and you have quite naturally only charged the customer once, those costs must be included. Rework time in an admin operation can be significant. Rework time in an admin, back office or head office operation often represents more than one-half of total labour hours. Confirm that it has been included in calculations.

Preparing a budget – forecasting specific costs

When total costs have been identified it is possible to relate all resource costs to specific revenues generated by those resources: you are now able to prepare a proper budget. What is needed is much more ambitious than the typical budget exercise. In the past this usually meant factoring whatever happened last year by a fixed percentage that correlates with the change in sales forecast. If you were to look over the shoulder of one of your middle managers during yearly budget preparation this is exactly what you would discover. It is crucial to the success of this effort that cost forecasts are developed with as much concern for accuracy and completeness as the master schedule. Work from the master schedule and cost analyses and develop detailed requirements for the next year for all resources, not just those for which the calculations are easy. The forecast must take into account specific volumes of identified product by individual controlling interval. Information from the capability studies we discussed in Chapters 2 and 3 are crucial for budget preparation. Remember, the objective is not to produce an accounting document, but to provide information to manage operations well.

The only process that will support long-range organization objectives is zero based budgeting built around accurate and complete information on what operations and activities really cost. Budget preparation must be taken seriously. It must be perceived as far more than a troublesome annual ritual to be completed with as little interference as possible with the real work of the unit. The ability to manage costs effectively will be in direct proportion to the commitment managers make to this process.

Evaluating current operating practices

A thorough evaluation of current methods and procedures is the first step in the investigation of options. To forecast a measurable improvement in resource utilization it must be possible to compare present practice accurately to a proposed change. One of the results of your tour is that you discovered a fair number of people either doing things they should not have, or not doing things they should have.

You must know what staff and managers are doing and be confident that what they are doing is what they should be doing. It is essential that operating practices, procedures and methods are published, readable, current, distributed and available to users.[10] Review the notes from your tour to evaluate how this is presently managed. A further step is to support processes that ensure that people are always in compliance with practices that support the job to be done. The role of the supervisor and first line manager in large part is to confirm that staff are provided, always, with every tool they need to do the work. Their most important tool is information of the kind provided by established standards, practices and procedures.[11]

Investigating options to current practices

Investigate options to the way you are presently doing things.[12] One that is relatively benign and easy to manage is the photocopier. If you examine photocopiers they are nearly always in the wrong places. Conduct a study of time spent walking to and from photocopying equipment throughout the facility. The total time will be equivalent to numbers of people and it will amaze you. Next to look at use to determine whether photocopies are appropriate for all present applications. It might be possible to eliminate some of the machines altogether. Remember, however, your action is to evaluate current practices and consider potential options; not to write memos directing people to stop using photocopiers.

Implementing and evaluating selected options

A change in procedures should enable you to either accomplish more for the same cost or accomplish the same for lower costs. The alternative depends on the specific situation. The combination of better accounting and reporting systems along with good documentation of practices, methods and procedures will enable you to forecast the impact of the proposed change.

Select the option of choice and implement it. Allow it to remain in operation for a reasonable time and evaluate it. If it has resulted in the predicted improvement make it a permanent part of standard practice. If it needs a bit of adjustment make the necessary revisions and extend the evaluation period. If it turns out to be totally unworkable, and this must happen occasionally if you are really trying, put everything back and begin again.

Accounting information versus operating information

Accounting practices can sometimes causes problems for operating managers with regard to the management of costs. The primary responsibility of the accountant to the organization is to account accurately for all assets within a very stylized, formal, statutory set of practices. The accountant can and should provide managers with information to assist them to manage operations effectively, but this must necessarily be a responsibility secondary to that of accounting for organization assets.[13] The problem is that information designed to support accounting systems and strategic financial decisions is not necessarily appropriate for tactical, operating decisions. One example is reporting labour hours. From the accountant's perspective, hours can be reconciled weekly or monthly; accuracy and completeness are more important than timeliness. From the operating manager's perspective accuracy beyond a reasonable level is not as important as timeliness if the information is to be useful to control daily operations. The operating manager has two choices. The first is to accept accounting information as it is provided and attempt to use it to manage operations with the knowledge that it has certain limitations. The second choice is to set up a parallel management operating system that provides appropriate operating information at the cost of some duplication or overlap with accounting information. My experience suggests the latter is preferable.

Given the importance of effective management of daily operations, the cost of some duplication and overlap of information generated by accounting and management operating systems is a small price to pay for improved control. In this book we will return to this principle several times, especially when discussing production scheduling systems and in-process quality management.

The balance between revenues and costs

Cost management is a balancing act. At one end of the spectrum you are faced with the powerful notion that, somehow, costs must be cut to the absolute minimum and this will contribute to improved profits. Our discussion thus far is based on the premise that your job is not to cut costs but to manage them. Good cost management, perceived as proactive utilization of organization resources, supports the achievement of long-range objectives better than does a series of cost cutting exercises.

The other extreme is the one expressed by the senior training manager and the aerospace operations manager in the quotations at the beginning of this chapter: ignore the costs – take care of the customer. If you think superficially about these quotations, in some circumstances they seem to make sense. If revenues are to be generated, the customer must be taken care of. That could mean on occasion that you disregard everything else, including costs, to deliver the order. Nobody can argue with this. If a key piece of equipment has broken down unexpectedly and production has been delayed, perhaps the only way you can meet the delivery schedule is to ship by courier, even if the cost of that service eliminates all profit for that particular order.

The word unexpectedly is important. If equipment failed because one of your cost cutting exercises eliminated preventive maintenance or the repair was delayed because the latest cost reduction programme reduced levels of spares, the breakdown was not unexpected. If the repair took longer than necessary because your latest cost control effort reduced the number of qualified repair staff on that particular shift, that delay could have been predicted. If order entries are late because a system enhancement was cancelled as part of the new cost containment policy, that situation was to be expected. Unexpectedly refers to those few real world situations that occur in spite of your best attempts at planning and control.

When taking care of the customer becomes a convenient excuse for poor planning, ineffective scheduling and incompetent tactical control, nothing has been accomplished except allowing the management team to abrogate responsibility for assertive and positive cost management. They have been permitted to walk away from half of their responsibility for the generation of profits.

The training manager is quoted to remind you that his way of thinking must cease to be part of the philosophy by which the business is managed. He was responsible for developing and delivering training for shop staff and managers, including induction courses for new employees. Regardless of the intended content of his sessions, the result was that people coming into the organization and were being told by a senior level manager at head office to 'Ignore costs, take care of the customers'. One of their first lessons concerning their contribution to the profit-making organization they recently joined was totally wrong.

The operations manager is quoted to remind you of a situation we find too frequently in the workplace. In this case, the operation for which he was responsible was operating at a loss on the order of $1,250,000 per week. While it is commendable that managers are concerned about the customer, it is an equally important part of their job to be concerned about costs. The two are not incompatible; indeed, that is what effective management is all about.

It is necessary to examine options and make decisions. You must promote throughout the organization the principle that costs and the management of costs are import elements of the profit equation. If the understanding of cost management in your team is anything like that of the two managers quoted above, then you have some serious work to do. The process must be formal and must become an integral part of your management philosophy, just as customer service and quality have become part of that philosophy. I talked in the Introduction about various things that interfere with the ability of managers to get on with taking actions to ensure the continual good health of the organization. Cost control programmes frequently interfere with effective cost management practices.

In many organizations supervisors, first line managers and even middle managers are not privy to information on revenues, costs or profits. I assume this is to discourage them from thinking they make any significant contribution to profits and thus prevent them from fantasizing about higher salaries if profits rise. The real result, however, is to take from them an awareness of their responsibilities for the management of costs. At the beginning of the year you hand them a budget. They have had no input for its preparation yet it intimately affects their every daily action. When equipment breaks down and delivery schedules slip you berate them for poor customer service. Then at the end of the month you chastise them for excessive overtime and high levels of scrap. Is it any wonder their understanding of their responsibility for the management of costs is muddled?

You will have noted that again I have said nothing in this respect about staff. They have always understood that you have to spend money to make money. They have never understood why, at the time they desperately need better tools and procedures to deliver the product, you, in the name of cost control, have attempted to either degrade or completely remove those tools.

Think about this

One problem with coming to terms with the principle of cost management is that while you think you have a process, in fact you do not. You have a marketing and sales team, a marketing strategy, a sales plan. You have, on the other hand, neither a cost management team, strategy nor plan. Cost management is something managers are supposed to do merely as part of being managers. You send them on courses and talk with them about communications, planning, motivation, meetings, stress management and many other management topics, but the perception is that cost management is something they should have acquired naturally somehow, somewhere along the way.

Review some present and past cost cutting exercises. Ask people whether they think anything was accomplished except to upset staff and interfere with operations. Before you try to implement a new process, review in detail some of the things that have gone on under the name of cost control – or the even sillier cost containment. Identify enough specific instances of misdirected actions to convince yourself the effort has been not only ineffective but counterproductive.

Discuss with staff how they perceive those cost cutting programmes. Ask each to show you specific examples of interference with their ability to maintain customer service and quality. Conduct an informal study of how the telephone memo[14] has made it more difficult to communicate well with customers. Talk with first-line managers about the training memo,[15] and how the reduction in budget for supervisory development training has made daily operations more difficult. Review with admin staff the recurring problems they encounter when the system slows down every afternoon because proposed systems enhancements have not been implemented.

Understand that effective cost management does not automatically mean a reduction in spending on resources, it means better utilization of resources. Again, you are not concerned with how much you spend, you are concerned about how much you have left over at the end. Think about how good cost management practice relates to organization health and long-range objectives. The object of the exercise is not to save money, it is to spend money effectively to achieve long-range organization goals.

Notes

1 Costs in this context is generic and refers to all the money you spend in the course of managing your operation.

2 This statement addresses a tactical issue, not accounting practice. If the board, for perhaps very good strategic reasons (or even for perhaps *not* very good reasons), make a decision to revalue certain assets and the result is a reported change in what you have left over at the end of the day, that changes nothing for you tactically. See the Coda; Concerning the Integrity of Stated Objectives.

3 You may think this statement is trivial, but why does it so often *not* happen according to plan?

4 James G. March and Herbert A. Simon, *Organizations*. 2nd Edn. (Oxford: Blackwell, 1993.) March and Simon consider a continuum of decisions in circumstances such as these under a process they define as satisficing.

5 Eliyahu M. Goldratt and Jeff Cox, *The Goal*. (Croton-on-Hudson, NY: North River Press, 1986.) Goldratt and Cox offer a detailed, entertaining and true-to-life illustration of the results of this kind of ineffective and misdirected action.

6 High staff turnover is not really a problem, it is the symptom of a higher order management problem. This example is appropriate, however, for this discussion.

7 This chapter is not intended to address specific actions taken to implement the processes discussed here. All of Part Two is about these tools.

8 The contribution of the master schedule to good tactical management practice will be examined in detail in Chapter 17.

9 This is sometimes characterized alternatively as: 'It costs us £1.50 to make it and we only sell it for £1.00, but that's okay, we'll make it up on volume'.

10 These are requirements fundamental to gaining BS5750/ISO9000 accreditation.

11 Chapter 17 will examine reporting systems and their relevance to this process.

12 Chapter 25 will address one formal process for managing methods improvements and Chapter 26 will consider the systematic investigation of options to present practices.

13 This is clearly a generalization and a simplification of a complex issue. It is, nevertheless, accurate in this context.

14 I know that at least one telephone memo has been written in your organization in the last year. There has been one written by a middle manager somewhere in *every* business in the UK in the last year.

15 I know about the training memo, too.

Elements of Management Theory: Somebody has to be in charge

And thou shalt teach them ordinances and laws, and shalt shew them the way wherein they must walk, and the work that they must do.

Exodus 18: 20

Don't ever be afraid to be the boss; somebody has to be in charge.

A senior production supervisor of a manufacturing company during a discussion about good supervisory practice

User-friendly management theory

The objective for this chapter is to offer you to a brief, user-friendly examination of management theory. The material presented here characterizes the Tactical Management model developed and tested in the workplace over the past twenty-six years. In my experience it is effective – consistently and for the long-term; this is what Tactical Management is all about. This treatment is not meant to be exhaustive either in breadth or depth. It does not have to be too complicated. What we want to do is to match just a little analytical enquiry with our own experience, both yours[1] and mine. Consistent with remarks in the Introduction about your own management model, this chapter will include very few definitions. If you feel the need to define a concept or principle under discussion that has not been defined, or if you are not comfortable with my definition, create your own. I think that is an important step in your professional growth. Any management model useful to you and your organization now and into the next century must admit this level of flexibility.

The reader working in organization development, the social sciences, human behaviour or industrial psychology may think this treatment naïve or primitive, although I hope neither simplistic nor superficial. The amount of literature available on management theory and related subjects is awesome. In this field there are even bibliographies of bibliographies. It ranges from very straightforward, general treatments found in airport bookstalls to tomes lining dusty university library stacks reporting the results of extremely arcane, narrowly constructed experiments conducted in the workplace or psychology laboratory. It includes material to suit all tastes and interests between the two extremes. The Recommended Reading at the end of this book will provide you with a long, long list of references covering a broad range of general and specific management topics. Those references will suggest enough further reading to last you the rest of your life.

Most issues of management theory relate to communications. This is true even for topics we characterize by more esoteric labels such as workplace behaviour, organization development or organization effectiveness. Accurate and complete information must be transmitted at the time it is needed to all those who need it. Within the context of a business organization, when a manager communicates with anybody – superior, peer or subordinate, it is nearly always with the intention of making something happen. Even those communications we think of as being merely to inform are aimed indirectly at making something happen; if only, for example, to confirm that a process continues to operate without change. Tactically, management theory consists of a body of principles intended to result in practices to ensure that when you communicate to somebody that you want something to happen, it happens. What you want is direction to help you go about getting the people you work with to do the things you want them to do.

This treatment is not restricted to people you manage; it also includes people at the same level as you on the organization chart and the people who manage you – those at higher levels:

1 Any meaningful body of management theory must be far more universal than simple prescriptions for giving orders.
2 Making things happen refers to *everybody* in the organization, not just subordinates.[2,3]

A brief history of management theory

From the large number of management models available to us in the literature I have chosen a few I feel are useful to illustrate this brief history. My choices are arbitrary, although I think they are representative. If your particular favourites are not included, enter them at appropriate places in the sequence.[4]

Scientific management

A convenient point to begin our discussion is with the set of principles known as scientific management. It began in the United States around 1880 and continued into the first part of the twentieth century. A number of management theorists and practitioners developed the scientific management model; their principal objective was to improve the output or productivity of individual factory workers and thereby reduce labour costs. This was happening at the time when owner-managers were relinquishing much day-to-day control to professional managers. Also during this period labour unions were becoming increasingly militant in their demands for improved wages and working conditions. The most prominent advocate of scientific management, Frederick W. Taylor, felt passionately that scientifically derived manufacturing methods and time standards would achieve two important results: in addition to improving labour efficiencies they would create a common framework within which labour unions and the new class of professional managers could peacefully resolve their differences.[5]

Operations managed under scientific management principles and practices may be characterized by these assumptions:

1 There is one 'best' method or most efficient way to perform each work activity.
2 The most cost effective way to perform each work activity is to break it down into its most elementary steps and to have each step or task performed by a single operator.
3 Task definition and best method can be determined through a detailed study of the job by a person especially trained in observation techniques.
4 Detailed studies will result in an objective, attainable, repeatable time standard for each task.
5 Operators can be selected and trained to enable them to perform each task according to the best method and to meet the time standard consistently.
6 Operators who meet standards should be rewarded through a bonus or piece-rate payment system.
7 The reward system will ensure that operators consistently strive to meet standards.
8 Operators, and by implication their labour unions, will support best methods and time standards because they are derived scientifically.
9 Professional managers are obligated to support both best methods and time standards for the same reason.
10 This total system will result in the most efficient production of manufactured products.

A thorough examination of one of the basic assumptions of the model resulted in a movement away from scientific management toward a more general theory. That assumption is that operators are simply extensions of the machines they operate. Thus improvements in the workplace environment and production equipment will necessarily result in corresponding improvements in worker output or production. Within a properly designed workplace, theoretically output is limited only by physical limitations of the worker.[6]

Since one factor limiting human performance is fatigue, that was the subject of a series of studies conducted in the United Kingdom beginning about the time of the First World War and continuing into the early 1920s. The original objective for the studies, consistent with some of Taylor's premises, was that a comprehensive study of fatigue would yield information on how to set faster paces for operations and schedule rest periods to achieve maximum individual output for an entire shift. Researchers, however, began to see that something other than fatigue was involved. They identified that boredom or monotony were important when evaluating operator performance. Monotony is clearly not a limitation on physical performance; therefore the human psyche must be considered when investigating how people behave in the workplace. The conclusion was that any theory of management useful to the practising manager must recognize this human factor of monotony. The general conclusion was that other as yet undefined human factors might also contribute to operator performance.

The Hawthorne experiments

In the 1920s and 1930s an extensive series of studies were conducted at the Hawthorne, Illinois, plant of the Western Electric Company in the United States to evaluate the effects of environmental factors on productivity. The stated purpose of the original studies was to evaluate the effect of specific environmental factors and working conditions on work output, and to identify correlations between the two. These studies overlapped those in the United Kingdom by several years. Today questions are raised about whether or not researchers in the US were aware of work done in the UK and how those studies might have influenced work at Hawthorne. In either case, human factors were not discovered by Hawthorne researchers, although many accounts now imply this was what happened. Most of us today informally, and probably incorrectly, refer to the importance of human factors in the workplace as the Hawthorne Effect. It is convenient but inaccurate jargon.

When attempts were made to evaluate the initial data, inconsistencies emerged which refuted the assumptions of scientific management and were also consistent with the work done in Britain. One particular series of studies involved the contribution of light levels to productivity.

Working under controlled conditions with a test group, light levels were increased with the predicted increase in productivity. The problem arose when productivity also increased for the control group for which light levels had not been increased. Research teams then modified the studies to include a range of light levels for both the test and control groups. Further investigation resulted in the hypothesis that improvements in productivity resulted not from the improvements in light levels that were forecast, but from the far more general condition of changes having been made in the environment.

A careful review of data resulted in the decision to conduct a series of interviews with test subjects. Conclusions were that it was not physical changes alone that caused productivity to increase; the perception that management was making an attempt to improve the workplace also contributed. During one of the experiments successive reductions in light levels resulted in continuous improvements in productivity. It was only when light was reduced to about the intensity of moonlight that productivity ceased to rise. One of the participants said during an interview: 'This was the best thing the company had ever done'. Work at the Hawthorne plant supported the hypothesis that human factors were far more important in understanding how people functioned in the workplace than was previously assumed. A large number of additional experiments conducted there over a ten-year period by a number of different researchers broadly supported that premise.

Theory X-Theory Y

The Hawthorne studies coincided with a major shift in emphasis concerning why people behave as they do in the workplace. Management theorists and practitioners developed a large number of models, all based on the increased importance of subjective factors such as motivation, access to information, levels of supervision, feedback on performance, involvement in decision-making processes and relationships amongst people.[7] One of the most quotable of these many hypotheses is the one known as Theory X-Theory Y. Traditional views such as those forming the basis for scientific management concerning the behaviour of workers in the workplace and how they should be managed are described as Theory X assumptions. Those based on premises derived from the work on fatigue in the UK, experiments such as the Hawthorne studies and similar work – that human factors are important considerations in the workplace, are described as Theory Y assumptions.

Theory X assumptions[8]

1 The average human being has an inherent dislike for work and will avoid it if he can.

2 Because of this human characteristic of dislike of work, most people must be coerced, controlled, directed, threatened with punishment to get them to put forth adequate effort toward the achievement of organizational objectives.
3 The average human being prefers to be directed, wishes to avoid responsibility, has relatively little ambition, wants security above all.

Theory Y assumptions

1 The expenditure of physical and mental effort at work is as natural as play or rest.
2 External control and the threat of punishment are not the only means for bringing about effort toward organizational objectives. Man will exercise self-direction and self-control in the service of objectives to which he is committed.
3 Commitment to objectives is a function of the rewards associated with their achievement.
4 The average human being learns, under proper conditions, not only to accept but to seek responsibility.
5 The capacity to exercise a relatively high degree of imagination, ingenuity, and creativity in the solution of organizational problems is widely, not narrowly, distributed in the population.
6 Under the conditions of modern industrial life, the intellectual potentialities of the average human being are only partially utilized.

Since the time of the Hawthorne experiments, the statement of Theory X-Theory Y and the development of similar models, most bodies of assumptions concerning how businesses should be organized and managed have shifted away from Theory X premises toward those of Theory Y. Look at the present structure of most business organizations and think about what you have read over the past few years in professional publications, books and periodicals, then review the content of management development courses and seminars you and your colleagues have attended during the past decade. Almost the entire content can be described as being based on Theory Y.

The Hawthorne Experiments demonstrated that when management are seen to be actively making changes in the workplace, and when operators are not only involved in those changes, but also consulted about the effects on daily working conditions, productivity increases – people produce more. A thoughtful comparison of the two theories suggests the total cost in resources to manage an operation under Theory Y should be lower. Staff should need less supervision and they should act more responsibly toward established practices and procedures, production standards and quality specifications. They should contribute more toward improvements in methods. Higher productivity should result in a lower unit cost. It would also appear that working in a Theory Y environment should be more pleasant for everybody.

A little observation, however, suggests some inconsistencies: go into the workplace and examine how you, other managers and your colleagues in other organizations really manage a business. You will discover an appreciable amount of actual practice is based on Theory X assumptions. In some situations the application is almost pure Theory X with little trace of Theory Y. How can this apparent discrepancy be explained?

If you review Theory Y carefully you will begin to question whether all of the assumptions are applicable *in toto* for all situations. They are not absolute, but open to interpretation of degree. How much self-direction and self-control will people exercise in the service of objectives to which they are committed? How much responsibility will the average human being not only accept but seek under proper conditions? In some circumstances an effective Theory Y management style requires substantially more time and effort by managers. In a perfect world this might be desirable, but what happens when the pressure is on to ship a big order: is Theory Y workable when you are well behind schedule? Are there not at least a few circumstances when external control and the threat of punishment seem to be the only practical means for bringing about effort toward organizational objectives?

The result of this is the discrepancy that, while much contemporary management theory claims to be based on Theory Y assumptions, much current management practice is carried out under Theory X assumptions. What you need is a model to resolve this contradiction.

A modern synthesis

You must go beyond a simple Theory X versus Theory Y process; you need an hypothesis to enable you to adapt or adjust the approach according to the circumstances of each particular situation.[9] For example, a new staff member, an inductee, probably needs more explicit direction and supervision in that position than suggested by Theory Y. If bad work practices, poor customer service and non-compliance with quality specifications have been allowed to flourish in one unit for some time, the actions you take initially will have to be more objective and assertive, and the control more circumscribed than that suggested by Theory Y. You might discover in another department, on the other hand, that restrictive management practices and inordinately close supervision have stifled creativity and placed artificial limitations on output. There you will have to assume a less inhibiting management approach – a style less like Theory X. Within another unit that has experienced a large number of trivial operating problems of late, managers must delegate some of their duties to supervisors. This is necessary for them to secure enough time to address the problems. Delegation is an element more appropriate to a Theory Y management style.

Developing a management approach to address each individual situation[10] demands that you look at a number of factors.

Your personal management style

Your personal management style is going to be an important factor in your approach to every situation. I submit that your style was fixed a long time ago and it is not something you can change fundamentally. It is part of you. Within that style, however, you can change practices, procedures, and timeliness and type of response for every situation:

1 If, for example, you consider your style akin to Theory Y, you may be uncomfortable making assignments to people under directions that are very narrowly defined, detailed and specific. Yet if objectives and deadlines are seldom achieved, you know that something must change. You can continue to manage within your own more open-ended and general style. You can improve your effectiveness by monitoring assigned work at shorter intervals and seeking more frequent feedback to keep work on schedule.
2 On the other hand, if you describe your style as Theory X, you are probably uneasy about assigning work with instructions that are loose, broad or non-specific. You may have experienced problems when objectives and deadlines were achieved but people were reluctant to demonstrate much innovation or go beyond the minimum effort necessary to get the job done. You can continue to manage within your more rigid and specific style. You can improve your effectiveness by increasing the interval of control and seeking less detailed feedback.

The specific situation

The specific details presented by each situation should suggest an appropriate approach. In the examples above, the unit with bad work practices and poor customer service presents you with a completely different situation than the department where creativity and innovation have been stifled. Look well beyond symptoms and excuses to identify root causes for problems. Organization culture can also be an important factor. One facility has a history of poor quality because of a culture of 'Ship it. It's good enough'. At another facility an equally poor quality record may result from the culture of a cost conscious management team that refuses to spend enough money to maintain tooling adequately. Superficially the problems appear to be the same, but the situations are completely different and need different approaches.

Needs of individuals in the context of the situation

Within the context of the situation the specific needs of individuals must be considered. The inductee above had different needs than the more experienced worker in the problem area. In some models this is referred to as a readiness level:[11] the inductee was not at the same readiness level as the experienced worker. Factors to be considered when evaluating readiness levels include time in the job, skill level, experience level and individual attitudes as reflected in behaviour. An important factor, although one sometimes not considered, is the readiness level of supervisors and managers. If all your team members are ready for a Theory Y approach but you are not, that must be part of your evaluation of the situation. It is also important to remember that readiness levels relate to individuals, not to groups or operating units.

Implications for individuals in the organization for the future

Your approach to every situation must also take into account how the readiness levels of people in the area are expected to change for the future. This is one of the primary objectives of *Tactical Management* and much of Part Two addresses efforts to examine the readiness levels of everybody in your organization and adjust them as necessary to meet various situations. For some situations a Theory Y approach will be effective and for a few situations Theory X is essential, but for most you will be challenged to identify the most effective balance between the two to manage the situation. One of my premises is that this will be crucial to meet the demands of an organization that is changing to face the challenges of the next century.

Finally, review several serious problems you have addressed recently and evaluate them with regard to how successful you consider the outcome. You will probably discover that with the successful efforts you adjusted your actions and approach to the specific needs of the situation, although maybe you did not consciously think about it. For those actions where you were not totally pleased with the results, it is possible you blundered through with an approach that worked well enough somewhere else, but was not appropriate for that particular situation.

General principles of management

Within the total body of management theory a number of hypotheses recur and seem to have nearly universal appeal. They seem to make sense in the real world of the workplace and therefore merit consideration as general principles. Read them carefully, however, with the understanding that this presentation is followed by some cautions on their use. From your reading you may be familiar with them worded differently and under different names.

In the context of the Tactical Management model, these principles are to be used to support your efforts to improve organization control. Recall our definition: you are in control when you are moving the organization, unit, department or area closer and closer to long-range objectives through your management of processes that support those objectives. Otherwise, your operation is out of control. Control has nothing to do with the manipulation of people, it is about managing work. Most of Tactical Management, as we have said, relates to communications: to your being able to ensure the actions you want taken happen according to plan. This is achieved through effective communications with people responsible for taking those actions. Improved communications have nothing to do with the manipulation of people.[12]

Another premise of Tactical Management is that effective management action follows good decision-making. A recurring theme in this book is that the responsibility for each decision must be vested in a single individual, and that person and everybody else in the organization must know who that person is. These general principles support this premise. Improved decision-making capabilities also have nothing to do with the manipulation of people.[13]

The principle of ultimate responsibility

While a manager may delegate authority for a subordinate to carry out a task, that manager still has full responsibility for proper completion of the task.

A department manager is responsible for all duties the department is charged with completing; the chief executive is responsible for the achievement of all organization objectives. This is an important general principle. Often when a manager has delegated authority for certain activities there is a feeling that thereafter he or she is absolved of all responsibility. The perception is that the delegate is totally responsible for the success or failure of the task. This is a particular problem when something goes wrong, a duty is not performed as it should have been and the inappropriate reply from the senior manager is: 'I'm not responsible'.[14]

The principle of the synchrony of authority and responsibility

Delegation of the responsibility to achieve any objective must be accompanied by the authority to manage all resources needed to achieve that objective.

This is an important general principle which is frequently ignored. An obvious example is the manager who is ostensibly given responsibility for the management of a cost centre but is encumbered with restrictions that, in fact, make it impossible to manage costs. There may be a requirement to purchase raw materials from another company in the group while having no authority to negotiate price. There may be an edict that photocopying paper must be obtained from Central Purchasing at £2.99 per ream when it can be secured from a nearby stationer for £1.99. The manager has been given responsibility for meeting cost centre objectives but not the authority necessary to carry them out.

The exception principle

As decisions required for the completion of a duty are determined to be routine, authority for those decisions should be delegated farther down in the organization.

This would seem to make sense. A production operator or maintenance craftsperson, for example, should have the authority to handle the routine order of standard hand tools; an admin clerk should have the authority to order standard stationery supplies. Department or middle managers should neither have to place these orders nor waste time approving them. If you feel this requirement is too obvious to be awarded the status of a principle, review the notes from your tour. You identified at least one *senior* manager ordering screwdrivers or pencils.

There is a related axiom usually stated as the principle of management by exception. A manager must evaluate an operation to determine which parts of it are functioning well – are achieving objectives, and which parts are not functioning well – are at variance with the plan. Resources should be assigned so the greater portion bears on the exception, on the process that is at variance.[15]

The principle of the synchrony of effectiveness and efficiency

Every operating procedure and human activity throughout the organization must meet two criteria: it must contribute to effectiveness – it must be the right thing to do, and it must contribute to efficiency – it must be a thing done right.[16]

In the Introduction reference was made to 'opportunities for improvement in productivity – doing things right, or methods – doing the right things'. Since then the terms effective and effectiveness have been used regularly in a general sense, but always in the context of the right thing being done.

Understanding the contribution of each and the difference between the two can result in spectacular differences in the utilization of resources:

Example

Several years ago we reviewed operations with the chief executive for a large admin centre for a government agency with the intention of implementing management systems and productivity improvement processes. Out of a total centre complement of 1300 people we identified a department with 94 staff responsible for correcting errors to documents created internally and processed in the centre. Had the decision been made to evaluate this department with respect to improving efficiency it would have been possible to develop systems and procedures to complete the work with about 75 people, for a net saving of 19 people. This would have been the result of doing things right. Had management elected, however, to change the entire process, had they chosen to do the right things – to eliminate the causes of errors and improve quality, department work could have been accomplished by about four people for a net saving of 90 people.

Most models, and common sense, support that all your efforts should be directed toward improving effectiveness. Examples such as the one above confirm that greater benefits can be achieved for the long-term. I agree. However, I think in some circumstances readiness levels for both managers and staff are such that actions to improve effectiveness should follow actions resulting in improvements in efficiencies. This will be examined at a number of points in this book. The point is that when evaluating activities in the organization both characteristics must be considered and every activity should be evaluated for its contributions to both effectiveness and efficiency.

The principle of unity of command

Every individual in the organization must take direction from one and only one person; and he or she, the person giving direction and everybody else in the organization must know who that person is.

If you think this notion is trivial ask any machine operator how often simultaneous, conflicting instructions are received from the supervisor, Somebody From Quality, Somebody From Production Planning and Somebody From the Toolroom. How often do *you* walk into accounts, bypass the entire management structure, walk up to a clerk and demand that the present job is stopped immediately so you can be provided with some information? Here you must make the distinction between taking direction and receiving information. It is perfectly acceptable, and indeed mandatory that the operator receives information from a number of different sources if work is to be managed effectively. But if that information makes it necessary for something different to be done, that change of direction must come from the supervisor.[17]

The principle of appropriate span of control

The number of people reporting directly to one person depends entirely upon circumstances, there is no theoretically efficient minimum or effective maximum.

In the early part of this century students of scientific management solemnly declared, then proved mathematically, that the appropriate number of people one person could supervise or manage was no less than five – in the interest of efficiency, nor more than ten – in the interest of effective control. This was sometimes stated as ranging from six to twelve and sometimes as exactly eight. You can also find references in Plato, writings about the Roman army and the Bible. The appropriate number may range from one to fifty according to the needs of the operation.[18] It depends totally on the situation and the readiness levels of people involved; it has nothing to do with Frederick Taylor or the Roman army. The criterion is whether a team is meeting all unit objectives or not. If they are, amongst other conditions, the span of control is probably about right.

The principle of integrity of command

Reporting lines, as formally defined in the organization chart and supported by operating practices, must be observed in letter and in spirit.

Information and direction must be communicated without skipping links in the chain of command. Consistent with the principle of unity of command, work or task assignments must be given by each individual's boss and nobody else. Similarly, upward communications must be channelled through one's immediate superior; links in the chain must not be skipped.

A note of caution

These principles, precisely because they are general principles, cannot be applied immediately and directly in the workplace, nor without consideration of the particular situation.

Compliance with these principles is neither a necessary nor sufficient condition for successful management. Rigorous obedience to them will not ensure the health of your organization, nor will disregarding them automatically condemn your organization to failure. Look critically, however, at those areas of the operation where management is not as effective as it should be. You will probably discover that some of these principles are being ignored, or are being incorrectly or incompletely applied.

Two, the unity of command, and integrity of command, merit special comment. It would seem that vigorous, consistent application of these would result in severe restrictions being placed upon operations, that I am advocating a management style straight out of Theory X. We have already discussed how you must consider each situation and the readiness levels of both the manager and the managed. Your approach might contain elements from anywhere in the spectrum ranging from pure Theory X to pure Theory Y:

- For the present you must consider that the readiness levels of most individuals in your organization require a relatively more strict compliance with the principles we have discussed here. This means that you and the entire team should probably operate, if perhaps only a little, toward the Theory X end of the spectrum.
- As you move into the future, as you and all the people in the organization become more comfortable with new ways of operating the business, as the readiness level for every individual changes it will be not only possible but essential that you shift your management style towards the Theory Y end of the spectrum.

A Theory X approach to management will not yield the flexibility and responsiveness that are crucial to the success of customer service, quality and cost management processes we discussed in the last three chapters. On the other hand, to move too quickly to a pure Theory Y approach before either you are anybody else on the team, whether staff or manager, is ready will not work.

It is really a matter of degree, a matter of judgement. It is, finally, what management is all about. It is about looking at a situation, evaluating it, recognizing that things are not going according to plan, identifying some options, then implementing the selected option based on your judgement as a manager as to what will be most effective. You are faced with the triple challenge of exercising a level of control appropriate to confirm that things happen as they should, while simultaneously taking assertive action to remove obstacles from the paths of people as they strive to achieve objectives, while allowing them ultimate freedom, flexibility and opportunities for creativity and innovation as they go about their work. Is it any wonder that being a good manager is difficult?

The Tactical Management model

The Tactical Management model is defined by the entire content of this book. It is not necessary, therefore, to provide you with another long list of elements. There are, however, several principles in addition to those already discussed that I want to offer as components central to *Tactical Management*.

The principle of unity of decisions

For every situation and every decision, one individual must be responsible for making that decision. That person and everybody else in the organization must know who that person is.

Somebody has to be in charge. This is presented as a principle because, especially in recent years, managers have attempted to change the organization to make it more responsive to changing requirements. They have tried to shift toward a more Theory Y approach and as this happens the identity of the decision maker or the person in charge has been lost. This happens when attempts are made to make the organization more democratic. Managers try to involve more people at more levels in decision-making processes and to provide more people with the opportunity to contribute to processes for improving customer service, quality, cost management and methods and procedures. The result, often, is decision by consensus – that is, *no* decision, leading to lack of effective control and under-utilization of resources. All of these ultimately result in poor customer service and quality, and higher than necessary costs. This has contributed to the observed discrepancy between the Theory Y theory and Theory X practice we discussed earlier. When Theory Y effort failed because of poorly judged readiness levels, managers compensated by applying a generous measure of Theory X. Neither committees, task teams nor workteams make decisions: individual people make decisions.

The principle of immediate response to performance

Management responses to the performance of every individual, whether staff or manager, good or poor, must follow immediately and focus directly on that performance. This is an important element of effective management action.[19]

If management action is to be effective, it must follow immediately and directly on the recognition that some action is necessary. This is particularly true for the management of that most precious of resources: people. When you recognize that either compliance or performance is at variance with the plan, it must be addressed – immediately and effectively. It is even more important that positive management action in response to compliance, performance, creativity and innovation beyond that required by plan or objectives is positively recognized: it is usually ignored. It must be celebrated and rewarded with enthusiasm at least of the scale of the denigration awarded to poor performance.[20]

The principle of work groups and teams as a basis for the organization

Most work should be organized on the basis of work groups and teams, rather than as linear processes or discrete activities. This is true for the principle work of the organization and for special assignments.[21]

Future competitive standards for customer service, quality and effective cost management will not be achieved unless the organization can deal very, very quickly with changing conditions, both inside and outside the organization. When the cycle time for new product development in your industry has been cut to one-quarter of what it is now, you must have a structure and culture in place to address this. When individual customer orders are one-quarter of present volume and order frequency has increased by a factor of four, your organization must be capable of responding competitively. If this evolution is to be successful, each individual must have full access to processes for creativity and innovation, communications channels and decision-making processes. Every individual in the organization must own responsibility for every organization goal. On the objective level this supports effective utilization of resources, and on a subjective level it supports efforts toward increasing job satisfaction.[22]

The traditional group of senior managers, wherein each individual was responsible for his or her own function will not succeed. Every manager must be part of a culture where every problem confronted by the organization is owned by the entire team. There will be no such thing as his problem or her problem, they will both be our problems. On the traditional assembly line, after you finished your step in the process and passed the product on to the next work station, your responsibility for the job was complete. If there was a problem down the line it was not perceived to be your problem even if your action caused it. Success will not be achieved unless everybody on the production line accepts, without qualification, that they are all members of a team that acknowledges any problem anywhere on the line as belonging to all of them.

Your management model

The accumulation of a useful body of management theory is a nebulous process. Throughout this book my objective is to offer you a number of tools I think will be effective for you in the workplace. My premise is that if you can consistently achieve daily, short term objectives you will be more likely to achieve long-range organization objectives. In my judgement this chapter is probably the most difficult of the entire book in this respect. Again, what is happening is that you are taking another step in the development of your own management model. Here, probably more than at any other point in this book, I must remind you to examine critically what I have said, what all the other authors referred to here have said; do a great deal of thinking about it within the framework of your own experience, then make up your own mind whether it makes sense or not. If it does not, make whatever changes you feel are necessary. Remember also that it is continually changing. What makes sense and is useful to you today will not necessary be useful to you in the organization in which you find yourself working five years from now, even if that organization has the same name as today. This is particularly true for these issues of management theory.

Notes

1 By this time you should be comfortable with the recurring comment: 'Review the notes from your tour'.

2 I use the terms subordinate, peer and superior with reluctance and then only for brevity. Subordinate and superior imply a division of people into categories of us and them. Peer sounds like something from a social worker's repertory. When I use these terms it is simply to indicate relationships within the formal organization or reflect reporting lines or channels of authority.

3 In Chapter 6 and especially in Chapter 27 we will emphasize changes to the organization that initially blur the distinctions between superior, peer and subordinate, and finally render them almost meaningless.

4 Michael Rose, *Industrial Behaviour: Theoretical Development Since Taylor.* (London: Penguin, 1978.) Rose's treatment of the evolution of management theory in this century is lucid and helpful.

5 Limited attempts to apply principles of scientific management to operations other than manufacturing were not generally successful for a number of reasons. No references to those efforts are included here.

6 This is admittedly a generalization, but reasonably accurate in the context of this discussion.

7 James L. Bowditch and Anthony F. Buono, *A Primer on Organizational Behavior*, 2nd Edn. (New York: John Wiley & Sons; 1990.) Bowditch and Buono's treatment of a number of management models is useful.

8 Douglas McGregor, *The Human Side of Enterprise.* (New York: McGraw-Hill, 1960.) McGregor introduced us to Theory X-Theory Y with this book. The theories are quoted verbatim and were used with the permission of the publisher.

9 In Chapter 6 we consider this a fundamental need for your organization for the future.

10 Paul Hersey and Kenneth H. Blanchard, *Management of Organizational Behavior*, 5th Edn. (London: Prentice-Hall International; 1988.) Hersey and Blanchard describe their management model as situational leadership.

11 *ibid.*, Readiness level is also a term developed by Hersey and Blanchard.

12 This issue will be examined in more detail in Chapter 11 when we discuss communications.

13 This issue will be examined in more detail in Chapter 10 when we discuss decision-making.

14 Chapter 20 discusses the implications of responsibility for achievement of objectives.

15 Dealing with exceptions is an important element of every effective operating system. This will be discussed in detail in Chapter 17.
16 Peter F. Drucker, *Managing For Results*. (Oxford: Heinemann, 1989.) Drucker articulated the importance of the difference between the right thing to do and a thing done right in the 1964 publication of this book.
17 In Chapter 10 this potentially serious impediment to effective operations will be examined in detail.
18 In Chapter 6 we will consider an appropriate span of control as a fundamental requirement for your organization for the future.
19 See Chapter 7.
20 In Chapter 6 we consider this as a fundamental requirement for your organization for the future.
21 There are a few exceptions which we can ignore for this discussion.
22 In Chapter 6 we will examine this fundamental requirement for your organization for the future in detail. We also examine task teams in Chapter 14 and workteams in Chapter 15. This change process has already begun in a number of healthy organizations and is well advanced in a few excellent companies.

An Organization for the Future: Catch-22

There was only one catch and that was Catch-22, . . . Orr would be crazy to fly more missions and sane if he didn't, . . . If he flew them he was crazy and didn't have to; but if he didn't want to he was sane and had to.

Joseph Heller
Catch-22

Simultaneous Loose-Tight Properties

Tom Peters and Robert H. Waterman, Jr.
In Search of Excellence

Catch-22

Business organizations must change dramatically in a number of ways if they are going to be successful in the immediate future and into the next century. This hpotheses is important to the Tactical Management model. Until now a number of references have been made to this, but we have not discussed it in any detail. My predictions for the design for an effective organization for the future are a convenient way to conclude Part One and prepare you for Part Two.

We need to contemplate an organization that will enhance the health of your business in a climate of increasingly rapid change. The organization must be amenable to that rapid change and at the same time be capable of conforming to some very strict tactical requirements. Successfully addressing both these demands is crucial to long-term health. You are faced with a dilemma that is easy to describe and difficult to resolve. Within the range of decisions you will need to make and the actions you will need to take there will be a large number that contradict each other and appear at times to be mutually exclusive:

- *Loose:* The organization must be flexible and responsive enough in this challenging new world to survive and to grow. The entire team – every executive, manager, and especially every staff member must be positively and assertively entrusted with endless opportunities to be adaptable and creative in the conduct of all activities. They must all be able to make contributions to decision-making processes. A culture in which there is one best way to do anything must be replaced by a commitment to one of continual improvement. You must support measures to confirm that every individual has access to these opportunities and utilizes them vigorously and routinely in the course of daily work.[1] You must agree this process and make that commitment to them. These efforts are based on a management style that is a paradigm of Theory Y.

- *Tight:* Objectives must be developed to support competitive commitments to customer service, quality and cost management practices. Consistent with our discussions in Chapters 2, 3 and 4, processes to meet these objectives have to be based on strict compliance with detailed standards. There must also be a mandate for accurate, timely, complete, open and honest communications throughout the organization. Deviations from these very narrowly defined, structured, ordered paths must be corrected immediately and effectively. If these objectives are to be achieved and if further results for these and similar processes are to be predictable with reasonable confidence, formal, comprehensive and consistent standards and procedures must be established to control these efforts. Procedures must be published and accessible, and everybody in the organization must agree them, commit to them and comply with them without exception. Mechanisms must also be established to keep them current, with revisions distributed immediately to all users. Resources must be allocated to ensure that everybody in the organization is fully trained in their use. These efforts are based on a management style that is the epitome of Theory X.

This dilemma will not be resolved. For the future, a never-ending sequence of decisions and actions to support these two contradictory demands will require an increasing proportion of every successful manager's work effort at the tactical level.

The organization as a system[2]

Organization theory can be as intricate and obscure as management theory. Most of my remarks in Chapter 5 concerning reading material and references are applicable, the difference here is that there are fewer of them. The literature is probably less extensive because organization theory is a newer formal discipline. The range of material available to you is just as wide and there is considerable overlap with management theory, particularly in recent writings. There is some diversity of opinions on what topics or issues organization theory should embrace.

Also consistent with my remarks in Chapter 5, we can achieve our objectives here without a treatment that attempts to be exhaustive either in breadth or depth. Again, it does not have to be too complicated. This presentation is different from Chapter 5 in one important respect. This chapter consists almost entirely of my predictions; my forecast of what the organization of the future should look like to succeed in the challenging environment of the late 1990s and into the twenty-first century.

Most issues pertaining to the concept of organization or an organization, certainly for a business organization, relate to good communications, as was the case with management theory. You are a participant in a body that at strategic or highest levels has been created and is maintained to deliver a primary or long-range objective. That may be a return on investment to an owner or number of owners, to defend the nation against all foreign enemies, to help children learn about the world they live in or provide a range of services to council residents. As you improve your ability to communicate expectations accurately to people in the organization, you increase the likelihood that objectives will be achieved. At the tactical level you are responsible for creating and maintaining a series of sub-organizations or unit organizations within the principal organization that will be capable of facilitating the delivery of that primary objective.[3] Unit organizations are established to provide mechanisms that ensure that things get done to move the organization continually closer and closer to long-range objectives. A significant part of that effort is support for effective communications.

When we refer to an organization as a system, we are talking about an entity that can be defined either by its structure or function. I might describe a system for you using a structural definition – by telling you what it looks like; or I might describe it functionally – by telling you how it works. If I were to describe a carburettor structurally, you would know what one looks like, but it would not help if you were trying to understand how it contributes to the workings of the internal combustion engine. For that you need a functional description. I might explain how air and liquid are drawn into the device by vacuum and are converted into petrol vapour that is made available to the engine for combustion. In system terminology I would be describing system function in terms of inputs, processes and outputs. You would have no idea what it looked like but the explanation would help you understand how the engine works. For most real world systems you need both structural and functional definition and this is eminently true when studying organizations.

Part of your job is to identify needs and design organizations to meet those needs. At the highest level objectives are ordinarily determined and the principal organization is created by a governing body such as a board or group of owners supported by a team of executives and senior managers. We are not concerned here with the creation of the principal organization; those efforts are usually defined as issues of strategy. We are interested in the structure and function of the sub or unit organizations that make up the primary organization. To create a new organization or revise an existing one you need to go through a series of ordered steps. You must:

1 identify outputs; specify what the organization is expected to achieve – what we describe as targets, aims or goals, but usually as objectives;
2 specify inputs – what you need to put into the organization to arrive at planned outputs or objectives;
3 specify processes to enable the organization to convert the inputs into outputs; and
4 develop structures to maintain the processes.

The first relates to function: what is it we want the organization to do? The second and third also relate to function: how do we expect the organization to do it? The fourth addresses structure: what do we want the organization to look like to function as we have proposed?

A thoughtful reading of this section suggests that function must be the first consideration. You must always begin the design effort by asking what you expect the organization to accomplish in the end. Once outputs or objectives have been determined, you can make decisions on inputs and processes. When this has been done, identifying a structure to accomplish this should be fairly straightforward. Your priorities are for process design, then structure should follow.

Realize, however, that the real world of the workplace can never be quite as tidy as I have presented it here. Inputs, outputs, processes, functions and structures are all wrapped up with one another throughout every organization design effort. They do not necessarily follow each other linearly. This statement is as applicable to the most ambitious primary organization as it is for the most modest unit organization. A slight shift in planned outputs can easily result in the need for major changes in processes or structure. For example, an environmental requirement to reduce pollution levels modestly may mandate that an entire production line is redesigned. A minor process change can make it necessary to revise inputs and structure drastically. The change of an admin activity to meet the requirements of a computerized accounting system can result in the demand for substantial revisions to job content, staff training and formal department organization structure. The entire process is very dynamic; no organization is static. As needs change, so must the organization. You must identify those changing needs and adjust both the function and structure to ensure the organization will be able to cope effectively. Following from my premise that needs are continually changing is that organization function and structure must also continually change.

An organization for the future

The problem facing you with rgard to the organization is not that you must manage change, but that the change will continue at an ever increasing pace. The organization that worked well enough in the past is probably not working very well now and will not work at all in the future. Because functions must change to meet the new needs, structures must change to support these new functions. The key attributes of the new organization at the tactical level must be rapid and flexible responses to changing customer requirements and the management of quality. Next in importance are mechanisms to deal with cost management issues effectively. These demand rapid and flexible responses by every part of the organization – every sub and unit organization. In addition to meeting customers' and cost management needs, there are two other important requirements. The organization must deal effectively with a chaotic environment and it must adapt to the changing needs of all of the people involved.

In Chapters 2, 3 and 4 we examined the management of customer service and quality, your relationship with customers, the issues you must manage well to keep them happy and cost management practices. There is no need to elaborate on matters raised in those three chapters. The other two, however, merit a closer look.

The environment

The organization has traditionally been pictured as having a nice, neat boundary, usually shown in diagrams as a solid black line encircling the system. This line was supposed to separate the internal environment – the organization, from the rest of the world – the external environment. For the future there can be no tidy partition between internal and external environments suggested by a bold line. There is only one environment and it exists both inside and outside the organization. Your design effort must account for this. In the past that line was perceived as a barrier, something protecting you and the organization; you could withdraw behind it and do things in your own way with little consideration for the way things were done outside, so long as ultimately you achieved objectives.

This was never a very good model. There is no bold, black line protecting you from the world outside. One example should be helpful:

Example

When you, your customers and suppliers were all working with manual, paper-based order entry systems, compatibility was not too much of a problem. What you did within the organization did not demand a really close liaison with those outside. Perhaps then it was possible to think in a limited fashion about internal and external environments. Later you and the others converted to free-standing mainframe or mini mainframe systems. Part of that process was to examine compatibility amongst systems as support for more effective communications. Then you were forecasting a life expectancy for mainframe systems of perhaps fifteen to twenty years. The distinction between internal and external environments was becoming blurred as you tried to design systems that not only met your needs but were convenient for customers and suppliers to use. Now you are contemplating linking your organization directly to customers and suppliers on line and in real time with either mainframes communicating through EDIs (Electronic Data Interchange systems) or fully integrated networked PCs. You are thinking of life expectancies for systems in terms of years rather than tens of years. Software life is measured in months rather than years. There is a requirement for systems that are totally compatible. Trying to separate the world into internal and external environments is meaningless under these circumstances.

If you are involved in the manufacture of a consumer product you are probably already aware of this single, ever more intrusive environment as product liability assumes more and more prominence as an element of organization responsibility. Accounting services now accept responsibility for the accuracy of audit reports, for example, but are also to accept responsibility for the implications of information that is deliberately *not* included in those reports. If some of the outputs of your operations are unusable waste products, the global impact of pollution has become part of the environment in which you must operate. Concern for the effect of the total environment on your organization and the effect of your organization on the total environment will assume greater importance for you and your team when you are looking at design changes in the coming years.

The people who comprise the organization

The organization consists of people – without them there is no organization. A good model for the future must include as material participants in the organization a group much wider than just employees and shareholders. In recent years this has been addressed by introducing the concept of a stakeholder. A stakeholder is any person affected by the way the organization functions. Stakeholders include employees, shareholders and customers, consumers (if different from customers), suppliers, people living nearby the facility and the newsagent outside the main gate whose livelihood depends on trade from people in the facility.[4] A full understanding of this principle also includes consideration of how the often conflicting needs of various stakeholders should be reconciled.

If you shift your perception from employees and shareholders to the much wider group of stakeholders, two important things happen:

1 The principle of one environment is reinforced. For example, if you consider where customers and suppliers should be placed in this scheme, the division into internal and external environments becomes meaningless.
2 A more mature model emerges with regard to the management of people in the organization. You become more aware of the difficulties when prioritizing the needs of all stakeholders. If you read through the business section of any current newspaper you are likely to find at least one article that reports the problem an executive or senior manager is having 'balancing the demands of the workforce with those of shareholders'. Effective organization design must take into account the needs of all stakeholders. One of the ways our world is changing dramatically is through an increasing awareness by almost everybody of what is happening to other people. This is a result of the impact of television on our lives, and changes in the ways we process and manage information. In the business world there is an almost universal increased competitiveness in a truly global economy. The results are that stakeholders are demanding more and more. This list is not complete, you can think of dozens more examples:
   (a) Staff want not only more pay and benefits but also more of a say in what happens to them in the workplace:
      i. to be consulted before a facility is relocated or
      ii. to be consulted before a major change in shift patterns is implemented;
   (b) first-line managers want more input into budgeting processes and matters of strategy;
   (c) shareholders want more and quicker returns on their investments;
   (d) the City want more impressive quarterly results;
   (e) professional business organizations and societies want you to invest more in staff training;
   (f) customers want more products and product variations with faster deliveries and at higher quality standards;
   (g) customers also want dramatically shorter product development cycles;
   (h) people living near the factory want reduced lorry traffic and lower pollution levels;
   (i) what people living near the factory really want is for the lorries and pollution to be moved elsewhere – at least 200 miles away;
   (j) consumer protection agencies and consumers want higher standards of product reliability;

(k) advertising standards agencies want the content of advertisements to reflect product or service performance more accurately; or
(l) The Government want higher safety standards and fewer occurrences of accidents.

Again, the old model never did work very well, but because things moved more slowly and communications were neither as graphic, as rapid or as ubiquitous, it appeared to work after a fashion. It will not work in the future. From now you must consider the needs, frequently expressed as demands, of all stakeholders. Your job is not only to consider all these needs, but to address the dilemmas resulting from efforts to reconcile them.

There is also an issue that addresses employees as one particular group of stakeholders and their role in the leaner organization of the future. This discussion includes everybody employed by the organization – staff, supervisors, managers and executives. Much effort is currently directed toward change relating to something variously called rightsizing, downsizing or rationalization. These three all mean the same thing: they are euphemisms for masses of redundancies and a demand that those remaining do at least all the work done previously by the larger group and probably more. Within some models apparently the only people capable of surviving, let alone thriving, in this brave new world are a minority of super-achievers. There seem to be no places for people of average ability. Think about this:

- An organization made up wholly of super-achievers is not likely to be successful in the long term. There is evidence from the workplace to suggest it is not effective even for the short term.[5]
- The world is made up of a large number of us ordinary people and only a few superachievers. There are not enough super-achievers to go around. You will thus have to staff your operation with a number of people of average ability if you are going to fill enough places to complete all the work.
- Working for very long with a group made up entirely of super-achievers is not much fun. In my experience, they generally tend to take themselves very seriously and they are impatient with the rest of the world. They make most of us very uncomfortable – and often themselves in the process. They tend to have difficulty communicating effectively with others in the organization who are not part of their immediate group.
- Raising the expectations of everybody in the organization, then leading them through the attainment of those higher expectations, is an exciting prospect for the manager of the future. Indeed, within some models this is the difference between management and leadership.

In the design of your organization you must make places for ordinary people. You will need them anyhow, and the workplace will be much more pleasant.[6]

With this preliminary work complete, we are now ready to present the twenty-four characteristics of an organization for the future based on the Tactical Management model. Some of these have been examined in the first five chapters, and thus there is no need for elaboration. A number of others are the subjects of entire chapters later in the book, and for those there is also no need for detailed discussion. In that sense, then, and certainly at the tactical level, this entire book is a prescription for the new organization.

Functional organization requirements

Throughout the new organization there must be:

1. Clearly defined tactical objectives

Every individual in the organization must have a clear understanding of what it is he or she is supposed to do. Each person – staff, supervisor, manager and executive, must know what his or her work is supposed to achieve, how it fits in with long-range organization objectives and how it supports short-range tactical objectives. Objectives, activity lists, assignments and job descriptions must be formalized, in writing, and agreed by both the assignor and assignee. People must know what is expected of them. This is a paradigm of loose versus tight and it presents you with a juggling act. If objectives and assignments are too delimiting they can be restrictive and interfere with the ability of assignees to complete work effectively. If they are not set out carefully and precisely they cannot accomplish their primary purpose which is to ensure support for organization objectives. You must continually evaluate the success of these processes as you wander around (see number 23 below and Chapter 18). Every expectation and objective must be evaluated according to the readiness levels of both assignor and assignee. Then decisions can be made to determine how detailed the statement of objectives and intensity of follow-up processes should be.

In Part Three we will examine long-range goals for organization health and growth. Later as changes you make begin to yield positive results it will be possible to reduce formality in some areas of task assignment and follow-up. In the perfect organization each person would be able to communicate perfectly with every other, each would fully understand plans, targets, goals and objectives and there would be no need for any written assignments or job descriptions. For now I think you must err on the conservative side. In the short term communicate expectations and objectives in great detail, and ask for concentrated feedback. This is particularly applicable to areas or units that are experiencing problems achieving targets. As readiness levels change and people in the unit demonstrate they are becoming better at meeting objectives, you can begin to communicate expectations with less precision and detail.[7]

2. Clearly defined operational practices and procedures

It is essential that operating practices, procedures and methods are published, readable, current, distributed and available to users. This need is based on the same arguments as in number 1 above. This is crucial to effective processes for all customer service, quality and cost management efforts and was discussed *ad nauseam* in Chapters 2, 3 and 4.

3. A comprehensive, organization-wide emphasis on customer service

This was examined fully in Chapter 2.

4. A comprehensive, organization-wide emphasis on quality

This was discussed in detail in Chapter 3.

5. A comprehensive, organization-wide emphasis on effective cost management

This was explored at length in Chapter 4.

6. Open, honest and complete communications

Open, honest and complete communications in the workplace are not so much a question of ethics as of practicality. If any individual is not provided with complete information it is *impossible* for that person to do a good job. If you deliberately provide partial, dishonest or incomplete information to anybody, that person inevitably receives conflicting signals. The consequences are ineffective or incorrect decisions and actions. The results are poor customer service and quality and high operating costs.

7. Total integrity in the conduct of all activities[8]

One seldom reads any meaningful discussion concerning integrity in the workplace. There is really very little to say on this subject. My strongly held belief is that this matter is so unequivocal that it is a waste of time to consider it in detail. If you want the people who work for you to believe you when you tell them what you expect, they must be able to conclude that what you tell them is, in fact, what you expect. You can never achieve the full potential benefits from a customer service process if you do not treat every customer, always, with total integrity.

8. Recognition of the significance of managing change

In Chapter 1 we discussed the importance of managing cultural change sensitively. Organization function must support a culture that ensures: sufficient involvement for participants during development and evaluation of change, adequate information to those involved during implementation, and ample time for participants to assimilate the change.

9. A comprehensive, organization-wide encouragement for innovation

It is essential that creativity and innovation are integral elements of the activities of each person in the organization, not just those responsible for new processes or new product development – everybody. This is your most valuable source for options and improvements to processes for customer service, quality, cost management, new products, entire new product lines, and improvements to practices, methods and procedures. This is another paradigm of loose versus tight. On one hand you must require that everybody comply in letter and spirit with standards and procedures, and on the other hand you must ask that everybody continually and vigorously seek better ways of doing things – look for better ways to do *everything*.[9]

10. A comprehensive, organization-wide encouragement for taking reasonable risk

The cost of assertive processes for creativity and innovation is risk. If you and the rest of the team are really being innovative you must experience some failures. If you never fail at anything you are not being genuinely innovative. Part of the function of a healthy organization is to achieve a climate where reasonable risk is encouraged, and an occasional failure is celebrated as an acceptable component of positive action. This is easy to talk about but not easy to manage. Failures inevitably increase short-term costs and you may inconvenience a customer, again for the short term. If you know your total costs, the occasional failure in pursuit of better health can be managed effectively. If you are truly close to customers, if they are actively involved with you in the entire customer service process and if you always treat them with integrity they, too, should be willing to absorb the occasional short-term failure with the long-term objective of improved service and quality.

11. An emphasis on appropriate task control mechanisms

The functional design of the organization must include appropriate emphasis on task control. This is important if work is to be managed and future results are to be forecast with confidence. The general principle, which I call short segment task control, involves breaking any task, whether a one-year business plan, a software enhancement, repair to a furnace or a daily production assignment, into manageable chunks – phases. The size of phases depends entirely on the nature of tasks and may range from one week for a software enhancement to two hours for a production assignment.[10] The principle is amenable to all organization work, both for routine tasks and one-off special assignments. It is applicable to the delivery of the primary products or services and to all support activities.

12. A comprehensive, organization-wide emphasis on effective management action

Effective action is the element in the management control cycle that closes the loop. It is the component of management activity that gradually brings the organization closer to ultimate objectives. No matter how effective you are at planning, assigning work, reporting on activities and evaluating results, unless management take appropriate corrective action to eliminate variances, objectives will never be achieved fully. It is the keystone of the Tactical Management model – without it there can be no effective management at the tactical level.[11]

13. An appropriate management approach to each situation

This was examined at length in Chapter 5.

14. Responses to performance that are immediate and focused

This was discussed in detail in Chapter 5.

15. The recognition that we should all try to enjoy our work

This requirement of organization function is not frivolous. It is based on several important considerations:

- Some kinds of work and parts of some jobs are boring. This is as true for the work of the chief executive as it is for those on the production line or those who sit in front of the admin input screen. This fact might as well be recognized so those assigned can get on with it. Supervisors and managers will address it according to requirements of particular jobs, readiness levels and individual management styles. The manager of a large admin department in a major UK bank, for example, requires his entire staff to complete all filing for the area each morning. They make a game of it and an onerous task is completed quickly under pleasant conditions.
- Economic conditions require most of us to work to earn a living. We should accept that fact and say little more about it – it is a condition of life in the real world.
- Recall our discussions in Chapter 1 concerning stability zones, and the requirement of dealing with novelty in the workplace. Consider that boring, repetitive tasks, if properly managed and appropriately assigned, might represent a bit of unchange in the chaos of a changing workplace.
- When linear processes and work formerly completed by staff support people are replaced by work groups and task teams, boring tasks can sometimes be reapportioned in a fashion similar to the filing discussed above (see number 20 below).
- Why should you not enjoy the work you do? There is nothing wrong with feeling good about your job. It makes the time pass quicker and probably aids digestion.[12]

Structural organization requirements

To support these functions, organization structure must be designed upon:

16. A broad, flat formal structure

If the organization is to become more responsive and flexible to deal with changing requirements, this process must begin with the formal organization as reflected by the organization chart. Layers in the organization must be eliminated if communications channels are to be simplified. When layers are eliminated, spans of control necessarily increase. In Chapter 5 we dismissed the five to ten rule as being useless for developing and evaluating structure. The number of levels and spans of control depend completely on the needs of each individual area or unit organization. You should seek over the next two years to achieve an organization with no more than five layers between production operator or admin clerk and chief executive. One year later this should be reduced to four. The span of control can range from one to fifty depending on need and readiness levels.

If this very broad, flat structure is going to work well, it will ultimately be necessary for individuals to routinely take direction from more than one source. My recommendation is that neither you nor your team are ready for that until you have worked under the new organization process for at least one full year.[13]

The structure must support the fifteen functional requirements discussed above. If you look carefully at those fifteen you realize that nearly all function consists finally of the transfer of information. Specifically, the structure must make it possible for information to be transmitted quickly, completely and unambiguously to those who need it. Examine your formal structure to see if it makes sense. This does not require any experience or background in organization development or industrial behaviour. Simply look at the organization chart and ask yourself how it might be revised to improve the flow of information. If what you propose seems reasonable, making the changes will probably result in better communications.

17. Decision-making at the lowest possible level

Decision-making, especially for daily operating decisions, must be made at the lowest level practicable in the organization. This also will increase the speed of response and improve flexibility. If, however, it is not handled with care and consideration for all consequences, the result can be a situation I call the millwright paradox. When this happens an individual can receive conflicting assignments from several sources resulting in the confusion we have already discussed. Decision-making processes must be developed fully and implemented sensitively.[14] The potential for this problem must not deter implementation of this important requirement.

18. Access to the decision-making process by all

If creativity and innovation are to be exploited fully, and ideas emanating from all sources are to be fed into the system so they can be presented for evaluation, every individual in the organization must have access to decision-making processes (see number 9 above). Understand that this is not the same thing as saying that decision-making should be by consensus.[15]

19. Clearly identified decision-makers

If decision-making is going to meet all organization needs two conditions must obtain:

- Decision-makers must be identified and recognized throughout the organization. Both the decision-maker and everybody else in the organization must be aware of who the decision-maker is, their sphere of authority, and that all decisions are final within that sphere. If this represents significant change – if decisions have in the past been made by consensus, it will need to be handled with some care.
- Appropriate structures must be in place to ensure that the decision-maker receives all relevant input. The decision-maker must be in possession of all material information from all applicable sources. Although decisions cannot be made by consensus, they must take into account information provided by everybody on the team (see number 18 above).

20. Groups, task teams and workteams as primary work units

Units responsible for completion of work must be structured as work groups or cells rather than being based upon linear assembly processes. In Chapter 2 we forecast that the customer who in the past placed one large order each month will now place smaller orders weekly for the same total order quantity. The product you supplied for many years in black will now be demanded in a profusion of colours. Production lines, processes and operators must be organized to respond to larger and larger numbers of smaller and smaller batches.[16] It is well beyond the scope of this book to discuss this particular issue in detail but it is included here because it is a necessary consideration for the future. You must review this aspect of your operation to determine whether work units are structured to meet future customer needs or if they must be changed. This is certainly a requirement for every manufacturing operation and I think the need will be at least as great for the delivery of services. This was discussed in Chapter 5.

Staff support groups must be replaced with task teams for the management of projects and special tasks. A task team structure is more effective for addressing many of the issues which in the past were handled by staff departments and middle management experts. Think, for example, about the reorganization of a large operating department. Before, this project would have been managed by a middle manager from the personnel department. The team would have consisted of personnel staff and managers, and technical expertise would have been provided by them. In a fortunate few cases a member of the user department would have been part of the project team. In most cases users would not have been informed until the reorganization was announced just prior to implementation. In the effective organization of the future this project will be managed and staffed by people from the user department. Expert input and technical support will be supplied by one or two team members from the personnel department.

Review your own experience; you can probably remember several projects that did not achieve satisfactory results because teams were staffed with specialists to the exclusion of users. The results were systems that were technically very elegant but either ineffective or inefficient from users' perspectives. Examples include computer systems development projects, particularly enhancements to existing systems, and production process and methods changes.

The important difference is that in the past staff support effort was broadly defined and open ended, whereas in the future the task team assignment will be closely defined and closed ended. Users will be actively involved from beginning to end. The overall result is a more effective and efficient utilization of resources, particularly staff and middle management hours, and systems that more closely meet the needs of users.[17]

21. *Staff as producers of value*

The structure must reinforce the principle that staff are producers: staff are the only people in the organization who convert anything or increase value. Everybody else, all of those whom we identify as management and those who reside in the executive suite, along with consultants and writers of management books, are costs.

22. *Supervisors as key providers of resources*

The structure must emphasize the nature of the supervisor and the importance of this person in the organization. Supervisors are the key to full utilization of all resources, in particular staff hours. The entire management team exists to support supervisors in this effort and the structure must reinforce this concept throughout the organization. Department structure must corroborate that the supervisor's job is not to do the work, not even the tricky bits, the supervisor's job is to see the work is done. In most organizations today this represents a significant change in the perception of the supervisory role.[18]

23. *Managers as providers of support*

The structure must emphasize the nature of managers as providers of support. At the tactical level the contribution of a manager to the health of the organization is support for the production or delivery process – managers themselves produce nothing. Results for the organization are achieved in direct proportion to the manager's positive, assertive and visible involvement and support for the operation.[19]

24. Supervisors and managers as facilitators

The structure must emphasize the functions of supervisors and managers as facilitators. The universal responsibilities of every supervisor and manager are to provide all the things staff need to do the job. They must set ambitious but reasonable targets based on tactical objectives then spend the balance of their time (this should represent most of their time) systematically removing all obstacles that interfere with staff as they attempt to achieve those goals. When they can do this, good customer service will be achieved, compliance with quality standards will be good and staff performance will be high. This is a paradigm of management action (see number 12 above).

Creating the new organization from the present

Creating the new organization is not an event, it is a never-ending process. It will end only when the organization ceases to exist. Think about all the things we have talked about here and in the past five chapters. Review your needs for customer service, quality and cost management. Begin to think about changes to the present organization that will make it more responsive to the new order:

Example

Some time ago I was responsible for the installation of a management operating system in a clerical area that consisted of 32 staff, eight section leaders, four supervisors, two assistant managers and one department manager. My final report included the recommendation that the positions of the two assistant managers be eliminated immediately and they be assigned to positions somewhere else in the organization. They added an unnecessary link to the communications chain, they were a cost that returned nothing for the investment and because they had no real work to do, their professional development was being stifled. It was clear that their removal would have no impact on the operation other than to reduce costs. The response from the department manager's boss, a middle manager was: 'Several years ago the manager was upgraded. After his [deserved] promotion, there existed too large a gap between his grade and the grades of supervisors. Personnel told us we must create the two assistant manager positions to span this gap.'

Spend a little time thinking about this story and how this chapter is applicable to that situation. That department boasted a management team of fifteen people. It required three: two supervisors and the department manager. It had four layers of management, it should have had two. Costs were significantly higher than they should have been. Communications were more complicated than they needed to be. No manager anywhere in the organization took any action to address this obviously absurd situation. Finally, structure was not based on department needs, it was based on what the personnel department told them they must do. The organization structure for an operating department had been designed by a staff support department totally divorced from workplace requirements and with no perceived responsibility for either customer service, quality or cost management.

Ask yourself if anything like this is happening anywhere in your facility. Review the notes from your tour. Use those notes, this story and this entire chapter as the starting point for creation of the new organization. Begin today.

Notes

1 In current vernacular this is described as empowerment.
2 Barnard, *The Functions of the Executive*; op. cit. This examination of organizations is consistent with Barnard's, although I have generalized and simplified parts of his work. This is particularly true for the concept of a sub or unit organization as an element of a larger organization. He presents this in much more detail.
3 It makes no difference whether you are creating a new organization or modifying an existing one. Our discussion is fully applicable in either case.
4 Rosabeth Moss Kanter, *When Giants Learn To Dance*. (London: Unwin 1990.) Kanter is one of a number of authors who examine the importance of the principle of stakeholders to organization development.
5 R. Meredith Belbin, *Management Teams: Why They Succeed or Fail*. (Oxford: Butterworth-Heinemann 1981.) Belbin has conducted experiments that demonstrate that super teams do not consistently achieve super results.
6 Much of Part Two addresses communicating high expectations to everybody in the organization. It turns out that all 'ordinary' people have the ability to achieve much more. Also, in Chapter 27 we will examine the performance of everybody in the organization in the chaotic environment of the future.
7 Peters, *Thriving on Chaos*; op. cit. Peters is one of the more visible of a number of authors who argue that you must eliminate formal organization charts and detailed job descriptions *now* in the interest of flexibility and speed of response. I disagree.
8 In the Coda we will examine business ethics briefly.
9 Managing creativity and innovation will be examined in detail in Chapter 26.
10 Short segment task control will be examined in Chapter 8.
11 Management action will be discussed in Chapter 7.
12 There are a few writers on management who state emphatically that there is no place for fun on the job, that it is unbusinesslike. I submit that these people do not enjoy their work, and therefore see no reason why you should.
13 Relaxing the unity of command principle will be examined in Chapter 27. It is an important requirement for the truly healthy company, but can cause problems if applied prematurely.
14 The millwright paradox will be examined in detail in Chapter 10.

15 The difference between universal input to decisions and decision-making by consensus will be examined in Chapter 10.
16 Nigel R. Greenwood, *Implementing Flexible Manufacturing Systems.* (Basingstoke: Macmillan 1988.) About 10 per cent of the GNP of most industrialized nations is represented by manufacturing batch quantities of 50 or less. Mass production accounts for less than one-half that amount. These figures will continue to shift in the direction of more and more batches of smaller and smaller quantities.
17 Task teams and workteams will be examined in detail in Chapters 14 and 15.
18 In Chapter 9 we will examine this key role of the supervisor.
19 See Chapter 18, Management by Wandering Around.

■ PART TWO ■

The practice

> I don't care if you are running 50 per cent scrap, I promised this order would ship today.
>
> The director of marketing in a manufacturing company giving instructions to a machine operator

This story is true and illustrates succinctly what the practice of Tactical Management is all about. As you read the following example, think about whether anything like this is happening in your organization:

Example

We were working in a manufacturing plant, a fabrication operation, on a project to implement management operating systems. The products were hand tools. The process I want to describe required an operator to assemble a blade and handle. The two parts were put together by hand then secured with rivets set by two strokes of a foot pedal. The metal blades were fabricated in the plant; the wooden handles were purchased. The blades had been inspected and approved for assembly; the handles had not. The operator recognized that about half the handles were bad and thus about 50 per cent of the tools he was producing were going to have to be rejected. He made a decision to stop the job and inform his supervisor.

The director of marketing had promised a customer that an order for 2000 units would be shipped that day. He by-passed production control, quality control, the manufacturing manager, the plant superintendent and the production supervisor. He walked out to the floor and issued his instructions directly to the operator as quoted above.

This situation was uncovered by the production supervisor about half-an-hour later when he and I were making a round on the floor.

Suppose that, instead of continuing to run the job when the bad handles had been identified, it had been stopped and somebody had been assigned to sort them.[1] What would have been the results?

1 Productivity for the operator would have doubled. Producing one good tool would have required two strokes of the pedal rather than four.
2 Machine utilization would have doubled. This may not seem too important for a fifty year old, fully amortized, foot-powered riveting machine. However, exactly the same thing is happening every day with your principal production line or process, the paint line, the mainframe and the free-standing minicomputer system in accounts.[2]
3 The operator would have been working neither faster nor harder to achieve the improved performance.
4 The operator would have completed the job in half the time. Doubling productivity and cutting fabrication time in half are not the same. Improving productivity relates to cost management and resource utilization. Reducing throughput time relates to customer service.
5 The cost of removing bad handles from good blades would have been eliminated.
6 Had the good blades not been attached to bad handles they would have been available immediately for assembly for the next order for this item. The importance of this may not be obvious. Typically a decision is made to purchase more material or use material allocated to another product, re-set the tooling and fabricate more parts rather than rework the bad ones. By that time the subsequent order is late and the whole silly cycle begins again. This is the origin, and a significant although hidden cost, of most of those bins of bad parts you noted on your tour.
7 The total cost to the organization for this change would have been zero.
8 Credibility for the management team would not have suffered. Recall the discussion in the Introduction concerning conflicting messages:

Example

Some time ago I walked up to a ticket counter and asked for a single to somewhere. The man behind the counter informed me that a return ticket would save me money. I replied that I was not anticipating a return soon.

He said: 'No, you don't understand. A single will cost you £3.60, a return will cost you £3.00'.

I commented: 'That doesn't make any sense at all'.

He responded: 'I know. They pay somebody in London £40,000 a year to think up things like this'.

Put yourself in the place of the operator. How seriously would you take the next solemn pronouncement from the director of marketing on the company's latest new and exciting customer service and quality programme?

Lest you feel none of this factory talk applies to your admin centre, look closely at the processes by which that operation is controlled. Examine the ways you create, process, batch, input and release to system the claims, vouchers, payments, advices, invoices and whatever you deal with in that unit. You will find exactly the same thing occurring. There is a mad dash to get those items processed and input to the system today, or this week or this month, regardless of the number of errors, so value is not lost. If you calculate total costs, you discover opportunities for improvements in productivity and reductions in throughput time in admin that are as least as great as in production operations, often much greater.[3]

The practice of Tactical Management consists of taking effective management action to eliminate situations such as the one discussed here from your operations and providing a culture that ensures they do not recur. As you do this, customer service and quality are improved and costs are reduced. The organization is healthier and this leads to excellence. The likelihood that long-range objectives will be achieved is increased. Part Two is all about that practice.

Notes

1 If effective quality processes had been in place the problem would not have occurred. The bad handles would not have left the receiving dock; or, even better, they would not have left the supplier's shipping dock. Review Chapter 3.
2 Review the notes from your tour.
3 I know of one UK company that is sitting on £500,000 in unmatched/unposted credits, all due to preparation or input errors. Some of those entries are four years old.

■ CHAPTER 7 ■

Management Action: The tactical closed-loop management cycle

Health attends the man who acts,
Wisdom guides him, Hope frees him, Joy helps him,
Power moves him, Progress marks him,
Fame follows him, Wealth rewards him, Love chooses him,
Fate obeys him, God blesses him,
Immortality crowns him.

Edward Earle Purinton
The Triumph of the Man Who Acts

To be both a speaker of words and a doer of deeds.

Homer
The Iliad

Management in an imperfect world

If the world were perfect, much of the work of managers would be straightforward. Most of your energies would go toward defining long-term strategic goals, developing business plans, converting these into short-term operational objectives and communicating them to other members of the team. Then you could retire to a beach in Tenerife with your salary cheques deposited, no doubt, in a bank in Barbados.

This is not a perfect world; after plans have been communicated to those responsible for completing the work, managers still have a great deal to do. In Part One we discussed some of the principles that comprise the Tactical Management model, all based on a fundamental thesis that you are more likely to achieve long-range organization objectives if you systematically meet a continuous sequence of sometimes prosaic short-range goals. Even in a perfect world this thesis would be useful. In the real world, however, problems of all sorts interfere routinely with the successful completion of work – according to specification, on schedule and within budget. Various things regularly disrupt the accomplishment of objectives, even when those objectives are based on thoughtfully constructed plans developed around reasonably accurate, timely and complete information. Tactically, managers are responsible for eliminating these problems and disruptions, and seeing they do not recur. For the real world of the workplace we need to expand the model to include formal mechanisms for addressing these problems. We need two more elements. First we need processes to identify and quantify operating problems. Second, and more importantly, we need processes to develop and implement actions to eliminate the problems effectively. In the Introduction we examined the issue briefly and said the components selected should enable us to create a closed-loop management cycle. We are considering two issues that are intimately linked: the concept of a closed-loop management cycle and a mechanism to close the loop. That mechanism is management action.

The tactical closed-loop management cycle[1]

Through your reading, during seminars you have attended and in discussions with your colleagues you have encountered a number of functional definitions for manager and management. You have considered a number of these descriptions – they are all similar and they all have one thing in common: they are linear. Examples of the responsibilities of a manager are shown in figure 7.1.

These prescriptions for management practice, because of their linearity, are not complete. What happens if the results of reporting processes in the first example reveal that plans have not been completed successfully? On the basis of our definition of control, what actions should be taken in the second or third examples if operations are deemed to be out of control? How are managers to respond when evaluation efforts in the fourth example suggest that assignment practices have been ineffective? If the model is going to work well in the workplace, it must include means for answering questions such as these. The loop must be closed.

The aim is to make things happen according to plan; when that happens the model is a good one. We are more concerned with the function of the complete cycle than we are with the specifications of individual components. Whether you choose to identify a specific element for control, as in two of the examples above, or whether you elect as we have done to define control as the ultimate aim of the complete process is a matter of personal choice. Tactical Management includes these elements in a closed-loop management cycle:[2]

Figure 7.1 Examples of the responsibilities of a manager

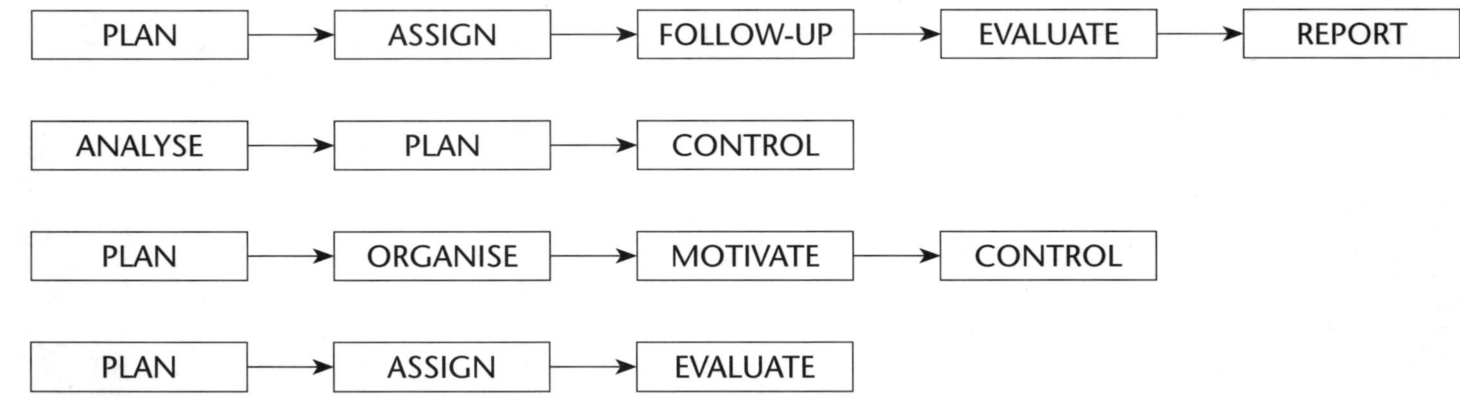

Figure 7.2 The tactical closed-loop management cycle

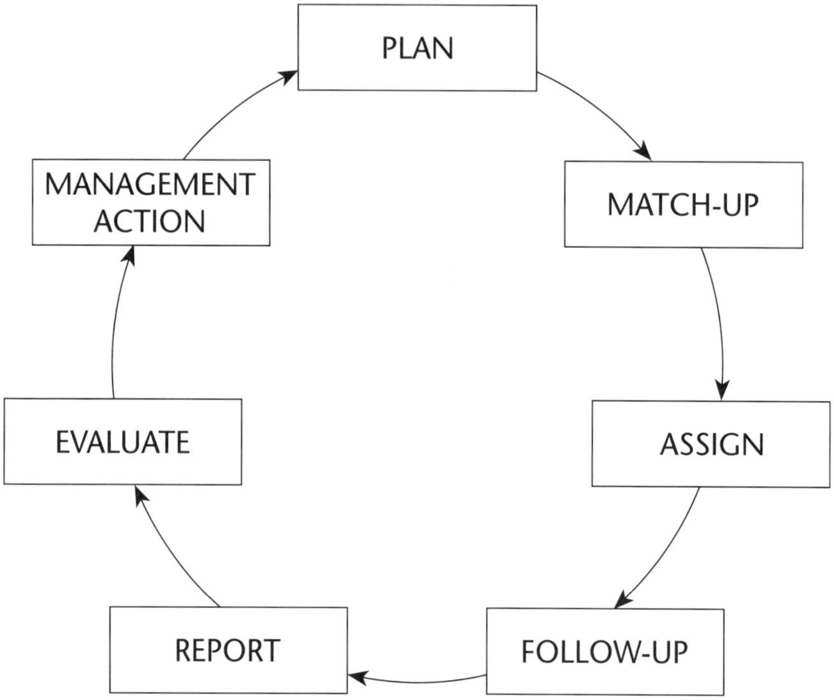

PLAN → MATCH-UP → ASSIGN → FOLLOW-UP → REPORT → EVALUATE → MANAGEMENT ACTION → PLAN

Plan

In the Introduction I described Tactical Management as encompassing all management decisions and actions that follow planning processes. The model is not concerned with planning as a specific management practice.[3] It is appropriate, however, to examine planning briefly here, since every management cycle must begin with a plan. This is true whether you are considering the construction of a complete, new manufacturing facility or a one hour work assignment for a two person housekeeping team. It is true whether the cycle is ambitious and formal or modest and informal. One useful definition for planning is that it is: 'the reasonable anticipation of future requirements'. The key word is reasonable. Every plan must be based on a reasonable forecast of what you hope to achieve if you entertain a reasonable hope of achieving it.[4] Several issues emerge from this definition.

- Two types of data are necessary:
  (a) those that define the plan – that specify what is to be accomplished; and

(b) those that define resources necessary to achieve the objective – commonly termed base data or standard data. These include materials, equipment availability and capacity, supplies, labour hours, time and information.[5] It must be possible to confirm from an examination of base data and the plan that the plan is reasonable: that resources are available and those resources are capable of accomplishing the required results.

- The plan must be expressed so that during the time work is being done it is easy to look at actual progress and compare results to the plan to determine if work is on schedule or if some variance has occurred.
- The plan must be flexible enough for adjustments to be made when a negative variance occurs. That is, if during the time work is being completed something has happened to interfere with its successful completion. For example:
  (a) a problem such as equipment breakdown or lack of correct material has caused the process to fall behind schedule;
  (b) the volume of work planned was not identified accurately because of inadequate or incorrect information; or
  (c) something outside your control such as a customer's changing a specification has caused a change in requirements.

In Chapter 8 we will examine a principle closely related to these planning requirements and the tactical closed-loop management cycle: short segment task control. When an ambitious activity is broken down into small, manageable chunks, what I call phases, the process is easier to control. When a big plan is broken down into a series of little plans, stating the objective, monitoring progress, identifying variances, quantifying these variances and taking effective management action to close the loop are all less demanding activities. The problems you face are easier to address because they are smaller. A crucial step in planning processes is to identify intervals of control appropriate to the work. Determining suitable intervals of control will be examined in the next chapter.

Match-up

The activity of match-up is the effort by which you first identify specific resources needed to complete the cycle, then commit those resources to the process. In Chapters 2 and 3 we said that an important element of effective quality management is the confirmation that you are capable of delivering a product before a commitment is made to the customer. In Chapter 4 we discussed identifying total process costs as contributing to good cost management practice. Both these activities are inseparable parts of the match-up process. Match-up as a discrete element in the management cycle is important because it is here that the availability of resources is verified and they are committed to a specific activity. If you are responsible for a manufacturing operation, how often have you failed a customer when a production order could not be run because you discovered too late that raw material had been used for another order or that equipment capacity was not available? If you work in a service industry, how often in the past year has service been below standard because labour resources were allocated to other projects and thus were not available? Match-up should be a straightforward process; either the resources are present or they are not. If they are not, do not commit them to *any* process. If the resources are available, commit them to a specific process, but do not then try to commit them somewhere else. This is an excellent example of the application of the criterion of reasonableness to planning. If your commitment to a customer is not based on a confirmed availability of resources but on wishful thinking, then the plan is not reasonable.

Assign[6]

In the assignment process objectives are communicated to those responsible for doing the work. Assignment activity requires that you:

1 Communicate the assignment to those responsible for achieving objectives. This is a process for transmitting expectations and two problems can be encountered. The first is based on the assumption 'They should know that'. What happens is that important information is omitted from assignments. The result is that expectations are not communicated accurately because, they, in fact, do *not* know 'that'; the process fails and it is unlikely that work will be done according to plan. The second problem occurs when assignors send conflicting signals, as we discussed in the Introduction. Assignments must be clear, thorough and unambiguous if work is to be completed according to plan.
2 Confirm the assignment has been understood – what we routinely describe as feedback.
3 Obtain commitments from assignees that they agree the assignment and will complete it according to specification and within the scheduled time. This is not the same as assignees assuring you they understand the assignment. Unless there is a specific commitment to completion it is possible that either it will not be completed at all or will not be completed according to plan. This is where many assignment practices fail.[7]
4 Communicate to assignees the details of follow-up processes. Make them aware of the assignor's schedule for follow-up activity (see Follow-up below).
5 Specify for assignees what actions they must take when any variances to the plan are identified. They must have specific instructions to either communicate variances to the assignor and continue to work,

stop the work, or take actions to address variances themselves. The actions they take will depend on the specific nature of individual assignments and the work to be done, but this process must be an integral part of every assignment.

When you consider assignment activity as we have described it here, you see that it is another example of a closed-loop management cycle. If it is to be successful, every assignment must include all the steps presented here. Specific details will vary according to the particular assignment and the readiness levels of both assignor and assignees, but if any step is omitted, the process is certain to fail. Review the notes from your tour for some specific examples of poor assignment practice resulting from a failure to communicate accurate and complete information to assignees.

Follow-up

Follow-up is the formal element in the management cycle that begins the process of accumulating information that finally drives management action. Follow-up is the process by which the person who implements a plan determines throughout the work sequence and at regular intervals how well objectives are being achieved. Follow-up must be formalized, it must be an integral element of the cycle and the follow-up schedule must be communicated assertively and positively to assignees. In most situations it is useful if assignees are actively involved in developing follow-up schedules. The mechanism for determining how frequently and where within the process evaluation points should occur is determined by the nature of the work.[8]

Follow-up is frequently misunderstood. On the most simplistic level it is perceived as checking up on people or treating them like children and is often seen as aimless interference with people trying to do a job. Follow-up is neither of these. It is a proactive, crucial component of every effective management effort. Without effective follow-up you can obtain no information on progress during any work sequence. All your information is received after work has been completed, when it is too late to take any effective corrective action. Follow-up must be understood to be a proactive, rather than reactive process.

Report

Reporting occurs during follow-up when actual results are compared with plans to determine whether objectives are being achieved and the work is on schedule, or something has interfered. The usual practice is to enter actual results beside planned values within a control mechanism – either on a paper control or into a computer system, then calculate attainment to plan, resources expended, and the details of any variances.

If plans have been developed in sufficient detail and if follow-up has been formalized as an integral element of the cycle, reporting should be a fairly straightforward process. There should be little need for judgement or decision-making: either you are on target or you are not, and if you are not, it should be easy for you to calculate the size of the variance.

Problems can occur in the design of operating reports and the format of reporting information.[9] We mentioned this briefly in Chapter 4 under a discussion of accounting versus operating information. My approach to this issue is that operating reports must be structured so that they are useful to the operating manager, even if this results in some duplication of the information provided to the accountant. The effectiveness of a closed-loop management cycle depends in part on the timeliness of operating information. Good management action follows from good information, and old information is useless in this respect. Reporting processes must provide information in time to resolve problems and adjust the plan so the original objective is delivered according to the original schedule.

Evaluate

Evaluation is not as straightforward as reporting. Planning processes must include mechanisms for reporting results and variances to plan. When a variance has been identified an evaluation must take place. The variance must be investigated to determine how serious it is – how it is going to impact on the achievement of objectives. Evaluation processes must enable you to identify causes. This demands judgement, and sometimes perseverance, if root causes and not symptoms of problems are to be identified. This is crucial to the success of management action. Evaluation is really the beginning of the process for closing the loop. Statements of operating problems and the causes of variances are the results of evaluation, and the results of statements of operating problems and the causes of variances are management actions.

Management action

We can now, finally, define management action:

> Management action is a structured action taken to eliminate an operating problem, usually but not necessarily a recurring problem, which has been identified and quantified as having a negative impact on a process or operation – which has caused a negative variance to occur during efforts to achieve an objective.

If management action is to be effective and close the loop, it must meet certain criteria. Management action must result in a formal action plan that consists of several rigorous steps:

- The problem must be identified – this may not be as obvious as it sounds. You must be certain the problem has been defined in terms of fundamental causes, not in terms of symptoms. If the problem is defined symptomatically, it will occur again and again.
  (a) For example: 'The Post Office is unpredictable. The post arrives at a different time every day, and this causes low productivity amongst my clerical staff'. The Post Office does not cause low productivity; poor scheduling and ineffective work assignment practices cause low productivity.

  It may well be that one of the options considered, and perhaps finally the one chosen, will be to negotiate with the Post Office to commit to a regular delivery schedule. If, however, you state the problem according to this example, you eliminate a number of potential options. If the root cause is poor scheduling, then low productivity will continue even when the post arrives at the same time every day.

  (b) Or: 'Punches keep breaking because our supplier continues to ship us out of spec material. It is often over-gauge and too hard'. The supplier does not cause punches to break, running the wrong material through the tooling causes punches to break.

  Again, if you state the problem as in this example, attention may be directed toward a symptom rather than the cause. One possible option is to install harder (and more expensive) punches. If use of this material always results in bad parts, however, harder punches are not going to accomplish anything more than longer, trouble free runs of bad parts.
- The problem must be quantified – the total cost must be identified. If lack of training has resulted in poor operator performance, well-designed management control systems should enable you to determine exactly what that lack of training is costing you in unproductive staff hours.
- A series of options must be identified. In Chapter 25 we will examine a system for addressing methods changes and in Chapter 26 we will discuss work simplification.[10] These closely related disciplines contribute to the identification of reasonable, viable options to present practices, processes and procedures. The original statement of the problem is important. The problem must be stated in a format that will encourage the creation of many options rather than restrict their number. An important part of the investigation of options is the cost of each. For the example above, the benefit derived from an operator training process in terms of improved performance must be offset with the cost of that training.
- An appropriate action must be selected from the options. This is the point in the process where management action truly begins. If

everything else has been done precisely according to our process but you stop here, the entire effort is a waste of time. This is the time for making a decision and also the time when the spectre of risk appears, the time when you are starting to use information you have developed to predict the future.

- The proposed action must be presented to all those who are involved in implementation, both managers required to support it and those who will actually operate the new process. Every management action demands change. If that change is to an established procedure, some resistance is to be anticipated from those who originated the procedure. If a particular problem has been apparent for a long time, and if in the past you have presented proposals for management action and they have been dismissed, perhaps several times, then you have some selling (or reselling) to do. You ensure a better reception than in the past for the proposal if you state the problem carefully, and if your cost/benefit information is accurate and reasonably complete.
- A commitment must be obtained from the decision-maker, that person in the organization who has first-line responsibility for managing the new process. This is the final step in the presentation to the individual responsible for approval of the action. As with any other sales transaction, unless you ask for the commitment you will not automatically receive it.
- The change must be implemented; the action must be taken. Implementation will receive better and more positive support from those affected by it if, as far as possible, they have all been intimately involved in the process throughout. This step carries even more risk than the selection effort presented above because this is the time when something actually happens in the workplace.
- The new procedure must be evaluated after it has been implemented and in use for a reasonable time. The original statement of the proposal must include objective means for evaluating results.
- All participants must be prepared to make adjustments to the new procedure. If the results of management action never require any adjustment, if no tweaking is ever necessary, then the team are not really trying – they are not being bold enough in their efforts. This should be the most challenging and exciting part of the cycle, and the most rewarding if properly done. If management action is to be truly effective for the long term – if this process is to deliver significant improvements, you and the entire team must be so vigorously and assertively involved that an occasional failure occurs. This is the ultimate test of the effectiveness of management action.
- Finally, each action must result in the organization moving closer to the objective that began that particular management cycle. Reporting and evaluation processes must confirm that the action is improving

control. When management action is totally effective the problem does not recur and the results are measurable with respect to improved attainment to the plan.

Example

Working in a manufacturing facility a few years ago we installed management operating systems that provided information not previously available to managers. Through this effort, production supervisors were able to demonstrate that the cost of not purchasing a pallet jack was £250 per day in material handling labour. The price of a pallet jack then was about £175 (when was the last time you had the opportunity to make a capital purchase with a 0.7 day payback?). For two years supervisors had been asking for two of these units and had been told by the plant superintendent: 'We can't afford them'. Material handling hours were defined as indirect and were not considered as a manufacturing cost. Thus the total cost of not purchasing this resource had never before entered the calculations.

Examine this story within the context of the entire Tactical Management model, and management action and closing the loop as principles of the model. Here the effective management action was not the obvious action of purchasing pallet jacks; that was only the final step. The effective management action, the specific action that made a material difference in daily operations, product throughput time, net labour costs and overall resource utilization was the complete series of positive steps taken by the supervisors, plant superintendent and plant manager to remove an obstacle to good labour utilization and throughput time. This distinction is important. For this improvement in operations to become a reality several critical steps had to take place.

1 The supervisors had to ask the superintendent for the jacks again knowing he had refused this request several times.
2 The superintendent had to reverse a decision he had made and confirmed several times in front of his subordinates.
3 The superintendent had to present to the plant manager a request for a change in his budget mid-way through the budget period.
4 The plant manager had to advise the head office two hundred miles away of his intention to spend money beyond budget.

If it is to be effective, management action must formally include all the steps we have outlined here.

There is one other factor to be considered: the timeliness of management action. The rule is that generally action should be taken immediately a problem or variance is recognized. When the problem is correctly identified and reasonable options are considered it is nearly always the case that the result is a net saving. When a proper analysis is conducted the cost of the improvement is almost always less than the short-term savings resulting from improved utilization of resources. My story is a good example of this. Think also about reductions in throughput time that result in improvements in customer service. When the cycle is managed effectively, the time for management action is now. Because the action frequently represents change – different work schedules for post clerks, revised material purchase specifications or the purchase of a previously rejected pallet jack, there is the anticipated resistance. The result is that actions are sometimes deferred or, too often, totally rejected.

Finally, because you are operating within a loop, as you work through the process you can gradually and continually shorten the cycle. When you shorten the increment of control you reduce the size of the task. When you reduce the size of the task you necessarily lessen the effort needed to control it and decrease the magnitude of proposed changes. This makes the process of evaluation easier, shortens the time span over which you have to manage information and reduces the cost of resources whenever further adjustments are necessary. An added advantage is that as you make the task smaller it is possible to assign it to people in the organization with less experience and less decision-making authority. This, as we discussed in Chapter 6, supports design criteria for the organization of the future.

Do this today

Look around your operation for an opportunity for a modest management action project. Somewhere in the facility somebody has been requesting a piece of equipment for a long, long time. You have turned down the request at least twice. Work through the process as we have described it here; do not omit any of the elements. Identify the total cost in under-utilized resources caused by not having the equipment. Find out what the delay is costing the organization in the next department down the line in the workflow. Determine what the cost is with regard to customer service and quality. A photocopier is a handy subject for this exercise, somebody is always asking for one of those. You can, however, accomplish the same thing with a request for a PC, racks for maintenance stores, a fax machine, a forklift truck or an additional telephone.

Cost out the new equipment. Now calculate the payback period. Is it one year, six months, one month? Or is it, as in my story, one day or less?

Notes

1. I am indebted to Steven Schroeder for this eminently useful characterization of tactical management activity.
2. This cycle is amenable to every level of management activity and all types of actions, but when discussing the tactical closed-loop management cycle here we will address tactical objectives – the support of daily, weekly and monthly operations, and our discussion of management action will also be at that level.
3. Planning at the tactical level be examined in more detail in Chapter 17 as an important part of every management operating system.
4. If you think this is a trivial observation, ask yourself how much of your planning in the past year was not successful because it was based on *unreasonable* expectations.
5. Standard data will be examined in Chapter 17 with particular emphasis on labour hours.
6. Assignment processes will be examined in detail in Chapter 17. We will also discuss assignment practice when examining delegation in Chapter 12 and when setting and achieving objectives in Chapter 20.
7. Obtaining feedback and obtaining a commitment to appropriate action will be examined as part of the Tactical Management communications model in Chapter 11.
8. Follow-up will be discussed in detail in Chapters 8, 11 and 17.
9. Operating reports will be examined in more detail in Chapter 17.
10. Edward de Bono, *The Use of Lateral Thinking*. (London: Penguin, 1967.) De Bono is the inventor of the term lateral thinking. His is one of a number of useful techniques for identifying many options to present practices and procedures.

■ CHAPTER 8 ■

Short Segment Task Control: Making molehills out of mountains

. . . they have succeeded in breaking up solar light into its rays, its elements, and to reconstruct it as a unity . . .

Edmond Duranty, *La Nouvelle Peinture*, 1876 quoted by Robert Katz and Celestine Dars in *The Impressionists In Context*

Question: How do you eat an elephant?
Answer: One bite at a time.

American Vaudeville routine

Introduction

Short segment task control[1] (SSTC) is the application of the principle that if you have a task to accomplish, you break it into small, manageable chunks – phases. The smaller the increment of control, the shorter the segment, the better will be your ability to manage it. This is because any variance to plan, the option identified to address it, the risk inherent in the forecast improvement, the cost of the selected management action and any necessary subsequent adjustment will be correspondingly small. I concluded Chapter 7 with the recommendation that as you work within the tactical closed-loop management cycle you should strive to make the loop smaller and smaller, and as you do, management control of operations will improve.

Short segment task control is applicable to every activity in the organization. In Chapter 17 we will examine this process as it applies to the principal work of the organization. Within this chapter, in addition to discussing the general principles of SSTC, we will examine applications not directly related to production or the primary work of the organization. These include such activities as project management for computer programming and systems development, maintenance and engineering, and special projects, accounting and admin management, sales management, and training for both technical skills and professional growth.

The need for improved control

At the tactical level the tactical closed-loop management cycle will tell you something about where you are and where you have been, but not where you think you would like to go. These actions must be a matter of judgement: you must, finally, make some decisions. No system will prioritize management actions. No process will examine a variety of proposed actions and tell you which it is better to do first and which may be deferred. The difficulty usually lies not in trying to make more things happen, but in working out how to make the right things happen at the right times.

A process that will do more than merely keep track of things is essential. You cannot necessarily reduce the number of actions, or the number of things happening, but if the actions to be taken can be simplified the job will be easier. Action plans must be based on a series of modest, straightforward and relatively small actions taken over time. This concept is important enough to attain the status of the eighth axiom of *Tactical Management*[2] and to merit a full examination in this chapter.

In some parts of the organization the record for consistent achievement of objectives – all work completed according to specification or plan, every time, on schedule and within budget, is typically not that impressive.

- Much of the work for which accounting and admin departments are responsible is produced to a deadline, either weekly, monthly or quarterly. When you look at the utilization of staff resources for those areas you discover a good positive correlation between deadlines and overtime usage. Each time a deadline approaches overtime increases dramatically.
- Examine major maintenance and engineering projects scheduled for completion in the past year. How many exceeded either target completion date or budget? How many exceeded both?
- Review total labour budgets for the entire organization for the past year. If you compare planned and actual staffing levels for full-time, permanent staff it is likely that you appear to have worked closely to budget. Examine, however, total hours used and total labour costs. Total hours and costs, inflated by part-time and temporary staff and overtime contributions, drove actuals well beyond the plan. Remember to include in this calculation the cost of all contract labour and work completed by outside resources that was not originally budgeted as such.
- Think about the success rate for computer systems and programming effort for projects completed on schedule. Calculate hours used against

project forecasts to determine how often actuals exceeded forecasts. Review the backlog of systems enhancements that were not only not completed according to commitments but never even begun.
- Review special projects you have assigned to either teams or individuals for completion in the past year. How many were completed according to your satisfaction and original specifications, on schedule and within budget?

Something is happening between the commitment to an objective, whether it is for a weekly admin deadline or a major engineering project, that is interfering with the ability of people in the organization to deliver what they promised to deliver. What is needed is a better process for controlling task effort.

A form of SSTC is now in use in some areas, although you probably do not call it by that name:

- Sales are forecast for the entire year then converted into monthly targets. The forecast also usually includes provisions to enter monthly actuals against the plan and compare the two. In a retail operation the monthly target may be further broken down into weekly or possibly even daily targets depending on the needs of the operation.
- Production planning may be driven by stock replacement levels or order requirements. In either case, for most operations planned production volumes are at some point converted into shift or hourly production targets. Monitoring of actuals may be upon order completion, but it may also be hourly or by shift for larger order quantities.

The keys to the success of SSTC effort are:

- the total task is clearly specified,
- the increment of control – the size of the chunk is defined and
- control points are identified.

When any one of these three elements is either incompletely developed or missing altogether the process will not work.

Short segment task control is usually not applied effectively in certain parts of the organization. The perception is that control in some areas cannot be as objective as elsewhere because activities are too soft, that is, it not possible to measure either activity content or performance accurately enough to establish detailed plans or monitor actuals, particularly over a short time span:

- Management of departments responsible for accounting functions and admin duties are famous for inadequate short term scheduling practices. As we have said, they are usually bailed out at the last moment by the application of massive doses of overtime:

Question: 'How do you assign work in this department?'
Answer: 'It's in the basket on the corner of the desk'
Question: 'How do individual staff members know how much work you expect them to accomplish today?'
Answer: 'The basket must be cleared by the end of the month'[3]

- Marketing projects are seldom, if ever, subject to detailed scheduling or monitored against interim or key event requirements (the exception to this is if the primary business of your organization is marketing services).
- A significant amount of maintenance work is typically not scheduled. The only difference between this situation and the admin department described above is that here the work requests, when they exist, are piled on the supervisor's desk instead of in a basket. Maintenance project work is sometimes scheduled, but usually without interim or key events specified (unless it is a REALLY BIG project).
- Yearly budgets are developed for some units but not for others, or for departments and sections within those units, and not at the level necessary to make SSTC fully effective.[4]
- Labour requirements are often forecast based on total numbers of full-time staff positions rather than a forecast of hours and total costs (see the comments above).
- Computer systems development and programming tasks are frequently managed under something referred to as a project. It is always given a clever name that suggests a fine level of short interval control. These efforts are not usually, in fact, subject to effective SSTC.
- Sales people are seldom, if ever, scheduled on a SSTC basis, sales people are usually not scheduled at all. Performance is evaluated a long time after the fact, and then only in terms of gross revenues generated, so far *post hoc* that no meaningful level of operational control is possible.
- Your assignment of special projects to teams or individuals within the organization always carries a completion date but seldom any intermediate checkpoints or key event schedules.

The application of short segment task control

Short segment task control is such an obviously useful management tool that little need be said in the way of explanation. There are two reasons why it is seldom used effectively to the benefit of the entire organization:

1 To apply short segment task control the activity must be scheduled on a short interval basis. This means that progress must be measured so you can both forecast and monitor actual results. If it is not clear how an activity is to be measured, or that it can be measured at all, then the applicability of SSTC will not be apparent.

2 The interval of control is purely a matter of judgement, a matter of degree. How much control is enough? How often should you look at actual progress?

Precisely because this is all a matter of judgement, it is not always necessarily obvious that a higher input of management resources – an investment in follow-up effort at more and closer control points – will yield higher immediate, short term improvements in customer service, quality and resource utilization. The suggestion is usually dismissed with 'I don't have time for that', or 'They should know that'.

When these two considerations are addressed it is possible to apply the principle of short segment task control effectively to every activity within the organization.

Every activity is amenable to short segment task control

All activity is measurable and therefore all activity is amenable to SSTC. It is *always* possible to specify an objective for a task, develop a plan, measure work content and define increments of control.[5]

Project management

This discussion addresses computer programming and systems development, maintenance and engineering projects, and special projects you might assign either to an individual or a team.[6] Needs are similar. (In fairness I must acknowledge that in many organizations some of these elements are present some of the time. If SSTC is to be effective, however, *all* the elements must be used *all* the time.)

The problem with managing a project of this nature is that you cannot realistically forecast resource and time requirements simply by looking at overall project objectives, the job is just too complex. To improve the ability to forecast accurately certain steps must be taken.

1 The entire content of the project must be defined. Specific, unambiguous objectives for both overall results and final completion date must be stated.
2 The project must then be phased: the work has to be broken down into discrete, definable increments. Each must have a clear start and finish so that everybody knows when a particular phase began and ended. Otherwise measurement is not possible. Identification of phases should develop logically from project content.
3 Control points must be identified. These are the times within the project when formal follow-up is undertaken to confirm that the phase is on schedule with respect to project specifications, completion dates

and resource utilization. For effect project management, control points within each phase must be established at intervals not greater that weekly. No phase should progress beyond one week without a check.

This element must also include formal identification of the individual responsible for monitoring progress and taking corrective action when a variance is noted.

Only after these formal steps have all occurred can the entire project be scheduled. The more effort put into this element of project management, the more likely it is that the final project will be achieved. Only then, after phases are defined, is it possible to forecast completion dates for each accurately, and only after accurate dates are established for each phase is it possible to forecast the final project completion date and realistic total resource requirements accurately. (You may, of course, reverse this sequence by establishing a scheduled completion date then identifying resources required to meet this final date.)

Accounting and admin management

Examine some of the monthly reports prepared by any accounting unit. Select a report for which source data are accumulated throughout the month. Establish a schedule to require that data are processed on a weekly interval as they are available. Each week has now become a phase: rather than looking at a one month assignment, people in the department are now looking at four, significantly smaller, one week assignments. Now any management action needed to address a variance is much less ambitious. If, for example, a problem has arisen in the second week, it is possible to make an adjustment in the third week, without the application of any overtime, to bring it back on schedule before the fourth week.

A further refinement is to establish a daily phase; if source data are available then it makes sense to process it daily. Now you are working with twenty very tiny phases, the management loop is correspondingly small, and the magnitude of any action needed is much less ambitious and therefore easier to manage.

You make the most effective use of short segment task control in this situation when you process a quarterly or even yearly report with phases of one day duration. This is what you try to do for production planning, why not in accounts?

This process obviously will not work if no data are available until shortly before the report is due. This is a totally different problem requiring another approach. A means must be developed to either level the workload (make procedural changes so that the data are available throughout the month rather than only at the end if this is possible) or co-ordinate work between a number of departments so that peak loads in one area correspond to valleys in another. Staff, supervisors and managers can then be assigned to move from peak to peak across department boundaries.[7]

Sales management

Sales management illustrates the use of short segment task control in a situation where the identification and measurement of results at short intervals are sometimes difficult. Results for a sales effort must be measured, ultimately, on sales generated – on revenues created. Depending on the nature of your particular business, however, the sales person may work for several weeks or even months and make no sales, then close a significant number within a very short time based on effective work done during those apparently unproductive times. In the long term he or she might achieve overall objectives. My argument here is that if the task can be controlled on a short segment basis, the sales person can achieve more.

The key to this can be found in an old routine, that you may be familiar with, developed by an insurance salesman. He calculated his earnings for the year and through a series of estimates arrived at the total number of times he dialled his telephone to generate that income. He divided total earnings by total dials. He now had an earnings value per dial: each time he picked up the telephone and dialled, regardless of whether the line was engaged, the party hung up, he made an appointment, the appointment was kept or whether he sold a policy or not, he generated a calculated portion of his yearly earnings.

Sales effort should be managed on a phase of one quarter day or one half day at most. Lay out a weekly schedule based on four phases per day. You and the sales people must jointly plan, specifically, what they are to be doing during each phase. They may be on the telephone making appointments, calling on established customers, cold calling, on the telephone at the Help Desk, doing administrative work or travelling.

Here the process is no different from the project management effort discussed above. The overall project objective in this case is to sell forecast amounts of specified product within a certain time period. If the sales person is to accomplish this, the project must be broken down into manageable phases and those phases will consist of all the various kinds of activities necessary to accomplish the final objective. Each phase successfully completed, whether it is cold calling or administrative duties, will move them closer to the ultimate objective. If through follow-up it is confirmed that he or she is always doing what is planned, then it is more likely the objective will be achieved.

Training[8]

Training for both technical skills and professional development is an area where it is sometimes difficult to correlate the final objective, improved performance, with the expenditure of resources, the time of both trainees and trainers. This is because improved performance may occur long after the training has taken place. Certainly the measure of an effective training process is that it results in significant improvements in performance long after delivery.

Effective short segment task control for training processes requires a somewhat different approach from that applied to earlier categories of activities we have discussed. There we were able to define a final objective, identify the specific tasks needed to achieve that objective, allocate appropriate resources, then schedule the entire project, phase-by-phase. Completion of phases then became our control intervals. Here, although the principle is the same, we are faced with the need for a somewhat different methodology.

- While we can state the final objective of improved performance it may not be possible to forecast a measurable level of improvement. For training in technical skills this is possible in many cases, but not necessarily for professional development. A significant element of the culture we want to engender using the Tactical Management model is that there are no limits on potential improvement.
- Although we have a final objective and we can identify the specific tasks required to meet that objective, those tasks are not a series of discrete actions that will lead us immediately to it – the tasks themselves are not parts of the result.
- The final objective is often some time away from the actions taken. It is not the case that completion of the last phase of the project results in immediate delivery of the objective.
- The connection between project phases and the final objective is not visible for training processes as it is, for example, with a project to install a new production line. We have no way of evaluating the effectiveness of phase activity during delivery of that phase to enable us to adjust processes or take corrective action to address any variances other than those of failure to deliver on time.

Treat the training process as you would any other special project. Begin by identifying who is to be trained and state, as accurately as possible, the objective for the training. Include measurable improvements in performance if these are part of the objective. Establish the time at which you expect to see results, including forecasts of gradual improvement over time if this is appropriate to the process. Next define the activities necessary to deliver the final objective. These have now become your tasks or phases. Identify resources needed to deliver those phases. These include not only the time of trainers and others such as supervisors and managers, but also training materials such as books, manuals and videos, venues, travel if required, any outside resources, and other needs such as use of a production line for skills training. Now specify the time when you plan to deliver the training.

You now have everything you need to schedule the project based on principles of short segment task control. You have:

1 a specification, a final objective
2 a list of tasks or phases
3 a list of resource requirements and
4 times for both the delivery of phases and the final objective.

Develop a project schedule in full detail as for any other project. Your control points now are at the completion of each task or phase and confirmation that training processes have been delivered to every delegate according to the project schedule. Your further control points are at the delivery of improvements in performance specified as final project objectives. You should monitor these with respect to the forecast time and level of improvement and also according to the project schedule.

While you have no means of monitoring the effectiveness of the delivery of the training during the delivery itself to enable you to take any corrective action to address variances, you can nevertheless support the project on a short interval basis by confirming that tasks are completed according to specification and on time. If all training processes are completed to specification and according to schedule, it is more likely that final project objectives will be achieved to specification and according to schedule.

The interval of control is always a matter of judgement

There is no formula or procedure that will identify the size of the interval or the point of control. This is a matter of judgement and will always require decisions. The content of the individual phases should emerge when you look carefully at the work content.

- The size of the phase depends entirely on the nature of the task, and may range from one week for a major computer programming project to one hour for the production or admin assignment. As a rule, for project assignments an individual phase should not be bigger than the equivalent of the work for one week for one person. The criterion for determining the size of the individual chunk is always manageability: if it seems to make sense it is probably about right.
- Control points must be specified. The exact points at which progress should be monitored must be identified. If phases are short enough, then an appropriate control point might be at phase completion. For

phases that are somewhat longer interim control points should be established. Judgement is always necessary.

In Chapter 7 we discussed how when you shorten the increment of control you reduce the size of the task at hand. Realize, however, that you are faced with another one of those juggling acts that keep complicating this business of management. Every situation must be examined according to its own requirement and a decision made on how big the phases should be, the content of each and precisely where the control points should be. The rule now, at this readiness level, is that you should strive to make the phases small, the intervals short and the control points frequent.

At the same time you should establish processes for review of the size of phases and the interval of control, especially for ongoing tasks such as production, admin operations and maintenance work. As it is demonstrated that the operation is under control, is regularly and consistently achieving objectives, as readiness levels shift in the direction of improved control, then the increment of control may be reduced.[9]

Think about this

In Chapter 6 we discussed an important requirement for the future: to push input to decision-making and creative processes farther down in the organization. In Chapter 7 we noted that as each task is made smaller it is possible to assign it to people in the organization with less experience and less decision-making authority. This enables the organization to gain more and more value from an increasing number of individual members.

Therefore the effort to make task phases smaller and less complex and of shorter duration, and the creation of more frequent control points accomplished two important aims: it results in the better level of operational control achieved with SSTC and it supports one of your long-term objectives for the future: that is, to drive decision-making for operational issues farther down in the organization. The two aims are totally consistent with both short- and long-term objectives.

Do this tomorrow

Identify two areas or departments in the organization that never seem to be able to achieve objectives – according to task specification, on time or within budget (remember that if any single element has not been completed according to specification and according to schedule, the primary objective has not been achieved). Select one department responsible for the delivery of one of the principal products or services of the organization and another responsible for one or another form of service or support. Conduct a thorough analysis of the way objectives are stated, then examine in detail how they are translated into work assignments, how those assignments are followed-up and progress evaluated, and how management actions are taken to address variances.

Develop an action plan for each area based on all the principles and practices discussed here and in Chapter 7. That action plan will consist of a project to revise the way that objectives are stated and the way that all subsequent management activity is directed to the achievement of them. Pay particular attention to the application of the principles of short segment task control, especially the delineation of phases and the identification of control points. Implement the revised processes to run for three months. Note that the objectives themselves are not to change. Indeed, the aim of this exercise is to see how much improvement can be made in the delivery of present targets.

Throughout the three month period you personally should follow-up on the project very closely using your own SSTC process for the effort. Evaluate the effectiveness of these changes. Adjust as needed (remember that if no adjustments are needed you are probably not trying hard enough). You will see a marked improvement in the ability of these two departments to complete tasks according to specification, on time and within budget.

Notes

1 Short segment task control must not be mistaken for a process with a similar name, short interval scheduling (SIS). Classical SIS is short segment task control sometimes taken to extremes. Although SIS is based on sound principles, its application is usually heavily Theory X oriented, cumbersome and ineffective for the attainment of long-range objectives. The positive elements of SIS will be examined in detail in Chapter 17.

2 See the Introduction to Part One.

3 If you think this does not occur in your organization, review the notes from your tour.

4 Recall our discussion in Chapter 4 about the company with retail shops throughout the UK for which the finest level of indirect cost monitoring is by region by quarter. It is *never* possible to identify the costs accrued to any individual retail outlet under any circumstances for any time period; yet each of these shops is deemed to be a cost centre.

5 We will not examine the specific needs of every individual activity and type of work within the organization. A number are presented here and you can easily generalize from these.

6 Project management as a distinct discipline will be examined in more detail in Chapter 14.

7 These processes will be discussed in Chapter 17 within the context of effective scheduling and in Part Three within the context of eliminating interdepartmental boundaries.

8 Training processes for both technical skills and professional development will be examined in detail in Chapter 21.

9 Much of Part Three has to do with reducing elements of overt control as readiness levels shift in the right direction.

What Have You Done For Your Supervisor Today?

The ballad of Ralph Hendershot

I'm right in the middle of this system.

A production supervisor of a manufacturing company during a *discussion about a proposed management operating system*

The role of the supervisor is sometimes describes as 'to control the people'. This is absurd. The role of the supervisor is to control the work; people are perfectly capable of controlling themselves.

Tactical Manager

The key role of the supervisor in the organization

In this chapter we examine the key role of the supervisor in the organization. Recall from Chapter 6 that the supervisor figures prominently in your design for the organization of the future. These needs relate to the staff as producers of value, the supervisor as provider of resources for the staff and the entire management team structured to support the supervisor in that effort. This premise requires a major shift of emphasis concerning supervisory practice.

Traditionally the supervisor was described as the one who communicated the 'needs of management' to the staff – whatever that was supposed to mean.[1] If the supervisor is to be fully effective, management thinking on this issue must change dramatically:

- Your entire body of management practice must reinforce the principle that staff are producers of value – staff are the only people in the organization who convert anything or add value.
- The supervisor is the singular key to effective utilization of all resources, but in particular, people.
- The primary role of every individual manager in the organization must be seen as a provider of support for the supervisor. Achievement of overall

organization objectives will be in direct correlation to each manager's positive, assertive and visible involvement and support for the supervisor.

There is another, closely related consideration: within the traditional organization the supervisor has usually been poorly prepared to perform duties. Because of the lack of real understanding of the function, the supervisor is seldom provided with either the tools or the support to do the job. Expectations of management are frequently never communicated. Even if the organization were not required to change for the future, significant effort would have to be put into altering these long held perceptions. With the changes that are essential to the long-term health of your organization, a full understanding of the supervisor's real role in the organization is crucial, both for now and later.

The Tactical Management model

The traditional organization chart was a pyramid shaped thing with the board and chief executive at the top, managers below that, followed by supervisors and a large number of staff at the bottom. Over the past few years a few innovative companies have decided that this communicates the wrong message. They, correctly, have inverted the pyramid. They put customers and staff at the top, with the Board and chief executive at the bottom.[2] To manage your operation effectively now and into the future this synthesis is required:

Figure 9.1 The Tactical Management model organization chart

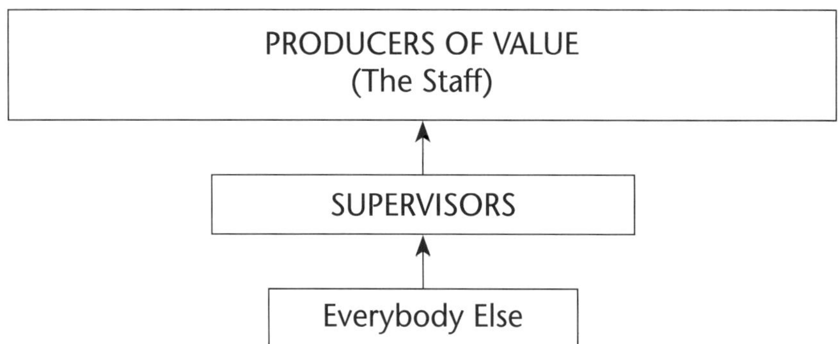

The traditional problem

The transition individuals must make to become totally effective supervisors is the most difficult required throughout a career in management.[3] Typically no preparation is made for this most important step; neither the new supervisors themselves, the managers to whom they report nor the people they manage are made aware of the significance. It usually happens like this:

Example

They were identified as ones who were dependable, worked hard[er than anybody else on the section], had good attendance records, were excellent technicians and, generally, deserved the promotions.

So . . . once upon a Monday morning they arrived at work and nothing, in fact, had changed beyond that they were now seated at [other] desks, had new titles (acting), new job grades (provisional) and the promise of pay rises. Perhaps they were sent on a three-day supervisory development course sometime within the first six months of promotion – probably not.[4] It is likely that nobody within the organization, neither their managers nor the chief executive, has ever taken the time to explain that their jobs are no longer those of workers, their jobs are now those of supervisors; they are managers and their jobs are not to do the work but rather to see that the work is done.

If you have not communicated to them, by your every word and action, your changes in expectations for them, then there have been no changes. At this moment they are out there working very hard trying to produce more to convince you that it was a wise decision to promote them.

Even with positive and extensive preparation for the new job, supervisors are still in an intrinsically difficult position within the organization. They, correctly, understand that sometimes they are managers: they plan, gives orders, make work assignments, counsel and discipline staff and do many of the things that managers are supposed to do. They, also correctly, understand that because of their experience and expertise sometimes they are part of the team responsible for getting the work out. They are often the only ones capable of completing the difficult task. This in itself is not unreasonable: part of their responsibility is to provide that kind of support for the team. They are also expected, not incorrectly, to pitch in to meet the difficult deadline. This dilemma is particularly apparent when they have been promoted from the ranks: when they are now responsible for supervising former colleagues.

Perhaps even more seriously, they are at the centre of the inevitable confusion resulting when any conflicting signals are sent by management. When a new and exciting quality programme has been introduced with the usual razzmatazz and then two days later the order is to: 'Ship it as it is,' supervisors are the ones who must explain this contradiction to the junior operator who has been bold enough to suggest another slight inconsistency between what management say and what management do. They are also the individuals who must stand to attention and be berated by their managers for excessive overtime two days after the latest No More Overtime memo was published; even though the overtime was a direct result of incompetent production planning or disingenuous promises by Somebody In Customer Service – they had absolutely no control over the situation.

This has all come about because of the way the promotions were handled, and that came about because of the faulty perceptions concerning the appropriate function of supervisors in the organization. Much, much more is required than seating new supervisors at desks and stating: 'Now you're supervisors'.

The new supervisory practice

It is crucial that all this changes. The transition to supervisor and entry into management, must be formalized. At the very minimum these structured processes must be developed and implemented:[5]

1 They must be provided with a comprehensive, unambiguous, formal, written job descriptions detailing precisely what is expected of the new positions. This must be supported by structured discussions with managers concerning expectations for the new positions.[6]

2 They must be intimately involved and have meaningful input into that portion of all business planning and budgeting, for any part of the organization, as those activities relate to their departments. This can yield important benefits. Through this process you will discover that they hold a great deal of useful information concerning what really goes on in their departments. Business planning and budgeting efforts will be far more effective with regard to overall organization objectives when supported by their inputs.

3 They must develop formal, written, jointly agreed yearly objectives with their managers. These will include those targets directly related to department objectives, improvements in operations, staff training and development, and their own technical and professional development.

4 They must have formal, quarterly[7] appraisals from their managers. The emphasis must be on their progress toward the attainment of all their yearly objectives. The appraisal should include positive recognition of achievement, and more importantly, recognition of those areas of non-achievement, and the specific support needed from their managers to address those deficiencies.

5 They must have the authority to determine both the organization structure and function for their areas, including identification of staff skills and experience levels that they determine are appropriate. Department structure must support close communications between them and their managers so that their area organization is consistent with overall department needs.

6 They must be given the appropriate support to develop staffing levels for their areas and they must have the final authority for those decisions.
7 They must have the authority for the selection of staff assigned to their areas. The personnel department may, if requested, provide an initial screening of candidates and their managers should no doubt be involved in a further evaluation but the final decision must be the supervisors'.
8 They must have the authority to set formal, written objectives for their staff and have the authority to appraise, counsel and discipline staff. This is an important opportunity for their managers to coach them and lead by example.
9 They must have the authority to schedule training for staff as they see fit.
10 They must have the authority to purchase routine materials and supplies for their departments. Their signing level must be appropriate for the scale of operations for which they are responsible.
11 They must have the authority to procure all resources necessary to address operating problems emanating from their departments relating to customer service, quality and cost management.
12 They must have the final authority to reject material when they recognize it cannot be used to make a good product.
13 They must have the final authority to refuse to run a job if the process is incapable of producing a good part. They must have the authority to refuse to commit to a schedule when they know it is impossible to complete a particular job on time because of other commitments.
14 They must have meaningful input into decisions relating to methods, practices and procedures for operations in their departments, and for options to current practices.
15 They must have substantial input into processes to evaluate present equipment and options to it. They must be contributing members of teams assigned to evaluate new equipment and processes.
16 They must be perceived as important members of any team involved in any new product development process, as that process relates to their areas or units. It is usually the case that their inputs are very useful in this respect, both for process capabilities and options to present products. This potential input has historically been ignored if the area was responsible for an early process step, part or subassembly.

When you examine these sixteen elements carefully, you realize that many of them are presently the responsibility of either the supervisor's manager, someone in middle management or one of the staff support functions such as personnel, production planning or procurement. Throughout *Tactical Management* and in particular in Chapter 6, I have talked about making the organization broader and flatter. That process means that many of these middle management and staff support functions are eliminated. This is your first opportunity to consider specifically how those kinds of changes in the organization might evolve. This is also your first exposure to the practical application of Eyes on-Hands off which we will examine in Chapter 12. If the department manager is truly effective in coaching and support, continual adjustment to the level of involvement with the supervisor for all these elements is essential.

Two optional models

Within the Tactical Management model I envision the role of the supervisor changing according to the sixteen steps discussed above. As we move to the broader and flatter organization of the future and place more responsibility for effective completion of work on self-managing workteams, the supervisor gradually shifts away from day-to-day responsibility for management of the team and becomes more of a facilitator – the primary link between the workteam and the rest of the world. Middle management and staff support ranks are reduced as the supervisor assumes responsibility for many of the activities previously performed by them. Where they remain, they provide expert support for the supervisor and the team. For example, in the past if a unit was to be re-organized, that process would have been managed by members of the personnel department. Similarly, training processes would have been designed and delivered by members of the training department and management system enhancements would have been developed and installed by the IT department. To continue with this example, in the future when there is a need for re-organization, training or revised management systems, the supervisor will facilitate a team consisting of unit members to manage those processes. Team makeup will include members from the personnel, training or IT according to the need for the technical support they can provide. Decisions relating to team objectives, however, are vested in the team; those responsible for completing the work are also responsible for deciding how it is to be organized and managed.[8]

There is another model: for some, the way forward is to eliminate the supervisor entirely. They hypothesize that truly self-managing teams do not need supervisors as facilitators; those workteams can collaborate directly as required with each other, middle management and staff support functions. They propose to flatten the organization by eliminating the entire supervisory layer, and later to simplify it further by eliminating senior supervisors and first line managers.

This argument is reasonable but not without problems. As the workplace of the future becomes more chaotic there is a need for a single individual to coordinate the myriad decisions needed throughout the day to keep everybody functioning effectively. Neither teams nor committees, whether permanent or temporary, formal or *ad hoc*, can make decisions. Only individuals can make decisions. Within the Tactical Management model, in the workplace that individual is the supervisor. Without a single, clearly identified decision maker to coordinate the activities of the unit with the large number of other, sometimes overlapping work units and teams, your most valuable resources – people and their time – will be under-utilized and therefore wasted.

Those who propose eliminating supervisors altogether argue that when the need for co-ordination between several units arises during the workday, conflict can be resolved by conducting an impromptu meeting among the parties involved and coming to a consensus. I disagree. In the real world of the workplace as we know it, this is impractical. In my experience this process is too cumbersome to address the rapid response demanded by the workplace of the future. Customer service and quality will suffer, and costs will be higher than necessary because time will be lost while discussions ensue concerning the allocation of carefully managed resources.[9] The present and near future readiness levels of most business organizations are not appropriate to this proposal.

Compare the two models. Review *Concerning theories and models* in the Introduction again. Examine your organization and what you think it will look like in the future. Talk with other members of your team. Talk with colleagues who are making the transition to workteams in their organizations and ask them how their supervisors are functioning within the new order. You, however, will have to make up your own mind.

It is probable that five years from now my argument will no longer be valid: then the readiness levels within many organizations will have shifted so that the optional model discussed here is appropriate.

The ballad of Ralph Hendershot

This story is true in every detail except for the name of our hero. Ralph Hendershot was a section leader responsible for a clerical unit of six people. I want to discuss his transition from worker to boss in detail to reinforce three important considerations:

- The improvement in operations resulting from this having been accomplished successfully can be spectacular.
- This will not happen without your direct involvement, active participation and positive support.
- The change is not necessarily easy for any supervisor.

This story is instructive because you can easily find parallel situations within your own organization:

Example

Several years ago I was responsible for installing management operating systems throughout a large admin operation. The system included daily individual performance reporting for all staff, section leaders and supervisors. The target was 85 per cent, calculated by accumulating standard hours earned for all work activity against total hours worked. Performances for section leaders and supervisors were measured against department work accomplished, but not for supervisory activities. Section and department performance were calculated daily by cumulating individual performance values.[10]

Two weeks after installation, performance in Ralph Hendershot's section had stabilized at about 70 per cent. Performance for Ralph himself, though, ranged daily from 92 to 97 per cent. It was obvious he was working very hard.

What was not obvious, however, was that requiring Ralph to reduce the amount of section work he performed and increase his supervisory effort would improve total section performance – total real output for the section.

The unit manager and I made the decision to take his desk away from him. Little preparation was made beyond telling him he could manage his section in any way he wanted but he could not sit down at his desk. It was also made clear to him that his manager was available throughout the implementation process should any problem arise as a result of this change, and that he would provide any other support needed.

The first day of implementation saw an improvement in total section performance to 78 per cent. Over the next few days it stabilized there. Ralph's individual performance dropped immediately to 52 per cent and thereafter varied daily from 50 to 55 per cent.

Think about this. The result of this change was an immediate improvement of 11 per cent in real performance not only at a net savings but at zero cost to the organization. This was the immediate and direct result of a supervisor shifting his activity from doing the work to seeing that the work was done. This supervisor's ability to support the people on the section not only increased the performance of individuals on the unit, but the cost to the unit for this supervisory time returned a higher yield in total resource utilization.

It is often argued that the supervisor must be involved in the work because he or she is the technical expert on the unit: the only person on the unit either available, experienced or authorized to perform certain work. That is sometimes the case. Here, the supervisor's 55 per cent performance reflected this.

Ralph was initially sceptical that this would work. He felt strongly that all necessary work would not be finished on time if he was not directly involved. However he worked very hard to make this change of practice a success. He later described his feelings that first morning as 'alien' and said he was not convinced it would result in an improvement until he saw it happen.

In this case both the supervisor and manager recognized that the change would not be easy. It was crucial to the success of this effort that the manager communicate his revised expectations to the supervisor. It was also crucial that the manager provide support for this change. In this particular case the supervisor was positive about improving his coaching and management skills. He was not reluctant to consider the change. In this sense it was not difficult for him to assume the new role although he was uncomfortable.

The supervisory and management development training discussed below is extremely important. A supervisor who has not been given the opportunity to develop these skills is often reluctant to assume the new way of operating because he or she is uncomfortable making proper work assignments, following up on them in a positive fashion and taking all the actions necessary to address problems. This frequently means the supervisor must now confront not only the people who work on the unit but supervisors in other departments with whom this team interacts and management at a number of levels.[11] When this occurs and the supervisor is not fully prepared, it is far easier to hide behind the work. If it is recognized that a problem is arising that requires attention but with which he or she is reluctant to deal, it is easier to reconcile a report or jump on a forklift truck – after all: 'the work needed to be done and we were busy'. The supervisor can do it quickly – quicker than anybody else on the unit because he or she used to do it every day and was very good at it.

There is one further consideration that is relevant to any change in process or procedure; the question of practice. Supervisory skills are not that much different from other sorts of things we learn to do: sailing, flying, playing football or cricket, the violin or piano – we get better with practice. This is probably the most important factor in the support you must provide for supervisors, both new and experienced, as they work their way into this new operational mode.

As they practice they will get better. As with the activities listed above, however, they will only improve if they push themselves until they make mistakes, otherwise they will never realize their full potentials. The same thing is true for the business of supervising: if supervisors in their new role are going to realize their full potentials, they are going to have to practise the new skills at a level that will push them until they make some mistakes. They must have your absolute, full, positive and continual support if they are going to be truly successful.

The supervisor in the organization of the future

If the needs of the present organization make this new way of functioning important for the supervisor, the organization of the future will make it essential. In this future organization the supervisor's work will be even more demanding. The span of control will increase dramatically and the people on the unit will be doing more and more different kinds of tasks. Product changes will be more frequent and there will be more products to track. The reaction to operating problems will have to become faster and faster. Diagnosis of operating problems and identification of options will assume more and more input from the people who do the work. The supervisor will need to make more frequent decisions and select many more options; the new charter will include much more emphasis on decision-making.[12]

Scheduling and work assignment practice will have to take into account that every staff member, at one time or another, will be leaving the area to attend task team meetings. The supervisor will no longer be responsible for ordering routine materials and supplies; that task will be performed by staff members. The supervisor's role will simply be to confirm that these orders support unit objectives. Regardless of unit objectives, whether they relate directly to the primary product of the organization or provide service or support, the supervisor will, at least part of the time, be working with other supervisors and managers from throughout the facility on tasks relating to improved customer service, quality and cost management processes. The supervisor will be responsible for managing his or her own time. One primary responsibility will be for saying 'No!' when resources are not available for performing an assigned unit task.[13]

If supervisors are poorly equipped to deal with the demands of the present organization, then they will most certainly fail when placed in the new environment. It is crucial that you prepare them for success.

Do this tomorrow

Review training plans for all supervisors. Confirm they have received at least a minimum of two weeks total formal, off-site training devoted to the subjects of effective supervision and the transition from worker to boss. Consider this as important as courses for middle and senior managers. If this has not been done, schedule it immediately.[14]

Make the commitment that in the future each person promoted to a supervisory position receives that training before assuming the new position – not six months after the promotion. This training should be scheduled soon after promotion to section or team leader.

Commit that every supervisor in the organization will receive a minimum of two weeks total formal management development – not technical – training yearly.[15]

Review with every supervisor the yearly objectives set for him or her by the unit manager or department head. If no objectives have been set, then clearly that manager has no understanding of the important role of the supervisor in the organization. Review with every unit manager or department head the objectives set for the year to develop and coach each supervisor. They must be specific and in writing. They must demonstrate continuous, progressive, substantive and realistic development. Insist that those managers who have not done this to do it immediately.

Spend at least half an hour, individually, with every supervisor in the organization. Devote this time to communicating the importance of this crucial position and your personal expectations. It is critical to the health of the organization that you allocate this time to the nurturing of one of your most important resources – second only in importance to staff as resources.

During your facility tours and your Management by Wandering Around, be alert for situations where supervisors are working when they should managing. When that practice is noted, stop it immediately. While you acknowledge that there are certain tasks the supervisor must perform as part of supervisory work, it is essential this does not become an excuse for not managing the unit. You understand this difference and so does the supervisor. Provide support for this change in practice.

Finally, be certain that everyone in the organization understands that the supervisor is the key individual immediately and directly responsible for providing staff with everything they need to meet operational objectives. Customer service, quality, cost management and profitability ultimately depend upon the effectiveness of the supervisor in this role. It must be made perfectly clear to everyone that the entire management structure and culture exist to support the supervisor in this role.

Do this over the next three months

Conduct a thorough review of practices for every supervisor in the organization. Work with each manager to develop and implement a productivity improvement process for each unit or department based purely on improved supervisory effectiveness similar to those changes realized by Ralph Hendershot. When this has been completed you will have made significant, real improvements in resource utilization at zero cost to the organization.

Notes

1 A text, published in 1969 and used during a graduate level course I attended on the practice of management, never mentioned the supervisor in any context; the supervisory function in the organization was totally ignored.
2 Peters, *Thriving On Chaos*; op. cit. – Peters cites a number of examples. Drawing a diagram will not change anything in itself, it must represent a commitment to a new model.
3 *Ibid.* – Peters recognizes the difficulty of this transition, and that it is frequently underestimated.
4 Check the records yourself.
5 This list is ambitious in the extreme; full implementation could require a year or more.
6 You are reminded again that much of this fomalization will be relaxed later. See Part Three.
7 Every quarter – not just the first one.
8 This is an essential requirement for any organization that seeks to become truly world class.
9 This important premise will be examined in detail in Chapter 10. I refer to it as the millwright paradox.
10 As we apply teamworking in more situations, there are fewer applications for daily, individual performance measurement. The principle of total unit performance and the contributions of individual team members, however, remains useful in the context of this story.
11 This will be discussed in detail in Chapter 11.
12 See Chapter 10 for some serious concerns about this aspect of the new supervisory practice.
13 See Chapter 16.
14 A three-day programme devoted to filling out little pieces of paper is *not* supervisory development.
15 Ask every supervisor about the time that has elapsed since his or her last management course. You will be appalled by the answers.

■ CHAPTER 10 ■

Decision-Making in the Real World: The millwright paradox

To be, or not to be – that is the question;

William Shakespeare
Hamlet

Business is not a democratic institution.

The director of operations of a D-I-Y retail company

Introduction

This chapter looks at some of the things that can interfere with the ability of people within the organization to make the many operational decisions demanded of them every day. This is not a discussion about the metaphysics of decision-making, nor is it a dissertation on the mental activity a person goes through while thinking about making a decision and then making it. We will examine a number of situations where a decision is not made either because no decision-maker has been identified, or the culture of the organization encourages decision by consensus.

In Chapter 6 we discussed the restructuring that must occur if the organization is not only to remain healthy but to grow. The impact of these changes will be particularly strong within the decision-making process. It must become less formalized, more responsive, open to more people at more levels and as free as possible from bureaucratic restrictions and limitations. In many organizations, possibly in yours, this is already happening: the shift to a team culture has resulted in a change in the way decisions are made; it has gradually and subtly changed to involve more people. Unfortunately this democratisation often carries with it the perception that because we are working as teams, decisions should be by consensus with the unanimous agreement of all involved. This is unworkable: decisions cannot be made by consensus. Further, when agreement cannot be secured, operations suffer because either a decision is not made at all, not made when it should have been or when it is made it is not the best for that particular situation:

- This is important for the present because within your organization certain things that should happen daily often do not because a decision has not been made.
- In the future this process will assume even more importance because the rate of change already experienced will continue to accelerate.

The millwright paradox

This story is instructive and you may be familiar with it, as it has been around for a while. If we take it to its logical conclusion, a paradox emerges relative to decision-making:

Example

Once upon a time there was a production operator running a machine on the line. Her machine broke down. She informed the production supervisor who informed the production manager who informed the maintenance manager who informed the maintenance supervisor. He directed a millwright to go out to the line to repair the machine.[1]

This is a paradigm of an occurrence within the traditional, vertical, authoritarian organization, and a perfectly reasonable situation. It has been proposed that as part of simplified and more responsive communication processes, the production operator should be able to leave her work station and go directly to the millwright and request his help. It makes sense: this is the kind of improvement you have been trying to make in your organization and perhaps have already made in some areas. Think, however, about what could happen next if this change is not managed properly. The saga continues:

Example

The millwright stopped midway through the work on his bench, a repair to equipment for another line the production control manager had scheduled to start up on the next shift. He collected his tools and left the shop. As he was walking out to the line he was met by the director of marketing who asked him to come to the short run department to adjust a die needed to fabricate some sample parts he was taking to an exhibition later that day. As he turned to walk to the short run department he was met by the director of engineering who asked him to come to the prototype department to deal with a problem with the development of the *New and Improved*. The bid to the MOD was due that day and he could not accurately cost out the *New and Improved* without at least one more trial run. As he moved toward the prototype department he was met by the PA to the chief executive. The air conditioner in the boardroom was making noise again . . . .

And herein lies the tale. To whom does the millwright respond first? How does he prioritize all the requests now on his list? Who is responsible for decisions *vis-à-vis* the millwright for these five requests?

What has happened here may not be obvious. What has occurred is that a sub or unit organization[2] has emerged spontaneously to meet a need, in this case the allocation of a limited resource, the millwright's time. This is the sort of situation that is encouraged in the new organization. In the interest of speeding up response times to address a range of problems from reducing production line downtime or waste to a customer's need for a new product or product variation, people are encouraged to create these sorts of impromptu groups or teams. The business organization of the future will be full of them. They may include from two to ten people and they may operate from a minimum of a few minutes, as in this case, to a few weeks. They will spring up in an instant and disappear immediately the issue is resolved.[3] The problem with this sort of *ad hoc* unit organization is that by the nature of its formation no single individual has either been given or assumed the responsibility for making decisions.

A business organization cannot be managed effectively on consensus, and when you try to do this the result is a situation such as the one in which the millwright found himself.[4] A team cannot make decisions, only one individual, the team leader, can make decisions. You might amuse yourself for an entire afternoon picturing the millwright, production control manager, director of marketing, director of engineering and the PA to the chief executive standing in a circle on the factory floor trying to reach agreement on which job the millwright should do first (who do you think would eventually win?).

This requirement is crucial:

> Within every group, whether formally or informally organized, whether permanent or temporary, somebody there must be identified – one individual – to make decisions. One of the principal activities of the supervisor and first line manager for the future must be that of arbiter, facilitator and *decision-maker*.

The millwright is not the appropriate person to make these decisions, nor is it reasonable to expect this group of five to come to agreement for prioritizing the millwright's work and work assignments. Work prioritizing and assignment must also achieve another important objective: effective and efficient utilization of all resources including labour hours. This cannot be achieved by consensus: for every situation one individual must be responsible for making decisions.

You might argue that with proper planning the four demands on the millwright's time other than the breakdown would not have the urgency described, you might even argue that with effective planned and preventive maintenance the impact of breakdowns can be minimized. Keep several things in mind, however:

- A primary objective for this new way of working is a faster response time. For example, the director of marketing may be in the position that he or she wants to respond quicker than one of your competitors to a recently identified customer need.
- This argument also applies for the scheduling of production for the next shift. When the production control manager and the team are functioning effectively they may not be able, nor indeed want, to schedule production more than one shift in advance.[5]
- Another objective is flexibility. The director of engineering may have just recently recognized a variation to the original design that would make the *New and Improved* a better product.
- Another requirement is the efficient utilization of resources, in particular labour hours. If we had five millwrights working on the bench there would be no problem except, of course, exorbitant labour costs. The objective is to staff the unit with no more millwrights than the entire department needs for long-term labour efficiencies. It is the job of the supervisor and manager to reconcile the needs of effective response time – short-term, and labour utilization – long-term.

Within the present business environment and certainly for the future, staff must assume more responsibility for customer service, quality and cost management, one element of which is labour utilization. This will require that they work as a team and that they, as a unit organization, provide information for the process. Under these circumstances there will inevitably arise situations where a number of courses of action are proposed and decisions must be made for the choice to be used. It does not make sense to propose that the group discuss the issue and achieve a consensus, decisions must be made by a single individual. For situations such as we are considering here, that person should probably be the supervisor or unit manager.

Decision-making within workgroups (service departments)

Since our story is about a millwright, we will look first at the decision-making process within a service department. Consider the millwright and his colleagues as a workgroup whose principal requirement is that they are able to respond quickly to demands for their services. This can be achieved if the person needing their assistance, in this case the operator, goes directly to the millwright. Think now about the role of the maintenance supervisor. If the paradox is to be resolved the supervisor must be included in the chain. The supervisor must be responsible for prioritizing work for the millwright and this is possible if the millwright, immediately upon receiving the request, informs the supervisor. However, for this to work the supervisor must be available to respond quickly. The problem will not be solved if the supervisor cannot be located quickly and easily and cannot be released from whatever he or she is doing at the moment to address the problem.

The supervisor can be available for this new way of working when appropriate delegation is in place.[6] If the millwright is now responsible for investigating new jobs, determining how they might be done, when they might be done, estimating hours needed for completion and ordering materials and supplies, all jobs that occupied the supervisor in the old organization, the supervisor now has time available to assume the new responsibilities. Under the old system, for example, the supervisor was responsible for ordering tools.[7] When the millwright orders tools the supervisor has been released from a duty. This is the beginning of the process to provide him or her with the time to decide and facilitate.

I know the manager of a back office department in a major UK bank who does all the filing for his group (his is a small department; admittedly this would not work for a large group). At first glance this seems like an extremely poor use of management resources. His rationale is this: during this activity he has the opportunity to examine every bit of work carried out in the department and thus he can monitor quality and identify potential problems. Germane to our argument is that he is available immediately to anybody needing his help. An interruption to the work he is doing will not cause a problem.

Decision-making within workgroups (production departments)

Decision-making relating to daily operations within a production department should be a fairly straightforward process. Consistent with the arguments presented above, the supervisor or unit manager is the individual designated to make decisions regarding work assignments, allocation of resources, approaches to the resolution of problems and similar issues. This is how it has been in the traditional business organization. There is, again, an important difference.

The process must be streamlined, made to respond faster and with more flexibility. When the machine goes down the operator's first action should be to inform the millwright: to set in motion immediately the process to ensure the machine is fixed quickly. The next action, however, must be to inform the supervisor, not simply to sit down beside the machine and wait for the repair. If the department is being properly managed a back-up job should be available for breakdown situations. In the interest of good labour utilization the operator should be reassigned immediately after speaking with the millwright. One option is to assist the millwright with the repair.

The supervisor must be the co-ordinator. The operator, for example, might not be aware that another machine has gone down at the same time.[8] Now a decision must be made and it makes no sense to expect the two operators to make it. The supervisor must have complete information concerning the entire unit operation so a decision can be made on the allocation of available resources, and this includes the millwright's time.

Please note that this discussion assumes your operation has not yet moved to fully self-managing workteams: the supervisor is still responsible for making work assignments, allocating resources and addressing operating problems. Here it is clear the supervisor is the focus of operating information such as how well lines and equipment are running, and is thus well placed to address problems such as those we have seen with prioritizing the millwright's work assignments. If self-managing workteams are functioning in your organization without the direct involvement of the supervisor, he or she must still be the focus for daily operating information to deal with problems such as we have examined here which cut across team and department boundaries. This approach is consistent with our discussions in Chapter 9 concerning the role of the supervisor.

Decision-making within task teams

The task team is a group of people who have been brought together to address a specific, closed-ended issue. Examples are the team responsible for collecting information and determining the specification for a new computer system or the team defining major revisions to the operating practices manual. The task team is by its nature multi-disciplinary and often composed of a number individuals on the same level on the organization chart. For these reasons it is often the understanding that decision-making is to be shared.

If you have worked with task teams in the past, you might not always have been satisfied with the results.[9] One of the reasons task teams have difficulty achieving objectives on time, if at all, is that typically it is not made clear when the team is commissioned that somebody must be in charge and responsible for making decisions. Without this, the implication for the team is that decisions will be achieved by consensus.

The person commissioning the team must:

1 identify the decision-maker,
2 make it clear to other team members that the decision-maker has the authority to make decisions,
3 make it clear the decision-maker has the full support of the commissioner in this respect and
4 the decision-maker's decisions are binding within the team's charter.

If your organization has experience with task teams, quality circles and workgroups, and if that experience has required consensus for decisions in the past, then this change in the process can be traumatic, perhaps extremely so for some. This will be especially awkward when team members are drawn from a group of peers and one is made responsible for decisions. It will be even more traumatic when the team leader, the decision-maker, is on a lower level on the formal organization chart than some other team members, and there is sometimes a need to overrule those others. This is not unreasonable – nothing in the methodology of task teams mitigates against appointing a team leader to manage a team composed of members some of whom are higher on the organization chart. Indeed, task team makeup is driven by the expertise, experience and talents of team members and by what they can contribute to the objective, not by their places on the organization chart (we must recognize, however, that organizing a task team with a subordinate in charge in the real world is a bit scary. Try it, you might have some fun with it).

I will close this section with an example of a situation where it almost went horribly wrong because no decision-maker had been clearly identified. Has anything like this ever happened to you?

Example

One of my recent projects involved working with an operating unit of a large UK based conglomerate engaged in the production of fresh chilled food products. I was using a desk next to that occupied by the manager for the test kitchen and new product development in an open plan office. This conversation took place between that manager and the engineering manager.

The work described here was a six month project to develop and manufacture a product entirely new to this operation, a vanilla and custard slice, for a major UK supermarket chain. Production of a cream slice is a rather complicated and fussy business and crucial to its manufacture is the slicer, a complex machine. Early in the project a preliminary order had been placed with a European manufacturer for the slicer, a bespoke machine. Partial payments had been made to the manufacturer with instructions to purchase materials and begin building the machine. Later during development work, as information became available, the product development team would forward it to the manufacturer so work would be completed in time for production trials.

Within this operation, any work that required the use of new or modified equipment involved the engineering manager as a member of the development team. His role was to coordinate the purchase, modification or in-house construction of any equipment needed, and submit and process any necessary capital requests.

Ten days before production trials were scheduled to begin, and twenty days before the customer was to arrive to view a prototype run, the following conversation took place:

'So, what is the scheduled delivery date for the slicer?' the engineering manager asked.

'I didn't order the slicer,' the new product development manager replied, 'I thought you ordered it'.

'No, I didn't order the slicer,' the engineering manager responded, 'I thought *you* ordered it'.

A mad scramble and a large number of very frantic telephone calls and fax messages to the slicer manufacturer to expedite delivery of the machine followed.

Think carefully about the implications of this situation. Here was a new product of potentially large volume, for a very important customer responsible for a majority percentage of gross revenues for this facility. The product had been treated in every respect as crucial to the long-term viability of this operation and its development had been given the stature of a very important project by everybody concerned. Yet even under these positive circumstances it came very close to being a major disaster for the business because too little thought had been given to the importance of clearly identifying the decision-maker.[10]

Decision-making within committees

The only difference between a task team and a committee is that the task team is assembled for a closed-ended, one time objective and the committee is a standing group, one that is permanent and is required to address a routine situation that is a regular and continual part of the operation. Examples of this include teams that are organized to monitor product or service quality, committees that oversee maintenance of procedure manuals, audit teams responsible for best practice within an admin centre and safety committees.

With regard to decision-making they are not that much different from task teams. Within many committees membership is on a rotating basis, perhaps a seat is filled by one individual for six months, one or two years then a colleague replaces him or her for the next term.

It is totally appropriate, indeed beneficial, for the position of leader or chair to be assigned to each member in rotation. It is particularly important here that the identification of the decision-maker is made clear to everybody within the committee itself and throughout the organization. Lack of a properly identified decision-maker is the reason why committee meetings go on for so long and seldom seem to achieve much (some committee meetings go on forever and never achieve anything).

Do this today

Identify one workgroup, team or committee in your organization whose members always seem to have difficulty achieving objectives. Be particularly receptive to the opportunity to work with one of the *ad hoc* groups that has emerged as a result of recent changes in the organization. It is probably the case that much of the difficulty they experience in achieving objectives is the result of the lack of decision-making authority that is the heart of this chapter.[11]

Review both the structure and function of the group. Work closely with them to develop processes to achieve the following.

- One person will be responsible for making decisions relative to group objectives. It is crucial that everybody within the group knows who that person is. This should be obvious: 'They should know that!' It seldom is obvious.
- Input to decisions must be from *all* group members. Each member must have unlimited access to the decision-making process, otherwise why is he or she part of the group? Identification of the decision-maker must in no way restrict information flow and constructive dialogue.
- These decisions will be *final* within the group charter. Unless, as sometimes happens, the requirement is to investigate a situation and present a series of options to somebody else empowered to make a decision, the charter must very clearly state that decisions are an integral element of objectives. Again: 'They should know that!'
- The group will receive direction from only one source. In Chapter 5 we referred to this as the principle of unity of command. If the group is receiving different assignments or different priorities, formally or informally, from several sources they will be hampered in their ability to make decisions. Identify the person to whom the team is responsible for achievement of objectives clearly, to everyone. All external direction to the group must be through this single channel.[12]

Be certain that everybody on the team fully understands the importance of all these elements in the new way of operating. Be equally certain that everybody else in the organization is aware that changes have been made in the way the group operates. Monitor efforts closely over the next few weeks as they work under the revised procedures.

Your strong and visible support will be needed for these predictable situations:

- The leader will now, from time to time, have to make decisions over the objections of some members. If he or she has not done this in the past, initially this will cause discomfort.
- People in the organization affected by a decision must accept it without qualification, so long as the group is operating within its charter. Throughout the organization decisions are binding, they are not optional. If this is not the case, why was the team established at all? As someone said, 'Moses, you recall, did not come down from Mount Sinai with the Ten *Suggestions*'.
- People who before had straightforward access to the group members in their team roles must now channel direction through the single facilitator. Some may object strongly to this change. For this first effort under the new procedure it would be beneficial for the entire operation if you act as facilitator. Whether you or somebody else was responsible for commissioning the team originally, your support will be critical for this phase of the change.

Finally, recognize this change will not be easy for many of those involved. There is comfort in consensus and relinquishing it will cause discomfort for almost everybody involved.

A word of caution

It is possible to create a minor monster with this process without too much difficulty. Team membership is based on the assumption that every member can make material contributions to the group objective. It is essential that nothing restricts individual input. Occasionally the decision-maker misunderstands the role and the flow of information will be ignored or inhibited if it appears to be in conflict with his or her approach. This can happen if the decision-maker is not very assertive or has difficulty with confrontation. It can also happen if he or she has identified this position as one from which to enhance personal visibility within the organization or to build a power base.[13] One of the reasons it is helpful for you to monitor team activities closely during these initial stages is to prevent this sort of problem.[14]

Do this over the next three months

Extend the experience you have gained in this exercise with the one group to the balance of the organization: from workgroups, task teams and safety committees to the management and executive committees. Look at the lack of effective decisions, not from the perspective of reluctance to make a decision (that is a separate problem), but as providing everybody within the organization with the clear understanding of *who* is responsible for making decisions, and the recognition that making decisions is not always popular. A business organization cannot be managed on consensus. Be mindful of the implications of the millwright paradox as you monitor the way decisions are made throughout your organization.

Notes

1 Toffler, *Future Shock*, op. cit. This is the earliest (1970) reference to this story. I am familiar with others.
2 See Chapter 6, The organization as a system, Page 87.
3 Peters and Waterman, *In Search of Excellence*; op. cit. Peters and Waterman discuss the emergence of these *ad hoc* teams or groups in detail and consider them essential in the excellent company.
4 Many banks in the US will not lend money to a 50–50 partnership for just this reason.
5 See the definition for customer service in Chapter 2, Page 33.
6 Delegation will be discussed in detail on Chapter 12.
7 Why is it we can trust the millwright to repair an annealing furnace worth £1,500,000 but we cannot trust him to order a screwdriver worth £1.50?
8 It could be argued that in this brave new world of ours we should not have all these machines breaking down but they are a fact of life at the best of times and in the best run organizations.
9 Task teams will be examined in detail in Chapter 14.
10 I can report happily that the machine arrived in time for successful trials that met the customer's schedule. This was not achieved, however, without many long hours of work by these two managers and many others.
11 There are several others that will be examined in Chapter 14.
12 In Part Three we will discuss the potential for relaxing this restriction later, when everybody in the organization has had the opportunity to work through these new processes for a year or more.
13 This issue is examined in slightly more detail in Chapter 14, A Cautionary Note, Page 199.
14 Rosabeth Moss Kanter, *The Change Masters*. (London: Unwin 1985.) Kanter discusses this problem with regard to team building in considerable detail.

■ CHAPTER 11 ■

A Positive Approach to Confrontation: The Brussels sprouts principle

What in the customer's behaviour appears to me totally irrational? And what therefore is it in *his* reality that I fail to see?

Peter Drucker
Managing for Results

Customer: 'This isn't a beefburger, this is liver'.
Waitress: 'I know. We're out of beefburgers'.
Customer: 'But I didn't order liver'.
Waitress: 'Eat it!'

Conversation overheard in a diner in Amanda, Ohio, USA

Introduction

The primary requirement for effective communications emphasized throughout *Tactical Management* is straightforward: the singular criterion for judging the effectiveness of any communication is that it causes the appropriate thing to happen. This chapter title does not include the word communications. What we will do is expand a traditional communications model in several ways, to improve the likelihood that the receiver will commit to compliance and achieve the results required by the message.

Nearly every act of communication you undertake as a manager involves an attempt to make something happen, and often what you want to happen is that something should change. Our test is pragmatic: we define the communication as having been successful if what happened is what you wanted to happen, and specifically when those things you wanted to change have changed. We will describe this type of communication as a confrontation[1] and when that information exchange has been deemed to have been successful, the confrontation will be described as positive.

The Brussels sprouts principle

Think about the last time you served Brussels sprouts to your family. Think about all the fuss when your children or grandchildren would not eat their vegetables:

- Items that are high on your priority list are not necessarily high on anybody else's list. In fact, they do not even appear on some lists.
- Positive confrontation is achieved when you move the items on the top of your list to the top of another person's list, and do this in a way that enables every individual involved in the transaction to feel that he or she has emerged as a winner.
- That you have directed somebody to do something, whether by written instruction, face-to-face conversation, established procedure or past practice will not, alone, ensure that it will be done – properly if at all.

If you think this idea is trivial, remember all the fuss about the sprouts. How could something as insignificant as a little green vegetable that smells funny and doesn't really even taste very good be the cause of so much turmoil that blows have been exchanged, crockery smashed and furniture destroyed?

Behaviour, attitudes and perceptions[2]

Until now I have used the word behaviour sparingly and only in contexts where the meaning was obvious. I have not used the word attitudes at all. Further, I have sometimes used the word perceptions in circumstances where I might have used the word facts. This is deliberate. These terms are used by psychologists and social scientists in a number of different ways according to individual choice and particular application. Also, they are routinely treated trivially, misused and abused in silly ways in the popular press. The purpose of this discussion is not to turn you into an expert on human behaviour, but to provide us with a basis for considering some of the things that go on in the workplace as people try to communicate with one another.

I will use these terms consistently according to the following practice:

Behaviour

Behaviour refers to those actions you can see a person taking during the day. This includes not only physical activity but spoken and written word, non-verbals – what we often call body language, dress, the choice of seats during lunch or at a meeting, the selection of reading material and all the other things that are unique to that person and that you can see. You cannot change behaviour.

We are not concerned with whether certain elements of behaviour might be described as conscious, unconscious or sub-conscious, nor are we concerned with the reasons, either objective or subjective, why a person behaves in a certain way. We are interested solely in what we can see.

You might argue that you can directly change a person's behaviour in the workplace. Perhaps you can, but only for the short term and only then on the most superficial level. For example, if you threaten to sack somebody for smoking in an unauthorized area, that person's behaviour will change: he or she will smoke in another unauthorized area, one unknown to you. You have not changed behaviour in any meaningful way. Our concern here is for consistent, very long-term, positive changes in behaviour that support organization objectives.

Attitudes

Attitudes will refer to all those things that cause a person to behave in a certain way. The single important property of attitudes is that they are totally internal to the person: you cannot see them, understand them in any meaningful way or change them.

Perceptions

Perceptions will refer to the ways all the external things that create attitudes or changes in attitudes within a person are seen by him or her. Perceptions are driven by occurrences outside the individual, they originate in the real world. But they are not facts, they are that person's interpretation of facts. If the same fact is presented to three people the result is going to be three distinct perceptions for the three individuals. You can to some extent influence perceptions and you do this by adjusting the information you want to present and your presentation of it – by adjusting *your* behaviour.

Consider our discussion in the Introduction about the operators who used out-of -date materials in the food processing operation.[3] We know a fact: we know that written quality and operating procedures stated that out-of-date materials were not to be used. Yet operators did not act on this. They did not comply with written procedure, but operated on their perceptions of it based on what they had either seen supervisors and managers do in the past or had themselves been ordered to do: to use out-of-date materials. What followed then, that the materials were used, regardless of the reasons operators might have given had they been asked, resulted in the perception by managers that they were not interested in doing a good job, that they did not care.

If you want to make something happen or if you want to make something different happen, a change must occur in the behaviour of the person who is supposed to take the appropriate action. According to our definitions you do this by altering a person's perception of certain facts, and you do this by changing your behaviour, by changing the way you present the information you wish to communicate. Altering perceptions will *perhaps* result in different attitudes that will *perhaps* result in changed behaviour. The process is very subjective.

This is complicated by several factors:

1 It is usually difficult to predict how a given change in your presentation is going to result in specific changes in behaviour for any individual. One of the principal purposes for consistent follow-up activity and Management by Wandering Around[4] is to enable you to observe how your behaviour is influencing the behaviour of others.
2 A person's perceptions are driven, in part, by your behaviour. This is really at the root of this business of sending conflicting signals: perceptions are influenced by all your behaviour, not just your memo, draft procedure or formal presentation speech.
3 A person's behaviour in the workplace is a result of attitudes derived not only by perceptions of things that happen on the job but throughout his or her life. Much as we wish it was not so, things that happen at home also influence behaviour at work. You have absolutely no control over perceptions created by events outside the workplace.

Elements of communications

We will review the elements of a traditional communications model, then add several of our own to support the application of the Brussels sprouts principle. Please be patient: much of this terminology derives from information theory that was originally concerned with explaining the dynamics of information flow within a telecommunications network or computer system. Some of it sounds very mechanical for describing communications between human beings.

Any information exchange must at minimum include these elements:

A sender

The sender is someone who has decided an information exchange must be initiated. It is crucial to the success of every communications process to remember that it begins when somebody makes a decision that certain information must be exchanged.

A message

The sender determines message content. A decision is made about what information is to be sent. For our purposes the sender must ask what specific results are expected to be achieved with the message. Unless he or she can articulate precisely what is hoped to be achieved by the communications effort, it will probably fail.[5]

An encoding process

This is the point at which the sender must begin to exercise judgement. The ability to forecast how the message will be perceived by the receiver will determine how it will be encoded, how it will be sent – the channel to be used, and how it will be received – how it will be decoded. The sender must decide what the message will look like: will it be in complex detail or general in scope, presented in a Theory X or Theory Y style, should it include examples and metaphors, should it be humorous or stern in tone, phrased in technical jargon or in everyday language? Unless the encoding process is carefully considered and thoughtfully developed, the information exchange is likely to fail.

A message channel

The choice of message channel requires another decision by the sender. Will the channel be a written procedure, a face-to-face conversation, a telephone call, by E-mail, a typed message sent by courier, the grapevine[6] or other available means? Choice of channel also has significant impact on how the message will be perceived. A decision to use a personal visit rather than a typed memo for a particular information exchange may shift the receiver's perception of the importance of the message. The decision of the sender must be based on a judgement of how the message will be perceived by the receiver. The choice of channel is critical to the success of any communication.

A receiver

The receiver is the person for whom the message is intended. This element should be fairly straightforward, frequently it is not. If, for example, the required action is to be taken by the supervisor, then he or she is the receiver, not the department manager. The message will probably be passed through the manager, but the choice of channel and the encoding process must be determined by the needs of the supervisor, not the manager.

A decoding process

The decoding process is crucial to the accuracy of the intentions of the sender as perceived by the receiver. The sender has no direct control over it, it is influenced by the choice of message content, encoding process and channel. The decoding process is affected by the entire set of

Figure 11.1 The basic communications model

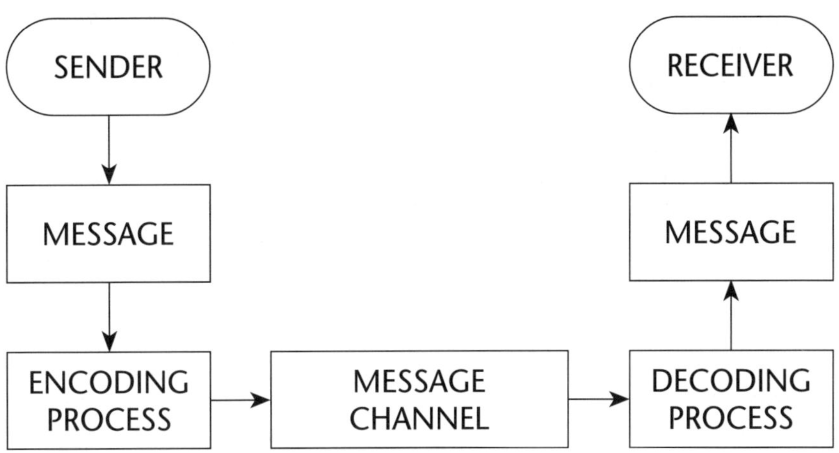

perceptions under which the receiver is operating at the time. You can think of numerous examples of decoding gone wrong. Recall our smoker who decoded your 'No smoking!' message as: 'Keep smoking, but do it somewhere else'.

These six elements are basic: without every one of them no information exchange can occur. However, the objective is not only that the message has been received but that it has been understood. Another element must be added:

A feedback channel

The feedback channel is established to attempt to confirm that the message has been received as intended by the sender. Feedback may range from the simple question: 'Do you understand?' to a request such as: 'Please repeat that back to me,' or the requirement for a twenty page, formal, written report.

The feedback process will tell you something about whether the message was received, but probably will not tell you much about whether it was understood, and it certainly will not tell you anything about the receiver's readiness to comply. Even the request that the receiver repeat the message back to the sender will provide no information about understanding. Your smoker, remember, promised never again to smoke in that particular area. Another element is needed:

A filter evaluation process

The filter evaluation is a process by which the sender evaluates information received through the feedback channel and uses this to make decisions about the accuracy of the information exchange effort. The term filter refers to the fact that the message is not received complete and intact by the receiver, it has been filtered through background noise and other interference (more information theory terminology). In our model the primary filter mechanism is that body of perceptions under which the receiver is operating at the time.

The sender uses this process to identify the specific kinds of things that could have interfered between the generation of the message and the correct, intended, interpretation.

Most traditional models consist of these eight elements, with the feedback channel and filter evaluation process closing the loop and creating a cyclic process. The Brussels sprouts principle suggests that the process can be made more effective with the addition of several elements. Our concern is not only that the message has been received and understood, but that the planned result has occurred, that the desired action has taken place. The Tactical Management communications model consists of four more elements:

A commitment channel

A commitment channel must be created parallel to the feedback channel. The purpose is to provide information to confirm not only that the message has been received and understood, but also that the receiver

Figure 11.2 The traditional communications model

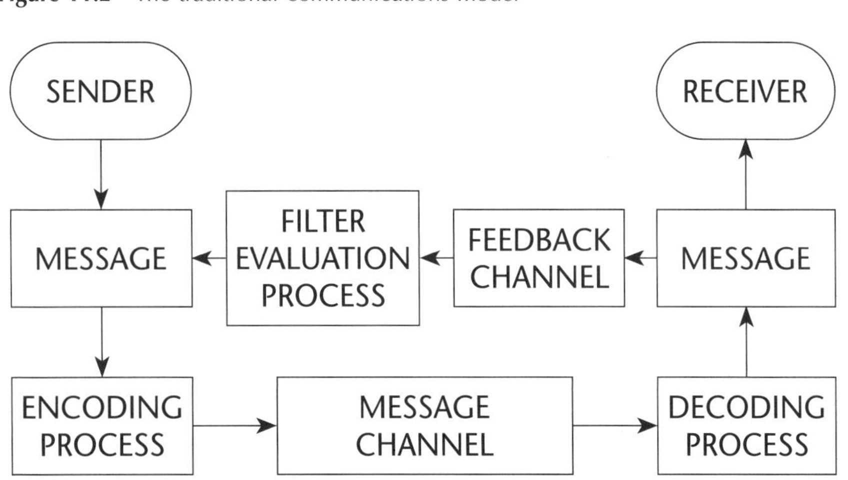

has made a commitment to take the actions required by the communications. Unless the sender has confirmed that the receiver has committed to taking the action required by the information exchange, that commitment has probably not been given and the communication is likely to fail.

The commitment may range from a simple: 'Yes, I will do as you requested,' to the series of formally identified control points throughout a project. The commitment will not be given unless the sender asks for it, it can never be assumed.

A message prioritizing process

This process is at the heart of the Brussels sprouts principle. To ensure effective compliance with the communication, something is needed to confirm that the required action is high on the receiver's priority list. The sender is responsible for providing information to communicate to the receiver that he or she must perceive this request to be of high priority.

The sender must evaluate message content, choice of channel and encoding process with respect to placing it high on the receiver's list of priorities. This is entirely a matter of judgement by the sender, these decisions are crucial to the success of this effort. The sender must further support this through evaluation of information received through feedback and commitment channels. Unless the sender succeeds in placing the objective of the information exchange high on the priority list of the receiver the communication effort is likely to fail.

A message evaluation process

The evaluation process makes use of the general principle of the tactical closed-loop management cycle and the specific elements of short segment task control to confirm during the action phase that the information exchange has been effective. These principles were considered at length in Chapters 7 and 8, and no further discussion should be needed. The message evaluation process must be made a formal, structured element of every communication effort.

A message revision process

It is consistent with the principles of the tactical closed-loop management cycle and short segment task control that every communication process must include an element to adjust the information exchange at any point during the transaction where it is identified that a revision will increase the likelihood of successfully achieving planned results. The message revision process must be a formal, structured element of every communication effort.

Figure 11.3 The Tactical Management Communications Model

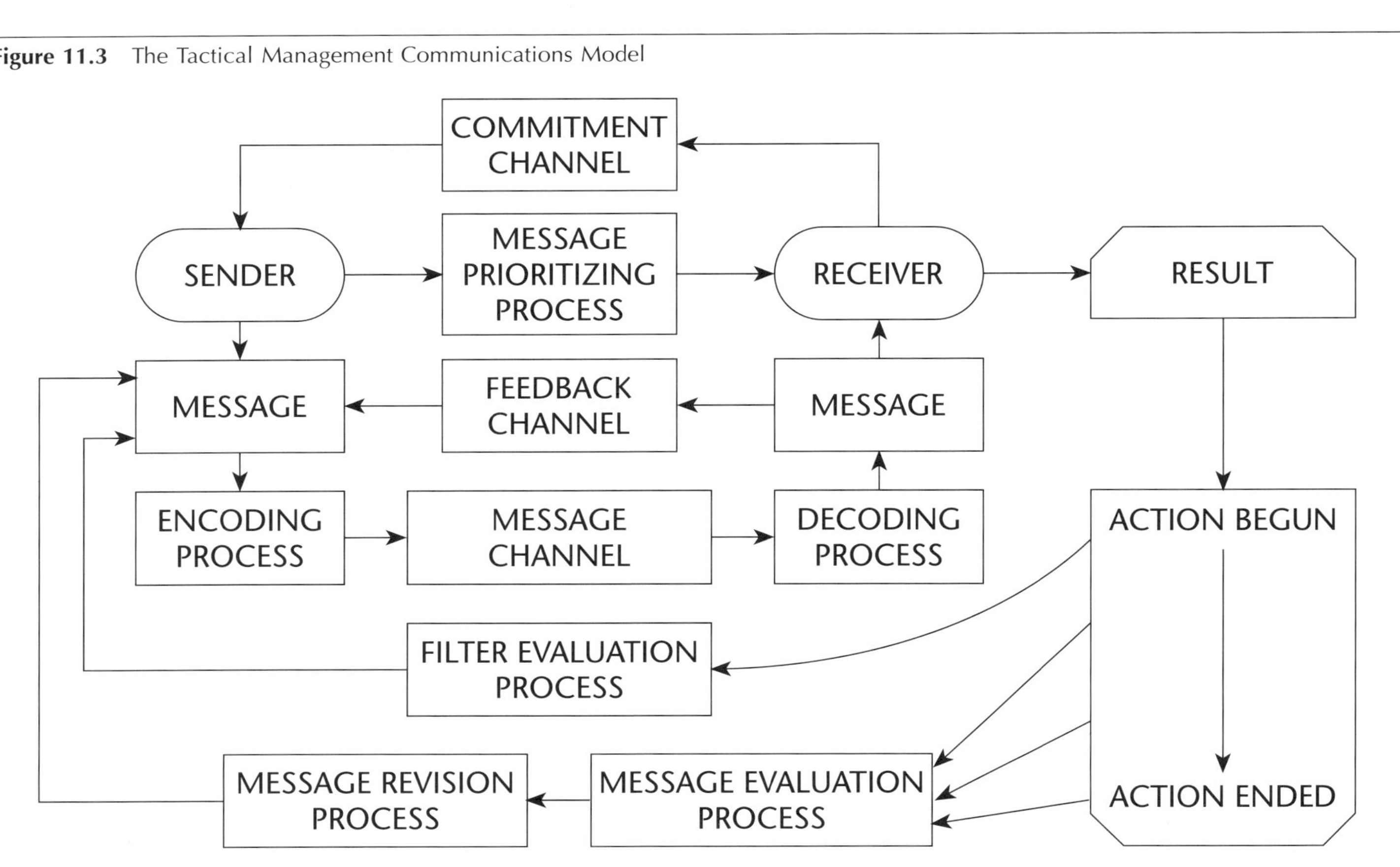

Think carefully about these twelve elements. Except for the decoding process all are fully within the control of the sender. If a communication fails it is because poor decisions were made regarding the choice of channel, encoding process, the message itself, the feedback channel and all the other elements necessary for an accurate information exchange.

Note also that in the Tactical Management model the filter evaluation process is no longer related to the message feedback element. Here the emphasis is on how well the intended result is being achieved. It is my belief that the sender cannot evaluate how the message has been filtered by the receiver until action has been taken in accordance with the original intentions of the sender.

Review our definition of behaviour. The one element over which the sender has no direct control is the decoding process, because it is part of receiver behaviour. If the information exchange is to result in the planned action correctly taken by the receiver, the sender must ensure correct receiver behaviour during the decoding process. Based on our definitions, the sender increases the potential for successful communications by adjusting his or her own behaviour – by careful selection of message content, choice of channel and encoding process, and by appropriate control over the balance of the effort through attention to the remaining elements, in particular message priority – Brussels sprouts.

Positive confrontation

Positive confrontation is any act of communication that results in a planned action or change in action having taken place successfully. Positive confrontation requires that the sender make carefully considered decisions throughout the communication process. There must be confirmation that each of the twelve elements has been developed to the extent that there is confidence that planned action will be effectively taken.

This fails if any single element is omitted:

Example

We were sitting with the managing director of a service company when he received a call from his head office. The call required that some immediate action be taken in response to a serious business emergency.

He interrupted our meeting and called a clerk to his office to give him verbal instructions to provide some information. Those instructions required the clerk to accumulate some operating data relating to agents, customer statistics and territories, quickly prepare some summaries and breakdowns, then colour code these against a map of territories covering the entire country. The complete mandate was fairly complicated.

The clerk stood inside the door while listening to all of this. He nodded, smiled and agreed throughout the conversation at appropriate times, as you would have expected. After receiving these instructions he moved to leave the office. He was nearly out the door when the managing director asked him if he understood what was needed. He turned and replied: 'No'.

Many would consider the managing director's final question superfluous. The usual response when the need for this action enters a discussion about communications is the remark: 'They should know that,' or: 'You're treating them like children'. In this case, however, had the sender not taken this action, this exchange would have failed. Moreover, had he written out his instructions, he would have further increased the likelihood of success for this communication.

For communications to be totally successful and positive confrontation to occur, two important criteria must be met.

A fully developed information exchange

The sender must develop and initiate the complete information exchange. All the elements must be included and all the elements must be fully developed. The sender has total responsibility for the ultimate success of the information exchange.

There are three distinct areas where this effort is typically not completely effective within the environment of a business organization:

1 A manager is sometimes reluctant to make proper work assignments and take all the actions necessary to address problems with the people he or she manages. This is especially true for follow-up effort, when there is a requirement to come face-to-face with subordinates and enquire why something was not done according to specification or completed on schedule. Unless the manager has been effectively coached and has had the opportunity to develop and practice the appropriate skills there is sometimes so much discomfort with this process that it is omitted from practice.[7]
2 Management action often requires a dialogue with peers, with managers in other departments with whom this team interacts. Certain operating problems can be fully resolved only if people in another department change something. Within the traditional business organization managers, particularly at department level, have not been encouraged to communicate the need for change with their peers in other parts of the organization.
3 Communication with superiors is often demanding, particularly when the subordinate is addressing change. Positive confrontation with bosses has never been favoured in our business culture. This type of communication is extremely difficult for most managers. Your active and positive support is necessary if this is to be successful.

Message prioritizing: Brussels sprouts

The sender must positively and assertively confirm that the action to be taken is high on the priority list of the receiver. The possibility of this being successful can be improved if certain considerations are addressed:

1 There must be absolutely no question about the integrity of the message. The sender must, in fact, be communicating the real objectives. If the sender is working with a hidden agenda or if the message disguises some secret intent, then the communication will ultimately fail. The sender may experience some short-term successes but long-term objectives will most certainly not be achieved. Review a few notable communications failures with which you are familiar (not necessarily your own) within your recent experience and ask yourself, honestly, about the true aims of those efforts.
2 Throughout the information exchange the sender must strive to convince the receiver that the planned action will result in a win-win situation. This is particularly important when the receiver has to make significant changes to the way something is done. When the sender can convince the receiver that the proposed change is to benefit both, the receiver will be far more likely to support the action and try to make it successful.
3 It is appropriate here to consider one additional issue: that of the degree of flexibility built into any communication involving the need for change. Throughout *Tactical Management* we have discussed a number of situations that required that specifications, practices and procedures be developed comprehensively and unambiguously. In Chapter 6 we referred to simultaneous loose-tight management control: that good management often requires a tight compliance with specifications and simultaneously a significant amount of flexibility concerning the way the people responsible for complying with those specifications go about their work.

   Any information exchange that is to result in some kind of action must be structured to provide the receiver with an amount of latitude concerning how action is to be taken consistent with the readiness levels of both of you. Communications efforts, particularly those concerned with work assignments and management actions must be delivered with the maximum flexibility and ambiguity to allow the receiver the opportunity to be creative and innovative in the pursuit of those objectives.

   This presents you with another one of those dilemmas we have several times alluded to. Fine judgement and decision-making are critical to the entire discipline of positive confrontation. If communications are to be effective in the achievement of long-range organization objectives this flexibility must be an element of all information exchanges at the operational level. As we have seen, this is extremely important now and will become crucial in the organization of the future.

Finally, it should be noted that the waitress quoted at the beginning of this chapter *did* achieve a positive confrontation: her customer ate the liver with no further complaint. (That she outweighed him by about four stone and was at least a head taller may have had something to do with both his readiness level and hers.)

Do this today

Review all the assignments you have made to individuals in the past six months for special actions to be taken, extraordinary information or reports to be prepared. Examine how many were completed fully according to your expectations with regard to thoroughness, accuracy, timely completion and within forecast costs. Analyse those that failed to meet your needs. Look at each specifically with respect to how well you communicated objectives; look at how fully you addressed all the elements of the communications process.

Now examine two of your special projects or requests currently in progress. Modify communications processes already underway for those assignments to enhance the effort. The revisions should result in better attainment of objectives. To keep this first exercise simple, review only assignments to individuals rather than teams. Once you are comfortable with this process, once you have practiced it a bit, generalize the assignments to include teams as well as individuals.

If any information exchange is to be totally successful, if the planned action is to be completed fully according to specification, on time and within budget, you must make all appropriate decisions to ensure that this item is as high on the message receiver's priority list as it is on yours – Brussels sprouts.

Notes

1 *Oxford Concise Dictionary*, CompLex for Windows, V2.0, 1993: **confront** *v.tr.*, face up to and deal with (a problem, difficulty, etc.)
2 See Bowditch and Buono, *A Primer on Organizational Behavior*; op. cit. and Hersey and Blanchard, *Management of Organizational Behavior*; op. cit. for examples of how different writers use these terms.
3 See page 14.
4 Management by Wandering Around will be discussed in detail in Chapter 18.
5 In Chapter 19 we will examine some situations where lack of clear objectives has resulted in unnecessary and costly communications failures.
6 The grapevine is an important communications channel which is often ignored.
7 Work assignment practice will be examined in detail in Chapter 17.

■ CHAPTER 12 ■

Delegation: Eyes on-hands off

The captain always delegates the preparation of the flight plan to his assistant, a task which requires from fifteen to thirty minutes . . . The remaining part of the hour he spends loading mail and baggage. These duties keep him busy and breathless until his captain arrives . . .

Ernest K. Gann
Fate Is The Hunter

The cost is the strength it requires to be vulnerable.

Kathleen Keating
The Little Book of Hugs

Introduction

Delegation is a bit like politics: everybody talks about it but nobody actually does anything. Enrolled in seminars about delegation, managers go out from the workplace to training centres. They return, look around, then say to themselves and their bosses: 'Delegation sounds really great, but I don't have anybody to delegate to', and that is about all there is to it.

We are constantly made aware of the subject – almost every contemporary supervisory or management development course includes a module on delegation. It is perceived by many to be nothing more than this year's, or last year's, favourite management buzzword. Finally, when you try to describe what delegation means, the explanation makes it sound so simple and obvious that you wonder what the fuss was all about.

> Delegation is the act of reassigning authority for the satisfactory completion of a specific activity or practice from one person to another, usually but not necessarily subordinate within the organization.

Delegation *is* really great, but like other topics addressed in *Tactical Management*, the application is sometimes difficult. It involves significant change, immediate and visible, for both the delegate and delegator. Delegation for activities related to daily operations can have an immediate and direct impact on customer service, quality and cost management, and if the change is not well managed or if unanticipated problems arise during implementation the short term results can be negative. Innovative or imaginative delegation usually meets with fierce objections from either Somebody From The Union or Somebody From Personnel – occasionally from both: 'You can't do *that*!'

Delegation

Delegation is crucial to organizational health now and for the future for several reasons:

- Good personal time management demands that you devote most of your energy to those tasks that require a level of authority, responsibility, training and experience consistent with your position. The exception principle states that as duties and decisions are determined to be routine they should be delegated farther down in the organization. Effective delegation enables you to spend more of your time on extraordinary needs and special tasks.
- Delegation is an important part of coaching and mentoring practices necessary to all well-managed supervisory and management development processes. When a subordinate is given the authority and responsibility for completing a duty previously done by you, he or she is being encouraged to grow professionally. A routine duty should be delegated down to the level in the organization at which it is no longer routine, to the level at which it becomes an attainable, reasonable challenge.
- When tasks are delegated appropriately they are being accomplished by people closer to the actual work. Their contributions are important and useful. For example, when a maintenance supervisor delegates to a craftsperson the task of estimating hours needed for a job, that person's experience, training and familiarity with the work are being better utilized. A clerk responsible for filing, because of daily exposure to the task, can often quickly and easily identify more effective and efficient methods of organizing the work.
- Finally, delegation is an important component of our general effort to make the organization broader and flatter. As the delegation for effective completion of any task is shifted farther down in the organization, the corresponding responsibility is also necessarily pushed downward. This helps you simplify the organization by reducing costly layers of management, especially middle management and staff support functions.

Here I want to remind you again of my reluctance to use terms like superior, subordinate and lower down in the organization. They seem particularly incongruous when we are preparing for the organization of the future when these terms will have less and less meaning until ultimately they will almost have disappeared. This seems, however, the only economic way to describe these structural relationships and reporting lines.

Why delegation is difficult

That is the way it has always been done

The practice of delegation is complicated by the fact that any particular duty has been assigned to a specific level or position in the organization as a result of past practice on a purely arbitrary basis. There is no logical reason why a department manager is authorized to approve expenditures up to a certain level and the boss approves those for some greater amount. You can offer no justification that scheduling an additional production shift or the decision to shut down a line may be approved by the department manager but not by the supervisor. These levels of authority have evolved over time – 'that is the way it has always been done'.

The person who originally established the practice made a decision; that is not being criticised. The decision you make now is identical except for the position or level of the delegate. What is important is that there is no valid reason why you may not change past practice. For some practices there might at one time have been a technical need for authority having been vested at a particular level, but there is a good chance that need has been abrogated by time. Review the notes from your tour. You will discover some examples of middle or even senior managers performing duties that should be handled by an operator or clerk. This is often the result of the evolution of information processing systems from manual to electronic: at some time in the past there was a technical need for a manager to examine a piece of paper and sign it; the paper has disappeared but the approval action has not.

History makes it difficult to manage this type of change. The practice, because it has been carried out in a certain way for such a long time, has assumed a permanence that cannot be annulled by reasoning alone. It has become formalized through job descriptions and has become an integral part of a specific job grade.

A duty recognized as belonging to a particular job grade or classification becomes a formal element of union agreements and contracts. Even when not agreed contractually, it often assumes the status of accepted practice. In most business organizations you do not assign duties or tasks of any kind downward in the organization without strenuous objections from the union.

Personnel departments can be even more conservative in approach than the union. When you review your experience in attempting to implement a change in any job description, and especially when you wished to shift a particular duty from one job classification to another, either up, laterally or down, you remember that personnel were extremely unhappy about it. How often when considering a proposal of this kind, have you been reminded by another member of the team that you had better check with personnel first?

Example

I recall sitting with a middle manager to develop the organization for a new department created from units drawn from several existing departments within a large admin centre. His first action was not to specify a possible section arrangement, planned duties for each and proposed staffing necessary for each to complete the forecast workload. His first activity was to draw a number of horizontal lines across the whiteboard we were using for our workshop and label them: CG1, CG3, S1, S2, M2/M3 and M5 to represent staff, supervisory and management grades. His priority was not to develop a staffing plan according to operational requirements, then identify the needed skills, his priority was to draw an organization chart with staff and management *levels* according to the requirements of personnel.

Please note that throughout this discussion I am not proposing that more and more responsibility be placed upon every individual without appropriate consideration for personal qualifications, total individual workloads, technical job requirements, contractual agreements or issues of compensation. What I propose is that you seek areas of opportunity where each individual can accept more responsibility within the existing framework of skills, workloads, experience, agreements and compensation schemes. I am not suggesting that you or anybody else in the organization ever act in violation of contractual agreements or even oral promises. The immense body of work following from the Hawthorne experiments demonstrates that people at every level in the organization are not only willing to accept more responsibility but welcome it – when it is properly managed. The primary force driving delegation is to remove artificial barriers to this process.

All objections must be addressed fully: every individual and group who argue against the changes must be convinced that the actions will result in not only a healthier organization but in increased challenges and job satisfaction for delegates. *Do not underestimate the magnitude of resistance*. This series of processes must be sold to everybody involved with as much enthusiasm as any other organizational change I have asked you to consider. Groups such as the union and personnel, those with institutionalized resistance, must be asked for a commitment to the changes. If the work is to be totally successful they must give that commitment positively.

Delegation must be universal

At the beginning of this chapter we quoted the usual objection to delegation: 'I don't have anybody to delegate to'. For many managers that may appear to be the case: people reporting directly to them may seem to be very busy. If delegation is to become a fully effective management tool it must occur at every level and throughout the organization.

Examine the alternatives: you may begin a series of delegations from the top downward. Each delegate is then going to be forced to delegate some of present duties if he or she is to have enough time to complete all routine work and achieve objectives. A better method is to start at the bottom: begin the delegation process with supervisors. There are two very good reasons for this:

1 When supervisors have delegated some of their duties they will then have time available to assume more duties as their department managers delegate to them. This process is led rather than being driven. Each successive phase is proactive rather than reactive and the phases can be made smaller, easier to manage and easier to evaluate.
2 The most difficult problems met throughout the organization with delegation will occur at this level:
   (a) The most serious objections from the union and personnel will arise when duties previously carried out by supervisors are delegated to staff. Experience gained here should assist the development of delegation in other areas. When problems have been successfully resolved at this level, acceptance for later phases elsewhere should not seem so formidable.
   (b) For the many reasons discussed in Chapter 9, the supervisor typically has a difficult time with the application of delegation. There is a feeling that he or she is the person responsible for completion of that particularly difficult assignment, and if it is delegated to somebody else on the section it might not be completed as well or as quickly as it might have been. The supervisor is correct in this assumption: it probably will not be done as well the first few times (see below, Risk). Some of this concern can be addressed if the initial duties selected for delegation are chosen for their simplicity and minimum impact on the product or service provided by the area.

Once it has been demonstrated that effective delegation is possible at the level of the supervisor, do exactly the same thing at the level of department manger. With the experience gained working with supervisors this next step should not be as difficult. Delegation must be applied throughout the operation, from section leader to chief executive, with nobody omitted from the process.

Risk

The risk associated with delegation is real and visible. In Chapter 1 we identified delegation as one specific area where resistance to change was most vigorous. A change in a method or procedure involves the risk inherent in your ability to forecast improvements in operations resulting from that change. Assuming that you have developed information in a reasonable fashion and planned the project carefully it should be possible to minimize this risk.

The risk involved in delegation is significantly different. Here you are looking at the same process or procedure but it is now to be performed by somebody who has not done it before. Learning and practice are part of that effort. The person doing the new activity will probably *not* be able to do it as well or as quickly as the one who had been doing it for a long time; there will be mistakes. In a production situation it is possible those mistakes will result in short term negative results for customer service, quality and cost management. So be it; this is part of the cost of improving the long-term health of the organization. If the process is well managed, if the principles of short segment task control are properly applied and if phases are small enough, any negative impact of the change should be small, of short duration and cause minimum disruption to the work of the unit.

Another element of risk follows from the principle of ultimate responsibility. When you delegate authority for a subordinate to complete a task, you still retain ultimate responsibility for successful completion. If the subordinate fails in this responsibility, you have failed in *your* responsibility. This is a genuine risk, not one that is merely perceived. Supervisors are particularly vulnerable to risk of this sort and they will need your strong and visible support. This risk, too, can be minimized when the delegation process is managed properly.

No doubt the unkindest element of risk for delegation, however, is that it is so visible: it is there for everybody in the world to see. If a methods change goes wrong, if it cannot be fixed and the only solution is to put it back the way it was before, you may be able to confine word of this to the immediate area. When you have delegated a duty and that process goes wrong, the entire organization will quickly learn about it. This is because you made this change over some strong objections from a number of people including, perhaps, the delegate. My only advice here is to remind you that this is what management is all about. Relax and try to have some fun with it.

People simply do not want to let go

There are two other issues to consider, the general matter of change and relinquishing ownership. These were both discussed in Chapter 1 and it is not necessary to address them in too much detail here, however:

- The general issue of change must be considered. Resistance to delegation is probably so strong because of the visibility and because the impact is upon regularly conducted, daily sorts of activities – delegation efforts will automatically upset stability zones.
- Delegation necessarily means that the delegator must relinquish ownership or at least part of the ownership for a process or activity. It has been recognized that this is difficult for every one of us. This is probably true for all levels within the organization, and this aspect of delegation is perhaps more difficult for the executive or senior manager than for the supervisor or department manager.

Elements of effective delegation

Eyes on-hands off

'Eyes on-hands' off refers to a management style that presents one more of those situations demanding that a manager continually juggle a number of conflicting needs. In Chapter 9 we introduced this concept when looking at the relationship between supervisors and the department manager. We outlined the dilemma that a manager faces when he or she must provide supervisors with strong, consistent, visible support while simultaneously allowing them the freedom and flexibility not only to manage the unit, but to try some things that will not necessarily work – to make some mistakes along the way (remember that if no mistakes are made, at least a few, they are not really trying).

This dilemma is nowhere more apparent than in the application of delegation, and it is true for people at every level in the organization. One of the objectives of this process is to free the delegator to assume more exceptional duties. If the delegator spends too much time following up on the delegate and becoming involved with the activities just delegated, the exercise has been a waste of time. When people delegate they must really let go.[1]

This means exactly what it says. The delegator must specify the task clearly and ensure the delegate has been fully prepared to perform it. Consistent with the principles of the tactical closed-loop management cycle and short segment task control, he or she must define phases, intervals of control, specific follow-up procedures and points of control. It must be clear to the delegate that the delegator is available on short notice should any problems arise that might require help. The delegate must be confident the delegator's full support is available for any matter relating to the task. The delegator must prevent interference from people outside the area who might have objections to the change in duties.

Finally the delegator must go away and leave the delegate to get on with it. Of all things I have recommended until now to improve the ability of a manager to manage, this is one of the most difficult to achieve. The delegate will never be able to assume ownership of the new task if the manager keeps interfering. The delegator will never be able to reduce involvement in the task, and improve his or her own time control and effectiveness, if there is continual interference.

And all this, of course, is complicated by the fact that as the delegator is walking away and leaving the delegate alone to get on with the work, there is the reminder that the delegator is responsible for successful completion of the work. The delegator is still ultimately responsible for total achievement of the objective – according to specification, on time and within budget.

No wonder people are reluctant to delegate.

Coaching for improved performance

A good eyes on-hands off relationship between a delegate and the delegator will come about only if the delegator understands how to use the technique; and this will only happen if he or she has been appropriately coached in the practice. The term coaching is used in different ways by different writers, but here it describes those specific actions a manager takes to support the professional development of a subordinate.[2]

Coaching is the process by which a department manager, for example, provides support for a supervisor who has just delegated some tasks to a subordinate, a section leader. If the section leader is to deal effectively with these new tasks, that effort must be well managed by the supervisor: by good use of eyes on-hands off practice. If the supervisor is to be able to use eyes on-hands off well he or she will need to have had the opportunity to learn the skills: to have been coached by the manager. It does not happen automatically or naturally, nor will it develop during formal training sessions. It is an example of a skill that can only be acquired and improved through one-on-one work between a manager and a subordinate – by coaching.

Coaching consists of a combination of agreed formal objectives, simultaneous loose-tight support for achievement of those objectives and a constant evaluation of the subordinate's professional needs. Be available when needed and do not look over the delegate's shoulder when the delegate wishes to test his or her limits by working a little close to the edge. It has nothing to do with the technical demands of the position; coaching has everything to do with helping the manager to become a better manager, to enable the delegate to be better at the present job and to prepare for further promotions. It must begin the moment it is recognized that somebody is to move from the ranks of staff to a position in management, when it is anticipated that he or she is soon to be promoted to section leader.

Delegation is an ideal subject for the coaching process. This is a further argument in favour of implementing delegation first at the lower end of the management structure rather than at the upper end.

Lateral reassignment of tasks

Consistent with the principles we have examined here, it is appropriate to consider whether a particular task is not only being performed at the correct level in the organization, but whether it is being performed by the appropriate person. When every activity in the operation is being evaluated for purposes of delegation a decision also should be made concerning which department or unit should be doing it.

During such an examination it often transpires that shifting responsibility for completion of a certain task from one unit to another makes sense. When you investigate, you discover no good reason why the work should be carried out where it currently is. You will also meet the same type of objections from the same people when you want to make a lateral change in duties. In most organizations the objection to relocating duties or tasks across department or unit boundaries is particularly acrimonious. Addressing those issues requires the same kind of patient effort you need to address issues of delegation.

Consider this

In one sense promoting delegation throughout the organization is easier than some of the other management actions proposed in this book. Any manager can begin by delegating the tiniest of duties. In an admin department, for example, something such as the administrative control of secure storage for items of value can be delegated one level lower. This might be a duty that takes a few minutes a day and can be carefully monitored by the delegator with a minimum of trauma. The ordering of a few routine supplies in a production unit can be delegated in the same way. These are both extremely small changes that can be well controlled and the delegator can respond quickly and easily to problems that may arise.

One of the additional and pleasant surprises resulting from universal application of delegation is that a number of duties and activities, when examined from this perspective, are identified as unnecessary to the operation. They can be eliminated immediately at zero cost to the organization.[3]

Delegation is a continuous process which should be applied to every duty and activity in the organization. The overall ability of the entire team to achieve organization objectives can be improved with the universal use of this management tool. Do not be discouraged by objections: answer each of them with a thoughtfully developed and carefully implemented process. The improved operational control will result in a healthier organization, and it will free you to work on some of those interesting things you would be working on if you were not encumbered with all of those onerous, routine tasks.

Do this tomorrow

Review achievements for four individual mangers within your operations. Select one section leader, supervisor, department manager and middle manager each of whom has been identified as having difficulty with personal time management because of an inability to delegate tasks effectively.[4]

Set up a three month project with each manager with objectives for delegating specific duties. Help each to create a fully developed plan to include properly structured processes for identification of delegates, presentation of objectives, preparation, implementation, follow-up and evaluation phases. Coach these four appropriately throughout. Support each visibly and assertively when the project meets resistance from Somebody In The Union or Somebody In Personnel. Remember, however, that it is the manager's responsibility to address all resistance from other sources: that is part of the experience.

Throughout the three month period evaluate your own effectiveness at delegation and make changes as needed. Lead by example. On completion of this pilot scheme generalize the experience to every other manager in the organization from section leader to executive.

Notes

1 Peters, *Thriving On Chaos*; op. cit. Peters vigorously supports the principle of *really letting go*. It must be carefully, thoughtfully and continually managed if it is to work well.

2 Some authorities argue that what I am describing as coaching should more appropriately be defined as mentoring. They confine coaching to narrowly defined, specific, focused tasks related closely to the job, and treat mentoring as the much broader, more general approach to professional growth and career progression. I see no need to make a distinction; both approaches ultimately support long-range objectives for both the delegate and the organization.

3 In Chapter 19 we will examine the elimination of obsolete and unnecessary activities in detail.

4 There are other reasons why managers experience poor time management, amongst them the inability to say no to you. This will be discussed in detail in Chapter 16.

■ CHAPTER 13 ■

The Metaphysics of Meetings

'Do you think they'll come? How long we going to wait, if they don't show up?' The older man stared at the open door. 'We ain't going to leave here before nine-thirty at the earliest. We got orders to hold this meeting'.

John Steinbeck
The Raid

Introduction

Meetings are like written reports: most are too long, are not structured properly, involve too many people or are unnecessary. People spend a great deal of time attending meetings and they spend a great deal of time complaining about the amount of time they spend attending meetings. Nothing is accomplished at many, and for those at which something is accomplished, the matter could have been handled in about one-quarter of the time. Everyone acknowledges this, yet keeps on going to meetings *ad infinitum*.

The issue of meetings is important because of their enormous cost: the expenditure of vast amounts of resources – staff, supervisory and management time. It is important for the present as is the implication for good utilization of every other resource. It will assume far more importance in the future. More and more of the work of the organization will involve the use of teams: workgroups and task teams. This will be true not only for the day-to-day effort to make the product or deliver the service, but also for special activities to address problems or examine options to current methods and procedures. In Chapter 10, for example, we discussed briefly the emergence of *ad hoc* teams and we said that much of their activity involved meetings. More people will be required to spend more time together in all sorts of meetings.

If you recognize that too much time is spent at meetings at which very little is accomplished, why do you continue to attend them, and why do you let them last so long? Why do you allow people throughout the organization to spend so many precious hours in meetings? Meetings are a useful element in communications processes. The goal should not necessarily be to eliminate meetings but to schedule and structure them properly to use this management tool effectively.

People want to attend meetings

Meetings are scheduled for various ostensible reasons: to communicate information to group members, to generate ideas and resolve a problem, to accumulate information and generate recommendations or to present recommendations to a project sponsor. Apparently people attend meetings for subtle and subjective reasons.[1] The full implications of the meeting as a mechanism for fulfilling various social or human needs are well beyond the scope of this book. It is not my intention to discuss them in detail. There is more to the dynamics of meetings than the need to address items on the agenda.

Meetings are sometimes perceived as status symbols: attending meetings in the boardroom regularly may reflect attainment of a certain rank in the organization. Within some organizations a kind of recognition is signalled when a person is elevated from that of dutiful listener to one permitted to express an opinion during a meeting. Chairing or even attending a prominent meeting can give one status and recognition not offered by the workplace.

A regularly scheduled meeting can function as a stability zone, a refuge from the chaos of the workplace. When the production schedule is in shambles you can postpone dealing with it for at least the next two hours while you attend the safety meeting. If the day has been a disaster so far, perhaps at the customer service meeting that misery can be shared with a manager from another unit who is having an even worse day than you are. An off-site meeting may be regarded as a reward, as a deserved break in the routine. Meetings can make you feel part of the group.

If a decision is needed, the decision-maker can obtain a certain level of comfort when the group comes to full agreement, or at least a consensus, on the issue. Disagreement within the group is a convenient excuse for postponing a particularly unpleasant decision.

Finally, scheduling plenty of meetings is often equated with good communications. It is somehow felt that if the organization is going to be properly contemporary in its business practice and its concern for the individual, it must arrange lots and lots of communications sessions. If managers spend a great deal of time in meetings talking to staff and other managers, they must be employing modern management technique. Meetings suggest group involvement, democratic management, listening and empathy.

Why meetings are scheduled

Every meeting should have a clearly identified purpose, to achieve a specific objective. If you ask an individual why he or she has scheduled a particular meeting and why certain people have been invited to attend, you must be provided with a definitive answer. Otherwise it is perfectly reasonable to question whether the meeting is necessary. If the response is something vague such as: 'Oh, it's about time we had another information workshop (or communications session or team briefing),' you can be confident the meeting will be a waste of time for everybody involved.

Meetings are scheduled for a number of reasons. You may be able to add several categories of your own. If, however, you cannot easily define the purpose, the meeting is probably unnecessary.[2]

To present information to a group

A decision has been made that certain information can be most effectively communicated to a number of people by presenting it to them as a group. Examples include an announcement to kick off a project, programme or new way of doing something, the introduction of new processes for customer service or quality management, regularly scheduled meetings to update people on the status of the business or of operations and information on such matters as changes in product lines or markets. This would be the meeting at which the chief executive announces major changes in the direction of overall objectives for the business.

The important factor here is that the meeting is strictly to announce something to a number of people collectively, it is not to engage in a dialogue or to obtain agreement or consensus. A decision has been made and this meeting is to announce it. The presentation may be extremely formal or rather informal. Depending on meeting format, questions and comments may or may not be entertained.

This is a necessary and useful meeting. The presentation must be based on all the considerations discussed in Chapter 11 for effective communications. One limitation is that there is no opportunity for immediate and detailed feedback. Nevertheless, the same question concerning session objectives must be asked: what results are expected from this communications effort? Again if the answer to that question is not easily stated, the meeting is probably a waste of everybody's time.

I have presented you with another dilemma. On one hand you are being asked to communicate intensively to keep everybody informed about what is happening. Occasionally this recommendation appears to be extreme – you seem to be being asked to overwhelm people with information. On the other hand you must be concerned about effective use of everybody's time. How much information is enough? As with every other management decision and action, the only answer is to evaluate it with respect to long-range results: is the action seen to be moving the organization closer to long-range objectives?

To announce good results

This meeting is to present special information to a group, specifically to announce good results or to recognize or reward individuals, teams or groups for good work. The significant difference between this meeting and other presentations to groups is that here the sole objective is to present good news, to support individual or group efforts through positive, visible recognition.

Here the trade-off between resource cost and results is even more tenuous than above. This type of recognition is a key component of *Tactical Management*: I urge you to consider this a good investment. This meeting must follow good work; it is under no circumstances a substitute for effective management action. Managers are continually faced with difficult choices. It is sometimes the case that a manager feels he or she can accomplish results without confronting issues simply by bringing people together and urging them, usually with a great deal of hyperbole, to get on with it. Examples include a reaction to serious product quality or customer service issues, or a recognized need to improve labour or line efficiencies. Gathering the workforce and exhorting them to change things, either positively or negatively, will not work. You must evaluate the use of this meeting very carefully.

To present information to an individual

This meeting is scheduled to enable a group of people or a team to provide information or data to an individual to enable him or her to make a decision. Included in this category are regularly scheduled meetings to update that individual. There is no dialogue or argument and the decision forthcoming will not necessarily be based on options proposed by group members. Input of every member is important, however, or the meeting has been a waste of that individual's time.

The purpose of this meeting is not to arrive at solutions or make decisions. This is the meeting that often degenerates into an open-ended problem solving exercise that goes on for hours and accomplishes nothing. Control must be very tight if it is to be effective.

To present a proposal

This is a meeting to present either interim findings or a final report for a project or other task team effort. The reason for this meeting is to enable the presenter to ask the project sponsor to sign off or otherwise approve either results, recommendations or findings.

This meeting must also be tightly controlled if it is not to turn into an open-ended workshop, problem solving session or forum for those who opposed the project from its inception. The objective is for the sponsor or buyer to approve findings or accept the recommendations. If this does not happen the meeting has been a failure and a waste of time. It is incumbent on the presenter to make adequate preparations and control the meeting so these results are achieved.

To communicate the status of operations

This category includes the daily or weekly customer service, quality or production planning session – sometimes a combination of all three, or a monthly meeting to evaluate sales or marketing activities. This is to address the requirement that a number of individuals simultaneously update each other on the status of several independent but related areas or units. Included in this category are also weekly staff meetings between a manager and a team of subordinate managers, and monthly board meetings.

It is typically difficult to control and always lasts at least twice as long as it should. It often ends up as a damage limitation session with myriad references to the FISH (first in-still here)[3] report on the status of customer orders. Evaluate this meeting very carefully. If it is scheduled daily, confirm that the same results might still be achieved if people met every other day or weekly; if it is presently scheduled weekly, perhaps monthly is a reasonable option.

This is not a problem solving session or workshop. What must happen is that each time an operating problem is isolated, a specific, closed-ended commitment is made by one of the attendants to deal with it. Look around this meeting and you will probably identify at least two individuals who never contribute anything. Eliminate them from the meeting; their time is being wasted.

Please note that reducing the frequency of this type of meeting seems contrary to the principles of the tactical closed-loop management cycle and short segment task control. Here again you are being asked to balance conflicting needs: on one hand for a number of people to receive current operating information and on the other to make most efficient use of their time.

To address issues before a standing committee

This category includes meetings scheduled regularly for those groups or teams usually referred to as committees. Examples are work to maintain manuals for operating practices or procedures, to monitor ongoing processes such as those for customer service or quality, or to evaluate tooling, safety or housekeeping.

These sessions are similar in conduct to update meetings. They usually last too long because they degenerate into unstructured problem solving sessions. They must be tightly controlled. What must occur is that problems are assigned to a group member for resolution. Resolution of that problem might require group effort, but that must be the subject of a subsequently chartered working party, not this meeting.

To address issues with a workshop or working party

This is a meeting where a number of people with different talents and experience come together to address one phase of a project: a problem, a change in methods or procedures, or to evaluate a proposal for something such as a new mainframe, production line or building. This is a working session rather than an information exchange. For example, if the project was a major revision to a procedures manual, this is the time when team members sit down to work together to draft the revisions. Workshops are a routine part of task team effort.[4] This category also includes brainstorming and other sessions to identify possible solutions to problems.

There are several critical requirements for good management of these meetings. The objective must be clearly stated and it must be appropriately phased so there is reasonable expectation for achievement in the stated time. No workshop or working party session should ever run for longer than two hours. If the work cannot be accomplished in two hours, then either the objective is too ambitious or the phase has been incorrectly structured. If it is necessary to schedule more that two hours, then arrange two sessions with a break in between. What typically happens if a break is not scheduled is that various members have to interrupt the session either to send or receive messages or telephone calls related to their other work.

You may argue reasonably there are some one-off sorts of workshops that cannot be conveniently fitted into my two-hour limitation. A good example might be an off-site session scheduled over several days for directors, executives and a number of high level managers to redefine strategic direction for the organization. Even here, however, you will probably achieve more if you schedule two-hour sessions with breaks at carefully defined points in the process.

To achieve a consensus or agreement

This is the meeting convened to achieve total agreement on an issue. The chairperson is charged with making a decision, is reluctant to do it and wants everybody in the group to concur with his or her choice.

A large number of meetings fall into this category and are a complete waste of time for everybody involved. Decisions are not made by committees, decisions are made by individuals.[5] Eliminate all of these from your organization – immediately.

To address issues with customers, suppliers and others outside the organization

We must also consider meetings involving people from outside the organization. These are different in that you do not necessarily have the same opportunities to sell improved meeting management processes as you do to people in the organization. A customer, for example, may insist that you and several other members of the team spend a full day at their factory working through revisions to product specifications. Even if you were confident the issue could be resolved in half the time by half the people working at your facility, you might not be able to tactfully propose a better way of managing the workshop.

For these meetings, particularly with customers, clearly you cannot exercise the same level of control as you can for meetings internal to your organization. If a customer is particularly demanding, you probably are going to have no option but to comply: in the real world that is sometimes the way things are. If costs are substantial and recurring, build them into the sales budget. However, remember that you are changing the way you do things and one of your objectives is improvements in customer service. Use your newly developed confrontation and communications skills to convince customers that compliance with your newly implemented meeting management practices will result in better service for them.

Effective meeting management

The meeting is a management tool. It is thus appropriate to establish formal processes to improve the utilization of the hours that staff, supervisors and managers spend at meetings. Requirements should be based on specific needs. Control of meetings should also take into consideration the subjective nature of some of the factors discussed above:

Purpose

The purpose for the meeting must be clear. Objectives or results must be defined. When the objective is being specified, the first important question is to ask whether a meeting is the best means of communicating the information. Is there a better use of resources: could the same thing be achieved with a memo, a telephone call, a personal visit or some other means? If the meeting requires the attendance of several people from widely scattered locations it might be effectively addressed by videoconferencing rather than jet flights and hotel accommodations. Justify this expenditure of resources with as much vigour as you demand for the purchase of a piece of capital equipment, because the cost of a single meeting of this type can exceed the cost of some capital projects.

Attendants

Identify who is to attend. Again, justify the expenditure in resources. If the same result can be achieved with the assistant manager from every department attending and returning to the department with the appropriate message for the manager and supervisors, significant savings have resulted over having had all managers, assistants and supervisors attend. Identify alternatives if the principal delegate is not available.

A further consideration is to examine whether the objective is better accomplished with one meeting attended by all or a series of meetings attended by subgroups. This is particularly true for working parties. Think back to some you have attended: you remember seven people sitting around for long periods of time watching another three working diligently.

Agenda

Agenda must be in writing. They must be in enough detail to enable those attending to understand fully what is to be accomplished and published far enough in advance to enable all those attending to prepare fully. They must include minutes from previous meetings where appropriate and any other statistics, data, information or reports that support the meeting's objective.

Schedule

The meeting should be scheduled so it is convenient for all attending. This should be obvious but frequently is not. For example, meetings for supervisors should not be scheduled for either the beginning or end of a shift when they are extremely busy with daily operational issues. The starting time and the scheduled completion time must be stated in the agenda. It must be accepted practice that anybody attending the meeting is free to leave at the scheduled end of the session. It is appropriate for the chairperson to stand up, turn and walk out; it is appropriate for the most junior attendant to make excuses and walk out.

Somehow through the years humankind has come to the conclusion that if you put enough people together in a room, leave them alone for a long time and provide them with coffee and biscuits great things will happen. This is not true.

Venue

The venue is important. The choice of location communicates much about the importance of the meeting. Schedule working parties in the workplace, not in the boardroom or off-site at a holiday retreat. Schedule kick-off meetings for important projects in the boardroom to communicate senior management support. Use your imagination. Think about how you respond to the choice of venue.

Select a format appropriate to meeting objectives. The needs might be for a conference style format with a podium and rows of chairs, a circle of people seated around a large table or a number of workgroups seated at individual tables. Consider this as part of the encoding process: how can the message be most effectively communicated to receivers?

Conduct

The meeting must be well controlled. The chairperson is responsible for confirming that presentations, discussions, questions and comments are relevant to the agenda. This is not always easy, particularly if issues are difficult, involve significant change or relate to extremely poor performance or serious operational problems. The chairperson must assertively maintain compliance with the agenda and the schedule. Objectives must be achieved. The meeting must finish on time. This is crucial to good resource utilization.

Unless the purpose for the meeting is purely to present information, everybody attending should participate in one way or another, otherwise they should not be in attendance and their time has been wasted.

Chairperson

The chairperson must be clearly identified and must control the meeting. It must be understood by all that he or she is fully in charge. This is one of those statements that seems obvious. Think, however, about all the meetings you have attended in the past six months. How often was the chairperson fully and comfortably in charge throughout the session? If the purpose for the meeting is to make a decision, it must be understood by all, but especially by the chairperson, that he or she is responsible for making it.

Outside needs of those attending

Provisions must be made so that there are *no* interruptions. It should not be the case that Somebody's Assistant or Somebody's Secretary runs into the room every five minutes to ask for advice or give the boss a message. Every person attending should appoint a deputy to handle all such matters until the meeting has been concluded. This is an element of good personal time management[6] and a further good argument for ending meetings on time.

Contingencies

For some meetings, particularly working parties, it might not be possible to specify the full agenda before the meeting because of the nature of the subject being examined. In these circumstances provide for those contingencies. One simple way to do this is to schedule the first meeting solely to set the agenda for the later meeting. This is one situation where good control can result in substantial time savings. What often happens because the agenda cannot be fully fixed in advance is that the meeting becomes open-ended. The result is the kind of session you are familiar with that goes on for three, four or five hours beyond scheduled time. This one is a real time waster; interruptions occur, people get tired, unhappy and sometimes downright ugly. If a workshop has gone on for four hours beyond scheduled completion they deserve to be angry.

Do this starting today

Begin today to apprise everybody in the organization that the use of meetings as a management tool must improve dramatically. To reinforce your concern for proper meeting management and control, and to make it visible for all, take these actions for every meeting you attend. Little preparation is required for any of these recommendations. There is no reason why you cannot start immediately:

- Bring your personal organizer to the next meeting you chair. At the beginning of the session, set the alarm to sound at the scheduled end of the session. Place the device in the middle of the table and state your intentions. Regardless of who is speaking and what has been achieved, when the alarm sounds, close your folio, stand up announce: 'Ladies and gentlemen, this meeting is ended', and walk out of the room.
- Look through your diary. Eliminate fully one-quarter of the meetings you are to attend. If it is your meeting, cancel it, if it is scheduled by someone else, decline to attend. For the remaining meetings reduce the scheduled time for each by half and support this decision with action. If you chair the meeting, use the alarm, otherwise excuse yourself and walk out at scheduled completion time.
- Deliberately miss one regularly scheduled meeting and see if anyone remarks on your absence. Do this again for the next session. If no comment is made after the second session stop attending – forever.
- Replace at least one scheduled meeting with a telephone call. Replace another with a hand-written memo.

- Schedule your most important meeting of the week for 7.00 am Monday or 5.00 pm Friday.
- Refuse to attend any meeting if you have received no comprehensive, written agenda, or if agenda were not received far enough in advance to allow you adequate preparation time.
- Cancel or end any meeting immediately anyone attending is not suitably prepared, even in the middle of it. Walk out if the meeting has not started within five minutes of scheduled starting time. In one month reduce this to two minutes.
- Refuse to permit any meeting you attend to be interrupted for any reason by anybody: 'I'm sorry, Mr. Grinch. I know you said you were absolutely positively not to be disturbed for *any* reason, but this is *really* important . . . !' Unplug the telephone in the corner of the meeting room; the caller is not part of the meeting.
- When the same item is discussed at two successive meetings and clearly no effective action has been taken, direct the appropriate person to resolve the matter. Inform him or her that you never want to see that item on the agenda ever again.
- Examine meetings and the number of people attending them, most are attended by too many. Discussion typically involves two or three individuals and everybody else just sits around and watches. When you recognize this happening, review it with the chairperson after the meeting. Direct him or her to schedule the next session for just those two or three, and to organize secondary meetings to update the others on results as needed.

Do this next week

First, determine precisely what meetings cost your organization. Conduct a study of the total time people throughout the organization spend in the preparation and attendance at meetings for one week. Convert this to total hours for staff, supervisors, managers and executives. Extend this by an average hourly cost for each. Include also the cost for word processing and photocopy resources to prepare and distribute agenda and minutes. Summarize this to understand the weekly cost in resources, then calculate the total cost for the year. Compare this with your total capital budget for the same year.

Then identify one unit that appears to spend an inordinate amount of time in meetings. Commission a task team from within that group. Establish practices for the effective use of meetings based on the content of this chapter. Require the team to implement these practices. Demand that managers justify the cost of meeting time with the same fervour they must use to justify any other resource. Evaluate the results over a three month period. Establish an objective to cut *total* costs for meetings in half. Remember, you are not concerned with the amount of time any individual spends in a particular meeting, you are concerned with the total time all people spend in all meetings. Generalize the results of this project to the rest of the organization over the subsequent three months.

Notes

1 Bowditch and Buono, *A Primer on Organizational Behavior*; op. cit. Bowditch and Buono provide a brief discussion of this thesis along with a number of primary references.
2 Training sessions are not considered here. They will be discussed in detail in Chapter 21. One-on-one coaching sessions, another type of meeting, have been examined in Chapter 12.
3 See the Coda for a discussion of the FISH report.
4 Task teams will be examined in detail in Chapter 14.
5 Review Chapter 10.
6 Personal time management will be examined in detail in Chapter 16.

■ CHAPTER 14 ■

The Task Team: Not just another pretty face

We are met to discuss our plans, our ways, means, policy and devices . . . It is a solemn moment. Our object is, I take it, well known to us all . . . the exact situation at the moment may require a little brief explanation –

J. R. R. Tolkien
The Hobbit

Introduction

The word team features prominently in management jargon these days. It is another axiom to which many people subscribe: those who organize and attend numerous meetings are usually the same people involved with lots of teams. In practice, however, in terms of results, team seems to be nothing more than another overworked management buzzword. Much contemporary experience demonstrates that teams, as they are presently structured and managed, do not consistently achieve objectives – according to specification, on time and within budget.[1]

The team is simply a management tool: a device to enable you to make good use of resources. It is a means for organizing work. Teams may be conveniently divided into two broad categories: to address a special project or unique problem, or to operate a process or meet an ongoing set of needs. In this chapter we will emphasize the former, which I have chosen to call a task team, although nearly everything in this discussion is fully applicable to teams in general. Not included in this examination of teams are workgroups currently described as workteams or self-managing workteams.[2]

A task team is a group of people assembled to address a special project or identified problem. The eminent characteristic of a task team is that it requires the amalgamation of a unique combination of disciplines, talents and experience not otherwise found working closely together elsewhere in the organization.

The basis for this chapter is that management of a successful team is not as obvious or straightforward as is sometimes assumed. Much team effort is wasted, and objectives are often not achieved, because the team is neither structured nor managed properly.

Why use a task team?

The importance of the task team is based on the assumption that organization requirements are changing; movement is in the direction of shorter production runs, more product lines, more variations within those lines, more specialized services and quicker response times. As this happens, people everywhere in the organization need a different kind of support. The number of occurrences of any particular activity will decrease, more and more work will become unique or nearly so, one-off or special. The task team is ideally suited to this situation.

A properly structured and directed team will improve use of management time. This is consistent with everything we have discussed in *Tactical Management* so far, but particularly with references to the manager as facilitator, the notion of delegation and the exception principle. For example, suppose you were responsible for a production unit and you had agreed a quarterly objective to improve process yield by a specified percentage, or you were an admin manager who had agreed to reduce cash exposure by a targeted amount. Consider two ways you might approach the objective:

1 You may *take* all the necessary actions. Calling upon subordinates, peers and superiors as needed to provide support, you identify needs, collect data, analyse those data, identify options, select an option, implement and evaluate results. You act – you *take* all the actions.
2 You may *direct* all the necessary actions. A task team is commissioned. Under your guidance and under the direction of the team leader, the same result can be achieved. You schedule frequent, very short meetings with the team to monitor progress, offer recommendations, evaluate results and make adjustments to the effort as you determine needs. You facilitate – you *direct* all the actions.

Of the two approaches, the second is in full correspondence with the entire Tactical Management philosophy. You are clearly now operating in the mode of facilitator and spending more of your time dealing with exceptions. The people doing the work are those closest to it. Hours for everybody are being more effectively and efficiently managed.

The task team is useful in a number of situations. At one end of the spectrum the assignment might be a minor change in a method or procedure requiring that three people work together through a few short meetings scheduled over one week. The other end of the spectrum might be defined by a fifteen member team assembled to develop and implement a new production facility requiring hundreds of hours of working party sessions extending over two years. In both cases the rationale is the same: to make the best use of precious staff and supervisory hours throughout the organization, to exploit every relevant bit of available expertise and experience, and to make the most effective use of management time.

Unless the function is fully understood and limitations are recognized, however, just as with any other management tool, the task team will not be effective. These requirements are not unlike those imposed on meetings: if the process is not appropriately managed, resources will be wasted. Success requires a stated practice applicable to the specific situation and strict compliance with that practice within the context of the work.

Task team requirements

One of the difficulties with efficient management of resources in certain areas or departments is the problem of levelling the workload – of confirming that all unit hours are efficiently employed for the long term. Consider accounts or maintenance: within those areas a number of different disciplines are gathered. Those various spheres of expertise are needed to accomplish overall unit objectives, but the different disciplines are needed at different times and at varying levels of involvement. The need is to maintain high standards for customer service and quality while simultaneously managing costs well. The attractiveness of the task team is that it is possible to bring into action all the resources needed, but only when they are needed, then remove them from the team when they are no longer required.

If a task team is going to achieve objectives – according to specification, on time and within budget, certain requirements must be fulfilled:

The sponsor must commission the action

The sponsor is the person who has decided a task team is the appropriate vehicle for addressing a situation. This role is critical to successful team effort. The sponsor has ultimate responsibility for managing the entire process and evaluating results, and is the caretaker of all resources used by the team to accomplish objectives. He or she is formally responsible for monitoring progress and providing all necessary support for the team. The sponsor is also specifically responsible for supporting any corrective action required to keep the process on schedule.

It is important to understand that the sponsor, as an individual, must be identified. while a committee may not sponsor a task team, the committee chairperson may. This is consistent with the unity of decisions principle.

The objective must be stated

The final objective for the team effort must be stated – clearly, unambiguously and with integrity. This is the responsibility of the sponsor.

In certain situations it might initially be impossible to identify the final objective. Consider, for example, the recognized problem that the mainframe is not meeting operational needs. Three possible options are to enhance present system, replace it with a new mainframe or replace it with networked PCs. Until the situation is adequately evaluated, that objective cannot be stated. The initial effort must be solely to diagnose the problem and offer potential solutions.

The team leader must be identified

This requirement is consistent with the unity of decisions principle: somebody has to be in charge. The team leader must be identified. He or she, all other team members and everybody else in the organization must know who the team leader is. The team leader is responsible for everything related to successful team management and results. Responsibility for effective liaison with the sponsor rests with him or her, and within the team charter his or her decisions are final.

The team leader is identified by the sponsor and selection is critical to success. The team leader must be somebody who has demonstrated an ability to deal comfortably with change, has the patience and empathy to assist others, is capable of moving easily within that part of the operation related to this project and can listen well. In addition, he or she should have a reputation for being good at wheedling, cajoling and obtaining commitments. He or she must be a good communicator and must be comfortable making decisions. The team leader must be capable of exercising tight control over the entire process.

Later, as everybody in the organization becomes more familiar with task team practice, it will be possible to assign the position of leader to those with less experience and less developed communication and management skills. Indeed, this is another example of a potentially good coaching opportunity.

One option is to identify team members and ask them to elect the team leader themselves. In my experience, people in most organizations are not now at readiness levels to make this a useful option. My suggestion is that within the present culture for most, it is best if the team leader is selected by the sponsor. Try managing task teams under this system for at least one year, then consider changing the process. However, look at your organization, think about it, then make up your own mind.

Team members must be identified

The leader, working closely with the sponsor, is responsible for identifying team members. Several considerations are critical to team success:

- Team members must be selected according to the talents they can bring to the project. That choice must be based solely on this consideration without regard to job title, level on the organization chart or department affiliation. This requirement is fundamental to the concept of a task team.
- An alternative must be identified for each member except for those projects with very short completion times. It must be understood that the work of the team will continue according to schedule whether the member is present or not. This consideration is particularly important for those projects that run over an extended period or require a great amount of members' time. It is reasonable to replace members at scheduled intervals, again for projects that run for a long time.
- All the required disciplines must be represented on the team. For example, a project for systems enhancement must include not only programmers and systems experts but also users and all others affected by results of the changes.

The project layout must be developed

The project must be comprehensively defined. According to specific requirements this might be accomplished by the sponsor and leader or the entire team. They must begin with the clearly articulated final objective and identify all the processes necessary to achieve it. Several things must be considered:

- A detailed specification must be created which unambiguously and completely specifies forecast results and the impact of those results, not only on those directly involved but everybody else in the organization.
- The project must be phased according to the principle of short segment task control. Resource requirements must be estimated and time requirements for team members forecast.
- The sequence of phases will follow logically from requirements of the final objective. Good time management practices might be well served if secondary teams are identified to handle certain phases of the project.

The project must be scheduled

The project must be comprehensively scheduled based on the layout:

- The schedule completion date is a crucial requirement for the statement of the final objective. The entire team, through the leader, must commit to it.
- An important provision is that the team will be disbanded upon completion of the project. This should seem obvious but it is not. If you review the notes from your tour you will discover at least one committee that meets regularly for no apparent purpose. Sometime in the dim and distant past this group met to address a problem. The problem was successfully resolved but the group has continued to meet every week or every month for years and years and years.
- Not all team members are required to attend the full agenda for every meeting. An individual member is only scheduled when he or she is needed – not required to sit through meetings watching others work.

Resource requirements must be fully identified

It is the responsibility of the team under the team leader to fully identify resource requirements. This is really part of the project layout. Depending on the nature of the particular project it might not be possible to identify requirements fully at the beginning. It might be necessary to complete early phases before later phases can be completely specified. When this is the case it must be clearly stated in the layout.

All necessary resources must be made available to the team

It is the responsibility of the leader to obtain all resources from every appropriate area in the organization where they are available. It is the responsibility of the sponsor to support the leader in this effort; he or she must confirm that resources are made available to the team. This includes releasing team members from home department duties to attend to team activities.

Team results must be final within the team charter

The sponsor is to confirm throughout the organization that team results are final within the team charter. If the objective is to select and implement a practice or action then this will receive compliance throughout, there will be no question that it is optional.

Management support for the team must be unequivocal

Management support for team effort must be full and unequivocal throughout the organization; otherwise the entire effort has been a failure and a waste of time for everybody.

Through the years much team effort has resulted in a great deal of time spent investigating something and the result has been an impressive report on a manager's desk but no alteration in operations – significant expense and nothing changed. When the sponsor commissioned the team it must have been because there was a recognition that present methods or practices required some revision, that some action must be taken. Task teams should not be commissioned to make recommendations, they should be commissioned to make something happen.[3]

Task team management

Requirements for task team structure and function have been identified. Successful team management must be achieved through actions based on all the practices we have discussed so far in *Tactical Management*: effective and appropriately applied management action, short segment task control, decision-making, communications, delegation and meeting management. Certain things are mandatory throughout the life of the team:

1 The primary reason why task teams fail is because the final objective is either not stated at all, or is vague or ambiguously articulated. If it is difficult to clearly and unambiguously define the objective, then you must seriously question why the team was commissioned.
2 The second most important cause for the failure of a team is that no leader has been clearly identified or the intention is to achieve aims democratically or by consensus. As we saw in Chapter 10, this is unworkable.
3 The third factor contributing to team failure is that no final project completion date was ever established – the effort was open-ended. In some cases the date was specified but it was either totally unreasonable or a commitment was never demanded from either the leader or the team.[4]
4 The sponsor must monitor all team activity appropriately. The mechanisms for this are careful attention to short-interval objectives and timely management action if there is a schedule variance. The sponsor is fully responsible for removing any obstacle faced by the team anywhere in the organization at any point in the process.
5 It is sometimes the case that the team cannot take appropriate action because their work has uncovered a bigger or more fundamental problem. This is because the original objective was in response to a symptom and not a root cause. It is the responsibility of the sponsor to

then evaluate the problem and redefine objectives This is a routine part of task team management and is to be anticipated. The flexibility of the process enables you to make this kind of adjustment with a minimum waste of resources.

6 Each team member must have full access to the entire project effort, including decision-making, everywhere that person's input is relevant. The leader must constantly seek to remove every obstacle to this process.

7 Tight control of workshops or working parties is essential. Schedule only those members involved in that particular phase of the work. Develop secondary teams where appropriate; there is no reason why a team leader cannot sponsor a task team. Do not waste any member's time having him or her sit during a session watching others work. Confirm that decisions are made by the leader when necessary. Be certain that he or she is not attempting to achieve consensus or unanimous agreement to the detriment of the overall effort.

8 People attending any meeting *must* be prepared. No work done at a workshop should be anything that an individual could accomplish working alone.

9 All relevant disciplines must be represented. One typical situation in this respect is the computer programming effort or systems enhancement that includes no user input of any kind. Another is the elegantly engineered production facility that is unworkable because no input from production people was considered.[5] Add members to the team at any point during the life of the project if it is recognized that different resources are required. Drop members from the team any time it is recognized that a particular resource is no longer making a contribution.

10 Management support for team efforts must be unequivocal. Unless the leader and the team are given the commitment that the work and decisions of the team will be implemented as policy, practice or procedure the entire effort is doomed to failure. *The role of the sponsor is crucial in this respect.*

You have been operating throughout your management career with a form of task team, although you might not have called it by that name. Computer programming and systems development, maintenance and engineering projects, and special projects you might assign to either an individual or a team are, in this sense, projects. Management of those efforts is no different from that for a task team; we have always referred to control of these processes as project management. It makes no difference whether the team is unique to one task, such as co-ordinating the move to a new building or they remain together continually, such as an engineering or design group. All the principles and practices presented here for the task team are immediately and directly applicable to project management.

Team roles

Over the past two decades, a number of management theorists have hypothesized that team dynamics, and ultimately team success, is influenced by the personalities of team members. Some propose that if teams are assembled from a number of different personality types that complement one another relevant to team needs, the likelihood of achieving good results is improved.

The argument is that the individual, for example, who is very good at thinking creatively and is thus capable of generating a large number of possible options to present practice will not necessarily be very good at focusing on the hard work needed to turn the proposal into a reality. On the other hand the hard working, self-disciplined individual who is good at managing all the detail necessary to turn an idea into action might not be very good at selling the change to those affected by it. When a team is organized, members should therefore be selected to include the range of personality types who will assume the various roles required for the work.

You are faced with another dilemma. For task teams, you need to select team members for the technical expertise and knowledge of specific parts of the operation they can bring to the team. According to team role theory, you should also be selecting team members based on the role they can potentially play in ensuring successful team results. You would be fortunate indeed were you to be able to match the two requirements perfectly every time.

My feeling is that consideration for technical expertise and area knowledge is the more important of the two: that you identify team members for what they can bring to the work. This is especially true when you consider that task team activity is closed-ended and the team disappears when objectives have been achieved. While I recognize the validity of the premise that individual personalities and the roles they play are important, I think this has more relevance for workteams or other groups such as committees and management teams that operate continually.

We will examine this issue in more detail in the next chapter when we examine self-managing workteams.

A cautionary note

Several conditions can interfere with successful team effort and cause significant damage, not only to the specific project, but also to the general image of the task team as a good management tool. They do not fit conveniently into the discussion above, and are matters that are seldom addressed in any meaningful way in management texts:[6]

- If a project is unpopular anywhere in the organization for any reason, management support from that area will at best be weak. At the worst the sponsor and the team can experience deliberate sabotage. Usually the subversion is fairly subtle, but occasionally it can be blatant in the extreme. This can have a negative impact on team effort in several ways:
  (a) Team members are not released from other duties to devote time to the project. The schedule cannot be maintained.
  (b) Other resources are not provided as requested. This also has a negative impact on the project schedule.
  (c) Managers will refuse to comply with actions or practices implemented by the team. The entire effort will ultimately be a failure.
  (d) Attempts will be made to disrupt the process through the dissemination of rumours, half truths or deliberate lies. Team credibility and therefore results will suffer.
  (e) Team members are ostracized from their primary groups or departments. This is probably the most insidious form of sabotage because it diminishes individual output to the point that the entire effort can fail.
- The leader can see the team as a means to promote his or her own agenda.[7] This may range from something fairly reasonable such as enhancing personal visibility in the organization to something ugly such as the deliberate destruction of career prospects for another individual. The extreme case, of course, is the complete destruction of the organization. This sounds preposterous, but think back through your time in the business community. You can recall at least one example of this type of behaviour.
- As we have noted, team membership is based on talents and experience, not on levels of the organization chart. It is totally appropriate for a leader to be managing a team consisting of some members who are higher in the organization than is the leader. Unless he or she is particularly comfortable in this role, it is to be expected that maintaining control of the process will sometimes be difficult. This is particularly true if he or she is not as assertive as some others on the team.
- Some team members may have an interest in promoting personal agenda over team objectives. The leader must be perceptive enough to recognize this and strong enough to address it. Forceful support from the sponsor may be necessary.

It is beyond the scope of this book, and it is not my purpose, to address relevant negative behaviour factors in detail.[8] These conditions are mentioned to reinforce the crucial contribution of the sponsor to successful team management. It is extremely important that the sponsor work closely with the team to identify these kinds of problems if they appear and to address them vigorously.

Support for the team leader by the sponsor is an important factor. This is an excellent opportunity to coach the leader in the workplace in a real life situation, there is nothing artificial or contrived about the problems faced in efforts to manage the team. These are situations where the ability of the sponsor to employ simultaneous loose-tight control, sensitive follow-up and appropriate, well-timed management action are crucial to project success.

Do this tomorrow

Locate a relatively uncomplicated, straightforward and small problem to address with a task team as a pilot scheme. Select an assignment that can be handled with perhaps no more than three disciplines, and which you estimate can be accomplished within one month and with relatively little team time. Sponsor the task team. Make certain throughout the effort that the entire process is in full compliance with all the requirements we have discussed in this chapter. Confirm that the leader, the team and you as sponsor are doing all the things you should be doing. Upon successful completion, compare results with past project efforts.

Over the subsequent three months, identify and sponsor four task teams: one for a computer systems enhancement, one maintenance engineering work such as an equipment rebuild, one admin objective such as a reduction in cash exposure or lost value, and one ambitious methods or procedures revision for a production or service unit. Identify tasks for which you would not ordinarily have been involved at this level. Take care not to violate either the unity of command or the integrity of command principles. Regard this as your coaching efforts for the appropriate managers in this respect; involve them as observers.

After start-up and preliminary work, maintain sponsorship of each task team with the expenditure of no more than half an hour of your time per week – one update meeting. If any team requires more than half an hour of your time, you must be doing something wrong. Consider your effectiveness as a manager when you can assume ultimate responsibility for four projects with the expenditure of only two hours per week.

Notes

1 Recall the story of the cream slicer. See Chapter 10, Page 151.
2 Self-managing workteams will be examined in detail in Chapter 15.
3 Occasionally the chosen option is to keep things the way they are. That is fine, if it is a positive decision and not simply avoiding making a decision.
4 In Chapter 16 we will examine the absurdity of either demanding or making commitments to unreasonable targets.
5 Review the notes from your tour.

6 Kanter, *When Giants Learn To Dance*; op. cit. Kanter is one of the few authors to address these issues. Her treatment is helpful.
7 See Chapter 10, Page 154.
8 See the Coda: On ultimatums and other disruptions.

■ CHAPTER 15 ■

Self-Managing Workteams: The whole *can* be greater than the sum of the parts

Within limits, each team could set its own pace. This was satisfying to its members and convenient to management from many points of view . . . . The deputy (first-line supervisor) stood largely in a service relationship to the group, which accorded well with the collier's independent, egalitarian spirit.

Michael Rose
Industrial Behaviour: Theoretical Development Since Taylor

It is team work that wins a football or baseball game; it is teamwork that enables a business organization to forge ahead; . . .

Arthur Capper
Citizenship

Introduction

Self-managing workteams are groups of typically from five to nine (in some literature, from four to ten and in other works, from two to fifteen) people who are responsible as a team for managing and performing all the short-term – daily to weekly – activities necessary to deliver a product or service. They are also responsible for managing medium- to long-term activities such as technical skills training, recruitment, process improvements and new product development. They work with the absolute minimum of close supervision or management control, but at the same time with adequate support as needed from the same supervisors and managers for the provision of all resources needed to deliver their objectives. As a team they plan, schedule, work, meet, discuss, problem solve, procure, scrounge, communicate, change or improve everything related to their work. They do this according to a contract they have agreed with management to deliver a planned volume of product or service according to a specification, on time and within budget. In exchange for this, from management they receive autonomy, meaningful support and agreed remuneration. As a team they take all actions necessary to manage a small business within the larger business we call the organization.

Within the context of this chapter we will not examine task teams, those teams commissioned to address one-off projects, change issues or process improvements, nor are we considering management teams, defined as teams of managers that have evolved to assume work formerly accomplished by a single manager.

Self-managing workteams have developed over the past thirty years or so in response to several conditions:

- With a shift to cellular manufacturing practices, there is the requirement that operators within a cell become multi-skilled to cope with all the tasks needed to produce a finished product or sub-assembly. Throughout the day as operators move product from one operation to the next within their cell, they thus become involved with an entire manufacturing process rather than each of them performing a single step in the process. It seems natural that people within a cell see themselves as a team responsible for the complete product or sub-assembly.
- Following the Hawthorne experiments a number of theories evolved that attempt to explain workplace behaviour in terms of human factors. Central to all these models is the principle that when people in the workplace are properly trained and provided with the right kind of support and direction, they can work productively without close supervision of the traditional sort.[1]
- Work with quality circles demonstrated the ability of people to work voluntarily and with the minimum of direct management involvement as a team, to complement each other's skills and abilities to identify and address operating problems. The idea of a team that can work without close supervision follows from this experience.
- We all are familiar with examples, typically in either the aerospace or computer industry, of teams that have achieved spectacular results when there was an urgent need to do so.[2] It is reasonable to generalize this to the workplace and conclude that a properly motivated team is capable of the same spectacular results for the everyday work of the organization.

Based on these situations it seems possible that a good way to organize the workplace is to set up small autonomous workteams responsible for an entire process, and to train and empower them to either get on with the work or call for help from management whenever they face a problem they cannot solve themselves.

Self-managing workteams are useful almost anywhere work is done by people. The most straightforward applications are in manufacturing and in administrative work. However, there is no reason why workteams could not be developed, for example, for the people who operate the switchboard, those who provide services such as word processing, photocopying or printing, those responsible for security services, or the people who develop, install and maintain computer hardware and software systems.

There is a recognized need in business and industry to develop work practices that support changing requirements for more flexibility in terms of number of products and product variations, all done at an ever increasing pace and at the lowest possible cost. The clear choice for an entity capable of achieving these new ways of working is a small, flexible, well-trained workteam qualified to respond quickly to changing requirements, similar to those we have in the past referred to as project teams, but with that methodology applied to the ongoing work of the organization.

However, the organization and operation of self-managing workteams require dramatic changes in the way people work, not just for those in the team but for everybody else with whom they interact. The move to the use of teams is not without significant trauma to any of those in the organization who are very comfortable with a traditional, hierarchical management structure and close control of daily work. It is necessary for you to consider carefully the readiness levels of people in your organization before embarking on this journey.

Team organization

Self-managing workteams do not have the same requirements for organization structure and function as those for task teams or project teams. There the need is for a combination of people with complementary skills and experience necessary for the achievement of a specific, closed-ended objective. Here the need is for a group of people capable of working closely together, each with the same combination of many skills required to deliver a series of products or services consistently over time to meet ongoing organization needs. There is the further requirement of self-management, that is, the team is responsible, as a team, for making decisions and taking actions to support short-term – daily to weekly – operational objectives that would formerly have been taken by a supervisor or manager. Involvement of the supervisor and manager, except for regular daily or weekly updates, when it occurs, is at the discretion of the team.

Elements of the self-managing workteam are these:

The team agrees team objectives with management

When the team is established team members meet with management and agree processes and team objectives to achieve the following:

- daily and weekly production targets,
- quality standards,
- rates of remuneration,
- the basis for team bonuses or incentives, if any, and
- the basis for measuring performance against targets.

They also establish and agree processes for the responsibility for:

- set-up and routine maintenance of equipment,
- procurement of supplies, raw materials or sub-assemblies,
- adjusting production schedules to deal with lack of stock or equipment breakdown,
- resolution of operating problems,
- process improvements,
- tightening quality standards for product and service specifications,
- new product development,
- assuming duties when team members are sick or on holiday,
- hiring team members,
- training team members and
- monitoring individual performance and addressing variances to it.

They further agree mechanisms to revise or adjust any of the above processes as organization and team needs change over time.

The team agrees and signs a contract with management

Team members and management jointly draft, agree and sign a contract that specifies a commitment that:

- the team will have the responsibility and the authority to manage all the above processes to deliver agreed levels of product or service according to specification, according to schedule and within budget, and
- management will provide all support the team requires to achieve those agreed targets.

The team performs all activities needed to manage daily work

These include:

- production scheduling,
- procuring supplies, raw materials or sub-assemblies,
- setting up machines and equipment,
- monitoring in-process quality,
- adjusting and making minor repairs to machines and equipment,
- monitoring team performance for output, quality and compliance with budget,

- addressing any variances to team performance,
- resolving operating problems,
- providing management with appropriate and timely performance reports,
- interacting with others in the organization as needed,
- providing or co-ordinating skills training for team members,
- screening, interviewing and hiring new team members, and
- monitoring individual performance and addressing variances to it.

The team operates without close direction from management

The team works without close supervision. Once the team and management have signed their contract, they operate with an absolute minimum of contact. The team is responsible for either delivering what members agreed to deliver or calling for help. Otherwise management leave them alone. When a team is functioning properly it should be possible for members to meet daily with their supervisor for a maximum ten minute update meeting each morning, and with their manager for a maximum half an hour meeting each week. Team members will call upon the support of their supervisor or manager as they identify a need.

Management operate without closely directing the team

Management do not manage the team, it is self-managing. Except for the daily and weekly update meetings noted above, there is no need for regular, formal contact. The team is responsible for contacting either the supervisor or manager when dealing with problems, or to ask for assistance to address an issue that cannot be resolved by them without outside help. The benefit for managers is straightforward: this arrangement removes the need for them to spend time with units that are operating well and leaves them time to deal with exceptions.

The team operates without a formal, identified leader

The team has no formal, identified leader. This requirement is fully in conflict with what I have said frequently about decision-making: that groups of people do not make decisions, only individuals make decisions. There are several points to consider:

- The team is a small, self-contained unit operating within a clearly defined work area. This is clearly unlike the position the millwright found himself in.[3]
- Team members have been specially trained to work as a team with the understanding that when a conflict arises amongst members that they cannot resolve, they ask their supervisor to intervene.

- When a team has been properly structured and appropriately coached, and is functioning well, often a natural leader emerges (see below: Team Roles).
- The supervisor becomes the arbiter when a conflict arises among members or they cannot arrive at a decision. In this sense, the team has *de facto* a single decision-maker.
- When you decide to establish self-managing workteams you have taken an ambitious stride toward the future. You are entering a new world where nearly everything we have said about organizations and the principles under which they seem to be able to operate effectively for the present comes into question. In the future, as readiness levels change, there will be less need for prescriptive principles of organization and a greater need for more relaxed, and some say chaotic, ways of managing all the human contacts occurring in the workplace.

The team agrees an individual identified as the single point of contact

If team members are to work with a minimum of interruption and without becoming involved in confusing and overlapping communications, it must be agreed that all minute-by-minute and day-to-day communications needed to connect the team with the rest of the organization are channelled through one individual. One team member is identified as the single point of contact. This is an important key to effective team dynamics. The position may be rotating, either daily, weekly or monthly within the team. The person assuming this position should be one who is very comfortable in confrontation and confident of achieving positive results with others in the organization outside the group (see below: Team Roles).

A single facilitator is identified to support team activities

The supervisor is the person to whom team members go when faced with a problem they cannot deal with themselves, and the person to whom other people in the organization come when they need to address issues other than daily work related activities managed through the single point of contact. This represents a dramatic shift in the role of the supervisor: he or she is no longer involved in managing work and directing people, that work is done by the team. The supervisor is responsible for providing technical support for the team and for making decisions when conflicts arise among team members. He or she is also responsible for communicating with the manager to whom the team reports when there is a need to address a problem between the team and others in the organization. He or she is responsible for assisting the team to obtain all resources needed to meet team objectives, particularly when they are in short supply and several units are competing for them. The supervisor has become a facilitator, arbiter, communicator and problem solver.

Here the Tactical Management model differs from some others who propose that first the supervisor, later the senior supervisor and eventually the first-line manager be eliminated when self-managing teams are operating well: that a properly functioning self-managing workteam is capable of assuming all these roles.[4] My feeling is that the supervisor functioning in this radically changed mode is vital to the success of the new organization. This is particularly true for a number of the organizations with which I have worked in recent years. In my experience, the readiness levels of both staff and managers were far from being capable of operating without clear, unbroken, unambiguous organizational lines of responsibility and decision-making authority. I accept, however, that some organizations exist today that are perhaps ready to eliminate up to the three levels of management immediately above the team and that my argument might not be valid five to seven years from now for many organizations.

Changes required in the traditional organization

If self-managing workteams are going to succeed, traditional perceptions of the relationship between the individual and the organization must change dramatically. Self-managing workteams break a number of rules concerning the way work is managed, decisions are made and good communications are ensured:

- Senior line management must be prepared to lead this new way of working and be seen to lead it. They must provide visible, meaningful, proactive support. This initiative is not something to be led by personnel, training, management services, quality control, production control or the manager for special projects.
- Senior line management must be prepared to initiate and monitor all training for team members in the new way of working.
- Senior line management must be prepared to support the team as required for any problems faced during start-up. For example, if the team has difficulty meeting operating standards, managers must:
  (a) initiate and monitor all additional training needed to bring the team up to standard,
  (b) be patient through this longer-than-anticipated learning process and
  (c) positively and assertively deal with all those in the organization who said from the beginning it would never work.
- Senior line management must be prepared to open the books to team members. They must be involved in budgeting, product costing, sales

revenues forecasts, overhead allocations, pay structures, raw material costs, yield percentages and other relevant accounting information related to the work of the team. Senior managers and accountants must be prepared to train team members as necessary to achieve this.

- Personnel must be prepared to relinquish authority to the team for interviewing, selecting, and hiring new team members. (Personnel will probably still be involved in the initial screening of applicants and will function as expert support for any issues of statutory requirements or policy). This includes processes for addressing negative performance variances for individual team members, and taking corrective action including removing consistently poor performers from the team. Personnel must be prepared to train team members for these elements of their work and lend support as needed.
- Personnel and others responsible for salary administration must be prepared to change the way team members are paid. In the ideal situation, team members contract for a weekly rate of pay and they are paid when they have delivered the agreed weekly production. If, for example, they have met the weekly target by 3.15 pm Thursday or 9.15 am Friday, they collect their cheques and go home. There are no time clocks.
- Team members must be prepared to work until schedule commitments are met, even beyond planned hours, for contracted pay when schedule variances were identified as having been within their control. There are no time clocks.
- Team members must be prepared to cover for sickness and holidays for other team members with no additional assistance when it is within their contract.
- Logistics must be prepared to ensure that supplies, raw materials or sub-assemblies are delivered according to schedule. They must be prepared to work closely with the team and acknowledge that, within the team contract, scheduling is now a team responsibility. The team, for example, may decide to move to a JIT (Just In Time) system. Logistics must not be talked into giving away raw materials allocated to the team to another part of the operation.
- Team members must be prepared to relinquish individual bonuses or piece rate payments in exchange for an agreed fixed salary or team bonus.
- The union must be prepared to abrogate any parts of contractual agreements or past practices that run contrary to team organization and operation.
- Personnel must be prepared to abrogate any parts of established company policy or past practices that run contrary to team organization and operation.
- Personnel and the union must be prepared to accept new pay grading structures and bases for incentive or bonus calculations. For example:

  (a) Individual bonuses or piece rate incentives are eliminated. Where agreed, these are replaced by a team bonus.
  (b) Individual grading ceases: within the team there is one grade of operator. A system is established whereby rates of pay increase as the number of specific tasks an individual team member is capable of performing increase according to an agreed schedule.
- Maintenance engineering must be prepared to allow team members to perform routine adjustments, minor repairs and lubrication tasks on equipment. They must be prepared to train team members in these skills.
- The toolroom must be prepared to allow team members to set up and adjust tooling and equipment. They must be prepared to train team members in these skills.
- Supervisors and first line managers in other parts of the organization must commit to not borrowing staff from the team simply because of a crisis in their area unless the team agrees to it following meaningful discussion. Likewise they must commit to not dumping staff who are excess to requirements.
- Quality assurance must be prepared to allow team members to perform all quality related tasks within the operation. They must be prepared to train team members in these skills. They include:
  (a) establishing process capability,
  (b) setting up and checking in-process quality monitoring equipment,
  (c) conducting in-process sampling, recording and comparisons with standards, and
  (d) identifying and taking corrective action for process variances.[5]

This is at the very minimum the number of substantial changes you and others in the organization will have to make, not only in the way you manage operations but in the way you perceive your roles as managers. These changes are ambitious and scary. When you make the decision to move to self-managing teams you must be prepared to plan the changes carefully and devote significant energy to selling these changes throughout the organization.

Team roles

In Chapter 14 we briefly discussed team roles in connection with task team dynamics.[6] I said that for task team operation, I felt the specific skills and expertise each individual brought to the team were more important than the particular personality role each was capable of assuming. With workteams, however, where a number of people with similar technical skills and experience work closely together continually to produce a product or deliver a service, it is appropriate to consider team roles.

Examples of team personality roles (these are after Belbin, you can find others[7]) are these:

Company worker

The company worker is a hard working and self-disciplined person with organizing ability and practical common sense. He or she is the person willing to take on the less glamorous, mundane or unpleasant jobs that nobody else wants to do.

Chairperson

The chairperson is one with a self-confident, controlled capacity to accept potential options and evaluate them objectively. He or she is capable of directing the team to make best use of its combined resources.

Shaper

The shaper is an outgoing, dynamic individual who is capable of challenging the team out of ineffectiveness or complacency. He or she is also capable of reminding the team of objectives and priorities.

Plant

The plant is the individual who has the imagination, intellect and knowledge to propose unorthodox solutions. He or she is capable of generating new ideas and helping the team shift direction if the present approach does not seem effective.

Resource investigator

The resource investigator is an enthusiastic, extroverted person who has the capacity to obtain resources necessary for team activities. He or she has an interest in exploring anything new.

Monitor-evaluator

The monitor-evaluator is a sober individual who exercises judgement and hard-headedness to keep the team on track. He or she is capable of examining a number of complex options and carefully selecting one that is likely to be the best for the situation.

Team worker

The team worker is a sensitive person who responds to people and promotes team spirit. He or she is able to intervene to avert potential friction and enable all team members to make positive contributions to team goals.

Completer-finisher

The completer-finisher is an orderly, conscientious perfectionist who fusses over team work and has the capacity for follow-up. He or she is able to maintain the same level of enthusiasm for completing a task as others have for starting it.

Work by Belbin suggests that when a team is assembled to include people capable of fulfilling all, or a significant majority in the right combination, of these personality roles, there is a better chance of consistently high levels of performance for the team. In an ideal world it would be possible to identify individuals with not only the technical skills and experience to deliver team objectives but also with the personalities to meet team needs. Most people writing about teams suggest that you put prospective team members through appropriate interviewing and testing processes to identify the particular role each is capable of playing, then select team members accordingly. I agree that at a greenfield site this might be workable.

There are, however, several factors to consider:

1 You are probably not starting with a greenfield site, you are starting with a group of technically competent people who are operating reasonably well within the present organization. Your objective is not to throw all these people away and start afresh, but to help them reorganize themselves into self-managing workteams and coach them so they will be able to deliver more than under their old organization.
2 Similarly, your objective is not to sift through the entire organization, identify the individuals who meet team requirements for technical skills and personality roles, build them into a team and leave the rest of the organization bereft of their talents. Your objective is to make the entire organization better at achieving long-range objectives by helping *everybody* improve the way they work.
3 One of my theses and a theme central to the Tactical Management model is that an important part of your job as a manager is to help people throughout the organization to be the best they can be. You do this by creating ambitious but reasonable expectations for every individual, then supporting their achievement through managing, training, coaching, leading by example, wheedling, cajoling, following-up and anything else it takes to enable them to realize their potential.

Having said all this, if workteams are not performing as well as you are confident they can, if they are not meeting expectations or delivering agreed objectives, you must investigate and take some action. If you have eliminated other possible factors such as the lack of clearly agreed objectives or your failure to provide adequate resources, it is appropriate to examine the combination of personalities within the team. If several of these personality types are missing from the team, it is possible this is contributing to the lack of team success. Even with good support and effective coaching it is likely that a team made up entirely, for example, of company workers will not be capable of the creativity and innovation necessary to make the team successful in a rapidly changing workplace. Similarly, while a team made up entirely of plants might be capable of generating plenty of innovative solutions to problems, they might not have the stamina to carry through with all the hard, sometimes mundane work needed to turn any of these potential solutions into results.

Think about this

It is difficult to quantify benefits resulting from a move to self-managing workteams. Much of the literature is either anecdotal[8] or proselytising[9] in presentation and scope. You can find articles and fragments in almost every current business or management periodical. Some promise impressive improvements in productivity – anywhere from 30 to 50 per cent. Most downplay the significant effort needed to change the present organization culture to make the process a success. My personal estimate is that, given positive and comprehensive support from the entire organization, a properly developed and well-trained self-managing workteam should be able to achieve initial improvements in performance of from 20 to 25 per cent over present operations, probably within the first six months. Reductions in levels of scrap and rework, and improvements in customer service and quality are impossible to quantify without a detailed analysis of the potential for your particular operation.

The real benefits, however go well beyond immediate gains in productivity. They are:

1. You now have in place in your organization a production team capable of maximum flexibility with respect to its ability to deal with rapidly changing customer needs. Those closest to the work are responsible for performing and managing it.
2. You have significantly reduced the workload of supervisors and first line managers to free them to spend more of their time working on meeting the challenge of helping you create an organization for the future.

Are you ready for self-managing workteams in your organization? There are two simple tests: are you and your organization ready to do away with time clocks and such humiliating practices as random bag searches and are you prepared to allow team members go home late Thursday afternoon or early Friday morning, with full pay for the week when they have delivered the weekly production target? If you are uncomfortable giving a positive answer to these two questions then you are not ready to start thinking about a move to self-managing workteams.

Realize, also, that you must be doing this for the right reasons. This is not a cost cutting or union bashing exercise, or an attempt to rid yourself of an outdated and unworkable piece rate incentive system. If an eight member team, for example, has demonstrated its ability to cope with sickness and holidays to the equivalent of one person for the year, do not cut the team to seven full time members for the following year and expect them not to be suspicious of your motives. If a team is not performing to standard, do not turn the management services department's video camera on the operation to discover who is under performing, as happened in one operation with which I am familiar. Do not unilaterally and secretly identify potential team leaders and send them into the workplace to, also unilaterally and secretly, identify potential members for 'their' teams. These practices are patently transparent to people in the workplace and will ensure the failure of any teambuilding effort.

Do this over the next three months

Identify three potential areas for the implementation of self-managing workteams. Select one production process, one admin process and one from another area such as a maintenance, engineering or computer systems operations. Conduct detailed analyses of the potential for improvement in these areas with respect to customer service, quality, labour utilization, scrap and rework. Meet with your senior management team and review opportunities for developing teams for these areas. Consider carefully everything we have discussed here. If you feel confident you and your organization are ready, then over the subsequent six months commission projects to create and install three teams, one in each of the areas identified in the study. Monitor their progress over a minimum one-year trial period. When this pilot scheme has proven to have been successful, generalize this experience to the rest of the organization.

Notes

1 See Chapter 5, Page 71–2.
2 Tracy Kidder, *The Soul Of A New Machine* (London: Penguin, 1982.)
3 Review Chapter 10.
4 This argument was considered at length in Chapter 9, Page 138; Two optional models, and is supported by discussions in Chapter 10, the millwright paradox.
5 In-process quality management will be examined in detail in Chapter 24.
6 Belbin, *Management Teams: Why they Succeed or Fail*; op. cit. Belbin's treatment is particularly helpful. While he addresses management teams rather than self-managing workteams, his work is nonetheless useful in this context.

7 For example, Mike Woodcock, *Team Development Manual* 2nd Edn. (Aldershot: Gower, 1989.)
8 See, for example, Peters, *Thriving On Chaos*; op. cit.
9 See, for example, Robert F Hicks and Diane Bone, *Self-Managing Teams*. (London: Kogan Page, 1991.)

CHAPTER 16

Realistic Personal Time Management: Saying 'no' can be good for you

'Well, now see here, Frank, that's a thing I want very much to talk to you about but I haven't the time right now. I haven't the time, have I, dear?' 'No, Mr. Baumbein, ...You certainly haven't the time'. 'You see. I just haven't the time'.

Evelyn Waugh
The Loved One

'I know I said I would do it but I didn't have the time'. 'If you tried saying "no" more often, you might not have to say "I know" so often'.

Tactical Manager

Introduction

Personal time management is another popular management topic these days. Count references to the subject in any recent management development syllabus, or calculate the cost in management hours your organization has scheduled in the past year for courses or seminars on time management. Examine the myriad imaginatively designed diaries, worksheets, boards, todo lists and personal electronic organizers people in the organization use in their attempts to organize personal time.

Personal time management is nothing more complicated than that you take charge of what is happening to you. You spend significant time and effort planning, scheduling and assigning work to others; you can benefit from applying the same practices to your own work.

Whenever you plan work for somebody on your team, once the job has been specified you match available resources to the task. You would not under any circumstances commit a staff member to perform work without reference to a standard – not necessarily a formal standard, but at least an estimate or rule-of-thumb projection. Yet when you commit to a task yourself you give no thought at all to the standard: you make no attempt to match up available resources to the work to be done. You blithely say 'yes' and add it to your endless list.

The result for you is not that you are unhappy about the total amount of time you spend working, although most of us would admit it would be nice to be able to spend a little less time on the job, but that you are frustrated because you never seem to be able to finish all the work you hope to accomplish in any given period.

My premise is that when you have identified all the work you are expected to do and matched up available resources – you – to perform that work, if there is more work to do than there is of you, something must change. Since your time is finite, options must be considered. This may seem so obvious that it needs no explanation. If that is the case, why send anybody on a time management course?

The problem is that usually you do not try to change anything; you neither look at your total workload in relation to your available hours, consider how you might revise priorities or delegate tasks, or discuss your dilemma with those whose requests fill your list. What you ordinarily do is continue to struggle, and in that effort you miss delivery dates, leave projects partially completed, perform work that does not meet your personal standard and continue to make promises you know in advance you cannot keep. You are continually frustrated and nothing changes.

Good practice

There is really little need for theoretical discussion. The fundamental requirement is to introduce good practice, then concentrate on establishing a consistent discipline.

You have a set of constantly changing claims made upon your time during the day. Some, such as the needs of the basic work of the unit, may be relatively easy to forecast.[1] Others, such as the demands of peers, requests from other units in the organization and your boss, may be extremely difficult to predict. Superimposed on everything else are the expectations you place on yourself.

You feel you are too busy to make any changes in the way you do things. If I were to suggest that you spend more time planning, for example, your reply would be that you do not have the time to plan. If I were to suggest that you delegate some of your work, you would reply that you have nobody to delegate to.[2] What you mean by this is that you do not feel you have time to take the steps I recommend or train a delegate.

If personal time management is to be effective, it is necessary to introduce some order into this process:

Capture the entire workload

Identify all the work you have to do. This is represented typically by the running, open-ended todo lists we all maintain. Be certain you make a clear distinction between all the things you *must* do and all the things you *would like* to do if you had more time. Consider desired completion dates. Make a distinction between the desired and the scheduled completion dates; they are not the same. The desired date is when the requester would like to have the result, the scheduled date is when you plan to complete the work. The desired date is not under your control, the scheduled date is.

Evaluate the entire workload

Assign time values to every task. Apply a time that reflects the hours you would need to complete the work if you were operating at a reasonable pace and without interruption. Be realistic: add 20 per cent to your original estimate for contingencies. After some practice reduce this to 10 per cent and next year to zero.

Eliminate unnecessary work

Review every task critically and ask whether it needs to be done at all. Do not be gentle; a modicum of ruthlessness is appropriate here.[3] Eliminate anything that is unnecessary from your workload. Sometimes a task will spawn other tasks. Review the list carefully for proposals that overlap and projects that might eliminate the need for other items on the list. Consider any work that might appropriately be assigned to a task team.

Delegate work as appropriate

Identify, then delegate all tasks for which that action is appropriate.

Prioritize the remaining work

Prioritize those tasks remaining on the list; sequence all work according to importance. Remember the Brussels sprouts principle: review priorities with those who assigned the work, especially the boss.

Match available time to the work

Match available time – your time – to the work to be done. This is where the traditional effort fails. If you usually work a ten hour day, do not presume to have ten hours available every day for tasks. You must allow time for routine work and emergencies.

Revise priorities as necessary

If there is more work than time to do it, review priorities critically. Examine requested and scheduled completion dates for opportunities to make revisions.

Say 'no' as required

Say 'no'. Do not commit to any task that you know in advance is not attainable. It makes no sense. Do not agree to unreasonable demands; do not force the people who work for you to make unrealistic commitments. It is a waste of time for everybody.

The correct action is to place the onus for prioritizing on the requester. Assume your boss has presented three demands, any one of which can be delivered on schedule, but all three cannot. It is crucial that you ask him or her to revise priorities: to sequence the tasks in order of importance and revise completion dates accordingly. If you cannot complete all work on time, the only meaningful response to those requests is 'no'. This is upward communications of the most demanding sort. If it is essential that all three are completed according to the original schedule, the only remaining options are that either you ask for more help or the boss makes the offer.

Many tasks are self-imposed. These demands are not only those that typically require a significant amount of time, but are also those over which you have full control. Managers responsible for computer systems development and maintenance operations are notorious for burying themselves with self-imposed work. These managers, in the most positive sense, strive to be all things to all people: they seek to solve every problem for the organization – today. They allow themselves and everybody in their departments to be interrupted at any stage of a task to deal with each new demand for service or support. They seldom say 'no' to any request. This is all fully within their control and it is self-imposed. When you examine their workloads, you discover that they go home at the end of the week with around fourteen projects unfinished, each about half an hour short of completion.[4]

This discussion has nothing to do with the appropriate, immediate reaction to systems crashes or equipment breakdowns, safety problems or the rapid response to a customer service or quality problem. I am referring here to those kinds of solicitations that regularly land on their desks solely because they and their departments have achieved the reputation for always seeming to be able to make something positive happen.

Do this today

In earlier chapters you were asked to go out to the shop floor or into the admin office and manage something: to direct somebody in the organization to make something happen. Before you introduce this effort for personal time management to anybody else, I will ask you to take some actions yourself. Success will be based wholly on practice; the mandate is that you make it happen the same way every day, day-after-day. Because this process requires change of the most personal nature, you will have to be totally comfortable with it before you can lead others with full credibility. Discipline and consistency are the factors that will ensure the effectiveness of this process:

- Spend ten minutes in the morning planning your day; it must be your very first activity every day. This is true whether you as a section leader or the chief executive. The plan must be realistic and must take into account both the routine sorts of things you expect to do and some allowance for emergencies. You must answer, without too much detail, the question: 'What can I *reasonably* expect to accomplish today?'
- We have already addressed the problem of dealing with one frequent emergency: that is that the boss places unreasonable demands at very short notice on your time. Emergencies arise from time-to-time and must not become an excuse for not planning. Your efforts will convince you it works; then sell it to everybody else.
- Design a DAILY PLAN. Make it simple; an A5 format is convenient:

Figure 16.1 A daily plan

DATE: **DAILY PLAN**

PR.	ACTIVITY DESCRIPTION	EST.	√

(a) Enter under ACTIVITY DESCRIPTION the four or five critical tasks you absolutely, positively must complete today. Enter nothing else; this is not your running todo list.
(b) Prioritize those tasks. Enter either 1, 2, 3, or A, B, C, under PR. according to their relative importance.
(a) Enter an estimated time under EST. Enter the time in which you could reasonably expect to complete the task if you could work without interruption.
(d) Examine your estimated times. If the total is more than three or four hours, you will not complete the work today. This step is the key to the success of this process. Most attempts at personal time management fail here because there are no allowances for contingencies of any kind. If the plan is to have solid credibility, if it is to work consistently, it must reasonably reflect your plans for the day. If you schedule thirteen or fourteen hours of tasks, as you do now, it will not work.
(e) Keep the DAILY PLAN in front of you during the day as a visible reminder. This can be especially helpful when it appears that a meeting will run beyond schedule. Often you need do nothing more than look down at your DAILY PLAN and scowl meaningfully to speed up a lagging presentation.
(f) Check each item when complete. It is useful to file completed DAILY PLANS for future reference for the date a particular task was completed.

Use this to manage your day. If you practice for five or ten days you will continue to use it for the long term.

- Spend the next hour or two, as your particular operation requires, to organize the day for your staff, deal with crises that have evolved since yesterday, make work assignments and handle enquiries.

  Do not schedule any meetings during this period. Your attention to the needs of the workplace is crucial in dealing with problems and issues while they are still relatively small and manageable. If you spend the entire morning in meetings without having spent time assisting your team to organize the workday, you will probably have to spend all afternoon dealing with problems that might never have occurred.
- Then isolate yourself from the rest of the world for a specified time. Make this a formal part of your daily routine; do it every day at about the same time. Depending on your workload, schedule a minimum of forty-five minutes to a maximum of one hour. Arrange for one specific individual to take your messages. The instructions must be explicit: the caller must be assured that his or her message will be forwarded in detail and must be told precisely when you will return the call. Do not

deviate from this schedule unless the building is on fire. All the people with whom you come in contact daily and who expect to see you at the moment, including your boss, must be made aware that you are not available, for any reason, during this time.

You are free to work on anything you choose. You will find that you can accomplish a great deal during this time when you can work without distraction. Relax, the place will run without you. Contrary to your hopes, the entire operation does not grind to a halt when you leave the building to go on holiday, for a seminar or if you are ill.

For the supervisor this recommendation may appear contrary to our discussion in Chapter 10, that he or she must always be immediately available to make decisions required by actions in the workplace. When the supervisor is isolated for these forty-five minutes, the authority to deal with any problems arising that cannot wait must be delegated to a section leader – a convenient coaching exercise – or another supervisor. In the absence of an appropriate delegate, the unit manager may assume this duty.

This is a very important component of effective personal time management, second only to daily planning. The rationale may not be obvious. When you can work completely free from interruption for a time, productivity is at least double what it would be otherwise. Again, you will convince yourself of this only when you have tried it. Do this for ten days before you try to evaluate its usefulness.

- Finish what you begin. If you are within thirty minutes of completing a task, do not stop when someone asks you for something. Send the person away. Tell him or her to go out, have a cup of coffee and return later.
- Photocopy this sign, enlarge it and mount it on a bit of card. Display it in a prominent location on your desk if in an open-plan office or otherwise on your office door when you need just a few more minutes undisturbed to complete a task.

Here you might argue that this discussion has made no reference to the use of computer based diaries or organizers, that I am promoting the use of little pieces of paper to do a job that should be accomplished with contemporary electronic information technology. Your argument is reasonable and must be addressed. I have not referred to electronic systems for several reasons:

- My central hypothesis is that the basic requirement for effective time management is a personal discipline, and this is totally separate from the mechanism you use to monitor the process. In this respect, the choice of PC-based system, personal electronic organizer or hand-written worksheet is entirely yours.
- Within our present culture there are till some circumstances where paper remains the preferred medium. You, for example, are now reading from a printed page, you are not looking at a PC screen. Many of us are more comfortable with paper for some applications and I think this is one of them.
- My other concern is this: I feel strongly that there are still certain circumstances where looking at information on a piece of paper has significantly more impact for a manager than calling up and viewing the same information on a PC screen. Consider, for example, the DAILY PLAN. In my experience the action of looking at this worksheet displayed prominently on your desk is more effective in reminding you of the time value of certain tasks than would be your calling up the same information on either a PC-based system or an electronic organizer.[5] Having made these comments, I recognize that paper versus electronic information management is an area not only within business but within our entire culture where events are changing very quickly. I would not necessarily expect my argument to be valid five years from now. I also recognize that for you personally and your particular operation, the argument may not be valid now. Make up your own mind.

Do this over the next four months

Developing and implementing a comprehensive personal time management process throughout the organization will involve intensive effort from you; it will not happen in any other way. Unlike other transformations taking place in the organization, it will be necessary for all supervisors and managers to make substantive changes in the way they conduct themselves nearly every minute of the workday. You are tampering with important stability zones. Because the entire day is affected by these changes the perception will be that the risk is colossal. The risk is not colossal; implementation can be phased as for most other change processes. The risk associated with delegation, for example, is far greater. Remember, however, it is not the fact that is important, it is perceptions of the fact. Some of the building blocks are already in place. The work you have done so far for control of meetings, delegation and the management of task teams all is directly related to improved management of personal time.

The first important step is to create, implement and execute your own personal time management process. Develop your project based on all the elements we have discussed in this chapter. Operate under this for one full month, evaluating and revising as necessary throughout that period. That month will give you the opportunity to practice working in the new way. Of far more importance, however, is that it will be the initial phase of the effort to train the entire management team. Your subordinates, peers and the individuals to whom you assign the job of taking messages when you are sequestered daily will also be learning. Training bosses is difficult, and your boss will not be happy the first few times you say 'no'. He will be even less pleased the first time he is told that you are in the facility but you are not to be disturbed for the next forty-five minutes. Be patient – your boss will learn. Do not forget that he, too, has a menacing carnivore lurking out there somewhere.

Use your own experience to create a process for the rest of the management team. Do not try this until you are totally comfortable with what you have learned. Your credibility will be crucial to the success of this effort. Unless you are able to communicate unqualified belief, it will fail. You must lead this process, you cannot drive it. It would be better to run your own scheme for another month rather than attempt to introduce this to others prematurely.

Identify four managers who report directly to you. Select those recognized to have difficulty with personal time management. Tell them what this is about. Conduct observations in the workplace: spend enough time to understand how each operates. Use the information gained during this analysis to develop processes for them.

Working jointly with them, create three-month objectives for improvements in personal time management. Obtain a positive commitment from each and implement the process. Follow up closely and provide all required support. Revise as necessary.

At the end of three months evaluate the results. If both you and all four of them are completely satisfied, coach all of them comprehensively as they develop and implement similar processes with four of their subordinates. You should then have the methodology and a qualified team in place to install the process throughout the organization.

Notes

1 In Chapter 17 we will examine work planning in detail.
2 Review Chapter 12.
3 We will discuss this practice in detail in Chapter 19.
4 Review the notes from your tour, then go back out and look at their desks.
5 In Chapter 17 we will consider this requirement for management reporting systems.

Management Operating Systems: Plan your work and work your plan

Once we were sure, however, that 47 tons was a proper day's work for a first-class pig-iron handler, the task which faced us as managers under the modern scientific plan was clearly before us . . .

Frederick W. Taylor
Principles of Scientific Management

Work expands so as to fill the time available for its completion.

C. Northcote Parkinson
Parkinson's Law

All work can be measured.

Tactical Manager

Introduction

This chapter addresses the design and installation of management operating systems to improve control of daily work and improve labour performance for the entire organization, including not just production and primary functions but support and service labour:

- Improved performance for a given number of labour hours immediately reduces throughput time and unit labour costs, which results in better customer service. Increased attention to work activity content immediately improves product or service quality.
- Good utilization of labour, that most precious of resources, makes an important contribution to organization health. Improvements in labour performance on the order of 20 per cent in real terms are relatively easy to achieve, quickly and at zero added cost – without capital expenditure.
- Correctly structured operating information will identify opportunities

for positive changes in methods, procedures and practices, and the recognition of training needs.

In the Introduction you were asked to conduct a ratio/delay study, then compare the performance you observed with that reported under your present operating system. The purpose of this exercise was to convince you that important opportunities exist for improvements in performance. Now conduct a similar study in another unit in the organization, one where performance reporting is not in place because you have been advised it is impossible to measure that type of work. There you will discover potential of at least the same magnitude, often greater.

My second reason for asking you to make that comparison is to demonstrate that existing performance reporting systems are frequently lacking in certain respects. If you observed 65 per cent performance during your tour, system reported performance is probably running between 90 and 95 per cent. It would appear some changes are in order.

I believe that every human activity within the organization can be specified and measured. All work can be planned, managed and evaluated, and the result when this is done is consistently better short-term operational control, improved labour utilization, and improved customer service, quality and cost management.

Special emphasis will be placed on implementation of operating systems in service and support areas, and other places where work specification and measurement is somewhat obscure. Because the perception has been that work measurement is either difficult or impossible, management control has frequently been neither as effective nor as efficient as it might have been. Significant opportunities for improvement exist in these units; that is one reason why this argument is important. Of greater importance, however, is that improvements in service and support functions *always* have an immediate positive impact for the delivery of the primary products or services of the organization.

Your accountant has always needed to distinguish costs under various headings such as direct, indirect, fixed or overhead. Many operating systems are fed by data structured to drive those accounting systems. We are concerned here about operating information – in reporting about what happens daily on the shop floor or in the office, and in using that information to improve management of the operation. We are interested, for example, in total hours, not whether those hours are classified by the accountant as direct or indirect. This will have an impact on system design in two ways:

1 the system must account for *all* staff and supervisory hours, and *all* products and services produced and accepted by the customer; and
2 it is likely this will result in a certain amount of duplication in the reporting effort.[1]

The management operating system

Review the tactical closed-loop management cycle. All those elements must be included in a properly structured management operating system. We also need one additional element, standard data, and one additional definition, performance:

- Standard data are all the information needed to convert a planned volume of products, parts, services or activities into equipment requirements, materials and hours necessary to deliver those products or services. Standard data include material and product specifications, procedures, routing sheets and, in particular, labour time standards or time values to identify all activities necessary to complete the work of the unit.
- Performance is defined as work done measured against hours required to accomplish that work. Performance is usually calculated by dividing standard hours earned or estimated hours completed, units or equivalent units of product, or some other measure of completed work by actual hours worked and stating the result as a percentage.[2]

The general structure for a management operating system consists of the following elements:[3]

Long range forecast

The long range forecast is a long-range plan stated in terms of revenues generated from the principal products or services delivered by the operation. For non-profit operations such as municipal governments or health authorities, forecasts are usually stated in terms of volumes of services to be delivered. It is typically developed around a one-year cycle and then broken down into months. It must be more than merely a single total for the year and it must reflect, as accurately as possible, the contribution from each product or service line for each month. It must include provision for entering actual monthly values against planned values and should also include a measure of attainment – the percentage of target achieved. It must also include arrangements for revision to the plan whenever variances are experienced. You are almost certainly already using some kind of long range forecast, although possibly not to the level of detail I propose.

The long range forecast is not strictly part of the management operating system, although long-range planning is the process that begins the cycle. Today most long range revenues or sales forecasts are system generated as one of the end products of strategic and business planning effort.

All effective planning for support services, admin, marketing, sales and units with similar functions must be driven by the long range forecast. Within these units the forecast is used to begin the process to identify what activities and efforts will be needed to support the delivery of the primary product or service of the business. It is crucial to effective and efficient utilization of all resources within service units that operational planning begins at this level.

Master schedule[4]

One objective for the master schedule is to convert revenues targets into specific volumes of products or services required to generate those revenues, and to define the contribution of each separate product or service to total forecast revenues by month.

The other, equally important feature of the master schedule is that it specifies resource requirements, especially labour and line or equipment hours. Hours requirements must be part of the master schedule: identification of hours must not be deferred until later in the planning process. Labour and equipment hours must directly relate to specific products or services.

Like the long range forecast, the master schedule must include provision for entering actual monthly values against planned values and should also include a measure of attainment – the percentage of target achieved. It must also include arrangements for revision to the plan whenever variances are met.

Within support and service departments the master schedule must be presented in measures of specific service levels planned, then extended to definitive resource requirements. In many organizations resource requirements for service units are not based on a long range forecast and a master schedule, they are simply a rehash of actual costs for the last year with perhaps a percentage added for a forecast total increase in sales. Why should a 20 per cent forecast increase in total revenues automatically mean a 20 per cent increase in word processing needs or accounts staffing?

Standard data

Standard data define all resources required to produce an individual product unit or activity occurrence. Properly structured standard data enable you to convert a required volume of product to total volumes of all resources necessary to produce that product, and to do this through a relatively simple and straightforward process. For the balance of this chapter we will not discuss equipment, materials or facilities; our concern is labour hours.

Labour hours requirements for a unit of product or service are referred to as standard times. Standard times can be developed from observations in the workplace or from a range of established work measurement techniques. My definition for a standard time is the time required for a trained operator working at a reasonable pace[5], without interruption, to complete one occurrence of an activity.

It is well beyond the scope of this book to discuss work measurement in detail. The important factors are that:

1 times are reasonable;
2 total activity content must be included – all work must be taken into account; and
3 the entire process must be uncomplicated and must not pose an undue clerical burden on those who use it.

Standard times must be an accurate reflection of reality. As such they can be used for realistic production planning, product or service costing and, when applied to a negative production variance, a measure of the cost of labour lost through an operating problem.

Staffing guide

The determination of staffing levels is a straightforward process if the long range forecast, master schedule and standard data have been developed accurately. Staffing requirements are simply the conversion of hours required from the master schedule translated into the right number of people scheduled in the right places at the right time.

Short range forecast

The short range forecast is just what the name implies: a portion of the long range forecast, usually a one month increment developed at the next level of detail appropriate to the shorter planning interval. It must also include the provision for entering actual values against planned values, a measure of attainment and arrangements for revision to the plan whenever variances are met.

Weekly plan

The weekly plan is driven by the short range forecast. Besides a planned volume of work for the entire week, it typically breaks the week down into daily or shift increments according to the needs of the particular workplace. It, too, should include the provision for entering actual values against planned values, a measure of attainment and arrangements for revision to the plan whenever variances are met. The weekly plan must also allow supervisors the opportunity to make final adjustments in staffing requirements.

Output of the weekly plan must be in a format that enables production planners and particularly unit managers and supervisors to schedule daily operations conveniently. Today many weekly plans are system generated by production planning or scheduling actions. They often include machine or equipment requirements but do not usually include labour hours requirements.

Production departments usually have weekly plans but it is safe to state that few service or support units engage in short-range planning in any depth, if at all.[6]

Daily schedule control–planned

The daily schedule control is the system element that converts the weekly plan into information to allow supervisors to procure materials, schedule equipment and make work assignments to people in the unit. It is two elements in one, a planning and reporting tool. It is the key component in any management operating system. We will discuss the planning aspects here and reporting below.

The structure of the daily schedule control will vary greatly according to workplace needs. In every application, however, certain elements are necessary. It general, it must make it possible for supervisors to make work assignments for all individual staff according to all the requirements of good communications discussed in Chapter 11.

- The daily schedule control must reflect the specific work to be accomplished for the day.
- It must reflect the total hours of the unit planned to accomplish that work.
- It must provide a format that enables supervisors to make effective work assignments (see below: Good work assignment practices).
- It must reflect the preferred interval of control: the time period which supervisors are going to use to establish schedules for follow-up. It may range from personal visits each hour in a production unit to telephone calls every half day for a sales team, from two hourly personal visits for computer programming effort to daily formal updates for design units or engineering projects.
- It must be prepared before the beginning of the day or shift; preparing a schedule after half the work is completed makes no sense whatsoever.

Daily schedule control–actual

Actual activity recorded on the daily schedule control is the beginning of the reporting process for any operating system. Because this drives the entire reporting process:

- Actual values entered on the daily schedule control must include *all* work to standard completed by every individual and *all* hours worked.
- It must require that either the individual or the individual and the supervisor jointly summarize all work for the day for that individual

and calculate his or her performance. The format will vary greatly. For example, in a production or maintenance unit all individuals are usually tracked on a single daily control. For admin, sales, material handling or toolroom work, each individual is typically monitored on a separate daily control.

- It must be completed immediately the day or shift is ended; critiquing actual daily activity three days after the event makes no sense at all.

Daily lost time report

The daily lost time report is maintained throughout the shift along with actual entries on the daily schedule control. This report is used to record all schedule variances, their magnitude and the reasons for them. It must record in specific detail those problems that interfered with the achievement of target performance. A useful way to highlight the contribution of operating problems to low performance is to calculate the number of lost production units, extend them by standard times and report the number of labour hours lost for each occurrence of the problem.

Daily/weekly operating report

The operating report is a daily summary of department operations and is prepared by supervisors at the end of the workday from actual entries on all daily schedule controls. It includes all work completed in the department and all hours used. A typical operating report merges daily summaries into a weekly format.

- Total department performance is calculated from individual performances. Total department performance is, in this sense, a measure of supervisory and management performance.
- The operating report also includes a calculation of attainment to plan – a measure of the percentage of planned work completed. This is important to monitor how closely daily operations are supporting short-range planning. When attainment is less than 100 per cent because problems were encountered, then action must be taken to either adjust the short range forecast or schedule extra production if long range objectives are to be achieved.

Daily lost time summary

The daily lost time summary is prepared by supervisors at the end of the shift or workday. It represents a summary of all lost time recorded on individual lost time reports. It is used in parallel with the daily/weekly operating report to qualify and quantify reasons for schedule variances. It is the element of the system that drives all management action to resolve operating problems.

Backlog report

The backlog report identifies all work in the department that is behind schedule. It is used to determine whether the department is accomplishing work at the level it should or is falling below targets. It is also used to support staffing requirements.

Weekly/monthly management report

The management report is a report that summarizes department operations for the week for senior management. It is driven from information on the operating report and backlog report. The purpose is to communicate to management whether department operations are supporting organization objectives or if adjustments must be made in the long range forecast to deal with variances. The ultimate purpose is to prepare senior management to support supervisors and first line managers in their efforts for management action. A typical management report merges weekly summaries into a monthly or quarterly format.

Weekly lost time summary

The weekly lost time summary is prepared by supervisors at the end of the week. It represents a summary of all lost time recorded on daily lost time summaries. It is used in parallel with the weekly management report to provide information on total lost time for the department for the week and the reasons for it. It supports management action.

Action plans

Action plans are formalized processes to address recognized and quantified variances in operations identified through the reporting system. They vary according to needs, and can range from a simple, one page, hand-written memo to a lengthy report specifying the need for a project for a ten member task team.[7]

Training plans

Training plans are driven by operating information and lost time summaries, and reflect training efforts designed to address variances caused by lack of training for individuals.[8]

Figure 17.1 Tactical Management short interval control system flow

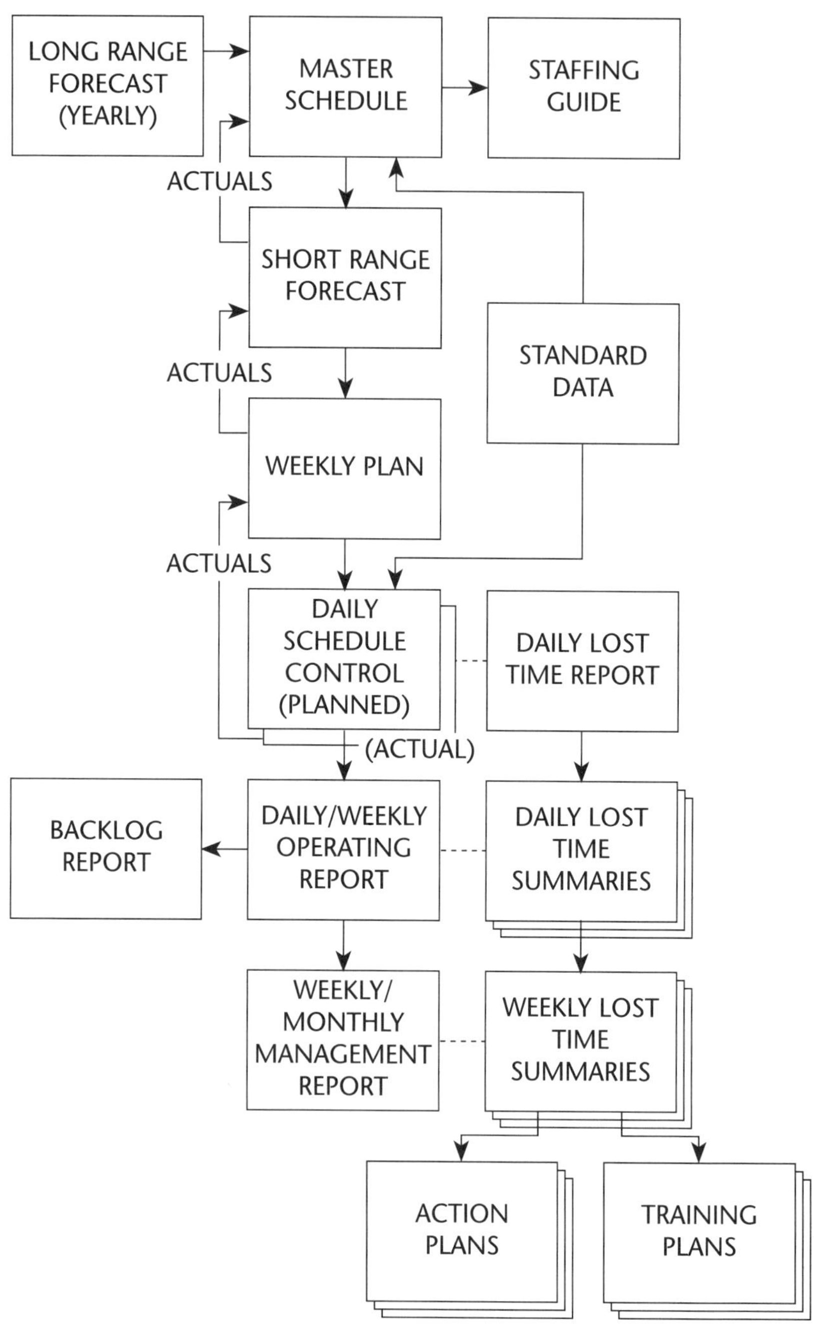

Functional requirements

Management of daily operations will be effective if that effort is conducted under operating system practices similar to those discussed here. That system, however, provides only a structure. If it is to be consistently effective for the long term and acceptable to changing conditions in the workplace, certain functional elements must also be considered:

Identification of work

Good daily work management is fundamentally nothing more than short segment task control applied formally and continually. The interval of control is a specified fraction of the day and the phase is represented by the activity of one individual. All the principles and practices examined in Chapter 8 must be part of any management operating system. If the practice is going to be effective, however, it must be possible to define work functionally. When work can be described in units of clearly identifiable activities, it is possible to manage it. It is helpful in this respect to offer an operational definition for an activity:

> An activity is a unit of work that is completed by one person at one sitting, that has an obvious beginning and end, and for which a logical unit of measure can be specified.

This definition makes it convenient to observe and establish a time standard, assign work, count units completed and monitor individual performance. It also makes it possible to phase such nebulous tasks, for example, as reconciling a report, developing a computer program, dealing with a customer query, conducting market research or repairing a piece of hydraulic equipment.

Reasonable standards

Standards must be reasonable, simply stated, easy to apply and not difficult to maintain. Most fully trained operators, working without problems or interruptions, should comfortably be able to attain the target performance (see Page 229: standard data).

> Improved performance will not be accomplished by setting tight standards and coercing assignees into trying to meet them, improved performance is achieved when management systematically remove all obstacles to the work.

Under this consideration there is nothing to be gained from setting standards either unreasonably tight or to too great a level of accuracy.

The first step is to flowchart the process you are going to observe. This is crucial to your ability to specify accurately the activities you want to observe and for which you want to establish standards. Use whatever flowcharting process is standard in your organization, or a process I recommend highly: Brown Paper systems analysis. In my experience, using the Brown Paper technique has a number of advantages over traditional processes. These will be discussed in detail in the Coda. Make up your own mind.

Standards can be established through any recognized work measurement technique or through a process known as direct observation.[9] Direct observation is straightforward, non-threatening to the person being observed since no stopwatch is necessary, and makes very efficient use of the observer's time. It is not quite so accurate as stop watch time study or MTM (Methods-Time Measurement) but the results fit system requirements very well.

The success of direct observation is contingent upon clearly specified activities. If activities are well defined, direct observation consists simply of observing several fully trained operators working over a series of occurrences of the activity, recording the total time, counting the number of occurrences and removing from the total time anything that is not part of that activity. The duration of the study is determined by the number of occurrences required to establish a reasonable time.

The advantage of direct observation over traditional work measurement practice is that the entire activity content is captured over a series of occurrences working with a number of fully trained operators. The result meets our needs for a reasonable standard that can be used for scheduling, monitoring performance and quantifying schedule variances or lost time. Another advantage is that it is not necessary to apply a factor such as a fatigue allowance to the standards because it is built into the observed times. You can use them as they are, in the form of pure work time, by setting the daily target at 85 rather than 100 per cent. The remaining 15 per cent will address personal time and rest allowances. The resulting system is much simpler to administer and maintenance of standards is far less complicated.

Your objective is to move from the present 65 per cent performance to the target of around 85 per cent. You are not concerned whether the precise number is 84.3 or 85.6 per cent, 'around 85 per cent' will accomplish the objective. Within this context, standards need not be any more accurate than necessary to achieve that aim. You are more concerned with the gap between where you are and where you want to be. Keep it simple.

A key element in successful application of standard times is that department supervisors and managers are involved in the studies and must then be responsible for agreeing – formally signing off – on those standards before they are used in the workplace. Area management must have ownership; it is a critical element of every operating system.[10]

Good work assignment practices

Good work assignment practices are nothing more than effective communications with heavy emphasis placed on the time value of the assignment. A good daily work assignment might look something like this:

> Here, Leslie (or Lesley), are 200 whatevers. I want you to ream the flanges according to spec. The standard for reaming flanges on whatevers is 100 units per hour, so this represents about two hours work. It's 9.00 am now so you should be finished at around 11.00 am if you have no difficulties. I'll be out to see how you're doing at about 10.00 am. Call me if you have any problems. Do you have any questions?

It is important that the assignee is aware of:

1 the assignment: what is to be done,
2 the volume: how many are to be done,
3 the time value: when the work is supposed to be completed,
4 that the supervisor will be following-up according to schedule,
5 that the supervisor is available if a problem occurs, and
6 that he or she has been offered the opportunity to ask questions concerning the assignment.

On the basis of our discussions in Chapter 11, the details would vary from this example according to the complexity of the assignment and Lesley's (or Leslie's) level of training and experience. It is important, nevertheless, that all these elements are included, in one form or another in every work assignment.

Lest you think this practice is overbearing or childish, recall my story in Chapter 11 about the managing director's work assignment to the admin clerk. You may adjust the presentation according to the readiness levels of both you and the assignee, but if any of these six elements is absent from the process, the effort will most certainly fail.

All work must be reported

This requirement should need little discussion. If performance is to have any meaning at all, it must consider all work done. This is usually not difficult to achieve in a production unit, but is not as easy in a maintenance or computer systems area, an admin department or for a sales team. Some creativity and innovation are needed to capture all the work in these units. Unless all work is reported, however, the entire effort is a waste of time: reporting only part of the work accomplishes absolutely nothing.

All hours must be reported

We can now explain the discrepancy between the performance you observed from the ratio/delay study and that reported under the current reporting system. Go back out to the area and collect some department level summaries: those worksheets that collate individual operating statistics to drive the report you receive each Tuesday morning. On those summaries you will see information recorded under at least three headings: work done – standard hours earned, total hours worked and hours worked on standard.

When you divide standard hours earned by total hours worked, the performance you calculate is the 65 per cent you observed during the ratio/delay study. When you divide standard hours earned by hours worked on standard, the performance you calculate is the 90 to 95 per cent you see every week on the report you receive.

The number your management team feeds you every week is performance with all the operating problems taken out. That number is meaningless; not only does it tell you absolutely nothing about the way the organization is performing, it communicates to everybody who sees it that things are wonderful. It discourages management action of any kind; it convinces everybody that problems are something they should do nothing about – they are part of the work.

The number you must be concerned about, the only number that has any meaning at all, is performance related to total hours worked. Multiply the differential, the 25 to 30 per cent, by total staff hours for the operation and extend that by the average hourly labour cost (total cost including burden) to understand what your operation is paying people to be unproductive. This is the true measure of how unwonderful things really are and the potential for improvements in performance in the organization.

Daily individual accountability must be universal

The operating system must provide daily individual accountability for *all* staff, section leaders and supervisors. Anybody performing work in the unit must be included in the system. There are a number of reasons for this:

- The purpose for performance measurement is not to beat up somebody who has not achieved the target but to trigger effective, short-term management action whenever a variance occurs. Daily individual accountability provides the best phase and interval of control for this purpose.
- Section leaders and supervisors are monitored to confirm that any unit work they do is included in reporting information. If a supervisor performs no hands-on work during the day this requirement may be omitted.

- Where a supervisor performs unit work it is important that the manager estimate a maximum performance target for him or her rather than a minimum. That maximum will depend on the needs of the area but probably should never exceed about 50 per cent. Remember Ralph Hendershot.
- Performance must only be calculated against good product generated. Poor performance resulting from the production of scrap or items not to specification must always be shown as a variance; that is, unless you ship your scrap to customers and they pay you full price for it. When this is done for individuals it provides immediate – within one day – information relating to a specific activity or work station to support customer service and quality management efforts.[11]

There are situations where individual accountability is strictly impossible. One example is a machine paced production or assembly line. It is still possible, however, to monitor the contributions of each operator to line performance. Typically, line speed is determined by the bottleneck or limiting machine. When that is established, then the line should be staffed so that all the operators along the line can work consistently at a 75 to 80 per cent rating – what I call a reasonable pace. These standards can be established using the direct observation technique discussed above. When any operator falls below the standard for any reason it will have a negative impact on output and thus on line performance. This variance can be identified and quantified on the lost time report and then investigated for resolution of the problem causing the variance.

Integrity of reporting information

Throughout the system, from individual daily schedule control entries to the management report, information must be reported with total integrity. The process of summarizing must not allow any material omissions to the information being reported or abstractions that only serve to camouflage problems. Do not permit poor performance to be adjusted somewhere within the information flow because: '. . . it's not their fault!'

A level workload

One of the benefits of an operating system such as that we are considering here is that it enables supervisors and managers to shift resources quickly if there is an uneven workload. An operator will not be able to achieve target performance if jobs are not available, regardless of how hard he or she works. When all the other obstacles have been removed and performance is still not up to target it is because people have run out of work.

Processes must be developed to either:

1 Level the workload. Make procedural changes so that work flows smoothly into the area rather than in peaks and valleys.
2 Co-ordinate work between a number of units or departments so that peak loads in one area correspond to valleys in another. Staff, supervisors and managers can then be assigned to move from peak to peak.[12]

Effective management action

Information provided by the operating system drives management action in a most visible way. When performance is reported against all unit hours it is impossible for problems to be buried: the operating report and lost time summaries are going to continue to display those problems for all the world to see until somebody does something about them. If the same problem occurs every week, supervisors and department managers are going to have to report it every week. The only action they can take to remove it from the report is to eliminate the problem.

Manual versus computerized reporting

In Chapter 16 we briefly mentioned manual versus electronic means for managing certain elements of communications processes.[13] Here is another situation where I feel that a system driven by manually calculated information has certain advantages. This is suggested by three considerations: the present culture under which most business organizations operate, the readiness levels of all people, including you, in the organization and my considerable experience with these systems.

When a staff member alone or a staff member and the supervisor are jointly responsible for manually calculating that staff member's performance at the end of the shift and entering it on the daily schedule control, this appears to be a factor that motivates him or her to want to improve performance. Similarly when a supervisor sits down at the end of the workday to summarize individual performances on the operating report manually and calculate a total performance for the section or department, he or she is motivated to initiate management action to attack operating problems.

In my experience these opportunities for motivation to improve are lost if primary statistics are entered into a computer and the machine automatically calculates performance either for the individual or the unit. I have worked with some systems where raw data from individual daily schedule control entries were handed to an input clerk without any review whatsoever. The clerk entered the data, and the operating report, lost time summary and management report were generated by the system, printed and distributed to supervisors and managers, and throughout that entire exercise *nobody looked at any of them.*

The singular reason for doing any of this is to trigger effective, timely, short-term management action. The sole purpose for preparing any reporting document within the operating system is to enable a manager to look at a variance, get excited/unhappy, and go out and do something about it. If an input clerk enters the data, the machine prints it and a messenger delivers it, possibly in the middle of the night, into the basket on the corner of your desk it is likely that nothing will happen. The entire effort has been a waste of time for everybody. This is precisely what occurs when you receive those reports that proclaim 95 per cent performance: nothing happens. You must want something to happen, otherwise you would not be considering this process.

One simple way to achieve both objectives is to first develop and install a manual system, then once you can confirm it is working according to plan and meeting your objectives, computerize it, but do in a special way. Develop a PC-based system with screens designed to simulate the paper controls and reports in use. This accomplishes two aims: it retains the requirement that supervisors and department managers review the information and enter it into the system and it eliminates the need for any manual calculations or the generation of hand-written reports.

Again I would not expect this argument to be valid in the workplace at some point in the future. As our business cultures and operating environments change and especially as the readiness levels of you and everybody else in the organization shift, this requirement will also change.

Variations on a theme

This system description has been for a typical production cycle. Recall these principles as several variations are examined. You should be able to generalize this presentation to every unit in the organization:

Admin department

In every situation where activities occur regularly, standards can be established through direct observation or other work measurement techniques. This technique can be used in any admin department or clerical operation. Problems are sometimes faced when trying to define activities. Use the definition presented above, along with a bit of imagination. When you can specify any activity according to that definition, observing and establishing a standard time is not difficult.

The usual procedure is to make a work assignment by passing a batch of work to the individual. The typical batch size is about two hours – this seems to be a reasonable control interval for this type of work. Differences can occur from one unit to another according to how far in advance the short range forecast or weekly plan can be developed. In an accounting area it may be possible to plan an entire week, in a customer service or query section it might not be possible to schedule work more than one day in advance. In those units where weekly planning is not possible, use recent history to estimate resource requirements.

Within a unit of this type it is convenient for each staff member to record all activities and variances on an individual daily activity report throughout the day. At the end of the day he or she is responsible for calculating performance, then passing the completed report to the supervisor and briefly discussing the day's work.

Maintenance department

The activities of a maintenance department can be broken down into three categories: planned or preventive maintenance, project work and emergency repairs and jobs needed immediately or reasonably soon. The critical factor for successful operational control of a maintenance unit is that all work must be captured. Paramount interest here is to support those departments responsible for the primary work of the organization. Better management control of the maintenance operation immediately translates into improved customer service, quality and cost management.

Planned and preventive maintenance can be planned, scheduled and assigned according to the general production model discussed above. Projects will be discussed below.

Emergency repairs, equipment breakdowns and work required immediately or soon can be effectively scheduled using estimates. The key to successful estimating is also activity definition. When phases, intervals and control point are clearly defined it is not difficult to estimate time requirements. Accuracy of estimates will be improved when those who actually do the work are involved in the estimating effort.

Assignment of this work is usually accomplished by passing detailed written work requests to the craftsperson along with an oral description of the work to be done and a statement of the estimated hours needed for completion. For jobs longer than two hours the supervisor should follow-up about halfway through the work. For shorter jobs this is not necessary, follow-up can occur when the next job is assigned. For very short jobs a batch of work requests can be assigned at one time.

Detailed short-range planning is not possible in this operation. It is necessary for the supervisor to carefully examine recent history to establish resource requirements. If about fifty hours have been required each day for the past month to complete emergency work, it is likely that about fifty hours will be needed tomorrow.

Performance is usually calculated by comparing estimated hours completed to actual hours worked. This is often done at the end of the shift when the supervisor and the individual craftsperson review all completed work requests and discuss results for the day. For this operation there is no formal daily schedule control, that function is accomplished by the craftsperson's batch of work requests, sometimes displayed on an assignment board.

Project management[14]

Project management is that collection of disciplines and practices used to address activities that occur only once or very infrequently. The designation 'project' is typically applied to those efforts that are fairly ambitious and require the work of more than one individual. This discussion is applicable to computer systems development, major maintenance and engineering works, market research or development, architectural and design work, and all task team effort.

Project management will fit conveniently into the general system model without too much difficulty:

- Overall management control must be monitored with a project schedule or progress chart. The form will vary from a one-page cover sheet or Gantt Chart[15] for a simple project, to a CPM[16] (Critical Path Method), PERT (Programme Evaluation and Review Technique) or network diagram covering an entire wall in the team leader's office for an ambitious effort. This is analogous in every respect to a master schedule. If it is to be truly effective it must contain detailed and complete information specifying objectives, resources and time requirements.
- Properly structured project phases compare nicely with short range forecasts or weekly plans when time requirements are stated in estimated hours.[17]
- Daily planning and work assignments should follow naturally from well-defined phases. Time values for assignments derive from phase estimates.
- No phase should be greater than the equivalent of the work of one person for one week. Follow-up depends entirely on the specific project: twice daily informal visits from the team leader and a formal review daily, weekly or at phase completion are appropriate.
- Reporting is also consistent with everything we have discussed. The one distinction is in the measure of performance and attainment. These calculations must be based upon estimated hours remaining rather than estimated hours completed. For example, if you began with 40 estimated hours remaining for a particular phase and the plan was to complete 30 hours this week, if at the end of the week there are 20

hours remaining, standard hours earned were 20, regardless of the actual time spent doing the work. Variances must also be based on estimated hours remaining. For this example the variance this week was 10 estimated hours lost.

There are many proprietary computerized project management systems available today. Use of such a software package can be effective if it meets all your needs: all the demands of good operational control, short segment task control and team management. One additional caution is that expressed above under manual versus computerized reporting. Automated systems must not become merely an excuse for supervisors and managers not having to follow-up and take meaningful management action because 'the system will take care of it'.

The Tactical Management system versus classical SIS systems

Earlier in this chapter we said the terminology we are using to describe elements in the management operating aystem follows that for classical SIS systems. It is appropriate to discuss SIS systems in some detail and examine where this system differs from them.

Positive characteristics of classical SIS systems, as they have been applied over the past 50 years or so are:

- They support the principle of short interval control. They enable you to begin with a yearly long range forecast and convert that plan, ultimately, into hourly work assignments.
- They support the concept of closed-loop management control. They include mechanisms for identifying schedule variances and initiating effective management action to eliminate those variances. They have provisions for adjusting long and medium range plans according to actual schedule attainment.
- They support the principle of individual accountability. This enables you to identify the specific problems that interfere with the ability of every individual to meet performance targets. They identify training needs for specific individuals.
- They support the principle of the key role of the supervisor in effective daily operations. They provide the supervisor with good operating information to enable him or her to make best use of labour hours.
- They provide very good operating information to improve communications between the supervisor and the first line manager, particularly concerning the manager's ability to provide support for the supervisor for the resolution of operating problems.
- They provide an effective and credible communications link between the supervisor and department manager, and senior management,

again particularly concerning the ability of senior management to provide high level support for the resolution of recurring operating problems.

Negative characteristics of classical SIS systems, as they have been encountered in my experience, are these:

- They are unduly complicated, with a reliance on complex forms and controls including, sometimes, much unnecessary detail and often higher than needed accuracy.
- They can be operated by the supervisor with no real understanding of the principles of short interval control and individual accountability. The emphasis is on compliance: if all the boxes are filled in and all calculations are done, then the supervisor is using the system well.
- They place enormous time demands on the supervisor. I have worked with systems that required the supervisor to spend one full hour before the beginning of the shift preparing the daily schedule control and one full hour after the end of the shift completing the daily operating report and lost time summary.
- They place high demands on the supervisor's time during the shift. Within some systems, the supervisor is required to spend three-quarters of every hour making schedule checks, calculating individual hourly performances and updating reports. This leaves him or her with very little time for training and positive management action.
- They place high emphasis on efficiency with no regard to effectiveness. One often quoted comment is: 'It doesn't matter if you're producing garbage, so long as you're doing it efficiently'. While the emphasis on eliminating operating problems is positive, there is no encouragement to experiment with options to present practice.
- They typically attempt to reduce labour content to the absolute minimum, leaving supervisors and department managers no opportunity to train operators for improved performance or to involve them in improvements to operations.

My objective for the Tactical Management operating system is to introduce you to a system that includes all the positive elements of classical SIS while eliminating all the negative. This is possible. Specific system requirements will vary according to the nature of the work being managed and the particular needs of your operation, but the following comments are helpful:

- Keep system design simple. If your current long-range planning document is working well, for example, continue to use it, do not revise it simply to meet the cosmetic requirements for the long range forecast.
- Keep standard data simple and free from unnecessary accuracy. Do not,

for example, enter a standard as 117 units per hour, enter it as either 115 or even better as 120 units per hour.

- Establish standards using the direct observation technique rather than more involved traditional work measurement techniques.
- Ensure that supervisors and department managers understand the rationale for the system. Seek good understanding rather than good compliance.
- Design the system so that supervisors and department managers need to spend the absolute minimum time entering either planning or reporting information. Their time is more productively spent planning, scheduling and assigning work, following up on that work, training staff for improved performance and eliminating operating problems through effective management action.
- Design the system so that calculations are simple and easy to understand. They only need to answer two questions for you:
  (a) How much good product did we make today against the plan? This is defined as schedule attainment and is a measure of customer service.
  (b) How many hours did it take us to do it against the plan? This is performance and it is a measure of how well you are managing costs.
- Concentrate on the gap between the 'around 65 per cent' where you are now and the 'around 85 per cent' target rather than on whether present performance is 64.8 or 65.2 per cent.

The need for short interval control and individual accountability

We have discussed throughout this book that your world, especially your business world is changing, and the Tactical Management model is one tool useful to you in your efforts to deal with some of that change. Most of the changes we are examining are in the direction of less close control of people in the workplace as they go about the work of the organization. The short interval control system presented here, and particularly daily individual accountability, appears to be in a direction contrary to the rest of our approach to this brave new world.

I believe that today, for most of the business world, certainly within my experience and for all the organizations for whom I have done work, including both manufacturing and service operations, there is still a need for the levels of control of work that we have examined in this chapter. This discussion has been prompted to some extent by a conversation I had recently with a consultant who was attempting to install a world class manufacturing culture in a large manufacturing facility. He feels there is no place in a world class organization for either short interval control, labour standards or daily individual accountability. I asked him three questions that he never answered for me:

1 How can you cost out any product accurately if you cannot determine the labour content and thus calculate one of the significant contributors to cost?
2 How can you schedule work and forecast delivery dates for any product if you cannot determine how long it will take to make it?
3 How can you quantify opportunities for lower costs and more competitive pricing if you have no current standards on which to gauge the improvements?

My answer is that unless you are already operating within a world class culture,[18] you need short interval control of work and either daily individual or small workteam accountability. At the readiness levels of you and others, for most of the work of the organization, you need to be able to operate a closed-loop management cycle on a daily interval. You need to know the time value of work if you are going to be able to schedule it well for good customer service. You are going to have to know the labour content of products and services, even if you are world class, if you are going to expect to remain competitive in a world market. I see no option for the present.

What will change, in my judgement, is that in the future people in the workplace will be capable of establishing their own standards and monitoring their own performance. Since they will be involved in product development and improvements to process control to a greater extent than they are now, they will be well placed to assist in costing out labour content and determining delivery schedules and dates. During production, when they note a schedule variance, they then either communicate with supervisors and managers for support to address the problem or solve it themselves. There will still, in fact, be elements of short interval control and individual accountability, it will simply be managed differently by those closest to the work.

Part of the objection by my colleague may be to warn us of the danger of time standards, scheduling systems and performance targets becoming ends in themselves rather than mechanisms for measurement and control of work.[19] This is a real danger. Short interval control systems based on carefully developed time standards and daily individual accountability are management tools that are no different in this respect from meetings, workteams or delegation practices. They must be used wisely and within the context of a dynamic and rapidly changing workplace.[20] You must establish an organization culture that celebrates the achievement of each new high attainment and performance target, not as an objective in itself, but simply as another step in your never-ending quest for health for your organization.

Do this over the next six months

It is not possible within the framework of *Tactical Management* and this chapter to provide you with all the detailed information necessary to design and install comprehensive management operating systems throughout the organization. Indeed, that effort would require an entire book. Rather it has been my intention to introduce the fundamentals and discuss what I regard as some of the important considerations. Information presented here, along with all the other elements we have examined throughout this book, should enable you to initiate a review of present practice. The objective for that review is to implement processes to improve current systems, then employ that experience to develop and install systems in those areas and units where they are not now in use.

Identify one unit for which an operating system is presently in place. Over three months, conduct an analysis of that system based on everything we have discussed throughout the book, and especially in this chapter. Evaluate the current system, revise as needs are identified, then install the redesigned system. Over the subsequent three months monitor improved performance. Involve everybody required to make this work. Pay particular attention to specific system elements. Confirm that:

- The system structure is not inordinately complicated and does not demand a great amount of clerical effort. The system must, however, include all elements – they are essential.
- Standards are reasonable, accurate and encompass all work of the unit; they are not extremely detailed or based on spuriously accurate calculations. For example, if a number of production standards are within one per cent of one another, treat them as one standard. Within an admin unit, group all telephone calls into one activity with one standard time. For maintenance work, estimate hours based on the total shift rather than taking out tea breaks or rest periods. Keep it simple.
- Supervisors are using the weekly plan and standard data to develop the daily schedule control and are, in fact, planning daily and scheduling work.
- Supervisors are making work assignments correctly, with time values, for all work.
- Supervisors are using operating information to update staffing plans. If performance is high and the backlog is increasing, the unit is understaffed; if performance is decreasing and the backlog is trending rapidly toward zero, the unit is overstaffed; if performance is low and the backlog is growing, you have serious, unresolved operating problems.
- All staff and supervisory hours are reported; performance is calculated against total hours. There is no such thing as adjusted performance – performance adjusted for downtime or other off-schedule conditions.

- Performance in real terms, in your accountant's measures of inputs versus outputs, is actually increasing. For some operations it might be difficult to confirm this independently in the short term. For example, actual unit cost figures may only be calculated at year end.
- Supervisors and managers are truly looking at operating information, understanding what that information is telling them about unit operations, and taking effective and timely management action.
- Other areas and departments are responding to requests for involvement and management action, and are supporting those requests quickly and effectively.
- Staff departments such as personnel, training and the union are not only not interfering with the attempts of supervisors and managers to effect reasonable sorts of changes and improvements in operations, but are assertively and positively supporting those changes.

Seek a modest goal for improvement in real performance: from the 65 per cent you observed under the ratio/delay study to 85 per cent. This can be achieved using present resources – at no additional cost. It has nothing to do with effectiveness, it can be accomplished solely through improvements to the efficiency of operations and practices now in place.[21]

At the end of the three month evaluation period, when you are comfortable with the results, and what you and the team have learned, extend the process to one other area. Identify a unit that currently does not have an operating system in place, one for which you have been told work measurement is either difficult or impossible. Design and install a management operating system in that unit. Evaluate that installation over the subsequent three months.

On satisfactory implementation in that unit, install similar processes in two more departments or areas over the next three months. You should then have the experience to extend the process to the entire organization.

Notes

1 This was discussed in some detail in Chapter 4, Accounting information versus operating information, Page 63.

2 This is one definition for performance and the one we shall use. Among the various models you will see, in addition, words such as efficiency, productivity and even effectivity are used to describe measures of performance. In the most general sense we are concerned simply with our ability to compare product or service output with labour input.

3 This terminology for system elements follows that for classical SIS systems (see Chapter 8, Page 122). The differences between the Tactical Management operating system and classical SIS system will be examined later in the chapter (see page 244).

4 In some models the master schedule is referred to as the capacity plan.
5 In formal work measurement terminology this corresponds to a 75 to 80 per cent rating.
6 Review the notes from your tour, then walk out to sales, the toolroom, maintenance stores or microfilm and ask to look at a weekly plan.
7 The tactical action system, one specific action plan, will be discussed in detail in Chapter 25.
8 Training plans will be examined in detail in Chapter 21.
9 Direct observation is not the same as time study or rated activity sampling as defined in formal work study terminology.
10 Peter Drucker, *The Practice of Management*. (Oxford: Heinemann, 1989.) Drucker's analysis of organizing work and the worker is particularly helpful here.
11 In Part Three we will discuss eliminating the requirement for universal, daily individual accountability. When the operation is effectively under control this system element can safely be modified. You are probably not ready, just yet, for that change. Also see below, The need for short interval control and individual accountability, Page 246.
12 This was discussed in Chapter 8, Accounting and admin management.
13 See Page 224.
14 There are many, many books available on project management with a range of detail to suit individual tastes and needs. Try: Dennis Lock, *Project Management* 5th Edn. (Aldershot: Gower, 1992.)
15 See the Coda for a discussion of the Gantt chart.
16 Also known as CPA (Critical Path Analysis).
17 Review Chapter 8 for essentials of effective phase identification.
18 A world class culture for your organization will be discussed in brief detail in the Coda.
19 Watson, *In Search of Management*; op. cit. Watson discusses the danger of means becoming ends in considerable detail.
20 Dr Walter E. Deming's 14 points for management, point number 10: 'Eliminate numerical goals, posters, and slogans for the workforce asking for new levels of productivity without providing methods'. As quoted in: John S. Oakland, *Total Quality Management*. (Oxford: Butterworth-Heinemann, 1989.)
21 Changes in effectiveness, in redesigning production processes for improved performance, will be examined in Chapter 26.

■ CHAPTER 18 ■

Management by Wandering Around

This open office concept is abysmal. We need traditional offices where we can isolate ourselves from the real world.

A senior marketing manager of a retail services company

Introduction

This book began with my mandate that you conduct an intensive, structured, unannounced tour of your operations. This action is a paradigm of Management by Wandering Around.[1] Management by Wandering Around is the follow-up element in the tactical closed-loop management cycle and at the same time, two components of effective communications processes: filter evaluation and message evaluation. It is the action by which you confirm, through observation of results and actions, how well you are communicating with people throughout the organization. It is short segment task control applied to all your communications efforts and confirmation of the accuracy of all the information you receive concerning operations. It is your support for everybody in the organization made highly visible.

Management by Wandering Around is an idea that is currently prominent in the business world; promoted by some, denigrated by others. It is perceived by many as aimless roaming about: Big Brother peeking around from behind filing cabinets or furnaces trying to discover somebody doing something wrong. It is seen as childishly checking up on people – not trusting them to be capable of doing their jobs. It is thought by others to be no more than briskly walking through the facility, superficially looking around and greeting everybody by first name with a wave and a smile.

Think about what you might have seen if you had made preparations for your *Tactical Management* introductory tour. Imagine that you had announced your intentions one week in advance, your secretary had accompanied you to take notes and a supervisor or department manager had been scheduled to conduct you through each area, with perhaps even a middle manager standing by to provide 'correct' answers to your really awkward questions. Do you believe your impressions about operations and the problems people face daily in their efforts to achieve objectives would have been as accurate? Think about the last time you conducted the board on a formal visit through the facility. Did they gain a realistic picture of how the operation functions every day?

The difference between what you see in the workplace when you wander around and what you see on a formal tour is well illustrated by the difference between the 65 per cent actual performance we discussed in Chapter 17 and you observed on your tour, and the 95 per cent reported to you weekly. Management by Wandering Around is no more complicated than this.

Chinese whispers (boy scout communications)

Chinese whispers still works with stupefying predictability. Think about the last time you were involved in this exercise to transmit a message through a number of people. Nearly every one of us has done this relatively recently at a training session or communications seminar. If you have not been through it within the past year, try it at the beginning of your next staff meeting to convince yourself the exercise is still eminently useful.

When you transmit the story through six people, a typical minimum number of levels between middle management and the people who do the work, the message is complete garbage by the time it is spoken back to you by the sixth person. Not only is the result total nonsense, what little bit comes through is frequently reported as a message exactly opposite to the original.

You must be continually concerned about effective communications in both directions. You must receive information about operations to make decisions and determine actions to be taken, and you must transmit information concerning actions you intend to take and things you want done.

Messages received – upward communications

In your attempts to obtain accurate and timely information concerning operations, several factors are important. Since messages must flow through several layers of the organization to reach you, all the experience of Chinese Whispers applies. The organization is awash with so much information that they cannot all be passed to you *in toto*:

- Information fed to you must be summarized. In that summarizing process it is to be expected that judgements are made according to what will forwarded and what will be eliminated. The result is a situation sometimes as spectacular as that experienced during the Chinese Whispers training exercise.

- People involved in any communications process necessarily filter[2] information – it is inevitable. Brussels sprouts applies here: those responsible for passing on information will, both consciously and unconsciously, emphasize those things they feel are important and de-emphasize those things they feel are not important.
- You are the boss, after all, and they are not going to tell you everything. If supervisors or managers have problems that might pose embarrassments for them, they are going to avoid telling you until they have had a chance to resolve them (you and I do exactly the same).
- Communications demand time and resources; information can get lost in the system from sheer overload. Brussels sprouts is at work again: when something must yield within the system it will be that datum the person processing it *at that moment* perceives is not important.
- The timing of actions is crucial in the organization today. Even under the faulty assumption the message can be transmitted to you accurately and completely, it might arrive too late for you to be able to respond most effectively.

Messages sent – downward communications

Equally you must consider communications in the other direction. Everything we have discussed applies to messages you want to send to others: the same filtering and prioritizing occurs. This is as important as for the information you receive:

- Your message often concerns a variance to plan: something that did not happen the way it should have. The principle of short segment task control demands that communications and subsequent actions be taken quickly – at short intervals. Frequent, regular wandering around supports this.
- Your message sometimes relates to uncertainty in the environment with potential negative impact on the organization. This might range from a modest downturn in the market to a potential decrease in sales and possible redundancies. This kind of information always generates serious doubts among people, and unanswered questions spawn rumours circulated through the grapevine. Your availability and visibility can be positive factors in answering those concerns.
- Your message is sometimes to describe a vision: something that is not only new, but that reflects significant change for the organization. Because this change is dramatic and far removed from present practice, it is crucial that you obtain immediate confirmation of how well your presentation was received and understood.

- Another *Tactical Management* theme is that if you are really trying, you must occasionally get it wrong; if you never fail, you are not really working hard enough – testing your limits and those of the organization. When you do get it wrong it is important that an adjustment is made quickly.
- Management support for the efforts of every individual in the organization must be made visible – people must *see* you. The formal presentation and written combination must be backed by a presence. Your personal visit vastly increases the likelihood that your message will be accurately received, correctly interpreted and effectively acted upon; your presence reinforces the importance of the communication.

This last element, the visibility of management, is crucial to organization health now and for the future. People everywhere in the organization must feel they are part of the bigger team: the team that includes you, them and everybody in between. If they are going to deal successfully with massive amounts of inevitable change, the 'us versus them' perception must be eliminated. The contribution of that perception to workplace behaviour can be drastically reduced by your continuing presence. Wandering around communicates to everybody your effort to understand what they face daily in their attempts to achieve objectives.

Elements of wandering around

The justification for Management by Wandering Around is to support improved communications; it is to confirm that messages are accurately received and result in anticipated actions. It is checking up on work; it is not checking up on people.

You may wander around in either of two ways: walk through the entire facility from one end to the other, daily at about the same time, or spend the same amount of time each day in a different part of the operation. Of the two, the latter reflects better use of your time:

1 You should be spending the greatest amount of your time in the area that you have identified to have the most serious problems. Working under the exception principle, the same amount of your time will never be required each day in every area.
2 The objective for this process is to evaluate activities in the workplace, not the occurrence of your visit. People should not expect to see you at the same time every day, or indeed each day at all.
3 This effort may be considered in this respect a random sample of activities in the workplace. Following the same routine every day places an artificial constraint on the process.

The requirements for effective wandering around are not all that complicated. Your introductory tour defines nearly everything you need to know about the practice. Recall the kinds of questions I suggested you ask and the types of enquiries you were directed to make. The only significant difference between that initial tour and wandering around is that now you are to a greater extent immersed in ongoing sorts of situations. A few additional comments may be helpful:

- Consistent with all the other changes we have discussed throughout this book, if wandering around is to result in improved communications, the effort must necessarily sometimes result in the discovery of activities that are not being conducted according to plan. When you meet this during a round, some confrontation is to be expected, and this is always uncomfortable for everybody involved.
- Initially, comments concerning Big Brother will be voiced. In my experience, staff will have less of a problem with wandering around than will department and middle managers. In fact, staff will become nonchalant about this practice long before you do. As with other actions we have considered, managers become better at wandering around and more relaxed when they have had the opportunity to practice it for a bit.
- Care must be taken to comply with the principles of unity of command and integrity of command. When you discover a variance during one of your visits, it is important that you comment, immediately, to the people involved. This is not the same as your giving direction to an individual without regard to the chain of command. Your follow-up must be consistent with good management practice, and organization structure and function.
- It is crucial to this process that you are totally and unequivocally consistent in your remarks and actions. You must never, ever, under any circumstances walk past another incident of substandard quality, poor housekeeping, inappropriate supervision, safety violation or incorrect procedure without making the appropriate comment and taking suitable action. This is at the heart of not sending conflicting signals. Precisely because you have made yourself so visible, that visibility must reflect total consistency with your written directives and other oral pronouncements, and the communications of every other manager in the organization.
- Wandering around can become an effective vehicle for short term positive recognition for individuals. It is totally appropriate to celebrate good work in the workplace, in front of peers, immediately it has occurred. If this is to be perceived as checking up on people at all, it is to catch somebody doing something right.[3]
- Management by Wandering Around must be seen as a management practice conducted with total integrity. The purpose of wandering

around is to evaluate the effectiveness of communications, it is not to berate somebody for not taking the correct action. It must never become a mechanism for reprimanding people in the workplace in front of peers.

- Concern for the principles of effective delegation and simultaneous loose-tight management control must be kept in mind all the time. We have discussed how work assignments should be made as flexible and ambiguous as possible within task requirements. As you observe work being done and actions taken, evaluate those efforts with this in mind. Be certain your comments during wandering around do not interfere with this important consideration. If it appears that a delegate or assignee will achieve his or her objective by a route somewhat different from the one you may have chosen, then so be it. Relax – you can both learn from the experience.

Wandering around must not be limited to those areas for which managers are directly responsible. Managers of service and support departments should wander around in every department that is a user of their services. From this experience, these managers can gain a better understanding of precisely how their products or services are used. Further, close examination of the ways that products or services are used often suggests opportunities for new products, variations on present services or changes in methods or procedures.

Invite suppliers to wander around within your facility, particularly in those areas where their products are in use. It makes visible for them the specific application for their products. If you experience problems with quality or delivery, their wandering around will communicate that to them. Understanding the precise nature of the applications for their products may provide them with the opportunity to recognize and suggest changes to the products or options to improve their ability to serve your organization. Make this a formal part of your relationship with suppliers. For all these reasons, customers should also be invited to wander around in your facilities.

You must mount an ambitious effort to make wandering around in your customers' workplaces an important element of customer service (review Chapter 2). It is to be expected that managers responsible for sales and marketing should visit customer facilities, but supervisors and managers responsible for production, quality, production planning and materials procurement must also be involved. Provide every new employee in the organization with a meaningful visit to a customer operation as a routine component of the induction process. This communicates to the new employee, far more graphically than any address by you, the importance of good customer service.

Effective coaching

Wandering around provides a convenient opportunity for coaching. Effective coaching ultimately rests upon supporting managers as they learn to do things in the harsh realities of the workplace rather than in the classroom. Indeed, this is one of the differences between coaching and teaching. When you spot variances to procedures during your rounds, it is often possible to use the action taken to address those variances as coaching exercises. Because you wander around regularly, you may repeat any part of the process with any individual manager as long as it is needed to achieve results.

Another essential element of effective coaching is that delegates are give the opportunity to fail, otherwise, they are never going to understand their limits. Management by Wandering Around allows those limits to be tested while the coach is nearby to step in before the situation becomes irretrievable.

Developing the ability to wander around effectively in others is in itself another coaching opportunity. Again, all the actions you take while wandering around relate to the real work of the organization. It is never necessary to invent case studies or create classroom exercises when you have the entire organization as your laboratory.

Serendipity

A serendipitous result of effective wandering around is that it makes hidden agenda more difficult to keep hidden. Calculate the total cost for security throughout the organization. This includes not only the obvious measures such as gate guards and audit teams, but also the demand for two or three signatures on certain documents, the need for middle or even senior managers to approve miniscule purchase orders, the requirement for outgoing telephone calls to be routed through the switchboard and all the waiting and delay time faced by individuals during compliance with these procedures. In spite of what seems to be close scrutiny and tight security, hidden agenda still sometimes prevail:

- At a factory in the American Mid-west, 20 steelworkers were observed to clock on at the beginning of the shift, walk the length of the building, exit at the far end and enter a factory nearby. There they clocked on and worked the shift. At the end of the shift they reversed procedure, clocking off in both factories and going home. For several years they had been receiving full pay from two businesses simultaneously. This was only discovered when supervisors began to wander around properly and truly observe what was happening daily in their organization.

- A production welder was discovered building a caravan on the night shift in a maintenance stores area in a manufacturing facility. His fabrication work was nearly complete and he was soon to remove it for finishing at home when his D-I-Y project was discovered by a maintenance superintendent making meaningful rounds – finally.
- Recall my remark in the Introduction to Part Two concerning the company holding £500,000 in unmatched/unposted credits. That situation was in part the result of the actions of a section manager. He simply stuffed advices into the file drawer in his desk when his section fell behind schedule in matching and posting credit entries. This problem had been going on for about two years. The root cause of the problem, of course, was input errors that created the backlog of unmatched credit advices; this manager did not cause the problem. Nevertheless, his failure to communicate with his manager when he had a problem meeting work schedules resulted in spectacular levels of value lost to the company. This was only discovered when the department manager began to look at the operation properly and ask the right questions.

Do this tomorrow

Beginning tomorrow, and for the next three months, spend a minimum of one hour every day wandering around some part of the operation. This time must be spent with staff, section leaders and supervisors – in those areas where the work is done – and not with managers. Conduct your rounds according to everything we have discussed in this chapter. Make this part of every day you are in the facility. From this experience evaluate how well you can correlate what you see in the workplace with the operating information you receive through reporting processes and the effectiveness of your personal communications: how well directions from you are turned into appropriate actions.

When you are reasonably comfortable with this, direct other members of the management team to do the same. Using practices similar to those under which you wander around, schedule the following for the subsequent three months:

- One senior level manager responsible for computer systems development and programming will spend a minimum of one hour per day within a user area.
- One senior level manager responsible for operations will spend a minimum of one hour per day within a computer systems development area.
- One senior level manager responsible for maintenance will spend a minimum of one hour per day within a user department.

- One senior level manager responsible for production planning will spend a minimum of one hour per day on the shipping dock.
- One senior level manager responsible for material procurement will spend a minimum of one hour per day in the receiving department.
- One senior level manager responsible for toolmaking and tooling maintenance will spend a minimum of one hour per day with quality management staff.
- One supervisor responsible for production or operations will spend a minimum of one full day in every two weeks in a customer service area answering telephone calls and written enquiries from customers.
- One supervisor responsible for production will spend a minimum of one full day every two weeks working directly with a craftsperson responsible for production equipment repair and maintenance.
- One middle level marketing manager will spend a minimum of one full day every two weeks within the facility of a satisfied customer, in an area where your product or service is used.
- One middle level marketing manager will spend a minimum of one full day every two weeks within the facility of an unhappy customer, in an area where your product or service is used.
- One middle level manager responsible for supervisory development and training will spend a minimum of two hours per day in the workplace with delegates.
- One middle level manager responsible for methods development, creating and publishing procedures or establishing work standards will spend a minimum of one hour per day in the workplace with users of his or her services. This time will be spent wandering around, not conducting studies.

Follow up weekly with all managers involved in this process. Confirm that all are, in fact, wandering around, not simply sitting in unit managers' offices talking about football or cricket. Verify that this time is useful in demonstrating to these managers how actions in their areas of responsibility impact other parts of the organization and how effectively they are communicating. Later, extend this experience to everybody on the management team.

Notes

1 Peters and Waterman, *In Search of Excellence*; op. cit. Management by Wandering Around features prominently in Peters' and Waterman's *Excellence* philosophy and is an important component of, for example, Hewlett-Packard management practice.

2 Review Chapter 11.

3 Kenneth Blanchard and Spencer Johnson, *The One Minute Manager*. (Glasgow: Fontana/Collins, 1983.) Catching somebody doing something right is a key element of One Minute Management.

■ CHAPTER 19 ■

How to Succeed in Business Without Really Trying

Reports Which Nobody Reads

Filing cabinet drawer title in a UK Bank Admin centre

You have not responded to my request for a decision. Unless I hear from you to the contrary, next Wednesday I shall take the action we discussed.

Tactical Manager
in a *memorandum to his or her boss*

Introduction

An important criterion for evaluating any action taken within the organization, even more basic than whether it is the right thing to do or a thing done right, is to ask whether it should be done at all.

One thing happening in the changing organization is that it places additional and different sorts of responsibilities on individuals throughout. Supervisors and first line managers are asked to perform many tasks previously done by people in support departments. Computer programmers, maintenance craftspeople, word processor operators and engineers are assigned to task teams. Production operators and admin clerks are asked to monitor their own quality and performance. Everybody is encouraged to spend time seeking improvements in methods, procedures and practices, and to strive for better communications. Each is required to do more, and more work necessarily demands more time.

An important element of Tactical Management is concern for the best use of the time of everybody in the organization. Every minute is precious, no individual should ever be expected to spend time doing anything that does not ultimately contribute to organization health. This is important because, within the context of this chapter, when you can eliminate an activity completely, the impact is an immediate improvement in the use of people's time, and the cost is zero.

Processes are needed to evaluate every activity, then make a decision: either confirm that it supports long-range organization objectives or revise it so that it does, or eliminate it entirely. These processes themselves must not demand inordinate amounts of time. One straightforward practice is simply to do away with the suspect activity for a time and examine the impact on operations. If no negative result is noted, eliminate that activity – forever.[1]

Reports which nobody reads

The quotation is not imaginary. There exists, within an admin centre in a UK clearing bank, a filing cabinet drawer with that title. The name accurately describes the contents: staff handling incoming internal post are instructed to file in that drawer certain correspondence that they know in advance will never be read or otherwise processed by anybody in the unit.

The question, then, is why somebody is generating reports that nobody is going to read. The situation ordinarily evolves over time as in this, typical, example:

Example

A chief accountant was asked by his head office to conduct a study that required the accumulation of detailed data on production. He requested that certain statistics be summarized and forwarded to him weekly for three months. That was done and he produced his report. We discovered that those statistics were still being prepared and delivered to his department weekly seven years later.

During a project several years ago I watched a computer centre manager conduct this exercise most elegantly:

Example

He quietly reviewed all reports his unit was responsible for printing and distributing according to a regular schedule. He identified those he judged were not being used by recipients. Each was printed on schedule, but instead of being delivered, was place on a shelf behind his desk. Regardless of whether the frequency of a report was daily, weekly, monthly or quarterly, when two successive issues had accumulated on the shelf, and nobody enquired, he simply ceased to produce it. During one year he was able to reduce paper consumption and printing time fully by half – at zero cost.

I am familiar with a related technique:

Action

Collect copies of all forms, controls, reports and worksheets used throughout the operation. Place samples on a wall regularly accessible to most people: near the canteen is usually convenient.[2] Under each form place three blank sheets of paper. Ask everybody to enter information according to whether: (1) they originate a form, (2) process it and forward it, and to whom, or (3) receive it, take some kind of action then file it.

Usually you discover that about 30 per cent of the total are originated by somebody but nobody anywhere uses them for anything, either for information or to drive some action. For about another 25 per cent, somebody receives them and files them, but again with no action being take according to the information received.

Consider that when such a report is eliminated there is absolutely no negative impact, and the positive effects are that a number of important costs are reduced. Identify one suspect report somewhere in the operation and calculate costs:

1 Preparation time is eliminated with a saving in labour.
2 Delivery time is eliminated with a saving in labour.
3 Receiving, handling and filing times are eliminated with a saving in labour.
4 Storage is eliminated. Depending on location, storage costs for one file drawer may be as high as £250 per year. Calculate the figure for your facility.
5 For computer generated reports, both printing time and paper consumption are eliminated. Include not only computer paper purchase, but inventory, handling and disposal costs.
6 For reports generated on the mainframe a further result must be considered. Whenever you eliminate a report you necessarily reduce system usage and memory requirements. Each time you do this you improve system utilization for other users because you reduce slowdown. That factor may very small for the elimination of one report. If you do it enough times, however, the impact can be significant. When response time is enhanced you improve labour utilization for every individual using the system at that moment.

Perhaps the most subtle benefit of all is if the purchase of the next mainframe can be deferred for a time, even for one year, through repeated application of this technique. Think about the savings to the organization when this becomes a reality.

An objection is sometimes raised that this appears to be a patently crude means of addressing this issue, that operations may suffer as a consequence – that the appropriate action is to conduct a 'comprehensive study of report usage, including interviews with users', and from that develop a revised report publication schedule:

- How can anything that positively saves time and money, and reduces information clutter, be regarded other than as good management practice?
- If steps similar to those above have been taken, most risk to users is eliminated. If the recipient has made no enquiry concerning the report after you have failed to deliver two issues in succession, what conclusions can you draw concerning the impact of that information on the operation?
- Do you and other members of your management team really have the time to conduct a 'comprehensive review of report usage', given all the other demands on your time? Have you not, in fact, accomplished that with the actions described above?

A report is, after all, information – a resource. What is being asked is nothing more than that a user proactively justify the requirement for a resource. This should be standard practice for information as it is for every other resource throughout the organization.

A memorandum to the boss

Ceasing to publish reports is a tidy example of a principle that is widely applicable in the organization. There is really no need to examine theoretical considerations, effective practice depends purely on management action – or in this case, management non-action. There are opportunities available throughout:

Dear boss

Occasionally you find yourself in a situation where you need approval for some action you must take to achieve objectives, or perhaps want to take as part of some project effort, but no response has been forthcoming. Usually you have discussed this with your boss, sometimes *ad nauseam*. Occasionally the boss has commented that he or she never wants to hear about that particular issue again, while nevertheless continuing to demand results. A foolproof means of either getting a response, or obtaining documented, albeit tacit, approval is to send a memorandum similar to the one quoted at the beginning of this chapter.

Multi-copy computer reports

During your tour you watched a clerk manually decollate at least one multi-copy computer report, then throw away the carbon copies. Print off suspect reports as single copies and note whether the computer centre receives any complaints. There are significant savings here in both paper and labour. A further benefit is in making the clerk very happy by eliminating a tiresome task.

Word processing rework

Review word processing unit statistics. About 30 per cent of final copy work is for revision to material that was initially produced correctly, but for which the originator decided to make changes or corrections (I am not referring here to draft copy typing).

Change the procedure. Require all those submissions to be routed to you upon revision. When the work is collected by the originator, he or she can explain why it was not possible to get it right the first time. This is an excellent example of good quality management practice applied to an internal operation. Total cost to the organization when the originator gets it right the first time is far less than the rework effort. Calculate the costs to convince yourself.

The concern here is not merely for the pure work time for a word processor operator to make revisions to the text. The more serious problem is that by the time a copy is returned, it has often acquired the status of a rush job. Now two jobs have to be interrupted to do the rework, the one being entered and the one being printed.

Word processing rush jobs

Examine work in the RUSH basket. Some of it, occasionally much of it, is more than a few hours old.

Change the procedure. Ask the unit supervisor to remove all work that has remained in the basket for more than one-half day and forward it to you. In two months reduce this to two hours. When the work is collected, the originator can explain to you why he or she was not in the same rush to redeem it as to submit it. This is a good case for communicating with integrity. When spurious rush requests are eliminated from the system, there is ordinarily ample time to deal with genuine emergencies.

Another way to deal with this problem is to ignore totally any request with a RUSH or ASAP entered for the collection date. Require every submission to include a specific date and time even if they are unreasonably tight. This practice is also useful for maintenance and computer systems emergency requests.

System enquiries

Within many admin operations there exists a routine practice for requests from outside the unit for information filed electronically. The requester forwards a hand-written worksheet with the items to be called up on the system and printed off. The worksheet is usually submitted in the morning, unit staff make the enquiries and the printouts are collected in the afternoon.

Change the procedure. Dedicate a terminal to external users. Now everybody making enquiries can do it at their convenience. Total enquiries will drop significantly. Although the reason might not be obvious, when you examine the process you discover the following:

- External users sit at their desks in the morning and review the files or enquiries they plan to action that day. They enter all those references on the hand-written worksheets and forward them to the admin department. During that initial review, they do not necessarily know whether they will need any particular file, but they might, so they request them all.
- As they are working through the lot, a better practice is to put aside all those that require a file reference. Now they are left with only those for which a system enquiry is necessary. The result is that total clerical effort and system usage are reduced. Further, they are ordinarily not so casual about the use of their own time as they are about the time of somebody in another department.

Microfilm and microfiche enquiries

Examine requests for microfilm and microfiche prints and you will discover a similar situation. Dedicate a unit to external users and implement a similar procedure. Total clerical effort and system usage will be reduced.

Meeting attendance

In Chapter 13 we examined this practice as it applies to meetings. If you honestly feel you can make no contribution to matters discussed at a meeting, and if you feel that you gain no benefit from your attendance, then what is achieved by that expenditure of your time? My suggestion that you do not attend is not an effort to promote anarchy in the organization, it is to force a proactive, zero base justification for that most valuable resource: personal time.

Manual paper and electronic systems running in parallel

Conduct a thorough review of units where work was converted from manual paper to electronic systems within the last year or two. You will often discover both systems running fully in parallel long after the manual system should have been eliminated.

This situation always demands a thorough evaluation for several reasons:

- The manual system may have been retained because the electronic system cannot meet operational needs. Here enhancements must be developed and implemented immediately to correct deficiencies in the computer system. Running parallel systems is inconsistent with effective customer service, quality and cost management.
- Unit supervisors and managers may be attempting to accomplish work under procedures and practices that are appropriate for the manual rather than the automated systems. For example, if staff do not have adequate keyboard skills, they will draft letters by hand, then move to the PC screen or mainframe VDU to enter them. In this instance they are using the computer system incorrectly – as nothing more than a very expensive typewriter.[3] Here no savings will be evident with the computerized system. Training is necessary.
- Work habits may reflect the old system. For example, batch sizes may be more appropriate for the manual system. No savings will be seen, and both staff and supervisors will be able to demonstrate clearly that the old system required less labour to operate.
- Conversion from a totally manual to fully computerized system represents massive change for everybody involved. If that transition has not been handled sensitively and with proper consideration for users, they will understandably be resistant to the change. If they have not been adequately trained in the new ways of working, this, too, will result in apparently unreasonable resistance.

Confirm that all these issues have been fully addressed. Then, however, the manual system must be eliminated.

Eliminate filing in sequence

Within admin operations there are a number of filing activities that require advices of some kind to be placed in order, by date, sequentially or alphabetically. It is important to examine the relative time required to file those compared to retrieval needs. Under certain conditions substantial time can be saved by revising the procedure.

Example

During system installation in a clerical operation in a large admin centre we noted that sequential filing of an advice note called the Yellow Peril into cardboard file boxes consumed about five hours per day. Daily retrieval was ordinarily about ten advice notes, and the standard for a single enquiry was about one minute.

The procedure was changed so that Yellow Perils were filed at random, with the provision that any single box contained them for only one month. Filing time dropped nearly to zero, while the retrieval time for one advice note increased to six minutes.

Net savings for the operation were four hours per day, with the additional benefit that an extremely boring task was eliminated.

Examine your operation carefully for opportunities of this nature. Review the notes from your tour; they will confirm that such opportunities exist.

Maintenance work requests and computer system enhancements

In Chapter 17 we discussed the importance of capturing all open work available to maintenance and computer systems development units. Much of that work is in the form of orders for service generated by user groups. That work must be formalized through a system of structured work requests and summarized in a backlog report. When evaluating resource requirements for these departments, all jobs on the backlog report must be examined critically.

It is necessary to purge the backlog regularly and frequently. The reason for this might not be obvious. Completion dates for maintenance work and system development projects are often scheduled as much as a full year after the initial request. Within the year between order and delivery it is not unusual for a request to be submitted for other work that renders at least part of the original order unnecessary. It is not uncommon to discover that a recent work request abrogates two, three or even four older ones in the backlog.

It is likely that the backlog of maintenance and systems development work can be reduced by between one-quarter and one-third when it is assertively purged. The benefits of this are twofold: staffing requirements are substantially reduced, and when lead times are shortened it is possible to improve management of the entire backlog.

Consider this

Actions we have examined here must be handled with sensitivity. Nearly every one relates to daily, visible change in the workplace:

- The elimination of reports must be handled quietly. If you interview people and ask them if they want to continue receiving reports, you are not going to achieve the same result as if you just stop publishing them. Telling people what you intend to do will only spoil the surprise.

- The computer centre manager will be extremely uncomfortable not printing reports; after all, that is perceived to be an important part of the job.
- The word processing supervisor will probably not be happy referring customers to you.
- Supervisors and managers in admin, microfilm and microfiche units will not be happy allowing outsiders access to their equipment and files.
- Staff and supervisors in admin units will feel that stuffing advices in cardboard boxes at random is untidy and ineffective.

There might be possible risk associated with some of these proposals. Software is sometimes designed so the command to print a report automatically updates a portion of the database. Eliminating that report may require an enhancement. Allowing external users access to the system without adequate training can results in errors, damage to equipment or degradation of information. Purging the maintenance backlog vigorously can result in the loss of an important work request. Not attending a meeting may mean that vital information is not received.

Nevertheless, these are powerful opportunities for improvements in operations. It might be conveniently compared to delegation: even with the associated risk and anticipated resistance to the changes, when properly managed the result is worth the effort.

Think, also, about the analysis of forms, controls, reports and worksheets you carried out on the canteen wall. Imagine being able to eliminate 55 per cent of the paper flowing through the operation – immediately and at zero cost.

Do this over the next six months

Work with appropriate managers in the organization to achieve these objectives over the next six months:

- Eliminate 25 per cent of all computer generated reports.
- Replace three multi-copy computer generated reports with single copies.
- Eliminate 25 per cent of all manually generated reports.
- Reduce word processing rework requests to five per cent of total unit workload. Reduce RUSH requests to five per cent of total unit workload.
- Eliminate two paper systems running fully and redundantly in parallel with electronic systems.
- Eliminate three externally driven enquiry processes and replace them with processes operated by users.

- Purge maintenance backlogs by 25 per cent through the elimination of overlapping or redundant work requests.
- Purge computer systems development and enhancement backlogs by 25 per cent through the elimination of overlapping or redundant requests.

Use this, also, as a coaching effort for the managers involved. Follow-up with them over the subsequent six months as they coach staff, supervisors and managers to apply these practices further within their units.

Notes

1 Drucker, *The Practice of Management*; op. cit. Drucker was applying this process in the early 1950s.
2 See the Coda, Brown paper systems analysis.
3 This will be discussed in more detail in Chapter 22.

■ CHAPTER 20 ■

Setting and Achieving Objectives: Management by objectives

The ultimate trust builder is delivering on promises.

Rosabeth Moss Kanter
World Class

I'm not responsible.

A cabinet minister, a chairman, a chief executive

You *are* responsible.

Tactical Manager

Introduction

Throughout *Tactical Management* 'objectives' has been used in connection with nearly everything we have discussed: achieving daily work targets, managing projects or meeting yearly production forecasts. In every case the term has referred specifically to managers managing the work of their units. In this chapter we examine an integrated set of practices to achieve better management of the work of managers.

Management by Objectives (MBO) was first articulated as a formal discipline in the 1950s.[1] The practice is based on: targets clearly set and agreed by both the manager and the delegate, mutually acceptable means of monitoring progress, open and honest communications and attention by both parties to a level of detail appropriate to effective completion of the task. The principles are extremely useful. In the past 20 years, however, MBO has attained a mystique from which many inferred that it could magically solve all their problems. This is about as likely as delegation solving all your problems. Management by objectives is nothing more or less than another management tool – useful when correctly applied. Unfortunately, those who attributed magical powers to the principle were very disappointed and the result is that now the term MBO is in disfavour with many.

Setting and achieving objectives, as an element of Tactical Management, is very close to the original MBO model. Review the tactical closed-loop management cycle, short segment task control, management operating systems and project management. Those disciplines contain nearly everything you need to know about setting and achieving objectives. The purpose of this chapter is to tailor those principles to the work of managers.

Managing the work of managers

In the most general sense setting objectives merely means telling the people who work for you exactly what you expect from them. Because the work of managers differs in a number of essential respects from that of staff, however, management of that work requires somewhat different tools:

- The interval of control for work assignments for staff is always very short, certainly less than one day. The interval of control for work or tasks assigned to section leaders, supervisors and managers will be longer, more than one day, occasionally much longer.
- Assignments for managers are typically less structured and demand less specific direction than those for staff. Generally the higher a manager is in the organization, the less structured is the assignment and less specific the direction (the objective itself, remember, is always very specific).
- Task assignments for managers often relate to matters other than the principal work of the unit – efforts to support that primary work.
- Staff people ordinarily have no people reporting to them, and because of this, their responsibilities do not extend beyond their individual work assignments. Managers are responsible for proper and timely completion of all work of their units and all the people in the unit. They are also responsible for effective and efficient utilization of all resources allocated to the unit, for specific levels of customer service, quality and cost management, and for safety, good housekeeping and good work practices.
- Coaching requirements are distinct. Coaching needs for staff people should emphasize preparing them to assume greater roles in customer service, quality and cost management efforts as those disciplines improve their abilities to contribute to organization health. Coaching for managers must focus on improving their abilities to provide support for staff and removing obstacles to effective operations, to widen their scope for planning and taking effective management action, and to increase their capacity to implement change.

There are some exceptions. Within a unit of only two or three people, for example, objectives may be set for each as deemed appropriate regardless of who was in charge. The staff person soon to be promoted to section leader or supervisor would also be expected to meet objectives as part of that preparation. This is one of those areas, too, where the distinction between staff and management will blur as the organization evolves; within your operation four years from now, people at every level will routinely be operating under this practice.

Setting and achieving objectives

Setting and achieving objectives is always a one-on-one process between a manager and a delegate; these discussions concern the interaction between a superior and one subordinate (this would not rule out, however, a delegate sponsoring a task team to assist with an objective). Setting and achieving objectives, as an element of Tactical Management, is based on the following requirements, all fully consistent with the constituents of classical MBO.

The goal is mutually agreed between manager and delegate

In an ideal world the manager and delegate sit down, and develop and mutually agree an objective. In the perfect world the delegate delivers to the manager an objective, already committed to it. In the real world it seldom happens that smoothly. The goal may be something the manager feels very strongly must be achieved and which he or she assertively tries to sell to the delegate. Or the objective may be one the delegate feels very strongly about and which he or she vigorously attempts to sell to the manager. In either case, both must commit fully to the objective in spirit and action.

The goal must be achievable. It should require work to a high standard and it should test the delegate, but it must be reasonable. Further, the delegate must feel that it is attainable with the determined support of the manager. There is no reason why an objective should not also test the manager. If, for example, the delegate forecasts that the alteration to a customer specification will result in a product of a higher standard at the same or reduced price, the powerful intervention of the manager could be needed to sell it to the customer.

The scheduled completion for the action must be an integral part of the statement of the objective and that also must be committed to by both.

The statement of the objective must be in writing, and agreement is to that written statement:

- The statement must be clear, simple and brief. If it cannot be contained on one A5 piece of paper, either the objective is muddled or you are looking at more than one. There must be absolutely no question about what is required.

- The completion date must also be clear and unambiguous. There must be absolutely no question about when it is required.
- The statement should contain the signatures of both manager and delegate.[2] Some may feel this requirement for a written statement and signatures is an unnecessary formality and additional, trivial paperwork. The Brussels sprouts principle is eminently useful here. How often in the past year has a manager not delivered on time something that was promised and that was important to you because he or she was 'too busy'?

The method for measuring attainment is mutually agreed

It is critical that the initial measure of attainment is an integral part of the primary statement of the objective. Indeed, if it seems impossible or even difficult to make this part of the primary statement, either the objective is still muddled or, in fact, you have no objective. The method for interim measurement or calculation of precise final attainment may be possible here, or may have to await the task layout.[3]

The means for achieving the goal is mutually agreed

Whereas the statement of the primary objective must be simple and brief, the means of achieving the goal must be stated at a level of detail appropriate to the task. The task must be phased according to good practices for project management and short segment task control. The first action taken by the delegate is to lay out the task in sufficient detail to ensure that both of them can jointly monitor progress. The first control point for the task is when the manager and the delegate sit down and review the layout. For some ambitious tasks it might not be possible for both to commit to the objective until the task has been laid out.

There is intense interaction between the manager and delegate

There is a requirement throughout the work for a high level of intense interaction and communications between the manager and delegate. This is the tactical closed-loop management cycle applied to an ongoing one-on-one situation.

Management support is universal and purposeful

The commitment for action is from the bottom up, support for the effort is from the top down. Management at every level, but especially at the top, must provide a climate that supports openness, integrity, willingness to change, reasonable levels of risk, creativity and innovation. Loose-tight management control is crucial. The overall objective is clearly stated (tight), the interaction between manager and delegate is close and intense (loose-tight) and within that framework the manager must allow the delegate a maximum amount of freedom to be innovative and take risk (loose). That freedom to take risk and exercise creativity and innovation must be a very visible component of management support throughout the organization.

Applicability

Setting objectives relates to almost all activities for every manager. Think of each objective set as a project; indeed, setting and achieving an objective is nothing more than a one-person project or task team effort. The time from initial signing of the contract to completion may range from three days for a minor management action or coaching exercise to two years for a major reduction in rework or development of a new product. This practice is amenable to almost every assignment made to each manager. The chief executive should be setting objectives for each director and the supervisor should be setting objectives for each section leader. The list is almost endless; the following are representative:

- Basic production, quality and cost management targets relating to the principal work of the unit may be set as objectives. This may be a requirement when a new manager or supervisor has assumed responsibility for an area that has had serious problems under previous management. The first task is to make the operation functional. This objective might cover a period as long as six months.
- Reductions in levels of rejections or rework, improvements in compliance with quality specifications and improved management of specific categories of costs can translate into objectives when control of unit operations is reasonably stable. These objectives may range from three months to one year according to magnitude.
- The professional development of managers must be of continuing concern. Set objectives for completion of specific courses, obtaining certificates and professional qualifications, both job-related and peripheral. Include in this category supervisory development courses for staff soon to be promoted to section leader or supervisor. In this case the requirement is for a continuous series of fairly short objectives.

- Ensuring appropriate and ongoing levels of staff training and development should be part of the objectives of every section leader and supervisor. These include technical and job-related skills, customer service awareness, quality management, and training to enhance an understanding of budgeting, cost management and profits. Time frames for individual objectives depend entirely on the demands of the unit and the readiness levels of staff.
- Objectives may be set for everybody, from new staff to middle manager, for improvements in unit safety or housekeeping. Here, also, the requirements are for a continuous series of fairly modest objectives.
- The introduction of methods and procedures changes to reduce throughput time or improve management of costs may be set as objectives for anybody within the area.
- Set objectives for supervisors to reduce paperwork or convert from manual to Computerized systems. This may be an excellent opportunity for a supervisor to learn how to sponsor a task team: a line supervisor will probably not have the background to evaluate computer applications for the unit and will have to enlist the help of systems people. Many objectives of this nature will be extremely ambitious.
- Objectives for the development of new products or services must not be confined to designers, development and marketing people. Supervisors and managers responsible for production and engineering should also be set objectives for product development and improved customer service.
- Set objectives for department managers to eliminate quality activities by external inspectors and convert to operator monitoring. Achievement of this type of objective will demonstrate the ability to manage significant change effectively.
- Involve admin section leaders and supervisors with objectives to reduce cash exposure, the age of the bought ledger or lost value. This work will improve understanding of the contributions these activities make to organization health.
- Convince supervisors and managers who are eager for promotion that they should develop subordinates to the point of their being qualified to replace them. Professional development of subordinates should be one of the principal objectives for every manager.
- Projects and assignments requiring specific management action to address unique operating problems may be used to set objectives for people everywhere in the organization. Any task that requires the effort and expertise of one individual may be used as the basis for a formal objective.

Setting objectives is also another opportunity for coaching. If a supervisor, for example, is having difficulty meeting production targets because he or she is not making effective work assignments, the department manager may set objectives for small, incremental improvements in output, and support the supervisor in this effort. This is an opportunity for the manager to coach. This may also be an opportunity for the manager's boss to develop his or her coaching skills. If a middle manager, for example, is not supporting subordinate department managers in demands for decisions nor providing adequate intervention for lateral communications, this is an excellent opportunity to set objectives and coach this middle manager to enhance his or her ability to take effective action.

The advantage here is that, as with delegation, the objective to be set can as bold or as modest as the delegate can handle. If the delegate is having a particular problem, tiny, tiny objectives can be set to bring him or her along. As the ability to achieve improves, objectives can be made more ambitious.

In no instance should an objective be set to write a report or provide somebody in the organization with a set of recommendations. This process is to generate action, not recommendations.

The principle of ultimate responsibility

When you commit to an objective, you accept full responsibility for completing and successfully achieving that objective.[4] When you accept a job as a manager, whether it is section leader or chief executive, you automatically accept full responsibility for proper completion not only of the duties you are charged with, but the duties of everybody you manage.

If you manage a production unit, for example, you are responsible for the production of every bad part; if you manage an admin unit, you are responsible for each error on a journal voucher (unless the bad part was caused by a hurricane or the error was the result of an earthquake).

Some discussion is appropriate: I have often heard supervisors or department managers say: 'I know I could reduce mistakes if I could train my people. But I'm not allowed to schedule it. I'm not responsible'. I have heard this comment more than a few times from senior managers and occasionally even from directors: 'I cannot meet production schedules with the tooling and equipment we have. I'm not allowed to upgrade either tooling or equipment. I'm not responsible'.

If the health of the organization is to be maintained, every manager must vigorously assert that responsibility that he or she has already assumed by acceptance of the position. It will no longer be tolerable for the production supervisor to let the job run and make bad parts because *they* told him or her to; the organization will eventually disappear unless that supervisor accepts the responsibility to shut the job down. If the error rate in the claims department is not trending to zero because the manager has not been able to obtain budgetary approval to train staff, the organization will die unless that manager accepts responsibility and takes whatever actions are needed to schedule training for staff.

This principle is most relevant to setting and achieving objectives. When you commit to an objective, you are responsible for successfully meeting that commitment. You cannot absolve yourself of responsibility because something interferes with your ability to manage the work.

The message for senior management should be clear: When a manager accepts responsibility for achievement of an objective, he or she also accepts responsibility for communicating with the boss when the ability to manage the task is lost – when something outside his or her immediate control has interfered. Of more importance, however, is that the boss has also accepted responsibility for providing whatever help is needed to enable the delegate to regain control. This process extends from the most junior staff members in the organization to Board members. If the organization is to survive, it will no longer be acceptable for anybody, any time to feel they are not responsible for attainment of objectives to which they have committed.

Concerning management performance appraisal

Consider the purpose for performance appraisal and how it is managed in your organization. Performance appraisal is supposed to be a formalized process to: (1) recognize and support actions that are consistent with organization goals, (2) be a factor for changing actions that are inconsistent with organization goals, (3) provide a consistent framework of reference for rewarding positive performance and not rewarding unsatisfactory performance, and (4) be perceived by everybody to demonstrate fairness – that a greater positive effort receives a proportionally greater positive reward. Few appraisal systems, where they exist at all, accomplish any of these aims.

Most appraisal systems work something like this: once every year the manager is supposed to sit down with each subordinate and conduct a formal performance review. Neither individual has any real idea why they are doing this, other, perhaps than that personnel requires it. Frequently this meeting occurs as much as six months later that scheduled, but: '. . . never mind. The important thing is to get this bit of paper into your personal file'. Recording the process follows either one of two forms: the appraiser enters an 'E' (for Excellent) after every question concerning achievement or the appraiser enters a number on a scale from one to ten in every category, and these numbers add to a certain minimum total that demonstrates excellent performance.

The pretence is that the appraisee is to be rewarded with a bonus or salary increase commensurate with good performance. The fact is that the increase is a fixed percentage, paid to everybody, having nothing to do with performance, having been determined by the board at the last monthly meeting. Except, of course, when the board have decided that no salary increases are to be awarded. In this case the appraiser enters an NS (for Not Satisfactory) in every blank, or numbers that do not total to the minimum for excellent performance.

If a performance appraisal process is to accomplish the aims outlined in the first paragraph above, it must meet, at minimum, two criteria: rewards or lack of rewards must be frequent and related to small, meaningful, understandable successes of failures. Rewards or lack of rewards must immediately follow the actions. Under a once-yearly appraisal programme, it is impossible to meet either of these requirements.

Setting objectives and measuring progress toward the achievement of them as we have discussed in this chapter accomplishes the aims of an effective performance appraisal system. Performance should not be appraised yearly, it must be evaluated continually. This is not difficult when both the appraiser and the appraisee can sit down any time and jointly review the attainment of objectives from a written record. If personnel demand a yearly summary, the appraiser can accurately and easily develop it from the written statements of the achievement or non-achievement of objectives.

Do this over the next three months

Identify four senior or middle managers whom you feel will be reasonably comfortable with setting and achieving objectives as the practice has been presented here. Sit down with the four and present the system.

Identify four objectives, one for each manager, and implement the process, considering carefully everything we have discussed. For this first effort, select objectives that can be accomplished in a relatively short time – one month perhaps – that are very simple and straightforward and for which measurement and attainment will be easy to monitor. Treat this as an exercise for you and the four to gain experience with this process.

On completion, evaluate the work and results. Then set four more, more ambitious objectives for these managers, while coaching them as they each set objectives for four of their subordinates.

With that experience you should be able to generalize setting objectives as a tool for managing the work of managers throughout the organization. Conduct this with the understanding that it is preparation for the next year when it will become a tool for managing work for everybody.

Notes

1 Drucker, *The Practice of Management*; op. cit. Drucker articulated this set of principles as a management tool in this book. Some references credit George S. Odiorne with first use of the term in his book: *Management By Objectives*, (New York: Pitman, 1965.)
2 In Part Three we refer to this as signing the contract.
3 Review Chapter 14, Page 195 for a discussion of the project layout.
4 Review Chapter 5, Page 77, the principle of ultimate responsibility.

■ CHAPTER 21 ■

Training and Development: The upward spiral path

> We have learned much, Siddhartha. There still remains much to learn. We are not going in circles, we are going upwards. The path is a spiral; we have already climbed many steps.
>
> Hermann Hesse
> *Siddhartha*

Introduction

The quotation is not romantic: technical and professional development for every individual in the organization must be understood to be a never-ending adventure, building upon what has gone before to prepare for the future. A total commitment must be made that training will be continual, comprehensive and continuous. If the organization is to survive and grow, training and development must be regarded as an element crucial to that enterprise. In this chapter we will examine processes to assist you to walk that path. There is no final objective; the path is indeed an upward spiral.

Training must be understood by everybody to be an integral part of the life of the organization. It is not a luxury tacked onto a list of items to be considered when you have a bit of money left over in the budget, nor should it be motivated by recent articles in management journals offering whatever new discovery about human behaviour is going to save the business this year. It most certainly is *not* the item to be cut automatically from the budget when money is tight. It should *never* be cut from the budget; if money is tight, that is probably a good sign that you should be investing more in training. Training and development resources as distinct entities, when they are thoughtfully conceived, wholly relevant to identified needs and professionally delivered, make vital contributions to the health of the organization.

Training is used here in the most general sense to include all the skills and types of knowledge you seek to impart to members of the team, ranging from induction and orientation sessions, through various technical disciplines to leadership and executive development seminars. The exception in this chapter is that we will not examine formal career growth processes such as graduate fast track or MBA schemes.

Measuring results

Training is one of the few elements in the Tactical Management model for which it is difficult to correlate costs and benefits easily. It is not always possible to relate the cost to direct, measurable results on a short interval basis. For some you can. Staff technical training, for example, will yield an obvious, immediate upward trend in daily performance. For others, however, the results will not be evident as quickly or as clearly. Supervisory development, for example, will contribute to improved section performance, but that will be happening at the same time as supervisors are doing a number of other things such as working toward a set of performance related objectives. For middle managers it is possible to relate training for management skills and communications to the statement of objectives, although the connection will be somewhat less immediate. Senior level management development effort will ordinarily be even less directly linked to improved operations performance for the short term.

Recall the example in Chapter 8 of the life insurance salesman who monitored his schedule attainment and performance on a short interval by the number of times he dialled the telephone. Retail organizations often use a similar technique for tracking the acquisition of product knowledge. Sales staff are responsible for achieving assigned levels of product knowledge through the review of circulars, video presentations or procedures. Somewhere in the canteen, restroom or training room you will find a matrix that includes names in rows and product categories in columns. Each individual is responsible for ensuring his or her own progress by studying the product information, then entering completion dates on the matrix according to a published schedule. This practice is sometimes supported by a combination of oral or written tests regularly scheduled by supervisors or unit managers.

For training effort, the short interval control mechanism must be session attendance and progress in meeting phased training objectives. Improvements in customer service, quality, cost management and profits resulting from training effort will finally be monitored for the longer term, yearly, when it is possible to compare revenues and total costs. This limitation must never inhibit the investment in training resources.

A comprehensive training plan

If training is to be totally effective, two conditions must be met: it must include everybody in the organization from the newest clerk or production operator to the group chief executive – everybody; and processes must address all the needs of each individual. Consider these as broad categories of training necessary to support long-term organization objectives:

Induction and general orientation to the organization

Induction training must be formal and must be more than a quick tour of the facility, one afternoon spent scanning a photocopy of the work rules, receiving a parking sticker and learning how to manipulate the timeclock. Inductees should be introduced to the basics of your particular business. The process should extend over a minimum of two weeks. It should include at least one full day in customer facilities with a salesperson.

At the conclusion of training inductees should be able to explain cogently what the primary work of the organization is and how their efforts in the department to which they have been assigned contribute to that final product. They should be able to find their way from one end of the facility to the other unassisted, and they should have a good working knowledge of safety and housekeeping procedures. They should be able to tell you what profits were for last year and how they compared to targets, who your principal competitors are and what typical problems interfere with meeting quality standards. They should recognize all department heads within the facility on sight.

Induction and orientation training must include everybody who joins the organization and must be conducted immediately each person enters, not sometime during the first six months.

Business management for staff

All staff must receive a minimum of one week yearly business training. This should include work to enhance the basic business skills introduced during induction. Every staff member should be capable of describing and quantifying the present state of operations with respect to forecast achievements in customer service, quality and cost management. This training should include the importance of planning, time management, corrective action and achieving objectives. Every staff member should spend one day each year with a salesperson within customer facilities.

Technical development for staff

Technical development for staff will very greatly according to the particular needs of their units and your business. This training must meet two objectives: it must enable the delegate to grow in performance and ability to make positive contributions to customer service, quality and cost management objectives, and it must enable him or her to grow professionally: to be able to assume more different kinds of responsibilities within the organization. Every staff member should spend a minimum of two full weeks yearly in technical development – probably more for most. Where possible this should be co-ordinated with efforts to obtain professional certification or other formal recognition.

Welcome to the world of management

This is most important for the transition from worker to boss. Include in this group supervisors, section leaders and senior operators soon to be promoted to one of these positions. It is important this training occurs before the new position is assumed, not nine months after. Review Chapter 9 for elements of this training.

Supervisory and management development

Supervisory and management development training must be provided at the minimum of two weeks each year for every supervisor and manager. It must address the real issues that managers at every level face in the workplace. The traditional sorts of subjects that comprise the needs for good management must be included such as communications, work assignment practices, time management, effective discipline, delegation, coaching and organizational development.

Specialized business skills

In preparation for the assumption of more responsibilities, managers must understand the importance of specialized business skills. These include strategic planning, business planning and budgeting, economics, the international business community, the impact of your industry on the environment, the responsibility of your organization for product or service liability, and health and safety requirements. After managers have acquired a core of supervisory and management development skills, these specialized business skills should be phased into their training.

Management development and leadership

As managers are promoted higher in the organization, the nature of assignments and responsibilities change. If we define management as making decisions and taking actions to keep the organization moving toward long-term goals, then we might define leadership as identifying what must be made to happen to achieve those long-term goals and obtaining commitments to action from those who must make it happen (this definition is not intended to be definitive).[1]

Leadership talents must be developed as any other body of management skills. Traditionally leadership was perceived to be part of the responsibility of senior managers and executives, and probably much emphasis will continue at that level. If you think, however, about the evolving organization, you realize that in the future leadership as a skill will be necessary at every level.[2]

Training in management development and leadership must enable managers to:

- identify when a change is crucial to organization health,
- design altered structures and practices to address it,
- introduce it to others and obtain a commitment to the new order and
- manage the change – implement the new order.

When effective delegation of management responsibilities has occurred, leadership skills will be required of people much lower on the organization chart than is the case today.

Interdepartmental communications

Barriers between departments, units, disciplines and functions must be eliminated. This is a crucial requirement for the future: the organization simply will not be able to respond quickly and effectively to changes in the environment if these barriers prevail. This represents a rather specialized form of communications and therefore demands a separate listing here. Systems training for people in user departments, and operations training for systems people, is probably the most obvious example of the need for this type of interdepartmental effort. People throughout the organization must be able to project how changes in their areas will affect other parts of the operation. They must also be able to influence changes in other units to support positive changes in their own units.

The training matrix

Review the notes from your tour. When you asked supervisors and managers about their most frustrating, recurring operating problems, their answers always included a global 'training'. When you asked each how much training was needed and in what particular skills, however, the typical response was: 'Lots of training'. You cannot drive truly effective management action with that sort of limited and unqualified information.

Throughout *Tactical Management* one of our premises has been that when a situation has been described objectively and quantified i.e.

measured, only then is it possible to address it adequately. This is particularly true for training needs. There is a need for a process to qualify and quantify training needs systematically for everybody in the organization.

Develop a matrix similar to Figure 21.1. Each row represents an individual to be trained and each column reflects a particular skill or training activity:

1 Create a separate plan for each unit, group of related activities or for people with similar skills requirements.
2 Enter the name of every individual in the unit. Do not omit anybody because they are fully trained.
3 Enter an activity description or skill identification for every discipline, skill or activity required to operate the unit or complete the list of skills.Under each individual and activity enter:
   (a) total hours required to enable the person to become fully proficient or qualified in that skill, and
   (b) the date he or she is scheduled to complete training for that activity.
4 For each individual, in the right column enter a grand total hours required to become fully trained on unit activities.
5 For each individual, in the right column enter a final date when all training is scheduled to be complete.
6 For every skill or activity enter at the bottom of the matrix the total hours required to fully train everybody presently in the unit on that particular activity.

There are a number of advantages to this process:

- When every individual and every activity is entered on the matrix, total unit requirements are summarized. This enables you to allocate resources not only for the total unit but according to each particular skill.
- When required hours are entered for each individual it is possible to quantify needs ranging from full training for a particular activity, through partial training to minor retraining or review of proficiency.
- Total organization requirements for outside resources can quickly and easily be summarized.
- Training needs for each individual can conveniently be converted into objectives. Training completion schedules can easily be co-ordinated with other objectives.

Development of a training plan drives both delegation and meaningful communications between superior and subordinate. The only two people who can accurately identify training requirements for an individual are the delegate and his or her immediate manager, working jointly. This is particularly true for those partially trained, for technical training,

Figure 21.1 The Tactical Management training plan

TACTICAL MANAGEMENT TRAINING PLAN

UNIT: PREPARED BY: DATE PREPARED:

NAME	ACTIVITY																TOTALS
HOURS																	
DATE																	
HOURS																	
DATE																	
HOURS																	
DATE																	
HOURS																	
DATE																	
HOURS																	
DATE																	
HOURS																	
DATE																	
HOURS																	
DATE																	
HOURS																	
DATE																	
TOTAL HOURS																	

refresher or retraining, and for supervisory and management development. The most important advantage for this plan, however, is that it enables each manager to quantify unit training needs fully. In the Introduction I remarked that a manger should be able to say 'I need X hours to train Y people in Z disciplines'. The matrix we have examined here enables every manager in the organization to do that.

Another advantage is that the matrix makes the entire process very visible. Treat each line entry on a training plan as an objective. Ask the individual to agree it with the manager, then commit to it, as would be done with any other objective. Make the delegate responsible for monitoring his or her own progress. When the entire process is made visible, for example, by hanging the matrix on the canteen wall as the retailers do, this appears to be a positive factor motivating people to achieve training and development objectives. This process could be computerized very easily. I personally feel that the visibility of the paper system outweighs the convenience of the computerized version. Make up your own mind.[3]

The venue

Much of this section addressed practices that have worked very well for me through the years. These are not the only approaches, nor necessarily the best. Treat them as recommendations and adjust them as they seem to meet your needs.

Venue, and session structure and content are important. I have never been in favour of throwing people off cliffs, dragging them through potholes or hurling them down swirling rapids in little rubber boats to promote teambuilding and engender *esprit de corps*, I feel the same kinds of pressures can be applied in the classroom and there the message is far more relevant to the workplace.[4] Training sessions, however, should be exciting and challenging, even a bit scary, and they should test delegates fully. People are capable of far more than we as managers generally expect from them and the carefully controlled atmosphere of the classroom is a safe place to test limits – safe for the tutor, delegates and the organization.

Delegates should not be drawn from more than two management levels for any session. When you schedule three or more levels, discussions, arguments, comments and questions are often inhibited which renders the effort a waste of time for everybody. If, for example, a session includes section leaders and supervisors, do not admit department managers. In my experience, in these circumstances the section leaders as those lowest in the management chain will not participate in front of the department managers, particularly to discuss any very sensitive issues. Except for strictly technical presentations, every session should include a mixture of people from various departments. This is important to break down barriers between units, and is a crucial requirement in those operations where serious problems between departments have been long-standing.

Sessions should be conducted jointly by a thoroughly experienced trainer and an operating manager familiar with the work of delegates. It is helpful if the manager is one level above delegate level on the organization chart, except in certain circumstances. For subjects such as accounting, budgeting, strategic planning, production design or mainframe capabilities, for example, the operating manager should be one recognized as the primary authority in the organization.

Facilities must be more than adequate; they must be appropriate, comfortable, well lighted, well equipped and generously supplied with coffee, tea and biscuits. Sessions should be held on site if possible; after all, that is where the work is done (this is not always possible; adequate facilities are sometimes not available). This is true even when the tutor is an outside resource. On site, one rule must be maintained: there are to be absolutely no interruptiuons – production supervisors or quality managers must not be dragged out every ten minutes or so because: '. . . something REALLY important has come up!' There are to be no telephones in the room.

Provide nicely designed namecards, and thoughtfully presented, colourful manuals. Notes and textbook extracts must be meaningful and relevant to the topic; even general material can be adapted with specific examples from the workplace. All visual aids, videos, overhead transparencies, equipment and supplies must be clearly dedicated to that session and that group. Never, under any circumstances provide delegates with shoddy photocopies of material pirated from another company or project with the name obviously obliterated. Pirate them certainly if you believe they will be useful – we all do it, but then redraw them; your people deserve that consideration. Make extensive use of games and exercises; there are many good ones available. Select from those that are not only fun but make the point. Create your own if you cannot find exactly what you want; it is not difficult.

Delegates should range from a minimum of 12, whenever possible to a maximum of 16. With any fewer you achieve too little interaction, and with any more each individual cannot always receive an appropriate amount of attention. Sessions must include heavy delegate involvement and significant dialogue between tutors and delegates. There are very few circumstances where a lecture format is appropriate. Make frequent use of role plays; they are instructive and they are fun. Role plays must, however, be well controlled by an experienced tutor. When delegates become truly involved in a well-developed role play, it can quickly go out of control as they work into their roles. If that occurs, the effects can be devasting – handle with care.

Tutors, both the professional trainer and operating manager, must be fully prepared. If a question cannot be adequately answered, the only response must be: 'I don't know. I'll find out and we'll discuss it at the next session'. Never lie to anybody if a question cannot be honestly answered for any reason.

I personally prefer not to video tape role plays. I feel it makes people nervous. Further, for purposes of critique, it seems that delegates tend not to observe as carefully when they know a tape can be reviewed.[5] If you do choose to use a video recorder, place it in a far corner of the room and let it run from the beginning of the session. It will cause less distraction.

Sessions must begin and end on time; that is one of the things you are supposed to be teaching. Sessions are not optional, any more than production schedules or service specifications are optional. Attendance is to be monitored – this activity is part of an objective for every delegate and scheduled attendance is a measure of your short interval control.

Training sessions are in every sense meetings, and therefore everything we considered in Chapter 13 concerning effective meeting management applies here. Do not let sessions run beyond schedule. If you are on site, delegates should have other commitments following completion time. Off site, under certain circumstances a session may be allowed to run over schedule, perhaps for a teambuilding exercise or to complete a special project. Generally, however, if more time is needed, an additional session should be scheduled.

Finally, the tutor and operating manager must make a commitment to delegates that everything discussed in the classroom remains in the classroom. The tutor may mention general attitudes, consistent behaviour patterns and perceptions to senior managers, but no specific problems or situations must ever be reported. Positive results may be reported if delegates agree. The entire process must be conducted with total integrity. Otherwise it is a massive waste of time and the credibility of the entire senior management group suffers serious damage. Training activity must never be used as the means for spying on delegates. The single purpose is for personal improvement and development, it is not to evaluate delegates either for fitness or promotion. If an attempt is made to use it for that purpose, the complete training and development function will utterly fail.

An important element of effective training is one-on-one work. This may be handled in several ways according to needs. The rule is that the tutor should spend a minimum of one hour in the workplace individually with each delegate for every hour spent in the classroom. There are some exceptions: for salespeople on the road, the tutor will spend time according to travel schedules – perhaps half-day increments are appropriate. For senior managers or executives, the tutor should spend a full half day observing each at work, then follow that with a comprehensive critique.[6]

The tutor must also be available for one-on-one counselling as needed. Delegates may not want to discuss things that are so sensitive they do not wish to bring them up in a general session in front of peers. Also, they may have particular problems with something such as work assignment practice, for which they will benefit from some individual role plays with the tutor. They may need to address a particularly difficult situation. For example, delegates may require preparation and some moral support from the tutor before confrontations with their bosses to resolve difficult issues. One-on-one time is an integral component of training processes. It is not something optional, to be used or not as convenient.

Do this over the next year

Over the next three months develop and implement training for every individual in the organization based on the elements we have discussed in this chapter. Consider all eight of the categories examined here. Pay particular attention to induction training for those who have been part of the organization for one year or less but have not received it, and supervisory and management development training for all present section leaders and supervisors who have never received it. Manage this process carefully to ensure that every training need is jointly identified and agreed by the delegate and his or her immediate manager.

While that is happening, establish reporting mechanisms to enable you to establish reasonably accurate cost/benefit analyses for the first full year this training process is in operation. Consider factors such as measurable improvements in performance, better achievement of objectives, reductions in scrap and rework, improvements in quality and reductions in customer complaints, increases in revenues related to improved customer service, reductions in cash exposure and lost value, and reductions in computer systems and production equipment slow-down and downtime. Correlate short-term attainment of objectives – meeting training schedules – with longer-term objectives such as lower unit production costs and improved profits.

Notes

1 Warren Bennis and Burt Nanus, *Leaders: The Strategies For Taking Charge.* (New York: Harper & Row, 1985.) Bennis and Nanus offer a particularly cogent definition of leadership. There are many others.
2 Review Chapter 6.
3 See the Coda, Brown paper systems analysis.
4 Abseiling, potholing and white-water rafting are nevertheless fun. I recommend them all.
5 I am grateful to Jeannette Dummeyer for bringing this phenomenon to my attention.
6 The work of M. Louise Meyer in development processes for senior managers and executives has been helpful to me in this respect.

■ CHAPTER 22 ■

Information Technology in the Workplace: Machines should work; people should think[1]

> The automating capacity of the technology can free the human being for a more comprehensive, explicit, systematic, and abstract knowledge of his or her work . . . Whether or not this new knowledge is achieved depends upon two crucial conditions: the presence of individual competence and the opportunity to express that competence.
>
> Shoshana Zuboff
> *In the Age of the Smart Machine*

> Send this by E-mail. Fax it, too, in case he doesn't check his E-mail. And mail the original so he has a clean copy.
>
> Scott Adams
> *Dogbert's Top Secret Management Handbook*

Introduction

In this chapter I want to examine briefly how well we seem to be managing the transition from manual record keeping and mechanical computing to electronic information processing, and in particular some of the ways we sometimes appear to be mismanaging it. My objective is not to turn you into an expert in information technology or information science, but to ask you to consider whether you are making best use of this relatively new management resource. We are concerned with the general use of computers for tasks that were formerly done manually such as accounting and financial record keeping, written communications, production scheduling, performance reporting and quality monitoring. We will not consider very specialized applications such as CAD (computer aided drafting), CAM (computer aided manufacturing) or CNC (computer numerically controlled) machining. Nor will we address esoteric applications such as economic or market modelling. Our concern is how you use electronic information processing resources to help you manage the day-to-day business of the organization.

In 1825 the Stockton and Darlington Railway first carried passengers and freight. Karl Benz drove his first internal combustion powered automobile on the streets of Paris in 1885. Two years later he sold the first automobile. Powered flight began when Orville Wright flew at Kitty Hawk, North Carolina, in 1903. In comparison, the first electronic digital computer was created in 1937 at Iowa State University in the United States. Around 1950 (the date is unclear) a total of eight Ferranti Mark I systems, the first commercial computers in the United Kingdom, were manufactured and sold. The US Bureau of Census purchased the first commercial computer manufactured in the United States, UNIVAC, in 1951 and a total of 46 units of that model were sold. Mainframes were beginning to be seen, rarely, from the mid-1950s and became more common in the early 1960s. The first commercial minicomputer was produced in 1956 in the United States by Digital Equipment. The first microprocessor, the 8080 was available in 1974, and PCs were not in widespread use until the late 1970s and early 1980s.

We have been making the transition from horse powered transportation to railway, automobile and aeroplane for 173 years. The transition is not yet complete – there are still quite a few horses around. In contrast we have been making the move to electronic information management for a mere 48 years. We are new to it. We are unfamiliar with it. Sometimes we are uncomfortable with it. In a few instances we are frightened by it. Another frustrating problem is that it is all changing so quickly. As soon as we become even moderately comfortable with some part of it, it becomes obsolete and is replaced by something new. The notebook computer on which this book was written is five years old. It is two generations out of date. It cannot support contemporary software, nor can it drive the new colour printers. It is frustratingly slow by present standards. I cannot obtain repair parts for it. I must buy another one soon, but I am reluctant to part with an old friend.

Computers do not think[2]

Computers do not think, any more than mechanical adding machines, hand-held calculators, or electric or electronic typewriters think. Computers automate[3] work. They perform tasks you could do manually, but instead have chosen to have machines do for you. They receive data, process them according to sets of instructions you have given them and provide you with the results of that processing activity. They are very fast, very accurate and very stupid. They will do exactly as you tell them to do, nothing more, nothing less.[4] If you tell them to do something useless they will do it without question. If you feed them inaccurate data they will process these according to your instructions and deliver inaccurate results; they cannot question the accuracy of data. They certainly have no ability to question the way you use or misuse the output you have instructed them to provide. If you tell them to generate reams of reports that nobody reads, they will obey.

You must see the computer as an information processing tool in the context of how you and other members of the team use information in the workplace. The computer does not generate information, you do that; the computer only makes letter and memo writing easier, keeps track of your diary entries and telephone numbers, crunches numbers, draws graphs and prints reports.

Misuses of information technology in the workplace

Presented here are a number of examples from my own experience of what I consider clearly inappropriate uses of information technology. Review the notes from your tour and you will be able to recall any number of similar situations:

- In a modern food processing factory, staff put on their wellies, wash their hands, then change into approved clothing. Before they enter their work area, they clock on using a bar-coded swipe card. Their presence on the factory floor has been recorded electronically: the computer knows they are at work. Immediately they enter their work area, a supervisor ticks their names on worksheets held in a large ring binder. Why? If it is simply to confirm they are at work, the computer has already done that. If it is to provide a list of people in the work area, for example, for a fire list, the computer has already done that, too. All that is needed is to ask the machine for a printout.
- A large manufacturing facility in the Midlands buys eight tons of computer paper each week. They print things on it, it is distributed, then somebody reads it (or does not read it, see Chapter 19, Page 261). Later each week a disposal company comes on site. They shred, then pulp eight tons of computer paper and haul it away. They are paid for this service. We know from the experience of the computer centre manager in Chapter 19 that approximately one-half of this paper could be eliminated at significant cost savings to the company.
- In the documentary credits department of a major UK bank, people, whose job title is opener, sit in front of their terminals and prepare letters of credit using the computer system. The next step is for others, called checkers, to call the letters up on system and review them for accuracy and statutory compliance. The documents are complex, so there is a need for checkers to review a number of screens to approve each credit. If they identify errors, they are to make the corrections on system, then approve and print letters. However, the software has been designed poorly: screens are not

sequenced appropriately to enable checkers to review documents conveniently, so openers print out the letters and pass them to checkers. These are documents of title valid across international borders; because of this they are printed on heavy, high standard paper, include a number of pre-printed designs to prevent counterfeiting and are produced as one original and six copies. Checkers receive printed letters, review them and either approve or mark them with corrections and pass them back to openers. Openers make the corrections on system, print them again and pass them back to checkers for approval. They repeat this process until they get them right. In some cases a letter may be printed four or five times before final approval. The cost in paper and printing time is high. Further, the queue at printers often causes delays resulting in poor customer service. Many documentary letters of credit are used in the movement of commodities or food crops, thus a delay of even one day during peak harvesting season can cause a customer to lose an order.

- On a recent project in a large manufacturing operation, I worked closely with a number of senior engineers attached to head office who were also assigned to the project. On most days their first activity when entering the office each morning was to check their E-mail. Typically they spent the first two to three hours of each day on this task. While I was not party to the details of most of their communications, it seemed that many of them involved flaming. Flaming is the act of replying to E-mail messages with nasty comments to the sender, often questioning the legitimacy of parentage or offering suggestions to perform a series of anatomically impossible acts. Serious flaming includes copying the original message and the reply to others in the organization either to make the originator look foolish, to score points with one's boss or both. These senior managers were not only wasting valuable equipment and network time, they were wasting between 25 and 38 per cent of their time producing nothing for their organization; their performance at best could never exceed 75 per cent. You would expect more from senior managers in a conglomerate with facilities world wide that likes to think of itself as world class.
- Within a number of organizations for which I have worked I have noted situations where staff and managers sit at their desks and draft letters or reports in pen or pencil on A4 pads. Next they move to computer terminals to input their work. This occurs routinely in query sections of back office operations in banks, insurance operations and pensions administrations where there are needs for large number of letters and reports. This is clearly a waste of their time: they are performing the same job twice.

- A recurring *Tactical Management* theme is that managers should spend most of their time on the shop floor or in the office where the work of the organization is actually done. In organizations where short-range operational control is poor, one of the symptoms is almost invariably the reluctance of managers, particularly middle and first line managers, but often supervisors also, to leave their offices and spend significant time on the floor understanding what goes on there. For these managers, the coming of computers has been a boon. Now they can manage their operations entirely without ever leaving their offices, with everything they need to know being provided by their computer terminals. This is the exact opposite of Management by Wandering Around.
- If you examine any admin operation of reasonable size you will discover at least one, and usually more, occurrence of an old manual paper system being run fully in parallel with a new computerized system.[5] Whatever the reasons for this situation, it must change. The work probably requires at minimum twice the time it should; this results in high labour costs and slower turn around time, resulting in poor customer service. Also, the manual system is more likely to introduce errors into transactions.
- Most operations of significant size have more than one computer system in use. They do not usually talk to one another. There is thus a need for output from one system to become input to another. It often occurs like this: output from one system is in the form of printed reports, often several inches thick. Staff take these unwieldy reports and sit down with them in front of a terminal on the other system. They scan the reports, identify an item, key it into the system, then mark it off in the report, usually with a yellow highlighter. The process is repeated and repeated and repeated, hour after hour, day after day – it never stops. It has to be one of the most boring, soul destroying tasks in any office and it is totally unnecessary.
- During a recent project in a back office operation for a major UK bank a senior manager spent approximately one full hour each morning checking her E-mail. She typically received between 80 and 90 messages each day. She had no network terminal at her desk, so she carried her notebook computer across the office to the desk of a special projects manager who worked for her and who had the required network line. She balanced her computer precariously on the intersection of two dividers in this open-plan office, unplugged the project manger's network connection from his computer, plugged it into hers and stood there in the middle of the aisle reading off her messages. All the time she was doing this, the project manager could do little work, and certainly nothing that involved use of the network. During this time she not only read all her messages but also sent off replies to some.

- Well-managed maintenance engineering operations use a system of work requests to capture the department workload, both for planning and recording of actual work done. A paper system works very well for this application, although in any but the smallest operation the number of work requests in various stages of completion can be large, and the clerical effort is onerous. This is an obvious application for a Computerized system, and there are a number of proprietary ones available. The process is driven originally by pieces of paper. These are either requests from user departments or those originating in the maintenance department itself for work such as projects, or planned or preventive maintenance. The next step is for an experienced person, either a craftsperson or a supervisor to review each job and estimate hours, tools and materials required for completion. Then the work orders are collected and input to the system; somebody has to sit down in front of a terminal and key them in. Of the systems with which I have experience the problem is this: the person usually assigned to input work requests is one of the more experienced craftspeople, the one who should spend his or her entire day on the floor. Time that should be spent reviewing work and estimating jobs is instead spent inputting to the system, a job that could be done by somebody without technical craft skills or with less experience.

These examples are representative. There are dozens more variations on these themes. What is happening may be summarized briefly as:

1 Users are wasting time making manual entries recording information already stored in the system.
2 Paper costs are excessive because large numbers of reports are generated.
3 Paper costs are excessive, users' time is wasted and customer service is suffering because system application software is not designed to be fully effective and convenient for users.
4 Senior managers' time is wasted because they are abusing the E-mail system in silly and unproductive ways.
5 Users' time is wasted because they have not been properly trained to make best use of computer systems.
6 Management control is not effective because managers are using the computer as a convenient excuse not to leave their offices to find out what is happening on the floor.
7 Users' time is wasted recording the same information twice because they have not been supported through the transition from the manual system to the new automated system.
8 Users are wasting their time on boring manual links between separate systems that are not enhanced to enable them to talk to one another.

9 A manager's valuable time is wasted by his or her not using good judgement to separate useful communications from the dross. A full hour of another manager's time is being wasted each day for want of one additional telephone line.
10 Skilled craft hours are wasted when the wrong people are assigned to systems related tasks.

Effective uses of information technology in the workplace

Review your operation, the notes from your tour and the examples of ineffective uses of information technology discussed above. Think about ways your operations could be improved. There are a number of things that might be done according to needs:

- People need to understand this relatively new resource, and that requires both training and coaching. Training includes theoretical work to understand what computer systems are all about and how they work, familiarity with the specific hardware and software in use, and such mundane subjects as keyboard skills and how to change a printer cartridge. Do not try to save money by limiting the delivery of training.
- In any application where an old paper system is running fully in parallel with a new computerized system designed to replace it, action must be taken. First confirm that the electronic system meets unit needs: that it has been demonstrated to do the job it was designed to do. Next confirm that all people in the unit – staff, supervisors and managers have been properly trained in its use. Then eliminate the paper system. Support people in the unit and coach then through the transition. Make the new system work.
- For those applications where the transition from paper to computer seems to be particularly difficult, examine those processes carefully. In my judgement there are some situations where a paper system will do a better job for you than an automated system.[6] Do not force the use of a computer where there is strong evidence that for now a manual system will do a better job for you. There are other circumstances where a new system is to be installed and you are faced with the choice of paper or computer. For some it might be useful to install is first as a paper system, then convert to computer after people have used it long enough to understand well how it works and why they are doing it.[7]
- Review the way people throughout the organization are using E-mail. It is supposed to be a communications tool. It is supposed to eliminate paper and ensure that information is distributed to people who need it to do their jobs, when they need it and in formats that are useful to

them. If middle level and senior managers are spending one, two or three hours each day reading, then replying to 80 or 90 messages, in my judgement that system is in serious need of purging. In the past they would not have spent the same amount of time reading and replying to 80 or 90 paper letters or memos each day.

- Examine rigorously those situations where there is a need for people to take the output from one system and input it directly, line-by-line into another system. That is precisely the sort of task this new resource is supposed to eliminate for us. Review the two systems, then develop and install enhancements to enable them to talk to one another. Calculate the total amount of time spent by staff on this activity, including total time spent correcting input errors, to justify the cost of the systems enhancements.
- Review those applications where people are hand writing drafts for letters and reports, then entering them into a system. The primary need here is for training. Users are clearly using the system inappropriately, but without proper training and support they will not make the change. Here, also, you must consider alternatives: the cost for a manager, particularly a senior manager, typing his or her own letters directly into the system versus the cost of dictation being passed to a secretary or skilled word processor operator. Conduct some studies, determine the relative costs, then make a decision.

Do this over the next six months

The first thing to do is sit quietly somewhere and ask yourself how well you understand this new technology. Are you comfortable with it? Are you still a little frightened by it? Are you concerned about the huge number of things you do not know about it? Do the arcane terminology and jargon sometimes make you feel left out of conversations? Do you feel at a disadvantage when discussing these matters with systems people? Relax, you are not alone.

Next conduct a detailed examination of your operation, looking specifically at the ways everybody – staff, supervisors, managers and executives, use or abuse computer systems. Forget the jargon. Ignore what any expert has told you can or cannot be achieved with the systems you have in place. Think about it from the perspectives of customer service, quality and cost management. Are your computers as they are presently configured supporting effective utilization of all the hours of people every day in the workplace?

Identify three opportunities for improved use of computer resources:

1 Select one unit where users are not making best use of their computer systems because they have not been properly trained. Develop a training plan to address their needs. Set a target of having everybody in

the unit fully trained and working to best practice within the six months.

2 Select one situation where substantial numbers of clerical hours are wasted in manual input activity because two or more systems do not talk to one another. Work with systems development people and programmers to install enhancements to link the systems electronically and eliminate the manual input activity.
3 Identify one process where a paper and computerized system are running fully in parallel. Develop a plan and take all actions necessary, including appropriate training and necessary systems enhancements, to eliminate the paper system.

Over the subsequent six months, use this experience to make improvements for the rest of the organization covering all ten of the opportunities for misuse of computer resources we have discussed. Involve both users and systems development people fully in all these projects. Place particular emphasis on improving the utilization of the time of staff, supervisors and managers using these systems through better understanding of this important new resource.

Notes

1 John Peers, President, Logical Machine Corporation.
2 I do not presume to offer a definition for thinking. While my comment that computers do not think probably applies in the workplace, it is not universally accurate. In laboratories and on university campuses, computers are being developed that attempt to simulate human thinking.
3 Most authorities make a distinction between mechanization and automation. If you routinely copy figures from a source document to an A4 pad and add them up manually using a pencil, then you change the task by entering the figures from your pad into a hand-held calculator, you have mechanized the process. You are still performing the activity of addition, but now with the assistance of the calculator. If, however, you enter figures from the source document directly into a computer, thus having the machine perform the activity of addition, you have automated the process.
4 Excluding mechanical breakdowns or electronic failures and under the assumption you have programmed them correctly.
5 This was discussed in some detail in Chapter 19, Page 265–6.
6 One example is the daily plan. See Chapter 16, Page 221.
7 One example is the operating system. See Chapter 17, Page 240, Manual versus computerized reporting.

CHAPTER 23

Cascade Communications: Eschew obfuscation

Over the past year personal use of telephones has been excessive and obviously this privilege has been abused and during this period I have written numerous memos and discussed this with many of you personally but in spite of this my requests have been ignored. I am therefore taking this opportunity to inform you that each month I shall personally review every itemized telephone bill in full detail and I shall hold each of you who abuse this privilege responsible for your inconsiderate actions.

Tactical Manager
A memorandum on the use of telephones (first draft)

Please limit your personal telephone calls.

Tactical Manager
A memorandum on the use of telephones (second draft)

ESCHEW OBFUSCATION!

Perennial American university graffiti
(undergraduate level)

Introduction

Within every organization there is a continual need for managers to communicate with the people who work for them to present information additional to that necessary for day-to-day operations. There is also a need for information to be passed not only from superiors to immediate subordinates, but downward through a number of management levels. We will refer to these types of messages as management communications.

It is a premise of *Tactical Management* that there are benefits to be gained from establishing formal processes to manage this kind of information and delivering it regularly. The purpose of this chapter is to examine some practices to increase the likelihood that such messages will be accurately interpreted by the ultimate receivers. Further, that this activity will be perceived as a positive effort by management to keep people informed about the state of the organization.

In Chapter 13 we discussed messages to kick off a project, introduce new processes for customer service or quality management, update people on the status of the business or of operations, and communicate such matters as changes in product lines or markets. Presentations may also be made about major changes in the direction of overall objectives for the business, positive results, or to recognize or reward individuals, teams or groups for good work.

In these circumstances, feedback cannot be immediate and direct, and the ultimate action triggered by the communication is usually distant from the communication itself. The sender must seek to increase the probability the message will be received and interpreted accurately. This can be accomplished through a process of regularly scheduled, frequent briefings:

- This type of meeting is intended to announce something to a number of people collectively, it is not to engage in a dialogue or to obtain agreement or consensus. A decision has been made and this meeting is to announce it. Questions and comments should be invited: the sender must establish feedback channels and message evaluation processes.[1]
- These kinds of messages are nearly always communicated through several people, they are re-encoded and filtered a number of times on their route to ultimate receivers. The sender must be able to examine how accurately the messages are being received.
- Managers have a fundamental obligation to answer questions, concerns, doubts, uncertainties, rumours, half-truths and misunderstandings inevitable in the operation of any organization, but especially within one subject to constant, significant change. These issues must always be addressed quickly.

When managers schedule regular communications sessions they obtain, through wandering around and the achievement of short-term objectives, feedback and information on commitment and appropriate action. If sessions are scheduled frequently, they have defined a short interval of control: the actions they are evaluating are those that have occurred since the last meeting.

In Chapter 11 we examined various problems that routinely interfere with effective communications. All these problems can probably be conveniently grouped into four categories:

1 conflicting signals have been broadcast by the sender;
2 the message is either inaccurate or incomplete;
3 the message has simply been misunderstood; or
4 the sender has failed to place the message high on the priority list of the receiver.

For the first, the message may have ended anywhere on the receiver's list of priorities, but possibly incorrectly decoded. For the second and third, it is unreasonable to expect any effective action. For the fourth, regardless of the accuracy of the decoding, it most certainly ended low on the receiver's list. The result in any case is that either the wrong thing is done or nothing is done at all.

Cascade communications

Cascade communications is designed to improve the delivery of management communications and systematically to reduce the interval of control to identify any problems with the process quickly. Think about how managers must act when it is necessary for them to communicate information to every individual in the units for which they are responsible:

- They must meet all the requirements of effective communications: messages must be received and understood by everybody, they must be placed at the correct level on each priority list and actions must occur as planned.
- They must meet these requirements while simultaneously complying with the principles of unity of command and integrity of command.
- They must accomplish this with practices that make most effective use of information resources including computer system time, word processing facilities and photocopiers, paper and especially the time of everybody involved.

Examine a cascade beginning with the group chief executive. He or she has made the decision to communicate to everybody information felt to be relevant to organization health and effective operations, and to do this regularly. The decision has been made this should be done monthly.[2]

The first echelon

All briefings must be conducted according to a regular, published schedule. The group chief executive begins the cascade with a briefing, for example, on the first Monday of every month. This presentation will be to all those people who report directly to him or her. The complete message, the cascade bulletin is in writing and copies are distributed to each delegate. The message is presented orally and delegates have the opportunity to ask questions concerning content. The meeting is limited to a maximum of one hour and the bulletin is limited to a maximum of two sides of one A4 page. At the conclusion of the briefing delegates return to their own units.

In Chapter 13 we discussed the importance of providing written agenda in advance to everyone attending a meeting. In this case that requirement is ignored. First, due to the nature of the briefing no preparation is necessary for delegates. Second, and of more importance, is that one of the purposes of cascade communications is to ensure that announcements concerning matters of sensitivity are communicated to everybody in the organization quickly and accurately. Publishing agenda in advance would interfere with that purpose.

The second echelon

Delegates-cum-managers next review the first echelon bulletin and any questions raised at the briefing. They then create their own bulletins, again limited to a maximum of two sides of one A4 page. Their information is additional, the original text is not edited. Their messages include:

- comments in reference to the first echelon text they feel will make that message more easily understood by people in their units,
- information supplementary to the original bulletin related to the specific needs of their units, and
- their own bulletins: information important to the operation of their units.

They assemble all their immediate subordinates and conduct a briefing according the same practice as for the first echelon: the meeting complies with the published schedule and it is limited to a maximum of one hour. At the conclusion of the briefing, delegates return to their units.

The third echelon

These delegates-cum-managers repeat the process with all their immediate subordinates.

Subsequent echelons

The cascade continues until finally all supervisors or section leaders in the organization have conducted a monthly, scheduled, one hour briefing with their entire teams and delivered the complete cascade bulletin. A monthly schedule seems to be about right for most organizations. If the first echelon briefing is on Monday morning, the last briefing at staff level should not occur later than Friday afternoon of the same week.

Benefits of cascade communications

An important benefit of cascade communications is that people, particularly staff, supervisors and department managers, are made to feel that executives and senior managers are genuinely trying to keep everybody informed about what is happening throughout the organization.

Review the notes from your tour. Recall that one recurring complaint was: 'Management never tell us anything'. This will become increasingly important as the organization is subject to more rapid and substantive change. People have a need to be informed and regularly scheduled cascade briefings can be a powerful stability zone in the chaos of the workplace.

Equally important is that meaningful information about the business is being communicated to people, and this is being done through a practice that seeks to ensure that everybody receives the same message. This will become increasingly important as more people move across unit and department boundaries more frequently to address changing organization needs. When a number of individuals from different departments come together on a task team, for example, it is helpful when they are all working from a common body of information.

An identical message can be communicated very quickly to everybody in the organization with a minimum of distortion (you must recognize that your message will never be communicated with absolute accuracy. Were this to be true, you could do your wandering around in Monte Carlo).

It is a premise of *Tactical Management* that there is a need for discipline for compliance with procedures and practices that is crucial to effective operations. Because cascade communications is such a visible process, you have the opportunity to communicate to everybody that this concern for discipline is universal and begins with executives and senior management. This enhances management credibility.

Remember that the accuracy of any communication effort can only finally be evaluated by looking at the action taken: no amount of oral feedback before that will enable you to forecast results. If you, for example, have implemented procedures to improve housekeeping, you need a mechanism to monitor progress against the objective. The combination of cascade communications and Management by Wandering Around creates a process to enable you to evaluate the effectiveness of your message concerning housekeeping efforts, and you do this with a minimum expenditure of your time.

You can continually evaluate the communications skills of the entire management team. As you wander around, for example, you might observe practices that seem to be at variance with your most recent cascade briefing. This indicates that your message has not been accurately received. The situation has resulted in an immediately identified coaching opportunity for the supervisors and managers involved for the improvement of communications skills.

A plethora of promulgations

Throughout this book I have constantly promoted the communication of more and more information to more and more people to deal with many of the changing needs of the organization. We have, at the same time examined a number of situations where too much information was being manipulated – too many meetings, too many reports – and investigated some ways of reducing that flood.

We are all keenly aware of the enormous amount of information it seems is needed to keep an organization functioning today. One is tempted to ask why more exists than in the past, and the typical, simplistic answer that we are now an information-based society is inadequate. When the situation is carefully analysed, however, it is entirely possible that it is not really more information we need now, but different kinds. I am not yet convinced, for example, that the person who programs a robot welder is a processor of information. I regard him or her as a set-up person working with tools different from the traditional sort. That we are inundated with information may merely be the result of the ease with which it can be generated, reproduced and delivered.[3] Whether, finally, more information is needed does not change the requirement that every bit of it must be evaluated critically and eliminated if it does not reflect good use of resources.

In either case it is the responsibility of all managers, but especially at senior level, to:

1 reduce the overall amount of information flowing through the organization when it can be clearly shown that information is unnecessary,
2 improve the accuracy and speed of delivery of essential information, and
3 ensure that necessary information is delivered to the people who need it.

Cascade communications is one process to assist you and your management team to do this.

Finally, the number of pages in the cascade bulletin increases with the number of management levels. This is a good argument in favour of reducing your present 12 level organization structure to four or five.

Some cautionary notes

Once you have fully implemented cascade communications it will be impossible for you ever to withdraw gracefully. Because you have rendered management communications proactive and so highly visible, you have committed yourself and your team to operate with total consistency and complete integrity. The first time you fail to deliver a briefing on schedule because you are 'too busy' or 'nothing much important happened this month', the credibility of the entire management team will be seriously damaged: '. . . there goes another new and exciting management programme that was going to solve all our problems. It lasted about three weeks and then disappeared without a trace'. Remember, attitudes are driven by perceptions, not facts.

Chinese Whispers is working here. It is crucial to success that the original bulletin is never edited, each echelon requires additional information, not a replacement. This is important so that people feel the communication is indeed from the originator, and to reduce the effects of Brussels sprouts, encoding and filtering.

Managers throughout must ask the right questions at briefings and convert them into meaningful messages. Through your wandering around you will observe how well the entire process is working, particularly whether the questions of staff, supervisors and department managers are truly being answered. Weaknesses in the communications chain will be highlighted. Ask clerks or operators to give you their copies of the latest bulletin. Examine how your original message has been interpreted for them through several echelons and how it has been tailored to their particular work units. Ask several to explain your message – ask them this trick question: 'What did your supervisor have to say about this?'

It is important that every immediate subordinate attend the briefing. Absolutely nothing is accomplished for all of this effort if a delegate merely drops into the secretary's office sometime after the briefing and collects a copy of the bulletin. When the delegate is not available for any reason, a designate must attend. This represents another useful coaching exercise for the soon to be promoted manager.

Every person who works for you, each person for whom you are responsible in the workplace, requires appropriate information to work effectively. More than that, however, everybody deserves honest and complete answers to questions related to their work and the questioner's place in the organization. If people ask the same question, and receive one answer from a supervisor, another from a middle manager and a third from you, how can they be expected to believe information coming from any source, and then be expected to use that information to perform effectively and efficiently? Believe me, they do ask the same question of several people; that is one of the subtle risks inherent in Management by Wandering Around.

Finally, under a comprehensive cascade communications process, it will be impossible for you to keep hidden agenda hidden:

Example

Some time ago I was a member of a team working within a large manufacturing operation. Our ostensible charter was to develop and implement management operating systems, improve process control and production planning practices, and to do all of this under a traditional project approach. The project had been commissioned by an executive at the head office, it had not been contracted by management at factory level.

We began using conventional practices: we conducted a thorough analysis of operations, then designed systems and procedures based on that analysis. Later, during implementation, as project actions began to require local managers to make commitments to change and senior managers support this change, it became apparent there were, in fact, hidden agenda.

The executive who commissioned the project had absolutely no interest whatsoever in improved management systems, process control or production planning. His sole objective in commissioning the project was to enforce a set of management practices he had developed and implemented. His package, as structured, was totally inappropriate for the needs of that operation – besides being inordinately cumbersome it was almost completely unworkable. Our hidden objective was to force compliance at local level over what may only be described as reasonable objections by staff, supervisors and managers.

Whenever properly designed operating systems are installed, a necessary consequence of that effort is that communications are vastly improved. In this situation, within that body of improved communications, discrepancies resulting from the executive's hidden agenda surfaced. What had been assumed by staff for some time became obvious to us when we attempted to implement systems and obtain commitment to them by managers in the factory. The entire effort collapsed. The project was a complete failure – the executive wasted his company's money, and his already extremely poor credibility with staff, supervisors and managers throughout the operation deteriorated even further.

The cascade process greatly improves management communications: every hidden agenda or inconsistency in management practice or approach will become highly visible.

Do this over the next six months

Implement a cascade communications system to include everybody in the organization based on all the requirements presented here. Keep in mind especially the cautions discussed above. Realize that even though both the principle and practice appear simple and straightforward, implications for the management team are serious. Spend enough time thinking about this to help you develop a process that will work well within your operation. Make yourself comfortable enough with it that you can assertively sell it to others. Design a standard bulletin format. Establish a monthly briefing schedule for the entire organization.

Use a cascade briefing to introduce the practice. Follow up closely at staff level immediately after the introductory cycle to confirm that everybody understands the process. If there appears to be even a minor problem, address it quickly with an extraordinary briefing. Cascade communications cannot be installed in phases, nor can a pilot scheme be considered; the initial effort must include everybody within the organization unit.

Monitor practices carefully over the six month period and make adjustments as needed. Remind everybody, especially middle managers, that no part of this effort is optional. Confirm, during all your wandering around and when evaluating the achievement of objectives, that cascade communications is contributing to improvements in operational control for the long term because of better communications for the short term.

Use a training effort procedure similar to that suggested in Chapter 21 to establish a cost/benefit analysis. Attempt to correlate short-term attainment of your objectives – meeting briefing schedules, with longer-term objectives such as lower unit production costs and improved profits resulting from enhanced management communications. Be patient; here the link between costs and benefits is even more tenuous than for training.

Do this over the subsequent six months

At the end of six months, the cascade process should be working well. During the following six months concentrate on the standard of the bulletin. In your wandering around examine copies of bulletins collected from staff to determine how they might be made more effective through improvements in either format or content. Make any revisions that seem appropriate. Be creative – use your imagination: if the basic cascade is working well it should be possible to experiment with this element of the process. Use this as a platform for coaching exercises where appropriate.

If your organization publishes a weekly or monthly newsletter, review it critically based on your experience with cascade communications to determine how it might be made a more effective vehicle for the distribution of management information.

Notes

1 Review Chapter 11.
2 It is simple to generalize this discussion to any level – any manager can initiate a cascade for his or her unit.
3 Review Chapter 19.

■ CHAPTER 24 ■

PQM (Process Quality Management): Doing it right the first time

To correct mistakes is a good work, but to prevent them is a far higher achievement.

Waldo Pondray Warren
Thoughts On Business

There is no such thing as a minor defect; every defect is a major defect.

Tactical Manager

Introduction

In Chapter 3 you were asked to consider the management of quality important enough to the health of the organization that it should be treated as a fundamental principle of management. In this chapter we examine some of the requirements for applying quality measures in the workplace – to define quality management practices capable of supporting effective operations and to apply those practices throughout the organization.

We will discuss elements of a number of disciplines you might know variously as quality control, quality assurance, statistical process control (SPC) and in-process quality control. The Tactical Management model contains many elements common to others, but equally important, does not include certain elements. To avoid confusion, I have chosen to call the inclusive discipline quality management and the specific elements related to managing quality during the manufacture of a product or the delivery of a service process quality management (PQM).

The first attempts to address quality systematically began in the 1920s in manufacturing operations. The application of truly effective, proactive, preventive quality management to other types of business operations has never been widespread, chiefly because of the perception that it is something that belongs in the factory. Nor has it generally been successfully applied in other business environments, principally because the emphasis has usually been on reactive inspection rather than prevention.

We will examine the application of PQM to every part of the organization. In fact, the use of PQM in an admin operation, for example, will often yield higher levels of improvements in customer service and the management of costs than in a manufacturing department.

It is not my intention to present all the intricacies of statistically based, in-process quality management, indeed, that effort would require an entire book. I am solely concerned with your achieving a good general understanding of the application of the principles to different types of activity in the organization.[1]

The axioms of quality

Review Chapter 3. With regard to the application of quality management principles to operations, it is possible to capture the fundamentals with these five axioms:[2]

1 Quality means compliance with the specification – nothing less. This definition for quality must be the basis for the entire practice.
2 Prevention rather than detection and correction is the only meaningful way to manage quality. Quality cannot be inspected into the product after it has been manufactured; it absolutely cannot be inspected into a service after it has been delivered.
3 The target, the objective, the ultimate goal for every quality management effort is zero defects; nothing less is acceptable.
4 The most cost effective way to manage quality is to get it right the first time. Every quality management activity must be evaluated according to the total cost of non-conformance.
5 Everything will submit to description, measurement and specification, and therefore every activity in the organization is amenable to quality management.

In this chapter, each element we examine will relate, in one way or another, to these five axioms. Your PQM practice must be based on these assumptions. They must become a way of life for the management of quality throughout your organization.

PQM definitions

Due to the technical nature of PQM it is necessary to define several terms and discuss them in some detail. Please be patient. These definitions are generally consistent with those you are familiar with from other models. As you examine these definitions, however, keep the following in mind:

1 There is no sequence in which to present these terms so that every one follows logically from the one before. Thus for some, the full meaning might not be clear until you have read further.
2 If you already have experience with SPC and a working knowledge of this discipline, several of them will appear not to be complete. I have deliberately simplified them to keep this presentation as non-technical as possible.
3 My objective for this section is to relate each of them specifically to PQM; to provide you with another tool to help you to improve short-term operational control.

Specification

The specification is that body of information that completely and unambiguously defines the product or service that is to be provided. The importance of a clearly defined specification was discussed in considerable detail in Chapters 2 and 3. If you are having any difficulty at all writing an unequivocal specification, the work must be carried no further until this can be done.

No effective quality management practice can be established unless everybody in the operation, including both suppliers and customers, is fully aware of what is expected, and without a specification this is impossible. Think about it. What is it you want to do, and how do you expect to measure it? If you cannot explain what you want to do, how can you cost it accurately and price it profitably?

Characteristic

A characteristic is the unique description of any single property or component that forms part of a product or service specification. It may be in the form of either a variable or attribute (see below). Every characteristic must be stated in language that makes it amenable to measurement.

Variable

A variable is any measurable characteristic that can be stated numerically. Examples of variables are: a linear dimension, weight, moisture content, capacitance, the age of a backlog or the value of unmatched credit transactions.

Attribute

An attribute is any characteristic other than a variable that can be described unambiguously in text or by comparison to a repeatable standard. The test for attribute measurement is either yes or no – either the characteristic meets the specification or it does not. Examples of attributes are: the requirement for a software package to perform a specified function, the absence of errors on a claims form, the phase of alternating current in a circuit or the direction of shaft rotation.

For purposes of process control it is often convenient, and totally appropriate, to convert a variable into an attribute. For example, a hole diameter may be compared to a go/no-go gauge, the angle of a wireform part may be evaluated according to whether it will fit a template or receiver gauge, or a fuse is acceptable if it does not fail when subject to a standard current.

When attributes are part of a specification they must be capable of objective verification. You, the person actually doing the work, and the customer must be able to examine the part or service and the specification, and agree whether it is in compliance or not. For example, how would you interpret a specification for steel reinforcing rods that states that they will be 'clean and free from excessive rust and scale', or how would you monitor a stamping operation so that parts will be 'free from burrs'?

When a gauge is required, the complete description must form an integral part of the specification. It is sometimes the practice for a customer to provide a gauge without any other information – with the requirement that parts must fit the gauge. This is unworkable. If a problem occurs when parts do not fit the gauge, how can you identify causes? Another problem is the attempt to communicate effectively with the customer when he or she has a problem with the item on their shop floor; how can you discuss characteristics over the telephone when you have not been provided with a specification?

Nominal dimension

A nominal dimension is the stated numerical value of a variable characteristic.

Tolerance

A tolerance is the stated range of acceptable values for a variable. Every variable must include a tolerance. Examples include: '25.600 mm ± 0.200 mm', '155.0 degrees C. ± 1.5 degrees C.', '100 parts per million ± 5 ppm', '3500 backlog hours ± 35 hours', or 'agreed within ± £0.05'. It is sometimes practical to specify a tolerance in one direction only; for example, '25.800 mm + 0.000 mm/−0.400 mm'. This is wholly acceptable.

Variation

A variation is the difference between the nominal dimension and the actual value of a variable observed for a particular characteristic. Variations necessarily exist for all physical measurements.

Chance (or normal) variation

A chance variation is a variation resulting from the behaviour of a process, a pattern based on randomly occurring events or a pattern not assignable to a specific cause. For example, if a process to turn shafts to a nominal diameter is under control, actual dimensions will cluster around the nominal diameter. Change variations obey the mathematical laws of statistics and are an inherent part of every process.

Normal distribution

Chance variations follow a statistically predictable pattern when a process is in control. From our example above, if we were to plot actual shaft diameters, we would record a large number very close to the nominal with some greater and some less than the nominal. The farther from the nominal, the fewer we would see. The result is the familiar bell-shaped curve we call the normal distribution.

Standard deviation

The standard deviation, σ (sigma) is a measure of the area under the normal distribution curve. For a normal distribution, when the process is under control, 99.73 per cent of the population will fall within $\pm 3\sigma$ of the mean. For most in-process quality management applications, 3σ is the standard to which we work, although for some applications practitioners work to $\pm 4\sigma$ (99.994 per cent of the population) and occasionally to $\pm 6\sigma$ (99.9999998 per cent of the population). The benefit of working to higher sigma levels is a reduction in inspection costs: if your process can meet a $\pm 6\sigma$ standard you can eliminate inspections altogether. This is offset by the higher costs of developing processes to control variables to substantially narrower distributions.

Assignable variation (or assignable cause)

An assignable variation is a variation resulting from an assignable cause: one that is not a chance variation. Assignable variations will show up as a deviation from the normal distribution curve. Quality management activity seeks to eliminate all assignable variations.

Population

The population is the totality of items of product or occurrences of a service to be considered when evaluating compliance with a specification.

Batch (or lot)

A batch is a convenient quantity of product used to control material movement and to manage an inspection process. Batch size is typically related to customer order quantities, or hourly or shift production volumes.

Inspection

Inspection is the act of examining a product or occurrence of a service to determine whether it conforms to the specification or not. Inspection must be a structured process that is at once a formal element of all quality management practice and an integral part of every specification.

100 per cent inspection

One hundred per cent inspection is the practice of inspecting every characteristic for every item in a batch. The technique is ordinarily used in three situations:

1 batch sizes are very low;
2 the cost of failure is high, for example, for parachutes or pacemakers; or
3 assignable causes have resulted in serious quality problems; and inspection activity must be intense until corrective actions have been determined to have been effective and the process is brought back under control.

There are several reasons why 100 per cent inspection should not be used except in special circumstances:

- the cost in labour is high: if batch sizes are large, a great deal of time is needed to inspect every item;
- when batch sizes are large it can be demonstrated that more defects are undetected with a 100 per cent inspection than with a properly managed, statistically based random sample. This is probably attributable to inspector fatigue and boredom;
- where destructive testing is a required part of the inspection process. For electric lamp life or shotgun shells, for example, 100 per cent inspection would be somewhat impractical.

Sampling

Sampling is the process of inspecting a small number of items within a population and inferring properties of the entire population from properties of the sample. Sampling is a critical element of PQM because it addresses the disadvantages of 100 per cent inspection.

Random sample

A random sample is a quantity of *n* units taken from a population so that any other combination of *n* units has an equal chance of being selected. The principle of random sampling is extremely important to PQM; if the sample is not truly random it will not accurately reflect the properties of the population. For example, if samples of claims forms input to the mainframe system are all drawn near the beginning of the shift, conclusions about error rates might be substantially different from a sample drawn late in the shift when operators are tired or response time is slower.

Acceptance sampling

Acceptance sampling is a statistically based sampling technique that permits the acceptance of batches of product if a certain number of defective items is not exceeded. Acceptance sampling is an integral element of classical SPC. This is inconsistent with the axiom of zero defects and thus has no place in Tactical Management PQM.

Defect (or defective)

A defect is a characteristic, either variable or attribute, of an inspected item that does not comply with the specification. An item is either defective or it is not.

Major/minor defect

Within some quality management models, defects are classified as either major or minor. Tactical Management PQM practice does not recognize any differences: as far as the customer is concerned there is no such condition as 'a little bit defective'. One of the crucial tenets of this philosophy that you must sell to your entire team, but especially to department and middle managers, is that there is no such condition as 'a little bit defective'.

There is a related principle which recognizes something referred to as a critical dimension. This means that as long as the critical dimension is within specification tolerance, the customer will accept the product when really desperate even if the rest of it is total rubbish.

Process in control

A process is in control if an inspection of the product demonstrates that the only variations occurring are chance or random variations.

Process out of control

A process is out of control if assignable variations are observed during an inspection of the product.

Capability study

A capability study is the action of formally confirming that a manufacturing or service process is capable of producing items that comply fully with the specification.

- **Variable** For a variable, the study must demonstrate that the process is capable of producing items so the mean dimension of items studied is very close to the nominal dimension and chance variations, typically measured to the $\pm 3\sigma$ level, are significantly less that the specification tolerance.
- **Attribute** For an attribute, the study must demonstrate that the process is capable of delivering the product or service entirely according to the specification and free from defects.

Every capability study for either variables or attributes must provide information on total costs.[3]

Statistical process control (SPC)

SPC is a body of quality management principles and practices designed to manage the quality of a product while it is being made:

- The initial phase of an SPC process is always a capability study to confirm that the process mean is very close to the nominal value and chance variations are well within specification tolerances (see below, Confirming capability). Following the calculation of the $\pm 3\sigma$ range, control limits are established. Control limits are somewhat greater that 3σ and somewhat less than specification tolerances,[4] and are used to assist monitoring the process during production runs.
- Inspection of parts in-process should demonstrate that they are falling within control limits: this ensures that they will always be within tolerance. Measurements of variables made using random, statistical sampling are entered on a control chart and monitored. The objective is to detect an assignable cause as represented by a shift or trend away from either the nominal dimension or the normal distribution, and to

identify this before actual values go outside control limits. If the job is stopped and corrective action taken, it is possible to bring the process back into control before any defective items are produced. Process charting may be done either manually on paper charts or with one of several proprietary computerized systems available.

- The emphasis for a properly managed SPC process is on prevention of defects rather than inspecting and sorting out defective items after completion.
- Under properly managed SPC it is possible to operate a truly zero defect process.

Process Quality Management is based largely on SPC. The notable exception is that the Tactical Management model does not admit acceptance sampling according to traditional SPC principles. A second significant exception is the application of PQM to work such as computer systems development, admin, accounts or design engineering where it has not universally been applied in the past. A third exception, as noted above, is that PQM does not admit the classification of defects into major and minor categories, or recognize dimensions as either critical or non-critical.

The Practice of process quality management

The practice of PQM follows directly from our discussions in Chapter 3 and above. Here I expand on those individual steps:

Obtain the specification

Everything important concerning obtaining the specification was discussed either in Chapter 3 or above.

Confirm capability

Confirmation of capability requires a comprehensive analysis of the process, to determine that it is possible to make the product or deliver the service according to the specification. A detailed examination of capability studies is beyond the scope of this book.[5]

Variables

Confirming capability for variables involves a statistical analysis of values for a number of occurrences, from an initial production run or a series of activity trials. The study results in the identification of the process mean, the $\pm 3\sigma$ band and control limits.

The next step is to confirm that the control limits demonstrated during capability studies are within a band that is narrower than the band required by the specification. It is extremely helpful if the specification tolerance is significantly wider than control limits (see below). This step is crucial to process capability: if control limits calculated from the capability study are wider than specification tolerances, the process by definition is not capable.

Attributes

Under a traditional SPC process for attributes, a similar statistical analysis of a trial run is made with the calculation for control limits based upon either a number or percentage defective parts or occurrences observed. This is wholly inconsistent with the zero defects axiom.

Within the PQM model, the requirement for capability for attributes will be that a trail run for the process demonstrates that it is capable of producing the characteristic fully according to the specification and totally free from error.

An integral requirement for all capability studies is that methods, procedures and practices for the process are fully documented to ensure that it will be kept under control during operation. A crucial element of this step also is that resource requirements are fully described and total costs are calculated.

Agree the specification

Everything important concerning agreeing the specification was discussed in Chapters 2 and 3.

Control the process

Effective Process Quality Management demands that inspection practices are established to ensure either that the process is under control or that it is stopped until appropriate corrective action can be taken to bring it back under control. An additional requirement is that no further work is performed on any individual item or batch until it has been confirmed that the entire batch is free from defects. The singular requirement for effective PQM is that defects are identified immediately they occur. A set of practices must be created that clearly establish the actions to be taken when inspection reveals that a process has gone out of control.

This administrative element requires that those people responsible for process control are allowed to control the processes. Procedures must enable operators or inspectors to take appropriate actions to either bring the process back under control or stop the line. They must also have the authority to refrain from restarting until it has been confirmed that the assignable cause has been addressed. It must be clear throughout the organization that these individuals have authority to make operating decisions *then and there* to accomplish this.

Identify defects

When inspection reveals the process has either gone out of control or is about to go out of control, corrective action must be taken to address identified assignable causes. Besides this corrective action, certain formal steps must be taken during operations for:

- the identification of defects and the removal of any defective items from the process; and
- revisions to the inspection process to monitor the effectiveness of corrective action.

The identification of defects

The specification and capability study should provide all the information needed to establish inspection requirements. The production cycle or service delivery sequence must be broken down into phases – usually called operations in a manufacturing environment. Inspections should be carried out throughout each operation in the cycle. No item or portion of a batch should be approved for the next operation until it has been confirmed that the batch is free from defects. This will ensure that no operation is ever performed on any item that may not be to specification because of a defect caused earlier.

Whenever a defect is identified, certain actions must be taken in the control process according to the nature of the defect:

A. Variables

For a variable characteristic, inspection will indicate either that:

1 The item is within specification and the process is under control – no assignable cause can be detected. The job will be permitted to run and the batch may be approved for the next operation.
2 The item is within specification but the process is going out of control – an assignable cause has been detected. The job must be stopped immediately and not restarted until the assignable cause has been identified and addressed. No defective items have been produced, so the batch may be approved for the next operation.
3 The item is outside of specification and the process is out of control – an assignable cause has been detected and a defective item has been identified. The job must be stopped immediately and not restarted

until the assignable cause has been identified and addressed. Defective items must be removed from the batch.

A further sample of the same size as the original must be taken. If no more defects are found, the batch may be approved for the next operation. If further defective items are found, a 100 per cent inspection must be performed on the batch.

B. Attributes

For an attribute characteristic inspection will indicate either that:

1 No defective items are identified – the process is in control. The job will be permitted to run and the batch may be approved for the next operation.
2 A defective item has been identified – the process is out of control. The job must be stopped and not restarted until the assignable cause has been identified and addressed. Defective items must be removed from the batch.
   A further sample of the same size as the original must be taken. If no more defective items are found, the batch may be approved for the next operation. If further defective items are found, a 100 per cent inspection must be performed on the batch.

Revisions to the inspection process

The inspection process is primarily to confirm that the process is in control. Accordingly, when that can be demonstrated, it is totally appropriate and cost effective to reduce levels of inspection (see below, Sampling).

- Begin any new inspection practice at the normal level. Begin with the tightened level only if control limits are very close to specification tolerances, or the process appears to be rather unpredictable for some other reason.
- If inspections are being conducted at the normal level, when ten successive batches have been free of defects, move to the reduced level. Similarly, if inspections have been at the tightened level, shift to normal after ten successive defect-free batches have been recorded.
- If it has been necessary to perform a 100 per cent inspection on a batch for any reason, then it is imperative that further inspections for that process are done at the tightened level. When it has been established that process control has been regained, reduce the level according to the recommendations in the above two paragraphs.

When you think about this process, these are good arguments in favour of reducing batch sizes and lowering in-process inventories. The overriding benefit from implementing JIT is that when a problem with the specification is discovered in a batch of one, the logistics of isolating bad product are reduced, and identifying the cause of the problem becomes much quicker and easier.

Take corrective action

Administrative procedures must be established to ensure that decision-making authority is vested in those people who are best able to take effective corrective action. For example, the production supervisor or the workteam must have the authority to stop a line, the admin supervisor must have the authority to require a change in procedure in another department when it is recognized to have a negative impact on the quality of his or her service, and the programmer must have the authority to request assistance from users to clarify a specification.[6]

Control material movement

Procedures must be implemented to ensure any item that is not to specification is removed from the process. This element needs little discussion. It should be the lowest cost step in the process; if you are doing everything else correctly, few resources will be needed.

Document the production process

Properly managed PQM will automatically result in full documentation of the entire production or service process. This will support, for both you and your customer, full compliance with the specification. Also, more and more customers are requiring continual monitoring of capability to increase the flexibility of quality specifications. Full process documentation helps to provide this.

Sampling

There are probably as many sampling plans as there are statisticians.[7] Entire days could be spent arguing relative merits. Because of the probabilistic nature of sampling, inferences made from a sample concerning properties of the population will always suffer from the flaw that the information derived will not be as accurate as if the entire population had been examined. You are faced with the trade-off between the increased accuracy of the inference drawn from a larger sample against the increased cost of obtaining that larger sample.[8] In contrast to the accuracies resulting from larger samples are the problems discussed above associated with continual 100 per cent inspection of large batches.

It is a postulate of *Tactical Management* that it is not the mechanics of the particular plan that are important. At the operational level it is far more important that:

1 whatever plan you select is used consistently throughout the organization as an integral element of universal quality management; and
2 the identification of defects results in effective corrective action and appropriate responses from everybody involved in the process.

Remember, the purpose of the inspection is not to identify defective items so that they can be rejected, the purpose of the inspection is to confirm that the process is in control so no defective items are produced. Under most circumstances this can be accomplished with any reasonable sampling plan, as long as the necessary discipline is maintained for management of the process.

If the practice is to be effective it must result in truly random samples. Samples must be drawn in ways that ensure that every member of the population has an equal chance of being selected. Techniques for ensuring that samples are truly random are beyond the scope of this book. However, a little common sense coupled, again, with a consistent discipline, should accomplish the objective. You would not, for example, attempt to make inferences about the average age of the people in your town by sampling the population outside a nursery school at 3.15 pm on a Wednesday. Not only must samples be random, they must occur at random times to avoid any influences from cyclic causes. Examples of cyclic causes are sampling from the same location in boxes of parts because they arrive at the workstation on a regular schedule, or inspecting parts each time immediately after a machine has been routinely lubricated or adjusted. When samples are truly random, inferences made from a relatively small sample size will yield surprisingly good information about the population.

The PQM sampling plans

These sampling plans are straightforward and easy to apply. If you are presently using plans that seem to be working well in your own operation, there is no valid reason to change. Make up your own mind.

These plans have been established for processes where batches can clearly be identified. For continuous processes, batches may be defined either as hourly or shift quantities. One convenient method is to initially treat each hourly quantity as a batch, then when the process is demonstrated to be consistently under control, to treat each shift quantity as a batch. In either case it is important that sampling be undertaken throughout the process, not merely upon batch completion. Sampling plans have been provided for both attributes[9] and variables.[10]

There are two ineffective sampling practices that are often used – sampling a constant number regardless of batch size, usually done each hour during a production run, and sampling a constant percentage regardless of batch size. A careful examination of these sampling plans suggests that constant sample sizes result in inspecting too many items at low batch size and too few at high batch size; and constant percentage sampling results in the same situation. Where these practices are used they unfortunately also usually include sampling at regular times, and this reduces their effectiveness even further.

N=2 Sampling

Since the purpose of inspection is to confirm that a process is under control, the more it can be demonstrated that the process is under control and likely to remain so, the less inspection should be necessary. We discussed reductions in inspection levels above. Consider the following two characteristics:

Figure 24.1 A Sampling Plan for Attributes

TACTICAL MANAGEMENT PQM SAMPLING PLAN FOR ATTRIBUTES					
BATCH SIZE			SAMPLE SIZE		
			REDUCED	NORMAL	TIGHTENED
2	to	8	2	2	3
9		15	2	3	5
16		25	3	5	8
26	to	50	5	8	13
51		90	5	13	20
91		150	8	20	32
151	to	280	13	32	50
281		500	20	50	80
501		1200	32	80	125
1201	to	3200	50	125	200
3201		10000	80	200	315
10001		35000	125	315	500
35001	to	150000	200	500	800
150001		500000	315	800	1250
500001	and	over	500	1250	2000

Figure 24.2 A Sampling Plan for Variables

TACTICAL MANAGEMENT PQM SAMPLING PLAN FOR VARIABLES					
BATCH SIZE			SAMPLE SIZE		
			REDUCED	NORMAL	TIGHTENED
3	to	8	3	3	4
9		15	3	3	5
16		25	3	4	7
26	to	40	3	5	10
41		65	4	7	15
66		110	5	10	20
111	to	180	7	15	25
181		300	10	20	30
301		500	15	25	35
501	to	800	20	30	40
801		1300	25	35	40
1301		3200	30	40	50
3201	to	8000	40	50	75
8001		22000	50	75	100
22001		110000	75	100	150
110001	to	550000	100	150	200
550001	and	over	150	200	200

A. *For a variable characteristic*

When it can be shown from capability studies that $\pm 3\sigma$ limits are less that ten per cent of specification tolerance, inspect only two items: the first piece and the last piece in the batch.

You would necessarily revert to tightened, normal then reduced sampling any time defects were identified under N=2 sampling. Reduced sampling levels would continue until another complete capability study demonstrated a return to the ten per cent condition.

B. *For an attribute characteristic*

When it can be shown from production runs that the process is capable of delivering a defect-free product or service for twenty successive batches, inspect only two items, drawn at random from the batch.

You would necessarily revert to tightened, normal then reduced sampling any time defects were identified under N=2 sampling. Reduced sampling levels would be continued until another twenty defect-free batches were demonstrated.

The elimination of sampling

The lowest cost inspection is, of course, no inspection at all. The ultimate objective of quality management should be to demonstrate that the process will remain forever in control. It is probably safe to assume that if it can be demonstrated that a process is fully in control – zero defects for either variables or attributes – over 100 consecutive batches inspected under an N=2 practice, inspections can be eliminated altogether.

Applications

Process Quality Management is suitable for every activity and kind of work in the organization. We will examine three distinctly different applications in some detail and you should be able to generalize this presentation to other types of operations:

A production unit

The application of PQM to a production unit should be easy. It should not be difficult to define capability then write the specification for a widget, nor should it be demanding to identify individual operations, establish batch sizes and inspection procedures, and create effective processes for controlling material movement.

The problems typically faced when attempting to apply PQM to a production operation are these:

- The specification is agreed with the customer before a capability study has been conducted, or the study has demonstrated that it is impossible to meet the specification, but the commitment to the customer has already been made.[11] It is entirely possible that no capability study of any kind was done. The result is that the manufacturing process will necessarily produce a certain, predictable number of defective items to complete the order. This inevitably leads to other problems:
  (a) Order quantities do not take rejections into consideration. As a result production is always behind schedule. If the operator, a production supervisor or quality inspector were to suggest that the job be shut down to deal with a problem, he or she would be overruled by Somebody From The Office.

(b) Material procurement procedures do not account for the rejected items. Because of this, material is not available to begin the order on schedule or material is 'borrowed' from another order and the other customer is made to suffer.
(c) Costs are substantially higher than anticipated – if costs are known at all – because of all these problems. The effect of this is that it is impossible to justify the additional costs of improved tooling, for example, that might solve the original problem.
(d) Finally, the credibility of all quality management effort is seriously impaired by this kind of wasteful activity.[12]

An admin unit

The application of PQM to an admin process should be no more difficult than for a production process. You will face two rather prominent objections that must be addressed before the work can continue:

1 'Quality control is something that belongs in the factory, not in the office. We don't run machines here; we work with our heads'.
2 'It is inevitable that a few mistakes will be made in a clerical environment. There is a law of diminishing returns when you consider the cost of getting it perfect'.

Recall the fourth quality axiom: the most cost effective way to manage quality is to get it right the first time (remember, right means according to the specification, it has nothing to do with being nice to people). Every quality management activity must be evaluated according to the total cost of non-conformance. This is as certain in an admin unit as in a manufacturing unit.

A thorough examination of rework costs for any admin operation will enable you to refute both these arguments with great vigour. If you are still not ready to do battle, discuss with the chief accountant the cost to the organization for lost value attributable to late posting for credit transactions due to internal errors.

Identify one admin procedure such as the processing of claims forms, the preparation, batching and inputting of journal vouchers, or the preparation and despatch of invoices. Review Chapter 17, especially that information concerning the identification of work content and activity steps. This should enable you to create a process flow, and operating specifications and procedures similar in nearly every respect to those for a production process. The one exception will be for inspection processes; rather than variables, quality will be managed using attributes: a voucher is either correct or defective.[13]

Quality management, where it has been applied at all in admin operations in the past, has typically been wholly reactive. For example:

an unacceptable level of errors or customer complaints triggers action by the quality control department. That action is to conduct a study that results in a report. The content of the report may be summarized something like: 'You would not have so many errors and customer complaints if you did not make so many mistakes. Stop making mistakes and the error rate will be reduced'.

There is usually a further recommendation for training, but the department cannot afford to invest in training because labour costs are already too high – because department staff are spending a lot of time correcting errors.

A computer systems development unit

Review Chapter 17, Project Management. If you and your team have succeeded in implementing an effective management operating system for systems development work, PQM should follow relatively easily. Properly defined phases are, for our purposes, analogous to individual production activities or operations.

The difficulty with systems development work is that under some circumstances it is impossible to evaluate a program fully, to identify every defect, until it has been completed, brought on line and run with live data. This must not become an excuse for not implementing a quality management process. Write specifications that will enable you to identify attributes that will submit to inspection on a short-interval basis:

- Write a specification for each phase that meets all the requirements we have discussed in this chapter. If problems are experienced in developing specifications, it may be necessary to return to the user to examine requirements and confirm precisely what is expected for this effort (if it is being managed properly, users should already be part of the project team). If all this seems to be difficult, remember that IBM *et al.* seem to be able to make a decent living doing this every day in a highly competitive industry.
- From the specification, identify attributes that will submit to test and inspection. Establish inspection procedures for these attributes. Use the same sort of criteria that are employed to create activity steps and estimate hours. Requirements may include an expert review of work done to date, or a test run of the program or sub-routine where possible.
- In many situations inspection may only be possible upon phase completion. Here the practice is that no further work is done on the project until it has been confirmed, as far as possible, that a particular phase has been satisfactorily completed.

Specific practice must depend entirely on the needs of each particular project. The overriding consideration, again, is not for the mechanics of the procedure but rather for the introduction and maintenance of a consistent discipline throughout the process.

If you doubt the value of implementing PQM for systems development, conduct a detailed review of user satisfaction for new programs and software enhancements delivered over the past two years. Calculate the percentage of users totally satisfied with the quality of service for that period.

Do this over the next year

Identify one production department where SPC is either in use or has been used at some time in the past. Working with all the principles and practices we have examined in this chapter, develop and implement a comprehensive PQM practice throughout that unit. It is entirely possible that SPC has never been used anywhere in the organization, but it is unlikely that quality management in some form has been wholly absent. Use whatever has been done as a beginning.

Manage the quality process in this unit until you and the rest of the team are completely convinced that full PQM is achievable, that it will contribute to improved customer service and that the goal of zero defects is, in fact, cost effective. Do not attempt to implement PQM in any other area until this has been demonstrated.

Next, designate an admin or clerical area and repeat the process: develop and implement a complete PQM practice for the unit. Again, spend enough time and effort to confirm it is working well and making positive contributions to the health of the organization.

Then repeat the process in one systems development, design engineering, marketing research or maintenance unit.

Finally, generalize this experience to every unit throughout the organization.

Recall some of the comments from Chapter 3 concerning the management of quality:

- Emphasis for quality management is entirely on the objective of getting it right. It should always be possible to specify the criteria to be evaluated and measure the results.
- A new culture of intensive quality management is typically not easy to develop and promote. The principle of zero defects as a cost effective approach to managing operations is one that is especially hard to appreciate until it has been demonstrated convincingly.
- Quality must become a way of life throughout the organization. Everybody must be totally committed, every person in the organization has a contribution to make, each person's every action is directly related to quality. You must ask for the commitment; it will not be given otherwise.

Notes

1 John S. Oakland and Roy F. Followell, *Statistical Process Control: A Practical Guide* 2nd Edn. (Oxford: Butterworth-Heinemann, 1990.) Oakland and Followell offer a comprehensive, readable reference work for SPC. There are others.
2 Crosby, *Quality Without Tears*; op. cit. The first four axioms are Crosby's; I have paraphrased them somewhat. Number five is unique to *Tactical Management*.
3 See Chapter 4, A Parable, Page 60.
4 This is a simplified explanation of control limits, but appropriate in the context of this discussion.
5 Oakland and Followell, *Statistical Process Control*; op. cit. Oakland and Followell discuss capability studies as an integral component of SPC.
6 Specific processes for taking effective corrective action have been discussed in a number of other chapters in *Tactical Management*.
7 J. M. Juran and Frank M. Gryna, Jr., *Quality Planning and Analysis: From Product Development through Use* 2nd Edn. (New York: McGraw-Hill, 1980.) Juran and Gryna discuss sampling in detail. They also provide a number of references to other works on the subject.
8 M. Louise Meyer's work has helped clarify my understanding of these sometimes difficult issues.
9 Adapted from MIL-STD-105D, *Sampling Procedures and Tables for Inspection by Attributes*. (Washington, DC: US Government Printing Office, 1964.) Sample sizes are based on single sampling plans: reduced inspection corresponds to general inspection Level I, normal to Level II and tightened to Level III.
10 Adapted from MIL-STD-414, *Sampling Procedures and Tables for Inspection by Variables for Per Cent Defective, Military Standard*. (Washington, DC: US Government Printing Office, US Department of Defence, 1968.) Sample sizes are based on single sampling plans: reduced inspection corresponds to inspection Level III, normal to Level IV and tightened to Level V.
11 Review Chapter 3, Page 48, Three Crucial Steps.
12 If you think this entire scenario seems absurd, carefully review the notes from your tour and calculate the *total* cost of not getting it right the first time.
13 Review Chapter 3. How many errors do your customers accept?

■ CHAPTER 25 ■

The Tactical Action System: You *are* they

He who would succeed in business, or in anything, must be methodical. No matter what his calling, he must master all its details and bearings, instruments and applications.

Henry Hardwicke
Self-Help And Success: Method

The next time someone asks you: 'Why don't *they* . . .?'
your response must be: 'You *are* they.'

Tactical Manager

Introduction

You need a formal process to manage systematically the ideas continually emerging during the workday when somebody looks at something that is not as it should be and asks: 'Why don't *they* . . .?' The question might be triggered by the identification of a specific operating problem, or simply the feeling there must be a better way to manage a particular task or element of the work. The purpose of this chapter is to examine a formal system for addressing those proposals, and ensuring they do not get lost somewhere in the flurry of daily routine activity.

The people who actually do the work and those who supervise it are always in a good position to recognize better ways of accomplishing it – of identifying better methods. Review the notes from your tour. When you discussed work with staff and supervisors they were willing to talk for most of the day. Some of their proposals were ambitious in the extreme but most were humble, some were obscenely costly but most would have cost very little, a few were downright impractical but many could have been implemented on the spot. A mechanism is needed to ensure that all these ideas and proposals are fully and fairly evaluated. Further, once a decision has been made for implementation, a system is needed to manage the process.

Why don't *they* . . .?

When any action needed is wholly within a single operating unit, it is reasonable to expect the manager of that unit to manage the process or delegate it to a subordinate. If on the other hand successful completion requires the co-ordination of efforts across several unit boundaries, management of the task becomes more complicated, and the complexity of the task increases with the number of units involved.

A simple system can be designed to monitor all 'Why don't *they* . . .?' proposals in progress and account for management actions involving several different units. This can be accomplished without requiring any direct involvement from the manager high enough in the organization to be responsible for all the units involved:

- Provisions must be made for effectively monitoring the status of all proposals in progress. All ideas and submissions have to be carefully managed so that none get lost.
- Responsibility for action must be assigned to the individual in the organization who can be most effective in identifying and implementing the best solution.
- Each person submitting a proposal should be periodically updated on its status. He or she should be apprised of the final disposition or result.
- A procedure must be provided for triggering additional action when the result of the initial action is the recognition of a more serious problem. A mechanism must be available to refer those proposals that can be better addressed by another process in the organization to the appropriate authority.
- Provisions should be made to address those proposals that are finally determined to be unworkable for any reason.

Some may argue that this entire sequence must not be tightly controlled: if it is managed too closely, that management control, of itself, will interfere with creativity and innovation – good ideas will be squelched by bureaucratic restrictions. Review Chapter 5, A Modern Synthesis, Page 74.

The need for a comprehensive tactical action system to manager this process is based on my estimate of the current readiness levels of staff, supervisors and managers in most organizations. I would argue strongly that if it is not adequately managed, too many potentially healthy ideas, especially those articulated by staff, will be lost forever. The benefits in improvements to the organization are, I feel, well worth the cost in additional systems. Later, perhaps four years from now, your organization will have evolved to the point that the tactical action system will not be necessary to meet this ongoing operational need.

The tactical action system

The tactical action system consists of a small number of controls and some very straightforward functional elements.[1]

The action request

The tactical action request is a one-page, A4 size form. Keep it simple; design it to be user friendly:

- It must include basic information from the originator: name, department and date of submission.
- Space must be provided for the reference number to be assigned by the committee secretary. When the request is prepared by a staff member, it should include a brief review and notation by his or her supervisor (see below, The practice).
- The first principal entry will be a description of the problem or present method.
- The second principal entry will be the proposed change. Any methods improvement must necessarily include the change proposed by the originator. Every identified problem should include proposed corrective action.
- Space must be provided to enable the originator to enter a brief statement of the cost of the present method or the forecast savings for the proposed change.
- The third principal entry will be for the action the assignee proposes to take to address the request. Note that this may or may not be the same action the originator proposed.
- The fourth principal entry will be that for the actual action taken. This may or may not be the same as the action the assignee originally proposed to take if investigation of the proposal results in identification of a better solution. This entry will also include the actual completion date and actual results such as cost savings or reduced throughput time.
- Space must be provided for notations for follow-up or evaluation dates.

The action request log

The action request log is a complete record of the status of all requests. The log will be maintained by the committee secretary. Immediately each request is received, it is assigned a reference number and entered in the log. The log must include the following information for each request:

- the reference number,
- the name and department of the originator,

- brief details of the proposal,
- forecast savings,
- the person to whom it was assigned for action,
- the date it was assigned and the date it was scheduled for completion,
- brief details of the action finally taken and the actual completion date,
- actual savings, and
- follow-up and evaluation dates as needed.

The thank you note

The secretary is responsible for acknowledging the receipt of each request by formally informing the originator that it has been received and entered in the log. The originator is also informed of the reference number for his or her own follow-up effort. The reference number is also used any time the secretary has a need to inform the originator of the status of the action request or the final disposition.

The thank you note is not a silly frill, it is a crucial element in this system. It is an expression of basic common courtesy to those in the organization who are trying very hard to make it better. It provides essential, positive feedback for the originator. It addresses the singular reason why so many traditional suggestion schemes fail so spectacularly: a lack of timely feedback.

The tactical action committee

The tactical action committee is the body that has the responsibility and authority to manage the system. The committee should consist of three to five (no more) members selected from throughout the organization. Members should be selected from those who are fairly comfortable moving around in the organization outside their own unit or area, and who have a good enough understanding of the operation and the politics to be able to evaluate proposals and identify specific individuals to assign for actions. The committee should represent a range of disciplines, skills and experience. Organization needs will suggest committee membership.

Membership should include staff, supervisors and managers. The committee is permanent, and therefore the member from a particular area might serve for six months or a year then be replaced by a colleague. The committee meets either weekly or fortnightly on a regular schedule depending on needs and the volume of requests to be processed. A chairperson should be identified to conduct meetings, and this position should be rotated throughout the committee.

You must communicate to everybody in the organization that committee decisions and actions are not optional. Committee functions are these:

- It must evaluate each proposal to determine that the tactical action system is the appropriate vehicle to address that issue (see below, The practice).
- It must forward each reasonable but unsuitable proposal to the authority that can best deal with it (see below, The practice).
- It is responsible for returning totally unworkable proposals to the requester. This should happen rarely, but in the real world it occurs occasionally. A cogent, polite, complete explanation must accompany the return (see below, The practice).
- It is responsible for identifying the appropriate person to address each proposal. It has the authority to make an assignment anywhere in the organization. It formally makes the assignment and establishes a proposed completion date. Depending on the scope or complexity of the request, the preliminary assignment might be to request a thorough analysis of the problem.
- It must establish review dates for proposals in progress and establish follow-up dates after completion to evaluate results.
- It is responsible for monitoring the progress of all projects and chasing those that fall behind schedule.
- It has the responsibility to reassign those proposals that are determined to require additional work, or those actions that identify other problems.
- It must confirm that originators are kept informed of the status of all action requests.

The committee secretary

The secretary is responsible for all administrative details necessary to manage the system. Significant effort and energy are needed to fill the position properly and therefore this assignment should also rotate among committee members. The secretary is responsible for logging all requests and assigning reference numbers, for making all administrative preparation for each committee meeting and for all committee correspondence.

The tactical action meeting

The purpose for the meeting is to evaluate proposals, make assignments and review the status of proposals in progress. It must be conducted under all the requirements for effective meeting management (review Chapter 13). It is not for the solution of problems. No meeting should ever last longer than one hour.

The status report

The status report is an internal control document used by the committee. It is prepared by the secretary before each meeting. The purpose is to summarize requests: the total submitted, the total completed, the number outstanding, the number overdue, and, most importantly, estimated savings to date for the entire process.

The reminder

The reminder is a formal correspondence emanating from the committee. It is used principally to remind assignees of approaching scheduled completion dates or dates missed. It may also be used to inform people about the reassignment of requests and for related needs.

The good news report

The good news report is a regular newsletter that promotes the tactical action system throughout the organization through recognition of good work accomplished by the process. Think about including this as a regular entry in cascade bulletins or existing newsletter.

The practice

Tactical action requests may be submitted by anybody in the organization at any level, but most proposals will be generated by staff and supervisors. Presentations, system structure and published procedures should be designed to ensure effective communications with these groups of people. Others have a number of suitable vehicles more readily available to them such as the authority to set formal objectives, delegate management actions and sponsor task teams.

As you introduce and promote this process, stress that the smaller and more discrete the proposal, the more likely it can be easily evaluated and quickly implemented. This is nothing more than the application of short segment task control to the resolution of operating problems and methods improvements. The request must be specific. It is not enough merely to discuss that the existing method is unsatisfactory, a proposed solution must be included with every submission. Action requests such as 'A better system is needed' or 'The existing line is too slow' will not accomplish anything – they are too vague and global to define effective corrective action.

Every proposal submitted by a staff person should be reviewed by the supervisor for two reasons:

Figure 25.1 The Tactical Action system flow

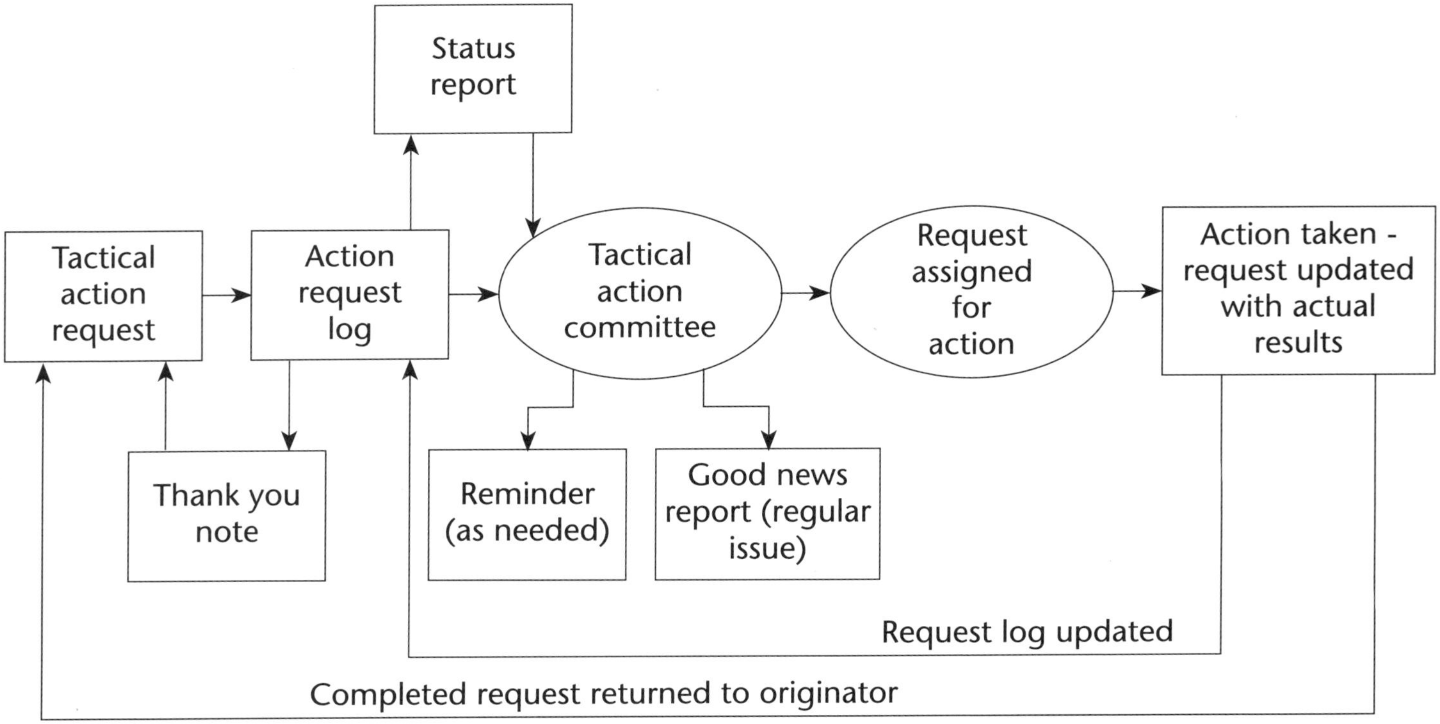

1 The proposal can probably be made stronger with a little help from the supervisor, especially if the originator is somewhat intimidated by the idea of writing out the idea and forwarding it to management. Recall from your tour that staff were very assertive when discussing their ideas with you, but asking them to put them in writing is a completely different matter.
2 The supervisor can help when developing the cost/benefit analysis, and he or she can make the presentation stronger and more positive. A fully implemented management operating system with daily individual accountability will provide an excellent source of information for potential methods improvements and forecast savings resulting from changes.

The original tactical action request is carried throughout the process, with photocopies being made as needed. The request thus becomes a convenient worksheet that documents the entire project on one piece of paper. On completion, the original is returned to the originator.

The entire tactical action system practice must be managed under all the principles of good task team management and effective project management. Clear assignments and reasonable schedule completion dates must be established, and commitments must be obtained for actions. The committee must not become a workshop or problem solving body.

The committee has the authority to assign action requests to anybody within the organization who is identified as the person with the appropriate expertise and authority to address the proposal effectively. The choice may range from the most junior operator or clerk to the group chief executive as deemed fitting. It is often appropriate, and indeed reasonable, for the originator to be assigned the proposal for action. This is especially effective when he or she possesses particular relevant technical skills. It is also appropriate to assign a request to two or more people if a number of skills are needed.

Recall the conversations you had with staff during your tour, and the number of ideas they discussed. Within an operation of even modest size – ranging from perhaps 250 to 500 people, it is not unusual to receive 100 proposals every week in the first few weeks of system implementation. Think about it. Even if 90 per cent must be rejected as being either impractical or too costly, you are still left with ten good ideas every week for improving the health of the organization. Many proposals will relate to work simplification and the elimination of unnecessary activity steps. These will result in immediate, net labour savings.[2] Make a game of it: celebrate spectacular improvements with prizes and recognition in the good news report.

An absolute commitment must be made that every request receives a thorough examination and every originator receives an answer to his or her proposal. This is crucial to the success of this process:

- A proposal can be totally appropriate but impossible or impractical to implement. It could be too costly to justify or is being addressed by another effort already in progress such as the revision to a production line or a new computer system. A complete answer is certainly in order, and this will encourage additional proposals from somebody already recognized as being capable of generating good ideas.
- A proposal can be reasonable but not suitable because it does not address either an operating problem or methods improvement. For example, it might be proposed that additional vending or coffee machines would make the workplace more pleasant. This request is certainly worthy of consideration but it is not an operating problem. The traditional suggestion scheme is probably a more effective vehicle for this type of proposal.
- A proposal can be totally inappropriate because it does not represent a constructive improvement, it is merely a complaint. Any submission of this type should be referred to the originator's manager for a polite, prompt and definitive answer. Realize, however, that this type of communication represents an expression of frustration by the originator. If you receive more than a few such submissions from any area it reflects a serious problem that has not been addressed through conventional management actions.
- A proposal can represent an attempt by an individual to bypass the chain of command and submit a message to people in the organization above his or her manager. Fortunately this is rare. Nevertheless the proposal must be answered. Again, this reflects a potentially serious problem that must be addressed.

Proposals that initially appear inappropriate might turn out to be workable after a thorough examination. Think about this:

Example

We were involved in the development and installation of operating systems with a large group of staff inputting financial data to a mainframe system. One of the proposals submitted through the action system we had implemented was that input operators be permitted to wear personal stereo headphone units while working. This proposal was rejected rather vigorously by client managers as being silly, childish, impractical and totally inappropriate for the workplace. Several months later a new department manager approved the original request. The result was an immediate 20 per cent improvement in productivity for input operators.

Finally, some resistance to this system will occasionally be seen from department or middle managers. Under no circumstances must any individual at any level ever be discouraged from submitting proposals. Sometimes, apparently, a manager feels that a significant number of proposals prepared by people in the department will reflect a criticism of his or her management ability or be perceived as attempts to circumvent his or her authority. Review the volume of proposals received from various departments and areas. If submissions from any particular unit are extremely low in comparison to those from other areas, or even totally absent, it would be prudent to make some enquiries.

In my experience I have even seen written memos from department managers ordering that no proposals were to be submitted from those departments. I sincerely hope you do not have to deal with this form of destructive behaviour.

Do this over the next two months

Develop and implement a tactical action system throughout your organization. Select committee members according to the requirements discussed above. Work with the committee to design system components and write procedures. Present the system through a cascade briefing. Schedule initial committee meetings weekly. Later change this to fortnightly if it seems appropriate. Monitor this process closely for two months to confirm it is working well. Ask to receive a copy of the status report regularly; monitor savings resulting from the actions. You should begin to see net savings well before the end of the two month period.

When you are convinced the process is working well, conduct a thorough review of any suggestion scheme in the organization. Resurrect the scheme if it is dormant, or revise it according to what you and the team have learned from your experience with tactical action. Structure the suggestion process to deal effectively with all requests other than operating problems and methods changes.

Example

Some years ago during a project we opened a suggestion box to examine the contents. This action was to support the chief executive's claim that he really listened to his people – all his people – all the time: that he truly communicated through an open-door policy. The latest submission was slightly more than two years old. It was unsigned and besides suggesting a patently impossible proposal, it stated rather rudely that the chief executive did not, in fact, listen well at all.

You *are* they

Keep a few blank copies of the tactical action request with you all the time. Each time someone asks: 'Why don't *they* . . .?' pull a request from your folio and respond with: 'You *are* they.'

Notes

1 This system is based, in part, on practices that have been around since the late 1940s or early 1950s, and have been known by various names such as Action Needed, Positive Action and Action Required.
2 Work simplification will be examined in detail in Chapter 26.

■ CHAPTER 26 ■

Work Simplification: Managing creativity

> The Electric Monk was a labour-saving device, like a dishwasher or video recorder . . . . Electric Monks believed things for you, thus saving you . . . believing all the things the world expected you to believe.
>
> Douglas Adams
> *Dirk Gently's Holistic Detective Agency*

> There is something I don't understand: why is it the last thing I do is staple this stack of advices together, and the first thing she does is remove the staple?
>
> An admin clerk (Y-T-S, age 16), a retail company (services) during a discussion about the content of her work activity

Introduction

Work simplification is a formal practice to examine work activity and systematically investigate ways of doing it better. Successful work simplification requires the ability not only to make minor adjustments to current procedures, but more generally to identify entirely new ways of doing things. We will call this creativity: the ability to bring into being by force of imagination something that did not exist before. The objective of this chapter is to examine work simplification as a management tool within the greater context of creativity.

Throughout this book we have discussed the need for change; that you develop and implement different ways of doing things. In a few cases the requirement was that somebody do something he or she should already have been doing – that work be done according to the original plan. In most situations, however, the demand was to identify a better way of doing something to improve it. It is a premise of *Tactical Management* that it is crucial to long-term organization health and growth that you establish a culture where creativity becomes a way of life for everybody.

When we talk about making specific changes in the way work is done, we are using practices which you might call as process reengineering.

I would not describe work simplification as presented here as process reengineering. Here the emphasis is on improvements to a current process, rather than the development of a totally new process to do the same job. I prefer to describe work simplification as a process for continual improvement.[1]

The term creativity is used in different ways by various authorities. The mental processes involved in bringing an entirely new idea into existence are complex; it is not my intention to examine them in detail. It is, however, my thesis that even though creativity occurs purely in the mind of an individual, it is possible to establish some procedures – to manage creativity. On the most fundamental level, of course, it is certainly no more possible to manage creativity than it is to manage behaviour. What you must seek is to establish a climate where creativity is to be encouraged, and the articulation of new ideas is continually celebrated with enthusiasm.

Creativity contributes nothing to the organization if it is not tied to the process of innovation. Innovation is action; the exercise of introducing something new or making a change – of bringing something new into use (again, various authorities use the term in slightly different ways). The subject of nearly all of *Tactical Management* has been making something happen, and in most cases to change something. It is fitting that Part Two ends with an examination of creativity – the effort required to identify what it is we want to change and how we plan to change it.[2]

Benefits of work simplification

Work simplification as a management tool has two principal operational objectives (they apply equally to both product and service operations):

1 to reduce process labour and improve the utilization of equipment and facilities, and
2 to reduce throughput time to support shorter delivery cycles.

While these both make important contributions to organization health, the full value of work simplification is far more substantial and not necessarily as obvious:

- Every time an activity step is eliminated an opportunity for error is removed. The ability to keep the entire process in control is enhanced and quality is improved.
- The simplification of any work activity increases flexibility and response time – the work becomes more manageable. This contributes in the short term to improved process control and in the long term to improved customer service.

- Improved management control and reduced throughput time for many admin or back office operations contributes immediately and directly to reductions in lost value or cash exposure.
- Any reduction in throughput time in a production operation reduces in-process inventories, with all the financial benefits this brings.
- Reduced in-process inventories improve the use of floor space, reduce material handling problems and product damage, and enhance housekeeping and safety.
- Simplified work content and activity steps reduce the complexity of planning processes. Less complicated planning processes necessarily contribute to more effective work scheduling and assignment practices.
- Simplified work activities need less complicated written procedures. This directly improves the management of these procedures and indirectly contributes to the improvement of all related communications.
- Work that has been simplified is work that makes more sense, especially to those who must perform it.[3] As jobs are perceived to make more sense, the entire process is seen to be more positive. This improves morale in the workplace and the credibility of the entire management team.
- Support for a universal culture of work simplification creates an ongoing awareness in everybody of work content and activity steps. This promotes an attention to detail in the workplace that contributes to good habits and better compliance with product and service specifications.
- Ongoing practices of work simplification result in a self-fulfilling prophecy for improvements in operations: the more of it that is done, and is being seen to be done, the more receptive are people to the idea of further improvements. The enthusiasm is contagious.

Questions to ask

Work simplification effort is directed at making activity less complicated, by identifying and implementing a number of different changes. Questions that drive the creative process to identify potential changes are these:

Can an activity be eliminated altogether?

The most important question to ask, and the easiest, is simply: 'Can this activity be eliminated altogether?' The admin clerk quoted at the beginning of this chapter could not understand why her final activity was to staple a batch of credit advices together and pass them to the clerk at an adjacent desk, whose first task was to remove the staple. Much of the content of Chapter 19 related to the complete elimination of certain activities.

Total elimination of an activity step is one of the most effective work simplification actions because it costs nothing and results in immediate savings to the operation.

Can the work be simplified?

After total elimination of an activity the next obvious step is to examine whether it can be simplified. An example of a simplified procedure is the two-bin material control system. With a two-bin system, parts staged for processing at a work station are stored in two bins. When the first bin has been emptied, this communicates that the reorder point has been reached and the next order for this operation is triggered. There is no need to examine production records or count volumes of parts, the presence of an empty bin automatically and visibly communicates the demand for a required action.

Can certain steps be rearranged?

The next question to be asked is if any steps in the process can be rearranged. Recall the story from the Introduction to Part Two about the riveting operation. Rearranging the sequence of activities so the handle was inspected before it was assembled to the blade doubled productivity and cut throughput time in half at zero cost to the operation.

Can some steps be combined?

Sometimes steps can be combined to improve the effectiveness of an activity. Consider, for example, combining production with quality inspection activity and making the operator responsible for both of them. The ostensible reason for this relates to the responsibility for producing work to the standard. There is a more subtle advantage, however. When the operator and inspector are two separate people, some communications must take place between the two each time the inspector performs an inspection. When the operator and inspector are one, steps in the communications chain have been eliminated. Each time this occurs it reduces the possibility for errors and garbled messages.

Can a single operation be separated into two or more steps?

It is sometimes possible to split or separate process steps to simplify the work. Examine processes for reconciling monthly financial reports, for example. Source documents should be processed in steps through the month as they become available. Then any problems are identified during the month rather than at the end. Systems development projects are far more manageable when they are clearly separated into diagnosis, design and installation phases.

Can the size of batches be changed?

Examine batch sizes carefully for manufacturing operations. Material movement costs are a significant factor for all operations. Are material batches on the factory floor the appropriate size for the operations: neither too large nor too small? They may be based on the sometimes fallacious assumptions of EOQ (economic order quantity – economical perhaps for volume purchase price breaks but not necessarily economical for production scheduling) or perhaps nothing more specific than the size of the last coil of steel the supplier delivered.

Review admin activities. You will often observe a clerk move from the work station to a computer terminal some distance away to conduct one file enquiry and return to the desk, then repeat this sequence again and again throughout the shift. In this case, is one the appropriate batch size?[4]

Work simplification practice

Work simplification practice is really fairly straightforward: we are more concerned with the creative processes needed to identify better ways of working. There are, however, a number of things to keep in mind:

- Every human activity within the organization is amenable to work simplification. Every job should be scrutinized critically and the six questions asked. Every step in every process must be challenged.
- Everybody throughout the organization must be encouraged to support an ongoing practice of work simplification.
- Use SSTC to examine tiny, discrete applications. Enough applications of the process in small matters will result in large overall improvements. The smaller the proposed change, the easier it will be to manage and the less intimidating the risk will appear.
- Many proposals for work simplification will come from operators and clerks. Encourage that effort and address it with patience. Recall what we said in Chapter 25: even if only one out of ten proposals results in positive action, the work has been worthwhile.
- Examine carefully how any change affects other departments and areas. You are not concerned with immediate, short-term savings in one area at the expense of another, you are concerned about long-term net savings for the entire organization.
- Evaluate all proposals fully. Within any good management operating system, standard data will provide a great deal of useful information about activity steps. When systems development, maintenance, or

market research projects are appropriately phased, these efforts will suggest many areas for work simplification.

- Finally, if any activity feels somehow 'wrong' to those people who are responsible for doing it every day, it probably is an excellent candidate for work simplification.

Consider this:

Example

Some time ago I was a member of a team responsible for the development and implementation of management operating systems within a head office admin centre for a large retail operation. Included in the project was the unit responsible for approving the disbursement of petty cash funds to retail shops and reimbursements to staff and managers for out-of-pocket expenses. During the project, staffing for the unit was reduced from the original fourteen to eleven through improvements in performance.

Work in this department, however, should have been examined more carefully. The existing practice was that personal expenses were paid by a cashier in each shop, then the vouchers were forwarded to the admin centre for approval. If vouchers could not be approved for any reason they were returned to payees with reminder letters. Payees, of course, ignored the letters – they already had their money. Department staff chased unapproved payments with a series of three different warning letters, and were routinely required to pursue shop personnel for months on end.

The process should have been changed – at zero cost to the business. The procedure should have been that all receipts were forwarded to admin and approved before payments were made. Through the application of some very obvious work simplification practice, I estimate that all the work of the department could have been done by four people instead of eleven. Beyond this, I did not have the opportunity to estimate what this practice cost the business in uncleared cash transactions.

Net savings of the scale described in this story are routinely achievable in every operation through the energetic and universal application of work simplification. Review the notes from your tour.

Managing creativity

It is possible to manage creativity without a detailed understanding of the complicated underlying mental processes. Identify a practice which will enable you to approach the subject systematically. You need:

1 a simple functional model of the creative process,
2 elimination of the obstacles that stand in the way of your being creative, and
3 an examination of some techniques to stimulate the flow of ideas.

A model of the creative process

A functional model of the creative process can be described. It is necessary to first formulate the problem, then bring the mind to focus on it. Next allow your mind to generate a number of ideas, examine and evaluate them, and finally refine them into a number of potential solutions to the problem or answers to the question.

Define the problem

Decide – what is the problem that you want to address or the question that is to be answered? The problem must be stated in such a way that it is amenable to solution. This is the singular key to success for any enquiry process (see below, A process to eliminate obstacles to creativity).

Collect relevant information

Collect as many of the facts and as much of the information about the problem as appears to be relevant to the solution (contrary to what they told us in school, it will never be possible to collect *all* the facts). The important consideration is that enough of the right information is examined to not exclude potential solutions.

Create a number of options

This is at the heart of the creative process; that of generating ideas. This is the activity that goes on inside the head of an individual. On a functional level we know nothing about it; we can only look at results. Two important cautions are: be certain that judgement does not interfere with the generation of ideas – first produce the ideas then evaluate them; second, confirm the process is not influenced negatively by others – an idea must not be eliminated from consideration because somebody might think it silly (recall the inputters' personal stereos in Chapter 25).

Nurture possible solutions

The creative process, again for reasons I do not claim to understand, is apparently assisted when you step back from it for a little time to allow the ideas to grow somewhere in the mind. It seems that the problem gets into the subconscious where the solution may come to you when you are bathing, eating, working, reading, listening to music or addressing another problem. It seems that while you are thinking about other things your brain is working on all the problems you have put there recently.

Evaluate tentative solutions

The final element in the process is to put the pieces together, formulate some of the ideas then evaluate them. This is also the point at which your ideas would be combined with those of others in the search for the best possible solution. Effective evaluation can only take place after the first four steps have received appropriate attention.

In the real world the process of creative thinking does not happen in the tidy one-two-three sequence we have outlined here. We may have ideas while we are examining the problem or gathering information. When we get to the nurturing phase we may discover more facts. The point to remember is that all these processes occur during creative thinking and although there may be a change in their order, each is essential.

A process to eliminate obstacles to creativity

There are a number of positive steps you can take to support the creative process. Every person can become more creative through the application of several simple practices:

- Relax and let the ideas flow; do not be concerned about the opinions of others. Little children are naturally creative; observe them when they remove a spectacular and complex – and expensive – toy from the carton, then play for hours with the carton.
- Allow yourself to be creative without attempting to judge any of the proposals at that time. Judgement is a separate process; do not mix the two. Do not let evaluation interfere with the generation of ideas.
- Define the problem in a way to make it solvable. Do not ask: 'How much more space is needed for this operation?' Instead, ask: 'How much space is really needed for this operation?' The difference between the two appears to be minor, but the impact on the creative process is significant.
- Do not be afraid to use your imagination. The cost will be a bit of your time and a few scraps of paper. The benefits to be gained, however, can be immense. Do not sabotage your own ability to be creative.

Techniques for generating ideas

There are any number of techniques for generating ideas. We will discuss four:

Question everything

The simplest technique for generating ideas is simply to question everything. Indeed, this book began with a series of questions. You were then asked to conduct a tour of your operations and question everything you saw:

- *Can it be put to other uses?* Could a van be turned into a caravan?
- *Can it be adapted?* Could military surplus gear be adapted to women's fashion clothing?
- *Can it be modified?* Could the principle of the compact laser disk be modified for use as a computer data storage device?
- *Can things be added?* Could a timer be added to an alarm clock to turn on a tea or coffee maker?
- *Can it be made smaller?* Could a stereo sound system be miniaturised to the point that it might be stuck in somebody's ear to irritate you on the underground?
- *Can a substitution be made?* Could plastic be substituted for steel to make an automobile lighter and more fuel efficient?
- *Can components be rearranged?* Could structural elements be placed on the outside of a building to increase the flexibility of the interior space?
- *Can elements be combined?* Could copper and tin be alloyed to form a new metal with entirely different properties?

Generalize

Throughout *Tactical Management* we have frequently considered the process of generalization. You, for example, have been asked several times to think about two departments, maintenance engineering and computer systems development, and to consider how they were similar with respect to requirements for management systems. You could then easily generalize this analysis to any unit whose majority work involves one-off sorts of activities: marketing research, design engineering, architectural projects or new product development.

Forced relationships

The forced relationship is a technique for investigating the number of ways in which two entities are related. This is often used in product development work when an investigator seeks to determine whether applications in one field might be useful in another. When I first asked you to consider the importance of similarities between functions of maintenance engineering and systems development in the paragraph above, we were using the forced relationship technique.

Free association

Free association is a technique you are familiar with as the activity we call brainstorming. Free association seeks to begin with the statement of a problem, then through a series of associated statements continue to redefine the problem in broader and more general terms. This process is usually most productively employed when a group of people work together: ideas generated by one person appear to stimulate another and it becomes an ever accelerating process. One example of free association is to start with the telephone system as a process for communicating the human voice over wires. Restate it as a system for transmitting information over wires with electrical impulses, then through free association arrive at the potential for transmitting computer data, facsimiles, television pictures, and even information on whether the baby upstairs in the nursery is awake or asleep.

Finally, realize that just because something you created happened to exist long before does not detract from your accomplishments or your creative abilities. Indeed, if the creative process is being universally and vigorously promoted, you should expect that from time-to-time several people will propose similar or even identical ideas.

Do this over the next six months

Over the next three months identify four specific, recurring work activities that are recognized to cause problems in the organization. Select one each from:

1 production or service delivery,
2 admin, accounting, personnel, training or procurement,
3 systems development and
4 maintenance, design engineering or marketing.

Implement practices for work simplification in these four areas using the techniques we have examined here. Establish three-monthly objectives based on measured improvement in either labour utilization, throughput time or both, for all four of the identified activities.

Work closely with staff, supervisors and the appropriate managers. Full and substantive staff involvement is essential to the success of this effort. Creativity is probably the most subjective topic we have considered in *Tactical Management*: all participants will need some practice before they become comfortable with it.

Over the following three months generalize this experience. Implement a comprehensive and ongoing process for work simplification throughout the organization. Establish measurable objectives in every department, unit and area.

Notes

1 In Chapter 27 and the Coda we will examine some of the distinctions between processes for continual improvement and reengineering in brief detail.
2 Steven Schroeder's work has helped to clarify my understanding of these subjects.
3 Review Chapter 25.
4 This is one of the principal reasons for the high mobility levels you observed in admin units during your tour.

■ PART THREE ■

The next year

'Over the Mountains
Of the Moon,
Down the Valley of the Shadow,
Ride, boldly ride,'
The shade replied, –
'If you seek for Eldorado!'

Edgar Allen Poe
Eldorado

You didn't need faith to fly, you needed to understand flying.

Richard Bach
Jonathan Livingston Seagull

A proposal

My proposal is that over the next year you achieve an improvement of 50 per cent in total labour utilization for your organization. That is, for a total labour budget equal to this year – including all wages, salaries, bonuses, fringe benefits, perks and other costs for all staff, supervisors, managers and executives; output, measured either as total finished goods produced, sales or revenues, will be equivalent to 150 per cent of this year. Further, that you accomplish this with no additional capital expenditures – that you do it using existing facilities, equipment and other resources.

You have come this far. You have read my message, pondered over it, thought about how it is relevant to your operation, then gone out and tried to apply it. Now, with this experience, you understand why I offered so many cautions concerning the challenges associated with the Tactical Management model.

Recall from the Preface:

> A productivity improvement goal of 100 to 200 per cent in the next two to four years is not only attainable but essential to the health of your organization.
>
> If you are a manufacturing organization you are spending 20 per cent or more of your sales revenues doing things wrong and doing them again; if you deliver a service you are spending 35 per cent or more of your total operating costs doing things wrong and doing them again. You must reduce operating costs by these factors if your business is to remain healthy.

Improvements such as these are not only possible within your organization but essential to its continual good health. The very survival of your business is at stake. What I am proposing is nothing less than a process to achieve improvements in your operations of the scale of those described in the two statements above:

- that you create a vision for your organization where such things are possible,
- that you develop the climate and provide the leadership, and finally
- that you provide your entire team with all the support and encouragement they need to make it happen.

Chapter 27 is all about the formal, fully integrated, comprehensive effort to accomplish this.

This proposal is extremely ambitious. It will involve monumental effort to develop and market it to your team, and implementation will demand energy, empathy and patience. You are introducing and managing massive cultural change throughout the organization.

You must sell this to managers, and especially staff, with as much enthusiasm as you do for a presentation for a new customer. Use flip charts, overhead transparencies, multi-media, stirring speeches and, yes, even lunches in the boardroom and weekend retreats.

From your experience so far, you know there will be some false starts and some risk: you will try some things that will not work as planned. I fully anticipate you will succeed – if you make the commitment and if you take the actions.

I am also confident that in the process you will have some fun; that next year this time you and the entire team will have matured dramatically in your changing roles. You will be able to walk out to the office or shop floor to follow up on an installation, and the most junior staff person will be able look you in the eye, smile and say: 'That didn't work at all, Boss.' And you will be able to look back at him or her, smile and say: 'You're absolutely right! What can we change to make this work?'

■ CHAPTER 27 ■

If You Seek For Eldorado

It is a far, far better thing that I do, than I have ever done;

Charles Dickens
A Tale Of Two Cities

There are two ways to improve profits: either increase output or cut costs. Increasing output is more fun.

Tactical Manager

Introduction

Throughout this book we have said nothing about how the Tactical Management model fits into other established change and growth processes such as continual improvement, process reengineering, TQM, BPR (business process reengineering) or world class manufacturing. Processes for change and growth in an organization may be divided conveniently into two categories: incremental improvement and quantum leap. Incremental improvement requires that we work with an existing process, operation or organization and gradually make it more effective through a series of structured changes. A quantum leap requires that we totally scrap an existing process, operation or organization and replace it with something more effective that did not exist before. The fundamental difference is not so much in the scale of the change but rather in the methodology. Although we should recognize that while processes for incremental improvement may be modest or ambitious, those for any quantum leap must necessarily be very ambitious. You cannot reengineer a business or implement a world class culture as a pilot scheme in one department, for one production line or for the delivery of one service.

The Tactical Management model is about incremental improvement, although sometimes on a very ambitious scale. Some argue that incremental improvements will not yield the level of growth necessary in time to keep your organization healthy and competitive in a rapidly changing world economy – that the only way forward is a quantum leap such as a total reengineering of all business processes or the move to a world class organization.[1] I accept this argument as reasonable, but in my experience most business organizations today are not ready to consider the move to world class immediately. If within your operation, for example, recurring operating problems routinely interfere with your ability to deliver all products or services to all your customers fully to specification, on time and in the volumes ordered, then that must be addressed before anything else. Reorganizing your business according to world class principles will not improve your ability to meet a manufacturing specification if you are now not capable of meeting it. BPR and implementing a world class culture are not about repairing an unhealthy organization, they are about preparing an already healthy organization for a challenging future. I feel strongly that before most business organizations are ready to begin the move to world class status, managers must spend significant time preparing foundations on which that quantum leap can be built. These include all the disciplines and practices discussed in Part Two of *Tactical Management*. My recommendation is that you work for one to two years, taking all the steps we have discussed in this book, before you consider a quantum leap. This chapter is about the first year of this process.

Before we discuss the next year in detail, however, it may be useful to think a bit about why I propose that you set increasing output rather than reducing costs as your objective.

Improved output versus reduced costs

I have proposed that you improve labour utilization by increasing output without increasing costs and by using present resources. This is contrary to the usual approach to performance improvement: the typical effort is to maintain output and reduce costs. My proposal must appear presumptuous under any circumstances, but particularly if you are in a market that for any reason is either static or declining.

It may well be that when all else has been tried, for reasons totally beyond your control you cannot increase sales; if you are to make the gains, you must reduce costs through practices that include management and staff reductions, shutting down lines and closing facilities.

Before you give up, however, think about several things:

- *How much more competitive will you be* – how much better can you price your product, when total labour utilization is improved by 50 per cent? How much more assertively can your marketing and sales team approach customers with a revised pricing structure based on vastly improved labour costs?
- *How much faster can you deliver the product* with reduced throughput time resulting from improved control of processes?

- *How much more product variety can you offer your customers* based on a far more responsive and flexible operation?
- *How many new markets can you exploit* with greatly improved cost management, flexibility and responsiveness under the new organization?

Conduct a campaign among everybody in the organization. Within the next two weeks you are required to produce a list of 1000 – no fewer – things that could be made in your facility or services your team could deliver that you are not now providing. No doubt about 975 will have to be rejected almost immediately as unworkable, but even if the result is only one item, that might be the entry into an entirely new market for you.[2]

Consider marketing your newly realized excess capacity, even to competitors. For example, take a walk through your local supermarket. Look at several items on the shelves including breakfast cereals, soap powders, pastas and tinned vegetables. For these products and others, you will see at least three different categories of labels: national or international brands, the store's own brand and a low priced or economy brand. It is likely that for some, all three labels were produced in the same factory, and it is even possible that for a few, all three were from the same production run – the only difference being that different labels were applied to the package. Those of you familiar with the banking industry know that certain services such as travellers' cheques and foreign currency processing are sometimes contracted between various high street banks. These means of utilizing production or service capacity are neither new nor inappropriate. If you are unable to sell all you can produce in the marketplace, perhaps there are opportunities to sell some of that capacity to others in your industry.

Even if you are a captive organization, for example, an admin centre, central purchasing unit or systems group, you still must consider the opportunity to market your products or services cost effectively. Why not? Why should it not be that central purchasing is managed as a business, that the manager of a manufacturing facility is encouraged to negotiate with central purchasing, and obtain materials and supplies there or elsewhere according to where the best price can be secured (consistent, of course, with quality and delivery specifications)?

Remember, also, that everything we have discussed throughout this book is applicable to the marketing and sales teams. Their effectiveness and efficiencies have been improving through the application of the principles and practices of Tactical Management too: they should be generating increased sales even in a static or declining market.

Therefore, throughout this chapter – my proposal for the next year, the emphasis on improved output rather than reduced costs. Maintain labour costs and increase the output; build a visible backlog for the sales team. Your selection of the alternative appropriate for your organization will not alter this proposal for our approach or process development.

The next year

To achieve this objective you will have to develop a systematic approach. If this effort is to be successful, a high degree of formalization is necessary. This is an ambitious project and management of it will demand the same intense levels of commitment, planning and control you expect to exercise over any other major project such as the construction of a new building, the development of a major new product or the installation of another mainframe system.

The master plan

Part Two of *Tactical Management* provided you with 20 separate tools for your kit. Until now, examples and situations discussed have generally been closed-ended, clearly defined, of modest proportion and specific. The recommendations were related to discrete operating problems. Now you are ready to go the other direction: to take the large number of small opportunities you have identified and put them together in the greater context of a universal process throughout your organization – something of a Gestalt theory of management.

Your first action might be to go away to a quiet place somewhere by yourself for a day and think about it. Remember, your very own menacing carnivore is still lurking out there somewhere, waiting to spring. During that day develop the outline for a master plan. The shape will evolve as preliminary information emerges during the analytical phase and will be specific to your particular operation. Apply estimated resource and time requirements, and potential completion dates.

The phases of the plan might look like the following:

- Identifying the opportunities.
- Setting the objectives.
- Signing the contract.
- Broadcasting the message.
- Organizing the teams.
- Implementing the processes and practices.
- Monitoring the actions.
- Adjusting the plan.
- Preparing for the following year.[3]

Next create a master task team responsible for overall project management. Choose team members carefully. Select from those who have demonstrated an ability to deal comfortably with change, have the patience and empathy to assist others, are capable of moving easily throughout the organization and can listen well. In addition, each should have a reputation for being good at obtaining commitments. This is not the place for those respected for their quiet, introspective approach to situations; there will be many opportunities for their particular talents later during development and implementation.

Assemble the team. This might be done off-site also. Plan the meeting to include not only an introduction to the subject, but allow plenty of time for comments, questions and explanations (what was *your* initial reaction when you first read my proposal?).

The 50 per cent improvement target *must* be kept confidential until after the contract is signed. Releasing this number without appropriate background information and preparation will accomplish nothing except to upset many people unnecessarily. In addition, nobody is yet sold on any of this, nor has anybody been asked to commit to it. Without that commitment, any discussion with people outside the team will most certainly communicate scepticism and doubt.

Identify yourself as team leader. This particular project is so crucial for the long-term health of the organization that you must monitor the entire effort closely, and you can do this best as leader. If you have been thinking ahead you will have realized that the principal activities of this team will be to monitor the progress, adjust the plan as needed and co-ordinate the work of may other, secondary teams.

Make it absolutely clear to everyone involved that you are available for support any time, and that you must be informed *immediately* of any variance to the plan or other problem. The reasons for this are:

1 The sensitive nature of this project makes it essential that you deal with any misunderstandings or garbled communications immediately.
2 That this effort will make substantial demands on the time of so many people mandates that time management is good throughout.
3 It is crucial that this most ambitious project is seen to be managed well; not that errors are not made (they are to be expected), but that those errors are addressed quickly and effectively.

Before the master team begins its work, hold preliminary meetings with both union leadership and personnel department senior management. Inform them both of your intention to enter into this major effort to improve the health of the organization. Ask for their full and unqualified support, and for their promise not to discuss this with others until you have formally announced the project. You will be unable, of course, to offer specific details before the analysis, but you should be able to provide general answers for the kinds of difficult questions you would expect in these circumstances. Present this project as an extension of the types of changes in the organization relating to Tactical Management they have experienced over the past few months. Do not make any material omissions or lie about the magnitude of potential changes. This endeavour must be managed with complete integrity.

Identifying the opportunities

The first project for the team is to confirm that the potential exists to achieve the objective. Through the master team, commission one or more teams to conduct a thorough study of labour utilization throughout the organization. This study must include everybody: all staff supervisors, managers and executives in every section, department and unit – everybody. This information is critical because it will drive the entire process.

Develop a plan and schedule for the analysis, and to make assignments:

- It is important that no opportunities are omitted. The total time and activity content for the work of every individual within the operation must be subject to this review.
- It is crucial that no attempt is made to evaluate conditions observed, especially concerning effectiveness. If the teams attempt to do this now, it will seriously interfere with data collection. You must conduct regular, frequent reviews of work as it progresses to confirm this is not happening.

These headings may be helpful:

Organization structure

Review the structure to identify ways it can be revised to make it more amenable to the new order. Most of that revision will take the form of simplification, either to reduce the number of layers, unclutter lines of communication or to bring the design into closer accord with changing needs.

Management effectiveness

Identify ways every manager can improve his or her personal effectiveness.

Supervisory effectiveness

Examine thoroughly the activities of all supervisors and section leaders concerning both personal effectiveness and efficiency, and their abilities to manage their units effectively and efficiently.

Quality and rework

These subjects have been so thoroughly dissected throughout Tactical Management that nothing remains to be discussed. My personal experience suggests that many operations should easily be able to achieve at least half of the 50 per cent proposed improvement from these areas alone (see Staff productivity below).

Customer service

Confirm that the customer service unit is appropriately structured and staffed. The addition of people here may result in net savings for the organization if, for example, more timely information would enable production planners to do a better job. Confirm that order entry procedures are timely, effective and free from the potential for error. Examine the entire body of customer service thinking and practice critically to determine that it is fully consistent with all the elements we discussed in Chapter 2.

Methods, procedures and practices

Conduct a comprehensive review of methods, procedures and practices throughout the organization. Usually this requires support from people with technical expertise in the various disciplines involved. Commission the required teams, co-ordinated by the master team, according to identified needs.[4]

Staff productivity

Staff productivity, along with quality, has been the subject of so much of Tactical Management that you should already be actively involved in a number of processes. One comment now is to caution you to review performance targets critically. Occasionally established targets will achieve the status of limitations. Be certain this has not happened anywhere. My experience suggests that most operations should be able to achieve the other half of the 50 per cent proposed improvement here (see Quality and rework above).

Information systems

Confirm that computer systems are being used to the fullest: that no task is being performed manually that should be automated. Conduct a thorough review of the backlog of requests for systems enhancements and new systems to determine that the time of programmers and development people is being used effectively.

Communications

Review the flow of technical information, data on customer orders, material requirements and similar bodies of hard information for opportunities. Evaluate the savings resulting from improving these processes. Examine how managers are rolling down expectations, communicating upward the need for support and other examples of soft information flow. Investigate how tasks require more time than necessary, or additional activity, to compensate for weaknesses in communications practices. Convert this into under-utilization of available hours.

Training and development

If you have not by this time created a comprehensive training plan for the entire organization, from the newest trainee clerk to yourself, then that must be done immediately. This must become one of the highest priority actions in this project. Identify specific situations where technical and skills training will improve the ability of staff and supervisors to improve the delivery of products and services according to specification, on time and to order.

Inventory levels

High inventory levels, besides the obvious problem of tying up cash and becoming obsolete while sitting on the shelf, contribute to poor safety and housekeeping practices, reduce material handling efficiencies, complicate storage records and increase set-up times (to replace finished goods damaged in storage). Higher than necessary inventory levels also, indirectly, increase the complexity of material planning and procurement functions.[5]

Tooling and equipment

Everything we have said about the potential for improved methods, procedures and practices is relevant to tooling and equipment. One or more secondary task teams with appropriate technical expertise will probably be needed. Realize this issue is relevant even if you are not responsible for a factory full of machines. This element of review must include office equipment, work stations, photocopying machines, microfilm facilities, the building itself, delivery vans and all the other hardware needed to support the operation. Look at the utilization of equipment, set-up time, machine-generated waste, scrap and rework, and extra staffing required to compensate for poorly managed machines or lines.

Equipment maintenance

The improved efficiencies resulting from improved response to breakdowns by engineers, the reduction in breakdowns resulting from improved planned and preventive maintenance, and the reduction in downtime resulting from appropriate spares inventories should be relatively east to forecast. Again, remember that photocopiers, work stations and office equipment must be subject to the same levels of maintenance as major production lines.

Planning and scheduling work

The work you have already done for improving planning and scheduling work throughout the operation, both for products and services, should make this phase of the analysis relatively easy. The improvements already documented through this effort should be one of the factors that convince you that my proposal is achievable.

Marketing and sales

Review your entire marketing and sales effort with the same degree of intensity with which you have examined production facilities and admin functions.

Reporting systems

You are well aware of my ongoing concern – some might say obsession – for the ways reporting data can be misused. An important element of this analysis should be a thorough review of all reporting systems. You should be able to identify situations where revised reporting procedures can contribute to improved performance by enhancing the responsiveness of supervisors and managers through the availability of better and more timely information on operating problems. More effective reporting can also reveal opportunities not evident under present procedures.

Setting the objectives

From this analysis work with the master task team to develop a detailed summary of the total opportunity for improvement in labour utilization. Structure this summary so the development of statements of secondary objectives will be straightforward. Be creative. Quantify the information so the total available improvement throughout the organization has been identified.

By this time you will have noted this chapter is remarkably short on specific instructions concerning what your master plan or your opportunities summary looks like. You should now be capable of defining actions and developing processes without much help from me. It is about time we cut the cord. You will soon be on your own.

If the result of all this work is less than the potential overall 50 per cent improvement I have proposed, then do the whole thing again. I know it is there, and you, by this time, must also know it. If you have not found it, then you have not really been looking.

You should now be ready to set specific secondary objectives. Start with the primary objective, the 50 per cent improvement in total labour utilization, and from that develop the phases and secondary objectives needed to achieve this. The plan must be specific in a number of respects. It is crucial to success that:

- the objectives are formalized,
- they are in writing,
- they are stated in a language rendering them amenable to agreement by everybody involved,
- they include specific timetables and definitive schedule completion dates,
- they are provided with short interval control points – short-term targets,
- they are measurable in the short interval,
- they include provisions for revisions to deal with variances, and
- they are ambitious but reasonable – attainable.

When the objectives have been formalized, examine them critically with regard to these eight requirements. If they do not submit easily to the eight criteria, if you or any other member of the master team is in any way uncomfortable with any of them, go no further until the matter has been resolved. This is crucial to success. If you are not comfortable with them, how can you expect to make people in the organization comfortable with them? How can you sell them to somebody else if you are not sold yourself?

Signing the contract

Schedule a weekend retreat for every manager reporting directly to you and all those reporting directly to them. Develop a presentation – again with the same level of preparation and degree of enthusiasm you would use for a presentation to a brand new customer. Deliver it to them *en masse*.

Prepare for this carefully and fully. If you are not successful in selling it to this group, if they do not buy into it, if you do not ask for the commitment and receive it from every individual, it is doomed to failure.

Everything in your experience relating to leadership must be brought to bear on this new way of organizing and managing the business. One distinction sometimes made between leadership and management is that leadership involves the creation of a vision, and a vision can only be of the future – with all the doubt and uncertainties that entails, and the talents and energy to cause others to believe in that vision. Unless you achieve this during your presentation, it will not succeed.

It is the singular objective of this meeting that you present this vision of the work of the organization for the next year to these members of the management team, that you ask everyone to commit to it and that each agrees his or her commitment to it by formally signing a contract. Symbols are important to all of us, and this formal contract is a symbol that I feel very strongly will make a significant contribution to the success of this effort.[6]

After the contract has been signed, the one remaining order of business will be to give the project a clever and memorable name. Be creative, have some fun with it. It is probably wise not to select a name that might easily become an acronym for something rude. You would probably not, for example, want to entitle this effort the Productivity Improvement and Systems Streamlining programme or the Total Organizational Systems Simplification project.

Broadcasting the message

The formal introduction to the project must consist of two distinct phases: a meeting with the union and personnel, and a meeting with the rest of the organization.

The union and personnel

Schedule a presentation for the same members of union leadership and personnel senior management with whom the previous meeting was held. Introduce the project, and again ask for complete and unqualified support. You should now be prepared to discuss the issues at the next level of detail, including your personal commitment to the primary objective and a preliminary project schedule. You will still, however, not be able to answer fully every difficult question. Remind each of them that you will be available to respond immediately to specific situations and questions as they arise during implementation.

The venue and style for this meeting must be consistent with the particular needs of your organization. Allow enough time to ensure that everybody attending is comfortable with the proposal. Ask for the commitment. Remember, however, that although you are asking for a commitment, you are not asking for a vote of approval.

Recall my comments in Chapter 12 concerning making changes in job-related responsibilities without proper regard for personal qualifications, technical job requirements, contractual agreements or the issue of compensation. This project will frequently require substantial revisions to job and activity content, and level of responsibility. It is important that these concerns are fully addressed, not only for the individuals directly involved, but also for those having either a perceived, contractual or institutionalized responsibility for monitoring these processes. Meaningful, proactive communications with both the union and personnel throughout this project will make it possible to address many potential problems of this nature before they become serious.

The entire organization

In that perfect world we have sometimes talked about you assemble everybody in the organization in one large room. You and those members of the management team who have signed the contract sit at the top table. You address the assembly and every question is satisfactorily answered. Every person in the organization leaves the meeting totally committed to this project.

This probably will not happen. It is, nevertheless, a condition to seek. Whether you choose to present the project to the entire group assembled or use a cascade briefing is really a matter of judgement. I have had the experience of seeing an entire shift consisting of 1000 people in a steel fabrication factory assembled in a warehouse and addressed as a group by the managing director. It is, indeed, spectacular. It very visibly communicates that the subject being addressed is extremely important to the organization.

It is important that:

1 Every individual in the organization is made fully aware of the objective of this project, and that this is communicated to everybody at the same time (or as quickly as possible).
2 Each individual has the opportunity to ask reasonable sorts of questions concerning the objective, and the role of both the individual and his or her unit in it.
3 Every person in the organization is made aware of the full commitment of you and the senior management team to the success of this effort.

After your address, follow up closely on the effectiveness of the presentation during your tours and wandering around activity. Ask questions; ask operators and clerks to repeat the objective back to you and ask them what they perceive to be their contributions to the result. Correct any misunderstandings immediately. If you sense any patterns that seem to indicate a general lack of understanding within any particular unit, address it quickly with the appropriate supervisors and managers.

Organizing the teams

Work with the master task team to develop a comprehensive project schedule for the primary objective, and preliminary schedules for all the secondary projects identified to meet the principal objective. Use whatever project management system you determine is appropriate for the needs of your operation. Develop a schedule that contains no interval of control greater than one week.

Next identify secondary task teams responsible for project implementation according to all the requirements discussed in Chapter 14. It might be convenient and time effective to assign sponsorship of each secondary team to a member of the master team.

The first assignments for these teams are to create detailed schedules for every secondary project. Again, no interval of control should be greater than one week. Now impose the additional requirement that no phase is greater than the equivalent of the work of one person for one week.

I hope that space is available to create a praetorium or project control centre. Structure it to include workrooms, and briefing and conference rooms. On the objective level it provides convenient areas for work, training and project related communications. Functionally it supports effective project management. On the subjective level it is a highly visible symbol of the project. Cover the walls with colourful schedules, charts and system flow diagrams.[7] It is extremely helpful if this centre can be located in the midst of the area where the primary work of the organization is done: in an unused supervisors' office or supply room. This will communicate more about the importance of this project than, for example, locating it in a marketing, research or training unit some distance away from the factory floor, principal offices or work centres.

When this work has been completed, amalgamate detailed secondary schedules into the master project schedule. With this preliminary work complete, it should now be possible to begin to make some positive things happen in the workplace.

Implementing the processes and practices

Implementing the various actions required by the project will derive from the secondary objectives. Specific activities will be determined by project content. Critical considerations are that:

- every planned change in process or practice includes, as an integral component of that implementation, appropriate preparation for all the people involved, and
- project schedules are scrupulously maintained.

The mechanics of implementation are based on all the disciplines examined in Part Two of *Tactical Management*. Work in this respect over the past few months should have prepared you and the team for this effort. If all work up to now has been done thoroughly, implementation should not be all that difficult.

Monitoring the actions

Follow-up for the project must be based on all the elements of the tactical closed-loop management cycle and short segment task control. Objectives must be stated so it is possible to monitor actions on a short interval, and quickly and easily evaluate short-term results.

Your role in this is important. Effective task team management requires that you are able to monitor progress without vast expenditures of your time. Statements of secondary objectives, intervals of control, specific control points, phase definitions, and means of evaluation and measurement techniques must be structured to enable you to identify exceptions quickly and easily. At the same time, you must be able to determine rapidly when phases are on schedule and under control so that you devote the minimum time to these areas. The prompt response to any required management action or change in action is also necessary to ensure effective and efficient use of the time of every person involved.

Adjusting the plan

Project definitions and statement of objectives must make specific provisions for adjustments to the plan. This is important for several reasons:

1 This project will result in a large number of significant changes in the way operations are structured and managed. It would be unrealistic to expect that all the opportunities and the full potential of each would have been identified initially. Under the dynamic conditions through which this project will be managed, you can expect that additional potential for improvement will be identified during implementation. Project management must be flexible enough to enable these opportunities to be exploited.
2 Any project of this scale must necessarily result in some action plans being based on incorrect assumptions or incomplete information. Project management must include provisions to adjust the plan when these situations are encountered.
3 During the one year of this project you will experience a number of the sorts of changes in markets, interest rates, customer needs and government regulations routinely driven by changes in the environment. Project management must be flexible enough to address then as they occur and integrate them into the primary objective.
4 I have said several times in this book that if you are really testing your limits you can expect an occasional failure: that you will sometimes simply get it wrong. Any project as ambitious as this in objective will necessarily entail this kind of risk. Project management must include:
   (a) the recognition that a failure will sometimes happen and
   (b) provisions to revise the plan to deal with that failure.

Expect that many adjustments will be needed throughout the year. Alterations will be made to schedules, task team membership will be revised from time-to-time according to newly identified needs, departments will be reorganized, some work activities will be added and others will be eliminated, and secondary objectives will be restated as further opportunities for improvement are identified. This is a necessary element of any project of this size.

Monitor task team membership carefully. Some assignments will demand far greater time than others. Rotate as many people as possible through task teams to keep time demands for each person to a reasonable level. Require *everybody* in the organization to make a positive contribution to this project in one way or another. Adjust team membership as particular talents emerge. You will experience some pleasant surprises as any number of previously quiet, introspective individuals offer substantial support for the effort. This is a paradigm of loose-tight management control, effective delegation, flexibility and really letting go.

Preparing for the following year

During this year you will achieve two specific objectives:

1 the primary aim: the 50 per cent improvement in total organization labour utilization and
2 an even more important long-term goal: to begin to acclimatize the organization to an entirely new way of working.

Throughout this book we have frequently alluded to future changes in both the structure and function of the organization. Toward the end of the year, as everybody is becoming more comfortable with the new style of operations, and as it becomes increasingly apparent that the primary objective will become a reality, begin to think about the following year:

Further simplification of the organization

Reduce management levels to an absolute maximum of five between operator or clerk and chief executive. After one full year of operation under this scheme reduce it to four. This will demand universal delegation and significant increases in spans of control:

1 Supervisors and managers must be formally trained and coached in appropriate management skills: each must be comfortable dealing with a large and ever increasing number of immediate subordinates. This demands good communications skills, the competence to set objectives and make good work assignments, and the confidence to initiate effective management action. These skills will not become realities without your assertive and positive support.
2 The organization structure must make sense in this respect. Eliminate any departments or unit whose primary work is to address rework, internal errors, customer complaints, queries[8] or *post hoc* quality problems. There is absolutely no place in the organization of the future

for an institutionalized team to sort finished product into categories of accept or reject, or to fix things that should never have been broken in the first place.

3 Reduce the size and complexity of staff support departments. The work of groups such as personnel, O&M, systems and training must be understood to provide specialized technical support for operations. Shift the emphasis of their activity away from that of setting policy and issuing mandates. The contributions of these disciplines to organization health must be managed by line managers and must be determined by operational needs. There is absolutely no place, for example, for a department whose sole responsibility is to write procedures for the entire operation. Any procedures should be written by those staff, supervisors and managers who developed them.[9]
4 Amalgamate, divide or eliminate as separate entities, units or departments as required to make the organization more effective and more responsive to changing needs. Again, the structure must make sense concerning future organization needs. Shift specific responsibilities from one department or unit to another according to operational needs, not according to bureaucratic requirements; the bureaucracy must conform to the demands of the organization, not the other way around.

No doubt the best way to initiate this process is to sit down in a quiet place with the present organization chart and simply look at it. If parts of it look right, they should probably be left intact, if other parts look inconsistent or out of place in the new order, they probably need to be changed.

The computerization of manual reporting systems

In this book I have asked you several times to consider the relative merits of manual versus computerized systems for such things as personal time management, project management and management operating systems. My recommendations were always that you initially develop a manual system because it is simple, inexpensive and quickly adjustable. Now it is time to review all those manual systems and consider computerizing them.

In Chapter 5 we discussed the concept of readiness levels: that management effort will be more effective when the style is adjusted according to the needs of the situation – according to the needs of the people involved, both the managers and those being managed. In practice this means that a management system should exercise no more control over a situation than is necessary to achieve the objective. In Chapter 17, in connection with operating systems I argued that the situation was best addressed with a manual reporting system: that a manual system supported an appropriate level of control, and in the early stages of implementation that level of control could not necessarily be provided by a computerized system.

Sometime during the second year of operation under Tactical Management, the situation will have changed so that a less intense level of control over daily work is necessary. Examine every management operating system with the intention of automating it when this change is appropriate. While the computerized system typically reduces the intensity of control it also reduces clerical effort and paperwork, and provides more systematic management of information.

The shift from individual to unit accountability

Consistent with the requirement for a less intense level of control over daily operations is a reduction in the need for daily, individual accountability. When it can be demonstrated that a unit is fully under operational control – when customer service, quality management and resource utilization are all consistently managed according to plan, it is reasonable to dispense with the requirement for daily, individual accountability. Individual daily plans may be eliminated and replaced with a daily section plan, for example, and this may later be further simplified to a weekly section plan.

When an operation is clearly under control, it is no longer necessary to monitor every occurrence of each individual activity: section performance and attainment may be monitored by tracking the principal products or activities of the unit. It is reasonably easy to relate recent information on total activity occurrences to the primary products. These principal products or activities are often referred to as key volume indicators. A discussion of the development of key volume indicators in beyond the scope of this book. The one caution is to confirm that the system must continue to monitor *all* unit hours.

It has been my experience that about 50 per cent of supervisors and first line managers working with operating systems similar to those examined in Chapter 17 choose to continue to control the work under a process of daily, individual accountability rather than shift to key volume indicators. They feel the detailed information provided by that system to address variances and operating problems is worth the higher cost in clerical effort. Personally I agree. Make up your own mind, however, after you have had the opportunity to work with both processes.

With a shift to unit accountability it is necessary to make some changes in emphasis for tracking performance and attainment. Since the individual can no longer distinguish his or her own performance, it is important to make unit performance more visible. Now is the time to create and display colourful charts and graphs in conspicuous places throughout the unit. Encourage contests of all kinds between units and departments. Celebrate good section and department performance and high unit attainment in the cascade bulletin.[10]

The relaxation of unity and integrity of command

In Chapter 5, I stressed the importance of these two principles: that any individual must receive all direction for work from one person – his or her boss, and that all communications, both upward and downward, must not skip any links in the chain of command. If compliance with these two principles is rigid, however, this will at some time interfere with the ability of people in the organization to respond to rapid change with the necessary speed and flexibility.

This situation, also, is related to the readiness levels of staff, supervisors and managers. As communications improve and as people become more comfortable in the shifting roles resulting from changes in the organization, it is perfectly reasonable to consider relaxing these requirements. At some time in the future you should expect the millwright to be able to prioritize the five demands on his time and make a decision, inform his supervisor of his decision and then get on with the work. Remember, however, there still must be an identified decision maker; that requirement will never be eliminated.

It should also be possible under certain circumstances for a staff person, for example, to be able to communicate directly with a middle manager, or vice versa, without directly involving the supervisor or department manager. In the organization of the future there will be a particular need for this kind of immediate communication, especially in matters of customer service and quality management.

If relaxation of these two practices is to be consistent with good management practice, three conditions must prevail:

1 All managers must be comfortable and confident in their roles. They must be able to respond appropriately, for example, when they discover upon their return from a task team meeting that something has changed on the unit as a result of information from another source delivered during their absence.
2 Communications practices throughout the organization must be wholly adequate to address these sorts of situations: mechanisms must be in place to ensure that everybody is fully informed when something has changed.
3 The entire organization must be managed with integrity. Elimination of the strict requirement for unity of command and integrity of command must not degenerate into opportunities for promotion of hidden agenda.[11]

The relaxation of formal job descriptions

One of the fundamental principles on which *Tactical Management* is based is that everybody must always understand what is expected of them: they must know what it is they are supposed to do. During the first year of your work under this model, one of the vehicles used to achieve this has been a formal, detailed, written, published and agreed job description for each individual in the organization.

One of the results of improved communications and the simplified organization structure is that each person gains a better understanding of these expectations. As this occurs it is important that the formal requirements are replaced with general guidelines: the detailed job description is exchanged for a broad statement of the expectations of the position. This shift, also, should occur as the readiness levels of individuals change in the direction of a need for less direct management activity.

The relaxation in the formality of work assignments

Consistent with the relaxation in the formality of job descriptions is a relaxation in the need for rigid formality in work assignments. It is important that the six elements of good practice examined in Chapter 17 are included in every assignment, but beyond these fundamental requirements, the assignment should become increasingly flexible. Every assignment should be open and somewhat ambiguous: it should allow the assignee the maximum opportunity for creativity and innovation in the completion of that assignment. This sounds glib and is not easily accomplished.

The objective is to provide just enough direction to the assignee to ensure that the work is completed according to at least the minimum specification, while encouraging him or her to consider not only the best method, but options that might improve on both the present method and standard of work. This is consistent with our discussions in Chapters 25 and 26.

The presentation and style of the assignment will be determined by the specific needs of the work, and by the readiness levels of both the assignee and the assignor. There is a need here for the assignor to practise at least the same degree of creativity and innovation as is expected from the assignee. There is also, of course, a degree of risk in this process.

One possible approach is to consider that the assignment is structured to include only any prohibitions: the assignee is free to consider any options he or she chooses except those expressly prohibited by practices or procedures, or the demands of customer service and quality specifications.

Performance targets as interim benchmarks, not objectives

It is another premise of *Tactical Management* that as we expect more and more from the people who work for us, they will do more and more, provided that we present them with appropriate opportunities and systematically remove any obstacles. Performance targets must be perceived as short-term benchmarks rather than objectives; they must never become limitations on output.[12]

Develop a climate throughout the organization where the potential level of output for every activity is open-ended: there is no artificial or arbitrary boundary placed on any process. Create an atmosphere where continual improvement in performance is the normal way of operating. This is another one of those practices that must be led rather than driven. If you drive it, perhaps with effort the standard will be achieved; if you lead it properly, there is almost no limit. Recall the story in the Introduction to Part Two concerning the riveting operation: three words and around ten seconds of the supervisor's time would have doubled productivity and cut throughput time by half. You must engender a culture wherein everybody involved in this type of situation automatically becomes indignant at the poor utilization of resources and immediately responds appropriately.

Example

I have had the experience of seeing a group of production operators working at *double* the minimum contractual standard – the rate which they were required to maintain to avoid disciplinary action. They did this under a system of straight time payment: there was no bonus for performance above the statutory standard. This was accomplished because their supervisors asked them to do it, in a climate of excitement for positive performance.

Create a sense of urgency. Through your personal example establish an atmosphere in the organization that leads each individual to become excited about the prospect of improving something, anything: a process output, his or her own professional development, a method, practice or procedure, a quality standard, or a level of customer service. Make this a fundamental element of all work of the organization. Recall from Chapter 6 the proposal that we should all try to enjoy this. There is absolutely no reason why you and the rest of the people in the operation should not have a bit of fun in the workplace and get excited about the work you are required to do.

More emphasis on effectiveness than on efficiency

In Chapter 5 we discussed the principle of the synchrony of effectiveness and efficiency; that although both are extremely important to the health of the organization, doing the right thing will typically contribute far more to the health of the organization than doing a thing right. Recall the example from the admin centre: an improvement in efficiency would have resulted in savings equivalent to 19 people, whereas an improvement in effectiveness would have resulted in saving 90 people.

There are at least three significant considerations here:

1 It is often quicker and easier to achieve improvements in efficiencies. Indeed, the development and installation of the operating systems we discussed in Chapter 17 can yield net labour savings quickly in those situations where there is a need for immediate improvements in the management of costs.
2 When comprehensive management systems are implemented, one of the results is a wealth of good operating information relevant to activity content and operating problems that provide a basis for management action and many methods changes. In this respect, then, the action of initially improving efficiencies drives the later action of improving effectiveness. Some would argue this is backwards: that we should try to do the right things before we seek to do them right – that it makes no sense to do the wrong thing better. That makes perfect sense in a perfect world. I argue that in the imperfect world in which we live it is often more practical to reverse the order. Ultimately you must make your decisions according to the needs of the particular situation.
3 Improving efficiencies will result in immediate reductions in throughput time and enhanced quality management, both of which contribute to improved customer service. Improving effectiveness will accomplish exactly the same thing, but on the greater scale illustrated by our example from the admin centre. When you think through this example, you realize, however, that achieving the improvements in effectiveness, saving 90 people, will required substantially more effort than accomplishing the improvements in efficiency.

Generally, then, it is probably reasonable to concentrate in this first year on improving efficiencies. Then, after many of the practices have been tested in the workplace and people are becoming accustomed to the new order, shift priorities during the second year to an emphasis on striving to improve effectiveness.

Finally

The kind of change we have talked about throughout *Tactical Management*, besides demanding massive amounts of energy, takes a long time.

To implement the processes and practices we have examined here fully, to the extent we have considered, will take years rather than months, according to the size and complexity of your organization.[13] Be patient; be patient with staff people, with supervisors and managers and especially with yourself. It should be obvious by now that, with the exception of that fortunately rather rare individual with ambitious hidden agenda, everybody in the organization wants this effort to succeed. Why should the goal of anybody else in this respect be any different from yours? If you can personally exhibit the degree of vigour and patience necessary to remove the obstacles, the effort will succeed.

We have discussed the occasional failure as evidence that you are truly testing your limits. There is a related issue. When you and the rest of the team begin practices to address matters relating to quality, rework and improved daily operational control assertively, you will often experience short-term drops in production output, increases in levels of rejected material or increases in unit production costs. This occurs as management actions purge the system of long-standing operating problems and flush unanswered queries, bad tooling, unreconciled credit entries, or substandard material out into the light of day. Again, be patient; the improvements to operations will generate net savings long before the chief accountant can note it in his or her quarterly reports.

Now is the time, also, to make a total commitment to the internal customer: to treat every department, area, work unit, workteam and process with the same level of attention and enthusiasm that you exhibit toward your biggest external customer.[14] Apply the same three-step process internally as you are doing externally:

1 obtain the specification,
2 confirm capability, then
3 agree the specification.[15]

One of the responsibilities of the supervisor, as we have said, is to confirm that materials, sub-assemblies and supplies are available to specification, on time and in the quantities needed if unit work is to be completed according to plan. It makes no difference whether these materials are coming from an outside supplier or from another area within the facility. You must lead a process to engender a culture where people in every department value the people in the next department down the line as their most important customer[16] and respond to specification or schedule variances with an appropriate sense of urgency. Canteen staff, supervisors and managers, maintenance engineers and computer systems people must treat each of the users of their facilities and services as their most important customer.

Tactical Management addresses issues of customer service, quality and cost management on an operational level. I have described the ultimate objective as being to ensure long-term health – profits, or more accurately, a consistent return on investment. The key phrase here is long-term. When evaluating any management action or decision, consideration must always be given to the long-term effects of those actions. This must necessarily translate into consideration for all stakeholders. Regardless of how it is described, the ultimate objective is the same.

> You will manage the way you have been managed.[17] It follows, then, that the people who work for you will manage the way they have been managed. If things are not happening the way you want them to happen, look the way you are managing the organization before you look any further for explanations.

Notes

1 See the Coda, World class manufacturing (even if you don't manufacture).
2 Drucker, *Managing For Results*; op. cit. Drucker cogently asks you to consider carefully how well you really know your customers, and your present and potential markets.
3 I expect you will want to create your own titles. I would be disappointed if you did not modify this list, at least a little.
4 Review Chapters 25 and 26.
5 See the Coda, The FISH method.
6 I will accede to your objection to this contract as an unnecessary and trivial formality the day you stop dressing exactly like everybody else for Board meetings.
7 See the Coda, Brown paper systems analysis.
8 I recognize that this is a generalization and there may be some exceptions. A pensions administration operation, for example, probably needs a structured query function.
9 In a large organization, or if there are widespread requirements for many written procedures, it is probably helpful to specify a minimum amount of input from somebody experienced in this craft to ensure continuity and consistency.
10 There are some who suggest this kind of visibility and glorification of positive results is demotivating for those who are not 'winners', and this contributes to a general lowering of morale. I have never found this to be the case when the process is properly managed. I imagine that those who subscribe to this premise have absolutely no sense of humour.
11 See the Coda, On the integrity of stated objectives, and On ultimata and other disruptions.
12 It is not uncommon for remuneration in a production operation, especially a bonus payment or piecework rate, to be based on a certain minimum level of output. Where this is the case, it is totally inappropriate to keep changing the target – to keep increasing the output required to meet the standard. This practice is dishonest, and it is utterly absurd to expect any person to respond to such a process with anything other than contempt. This is not at issue here.
13 Rensis Likert, *New Patterns of Management*. (New York: McGraw-Hill, 1961.) Likert suggests the time might range from three to seven years. I agree

with him. There are others, for example, Sid Joynson, 'A Journey to Enlightenment,' *Management Services*, October 1997, who think the time frame is much less. I disagree that the scale of change we are talking about here can be achieved in any organization in 'less than nine months'.

14 Review Chapter 2, The internal customer.

15 Review Chapter 3, Quality Management.

16 Remember, there is no such person as the most important customer, *every* customer is the most important customer.

17 I do not know the author of this quotation. I wish I had said it.

The Coda

Introduction

Throughout *Tactical Management* we have examined specific issues as they support your efforts to improve and maintain the health of your organization. Consistent with the elements of effective, positive action and 'do it now', I have tried to keep discussions of theories and broad principles to a minimum. There are, however, some principles that I feel provide support for these processes, but that do not fit conveniently anywhere else within the sequence. They are included here for your consideration.

World class manufacturing (even if you don't manufacture)

In our current business vocabulary, 'world class' is used to describe two distinctly different processes. The later use has to do with an organization that is comfortable seeing itself as operating within an environment that covers the entire world. It thinks globally in terms of its suppliers and its markets. Whether it is large, medium or small makes no difference. Whether it, in fact, works with suppliers from the other side of the earth or just up the street is of no concern. And whether its customers are near or far away does not matter, the point is that it sees itself as a cosmopolitan, global player.[1]

The earlier use of world class has been around for perhaps 15 years to describe operations, usually involved with manufacturing, that are organized in very specific ways. The complete phrase is usually read as world class manufacturing, although the principles are applicable *in toto* to service businesses as well as manufacturing. This section addresses this older use of world class.

You can develop a world class manufacturing culture within every business, it is not limited to manufacturing. World class manufacturing is a state of mind – it is a commitment to a carefully nurtured organization culture. World class manufacturing is defined by a set of principles and practices that support your efforts to place your organization in the most competitive position in your industry, world wide, with respect to quality, price, delivery and, ultimately, profitability.

World class manufacturing defined

To achieve a world class manufacturing culture, you totally reengineer the function and structure of the organization around certain principles and apply them consistently. They become key elements for short-term tactical management and especially for long-range strategic management from one end of the organization to the other, from bottom to top. You cannot implement world class manufacturing in one department.

In this, however, we face a problem – the application is so specific to the organization and its environment it is impossible to prescribe; the way forward has to be built on a detailed and thoughtful analysis of the precise needs of your organization within your industry. In addition, two factors tend to obscure this analysis. The first is that a number of these principles are already familiar to us under the heading of TQM. The second is that others are so fundamental they appear as platitudes when used to address significant organization needs.

There is no cookbook approach to becoming world class. Ultimately you make selections from this menu. In a pure service business, for example, inventory management is not a high priority concern. Nevertheless, it is possible to present the general principles. When you examine these thoughtfully it is not difficult to adjust them to apply to every business organization, public or private, profit or non-profit, whether delivering a manufactured product or a service. With a few changes in our choices of words, all these principles are applicable to both a manufacturing operation and an organization delivering a service:[2]

- The entire organization, but particularly operating units, are based on the needs of the process, not on functional considerations. Separate manufacturing, quality and maintenance departments, for example, no longer exist; there is a single product business unit that includes these formerly distinct specialities. The organization is flat. Specialists operate within business units, not in separate departments. It is no more difficult to identify and chart a process for the delivery of a service than it is for a manufacturing operation. If you have achieved, or are working toward BS5750 or ISO9000, you are already doing this. Eliminate separate functional departments or sections and allocate those resources to the business units according to process needs. Devolve all functions into processes. Within your business you really have only three processes: you either buy something, make something or sell something.

- The total focus of the organization is on the customer. There is a clear understanding of what it is you have committed to delivering to the customer. There is a total commitment throughout the organization to delivering it – according to specification, in the correct quantity and on time. Every word and action supports this commitment. There is, also, this level of support for every internal customer. Every team and business unit within the organization has a customer. Every individual within the organization has a customer. This principle clearly applies equally to a manufacturing and a service organization. The one problem here for a service organization is that it is sometimes a bit more difficult to measure customer service performance accurately.
- Production planning and scheduling are based on JIT practices. Pallets of parts staged between operations add no value to the product. Three important contributions of JIT to this process are a substantial reduction in in-process inventories, a clear identification of bottlenecks and an immediate signal of almost every in-process quality problem. We usually associate JIT with the movement of parts through a factory. The philosophy, however, has less to do with the movement of parts than it has to do with effective planning and scheduling. You seek to deliver just the right amount of service to the customer just in time – neither more nor less than required, neither too late nor too early. If you deliver too little too late, you are providing poor customer service. If you deliver too much too early, you are not managing your operation most cost effectively. JIT applies equally to every internal customer also.
- Work units are organized around self-managing teams rather than traditional superior/ subordinate relationships. The people responsible for making parts are responsible, as a team, for budgeting, scheduling, set-ups, manufacture, maintenance, quality, performance monitoring, problem solving, process improvement and product improvement. Supervisors function as facilitators and arbiters between the business unit and the rest of the world. Here there is no distinction between manufacturing and service organizations. Empower every individual at business unit level – this means at team level, to make all decisions necessary to operate his or her business unit at a profit and deliver services at committed levels of customer service to meet organization objectives.
- There is a total and meaningful commitment to value-managed relationships and partnership agreements with vendors. The traditional adversarial culture ceases. You work closely with them to design cost out of raw materials, parts, supplies and sub-assemblies. You work with them to implement their own world class manufacturing culture. Their successes will be your successes. This principle applies for a service organization whether vendors provide you with

materials or services. Form close, open, honest, value-managed relationships and partnership agreements with all your vendors. Work with them to support their efforts toward a world class culture. Some argue that you cannot become truly world class until all your vendors are world class.

- The entire manufacturing process, from the initial specifications for purchased materials through final inspection, delivery and management of customer service is organized to support consistent, effective process control. Many of the tools and practices to achieve this are elements of the discipline we discussed in Chapter 24 as PQM. Process control is applicable to every service process also. When you can describe the process you can manage it. What is it you put on your brochures and tell prospective customers on the telephone that you do? The only difference is that in a manufacturing environment we can usually count and measure things easily, while the evaluation of a service can be a little more difficult. It is possible, however. If your customer is happy with the service and the team is happy with actual costs, the process is under control, otherwise the process is out of control.
- Every activity throughout the organization is evaluated with regard to how it adds value to the finished product. Strategic objectives for the organization include efforts to eliminate all non-value adding activities. Within service organizations, particularly in admin centres, rework and the correction of internally generated errors can represent up to one-half of total operating costs. These are clearly non-value adding activities and must be eliminated.
- Cost management initiatives are developed to design cost out of the product and proactively eliminate non-value adding activities. Negative and reactive cost reduction, cost containment and cost control programmes contribute nothing to the value of the finished product.
- Inventory management is based on strategic sourcing, zero stores and JIT procurement. Raw materials, parts, supplies and purchased subassemblies move in a straight line from suppliers' shipping docks to manufacturing cells without stopping. Incoming inspections are eliminated and replaced by suppliers' improved process control and documentation. Warehouses and stores are eliminated. This principle is perhaps the least lucid for this generalization from manufacturing to service organizations. Think about services you sub-contract. These resources can, and should, be managed as carefully as the manufacturer's raw materials and parts inventories.
- Organization objectives, both short-term and long-range, are explicit, attainable and capable of convenient short interval monitoring. There is an emphasis on the generation and use of knowledge and information, not the collection of data. This principle is clearly applicable to your service organization and needs no further explanation.

- Strategic objectives include a culture of benchmarking every activity in the organization against recognized world leaders. This, also, is clearly applicable to a service organization.
- The entire organization nurtures a culture of continual improvement. This is crucial if you are to remain world class, because you must assume that everybody else in your industry is chasing you in this respect. If you are the leader, all of them already are. Examples of continual improvement include the following. You are familiar with most of these.

This list is representative; it is not exhaustive:

- work organized around process-specific manufacturing cells rather than function-specific, linear assembly steps,
- set-up times reduced to the point that production volumes of one unit are economic,
- the elimination of time clocks,
- open, honest and comprehensive communications throughout the organization,
- operating specifications and procedures that are current, published, readable and available to users,
- a meaningful company mission statement that is easily translatable into both short-term expectations and long-range objectives,
- zero based budgeting,
- activity based accounting,
- the elimination of paper wherever possible,
- a total, organization-wide commitment to quality,
- a total, organization-wide culture of creativity, innovation and work simplification,
- a total, organization-wide culture of training, training then more training,
- a culture that encourages a reasonable degree of risk in the pursuit of excellence, and
- people throughout the organization empowered to support the new culture.

Here, too, everything we discussed is applicable throughout your service organization. The possible exception is set-ups. Even here, if you consider waiting time, poorly balanced capacities and delays between work batches in any admin area, you will identify many opportunities for continual improvement with resulting improvements in customer service and the management of costs.

Conclusions

A world class culture for your organization is not a programme, it is a journey. Even more than continual improvement it is a never-ending search for better and better ways to organize and manage the business. Even more than TQM it must be led by a visionary and implemented by people throughout the organization empowered to the extent that they no longer are recognizable as staff and it is meaningless to describe them as such. Like zero defects, you will never fully achieve it – therein is the journey.

In a service organization there is one further, crucial consideration: for many manufacturing operations, while there are always opportunities for vast improvements in customer service, quality and cost management, there are often theoretical limits imposed by line speeds or process capabilities. For service organizations there are no corresponding theoretical limitations to process improvement. For you the opportunities for improvement are limitless.[3]

The Blitz Team

Imagine you are faced with an operation that is in need of massive change to make it healthy. Throughout the facility – across a large number of departments and units, deliveries are late, quality is poor, customers are unhappy, downtime is high, scrap and rework are excessive, operating costs are rocketing, overtime is obscene, in-process inventories are enormous, morale is rock-bottom, and absenteeism and staff turnover are embarrassing. The task appears overwhelming, particularly if you need to make improvements quickly to satisfy the board, the owners, the City or simply to keep your job. Where do you begin?

Your typical approach always has been to analyse the situation, then begin a number of initiatives nearly simultaneously to address specifically identified needs. This is the approach advocated throughout *Tactical Management*. There is, however, another approach that is worth considering: the use of a Blitz Team.[4]

Using a Blitz Team to address situations such as these we have hypothesized follows from the exception principle: to concentrate great amounts of time, energy and resources where the most serious variances or problems occur.

The idea is straightforward:

- Conduct a detailed analysis of the operation and identify the single area, unit, process or production line where you think you can achieve the biggest improvements quickly. It may be, for example, one troublesome line, a specific product for one high volume customer or a particular quality or waste issue.
- Commission a Blitz Team consisting of enough people with appropriate skills, experience and energy to address all the identified problems across that entire area.

- Manage the project under all the requirements of effective task team management and best project management practice. Using a very rigorous, structured approach, eliminate totally all the causes of problems in that one area and bring it fully up to standard. Work very quickly by concentrating wholly on the issues that are important, to the exclusion of everything else.
- When that has been achieved, identify the area or process causing the next most serious problem for the operation, commission another Blitz Team and repeat the process. The new Blitz Team will probably not consist of the same members as the first because of the specialized skills needed to achieve results in each separate area.
- Repeat this process across the facility until entire operation is properly under control.

When you are faced with a number of serious issues, your efforts can become fragmented. You jump from task to task, never really completing anything, merely damping down one fire and moving on to the next. In the meantime, the trail of smouldering ashes you left behind often bursts into flames again. Use of the Blitz Team ensures that the fire has been put out forever. As you work systematically across the organization, control of operations improves.

The process is very visible. People, not just in the area involved but across the organization, see a flurry of activity in one area and then see positive results following these actions. While other parts of the operation still have serious problems, at least one very obvious success has been achieved. The process feels manageable, and is seen to be manageable by everybody involved because of the very clear focus of the effort.

Things happen very quickly. People see results in weeks rather than months. You and the rest of the team build on your positive results. The enthusiasm becomes contagious as success follows success. Positive actions become a self-fulfilling prophecy for further positive actions.

Although the benefits to be achieved with a Blitz Team can be impressive – sometimes bordering on spectacular – you can experience some problems:

- The entire process results in turmoil and chaos for those involved, both supervisors and managers, but especially operators or clerks who have to work through the very rapid change. Remember, these are the same people who have suffered for a long time under the old, out-of-control system. When dealing with significant change, one of our cautions is always to be patient. When a Blitz Team is in full operation, there is little time to be patient with those uncomfortable with the change.
- When you are implementing massive change very quickly, there is often not sufficient time to measure results accurately against earlier

performance. Activity descriptions and work standards for the new system sometimes have to be estimated. Operating system elements such as weekly/daily plans and daily schedule controls are put together very quickly, sometimes even hand-drawn, with the result that some low volume or infrequently occurring activities are omitted. This should not be a problem so long as everybody involved understands the limitations of such information. Those individuals, however, who are careful with details and concerned about tying up all loose ends may be extremely uncomfortable with this process.

- Unless the process is rigorously managed, furious activity can be mistaken for positive action. Perhaps here more than anywhere else, there is a need for clear objectives and close short-interval control.
- The use of the Blitz Team must not become an excuse for delivering sub-standard product or services below specification. The objective of all this effort is improved operational control resulting in improved customer service, quality and cost management. Within the prevailing chaos, you must continue to remind people that compliance with standards for customer service and quality must remain the forces driving this hectic change.
- When an operation is dramatically out of control and has been for some time, the frustrations of people involved tend to focus on symptoms rather than the root causes of problems. For example, a problem that is causing quality problems may be identified with tooling. This would appear to be something operational that the Blitz Team could address quickly and effectively. When the issue is examined fully, the root cause of the problem might turn out to be out-of-spec material. The problem has now become external to the operation, one that will probably need more resources and time than earlier forecast. Because the Blitz Team is committed to quick and effective results, there now is a need for the re-focus of some Team resources, possibly some adjustments to project schedules and perhaps even an immediate requirement for additional resources. This kind of change always results in further chaos in an already chaotic situation.

Use of a Blitz Team is fully consistent with all the principles included in the Tactical Management model. It is merely a choice of whether to work in a number of areas with a number of processes at the same time, or concentrate efforts on one particular problem to the exclusion of others. This is probably the clearest example of considerations for the differences between doing things more efficiently and doing things more effectively. My feeling is that the Blitz Team is useful in improving efficiencies fast when there is an urgent need to improve customer service and quality very quickly. First Blitz an area and improve efficiencies dramatically to bring the operation is under reasonable control and make customers happy (or happier), and begin to show some savings through reduced labour and machine time, and scrap and rework. You should always be able to manage a Blitz Team under a scheme showing net savings for any costs incurred during the project. This is neither the time nor place for massive capital or ambitious reengineering projects, this a comprehensive, lightning effort to bring an existing process or operation back under good control. When that has been achieved, then you can set about a longer, more studied process for improving effectiveness.

Whether you decide to blitz a specific problem area or begin a number of separate tactical initiatives across the entire operation depends on your needs. You decide.

Concerning the integrity of stated objectives

There is one topic that I challenge you to find discussed in any book on management, either theory or practice: that is an cxamination of the integrity of stated objectives.

Think about the following. Although this example is based on a situation I experienced during a project, I have chosen to modify it so that it must be described as a fictitious case:

Example

You are a unit manager responsible for a cost centre. You have been struggling diligently for some time to meet revenue and cost management targets to achieve planned margins and profits.

You have identified that if more space could be found in the warehouse the operation could be improved in several ways that would move you much closer to your objectives:

- Shipping staff driving forklift trucks could move about faster and this would improve the efficiency of loading activities, lower costs and improve customer service.
- Shipping staff could locate goods to be shipped quicker and this would further improve the efficiencies of loading activities, lower costs and improve customer service.
- Less crowding in the warehouse would result in less damage to stored finished goods and this would reduce operating costs and improve throughput times.
- Less damage to finished goods would result in a reduction of set-up times (to replace the damaged finished goods) and this would further lower operating costs.
- Less crowding in the warehouse would result in improved housekeeping and safety and this would further improve operating costs and improve morale.

> You went to your boss with a plan to recover a significant amount of space by scrapping out a large quantity of damaged, unshippable finished goods. This product had been in the warehouse for a long, long time.
>
> Your boss tabled your proposal and told you she had to think about it a bit. At her next staff meeting she berated you mercilessly – again – for continual late deliveries and excessive overtime in your unit. You asked her about your proposal for the warehouse but she did not respond.
>
> Finally you demanded an answer and she was forced to give you one. It was: 'Leave it. We have been carrying that on the books as finished goods for several years now. We can't afford to show the write-off this year. We are already operating at a loss and that would increase it substantially'.

Now ask yourself what you should make of her answer. Do you *really* have the authority to manage a cost centre: are you, in fact, permitted to make decisions that matter? What kind of messages is she really sending? Why should levels of customer service, quality and profitability of your operation be subject to an accountancy convenience? How do you think *she* would respond if placed in these circumstances?

Please do not interpret this as an anti-accountancy tirade, read it as a pro-organizational health tirade. Calculate the true costs resulting from the crowded warehouse. You will probably find that the costs of writing off the damaged finished goods are more than offset by the savings.

One of the cardinal requirements for the success of the processes we have examined in this book is that objectives must be stated with integrity. There must be no hidden agenda. At every level within the organization, objectives must be stated fully, honestly, openly and unambiguously. There is no option.

One matter that is not at issue concerns processes for delegation and work assignments. As we have said, when these are done properly, a necessary part of that effort is that directions are given somewhat incompletely and ambiguously to permit the delegate a degree of flexibility and opportunity to be innovative in work toward the objective. This has absolutely nothing to do with hidden agenda.

Finally, if the situation does not change, if you continue to face equivocally stated objectives or hidden agenda, I can offer little advice. You might give your boss or the board a copy of this book (it would probably be considered *gauche* to highlight this section). You might attempt to confront the issue assertively – head-on. Then again, you may have to go looking for another job.

The Gantt chart

Henry L. Gantt was a contemporary of Taylor, Urwick, Gilbreth, Fayol *et al.* who created the chart named for him around the time of World War I.

It was originally developed for production scheduling. It is an extremely simple, useful tool for project scheduling. Unless you are responsible for either digging the Channel Tunnel or constructing Canary Wharf, it may be the only scheduling tool you need. Through the years is has been modified in all sorts of clever ways. This presentation is one of its simplest manifestations. There are computerized variations of it available as elements of many project management software packages. Without a computer program, you can create your own version with any available spreadsheet module. I have included it here because in the past few years I have been a little surprised by the number of people who are not familiar with this most useful management tool.

On the Gantt Chart, columns represent time periods,[5] either months, weeks or days, and rows represent activities. Planned and actual time requirements are represented by horizontal bars or lines.

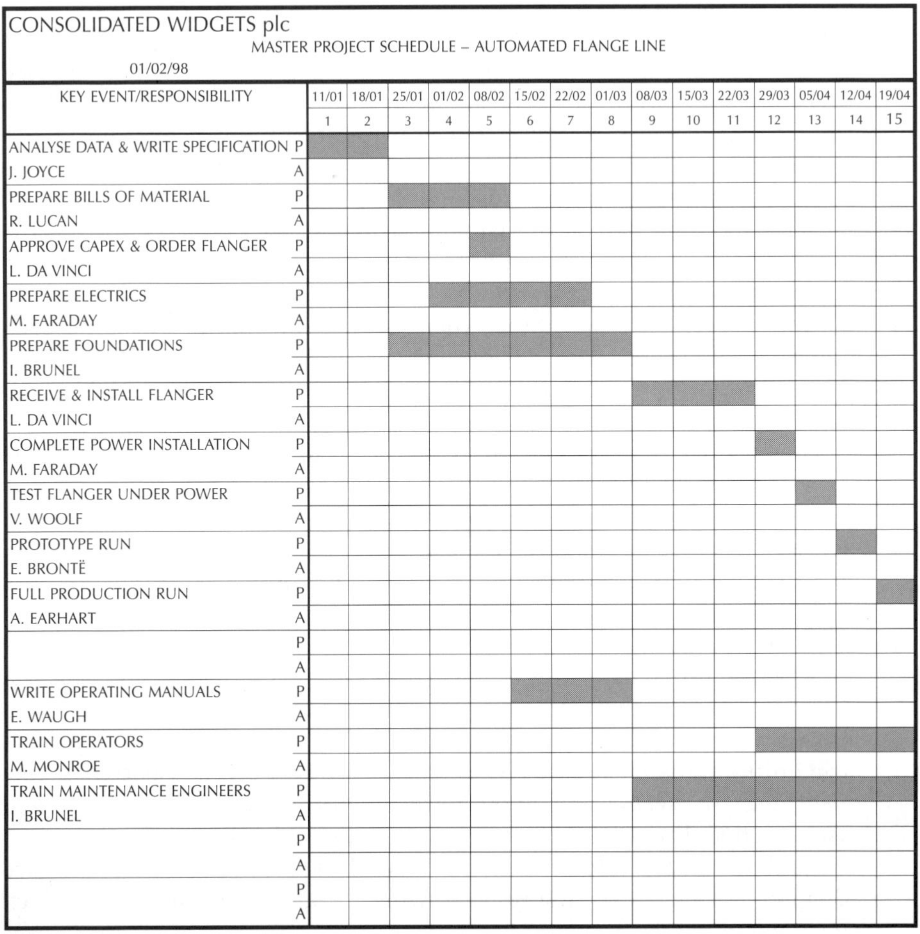

CONSOLIDATED WIDGETS plc

MASTER PROJECT SCHEDULE – AUTOMATED FLANGE LINE

01/02/98

KEY EVENT/RESPONSIBILITY		11/01	18/01	25/01	01/02	08/02	15/02	22/02	01/03	08/03	15/03	22/03	29/03	05/04	12/04	19/04
		1	2	3	4	5	6	7	8	9	10	11	12	13	14	15
ANALYSE DATA & WRITE SPECIFICATION	P															
J. JOYCE	A															
PREPARE BILLS OF MATERIAL	P															
R. LUCAN	A															
APPROVE CAPEX & ORDER FLANGER	P															
L. DA VINCI	A															
PREPARE ELECTRICS	P															
M. FARADAY	A															
PREPARE FOUNDATIONS	P															
I. BRUNEL	A															
RECEIVE & INSTALL FLANGER	P															
L. DA VINCI	A															
COMPLETE POWER INSTALLATION	P															
M. FARADAY	A															
TEST FLANGER UNDER POWER	P															
V. WOOLF	A															
PROTOTYPE RUN	P															
E. BRONTË	A															
FULL PRODUCTION RUN	P															
A. EARHART	A															
	P															
	A															
WRITE OPERATING MANUALS	P															
E. WAUGH	A															
TRAIN OPERATORS	P															
M. MONROE	A															
TRAIN MAINTENANCE ENGINEERS	P															
I. BRUNEL	A															
	P															
	A															
	P															
	A															

A Gantt Chart for a master project schedule

This is the master project schedule for a 15 week project to install a new flanger on the automated flange line. Each column represents one week. Information heading each column includes the week ending date and the project week number. Row information includes the key event or primary activity and the person responsible for delivering it. The planned time for each key event is represented by a horizontal bar. The blank line below each planned bar is where you enter another bar or line to represent the actual beginning and completion date for that activity.

To keep this presentation simple, I have not shown any entries at the top of the schedule except for the project name. You may naturally include here any information useful to the project team such as capex approval numbers, the name of the project sponsor or references to related projects.

I have, however, included a date. I recommend that for every project schedule, somewhere in the heading you insert a system date. A system date is a date you instruct the computer to display automatically each time the schedule is printed, and it is always the date of printing. It is useful because for every project, schedules will go through myriad revisions and updates; it is an expected part of the process. It is impractical to try to assign a revision number to each one. If you are sitting around the table during a workshop or project review and various team members hold different issues of a project schedule, the one with the latest system date is the latest revision.[6]

Opposite is a detailed area schedule for one phase of the automated flange line project, preparation of bills of material. For this schedule, columns represent days rather than weeks. Information heading each column includes the date, day of the week and the project week number. Row information includes the activity and the person responsible for it. This detailed schedule also includes a system date in the heading.

The area where the Gantt Chart is weak is in displaying dependencies. By that we mean that whereas some activities may be started whenever it is convenient to schedule them, others cannot be started until something else is complete. We can show dependencies by the simple expedient of a vertical line representing the completion of one activity and the beginning of another. If your project is very complicated, with a large number of activities that are dependent on the completion of a large number of other activities, many activities overlap one another and scheduled completion dates for many activities are very tight, then you probably need to consider one of the more sophisticated project scheduling tools such as CPM or PERT.[7] They are much better in this respect than the Gantt Chart. Nevertheless consider this simple and useful scheduling tool the next time you are laying out a project.

Finally, shortly after the incident with the cream slice slicer (see Chapter 10, Page 151), many interesting variations on the Gantt Chart appeared on walls throughout that facility.

CONSOLIDATED WIDGETS plc
DETAILED AREA SCHEDULE – PREPARE BILLS OF MATERIAL
01/15/98

ACTIVITY/RESPONSIBILITY		3	3	3	3	3	4	4	4	4	4	5	5	5	5	5
		19/01	20/01	21/01	22/01	23/01	26/01	27/01	28/01	29/01	30/01	02/02	03/02	04/02	05/02	06/02
		M	T	W	T	F	M	T	W	T	F	M	T	W	T	F
REVIEW DATA & SPECIFICATIONS	P	■	■													
R. LUCAN	A															
PREPARE BILLS OF MATERIAL - DRAFT	P			■	■	■	■	■	■							
	A															
REVIEW WITH PRODUCT	P									■						
DEVELOPMENT	A															
REVIEW WITH ENGINEERING	P									■						
	A															
REVIEW WITH USERS	P									■						
	A															
PREPARE BILLS OF MATERIAL - FINAL	P										■	■	■	■		
	A															
REVIEW & APPROVE - PRODUCT DEV.	P														■	
	A															
REVIEW & APPROVE - ENGINEERING	P														■	
	A															
REVIEW & APPROVE - USERS	P														■	
	A															
ISSUE BILLS OF MATERIAL	P															■
	A															
	P															
	A															
	P															
	A															
	P															
	A															
	P															
	A															
	P															
	A															
	P															
	A															

A Gantt Chart for a detailed area schedule

Good housekeeping

Standards of housekeeping within a business environment are a powerful reflection of the perception of self – both for the individual and for the organization. Good housekeeping is an ever-present, visible reminder to everybody of how the organization and the people who comprise it see themselves. We operate our lives, as we have said, for the most part on perceptions rather than facts, and many of these perceptions are based on symbols. Housekeeping is, in this sense, an important symbol which affects how people perceive the organization and their places in it.

Take a critical look at housekeeping throughout your organization:

- Look at canteens, toilets and washrooms. Walk through the shower and locker rooms. Ask yourself if you would be comfortable using these facilities every day in their present state. What impression do you think your biggest customer would form if he or she were to walk through there?
- Look at storage facilities for raw materials, goods in process, finished goods, materials and supplies. Is the state of housekeeping consistent with safe material handling practices and efficient operator movement through these areas?
- Look at production lines and admin areas. Do conditions there reflect your words about quality and productivity?
- Look at the programmers' cubby-holes, the state of desks and benches of supervisors and senior staff members, the condition of your secretary's desk and your assistant's office. Walk through the microfilm and word processing units, and examine the chief accountant's desk. What conclusions can you draw concerning the morale of the people who use these facilities every day?
- Get into your car, go up the road a short distance, then drive past the facility. Ask yourself what impressions you form about the people inside from what you see from the road. Park in the visitors' car park and walk into the main lobby or reception area. What kind of impression do you honestly think it communicates to outsiders about the inhabitants and the work they do?
- Look at the way people are dressed, especially those in boiler suits, uniforms or other clothing provided by the company. Look at the way, in particular, that supervisors dress. Does this reflect pride in the organization they work for and in the product they deliver?
- Do you spend considerable time and cost to clean up the facility before a tour by the board? If so, why? Why should it be cleaner and tidier for the board than it is for the people who work there every day?

So far the tour has been general. Now look at specifics. Identify one individual or unit that always performs well and one that always performs poorly. Examine both and note the relationship between levels of housekeeping and performance. A good correlation between the two nearly always exists.[8]

Where you identify opportunities for improvements in housekeeping, take appropriate action. Either the problem is slight or extremely serious throughout the organization, it is unusual to find anything in between.

If the problem is relatively minor, either confined to one area or widespread but not serious, you can address it without too much effort. Start with a mention during your next cascade briefing and a note in the newsletter, follow that with inclusion in quarterly objectives for those concerned and support the entire effort during your wandering around.

If the problem is serious then it will demand some effort. This, as with major commitments to improved customer service or quality, will require that you lead the organization through significant cultural change. Some time and patience will be needed. Task teams will have to be commissioned to identify opportunities and the change will have to be sold throughout the organization. The change will involve everyone, and the positive, visible support of you and the entire management team will be necessary.

Good housekeeping is consistent with pride of workmanship, and high levels of customer service, quality, morale and safety throughout the organization. These all contribute, ultimately, to higher profits. Your efforts to facilitate high standards of housekeeping will begin to pay dividends, in real terms, almost immediately.

If the entire facility is not as clean, neat, tidy and well organized as your office, clean it up. Begin today.

On ultimatums and other disruptions

When a person agrees to become part of nearly any social system, he or she does so with the tacit commitment that personal objectives and those of the group are, for the most part, compatible (there are a few exceptions: going to prison, for example). A business organization cannot operate successfully otherwise, although seldom is this assumption stated. Throughout this book we have discussed the confusion that arises when organization objectives are not stated clearly. We have examined situations where an individual has difficulty with this reconciliation, either through too much change, inadequate direction or conflicting messages. Addressing these problems is an important part of every manager's job and this is not at issue.

My concern is the situation that you are faced with occasionally when an individual somewhere in the organization deliberately develops agenda of his or her own that are totally divorced from organization objectives. These may range from the simple theft of small amounts of supplies to organized removal of substantial assets. They may include the manipulation of information for material gain, lying or falsification of information for some other reason. The motivation might be a desire for money, personal power, the promotion of a friend, or the elimination or destruction of career prospects of somebody else. Occasionally the objective is the destruction of the organization itself.

The actions a person takes in such circumstances can extend from rather innocuous lies and omissions of the truth to elaborate schemes and plans covering an entire unit and a schedule extending over many years. I am familiar with a manager responsible for a unit of 300 people who developed a highly detailed, complicated five-year programme to inflate his performance bonuses by artificially manipulating job standards.

This behaviour is always disruptive. It is upsetting to those nearby – who nearly always know that something is seriously wrong even though they cannot prove it. It reduces effectiveness and efficiencies, it adversely affects customer service and quality – and therefore profits, and it causes severe morale problems among staff, supervisors and managers. It requires your time and the valuable time of your managers: time you should be spending managing the business. In the long term it is destructive for the entire organization.

The most visible action this person can take is to offer you an ultimatum. He or she feels confident enough to state: 'Either do it my way or else'. The 'or else' might be to resign, go to the board with information thought to be damaging to you, leave with some of your customers to establish a competing business, subvert computer systems or report to an appropriate regulatory body that the business is in violation of regulations.

Several things can be done to prevent this:

- Manage the operation properly. Set the right kinds of objectives, establish appropriate benchmarks, ask the right questions and follow-up effectively. When you do this, you should be able to spot potential problems of this kind early.
- Confirm this person is fully occupied doing the job he or she is supposed to be doing. Confirm that he or she has enough to do. If so, there will not be much time to engage in surreptitious activities. If a person is consistently not delivering what has been promised, and if you have eliminated all other reasonable kinds of obstacles, then look closely for a potential problem.
- If you have been properly wandering around, if you have really been looking at your operation, you should notice when things are not what they should be.
- Examine your own agenda. Have you been doing things you should not – or not doing things you should? This has already been discussed above under the integrity of stated objectives.

Suppose, however, that either you have missed the problem or chosen to ignore it. Perhaps the person is a long time associate and you suspect, but do not really want to admit that a problem exists. Maybe you are aware of it but you feel it is just too unpleasant, or too embarrassing, to face.

Action must be taken. You have no option but to dismiss the individual, immediately, today. He or she must be out of the building and off the premises before you leave this evening. Pay whatever severance pay you must. Accept whatever aggravation you must from personnel, the union or legal. You have no option: the health of the organization is at stake. You have allowed yourself to be placed in a no-win situation; the sooner you take action, the better it will be for both the entire organization and you personally.

> Your integrity and personal credibility are two of the most important qualities you bring to the organization. At the time when you fail to act on an ultimatum delivered in this way, you have totally destroyed these two resources as management tools.

If you have been remiss in taking action, you will have to swallow your pride, go to the board and address it honestly. But do it now. Usually the entire team, and certainly all the people in the unit, already know about the situation. Many people in the organization are suffering because of this destructive behaviour. In the case of an ultimatum, it was probably delivered orally, and even though from behind closed doors, some will have heard it. Even those who did not hear it 'heard' it.

Be assured of this, however, because of the nature of this agendum, you only have two choices: whether to deal with it now or later. The time for coaching and empathy are past. The only result of your delaying action is to dig a deeper and deeper hole in which this person will eventually, if unchecked, bury you and possibly the entire organization.

Status symbols: the earnestness of being important

I recall a luncheon some time ago with the chief executive and directors of a prominent UK company:

Example

This took place in the boardroom and was complete with a chef in a tall white hat, wine, a wine steward and a selection of brandies and cigars served up by the *maître d'*. Profits for this business for the previous year were 16 per cent of target and that year things were getting worse. As these people were comfortably seated for this very pleasant meal their business was rapidly going down the drain. They dined here every day.

My objections to this are not based on any Philistinean aversion to brandy and a good cigar. My concerns are these:

- This setting totally insulated them from the realities of their operations. There was no sense of urgency, no feeling that they must get excited about changing anything. They were not motivated to go out to the floor or into the marketplace and fix those things that so obviously needed to be fixed.
- While they were enjoying this costly appurtenance, staff one floor up were being instructed to stop making telephone calls to customers and to communicate instead by second class post to cut costs. What is your reaction when you receive an important correspondence sent by second class post?

- Finally, and my greatest objection: this meal was perceived as a perquisite of office and a reward for performance. The prize for nearly succeeding in destroying the business, along with the livelihoods of 4,000 people, is to get to eat lunch in the boardroom every day with the directors.[9]

The owners of your business are not paying people to *be* executives and managers, they are paying them to execute plans and manage the business. Inherent in this statement is that the executive or manager is paid for results, for making the appropriate things happen to achieve objectives, he or she is not being paid merely for assuming the title of office.

It is not my intention to address the general subject of compensation, nor am I suggesting that it should ever be possible, or necessarily even desirable, to pay every individual in the organization exactly what he or she is 'worth'. However, review your practices for perks, bonuses and status symbols:

- They should not isolate the individual from the workplace. If the director of engineering is sitting in an opulent office when, to achieve objectives, she should be inside the 500 ton press alongside the senior toolmaker, you have accomplished nothing for the organization by providing that office. She should be able to achieve objectives and occasionally enjoy the office.
- They must be totally consistent, and be seen to be consistent with other cost management practices. Is it really reasonable to tell the staff in accounts, again, that they must wait until next year for three additional PCs because of cost control measures, then approve the Axminster for the chief accountant's office the next day? Is this decision cost effective and consistent with your newly announced productivity improvement goals? If you are managing properly you should be able to afford the PCs *and* the Axminster.
- They should be awarded on satisfactory performance, and should not be given until results are achieved. You do not pay a supplier for trying or talking hopefully about it, you pay for delivery. Why should you reward the director of marketing and sales with a bigger and shinier car, this one with dive brakes, when revenues this year were only 75 per cent of what they should have been? What kind of car are *you* going to be driving this year?
- There must be an attempt to make them correlate, even if imperfectly, in some reasonable way with contributions to overall effort and results. If task team members are required to travel economy on the trip back from a spectacular, and successful, presentation to the board, why should the team leader travel first class? Has his or her contribution to the project been that much more important? If budgetary requirements mandate that some must travel economy, all should travel economy.[10]

Confirm that perks, bonuses and status symbols are consistent with long-term organization objectives.

Try this as a pilot scheme: remove names from the five most senior parking places in the car park and replace them with the names of the five most junior operators or clerks in the facility. Change them as new people come into the organization. Make places for these five each work day in the executive dining room and see they are served, free of charge, the same meal you are served. If you really believe they are important – remember that is what you told them in your brief talk during their induction training – make that belief visible.

And the last shall be first: the *FISH* method[11]

FISH is an acronym for first in-still here. It is a method used by many businesses to schedule production and prioritize work. In practice it looks like this, although your particular circumstances may vary somewhat:

> The order entry system contains a backlog of orders waiting to be processed. Some are easy to make, which means that maybe you have process capability, and some are difficult, which means that probably you do not. Some are large volume and some are low volume. Some are for important customers (see below for the definition of important) and some are for unimportant customers (see Chapter 2 for the definition of unimportant).

Production planners make a list of orders that are easy to make and are for important customers. Then they look at volume requirements. High volume orders are separated and scheduled for production, unless, of course, not enough material is available to run the order. In these cases, partials are scheduled. All orders remaining on the books, including the balance due against all partials, are placed on the FISH report. Now that many order entry systems are automated, the FISH report has become a very impressive computer generated document in most organizations, sometimes as much as five or six inches thick. If any production capacity remains, it is filled by medium to low volume easy orders for important customers. It is crucial to the success of the FISH method that all delivery dates are *totally* ignored.

The FISH report is now put to one side and no further reference is made to it. When the next order entry cycle begins, a new report is prepared. This report includes all orders on the previous report and new entries accrued from the latest production planning effort. The old report is now filed. It is extremely important that it is not discarded. If your order entry system is fully computerized, old FISH reports are placed in those salmon-coloured cardboard or vinyl binders with the clasps that always hurt your fingers and are suspended on special racks.

We can now define an important customer:

> An important customer is one who rings you at unreasonable times and demands, often in an ugly tone of voice and occasionally accompanied by threatening gestures, that you remove one of his or her orders from the FISH report, interrupt production schedules and run it *immediately*.
>
> The unimportant customer is, of course, the one who does not ring you to demand that his or her orders are removed from the FISH report.

The elegance of this practice is obvious. If production planning is properly managed under the FISH system, the ages of orders in the FISH report grow older and older. Also, the process is self-perpetuating: when production is interrupted to run an order for an important customer, the order that was interrupted is automatically transferred to the FISH report. Indeed, with a system adroitly managed using FISH you can accumulate a backlog of orders up to two years old.

An alternative option to FISH

Recently some managers have sought an alternative option to FISH. There is a relatively simple technique for accomplishing this. It does, however, require a rather strict discipline:

> When scheduling production, always be certain the single oldest order on the books is scheduled first; regardless of the difficulty, the volume of the order or the importance of the customer.

If every production cycle includes this single oldest order, then remaining capacity may be used according to any other appropriate customer service requirement. If the oldest order is always scheduled first, the volume of work on the FISH report must necessarily diminish and over time decrease to zero.

There are two important considerations:

1 That oldest order must always be scheduled first, regardless of difficulty or volume.
2 This discipline must not be interrupted by important customers: every order must be scheduled according to delivery date.

If these requirements are met, the process will be effective: the FISH report will eventually be eliminated.

It is not usually necessary to engage in ambitious and costly backlog reduction schemes, nearly always requiring massive amounts of overtime, unless the situation is extremely serious. Unless you have a very large number of very important customers, the FISH report can be eliminated gradually over time using ordinary resources. The very first time this discipline is ignored, the FISH report will begin to grow again.

Business ethics

Ethics in business is a difficult subject to address, probably because every one of us has a different idea of what the word means or should mean. Aside from creating a workable definition, the topic raises strong emotions. The more conservatively oriented individual feels that ethics has no place at all in the world of business, that the only requirement is that the business is managed according to prevailing laws (I have talked with a few individuals recently who feel even this requirement is inappropriate: 'as long as you can get away with it'). The less conservative individual feels that ethics is very important, that even in a business organized to profit the owners, considerations for ethical behaviour must take precedence over profits. The subject is complicated even further by exercises or case studies you have probably gone through during a recent training session or seminar: 'You boss has ordered you to ship a consignment of faulty artificial heart valves you know will fail the day after they are implanted . . . What would you do?'

What we need first are some definitions, then we can consider how to develop a measure for whether a business is behaving ethically or not. Hopefully the definitions I offer and the tests I propose will satisfy both the individuals cited above.

Ethics may be defined as 'moral principles; rules of conduct'. Values may be defined as 'one's judgement of what is valuable or important in life',[12] or 'ideas about what is good and bad, right and wrong'.[13] Working with these two definitions I propose the following:

Values: the set of ideas that govern how you decide whether particular ways of behaving are right or wrong for your organization.

Ethics: the set of standards, rules, practices and procedures you use to ensure your organization is complying with your values, both stated and implied.

The question of whether there is a place for ethics in the world of business remains. Personally, I think there is. It is not so much a question of being nice to people, it comes down to the question of your ability to manage effectively. This, ultimately, is based on trust – on your credibility, both personal and that of the organization. To repeat a statement I made in Chapter 6: if you want the people who work for you to believe you when you tell them what you expect, they must be able to conclude that what you tell them is, in fact, what you expect. You can attempt to bind up every transaction you propose to make – internally with subordinates, peers and superiors, externally with suppliers, customers and other stakeholders – with some sort of formal contract, but at some point you are going to want somebody to believe you when you tell them something. If you want to get anything done at all without reference to a formal, written contract, you are going to want somebody to *trust* you. In my judgement, that trust can only be built on consistent behaviour: people must know what to expect.

Values

Values are purely arbitrary, and they emerge from somebody's head and heart as feelings about the way people should behave and the way things should be in the world. Because they are internally driven, there is no such thing as a right or wrong value except in the head and heart of the originator. If you, for example, choose not to sell toy weapons in your shop, I cannot argue the rightness or wrongness of that decision; if you choose to ignore that a particular piece of furniture has been made from a non-renewable tropical hardwood, that is your decision. That I may make a different decision in the same circumstances has nothing to do with the issue, and I have absolutely no moral authority to impose my values over yours.

The question is how can we apply this to business organizations? My conclusion is that there is a test we can use that is consistent, which is to ask whether what you are doing is within the letter of prevailing law. This solves several problems for us:

- It enables you total freedom and flexibility to work within whatever set of values you offer as being the appropriate ones for your organization so long as they are in compliance with the law.
- It is easy to test: your values, as manifest in the behaviour of individuals acting for the organization, are either in compliance with the law or they are not.
- It separates completely the two distinct issues of whether your values are acceptable in our culture – by my definition they are if they comply with the law, and whether my values are different from yours.
- It enables you to disseminate your organization values consistently with formally published vision statements, mission statements, operating procedures, best practice manuals, codes of practice or general recommendations on how various organization members are to deal with potential problems such as chemical leaks, television interviews or product recalls. It enables you further to support those published values consistently through informal channels such as the organization culture, the informal organization, the general 'way we do things here', and coaching and mentoring practices.
- It enables you to reconcile the requirements of profits and ethics. If you set strategic objectives that include specified levels of profits, and can do this within the framework of published and informal organization values, then there can be no argument that you are operating outside your set of values or unethically.

- The requirement that the test is to the letter rather than the spirit of the law removes a further, value-driven test that some may attempt to apply. This may sound a little harsh to those of us who happen to think that being nice to people is not such a bad idea, but remember what we are seeking here is the ability to measure compliance. Personally, I expect some people to push beyond the spirit of the law to the letter. In my judgement this is often the way that new, and often better, ways of doing things are discovered.

Ethics

If we apply this test to the values you propose for your organization, then the test for whether you are behaving ethically is easy: are you complying with your published, formal values and informal values or not?

We may pose the same questions informally:

- Are you operating your business within the prevailing letter of the law?
- Are you doing what you said you were going to do?

Ethics has nothing to do with being nice to people, that is part of somebody's set of values. Ethics has to do with keeping your promises.

Brown paper systems analysis

Brown paper systems analysis is an effective technique for making the structure and function of any system highly visible, and is useful when you want to critique current practice or methods.

The practice originated in the circumstance that nearly every business organization in the world has a generous supply of brown kraft paper somewhere in the building. In manufacturing facilities it is found in the shipping department, in other operations it is found in the mailroom. In those few situations where it is not available in-house, the nearest stationer can probably help. In extreme emergencies white kitchen shelf lining paper will do, but the presentation is not nearly so spectacular.

When you are ready to analyse any system: a production flow, paper process, communications chain, manual/computer interface or organization, your first step is to visit the shipping floor or mailroom. Return with a roll of brown paper around 200 feet long. The standard width is about 30 inches. You will also need a number of felt-tipped markers in various colours and weights, and a generous supply of paper glue.

Unroll a convenient length of paper on a large worktable. Develop the flow by pasting up full size copies of all forms, worksheets and documents in the system. Allow plenty of space between individual forms for flow arrows and explanatory text. It is helpful if the documents are live and an audit trail for a particular transaction can be followed through the system. Use your imagination to draw cute pictures of mailbags, telephones, PCs, franking machines, lathes, filing cabinets, milling machines and other sorts of items as they apply. Meetings and events such as actions and decision points are always represented by clouds. A standard cloud can be created from a piece of A4 photocopy paper. This can be duplicated as needed.

There are a number of advantages to this technique:

- A live copy of a document communicates much more information about utility than a small square drawn on an A4 system flow diagram.
- The space around individual documents enables the analyst to enter descriptions, questions and comments about the process and document function.
- The entire system can be placed on a conference or workroom wall for presentation or critique. It is often more convenient for a number of users to be able to view the system and question the analyst than were the same information presented in a report format, on overhead transparencies or from a video display driven from a notebook computer. If the system is of interest to a large number of organization members, it can be placed on a wall in a high traffic area, such as the entry to the canteen, to stimulate interest in the project for which it was created.
- Except for the most simple situation, a number of users typically use particular system elements in different ways. This is made clear with this type of analysis. The accuracy of the presentation can be appraised by any number of users before completion and adjustments made as needed.
- It is possible to colour code various elements of the flow to assist in explanation or evaluation. Indeed, the elegance of brown paper development is limited only by your imagination.
- The critique can be made on the brown paper itself, either by writing comments directly on the paper, or with notes or cards pasted on.
- Options to the present system can be drafted on notes or cards and moved about on the paper.
- A revised or optional system can be prepared on another brown paper and the two can be displayed beside one another. A point-by-point comparison can be made.
- Brown papers can be rolled up and transported easily to another location for further work or additional presentations.

Try this the next time you have a system to evaluate or propose. It is fast, convenient and economical. The open-ended feature offered by the roll of paper allows a great deal of flexibility in the layout. Establish a brown paper culture within your organization. It encourages a very visible type of systems analysis that can be understood by everybody.

Listening[14,15]

Listening is the mental process of receiving information aurally, hearing is the physical perception of sound. Within the Tactical Management model the sender is responsible in every respect for ensuring the message has been received and the desired action has been taken. Nevertheless, there are some practices that every listener can use to improve the effectiveness of this effort. Each individual has an obligation to enhance communications through effective listening. This supports improved organization health and makes life in the workplace easier.

Listening is a complex mental process. It is not necessary that I discuss it in detail. As with creativity, it is possible to improve the effectiveness of listening with a few simple rules:

Recognize your personal communications barriers

Understand that every message you receive is processed by your personal filters and decoding devices. These barriers may conveniently be divided into two categories:

- **Personal Prejudices** No matter how much we wish it were otherwise, our reception of the oral message is influenced by what we think of the sender. It may be something as obvious as that you do not like her. Or it may be something as subtle as that he is wearing a necktie that somehow reminds you of a particularly bad experience you had in the past. Since you cannot eliminate this filtering, it is important that you recognize it for what it is. You must keep the messenger and the message separate.
- **Emotional Words** 'When you are made redundant, we are in a recession; when I am made redundant, we are in a depression'. Emotional words affect the decoding process in the same way that personal prejudices do. The sender will use particular words that have an intended meaning for him or her, and you will listen to these words according to *your* intended meaning. Again, you cannot eliminate this decoding, but you must recognize the impact it has on all listening. Be alert for emotional words.

Listen critically

Many people have a tendency to think ahead while listening. Some have the very annoying habit of finishing sentences for speakers. When this happens, the obvious assumption is that the person is not really listening to the speaker, his or her conclusions have already been drawn. This can be a particular problem if the communication relates to an ongoing, highly emotional issue such as a personal discipline problem or negotiations with the union. Listen completely and carefully to what the speaker has to say. You cannot listen effectively while you are talking.

Ask questions

Make certain you understand the speaker. Ask questions any time you feel the message is not clear. There are two helpful types of questions:

1 'Will you repeat that for me, please?'.
2 'Would you please expand on that for me? Will you give me several more examples?'

Be patient

There are some things that can be done to reduce the negative impact of physical barriers to effective listening. Put the speaker at ease. If a staff member is extremely nervous in your office, listen to him or her in the canteen or at the workstation. Eliminate distractions: close the door and do not shuffle papers. Give the speaker your undivided attention. Concentrate on the message. Listen patiently.

Do not interrupt

Do not argue with the speaker while he or she is speaking, wait until the presentation is finished. Do not interrupt with a poorly timed question, wait for a pause. Do not use questions as a forum to express your own opinions. All three of these actions will upset the speaker's delivery unless he or she is particularly skilled and experienced at speaking. Disruptions of this kind will interfere with the ability to deliver a cogent message and your ability to listen to it.

Practise the skill

Effective listening is a skill that will be improved with practice. During the next meeting you attend, do two things:

1 Observe how others listen. Note occurrences of both good and poor listening practices based on this discussion.
2 Observe your own listening behaviour. Examine how prejudices, emotional words, interruptions, distractions and failure to concentrate critically affect your ability to listen effectively.

Finally, practice good listening. After every verbal encounter, ask yourself how well you really listened. Any time a communications effort has failed to achieve the desired result, ask yourself if you could have listened better. Make a positive, structured effort to improve your ability to listen.

Notes

1 Rosabeth Moss Kanter, *World Class: Thriving Locally in the Global Economy*. (New York: Simon & Schuster, 1995.) Kanter's treatment of this subject is helpful.
2 Many of these appear to be repetitions of things already presented in Part Two. Review the Introduction to Chapter 27 and remember that here we are talking about total reengineering of the organization, rather than the incremental improvements proposed throughout *Tactical Management*.
3 The body of literature on world class manufacturing and implementing a world class culture is growing. Begin with these three and supplement them according to taste and the needs of your organization:
Richard J. Schonberger, *World Class Manufacturing: The Lessons of Simplicity Applied*. (New York: The Free Press, Macmillan, Inc., 1986.)
Michael Hammer and James Champy, *Reengineering the Corporation: A Manifesto for Business Revolution*, Revised edn. (London: Nicholas Brealey Publishing, 1995.)
Oakland, *Total Quality Management*; op. cit.
4 Robert H. Schaffer, *The Breakthrough Strategy: Using Short-term Successes to Build the High Performance Organization*. (New York: HarperCollins, 1988.) Schaffer's approach to these sometimes daunting situations is useful.
5 On the original Gantt Charts column widths sometimes represented unit volumes of work or hourly machine capacities graphically.
6 This an excellent, although admittedly simple, example of letting the machine do the work for you. Review Chapter 22.
7 Lock, *Project Management*; op. cit. Consult Lock or any other good book on project management for a discussion of CPM and PERT project scheduling tools.
8 In every organization there is at least *one* high performer whose housekeeping is abysmal: the desk or bench is a tip, the bin is overflowing, the back of the chair is broken and the PC and keyboard are covered with coffee stains (until a few years ago this nearly always also included an overflowing ashtray and cigarette ash everywhere). Frequently the owner of this mess is the most productive individual in the entire facility. This is the exception, and the confident manager will isolate this individual (only to the extent that the untidiness ceases to be a disruption to those nearby) and let him or her get on with continuing to out-perform everybody else. This aberration does not obviate my argument.
9 Since that luncheon this practice has been stopped by a new chief executive and most, if not all, of the previous directors are gone while profits are increasing. *That* group never succeeded in fixing things.
10 I personally believe everybody should travel first class (I told you I was no Philistine).
11 David L. Johns, Personal communication to the author, 1982. This is my earliest reference to the FISH method. It is sometimes alternatively stated as: 'Those Riley people are really patient. They hardly ever ring to complain about late deliveries'.
12 *Oxford Concise Dictionary*; op. cit.
13 Watson, *In Search of Management*; op. cit.
14 Steven Schroeder's work has helped clarify my understanding of this subject.
15 Vincent Nolan, *The Innovator's Handbook: The Skills of Innovative Management*. (London: Sphere, 1989.) Nolan's treatment of the listening process is useful.

Epilogue: Do it now

Sometimes I sits and thinks, and sometimes I just sits.

Anonymous

Do it now

There are myriad excuses why now is not the time. Here are eleven, ten specific and one general:

- My key people are on holiday. When they return I will consider it.
- This is our low volume period. Data we collect now would be unrepresentative.
- This is our high volume period. Data we collect now would be unrepresentative.
- The new computer will take care of it.
- We are in the midst of a management reorganization. After the dust has settled I will have the time to think about it.
- After the move to the new building is complete, I will review the situation.
- We just completed the merger 18 months ago. We must assimilate the cultural changes before we can embark on a programme like this one.
- Our market is changing too quickly right now to consider a programme like this one.
- The board would not approve it.
- The union would not agree to it.
- You simply don't understand, my problem is different.

In over 26 years in this business I have been offered some superbly creative excuses as to why 'now is not the time'. My list currently runs to more than 70 entries, and nothing totally original has been heard for quite some time.

> There is absolutely no excuse for not embarking on this journey to improve customer service, quality, utilization of resources and cost management *today.*

Now perhaps one of three things has happened:

1 You have read *Tactical Management* and you have tried to take some of the actions I recommend, probably with some success but also probably with some difficulty. Remember, I told you parts of it wouldn't be easy.
2 You think some of this might have relevance for you, but you just haven't had the time to try it.
3 You read this book because one of your colleagues suggested it, but you don't believe any of it is applicable to your operation. Besides, you are too busy managing the business to get involved with this sort of thing.

If you have tried to take some of these actions and you have met with success, good. Keep building on that effort – there is *no limit* to what you and your team can do. You now understand the process and what it can do for you: there is no more I need say. Parts of it have been exciting, haven't they?

If you are experiencing some difficulty, then stay with it. Managing well, as we have said, is no different from other sorts of skills we develop: playing football, cricket, the violin or piano, flying or sailing. Practice will improve the effort; do it, do it again, then do it some more.

If you have not yet taken any of these positive steps for the health of your organization because you think you don't have the time, then my reply, as you may have guessed already, is that you don't have the time not to. Recall The Ballad of Ralph Hendershot: take the time. It is what you are being paid to do.

Finally, if you honestly believe this process has no relevance for your organization, you have not really been looking. Go back out there to the shop floor or office where the work is actually done and look again.

Whether you elect a quantum leap, and reengineer the entire business in one massive effort, or the incremental approach introduced here in *Tactical Management* that might extend over several years, in either case, do it today. Do it now.

Recommended Reading

He reads much;
He is a great observer, and he looks
Quite through the deeds of men.

William Shakespeare
Julius Caesar

This is a list of books I recommend you read, digest, ponder over, reread then keep for convenient reference on the shelf behind your desk alongside the books already there. I recommend them whether you are section leader or chief executive. Several are difficult and somewhat arcane. Their application to your particular operation may not always be apparent, but your examination of *Tactical Management* should have helped prepare you for them. Each will in its own way support your efforts to maintain the health of your organization. Most include extensive notes, bibliographies and recommendations for further reading. The eventual extent of your library is limited only by your stamina and the length of your bookshelf. As with *Tactical Management* itself, this list is not the end of anything, it is only another step in your journey.

You will not agree with everything you read here, not all of it will be useful and you will often encounter discrepancies between statements made by different authors. If you are still uncomfortable with this, recall what we discussed in the Introduction under Concerning theories and models. Think about it, then make up your own mind.

My good friend and associate Peter Brown has commented: 'If you read an entire book and from it discover only one paragraph, or even one phrase, that helps clarify your thinking on some important issue, that reading has been worthwhile'.

Some of these have already been cited in chapter notes and are included here for your convenience.

Management and business

Ansoff, H.I. (1987) *Corporate Strategy*, Revised edn. London: Penguin.
Argyris, C. (1957) *Personality and Organization*, New York: Harper & Row.
Barnard, C.I. (1968) *The Functions of the Executive*, 30th anniversary edn. Cambridge: Harvard University Press.
Belbin, R.M. (1981) *Management Teams: Why They Succeed or Fail*, Oxford: Butterworth Heinemann Ltd.
Bennis, W. (1992) *On Becoming a Leader*, London: Century Business.
Bennis, W. and Nanus, B. (1985) *Leaders: The Strategies For Taking Charge*, New York: Harper & Row.
Bentley, T.J (ed.) (1991) *The Management Services Handbook*, 2nd edn. London: Pitman.
Blethyn, S.G. and Parker, C.Y. (1990) *Designing Information Systems*, London: Butterworth Heinemann.
Bowditch, J.L. and Buono, A.F. (1990) *A Primer on Organizational Behavior*, 2nd edn. New York: John Wiley & Sons.
Bergin, F.J. (1981) *Practical Communication*, 2nd edn. London: Pitman.
Crosby, P.B. (1980) *Quality Is Free*, New York: New American Library.
Crosby, P.B. (1985) *Quality Without Tears*, New York: New American Library.
Donaldson, J. (1992) *Business Ethics: A European Casebook*, London: Academic Press.
Drucker, P.F. (1955) *The Practice of Management*, Oxford: Heinemann.
Drucker, P.F. (1964) *Managing For Results*, Oxford: Heinemann.
Feigenbaum, E., McCorduck, P. and Nii, H.P. (1988) *The Rise of the Expert Company: How Visionary Companies Are Using Artificial Intelligence To Achieve Higher Productivity and Profit*, London: Macmillan.
Friedmann, G. (1961) *The Anatomy of Work: The Implications of Specialization*, trans. W. Rawson, London: Heinemann Educational.
Fournies, F.F. (1978) *Coaching For Improved Work Performance*, New York: Van Nostrand Reinhold.
Gellerman, S.W. (1963) *Motivation and Productivity*, New York: American Management Association, Inc..
Goldratt, E.M. and Cox, J. (1986) *The Goal*, Croton-on-Hudson, New York: North River Press.
Golembiewski, R.T. (1989) *Organization Development: Ideas and Issues*, New Brunswick, New Jersey: Transaction Publishers.
Greenwood, N.R. (1988) *Implementing Flexible Manufacturing Systems*, Basingstoke: Macmillan Education.
Hammer, M. and Champy, J. (1995) *Reengineering the Corporation: A Manifesto for Business Revolution*, Revised edn. London: Nicholas Brealey Publishing.
Handy, C. (1991) *The Age of Unreason*, 2nd edn. London: Random Century Ltd.
Harvey-Jones, Sir J. (1989) *Making It Happen: Reflections On Leadership*, London: Fontana/HarperCollins.
Harvey-Jones, Sir J. (1990) *Trouble Shooter*, London: BBC Books.
Hersey, P. and Blanchard, K.H. (1988) *Management of Organizational Behavior*, 5th edn. London: Prentice Hall International.
Herzberg, F., Mausner, B. and Snyderman, B.B. (1959) *The Motivation to Work*, 2nd edn. New York: Wiley.
Heyel, C. (ed.) (1982) *The Encyclopedia of Management*, 3rd edn. New York: Van Nostrand Reinhold.
Juran, J.M. and Gryna, F.M. Jr., (1980) *Quality Planning and Analysis: From Product Development through Use*, 2nd edn. New York: McGraw Hill.

Kanter, R.M. (1985) *The Change Masters*, London: Unwin.
Kanter, R.M. (1990) *When Giants Learn To Dance*, London: Unwin.
Kanter R.M. (1995) *World Class: Thriving Locally in the Global Economy*, New York: Simon & Schuster.
Kelly, J.E. (1982) *Scientific Management, Job Redesign and Work Performance*, London: Academic Press.
Krajewski, L.J. and Ritzman, L. P.(1987) *Operations Management, Strategy and Analysis*, Reading, Massachusetts: Addison Wesley.
Liebfried K.H.J. and McNair, C.J. (1992) *Benchmarking: A Tool for Continuous Improvement*, New York: HarperCollins.
Likert, R. (1961) *New Patterns of Management*, New York: McGraw Hill.
Lock, D. (1992) *Project Management*, 5th edn. Aldershot: Gower.
March, J.G. and Simon, H.A. (1993) *Organizations*, 2nd edn. Oxford: Blackwell Publishers.
Martin, A. (1994) *Infopartnering: The Ultimate Strategy for Achieving Efficient Consumer Response*, Essex Junction, VT: omneo, Oliver Wight Publications. Do not be put off by the jargon. Although this book addresses retail supply chain management, there are lessons here for anybody responsible for the movement of goods from manufacturer to user.
Maslow, H.A. (1970) *Motivation and Personality*, 2nd edn. New York: Harper & Row.
Mayo, E. (1946) *The Human Problems of an Industrial Civilization*, 2nd edn. Cambridge, Mass.: Harvard University Press.
McConkey, D.D. (1986) *No Nonsense Delegation*, Revised edn. New York: Amacon, American Management Association.
McGregor, D. (1960) *The Human Side of Enterprise*, New York: McGraw Hill.
Mensching J.R. and Adams, D.A. (1991) *Managing An Information System*, Englewood Cliffs, NJ: Prentice Hall International Editions, Simon & Schuster.
Moore P.G. and Thomas, H. (1988) *The Anatomy of Decisions*, 2nd edn. London: Penguin.
Morton, M.S.S. (1991) (ed.) *The Corporation of the 1990s: Information Technology and Organizational Transformation*, New York: Oxford University Press.
Nolan, V. (1989) *The Innovator's Handbook: The Skills of Innovative Management*, London: Sphere Books Ltd.
Oakland, J.S. (1989) *Total Quality Management*, Oxford: Butterworth Heinemann Ltd.
Oakland, J.S. and Followell, R.F. (1990) *Statistical Process Control: A Practical Guide*, 2nd edn. Oxford: Butterworth Heinemann Ltd.
Parkinson, C.N. (1961) *Parkinson's Law or The Pursuit of Progress*, London: John Murray.
Peter, Dr L.J. and Hull, R. (1969) *The Peter Principle: Why Things Always Go Wrong*, London: Souvenir Press Ltd..
Peters, T.J. (1988) *Thriving On Chaos*, New York: Harper & Row.
Peters, T.J. and Waterman, R.H.Jr., (1982) *In Search of Excellence*, New York: Harper & Row.
Peters, T.J. and Austin, N. (1986) *A Passion For Excellence*, Glasgow: Fontana/Collins.
Porter, M.E. (1985) *Competitive Advantage: Creating and Sustaining Superior Performance*, New York: The Free Press.
Pugh, D.S. (1990) (ed.) *Organization Theory: Selected Readings*, London: Penguin.
Roethlisberger, F.J. and Dickson, W.J. (1939) *Management and the Worker*, Cambridge, Mass.: Harvard University Press.

Rose, M. (1978) *Industrial Behaviour: Theoretical Development Since Taylor*, London: Penguin.
Rushton, A. and Oxley, J. (1991) *Handbook of Logistics and Distribution Management*, London: Kogan Page.
Schaffer, R.H. (1988) *The Breakthrough Strategy: Using Short term Successes to Build the High Performance Organization*, New York: HarperCollins.
Schonberger, R.J. (1982) *Japanese Manufacturing Techniques: Nine Hidden Lessons In Simplicity*, New York: The Free Press.
Schonberger. R.J. (1986) *World Class Manufacturing: The Lessons of Simplicity Applied*, New York: The Free Press.
Sloan, A.P. Jr., (1964) *My Years with General Motors*, New York: Doubleday.
Taylor, F.W. (1947) *Principles of Scientific Management*, New York: Harper & Row.
Toffler, A. (1971) *Future Shock*, London: Pan Books Ltd. **If you read only one book from this entire list it should be this one.**
Toffler, A. (1981) *The Third Wave*, London: Pan Books Ltd
Toffler, A. (1984) *Previews And Premises*, London: Pan Books Ltd.
Toffler, A. (1991) *Power Shift: Knowledge, Wealth, and Violence at the Edge of the 21st Century*, London: Bantam.
Townsend, R. (1971) *Up The Organization: How to stop the company stifling people and strangling profits*, London: Coronet Books.
Vroom, V.H. and Deci, E.L. (eds.) (1970) *Management and Motivation: Selected Readings*, London: Penguin.
Watson, T.J. (1996) *In Search of Management: Culture, Chaos & Control in Managerial Work*, London: International Thomson Business Press.
Whyte, W.H. (1956) *The Organization Man*, London: Penguin.
Wickens, P.D. OBE, (1995) *The Ascendant Organization: Combining Commitment and Control for Long term, Sustainable Business Success*, Basingstoke, Macmillan Business.
Wight, O.W. (1981) *MRP II: Unlocking America's Productivity Potential*, Williston, Vermont: Oliver Wight Limited Publications.
Woodcock, M. (1989) *Team Development Manual*, 2nd edn. Aldershot: Gower.
Woolsey, R.E.D. and Swanson, H.S. (1975) *Operations Research for Immediate Application: A Quick & Dirty Manual*, New York: Harper & Row.
Zaleznik, A. (1966) *Human Dilemmas of Leadership*, New York: Harper & Row.
Zuboff, S. (1988) *In the Age of the Smart Machine: The Future of Work and Power*, New York: Basic Books.

Further reading

These are books you might not ordinarily categorize as directly related to your work as a manager. I have found them helpful in my work. I have included appropriate comments for some where the link with management practice is tenuous.

Ardrey, R. (1961) *African Genesis: A Personal Investigation into the Animal Origins and Nature of Man*, New York: Dell Publishing Co., Inc.. Later research into a number of theses examined by Ardrey in these books raises some serious questions about some of his conclusions. My experience, however, supports his fundamental argument about the importance of territory in our lives.
Ardrey, R. (1966) *The Territorial Imperative: A Personal Inquiry into the Animal Origins of Property and Nations*, New York: Dell Publishing Co., Inc..

Ardrey, R. (1970) *The Social Contract: A Personal Inquiry into the Evolutionary Sources of Order and Disorder*, New York: Dell Publishing Co., Inc..
Argyle, M. (1988) *Bodily Communication*, 2nd edn. London: Methuen & Co. Ltd.
Berne, E. (1968) *Games People Play: The Psychology of Human Relationships*, London: Penguin.
de Bono, E. (1967) *The Use of Lateral Thinking*, London: Penguin.
de Bono, E. (1970) *Lateral Thinking: A Textbook of Creativity*, London: Penguin.
de Bono, E. (1969) *The Mechanism of Mind*, London: Penguin.
de Bono, E. (1990) *I Am Right You Are Wrong: From This To the New Renaissance, From Rock Logic To Water Logic*, London: Penguin.
Davis, M.D. (1973) *Game Theory: A Nontechnical Introduction*, New York: Basic Books.
Flew, A. (1975) *Thinking About Thinking (Or, Do I sincerely want to be right?)* London: Fontana.
Gall, J. (1979) *Systemantics: How Systems Work And Especially How They Fail*, Glasgow: Fontana/Collins, 1979. Try reading this interesting little book soon after you have read (or reread) Parkinson's Law.
Howard, P. (1986) *The State of the Language: English Observed*, London: Penguin. This book reinforces my premise that careful use of language always improves our ability to communicate.
Huff, D. (1973) *How To Lie With Statistics*, London: Penguin.
Kidder, T. (1982) *The Soul Of A New Machine*, London: Penguin. This interesting book can be read on several levels. If you are still terrified of computers, it may help. It is also an interesting case study of successful leadership and teamworking under great pressure.
Molloy, J.T. (1976) *Dress For Success*, New York: Warner Books. A careful reading of this book reinforces the importance of symbols in our lives and particularly in the business world.
Molloy, J.T. (1983) *Molloy's Live For Success*, New York: Bantam/Perigord Press. This book broadens Molloy's thesis of the power of symbols in our lives.
Morris, D. (1968) *The Naked Ape*, London: Corgi.
Packard, V. (1981) *The Hidden Persuaders*, London: Penguin.
Raggett, J. and Bains, W. (1992) *Artificial Intelligence from A to Z*, London: Chapman & Hall.
Stewart, V. and Stewart, A. (1981) *Business Applications of the Repertory Grid*, London: McGraw Hill.
Wainwright, G.R. (1985) *Body Language*, Sevenoaks: Hodder and Stoughton Ltd.

Index